THE MICRO
ECONOMY
TODAY

13e

The McGraw-Hill Series Economics

ESSENTIALS OF ECONOMICS

Brue, McConnell, and Flynn
Essentials of Economics
Second Edition

Mandel
Economics: The Basics
Second Edition

Schiller
Essentials of Economics
Eighth Edition

PRINCIPLES OF ECONOMICS

Colander
Economics, Microeconomics, and Macroeconomics
Eighth Edition

Frank and Bernanke
Principles of Economics, Principles of Microeconomics, Principles of Macroeconomics
Fifth Edition

Frank and Bernanke
Brief Editions: Principles of Economics, Principles of Microeconomics, Principles of Macroeconomics
Second Edition

McConnell, Brue, and Flynn
Economics, Microeconomics, and Macroeconomics
Nineteenth Edition

McConnell, Brue, and Flynn
Brief Editions: Microeconomics and Macroeconomics
Second Edition

Miller
Principles of Microeconomics
First Edition

Samuelson and Nordhaus
Economics, Microeconomics, and Macroeconomics
Nineteenth Edition

Schiller
The Economy Today, The Micro Economy Today, and The Macro Economy Today
Thirteenth Edition

Slavin
Economics, Microeconomics, and Macroeconomics
Tenth Edition

ECONOMICS OF SOCIAL ISSUES

Guell
Issues in Economics Today
Sixth Edition

Sharp, Register, and Grimes
Economics of Social Issues
Nineteenth Edition

ECONOMETRICS

Gujarati and Porter
Basic Econometrics
Fifth Edition

Gujarati and Porter
Essentials of Econometrics
Fourth Edition

MANAGERIAL ECONOMICS

Baye
Managerial Economics and Business Strategy
Seventh Edition

Brickley, Smith, and Zimmerman
Managerial Economics and Organizational Architecture
Fifth Edition

Thomas and Maurice
Managerial Economics
Tenth Edition

INTERMEDIATE ECONOMICS

Bernheim and Whinston
Microeconomics
First Edition

Dornbusch, Fischer, and Startz
Macroeconomics
Eleventh Edition

Frank
Microeconomics and Behavior
Eighth Edition

ADVANCED ECONOMICS

Romer
Advanced Macroeconomics
Fourth Edition

MONEY AND BANKING

Cecchetti and Schoenholtz
Money, Banking, and Financial Markets
Third Edition

URBAN ECONOMICS

O'Sullivan
Urban Economics
Eighth Edition

LABOR ECONOMICS

Borjas
Labor Economics
Fifth Edition

McConnell, Brue, and Macpherson
Contemporary Labor Economics
Ninth Edition

PUBLIC FINANCE

Rosen and Gayer
Public Finance
Ninth Edition

Seidman
Public Finance
First Edition

ENVIRONMENTAL ECONOMICS

Field and Field
Environmental Economics: An Introduction
Fifth Edition

INTERNATIONAL ECONOMICS

Appleyard, Field, and Cobb
International Economics
Seventh Edition

King and King
International Economics, Globalization, and Policy: A Reader
Fifth Edition

Pugel
International Economics
Fifteenth Edition

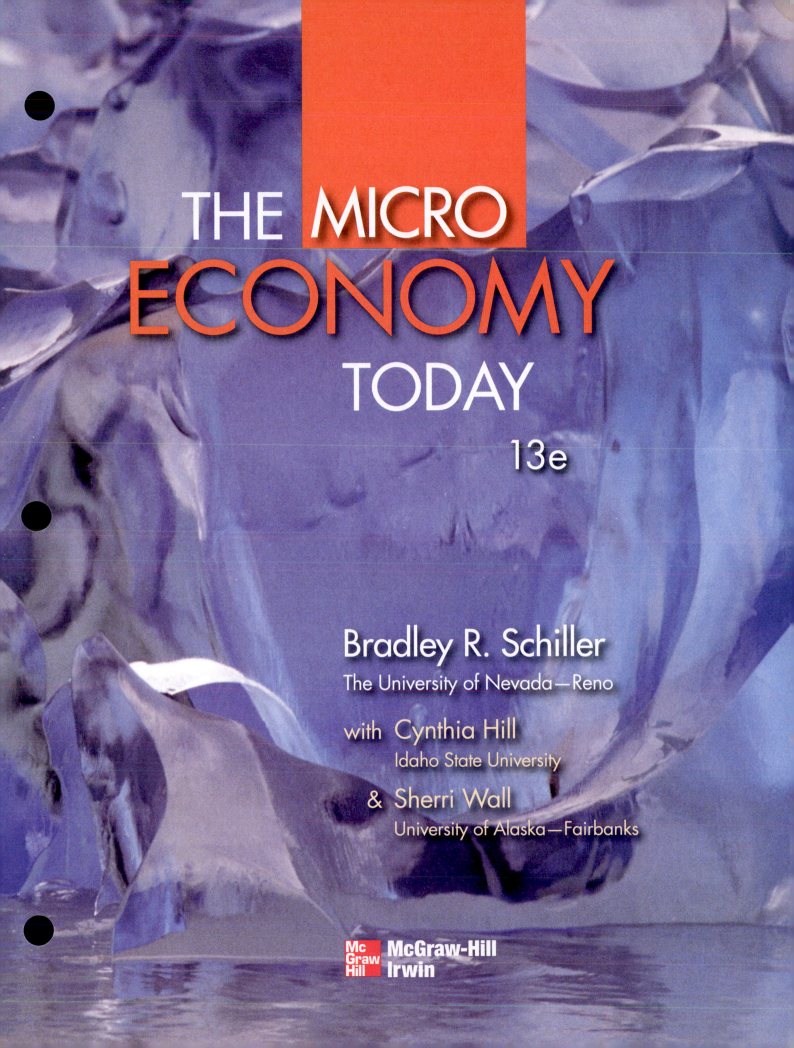

THE MICRO ECONOMY TODAY

13e

Bradley R. Schiller
The University of Nevada—Reno

with Cynthia Hill
Idaho State University

& Sherri Wall
University of Alaska—Fairbanks

McGraw-Hill Irwin

THE MICRO ECONOMY TODAY
Published by McGraw-Hill/Irwin, a business unit of The McGraw-Hill Companies, Inc., 1221 Avenue of the Americas, New York, NY, 10020.
Copyright © 2013, 2010, 2008, 2006, 2003, 2000, 1997, 1994, 1991, 1989, 1986, 1983, 1980 by The McGraw-Hill Companies, Inc. All rights reserved.
Printed in the United States of America. No part of this publication may be reproduced or distributed in any form or by any means, or stored in a database or retrieval system, without the prior written consent of The McGraw-Hill Companies, Inc., including, but not limited to, in any network or other electronic storage or transmission, or broadcast for distance learning.

Some ancillaries, including electronic and print components, may not be available to customers outside the United States.

This book is printed on acid-free paper.

3 4 5 6 7 8 9 0 DOW/DOW 1 0 9 8 7 6 5 4 3

ISBN   978-0-07-741653-9
MHID   0-07-741653-8

Vice president and editor-in-chief: *Brent Gordon*
Publisher: *Douglas Reiner*
Sponsoring editor: *Scott Smith*
Director of digital content: *Douglas Ruby*
Executive director of development: *Ann Torbert*
Development editor: *Marianne L. Musni*
Vice president and director of marketing: *Robin J. Zwettler*
Director of marketing: *Bradley Parkins*
Senior marketing manager: *Melissa Larmon*
Vice president of editing, design, and production: *Sesha Bolisetty*
Lead project manager: *Harvey Yep*
Senior buyer: *Michael R. McCormick*
Lead designer: *Matthew Baldwin*
Senior photo research coordinator: *Keri Johnson*
Photo researcher: *Michelle Buhr*
Lead media project manager: *Allison Souter*
Media project manager: *Ron Nelms*
Interior designer: *Matthew Baldwin*
Cover designer: *Laurie Entringer*
Cover image: *© Getty Images*
Typeface: *10/12 Times New Roman*
Compositor: *Aptara®, Inc.*
Printer: *R. R. Donnelley*

Library of Congress Cataloging-in-Publication Data

Schiller, Bradley R., 1943–
    The micro economy today / Bradley R. Schiller, Cynthia Hill, Sherri Wall.—13th ed.
       p. cm.—(The McGraw-Hill series economics)
    Includes index.
    ISBN 978-0-07-741653-9 (alk. paper)
    ISBN 0-07-741653-8 (alk. paper)
    1. Microeconomics. I. Hill, Cynthia. II. Wall, Sherri. III. Title.
  HB172.S3625 2013
  338.5—dc23
                                                      2011046890

www.mhhe.com

Bradley R. Schiller has over four decades of experience teaching introductory economics at the University of Nevada, American University, the University of California (Berkeley and Santa Cruz), and the University of Maryland. He has given guest lectures at more than 300 colleges ranging from Fresno, California, to Istanbul, Turkey. Dr. Schiller's unique contribution to teaching is his ability to relate basic principles to current socioeconomic problems, institutions, and public policy decisions. This perspective is evident throughout *The Micro Economy Today.*

Dr. Schiller derives this policy focus from his extensive experience as a Washington consultant. He has been a consultant to most major federal agencies, many congressional committees, and political candidates. In addition, he has evaluated scores of government programs and helped design others. His studies of poverty, discrimination, training programs, tax reform, pensions, welfare, Social Security, and lifetime wage patterns have appeared in both professional journals and popular media. Dr. Schiller is also a frequent commentator on economic policy for television and radio, and his commentary has appeared in *The Wall Street Journal, The Washington Post, The New York Times,* and *Los Angeles Times,* among other major newspapers.

Dr. Schiller received his Ph.D. from Harvard and his B.A. degree, with great distinction, from the University of California (Berkeley). He is now a professor of economics at the University of Nevada in Reno, where he hosts McGraw-Hill's annual West Coast Teaching Economics Conference. On his days off, Brad is on the tennis courts, the ski slopes, or the crystal-blue waters of Lake Tahoe.

Cynthia D. Hill is a professor of economics at Idaho State University, where she has dedicated herself to helping students develop as thinkers and scholars. Her academic research is primarily focused on economic education and the advancement of classroom pedagogy. Over the past decade Professor Hill has undertaken many administrative roles, which focus on student success and educational advancement. These positions include director of the University Honors Program, director of the Center for Teaching and Learning, and currently the position of executive director of the Student Success Center.

Professor Hill has won numerous teaching and public service awards over her 14-year tenure at Idaho State University, including the Carnegie Foundation for the Advancement of Teaching Idaho Professor of the Year, two-time Master Teacher, five-time Most Influential Professor, two-time Outstanding Public Servant, and Distinguished Public Servant. She earned her bachelor's degree from the University of Montana and her Ph.D. from Washington State University.

Sherri L. Wall has taught economics in the School of Management at the University of Alaska—Fairbanks since 2006. She is the founding faculty advisor for two student organizations at UAF: SWEET (Students Who Enjoy Economic Thinking) and SIFE (Students in Free Enterprise). The UAF SIFE team has won three Regional championships, and in 2011, were 2nd runner up in the opening round of competition at the National Exposition. Sherri was a finalist in the Market-Based Management Institute's Economic Communicators contest at the Association of Private Enterprise Conference in 2008. In that same year, she was recognized as Outstanding Faculty Member of the year by the UAF student body, and in 2010, Outstanding Student Organization Advisor.

©Kelly Atlee Photography.

Sherri has a Master's of Science in Resource and Applied Economics, and is completing her Ph.D. through a National Science Foundation fellowship. Her research interests include economic issues of climate change in Alaska, institutional economics and economic education. She has presented her research at universities and conferences around the world. In her spare time, she finds great utility in the outdoor recreational opportunities in Alaska including, flying with her husband, hiking, fishing, hunting, skiing, and trail running.

The Great Recession of 2008–2009 lingered for far too long. But that devastating experience had at least one positive effect: it revitalized interest in economics. People wanted to know how a modern economy could stumble so badly. And why it took so long to recover. Public debates about economic theory became increasingly intense and partisan. Everything from Keynesian theory to environmental regulation became the subject of renewed scrutiny. These debates increased the demand for economic analysis and for principles instruction as well. Indeed, one could argue that the Great Recession proved that economics instruction is an inferior good: as the economy contracts, the demand for economics courses increases.

While we might take offense at the thought of producing an inferior good, we should certainly rise to the occasion. This means bringing the real world into the classroom as never before: relating basic micro principles to the policy debates over taxes, regulation, energy, climate change, poverty, and trade; and getting students to appreciate why and how economic issues were the central focus of the 2012 election campaigns.

The Micro Economy Today has always been a policy-driven introduction to economic principles. Indeed, that is one of its most distinctive features. This 13th edition continues that tradition, with even more fervor. It challenges students to think more critically about the dominant policy issues of the day. Take solar energy, for example. Students overwhelmingly embrace the potential of "clean" solar energy to replace "dirty" fossil fuels, thereby saving the environment, breaking the power of "Big Oil," and achieving energy independence. But what about opportunity costs? Economists preach that there is neither a "free lunch" nor "free" solar panel. The first chapter of this text tries to get students thinking more like economists—that is, about resource constraints and implied trade-offs. The same critical thinking is applied in Chapter 1 to the "guns versus butter" debate that soaring budget deficits have brought to the fore once again (that is, which to cut). Then there is the renewed debate over "taxes on the rich," which relates both to equality (what is a "fair" distribution of the deficit–cutting burden) and to efficiency (production and investment disincentives).

A section titled, "The Economy Tomorrow" at the end of every chapter focuses on these kinds of front-page policy issues. But the real-world emphasis of this text is not confined to that feature. Every chapter has an array of In the News and World View boxes that offer real-world illustrations of basic economic principles. And the body of the text itself is permeated with actual companies, products, people, and policy issues that students will recognize. There are no mythical widgets or Jack & Jill water companies in this textbook. Students will see and appreciate the links between core principles and real-life events. They will also learn and remember those principles far longer.

DIFFERENTIATING FEATURES

The policy-driven focus of *The Micro Economy Today* clearly differentiates it from other principles texts. Other texts may claim real-world content, but none comes close to the empirical perspectives of this text. Beyond this unique approach, *The Micro Economy Today* offers a combination of features that no other text matches, including the following:

Markets versus Government Theme

We all know there is no such thing as a pure market-driven economy and that markets operate on the fringe even in the most centralized economics. So "markets versus government" is not an all-or-nothing proposition. It is still a central theme, however, in the real world. Should the government assume *more* responsibility for managing the economy—or will *less* intervention generate better micro outcomes? Public opinion is clear: as the accompanying News reveals, three out of four Americans have a negative view of federal intervention. The challenge for economics instructors is to enunciate principles that help define the boundaries of public and private sector activity. When do we expect **market failure** to occur? How and why do we anticipate that government intervention might result in **government failure?** Can we get students to think critically about these central issues? *The Micro Economy Today* certainly tries, aided by scores of real-world illustrations.

market failure: An imperfection in the market mechanism that prevents optimal outcomes.

government failure: Government intervention that fails to improve economic outcomes.

IN THE NEWS

Government Failure?

An August 2011 *Washington Post* poll asked a cross-section of Americans the following question:

Question: "In general, when the government in Washington decides to solve economics problems, how much confidence do you have that the problem actually will be solved?"

Responses:

A lot — 5%
Some — 21%
Little — 34%
None — 39%

Source: The Washington Post, © August 9, 2011. All rights reserved. Used with permission.

Analysis: "Government failure" occurs when government intervention fails to improve economic outcomes—that is, solve economics problems. Three out of four Americans expect such failures to occur.

The staples of introductory economics are fully covered in *The Micro Economy Today*. Beyond the core chapters, however, there is always room for additional coverage. In fact, authors reveal their uniqueness in their choice of such chapters. Those choices tend to be more abstract in competing texts, offering "extra" chapters on pubic choice, behavioral economics, economics of information, uncertainty, and asymmetric information. All of these are interesting and important, but entail opportunity costs that are particularly high at the principles level. The menu in *The Micro Economy Today* is more tailored to the dimensions and issues of the world around us. Chapter 2, for example, depicts the dimensions of the U.S. economy in a comparative global framework. Where else are students going to learn that China is *not* the world's largest economy, that U.S. workers are the most productive, or that income inequality is more severe in poor nations than rich ones?

Unique Topic Coverage

The emphasis on contemporary policy issues is evident in micro. The parallel chapters on taxes (19) and transfers (20) underscore the central conflict between equity and efficiency concerns that impedes easy solutions to important policy questions. The analysis of President Obama's own 2010 tax return (p. 415) enlivens the discussion of tax "loopholes."

The extensive coverage of market structure includes *two* chapters on competition. The first (8) presents the standard, static profit-maximization model for the perfectly competitive firm. The second chapter (9) adds real-world excitement. Chapter 9 focuses on market dynamics, emphasizing how competitive *forces* alter both market structures and market outcomes. The core case study takes students from the original Apple I (see photo on p. 195!) all the way to the iPad. Along the way, the effects of continuous entry, exit, and innovation are highlighted. Students come away with an enhanced appreciation of how competitive markets generate superior outcomes—one of the most important insights of the micro sequence.

Also noteworthy in the micro sequence is the Chapter (13) on natural monopoly. We know that natural monopoly presents unique challenges for antitrust and regulatory policy. This chapter first assesses the goal conflicts that complicate government intervention, then reviews regulatory history and outcomes in the rail, telephone, airline, and cable industries.

Global Perspective

"Global perspective," along with "real-world" content is promised by just about every principles author. *The Micro Economy Today* actually delivers on that promise. This is manifestly evident in the titles of Chapter 2 (global comparisons) and Chapter 23 (global poverty). The global perspective is also easy to discern in the boxed World Views features embedded in every chapter. More subtle, but at least as important, is the portrayal of an open economy from the get-go. While some texts start with a closed economy—or worse still, a closed, private economy—and then add international dimensions as an afterthought, *The Micro Economy Today* depicts an open economy from start to finish. These global linkages are a vital dimension of micro issues (e.g., effective competition, oil prices).

YouTube Content!

YouTube content has come to *The Micro Economy Today*! Students are always checking things out on YouTube and even forwarding occasional videos they think relate to economics. So we decided to integrate YouTube videos into *The Micro Economy Today*. Professors Sherri Wall (University of Alaska—Fairbanks) and Cindy Hill (Idaho State) identified scores of YouTube videos that do, indeed, illustrate basic economic concepts. These were then annotated to explain that economic content, highlighting key terms from the text. Sherri and Cindy also provided questions to test student comprehension of the economic principles covered. The result is a new and exciting student supplement to *The Micro Economy Today*—a catalog of chapter-specific, engaging, and instructive YouTube videos. They are available in the book-specific *Connect* software system and the book-specific Online Learning Center.

WHAT'S NEW IN THIS 13TH EDITION

Every edition of *The Micro Economy Today* introduces a wealth of new content and pedagogy. This is critical for a text that prides itself on currency of policy issues, institutions, and empirical perspectives. Every page, every example, and all the data have been reviewed for currency and updated where needed. Beyond this general upgrade, previous users of *The Micro Economy Today* will notice some specific revisions, including the following.

New Chapters on Consumer Choice and Elasticity

The previous chapter on "Consumer Demand" has been expanded into two new chapters. Chapter 5 on "Consumer Choice" now includes an extensive discussion of consumer surplus. All coverage of elasticity has been moved into the new Chapter 6, where the various elasticity concepts get more detailed coverage.

New "Economy Tomorrow" Topics

Each chapter ends with a feature called "The Economy Tomorrow" that challenges students to apply key concepts to current policy issues. There new Economy Tomorrow features range from "Harnessing the Sun" (the opportunity costs of solar energy) in Chapter 1 to "Policing World Trade" (international trade disputes) in Chapter 21.

New "World Views"

The boxed World Views in each chapter are designed to showcase the global reach of economic principles. There are various new World Views in the 13th edition, including the 2010–2011 surge in oil prices (supply and demand shifts) in Chapter 3, OPEC quota setting (oligopoly price-fixing) in Chapter 11, and Walmart's epic union battles in Chapter 17. All of the World Views are annotated, are referred to in the body of the text, and often are the subject of end-of-chapter questions. These added dimensions help ensure that students will actually read the boxed material.

The boxed In the News features highlight domestic applications of basic principles. In Chapter 3 alone there are three new ones on selling human organs (supply and demand); the BP oil spill and shrimp prices (supply shift); and ticket scalping (disequilibrium prices). The News in Chapter 4 about firefighters watching a house burn to the ground in Tennessee is a vivid introduction to the concepts of public goods and externalities. Some of my new favorites are the competitive chase in the tablet market (p. 209) underscores how market dynamics offer continuous product improvements and lower prices. The News on Google's (p. 235) and AT&T's (p. 260) alleged anticompetitive practices may get students thinking more critically about "fair" and "unfair" business behavior. Scrutiny of President Obama's own tax return (p. 415) should spark debate on "fair" taxation as well.

New "In the News" Content

At the end of every chapter there are both questions for discussion and a separate set of numerical and graphing problems. The problem set is designed so that students can answer and submit manually if desired. The same problems are also embedded in the course management system *Connect* to facilitate online submissions, automatic grading, and course monitoring. Both the questions for discussion and problems utilize tables, graphs, and boxed material from the body of the chapter, requiring the students to read and process core content. As a result, the end of chapter material has to be updated along with the text itself.

New Problems & Questions for Discussion

We are pleased to welcome Cynthia Hill (Idaho State University) and Sherri Wall (University of Alaska—Fairbanks) to the author team. Both are active instructors at their respective institutions and are dedicated to teaching and using technology as an innovative part of their courses. Cindy and Sherri have been brought into the Schiller franchise as digital coauthors. They have made important contributions to the 13th edition, including revising the end-of-chapter content, streamlining learning objective pedagogy, and most notably updating the technology features of the text. Working directly with the content in McGraw-Hill's homework management system, *Connect,* they have each created algorithmic problems, provided datasets, and accuracy–checked the content, ensuring correct and accurate material.

New Digital Coauthors and Enhanced Digital Content

YouTube Videos. The YouTube videos added to *The Micro Economy Today's* instructional package is the most visible contribution to this edition made by Cindy and Sherri. These short, engaging videos are annotated to highlight basic economic concepts. They can be used independently by students or used as visual aids in the classroom. In either case, they will enhance the learning experience.

CHAPTER-BY-CHAPTER CHANGES

The Micro Economy Today, 13th edition, features improved and expanded learning objectives, end-of-chapter content, and up-to-date material and data reflecting today's economy in every chapter. Changes include the following.

Chapter 1 focuses on respective powers of market and government to fashion economic outcomes, reinforcing the market versus government theme of the text. A new discussion of normative versus positive analysis, an In the News article on unemployment in 2011, and illustrations of opportunity cost have been added, including a new Economy Tomorrow section discussing solar power and the opportunity costs of development.

Chapter 2 is thoroughly updated with global and domestic comparison data, such as comparative output (GDP); GDP per capita around the world; GDP growth versus population growth; the education gap between rich and poor nations; income share of the rich; U.S. output and population growth; and U.S. distribution of income.

Chapter 3 emphasizes comparative advantage and specialization and features In the News and World View articles such as; AT&T's price cuts on the iPhone to illustrate the law of demand; BP's oil spill and its effects on shrimp prices to show supply-curve shifts; ticket scalping to exemplify market shortages; the 2011 gasoline price surge to demonstrate changing equilibrium; and the selling of human organs to describe a zero price ceiling.

Chapter 4's revisions include updated domestic data, new In the News and World View articles on fire protection in regards to public goods and the free-rider dilemma, externalities described by deaths due to secondhand smoke, and a new Economy Tomorrow section on public choice theory in "right-sizing government."

Chapter 5, re-titled to "Consumer Choice," contains new content, such as the 2011 data on spending patterns; a new discussion of price discrimination and consumer surplus and an expanded discussion of marginal utility; the introduction of two new key terms "consumer surplus" and "price discrimination;" and a new Economy Tomorrow section with new LeBron James examples.

Chapter 6 is a new stand-alone chapter that focuses on various elasticities. Examples include a new segment on the elasticity of supply; a new key term "price elasticity of supply;" numerous In the News and World View articles that cover the elasticity of iPhone demand; the impact of iPhone price cuts on substitute and complementary goods; the idea of alligator skins becoming a normal good due to the decline in income and demand; SUV sales declining and gas prices, rising showing that they are complimentary goods; price elasticity of gold supply; and a new Economy Tomorrow section, "Achieving Energy Independence."

Chapter 7 has new data on global competitiveness and a new In the News article on Ford's investment decision in a new plant in Kansas City to illustrate long-run and short-run costs.

Chapter 8 includes a new figure that illustrates differing output goals, a new poll on public distrust of the profit motive, and an In the News piece on rising marginal cost in the catfish industry.

Chapter 9 features an updated introduction on the 2009–2011 price and cost pressures of the catfish industry shutdowns and exits, as well as a new Economy Tomorrow section about competition in the tablet market that includes an In the News article exemplifying the economics behind innovation and pricing.

Chapter 10's updates include a new key term "consumer surplus" and In the News articles on Ticketmaster's 2011 "dynamic pricing" strategy to show price discrimination and Intel's monopoly practices and entry barriers. To end the chapter, the Economy Tomorrow section is centered on Microsoft and Google's business practices.

Chapter 11 is updated with new data on U.S. product markets and global market power and highlights new In the News and World View cases on 2011 airplane fare hikes; OPEC's decision to hold production, causing oil prices to jump; and AT&T's proposed purchase of T-Mobile.

Chapter 12 has resequenced short- and long-term graphs, has updated data on advertising and brand values, and incorporates a new key term "cross-price elasticity of demand."

Chapter 13, retitled to "Natural Monopolies: (De)Regulation," includes a new discussion of substitute goods (cable versus satellite) and two additional key terms: "substitute goods" and "price ceiling."

Chapter 14 covers the 2009 Copenhagen Accord, BP oil spill, and In the News pieces on the efficiency decision of a New York nuclear plant and its thermal pollution and on job losses due to the 2011 mining regulation.

Chapter 15 previews the 2012 Farm Act, covers 2011 commodity inflation, and includes discussion of basic economics of farm subsidies in an In the News piece.

Chapter 16 contrasts Larry Ellison's salary (at Oracle) with average wage and MRP, along with Joe Maurer's (from the Minnesota Twins) baseball contract and MRP expectation. This chapter also adds a new key term, "market surplus," and updated data on 2010 MBA starting salaries.

Chapter 17 details the growth of public sector unions, presents a new figure on private versus public unions, covers the 2011 NFL lockout, and describes Walmart's collective bargaining situation in a new World View.

Chapter 18 discusses the origins and financing of Facebook and has a new In the News article on Google's reduced market share and stock price to illustrate the value of information in financial markets.

Chapter 19 starts with a new introduction that highlights disparity between poverty budgets and Google executive salaries, discusses updated data on global top tax rates, and has In the News articles on Obama's 2010 tax return "loopholes" and his 2011 proposal to raise the top marginal tax rates.

Chapter 20 showcases new Social Security benefit calculations and has updated data on poverty thresholds, Social Security finances, wage replacement rates, and declining labor supply throughout the chapter.

Chapter 21 includes updated export ratio and trade balances data. New World View and In the News articles explore tariffs on Chinese tires and sugar import quotas, discuss the Mexican trucking dispute, and focus on "Policing World Trade" in the Economy Tomorrow section.

Chapter 22 contains updated data on foreign exchange rates, 2010 data for the U.S. balance of payment summary statement and a World View about China's deliberate attempt to keep the value of the yuan low by purchasing foreign currency.

Chapter 23 is thoroughly updated with global data such as poverty thresholds and population, income distribution, foreign aid, growth rates, agriculture share of total output and productivity, and business climates.

EFFECTIVE PEDAGOGY

Despite the abundance of real-world applications, this is at heart a *principles* text, not a compendium of issues. Good theory and interesting applications are not mutually exclusive. This is a text that wants to *teach economics,* not just increase awareness of policy issues. To that end, *The Micro Economy Today* provides a logically organized and uncluttered theoretical structure for micro and international theory. What distinguishes this text from others on the market is that it conveys theory in a lively, student-friendly manner.

Clean, Clear Theory

Student comprehension of core theory is facilitated with careful, consistent, and effective pedagogy. This distinctive pedagogy includes the following features:

Concept Reinforcement

Chapter Learning Objectives. Each chapter contains a set of chapter-level learning objectives. Students and professors can be confident that the organization of each chapter surrounds common themes outlined by three to five learning objectives listed on the first page of each chapter. End-of-chapter material, including the chapter summary, discussion questions, and student problem sets, is tagged to these learning objectives, as is the supplementary material, which includes the Test Bank, and Instructor's Resource Manual.

Self-Explanatory Graphs and Tables. Graphs are *completely* labeled, colorful, and positioned on background grids as the graph on the next page illustrates. Because students often enter the principles course as graph-phobics, graphs are frequently accompanied by synchronized tabular data. Every table is also annotated. This shouldn't be a product-differentiating feature but, sadly, it is. Putting a table in a textbook without an annotation is akin to writing a cluster of numbers on the board, then leaving the classroom without any explanation.

Reinforced Key Concepts. Key terms are defined in the margin when they first appear and, unlike in other texts, redefined in the margin as necessary in subsequent chapters. Website references are directly tied to the book's content, not hung on like

FIGURE 3.3
Shifts vs. Movements

A demand curve shows how a consumer responds to price changes. If the determinants of demand stay constant, the response is a *movement* along the curve to a new quantity demanded. In this case, the quantity demanded increases from 5 (point d_1), to 12 (point g_1), when price falls from $35 to $20 per hour.

If the determinants of demand *change*, the entire demand curve *shifts*. In this case, a rise in income increases demand. With more income, Tom is willing to buy 12 hours at the initial price of $35 (point d_2), not just the 5 hours he demanded before the lottery win.

		Quantity Demanded (Hours per Semester)	
	Price (per Hour)	Initial Demand	After Increase in Income
A	$50	1	8
B	45	2	9
C	40	3	10
D	35	5	12
E	30	7	14
F	25	9	16
G	20	12	19
H	15	15	22
I	10	20	27

ornaments. End-of-chapter discussion questions use tables, graphs, and boxed news stories from the text, reinforcing key concepts, and are linked to the chapter's learning objectives.

Boxed and Annotated Applications. In addition to the real-world applications that run through the body of the text, the new design of *The Micro Economy Today* intersperses boxed domestic (In the News) and global (World View) case studies intertextually for further understanding and reference. Although nearly every text on the market now offers boxed applications, *The Micro Economy Today*'s presentation is distinctive. First, the sheer number of In the News and World View boxes is unique. Second, and more important, *every* boxed application is referenced in the body of the text. Third, *every* News and World View comes with a brief, self-contained explanation as the following example illustrates. Fourth, the News and World View boxes are the explicit subject of the end-of-chapter discussion questions and student problem set exercises. In combination, these distinctive features assure that students will actually *read* the boxed applications and discern their economic content. The Test Bank provides subsets of questions tied to the News and World View boxes so that instructors can confirm student use of this feature.

WORLD VIEW

Gas Prices High—and Might Get Higher

NEW YORK (CNNMoney)—Strong worldwide oil demand and lack of supply are to blame for steadily rising gasoline prices in the United States, an oil industry group said Friday. . . .

Felmy said worldwide oil demand in 2010 hit a record of more than 87 million barrels a day, driven largely by strong growth in India, China, and the Middle East.

Supply, meanwhile, was constricted by the drilling moratorium in the Gulf of Mexico following the BP disaster, slow production growth in non-OPEC countries, and OPEC production controls. . . .

Over the last year, prices are up 39 cents a gallon or 14 percent. Crude oil is up by a similar percentage, currently trading at just under $90 a barrel.

—Steve Hargreaves

Source: CNNMoney.com, January 21, 2011. © 2011 Time Inc. Used under license.

Analysis: Equilibrium prices change whenever market demand or supply curves shift. In this case, both curves are shifting, and the equilibrium price is rising.

Photos and Cartoons. The text presentation is also enlivened with occasional photos and cartoons that reflect basic concepts. The photos on page 40 are much more vivid testimony to the extremes of inequality than the data in Figure 2.3 (p. 39). The contrasting photos of the original Apple I (p. 195), the iMac, and the iPhone (p. 205) underscore how the "animal spirits" of competitive markets spur innovation. Every photo and cartoon is annotated and referenced in the body of the text. These visual features are an integral part of the presentation, not diversions.

Readability

The one adjective invariably used to describe *The Micro Economy Today* is "readable." Professors often express a bit of shock when they realize that students actually enjoy reading the book. (Well, not as much as a Stephen King novel, but a whole lot better than most textbooks they've had to plow through.) The writing style is lively and issue-focused. Unlike any other textbook in the market, every boxed feature, every graph, every table, and

© Santokh Kochar/Getty Images/DAL

Gene Alexander, USDA Natural Resources Conservation Service/DAL

Analysis: An abundance of capital equipment and advanced technology make American farmers and workers far more productive than workers in poor nations.

every cartoon is explained and analyzed. Every feature is also referenced in the text, so students actually learn the material rather than skipping over it. Because readability is ultimately in the eye of the beholder, you might ask a couple of students to read and compare a parallel chapter in *The Micro Economy Today* and in another text. This is a test *The Micro Economy Today* usually wins.

Student Problem Set

I firmly believe that students must *work* with key concepts in order to really learn them. Weekly homework assignments are *de rigueur* in my own classes. To facilitate homework assignments, I have prepared the student problem set, which includes built-in numerical and graphing problems that build on the tables, graphs, and boxed material that align with each chapter's learning objectives. Grids for drawing graphs are also provided. Students cannot complete all the problems without referring to material in the chapter. This increases the odds of students actually *reading* the chapter, the tables, and the boxed applications.

The student problem set at the end of each chapter is reproduced in the online student tutorial software (*Connect® Economics,* discussed in the following pages). This really helps students transition between the written material and online supplements. It also means that the online assignments are totally book specific.

NEW AND IMPROVED SUPPLEMENTS

Instructor Aids

Test Bank. William Aldridge of the University of Alabama—Tuscaloosa and Diane Keenan of Cerritos College, with the help of Mack Bean of Franklin Pierce University and Steve Abid of Grand Rapids Community College, have thoroughly revised the Test Bank for the Thirteenth edition. This team assures a high level of quality and consistency of the test questions and the greatest possible correlation with the content of the text. All questions are coded according to chapter learning objectives, AACSB Assurance of Learning, and Bloom's Taxonomy guidelines. The computerized Test Bank is available in EZ Test, a flexible and easy-to-use electronic testing program that accommodates a wide range of question types including user-created questions. Tests created in EZ Test can be exported for use with course management systems such as WebCT, BlackBoard, or PageOut. The program is available for Windows, Macintosh, and Linux environments.

PowerPoint Presentations. Mike Cohick of Collin College, with the help of Susan Glanz of Saint John's University, created new presentation slides for the Thirteenth edition. Developed using Microsoft PowerPoint software, these slides are a step-by-step review of the key points in the book's 23 chapters. They are equally useful to the student in the classroom as lecture aids or for personal review at home or the computer lab. The slides use animation to show students how graphs build and shift.

Digital Image Library. All of the text's tables and graphs have been reproduced as full-color images on the website for instructor access.

Instructor's Resource Manual. Jan Ojdana of the University of Cincinnati, with the help of Stephanie Campbell of Mineral Area College, has prepared the Instructor's Resource Manual. The Instructor's Resource Manual is available online, and it includes chapter summaries and outlines, "lecture launchers" to stimulate class discussion, and media exercises to extend the analysis.

News Flashes. As up-to-date as *The Micro Economy Today* is, it can't foretell the future. As the future becomes the present, however, I write two-page News Flashes describing major economic events and relating them to specific text references. These News Flashes provide good lecture material and can be copied for student use. Adopters of *The Micro Economy*

Today have the option of receiving News Flashes via fax or mail. They're also available on the Schiller website. Four to six News Flashes are sent to adopters each year. (Contact your local McGraw-Hill/Irwin sales representative to get on the mailing list.)

At the instructor's discretion, students have access to the News Flashes. In addition, the following supplements can facilitate learning.

Student Aids

Built-in Student Problem Set. The built-in student problem set is found at the end of every chapter of *The Micro Economy Today*. Each chapter has 8 to 10 numerical and graphing problems tied to the content of the text. Graphing grids are provided. The answer blanks are formatted to facilitate grading and all answers are contained in the end-of-chapter Solution's Manual. For convenience, the student problem set pages can also be found on the textbook's website in exactly the same order and format. This facilitates either manual or electronic retrieval of homework assignments.

Study Econ Mobile App. McGraw-Hill is proud to offer a new mobile study app for students learning economics from Schiller *The Micro Economy Today*, 13th edition. The features of the Study Econ app include flashcards for all key terms, a basic math review, customizable-self quizzes, common mistakes, and games. For additional information, please refer to the back inside cover of this book. Visit your mobile app store and download a trial version of the Schiller Study Econ app today!

DISTINCTIVE WEB SUPPORT

The Thirteenth edition of *The Micro Economy Today* continues to set the pace for web applications and support of the principles course.

A mini website directory is provided in each chapter's marginal Web Analysis boxes, created and updated by Mark Wilson of West Virginia University Institute of Technology. These URLs aren't random picks; they were selected because they let students extend and update adjacent in-text discussions.

Web Analysis Boxes

The Micro Economy Today's website now includes even more features that both instructors and students will find engaging and instructive. The Online Learning Center is user-friendly. Upon entering the site at **www.mhhe.com/schiller13e,** students and instructors will find detailed information on the new edition and links to the specific site for the version of the book they are using.

Online Learning Center www.mhhe. com/schiller13e

Proceeding into the Student Center, students will find lots of brand-new interactive study material. Mark Wilson, with the help of Rondi Schei of Portland State University, has revised 10 self-grading multiple-choice questions per chapter, which are ideal for self-quizzing before a test. In addition, they have enhanced the Auxiliary Problem Sets for the site through updating the problems for added practice. Professors can assign these extra problems as homework or students can access them for additional skills practice. Answers can be found on the password-protected Instructor's Edition of the website. Mark and Rondi have also revised and created new Web Activities for each chapter. On top of all that, students have access to my periodic News Flashes along with my e-mail address to ask me any questions directly, under "ask Brad."

The password-protected Instructor Center includes some wonderful resources for instructors who want to include more interactive student activities in their courses. The downloadable Instructor's Resource Manual, end-of-chapter Solutions Manual, Test Bank, PowerPoints, Auxiliary Problem Sets and answers, Web-Based Activities and answers, and YouTube Activity answers are available to provide guidance for instructors who collect these assignments and grade them.

Premium Content. The Online Learning Center now offers students the opportunity to purchase Premium Content. Like an electronic study guide, the OLC Premium Content enables students to download Schiller-exclusive iPod content including podcasts by Brad

Schiller, Paul Solman videos, and chapter summaries—all accessible through the student's MP3 device.

McGraw-Hill *Connect®* Economics

McGraw-Hill *Connect®* Economics Features

Less Managing. More Teaching. Greater Learning. McGraw-Hill *Connect® Economics* is an online assignment and assessment solution that connects students with the tools and resources they'll need to achieve success.

McGraw-Hill *Connect® Economics* helps prepare students for their future by enabling faster learning, more efficient studying, and higher retention of knowledge.

Connect® Economics offers a number of powerful tools and features to make managing assignments easier, so faculty can spend more time teaching. With *Connect® Economics,* students can engage with their coursework anytime and anywhere, making the learning process more accessible and efficient. *Connect® Economics* offers you the features described below.

Simple Assignment Management. With *Connect® Economics,* creating assignments is easier than ever, so you can spend more time teaching and less time managing. The assignment management function enables you to:

- Create and deliver assignments easily with selectable end-of-chapter questions and test bank items.
- Streamline lesson planning, student progress reporting, and assignment grading to make classroom management more efficient than ever.
- Go paperless with the eBook and online submission and grading of student assignments.

Smart Grading. When it comes to studying, time is precious. *Connect® Economics* helps students learn more efficiently by providing feedback and practice material when they need it, where they need it. When it comes to teaching, your time also is precious. The grading function enables you to

- Have assignments scored automatically, giving students immediate feedback on their work and side-by-side comparisons with correct answers.
- Access and review each response; manually change grades or leave comments for students to review.
- Reinforce classroom concepts with practice tests and instant quizzes.

Instructor Library. The *Connect® Economics* Instructor Library is your repository for additional resources to improve student engagement in and out of class. You can select and use any asset that enhances your lecture. The *Connect® Economics* Instructor Library includes

- eBook.
- PowerPoint presentations.
- Test Bank.
- Solutions Manual.
- Instructor's Manual.
- Auxiliary Problem Sets and answers.
- YouTube Activity answers.
- Web-Based Activities and answers.
- Digital Image Library.
- Video Cases.
- Logic Cases.

Student Library. The *Connect® Economics* Student Library is the place for students to access additional resources. The Student Library:

- Offers students quick access to lectures, practice materials, eBooks, and more.
- Provides instant practice material and study questions, easily accessible on-the-go.
- Gives students access to the Self-Quiz and Study described on the next page.

Self-Quiz and Study. The Self-Quiz and Study (SQS), updated by Tim Kochanski of Portland State University with the help of Rondi Schei, connects each student to the learning resources needed for success in the course. For each chapter, students

- Take a practice test to initiate the Self-Quiz and Study.
- Immediately upon completing the practice test, see how their performance compares to content by sections within chapters.
- Receive a Study Plan that recommends specific readings from the text, supplemental study material, and practice work that will improve their understanding and mastery of each learning objective.

Diagnostic and Adaptive Learning of Concepts. LearnSmart Students want to make the best use of their study time. The *LearnSmart* adaptive self-study technology within *Connect® Economics* provides students with a seamless combination of practice, assessment, and remediation for every concept in the textbook. LearnSmart's intelligent software adapts to every student response and automatically delivers concepts that advance the student's understanding while reducing time devoted to the concepts already mastered. The result for every student is the fastest path to mastery of the chapter concepts. LearnSmart

- Applies an intelligent concept engine to identify the relationships between concepts and to serve new concepts to each student only when he or she is ready.
- Adapts automatically to each student, so students spend less time on the topics they understand and practice more those they have yet to master.
- Provides continual reinforcement and remediation, but gives only as much guidance as students need.
- Integrates diagnostics as part of the learning experience.
- Enables you to assess which concepts students have efficiently learned on their own, thus freeing class time for more applications and discussion.

Student Progress Tracking. *Connect® Economics* keeps instructors informed about how each student, section, and class is performing, allowing for more productive use of lecture and office hours. The progress-tracking function enables you to

- View scored work immediately and track individual or group performance with assignment and grade reports.
- Access an instant view of student or class performance relative to learning objectives.
- Collect data and generate reports required by many accreditation organizations, such as AACSB.

Lecture Capture. Increase the attention paid to lecture discussion by decreasing the attention paid to note taking. For an additional charge Lecture Capture offers new ways for students to focus on the in-class discussion, knowing they can revisit important topics later. Lecture Capture enables you to

- Record and distribute your lecture with a click of button.
- Record and index PowerPoint presentations and anything shown on your computer so it is easily searchable, frame by frame.
- Offer access to lectures anytime and anywhere by computer, iPod, or mobile device.
- Increase intent listening and class participation by easing students' concerns about note-taking. Lecture Capture will make it more likely you will see students' faces, not the tops of their heads.

McGraw-Hill Connect® Plus Economics. McGraw-Hill reinvents the textbook learning experience for the modern student with *Connect® Plus Economics*. A seamless integration of an eBook and *Connect® Economics*, *Connect® Plus Economics* provides all of the *Connect® Economics* features plus the following

- An integrated eBook, allowing for anytime, anywhere access to the textbook.
- Dynamic links between the problems or questions you assign to your students and the location in the eBook where that problem or question is covered.
- A powerful search function to pinpoint and connect key concepts in a snap.

In short, *Connect® Economics* offers you and your students powerful tools and features that optimize your time and energies, enabling you to focus on course content, teaching, and student learning. *Connect® Economics* also offers a wealth of content resources for both instructors and students. This state-of-the-art, thoroughly tested system supports you in preparing students for the world that awaits.

For more information about *Connect,* go to **www.mcgrawhillconnect.com,** or contact your local McGraw-Hill sales representative.

Tegrity Campus: Lectures 24/7

Tegrity Campus is a service that makes class time available 24/7 by automatically capturing every lecture in a searchable format for students to review when they study and complete assignments. With a simple one-click start-and-stop process, you capture all computer screens and corresponding audio. Students can replay any part of any class with easy-to-use browser-based viewing on a PC or Mac.

Educators know that the more students can see, hear, and experience class resources, the better they learn. In fact, studies prove it. With Tegrity Campus, students quickly recall key moments by using Tegrity Campus's unique search feature. This search helps students efficiently find what they need, when they need it, across an entire semester of class recordings. Help turn all your students' study time into learning moments immediately supported by your lecture.

To learn more about Tegrity, watch a 2-minute Flash demo at **http://tegritycampus. mhhe.com.**

Assurance-of-Learning Ready

Many educational institutions today are focused on the notion of *assurance of learning,* an important element of some accreditation standards. *The Micro Economy Today* is designed specifically to support your assurance-of-learning initiatives with a simple, yet powerful solution.

Each test bank question for *The Micro Economy Today* maps to a specific chapter learning outcome/objective listed in the text. You can use our test bank software, EZ Test and EZ Test Online, or *Connect® Economics* to easily query for learning outcomes/objectives that directly relate to the learning objectives for your course. You can then use the reporting features of EZ Test to aggregate student results in similar fashion, making the collection and presentation of assurance of learning data simple and easy.

AACSB Statement

The McGraw-Hill Companies is a proud corporate member of AACSB International. Understanding the importance and value of AACSB accreditation, *The Micro Economy Today,* 13th edition, recognizes the curricula guidelines detailed in the AACSB standards for business accreditation by connecting selected questions in the text and the test bank to the six general knowledge and skill guidelines in the AACSB standards.

The statements contained in *The Micro Economy Today,* 13th edition, are provided only as a guide for the users of this textbook. The AACSB leaves content coverage and assessment within the purview of individual schools, the mission of the school, and the faculty. While *The Micro Economy Today,* 13th edition, and the teaching package make no claim of any specific AACSB qualification or evaluation, we have labeled within *The Micro Economy Today,* 13th edition, selected questions according to the six general knowledge and skills areas.

McGraw-Hill Customer Experience Support Team

At McGraw-Hill, we understand that getting the most from new technology can be challenging. That's why our services don't stop after you purchase our products. You can e-mail our Product Specialists 24 hours a day to get product-training online. Or you can search our knowledge bank of Frequently Asked Questions on our support website. For Customer Support, call **800-331-5094,** or visit **www.mhhe.com/support.** One of our Technical Support Analysts will be able to assist you in a timely fashion.

CourseSmart is a new way for faculty to find and review eTextbooks. It's also a great option for students who are interested in accessing their course materials digitally. CourseSmart offers thousands of the most commonly adopted textbooks across hundreds of courses from a wide variety of higher education publishers. It is the only place for faculty to review and compare the full text of a textbook online. At CourseSmart, students can save up to 50% off the cost of a print book, reduce their impact on the environment, and gain access to powerful web tools for learning including full text search, notes and highlighting, and email tools for sharing notes between classmates. Complete tech support is also included in each title.

Finding your eBook is easy. Visit **www.CourseSmart.com** and search by title, author, or ISBN.

ACKNOWLEDGMENTS

This Thirteenth edition is unquestionably the finest edition of *The Micro Economy Today,* and I am deeply grateful to all those people who helped develop it. Marianne Musni was my faithful, fastidious, and cheerful development editor, who checked every word and feature in the text, prompting scores of corrections. Harvey Yep, the Project Manager, once again did an exceptional job in assuring that every page of the text was visually pleasing, properly formatted, error-free, and timely produced. Douglas Reiner served as the Publisher, offering sage advice and savvy leadership. Scott Smith joined the team as editor late in the game but contributed as well. The design team, led by Matt Baldwin, created a vibrant pallette of colors and features that enhanced *The Micro Economy Today*'s readability. My thanks to all of them and their supporting staff.

Special appreciation is extended to Cindy Hill and Sherri Wall, who together assumed responsibility for the digital content of the teaching package. The chapter-specific library of annotated YouTube videos is their most visible contribution to this Thirteenth edition. But their efforts in integrating and upgrading the learning objectives, discussion questions, and problem sets in both the print and digital platforms will yield even greater pedagogical value.

I also want to express my heartfelt thanks to the professors who have shared their reactions (both good and bad) with me. Direct feedback from these users and reviewers has always been a great source of continuing improvements in *The Micro Economy Today:*

Reviewers

Cynthia E. Abadie
Southwest Tennessee Community College

Mark Abajian
San Diego Mesa College

Steve Abid
Grand Rapids Community College

Ercument G. Aksoy
Los Angeles Valley College

Mauro Cristian Amor
Northwood University

Catalina Amuedo-Dorantes
San Diego State University

Gerald Baumgardner
Penn College

Mack A. Bean
Franklin Pierce University

Adolfo Benavides
Texas A&M University-Corpus Christi

Anoop Bhargava
Finger Lakes Community College

Joerg Bibow
Skidmore College

Eugenie Bietry
Pace University

John Bockino
Suffolk County Community College

Peter Boelman
Norco College

Walter Francis Boyle
Fayetteville Technical Community College

Amber Brown
Grand Valley State University

Don Bumpass
Sam Houston State University

Suparna Chakraborty
Baruch College, CUNY

Stephen J. Conroy
University of San Diego

Sherry L. Creswell
Kent State University

Manabendra Dasgupta
University of Alabama at Birmingham

Antony Davies
Duquesne University

Diane de Freitas
Fresno City College

Diana Denison
Red Rocks Community College

Alexander Deshkovski
North Carolina Central University

John A. Doces
Bucknell University

Ishita Edwards
Oxnard College

Eric R. Eide
Brigham Young University

Yalcin Ertekin
Trine University
Kelley L. Fallon
Owensboro Community & Technical College
Frank Garland
Tri-County Technical College
Leroy Gill
The Ohio State University
Paul Graf
Indiana University
Barnali Gupta
Miami University
Sheila Amin Gutierrez de Pineres
University of Texas at Dallas
Jonatan Jelen
City College of New York
Hyojin Jeong
Lakeland Community College
Barbara Heroy John
University of Dayton
Tim Kochanski
Portland State University
David E. Laurel
South Texas College
Raymond Lawless
Quinsigamond Community College
Richard B. Le
Cosumnes River College
Jim Lee
Texas A&M University-Corpus Christi
Sang H. Lee
Southeastern Louisiana University
Minghua Li
Franklin Pierce University
Yan Li
University of Wisconsin-Eau Claire
Paul Lockard
Black Hawk College
Rotua Lumbantobing
North Carolina State University
Paula Manns
Atlantic Cape Community College

Jeanette Milius
Iowa Western Community College
Norman C. Miller
Miami University
Stanley Robert Mitchell
McLennan Community College
Stephen K. Nodine
Tri-County Technical College
Phacharaphot Nuntramas
San Diego State University
Seth Ari Roberts
Frederick Community College
Michael J. Ryan
Western Michigan University
Craig F. Santicola
Westmoreland County Community College
Rolando A. Santos
Lakeland Community College
Theodore P. Scheinman
Mt. Hood Community College
Marilyn K. Spencer
Texas A&M University-Corpus Christi
Irina Nikolayevna Strelnikova
Red Rocks Community College
Michael Swope
Wayne County Community College
Gary Lee Taylor
South Dakota State University
Deborah L. Thorsen
Palm Beach State College
Ngoc-Bich Tran
San Jacinto College
Markland Tuttle
Sam Houston State University
Kenneth Lewis Weimer
Kellogg Community College
Selin Yalcindag
Mercyhurst College
Erik Zemljic
Kent State University

Finally, I'd like to thank all the professors and students who are going to use *The Micro Economy Today* as an introduction to economics principles. I welcome any responses (even the bad ones) you'd like to pass on for future editions.

—Bradley R. Schiller

CONTENTS IN BRIEF

PREFACE VIII

PART 1: THE ECONOMIC CHALLENGE

CHAPTER 1: ECONOMICS: THE CORE ISSUES 2

Appendix: Using Graphs 22

CHAPTER 2: THE U.S. ECONOMY: A GLOBAL VIEW 30

CHAPTER 3: SUPPLY AND DEMAND 45

CHAPTER 4: THE ROLE OF GOVERNMENT 70

MICRO

PART 2: PRODUCT MARKETS: THE BASICS

CHAPTER 5: CONSUMER CHOICE 92

Appendix: Indifference Curves 107

CHAPTER 6: ELASTICITY 116

CHAPTER 7: THE COSTS OF PRODUCTION 136

PART 3: MARKET STRUCTURE

CHAPTER 8: THE COMPETITIVE FIRM 164

CHAPTER 9: COMPETITIVE MARKETS 190

CHAPTER 10: MONOPOLY 213

CHAPTER 11: OLIGOPOLY 239

CHAPTER 12: MONOPOLISTIC COMPETITION 265

PART 4: REGULATORY ISSUES

CHAPTER 13: NATURAL MONOPOLIES: (DE)REGULATION? 282

CHAPTER 14: ENVIRONMENTAL PROTECTION 302

CHAPTER 15: THE FARM PROBLEM 325

PART 5: FACTOR MARKETS: BASIC THEORY

CHAPTER 16: THE LABOR MARKET 342

CHAPTER 17: LABOR UNIONS 366

CHAPTER 18: FINANCIAL MARKETS 386

PART 6: DISTRIBUTIONAL ISSUES

CHAPTER 19: TAXES: EQUITY VERSUS EFFICIENCY 408

CHAPTER 20: TRANSFER PAYMENTS: WELFARE AND SOCIAL SECURITY 427

INTERNATIONAL

PART 7: INTERNATIONAL ECONOMICS

CHAPTER 21: INTERNATIONAL TRADE 444

CHAPTER 22: INTERNATIONAL FINANCE 470

CHAPTER 23: GLOBAL POVERTY 490

Glossary   G-1
Index   I-1
Reference Tables   T-1

CONTENTS

PREFACE   VIII

PART 1: THE ECONOMIC CHALLENGE

CHAPTER 1: ECONOMICS: THE CORE ISSUES   2

The Economy Is Us   3
Scarcity: The Core Problem   4
Opportunity Costs   6
Production Possibilities   7
Three Basic Decisions   12
The Mechanisms of Choice   13
What Economics Is All About   18

Summary   21

Appendix: Using Graphs   22

THE ECONOMY TOMORROW:
Harnessing the Sun   20

IN THE NEWS
Job Market Loses Momentum   11

WORLD VIEW
Chronic Food Shortage Shows Despite Efforts by
    North Korea to Hide It   10
Rocket Launch Cost Enough to End Famine in
    North Korea for a Year   10
Market Reliance vs. Government
    Reliance?   15
Index of Economic Freedom   16

CHAPTER 2: THE U.S. ECONOMY: A GLOBAL VIEW   30

What America Produces   31
How America Produces   35
For Whom America Produces   38

Summary   41

THE ECONOMY TOMORROW:
Ending Global Poverty   41

WORLD VIEW
Comparative Output (GDP)   31
GDP per Capita around the
    World   32
The Education Gap between Rich and
    Poor Nations   36
Income Share of the Rich   40

CHAPTER 3: SUPPLY AND DEMAND   45

Market Participants   46
The Circular Flow   47
Demand   48
Supply   55
Equilibrium   59
Market Outcomes   63

Summary   66

THE ECONOMY TOMORROW:
Deadly Shortages: The Organ-Transplant Market   64

IN THE NEWS
AT&T Cuts Price on iPhone 3GS to $49   51
Seafood Prices Rise on BP Oil Spill   58
Students Struggle to Find Final Four Tickets   61
Study: People Would Donate Kidneys for Payment   66

WORLD VIEW
Gas Prices High—and Might Get Higher   63

CHAPTER 4: THE ROLE OF GOVERNMENT   70

Market Failure   71
Growth of Government   78
Taxation   79
Government Failure   82

Summary   86

THE ECONOMY TOMORROW:
"Right"-Sizing Government?   84

IN THE NEWS
Firefighters Watch as Home Burns to the Ground   73
Perpetuating Poverty: Lotteries Prey on the Poor   82
Persistent Doubts about Government Waste   83

WORLD VIEW
Secondhand Smoke Kills 600,000 People a
    Year: Study   74

PART 2: PRODUCT MARKETS: THE BASICS

CHAPTER 5: CONSUMER CHOICE   92

Determinants of Demand   93
The Demand Curve   95
Market Demand   99
Consumer Surplus   99

Price Discrimination 101

Choosing among Products 101

Summary 106

Appendix: Indifference Curves 107

THE ECONOMY TOMORROW:
Caveat Emptor 105

IN THE NEWS
Men vs. Women: How They Spend 93

CHAPTER 6: ELASTICITY 116

Price Elasticity 117

Price Elasticity and Total Revenue 123

Cross-Price Elasticity 126

Income Elasticity 128

Elasticity of Supply 130

Summary 132

THE ECONOMY TOMORROW:
Achieving Energy Independence 131

IN THE NEWS
Federal Cigarette Tax Going Up 121
After iPhone Price Cut, Sales Are Up by
   200 Percent 121
PlayStation 3 Sales More Than Double after
   Price Cut 122
Professor Becker Corrects President's Math 123
iPhone Price Cut a Blow to Palm, Motorola 127
SUV Sales Drop with Gasoline Price Rise 128
Recession Eats into Gator Market 130

WORLD VIEW
High Gold Price Swells Ranks of Illegal Miners 131

CHAPTER 7: THE COSTS OF PRODUCTION 136

The Production Function 137

Marginal Productivity 140

Resource Costs 141

Dollar Costs 143

Economic vs. Accounting Costs 151

Long-Run Costs 152

Economies of Scale 154

Summary 158

THE ECONOMY TOMORROW:
Global Competitiveness 156

IN THE NEWS
Ford Pumps $400 Million in Kansas
   City Plant 152
Funeral Giant Moves In on Small Rivals 154

WORLD VIEW
United States Gains Cost Advantage 157

PART 3: MARKET STRUCTURE

CHAPTER 8: THE COMPETITIVE FIRM 164

The Profit Motive 165

Economic vs. Accounting
   Profits 166

Market Structure 169

The Nature of Perfect
   Competition 170

The Production Decision 172

Profit-Maximizing Rule 174

The Shutdown Decision 180

The Investment Decision 181

Determinants of Supply 182

Summary 186

THE ECONOMY TOMORROW:
Internet-Based Price Competition 186

IN THE NEWS
Are Profits Bad? 165
Strawberry Fields Forever? 167
T-Shirt Shop Owner's Lament: Too Many T-Shirt
   Shops 169
Southern Farmers Hooked on New
   Cash Crop 177
GM to Close 15 Plants for 9 Weeks 182
Dell Plans to Close Plant in Texas 182
As Price of Grain Rises, Catfish Farms
   Dry Up 184

CHAPTER 9: COMPETITIVE MARKETS 190

The Market Supply Curve 191

Competition at Work: Microcomputers 194

The Competitive Process 204

Summary 209

THE ECONOMY TOMORROW:
$99 iPads? 208

IN THE NEWS
IBM to Halt PCjr Output Next Month 204
Tablet Brigade 209

WORLD VIEW
Economy Threatens Catfish Industry 191
Flat Panels, Thin Margins 194
Wireless-Phone Rates in India Declining As
   Competition Grows 206

CHAPTER 10: MONOPOLY 213

Market Power 214

Market Power at Work: The Computer Market
Revisited 217

A Comparative Perspective of Market Power 223

Pros and Cons of Market Power 228

Summary 235

THE ECONOMY TOMORROW:
Microsoft and Google: Bullies or Geniuses? 232

IN THE NEWS
Ticketmaster—Live Nation: A Sour Note 223
U.S. Sues over Drug's Price Hike 225
Ticketmaster Rolls Out "Dynamic" Pricing 226
Intel's Concessions Settle Antitrust Suit 228
Jury Rules Magnetek Unit Is Liable for Keeping
Technology off Market 229
Rocket Monopoly Approved 230
XM-Sirius Merger Made Simple: One Is Always Less
than Two 231
Judge Says Microsoft Broke Antitrust Law 233
Microsoft: Google Stifles Competition 235

WORLD VIEW
Foxy Soviets Pelt the West 218

CHAPTER 11: OLIGOPOLY 239

Market Structure 240
Oligopoly Behavior 243
The Kinked Demand Curve 247
Game Theory 249
Oligopoly vs. Competition 251
Coordination Problems 253
Barriers to Entry 255

Summary 261

THE ECONOMY TOMORROW:
Antitrust Enforcement 258

IN THE NEWS
Pop Culture: RC Goes for the Youth Market 246
Major Airlines Match Southwest's Fare Cuts 248
Major U.S. Airlines Roll Back Latest Fare Hike 248
Coke and Pepsi May Call Off Pricing Battle 251
Eliminating the Competition 255
Frito-Lay Devours Snack-Food Business 256
AT&T to Buy T-Mobile Means Higher Prices,
Fewer Phones 260

WORLD VIEW
Putting Size in Global Perspective 243
OPEC Leaves Output on Hold, Causing Oil
Price Jump 252

**CHAPTER 12: MONOPOLISTIC
COMPETITION 265**

Structure 266
Behavior 268
Summary 276

THE ECONOMY TOMORROW:
No Cease-Fire in Advertising Wars 274

IN THE NEWS
What's Behind Starbucks' Price Hike? 267
Water, Water Everywhere; Coke, Pepsi Unleash Flood of
Ad Muscle 269
Fast-Food Rivals Suit Up for Breakfast War 270
Premium Coffee Shops May Be Nearing
Saturation Point 273
The Cola Wars: It's Not All Taste 274

WORLD VIEW
The Best Global Brands 276

PART 4: REGULATORY ISSUES

**CHAPTER 13: NATURAL MONOPOLIES:
(DE)REGULATION? 282**

Antitrust vs. Regulation 283
Natural Monopoly 283
Regulatory Options 285
The Costs of Regulation 288
Deregulation in Practice 291

Summary 298

THE ECONOMY TOMORROW:
Deregulate Everything? 297

IN THE NEWS
Costs of Trucking Seen Rising under New
Safety Rules 290
Bell Monopolies Push to Disconnect Competition 292
The JetBlue Effect 294
Financial Woes Heating Up 297

**CHAPTER 14: ENVIRONMENTAL
PROTECTION 302**

The Environmental Threat 303
Pollution Damages 305
Market Incentives 306
Market Failure: External Costs 308
Regulatory Options 311
Balancing Benefits and Costs 315

Summary 321

THE ECONOMY TOMORROW:
The Greenhouse Threat   319

IN THE NEWS
Kaua'i Beach among Most
    Polluted   304
Dirty Air Can Shorten Your Life   306
Study Finds Net Gain from
    Pollution Rules   316
Forced Recycling Is a Waste   317
New Rules Would Cut Thousands of
    Coal Jobs   318

WORLD VIEW
Polluted Cities   303
Paying to Pollute   314
Evidence Is Now "Unequivocal" That Humans Are
    Causing Global Warming   319

CHAPTER 15: THE FARM PROBLEM   325

Destabilizing Forces   326
The First Farm Depression, 1920–1940   329
U.S. Farm Policy   330
The Second Farm Depression,
    1980–1986   335

Summary   338

THE ECONOMY TOMORROW:
Farmers on the Dole   335

IN THE NEWS
Corn Acres Expected to Soar in 2007, USDA Says
    Ethanol, Export Demand Lead to Largest Planted
    Area in 63 Years   329
Farm Subsidies Ripe for Reform   337

WORLD VIEW
EU Farm Subsidies   333

**PART 5: FACTOR MARKETS:
BASIC THEORY**

CHAPTER 16: THE LABOR MARKET   342

Labor Supply   343
Market Supply   346
Labor Demand   347
A Firm's Hiring Decision   352
Market Equilibrium   355
Choosing among Inputs   357

Summary   362

THE ECONOMY TOMORROW:
Capping CEO Pay   360

IN THE NEWS
Job Fairs: Long Lines and a Ray of Hope   343
Challenging Work and Corporate Responsibility Will
    Lure MBA Grads   344
Mauer, Twins Agree to Eight-Year, $184 Million
    Extension   353
Obama Wants $9.50 Minimum Wage   357
Obama Talks Tough on CEO Pay   361

WORLD VIEW
Your Money or Your Life   346

CHAPTER 17: LABOR UNIONS   366

The Labor Market   367
Labor Unions   368
The Potential Use of Power   369
The Extent of Union Power   372
Employer Power   374
Collective Bargaining   377
The Impact of Unions   380

Summary   382

THE ECONOMY TOMORROW:
Merging to Survive   382

IN THE NEWS
The GM-UAW Deal   369
A Win for the Graduate(s)   375
Free Agents in Sports: A Threat to
    Monopsony   375
Caterpillar vs. the UAW   378

WORLD VIEW
Union Membership   373
Walmart Chief Defends Closing
    Unionized Store   380

CHAPTER 18: FINANCIAL MARKETS   386

The Role of Financial Markets   387
The Present Value of Future Profits   388
The Stock Market   392
The Bond Market   398

Summary   402

THE ECONOMY TOMORROW:
Venture Capitalists—Financing Tomorrow's
    Products   401

IN THE NEWS
Yahoo, Microsoft Gain Slim Search Share from
    Google—ComScore   396
Where Do Start-Ups Get
    Their Money?   402

PART 6: DISTRIBUTIONAL ISSUES

CHAPTER 19: TAXES: EQUITY VERSUS EFFICIENCY   408

What Is *Income*?   409
The Size Distribution of Income   409
The Federal Income Tax   411
Payroll, State, and Local Taxes   417
Taxes and Inequality   419
What Is *Fair*?   420

Summary   423

THE ECONOMY TOMORROW:
A Flat Tax?   422

IN THE NEWS
The Obamas' Taxes   415
Obama Pitches Tax Hike on the Rich   417

WORLD VIEW
U2 Avoids Taxes, Raising Ire in Ireland   413
Top Tax Rates   421

CHAPTER 20: TRANSFER PAYMENTS: WELFARE AND SOCIAL SECURITY   427

Major Transfer Programs   428
Welfare Programs   430
Social Security   435

Summary   440

THE ECONOMY TOMORROW:
Privatize Social Security?   438

PART 7: INTERNATIONAL ECONOMICS

CHAPTER 21: INTERNATIONAL TRADE   444

U.S. Trade Patterns   445
Motivation to Trade   448
Pursuit of Comparative Advantage   452
Terms of Trade   453
Protectionist Pressures   455
Barriers to Trade   458

Summary   466

THE ECONOMY TOMORROW:
Policing World Trade   465

IN THE NEWS
California Grape Growers Protest Mixing
  Foreign Wine   456
End the Import Quotas on Sugar   463
NAFTA Reallocates Labor: Comparative Advantage
  at Work   466

WORLD VIEW
Export Ratios   446
China Accuses Corning of "Dumping"   458
Meat Imports "Threaten" Farmers   459
"Beggar-Thy-Neighbor" Policies in the 1930s   461
Mexico Retaliates for Loss of Truck Program   464

CHAPTER 22: INTERNATIONAL FINANCE   470

Exchange Rates: The Global Link   471
Foreign-Exchange Markets   471
Market Dynamics   475
Resistance to Exchange-Rate Changes   478
Exchange-Rate Intervention   480

Summary   486

THE ECONOMY TOMORROW:
Currency Bailouts   485

WORLD VIEW
Foreign-Exchange Rates   474
Weak Dollar Helps U.S. Firms   477
Dollar's Fall Puts Big Crimp in European Tourism   477
Nobel Prize Was Nobler in October   479
Analysis: China's $3 Trillion in Reserves More Bane
  Than Boon   483

CHAPTER 23: GLOBAL POVERTY   490

American Poverty   491
Global Poverty   492
Goals and Strategies   494
Income Redistribution   494
Economic Growth   497

Summary   509

THE ECONOMY TOMORROW:
Unleashing Entrepreneurship   508

WORLD VIEW
Glaring Inequalities   495
The Way We Give   497
The Female "Inequality Trap"   499
Dying for a Drink of Clean Water   500
Muhammad Yunus: Microloans   502
Jeffrey Sachs: Big Money, Big Plans   503
Chávez Sets Plans for Nationalization   505
African Sugar Production Ramps Up   508

Photo Credits   PC-1

Glossary   G-1

Index   I-1

Reference Tables   T-1

THE MICRO

ECONOMY

TODAY

13e

The Economic Challenge

People around the world want a better life. Whether rich or poor, everyone strives for a higher standard of living. Ultimately, the performance of the economy determines who attains that goal.

These first few chapters examine how the *limits* to output are determined and how the interplay of market forces and government intervention utilize and expand those limits.

Economics:
The Core Issues

"The Economist in Chief"

People understand that the president of the United States is the Commander in Chief of the armed forces. The president has the ultimate responsibility to decide when and how America's military forces will be deployed. He issues the orders that military officers must carry out. He is given credit for military successes and blame for military failures. He can't "pass the buck" down the line of command.

Less recognized is the president's role as "Economist in Chief." The president is held responsible not just for the *military* security of the United States, but for its *economic* security as well. Although he doesn't have the command powers in the economic arena that he has in the military arena, people expect him to take charge of the economy. They expect the Economist in Chief to keep the economy growing, to create jobs for everyone who wants one, and to prevent prices from rising too fast. Along the way, they expect the Economist in Chief to protect the environment, assure economic justice for all, and protect America's position in the global economy.

That is a tall order, especially in view of the president's limited constitutional powers to make economic policy decisions and the array of forces that shape economic outcomes. But no matter. Voters will hold the Economist in Chief responsible for economic misfortunes, whether or not he is able to single-handedly prevent them. That's why President Obama was so worried about his reelection prospects in 2012. The Great Recession of 2008–2010 left millions of Americans jobless, homeless, and hopeless. They had voted for Obama in 2008 on the promise of better economic times. In 2012 their disappointments threatened President Obama's reelection.

What everyone ultimately wants is a prosperous and growing economy: an economy in which people can find good jobs, enjoy rising living standards and wealth, pursue the education they desire, and enjoy the creature comforts of a prosperous economy. And we want to enjoy all these material comforts while protecting the environment, caring for the poor, and pursuing world peace.

We may know what we want, but how do we get it? Is "the economy" some sort of perpetual motion machine that will keep churning out more goods and services every year? Clearly not. During the Great Recession of 2008–2010 the economy churned out less output, eliminated jobs, and reduced living standards and wealth. A lot of college graduates had to move back home when they couldn't find jobs. What went wrong? Are there mechanical defects in the economic machine? If so, can they be fixed?

Why didn't the Economist in Chief fix these problems? What powers does a president have to prevent economic downturns? If governments had enough power to shape economic outcomes, why would we ever suffer economic setbacks? Would the government—led by the Economist in Chief—really make such colossal mistakes?

Just raising these questions begs the fundamental issue of what makes an economy tick. How are prices, wages, employment, and other economic outcomes actually determined? Does Wall Street run the system? How about selfish, greedy capitalists? Or maybe foreign nations? Are incompetent bureaucrats and self-serving politicians the root of our occasional woes? Who, in fact, calls the shots?

The goal of this course is to understand how the economy works. To that end, we want to determine how *markets*—the free-wheeling exchange of goods and services— shape economic outcomes—everything from the price of this textbook to the national unemployment rate. Then we want to examine the role that government can and does play in (re)shaping economic performance. Once we've established this foundation, we'll be in a better position to evaluate what the Economist in Chief *can* do—and what he should do. We'll also better understand how we ourselves can make better economic decisions.

We'll start our inquiry with some harsh realities. In a world of unlimited resources, we could have all the goods we desired. We'd have time to do everything we wanted and enough money to buy everything we desired. We could produce enough to make everyone rich while protecting the environment and exploring the universe. The Economist in Chief could deliver everything voters asked for. Unfortunately, we don't live in that utopia: we live in a world of limited resources. So we have to make difficult decisions about how best to use our time, our money, and our resources. The Economist in Chief has to decide how best to use the nation's limited resources. These are *economic* decisions.

In this first chapter we'll examine how the problem of limited resources arises and the kinds of choices it forces us to make. As we'll see, **three core choices confront every nation:**

- **WHAT to produce with our limited resources.**
- **HOW to produce the goods and services we select.**
- **FOR WHOM goods and services are produced—that is, who should get them.**

We also have to decide who should answer these questions. Should people take care of their own health and retirement, or should the government provide a safety net of health care and pensions? Should the government regulate airfares or let the airlines set prices? Should Microsoft decide what features get included in a computer's operating system, or should the government make that decision? Should Facebook decide what personal information is protected, or should the government make that decision? Should interest rates be set by private banks alone, or should the government try to control interest rates? The battle over *who* should answer the core questions is often as contentious as the questions themselves.

THE ECONOMY IS US

To learn how the economy works, let's start with a simple truth: *the economy is us.* "The economy" is simply an abstraction referring to the grand sum of all our production and consumption activities. What we collectively produce is what the economy produces; what we collectively consume is what the economy consumes. In this sense, the concept of "the economy" is no more difficult than the concept of "the family." If someone tells you that the Jones family has an annual income of $42,000, you know that the reference is to the collective earnings of all the Joneses. Likewise, when someone reports that the nation's income is $15 trillion per year—as it now is—we should recognize that the reference is to the grand total of everyone's income. If we work fewer hours or get paid less, both family income *and* national income decline. The "meaningless statistics" (see the cartoon on the next page) often cited in the news are just a summary of our collective market behavior.

"Meaningless statistics were up one-point-five per cent this month over last month."

Analysis: Many people think of economics as dull statistics. But economics is really about human behavior—how people decide to use scarce resources and how those decisions affect market outcomes.

The same relationship between individual behavior and aggregate behavior applies to specific outputs. If we as individuals insist on driving cars rather than taking public transportation, the economy will produce millions of cars each year and consume vast quantities of oil. In a slightly different way, the economy produces billions of dollars of military hardware to satisfy our desire for national defense. In each case, the output of the economy reflects the collective behavior of the 310 million individuals who participate in the U.S. economy.

We may not always be happy with the output of the economy. But we can't ignore the link between individual action and collective outcomes. If the highways are clogged and the air is polluted, we can't blame someone else for the transportation choices we made. If we're disturbed by the size of our military arsenal, we must still accept responsibility for our choices (or nonchoices, if we failed to vote). In either case, we continue to have the option of reallocating our resources. We can create a different outcome the next day, month, or year.

SCARCITY: THE CORE PROBLEM

Although we can change economic outcomes, we can't have everything we want. If you go to the mall with $20 in your pocket, you can buy only so much. The money in your pocket sets a *limit* to your spending.

The output of the entire economy is also limited. The limits in this case are set not by the amount of money in people's pockets, but by the resources available for producing goods and services. Everyone wants more housing, new schools, better transit systems, and a new car. We also want to explore space and bring safe water to the world's poor. But even a country as rich as the United States can't produce everything people want. So, like every other nation, we have to grapple with the core problem of **scarcity**—the fact that there aren't enough resources available to satisfy all our desires.

scarcity: Lack of enough resources to satisfy all desired uses of those resources.

factors of production: Resource inputs used to produce goods and services, such as land, labor, capital, and entrepreneurship.

Factors of Production

The resources used to produce goods and services are called **factors of production.** *The four basic factors of production are*

- *Land.*
- *Labor.*
- *Capital.*
- *Entrepreneurship.*

These are the *inputs* needed to produce desired *outputs*. To produce this textbook, for example, we needed paper, printing presses, a building, and lots of labor. We also needed people with good ideas who could put it together. To produce the education you're getting in this class, we need not only a textbook but a classroom, a teacher, a blackboard, and maybe a computer as well. Without factors of production, we simply can't produce anything.

Land. The first factor of production, land, refers not just to the ground but to all natural resources. Crude oil, water, air, and minerals are all included in our concept of "land."

Labor. Labor too has several dimensions. It's not simply a question of how many bodies there are. When we speak of labor as a factor of production, we refer to the skills and abilities to produce goods and services. Hence both the quantity and the quality of human resources are included in the "labor" factor.

Capital. The third factor of production is capital. In economics the term **capital** refers to final goods produced for use in further production. The residents of fishing villages in southern Thailand, for example, braid huge fishing nets. The sole purpose of these nets is to catch more fish. The nets themselves become a factor of production in obtaining the final goods (fish) that people desire. Thus they're regarded as *capital*. Blast furnaces used to make steel and desks used to equip offices are also capital inputs.

> **capital:** Final goods produced for use in the production of other goods, such as equipment and structures.

Entrepreneurship. The more land, labor, and capital available, the greater the amount of potential output. A farmer with 10,000 acres, 12 employees, and six tractors can grow more crops than a farmer with half those resources. But there's no guarantee that he will. The farmer with fewer resources may have better ideas about what to plant, when to irrigate, or how to harvest the crops. *It's not just a matter of what resources you have but also of how well you use them.* This is where the fourth factor of production—**entrepreneurship**—comes in. The entrepreneur is the person who sees the opportunity for new or better products and brings together the resources needed for producing them. If it weren't for entrepreneurs, Thai fishers would still be using sticks to catch fish. Without entrepreneurship, farmers would still be milking their cows by hand. If someone hadn't thought of a way to miniaturize electronic circuits, you wouldn't be able to text your friends.

> **entrepreneurship:** The assembling of resources to produce new or improved products and technologies.

The role of entrepreneurs in economic progress is a key issue in the market versus government debate. The British economist John Maynard Keynes argued that free markets unleash the "animal spirits" of entrepreneurs, propelling innovation, technology, and growth. Critics of government regulation argue that government interference in the marketplace, however well intentioned, tends to stifle those very same animal spirits.

Limits to Output

No matter how an economy is organized, there's a limit to how much it can produce. The most evident limit is the amount of resources available for producing goods and services. One reason the United States can produce so much is that it has nearly 4 million square miles of land. Tonga, with less than 300 square miles of land, will never produce as much. The United States also has a population of over 300 million people. That's a lot less than China (1.4 billion) but far larger than 200 other nations (Tonga has a population of less than 125,000). So an abundance of raw resources gives us the potential to produce a lot of output. But that greater production capacity isn't enough to satisfy all our desires. We're constantly scrambling for additional resources to build more houses, make better movies, and provide more health care. That imbalance between available resources and our wish list is one of the things that makes the job of Economist in Chief so difficult.

The science of **economics** helps us frame these choices. In a nutshell, economics is the study of how people use scarce resources. How do you decide how much time to spend studying? How does Google decide how many workers to hire? How does Ford decide whether to use its factories to produce sport utility vehicles or sedans? What

> **economics:** The study of how best to allocate scarce resources among competing uses.

share of a nation's resources should be devoted to space exploration, the delivery of health care services, or pollution control? In every instance, alternative ways of using scarce labor, land, and capital resources are available, and we have to choose one use over another.

OPPORTUNITY COSTS

Scientists have long sought to explore every dimension of space. President Kennedy initiated a lunar exploration program that successfully landed men on the moon on July 20, 1969. That only whetted the appetite for further space exploration. President George W. Bush initiated a program to land people on Mars, using the moon as a way station. Scientists believe that the biological, geophysical, and technical knowledge gained from the exploration of Mars will improve life here on Earth. But should we do it? In a world of unlimited resources the answer would be an easy "yes." But we don't live in that world.

Every time we use scarce resources in one way, we give up the opportunity to use them in other ways. If we use more resources to explore space, we have fewer resources available for producing earthly goods. The forgone earthly goods represent the **opportunity costs** of a Mars expedition. *Opportunity cost is what is given up to get something else.* Even a so-called free lunch has an opportunity cost (see the below cartoon). The resources used to produce the lunch could have been used to produce something else. A trip to Mars has a much higher opportunity cost. President Obama decided those opportunity costs were too high: he scaled back the Mars programs to make more resources available for Earthly uses (like highway construction and energy development).

Your economics class also has an opportunity cost. The building space used for your economics class can't be used to show movies at the same time. Your professor can't lecture (produce education) and repair motorcycles simultaneously. The decision to use these scarce resources (capital, labor) for an economics class implies producing less of other goods.

Even reading this book is costly. That cost is not measured in dollars and cents. The true (economic) cost is, instead, measured in terms of some alternative activity. What would you like to be doing right now? The more time you spend reading this book, the less time you have available for other uses of your time. The opportunity cost of reading this text is the best alternative use of your scarce time. If you are missing your favorite TV show, we'd say that show is the opportunity cost of reading this book. It is what you gave up to do this assignment. Hopefully, the benefits you get from studying will outweigh that cost. Otherwise this wouldn't be the best way to use your scarce time.

opportunity cost: The most desired goods or services that are forgone to obtain something else.

Opportunity Cost

"There's no such thing as a free lunch."

© Dana Fradon/The New Yorker Collection/ www.cartoonbank.com.

Analysis: All goods and services have an opportunity cost. Even the resources used to produce a "free lunch" could have been used to produce something else.

Guns vs. Butter

One of the persistent national choices about resource use entails defense spending. After the September 11, 2001, terrorist attacks on the World Trade Center and Pentagon, American citizens overwhelmingly favored an increase in military spending. Even the unpopularity of the war in Iraq didn't quell the desire for more national defense. But national defense, like Mars exploration, requires the use of scarce resources. The 1.4 million men and women who serve in the armed forces aren't available to build schools, program computers, or teach economics. Similarly, the land, labor, capital, and entrepreneurship devoted to producing military hardware aren't available for producing civilian goods. An *increase* in national defense implies still more sacrifices of civilian goods and services. How many schools, hospitals, or cars are we willing to sacrifice in order to "produce" more national security? This is the "guns versus butter" dilemma that all nations confront.

PRODUCTION POSSIBILITIES

The opportunity costs implied by our every choice can be illustrated easily. Suppose a nation can produce only two goods, trucks and tanks. To keep things simple, assume that labor (workers) is the only factor of production needed to produce either good. Although other factors of production (land, machinery) are also needed in actual production, ignoring them for the moment does no harm. Let us assume further that we have a total of only 10 workers available per day to produce either trucks or tanks. Our initial problem is to determine the *limits* of output. How many trucks or tanks *can* be produced in a day with available resources?

Before going any further, notice how opportunity costs will affect the answer. If we use all 10 workers to produce trucks, no labor will be available to assemble tanks. In this case, forgone tanks would become the *opportunity cost* of a decision to employ all our resources in truck production.

We still don't know how many trucks could be produced with 10 workers or exactly how many tanks would be forgone by such a decision. To get these answers, we need more details about the production processes involved—specifically, how many workers are required to manufacture either good.

The Production Possibilities Curve

Table 1.1 summarizes the hypothetical choices, or **production possibilities,** that we confront in this case. Suppose we wanted to produce only trucks (i.e., no tanks). Row *A* of the table shows the *maximum* number of trucks we could produce. With 10 workers available and a labor requirement of 2 workers per truck, we can manufacture a maximum of five trucks per day.

Producing five trucks per day leaves no workers available to produce tanks. Our 10 available workers are all being used to produce trucks. On row *A* of Table 1.1 we've got "butter" but no "guns." If we want tanks, we'll have to cut back on truck production. The remainder

production possibilities:
The alternative combinations of final goods and services that could be produced in a given time period with all available resources and technology.

TABLE 1.1
A Production Possibilities Schedule

As long as resources are limited, their use entails an opportunity cost. In this case, resources (labor) used to produce trucks can't be used for tank assembly at the same time. Hence the forgone tanks are the opportunity cost of additional trucks. If all our resources were used to produce trucks (row *A*), no tanks could be assembled. To produce tanks, we have to reduce truck production.

		Production Options	
		Output of Trucks per Day	Output of Tanks per Day
	A	5	0
	B	4	2.0
	C	3	3.0
	D	2	3.8
	E	1	4.5
	F	0	5.0

of Table 1.1 illustrates the trade-offs we confront in this simple case. By cutting back truck production from five to four trucks per day (row *B*), we reduce labor use in truck production from 10 workers to 8. That leaves 2 workers available for other uses, including the production of tanks.

If we employ these remaining 2 workers to assemble tanks, we'll assume we can build two tanks a day. We would then end up on row *B* of the table with four trucks and two tanks per day. What's the opportunity cost of these two tanks? It's the one additional truck (the fifth truck) that we could have produced but didn't.

As we proceed down the rows of Table 1.1, the nature of opportunity costs becomes apparent. Each additional tank built implies the loss (opportunity cost) of truck output. Likewise, every truck produced implies the loss of some tank output.

These trade-offs between truck and tank production are illustrated in the production possibilities curve of Figure 1.1. ***Each point on the production possibilities curve depicts an alternative mix of output*** that could be produced. In this case, each point represents a different combination of trucks and tanks that we could produce in a single day using all available resources (10 workers in this case).

Notice in particular how points *A* through *F* in Figure 1.1 represent the choices described in each row of Table 1.1. At point *A*, we're producing five trucks per day and no tanks. As we move down the curve from point *A* we're producing fewer trucks and more tanks. At point *B*, truck production has dropped from five to four vehicles per day while tank assembly has increased from zero to two. In other words, we've given up one truck to get two tanks assembled. The opportunity cost of those tanks is the one truck that is given up. A production possibilities curve, then, is simply a graphic summary of production possibilities, as described in Table 1.1. As such, ***the production possibilities curve illustrates two essential principles:***

- ***Scarce resources.*** There's a limit to the amount of output we can produce in a given time period with available resources and technology.
- ***Opportunity costs.*** We can obtain additional quantities of any particular good only by reducing the potential production of another good.

FIGURE 1.1

A Production Possibilities Curve

A production possibilities curve (PPC) describes the various output combinations that could be produced in a given time period with available resources and technology. It represents a menu of output choices an economy confronts.

Point *B* indicates that we could produce a *combination* of four trucks and two tanks per day. By producing one less truck, we could assemble a third tank and thus move to point *C*.

Points *A*, *D*, *E*, and *F* illustrate still other output combinations that could be produced. This curve is a graphic illustration of the production possibilities schedule in Table 1.1.

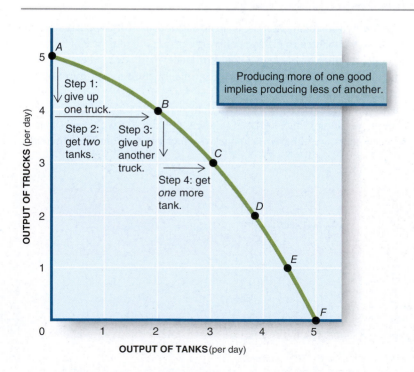

Increasing Opportunity Costs

The shape of the production possibilities curve reflects another limitation on our choices. Notice how opportunity costs increase as we move along the production possibilities curve. When we cut truck output from five to four (step 1, Figure 1.1), we get two tanks (step 2). When we cut truck production further, however (step 3), we get only one tank per truck given up (step 4). The opportunity cost of tank production is increasing. This process of increasing opportunity cost continues. By the time we give up the last truck (row *F*), tank output increases by only 0.5: we get only half a tank for the last truck given up. These increases in opportunity cost are reflected in the outward bend of the production possibilities curve.

Why do opportunity costs increase? Mostly because it's difficult to move resources from one industry to another. It's easy to transform trucks to tanks on a blackboard. In the real world, however, resources don't adapt so easily. Workers who assemble trucks may not have the right skills for tank assembly. As we continue to transfer labor from one industry to the other, we start getting fewer tanks for every truck we give up.

The difficulties entailed in transferring labor skills, capital, and entrepreneurship from one industry to another are so universal that we often speak of the *law* of *increasing opportunity cost*. This law says that we must give up ever-increasing quantities of other goods and services in order to get more of a particular good. The law isn't based solely on the limited versatility of individual workers. The *mix* of factor inputs makes a difference as well. Truck assembly requires less capital than tank assembly. In a pinch, wheels can be mounted on a truck almost completely by hand, whereas tank treads require more sophisticated machinery. As we move labor from truck assembly to tank assembly, available capital may restrict our output capabilities.

The Cost of North Korea's Military

The production possibilities curve illustrates why the core economic decision about WHAT to produce is so difficult. Consider, for example, North Korea's decision to maintain a large military. North Korea is a relatively small country: its population of 24 million ranks fortieth in the world. Yet North Korea maintains the fourth-largest army in the world and continues to develop a nuclear weapons capability. To do so, it must allocate 16 percent of all its resources to feeding, clothing, and equipping its military forces. As a consequence, there aren't enough resources available to produce food. Without adequate machinery, seeds, fertilizer, or irrigation, Korea's farmers can't produce enough food to feed the population (see the World View on the next page). As Figure 1.2 illustrates, the opportunity cost of "guns" in Korea is a lot of needed "butter."

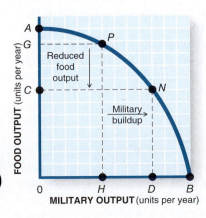

FIGURE 1.2
The Cost of War

North Korea devotes 16 percent of its output to the military. The opportunity cost of this decision is reduced output of food. As the military expands from 0*H* to 0*D*, food output drops from 0*G* to 0*C*.

WORLD VIEW

Chronic Food Shortage Shows Despite Efforts by North Korea to Hide It

NAMPO, North Korea—Along the sides of the road, people comb through the grass looking for edible weeds. In the center of town, a boy about 9 years old wears a tattered army jacket hanging below his knees. He has no shoes.

Sprawled on the lawn outside a bath house, poorly dressed people lie on the grass, either with no place better to go or no energy to do so at 10 a.m. on a weekday.

Despite efforts to keep North Korea's extreme poverty out of view, a glance around the countryside shows a population in distress. At the heart of the problem is a chronic food shortage. . . .

The UN World Food Program reached similar conclusions. In a recent survey of 375 North Korean households, more than 70 percent of North Koreans were found to be supplementing their diet with weeds and grasses foraged from the countryside. Such wild foods are difficult to digest, especially for children and the elderly.

The survey also determined that most adults had started skipping lunch, reducing their diet to two meals a day to cope with the food shortage.

These are some of the same signs that augured the mid-1990s famine that killed as many as 2 million people, 10 percent of the population.

—Barbara Demick

Source: "Hunger gnaws at N. Korea's facade," *Los Angeles Times*, November 2, 2008. Used with permission.

Rocket Launch Cost Enough to End Famine in North Korea for a Year

SEOUL—The rocket launched by North Korea on Sunday is believed to be an upgraded version of the country's Taepodong-2 missile, which was used in a failed missile test in 2006, according to a report by the South Korean military. . . .

A researcher at the National Intelligence Service estimated the cost of developing the missile at 300–500 million dollars, based on a previous statement by North Korean leader Kim Jong Il that the Taepodong-1 missile launched in 1998 cost 200–300 million dollars.

Insiders close to South Korean President Lee Myung-bak say the launch itself cost around 300 million dollars, enough to break the famine sweeping much of the nation for a year.

Source: *The Mainichi Daily News*, April 6, 2009. Used with permission.

Analysis: North Korea's inability to feed itself is partly due to maintaining its large army: resources used for the military aren't available for producing food.

During World War II, the United States confronted a similar trade-off. In 1944 nearly 40 percent of all U.S. output was devoted to the military. Civilian goods were so scarce that they had to be rationed. Staples like butter, sugar, and gasoline were doled out in small quantities. Even golf balls were rationed. In North Korea, golf balls would be a luxury even without a military buildup. As the share of North Korea's output devoted to the military increased, even basic food production became more difficult.

Figure 1.3 illustrates how other nations divide available resources between military and civilian production. The $740 billion the United States now spends on national defense absorbs only 4.7 percent of total output. This made the opportunity costs of the post-9/11 military buildup and the wars in Iraq and Afghanistan less painful.

Efficiency

Not all of the choices on the production possibilities curve are equally desirable. They are, however, all *efficient*. Efficiency means squeezing *maximum* output out of available resources. Every point of the PPC satisfies this condition. Although the *mix* of output changes as we move around the production possibilities curve (Figures 1.1 and 1.2), at every point we are getting as much *total* output as physically possible. Since **efficiency** in

efficiency: Maximum output of a good from the resources used in production.

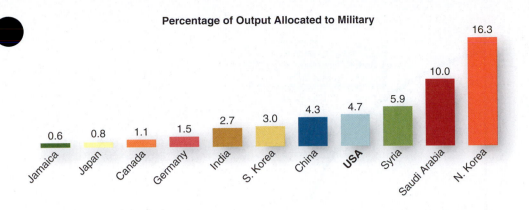

Percentage of Output Allocated to Military

Jamaica 0.6 | Japan 0.8 | Canada 1.1 | Germany 1.5 | India 2.7 | S. Korea 3.0 | China 4.3 | USA 4.7 | Syria 5.9 | Saudi Arabia 10.0 | N. Korea 16.3

FIGURE 1.3
The Military Share of Output

The share of total output allocated to the military indicates the opportunity cost of maintaining an army. North Korea has the highest cost, using 16 percent of its resources for military purposes. Although China and the United States have much larger armies, their military *share* of output is much smaller.

Source: U.S. Central Intelligence Agency (*WorldFactbook*, 2011).

production means simply getting the most from what you've got, **every point on the production possibilities curve is efficient.** At every point on the curve we are using all available resources in the best way we know how.

Inefficiency

There's no guarantee, of course, that we'll always use resources so efficiently. *A production possibilities curve shows* **potential** *output, not necessarily* **actual** *output.* If we're inefficient, actual output will be less than that potential. This happens. In the real world, workers sometimes loaf on the job. Or they call in sick and go to a baseball game instead of working. Managers don't always give the clearest directions or stay in touch with advancing technology. Even students sometimes fail to put forth their best effort on homework assignments. This kind of slippage can prevent us from achieving maximum production. When that happens, we end up *inside* the PPC rather than *on* it.

Point *Y* in Figure 1.4 illustrates the consequences of inefficient production. At point *Y*, we're producing only three trucks and two tanks. This is less than our potential. We could assemble a third tank without cutting back truck production (point *C*). Or we could get an extra truck without sacrificing any tank output (point *B*). Instead we're producing *inside* the production possibilities curve at point *Y*. Whenever we're producing inside the production possibilities curve, we are forgoing the opportunity of producing (and consuming) additional output.

Unemployment

We can end up inside the production possibilities curve by utilizing resources inefficiently or simply by not using all available resources. This happened in 2008–2010. In mid 2011, 14 million Americans were still unemployed (see the News below). These men and women

FIGURE 1.4
Points Inside and Outside the PPC Curve

Points outside the production possibilities curve (point *X*) are unattainable with available resources and technology. Points inside the PPC (point *Y*) represent the incomplete use of available resources. Only points on the PPC (*A, B, C*) represent maximum use of our production capabilities.

IN THE NEWS

Job Market Loses Momentum

Employers spooked by a sputtering economy hit the brakes on hiring last month, postponing the upswing needed to put 14 million unemployed Americans back to work.

The government's snapshot of the labor market showed the U.S. added only 54,000 jobs in May, the fewest since September. With employment gains failing to keep up with a growing population and people re-entering the work force, the unemployment rate ticked up to 9.1%, from 9% in April.

—Justin Lahart

Source: *The Wall Street Journal*, www.wsj.com, June 4, 2011, p. A1. Used with permission of Dow Jones & Company, Inc. via Copyright Clearance Center, Inc.

Analysis: In the years 2008–2011 the U.S. economy was producing *inside* its production possibilities curve (like point *Y* in Figure 1.4), leaving millions of workers jobless.

Growth: Increasing Production Possibilities

A production possibilities curve is based on *available* resources and technology. If more resources or better technology becomes available, production possibilities will increase. This economic growth is illustrated by the shift from PP_1 to PP_2.

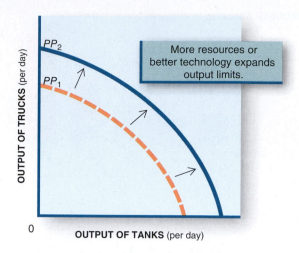

economic growth: An increase in output (real GDP); an expansion of production possibilities.

were ready, willing, and available to work, but no one hired them. As a result, we were stuck *inside* the PPC, producing less output than we could have. The goal of U.S. economic policy was to create more jobs and get the United States back on its production possibilities curve.

Economic Growth

The challenge of getting to the production possibilities curve increases with each passing day. People are born every day. As they age, they enter the labor force as new workers. Technology, too, keeps advancing each year. These increases in available labor and technology keep pushing the producing possibilities curve outward. This **economic growth** is a good thing in the sense that it allows us to produce more goods and raise living standards. But it also means that we have to keep creating more jobs every year just to stay on the PPC.

Figures 1.4 and 1.5 illustrate how economic growth raises our living standards. Point X in Figure 1.4 lies outside the PPC. It is an enticing point because it suggests we could get more trucks (five) without sacrificing any tanks (two). Unfortunately, point X is only a mirage. *All output combinations that lie outside the PPC are unattainable in the short run.*

In the long run, however, resources and technology increase, shifting the PPC outward, as in Figure 1.5. Before the appearance of new resources or better technology, our production possibilities were limited by the curve PP_1. *With more resources or better technology, our production possibilities increase.* This greater capacity to produce is represented by curve PP_2. This outward shift of the production possibilities curve is the essence of economic growth. With economic growth, countries can have more guns *and* more butter. Without economic growth, living standards decline as the population grows. This is the problem that plagues some of the world's poorest nations, where population increases every year but output often doesn't (see Table 2.1).

THREE BASIC DECISIONS

Production possibilities define the output choices that a nation confronts. From these choices every nation must make some basic decisions. As we noted at the beginning of this chapter, the three core economic questions are

- *WHAT to produce.*
- *HOW to produce.*
- *FOR WHOM to produce.*

WHAT

There are millions of points along a production possibilities curve, and each one represents a different mix of output. We can choose only *one* of these points at any time. The point we choose determines what mix of output gets produced. That choice determines how many guns are produced, and how much butter—or how many space expeditions and how many sewage treatment facilities.

The production possibilities curve doesn't tell us which mix of output is best; it just lays out a menu of available choices. It's up to us to pick out the one and only mix of output that will be produced at a given time. This WHAT decision is a basic decision every nation must make.

HOW

Decisions must also be made about HOW to produce. Should we generate electricity by burning coal, smashing atoms, or harnessing solar power? Should we harvest ancient forests even if that destroys endangered owls or other animal species? Should we dump municipal and industrial waste into nearby rivers, or should we dispose of it in some other way? Should we use children to harvest crops and stitch clothes, or should we use only adult labor? There are lots of different ways of producing goods and services, and someone has to make a decision about which production methods to use. The HOW decision is a question not just of efficiency but of social values as well.

FOR WHOM

After we've decided what to produce and how, we must address a third basic question: FOR WHOM? Who is going to get the output produced? Should everyone get an equal share? Should everyone wear the same clothes and drive identical cars? Should some people get to enjoy seven-course banquets while others forage in garbage cans for food scraps? How should the goods and services an economy produces be distributed? Are we satisfied with the way output is now distributed?

THE MECHANISMS OF CHOICE

Answers to the questions of WHAT, HOW, and FOR WHOM largely define an economy. But who formulates the answers? Who actually decides which goods are produced, what technologies are used, or how incomes are distributed?

The Invisible Hand of a Market Economy

Adam Smith had an answer back in 1776. In his classic work *The Wealth of Nations,* the Scottish economist Smith said the "invisible hand" determines what gets produced, how, and for whom. The invisible hand he referred to wasn't a creature from a science fiction movie but, instead, a characterization of the way markets work.

Consider the decision about how many cars to produce in the United States. Who makes that decision? There's no "auto czar" who dictates how many vehicles will be produced this year. Not even General Motors can make such a decision. Instead the *market* decides how many cars to produce. Millions of consumers signal their desire to have a car by browsing the Internet, visiting showrooms, and buying cars. Their purchases flash a green light to producers, who see the potential to earn more profits. To do so, they'll increase auto output. If consumers stop buying cars, profits will disappear. Producers will respond by reducing output, laying off workers, and even closing factories as they did in 2008–2009.

Notice how the invisible hand moves us along the production possibilities curve. If consumers demand more cars, the mix of output will include more cars and fewer of other

market mechanism: The use of market prices and sales to signal desired outputs (or resource allocations).

goods. If auto production is scaled back, the displaced autoworkers will end up producing other goods and services, changing the mix of output in the opposite direction.

Adam Smith's invisible hand is now called the **market mechanism.** Notice that it doesn't require any direct contact between consumers and producers. Communication is indirect, transmitted by market prices and sales. Indeed, *the essential feature of the market mechanism is the price signal.* If you want something and have sufficient income, you can buy it. If enough people do the same thing, the total sales of that product will rise, and perhaps its price will as well. Producers, seeing sales and prices rise, will want to exploit this profit potential. To do so, they'll attempt to acquire a larger share of available resources and use it to produce the goods we desire. That's how the "invisible hand" works.

The market mechanism can also answer the HOW question. To maximize their profits, producers seek the lowest-cost method of producing a good. By observing prices in the marketplace, they can identify the cheapest method and adopt it.

The market mechanism can also resolve the FOR WHOM question. A market distributes goods to the highest bidder. Individuals who are willing and able to pay the most for a product tend to get it in a pure market economy.

Adam Smith was so impressed with the ability of the market mechanism to answer the basic WHAT, HOW, and FOR WHOM questions that he urged government to "leave it alone" **(laissez faire).** In his view, the price signals and responses of the marketplace were likely to do a better job of allocating resources than any government could.

laissez faire: The doctrine of "leave it alone," of nonintervention by government in the market mechanism.

Government Intervention

The laissez-faire policy Adam Smith favored has always had its share of critics. The German economist Karl Marx emphasized how free markets tend to concentrate wealth and power in the hands of the few at the expense of the many. As he saw it, unfettered markets permit the capitalists (those who own the machinery and factories) to enrich themselves while the proletariat (the workers) toil long hours for subsistence wages. Marx argued that the government not only had to intervene but had to *own* all the means of production—the factories, the machinery, the land—in order to avoid savage inequalities. In *Das Kapital* (1867) and the revolutionary *Communist Manifesto* (1848), he laid the foundation for a communist state in which the government would be the master of economic outcomes.

The British economist John Maynard Keynes offered a less drastic solution. The market, he conceded, was pretty efficient in organizing production and building better mousetraps. However, individual producers and workers had no control over the broader economy. The cumulative actions of so many economic agents could easily tip the economy in the wrong direction. A completely unregulated market might veer off in one direction and then another as producers all rushed to increase output at the same time or throttled back production in a herdlike manner. The government, Keynes reasoned, could act like a pressure gauge, letting off excess steam or building it up as the economy needed. With the government maintaining overall balance in the economy, the market could live up to its performance expectations. While assuring a stable, full-employment environment, the government might also be able to redress excessive inequalities. In Keynes's view, government should play an active but not all-inclusive role in managing the economy.

Continuing Debates

These historical views shed perspective on today's political debates. The core of most debates is some variation of the WHAT, HOW, or FOR WHOM questions. Much of the debate is how these questions should be answered. Conservatives favor Adam Smith's laissez-faire approach, with minimal government interference in the markets. Liberals, by contrast, think government intervention is needed to improve market outcomes. Conservatives resist

WORLD VIEW

Market Reliance vs. Government Reliance?

A public opinion poll conducted in countries from around the world found a striking global consensus that the free market economic system is best. In all but one country polled, a majority or plurality agreed with the statement that "the free enterprise system and free market economy is the best system on which to base the future of the world."

Source: GlobeScan Toronto—London—San Francisco 2010.

The free enterprise system and free market economy is the best system on which to base the future of the world.

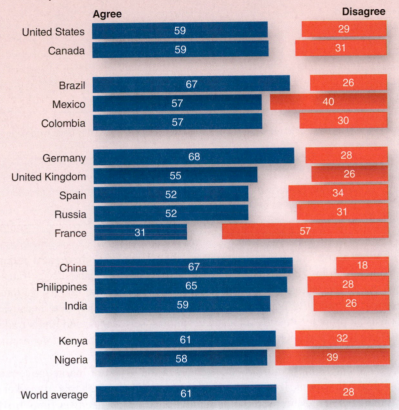

	Agree	Disagree
United States	59	29
Canada	59	31
Brazil	67	26
Mexico	57	40
Colombia	57	30
Germany	68	28
United Kingdom	55	26
Spain	52	34
Russia	52	31
France	31	57
China	67	18
Philippines	65	28
India	59	26
Kenya	61	32
Nigeria	58	39
World average	61	28

web analysis

Comparative data on the percentage of goods and services the various national governments provide are available from the Penn World Tables at **www.pwt.econ.upenn.edu**.

Analysis: People around the world believe that markets can do a good job of fostering economic growth.

workplace regulation, price controls, and minimum wages because such interventions might impair market efficiency. Liberals argue that such interventions temper the excesses of the market and promote both equity and efficiency.

The debate over how best to manage the economy is not unique to the United States. Countries around the world confront the same choice between reliance on the market and reliance on the government. Public opinion clearly favors the market system, as the above World View documents. Yet few countries have ever relied exclusively on either the markets or the government to manage their economy.

WORLD VIEW

Index of Economic Freedom

Hong Kong ranks number one among the world's nations in economic freedom. It achieves that status with low tax rates, free-trade policies, minimal government regulation, and secure property rights. These and other economic indicators place Hong Kong at the top of the Heritage Foundation's 2011 country rankings by the degree of "economic freedom." The "most free" and the "least free" (repressed) economies on the list of 179 countries are listed here:

Greatest Economic Freedom	Least Economic Freedom
Hong Kong	North Korea
Singapore	Zimbabwe
Australia	Cuba
New Zealand	Eritrea
Switzerland	Venezuela
Canada	Myanmar (Burma)
Ireland	Libya
Denmark	Congo
United States	Iran
Bahrain	Timor-Leste

Source: Heritage Foundation, *2011 Index of Economic Freedom,* Washington, DC, 2011. Used with permission. **www.heritage.org**.

Analysis: Nations differ in how much they rely on market signals or government intervention to shape economic outcomes. Nations that rely the least on government intervention score highest ("most free") on this Index of Economic Freedom.

web analysis

To learn how the Heritage Foundation defines economic freedom, visit its website at **www.heritage.org/index**.

The World View above categorizes nations by the extent of their market reliance. Hong Kong scores high on this "Index of Economic Freedom" because its tax rates are relatively low, the public sector is comparatively small, and there are few restrictions on private investment or trade. By contrast, North Korea scores extremely low because the government owns all property, directly allocates resources, sets wages, and limits trade. In other words, Hong Kong is the most market-reliant; North Korea is the most government-reliant.

The Heritage rankings simply *describe* differences in the extent of market/government reliance across different nations. By themselves, they don't tell us which mix of market and government reliance is best. Moreover, the individual rankings change over time. In 1989 Russia began a massive transformation from a state-controlled economy to a more market-oriented economy. Some of the former republics (e.g., Estonia) became relatively free, while others (e.g., Turkmenistan) still rely on extensive government control of the economy. China has greatly expanded the role of private markets in the last 20 years, and Cuba is moving in the same direction in fits and starts.

In the United States, the changes have been less dramatic. The most notable shift was President Franklin Roosevelt's New Deal, which greatly expanded the government's role in the economy. In more recent times, the tug-of-war between laissez faire and government intervention has been much less decisive. Although President Reagan often said that "government *is* the problem," he hardly made a dent in government growth during the eight years of his presidency. Likewise, President Clinton's very different conviction that the government can *fix* problems, not cause them, had only minor effects on the size and scope of government activity. President George W. Bush not only lowered taxes but also lessened government regulation of HOW goods are produced. By the time President Obama took office, the economy was in such a mess that people demanded more government intervention to help fix the market's problems.

A Mixed Economy

No one advocates *complete* dependence on markets, nor *total* government control of economic resources. Neither Adam Smith's invisible hand nor the governments' very visible hand always works perfectly. As a result, *the United States, like most nations, uses a combination of market signals and government directives to direct economic outcomes.* The resulting compromises are called **mixed economies.**

The reluctance of countries around the world to rely exclusively on either market signals or government directives is due to the recognition that both mechanisms can and do fail on occasion. As we've seen, market signals are capable of answering the three core questions of WHAT, HOW, and FOR WHOM. But the answers may not be the best possible ones.

mixed economy: An economy that uses both market signals and government directives to allocate goods and resources.

Market Failure

When market signals don't give the best possible answers to the WHAT, HOW, and FOR WHOM questions, we say that the market mechanism has *failed.* Specifically, **market failure** means that the invisible hand has failed to achieve the best possible outcomes. If the market fails, we end up with the wrong (*sub*optimal) mix of output, too much unemployment, polluted air, or an inequitable distribution of income.

In a market-driven economy, for example, producers will select production methods based on cost. Cost-driven production decisions, however, may encourage a factory to spew pollution into the environment rather than to use cleaner but more expensive methods of production. The resulting pollution may be so bad that society ends up worse off as a result of the extra production. In such a case we may need government intervention to force better answers to the WHAT and HOW questions.

We could also let the market decide who gets to consume cigarettes. Anyone who had enough money to buy a pack of cigarettes would then be entitled to smoke. What if, however, children aren't experienced enough to balance the risks of smoking against the pleasures? What if nonsmokers are harmed by secondhand smoke? In this case as well, the market's answer to the FOR WHOM question might not be optimal.

market failure: An imperfection in the market mechanism that prevents optimal outcomes.

Government Failure

Government intervention may move us closer to our economic goals. If so, the resulting mix of market signals and government directives would be an improvement over a purely market-driven economy. But government intervention may fail as well. **Government failure** occurs when government intervention fails to improve market outcomes or actually makes them worse.

Government failure often occurs in unintended ways. For example, the government may intervene to force an industry to clean up its pollution. The government's directives may impose such high costs that the industry closes factories and lays off workers. Some cutbacks in output might be appropriate, but they could also prove excessive. The government might also mandate pollution control technologies that are too expensive or even obsolete. None of this has to happen, but it might. If it does, government failure will have worsened economic outcomes.

The government might also fail if it interferes with the market's answer to the FOR WHOM question. For 50 years, communist China distributed goods by government directive, not market performance. Incomes were more equal, but uniformly low. To increase output and living standards, China turned to market incentives. As entrepreneurs responded to these incentives, living standards rose dramatically—even while inequality increased. That surge in living standards made the vast majority of Chinese believers in the power of free markets (see the World View on page 15).

Excessive taxes and transfer payments can also worsen economic outcomes. If the government raises taxes on the rich to pay welfare benefits for the poor, neither the rich nor the poor may see much purpose in working. In that case, the attempt to give everybody a "fair" share of the pie might end up shrinking the size of the pie. If that happened, society could end up worse off.

government failure: Government intervention that fails to improve economic outcomes.

Seeking Balance

None of these failures has to occur. But they might. *The challenge for society is to minimize economic failures by selecting the appropriate balance of market signals and government directives.* This isn't an easy task. It requires that we know how markets work and why they sometimes fail. We also need to know what policy options the government has and how and when they might work.

WHAT ECONOMICS IS ALL ABOUT

Understanding how economies function is the basic purpose of studying economics. We seek to know how an economy is organized, how it behaves, and how successfully it achieves its basic objectives. Then, if we're lucky, we can discover better ways of attaining those same objectives.

Ends vs. Means

Economists don't formulate an economy's objectives. Instead they focus on the *means* available for achieving given *goals*. In 1978, for example, the U.S. Congress identified "full employment" as a major economic goal. Congress then directed future presidents (and their economic advisers) to formulate policies that would enable us to achieve full employment. The economist's job is to help design policies that will best achieve this and other economic goals.

Normative vs. Positive Analysis

The distinction between ends and means is mirrored in the difference between *normative* analysis and *positive* analysis. Normative analysis incorporates subjective judgments about what *ought* to be done. Positive analysis focuses on how things might be done without subjective judgments of what is "best." The Heritage Index of Economic Freedom (World View, page 16), for example, constitutes a *positive* analysis to the extent that it objectively describes global differences in the extent of market reliance. That effort entails collecting, sorting, and ranking mountains of data. Heritage slides into *normative* analysis when it suggests that market reliance is tantamount to "economic freedom" and inherently superior to more government intervention—that markets are good and governments are bad.

Debates over the core FOR WHOM question likewise reflect both positive and normative analysis. A positive analysis would observe that the U.S. incomes are very "unequal," with the richest 20 percent of the population getting half of all income (see Figure 2.3). That's an observable fact—that is, positive analysis. To characterize that same distribution as "inequitable" or "unfair" is to transform (positive) fact into (normative) judgment. Economists are free, of course, to offer their judgments but must be careful to distinguish positive and normative perspectives.

Macro vs. Micro

macroeconomics: The study of aggregate economic behavior, of the economy as a whole.

The study of economics is typically divided into two parts: macroeconomics and microeconomics. **Macroeconomics** focuses on the behavior of an entire economy—the 'big picture.' In macroeconomics we worry about such national goals as full employment, control of inflation, and economic growth, without worrying about the well-being or behavior of specific individuals or groups. The essential concern of macroeconomics is to understand and improve the performance of the economy as a whole.

microeconomics: The study of individual behavior in the economy, of the components of the larger economy.

Microeconomics is concerned with the details of this big picture. In microeconomics we focus on the individuals, firms, and government agencies that actually compose the larger economy. Our interest here is in the behavior of individual economic actors. What are their goals? How can they best achieve these goals with their limited resources? How will they respond to various incentives and opportunities?

A primary concern of *macro*economics, for example, is to determine how much money, *in total,* consumers will spend on goods and services. In *micro*economics, the focus is much narrower. In micro, attention is paid to purchases of *specific* goods and services rather than just aggregated totals. Macro likewise concerns itself with the level of *total* business investment, while micro examines how *individual* businesses make their investment decisions.

Although they operate at different levels of abstraction, macro and micro are intrinsically related. Macro (aggregate) outcomes depend on micro behavior, and micro (individual) behavior is affected by macro outcomes. One can't fully understand how an economy works until one understands how all the individual participants behave. But just as you can drive a car without knowing how its engine is constructed, you can observe how an economy runs without completely disassembling it. In macroeconomics we observe that the car goes faster when the accelerator is depressed and that it slows when the brake is applied. That's all we need to know in most situations. At times, however, the car breaks down. When it does, we have to know something more about how the pedals work. This leads us into micro studies. How does each part work? Which ones can or should be fixed?

Our interest in microeconomics is motivated by more than our need to understand how the larger economy works. The "parts" of the economic engine are people. To the extent that we care about the well-being of individuals, we have a fundamental interest in microeconomic behavior and outcomes. In this regard, we examine how individual consumers and business firms seek to achieve specific goals in the marketplace. The goals aren't always related to output. Gary Becker won the 1992 Nobel Prize in Economics for demonstrating how economic principles also affect decisions to marry, to have children, to engage in criminal activities—or even to complete homework assignments in an economics class.

Theory vs. Reality

The distinction between macroeconomics and microeconomics is one of many simplifications we make in studying economic behavior. The economy is much too vast and complex to describe and explain in one course (or one lifetime). Accordingly, we focus on basic relationships, ignoring annoying detail. In so doing, we isolate basic principles of economic behavior and then use those principles to predict economic events and develop economic policies. This means that we formulate theories, or *models,* of economic behavior and then use those theories to evaluate and design economic policy.

Our model of consumer behavior assumes, for example, that people buy less of a good when its price rises. In reality, however, people *may* buy *more* of a good at increased prices, especially if those high prices create a certain snob appeal or if prices are expected to increase still further. In predicting consumer responses to price increases, we typically ignore such possibilities by *assuming* that the price of the good in question is the *only* thing that changes. This assumption of "other things remaining equal" (unchanged) (in Latin, *ceteris paribus*) allows us to make straightforward predictions. If instead we described consumer responses to increased prices in any and all circumstances (allowing everything to change at once), every prediction would be accompanied by a book full of exceptions and qualifications. We'd look more like lawyers than economists.

ceteris paribus: The assumption of nothing else changing.

Although the assumption of *ceteris paribus* makes it easier to formulate economic theory and policy, it also increases the risk of error. If other things do change in significant ways, our predictions (and policies) may fail. But like weather forecasters, we continue to make predictions, knowing that occasional failure is inevitable. In so doing, we're motivated by the conviction that it's better to be approximately right than to be dead wrong.

Politics. Politicians can't afford to be quite so complacent about economic predictions. Policy decisions must be made every day. And a politician's continued survival may depend on being more than approximately right. Barack Obama won votes in 2008 by tying his opponent's economic views to those of President George W. Bush. He argued that Senator John McCain, like President Bush, was too optimistic about the ability of markets to self-correct. He insisted that more government intervention was needed to get the economy back on track.

After he took office, President Obama introduced a massive stimulus program of tax cuts and increased government spending, especially on infrastructure (roads, rails, bridges, etc.). Were these the right choices? Economic theory can't completely answer that question. Choices about the mix of output are ultimately political—decisions that must take into account not only economic trade-offs (opportunity costs) but also social values. "Politics"—the balancing of competing interests—is an inevitable ingredient of economic policy.

Imperfect Knowledge. One last word of warning before you read further. Economics claims to be a science in pursuit of basic truths. We want to understand and explain how the economy works without getting tangled up in subjective value judgments. This may be an impossible task. First, it's not clear where the truth lies. For more than 200 years economists have been arguing about what makes the economy tick. None of the competing theories has performed spectacularly well. Indeed, few economists have successfully predicted major economic events with any consistency. Even annual forecasts of inflation, unemployment, and output are regularly in error. Worse still, never-ending arguments about what caused a major economic event continue long after it occurs. In fact, economists are still arguing over the primary causes of the Great Depression of the 1930s!

In view of all these debates and uncertainties, don't expect to learn everything there is to know about the economy today in this text or course. Our goals are more modest. We want to develop a reasonable perspective on economic behavior, an understanding of basic principles. With this foundation, you should acquire a better view of how the economy works. Daily news reports on economic events should make more sense. Congressional debates on tax and budget policies should take on more meaning. You may even develop some insights that you can apply toward running a business, planning a career, or simply managing your scarce time and money more efficiently.

THE ECONOMY TOMORROW

HARNESSING THE SUN

Powering our homes with solar power is an exciting prospect. At present, over 50 percent of our electricity is generated from the burning of oil and coal. These fossil fuels pollute the air, damage the land, and, as we saw in the 2010 BP oil spill, damage marine life as well. By contrast, we don't have to burn anything to generate solar power. We just need to harness that power by absorbing it in solar panels that convert solar radiation into electricity. The U.S. Department of the Interior says solar stations built in the deserts of the southwestern states could deliver 2,300 gigawatts of energy, more than double America's entire electricity consumption. The substitution of solar power for fossil fuels would also reduce America's enormous dependence on imported oil.

Solar power could also be used to fuel our cars. When automakers peer into the future, they see fleets of electric cars. Those fleets will have to be continuously charged with electricity. Why not solar-powered recharging stations? Just think how much that gasoline-to-solar conversion would help clean up the air we breathe!

Opportunity Costs

It's hard not to get excited about a solar-powered future. But before we jump on the solar bandwagon, we have to at least consider the costs involved. Sure, the sun's rays are free. But you need a lot of capital investment to harness that solar power. Solar panels on the roof don't come free. Nor do solar-powered electrical charging stations, solar power plants, or the electrical grids that distribute electricity to users. President Obama set aside $300 million in the 2011 budget as a mere down payment on the development of solar power. The full-scale development of solar power infrastructure would cost *trillions* of dollars.

web analysis

The largest solar thermal power station in the United States is located in the Mojave Desert of California. For more information, see the National Renewable Energy Laboratory (NREL) at **www.nrel.gov,** then click the "Science and Technology" tab.

Remember, economists think in terms of real resources, not money. Paper money doesn't build solar panels; it takes real factors of production—land, labor, capital, and entrepreneurship. Those resources—worth trillions of dollars—could be used to produce something else. If we invested that many resources in medical technology, we might cure cancer, find an antidote for the AIDS virus, and maybe even eradicate the flu. Investing that many resources in education might make college not only more enjoyable but a lot more productive as well. To invest all those resources in solar development implies that solar development trumps all other social goals. In deciding whether and how intensively to develop solar power, we have to assess opportunity costs—what goods and services we implicitly forsake in order to harness the sun.

SUMMARY

- Scarcity is a basic fact of economic life. Factors of production (land, labor, capital, entrepreneurship) are scarce in relation to our desires for goods and services.   LO1-1
- All economic activity entails opportunity costs. Factors of production (resources) used to produce one output cannot simultaneously be used to produce something else. When we choose to produce one thing, we forsake the opportunity to produce some other good or service.   LO1-1
- A production possibilities curve (PPC) illustrates the limits to production—the various combinations of goods and services that could be produced in a given period if all available resources and technology are used efficiently. The PPC also illustrates opportunity costs—what is given up to get more of something else.   LO1-2
- The bent shape of the PPC reflects the law of increasing opportunity costs: Increasing quantities of any good can be obtained only by sacrificing ever-increasing quantities of other goods.   LO1-2
- Inefficient or incomplete use of resources will fail to attain production possibilities. Additional resources or better technologies will expand them. This is the essence of economic growth.   LO1-2

- Every country must decide WHAT to produce, HOW to produce, and FOR WHOM to produce with its limited resources.   LO1-3
- The WHAT, HOW, and FOR WHOM choices can be made by the market mechanism or by government directives. Most nations are mixed economies, using a combination of these two choice mechanisms.   LO1-4
- Market failure exists when market signals generate suboptimal outcomes. Government failure occurs when government intervention worsens economic outcomes. The challenge for economic theory and policy is to find the mix of market signals and government directives that best fulfills our social and economic goals.   LO1-4
- The study of economics focuses on the broad question of resource allocation. Macroeconomics is concerned with allocating the resources of an entire economy to achieve aggregate economic goals (e.g., full employment). Microeconomics focuses on the behavior and goals of individual market participants.   LO1-3

Key Terms

scarcity
factors of production
capital
entrepreneurship
economics
opportunity cost

production possibilities
efficiency
economic growth
market mechanism
laissez faire
mixed economy

market failure
government failure
macroeconomics
microeconomics
ceteris paribus

Questions for Discussion

1. What opportunity costs did you incur in reading this chapter? If you read another chapter today, would your opportunity cost (per chapter) increase? Explain.   LO1-1

2. How much time could you spend on homework in a day? How much do you spend? How do you decide?   LO1-1

3. What's the real cost of the food in the "free lunch" cartoon on page 6? LO1-1

4. How might a nation's production possibilities be affected by the following? LO1-2
   a. A decrease in income taxes.
   b. An increase in immigration.
   c. An increase in military spending.
   d. An increase in college tuition.

5. What are the opportunity costs of developing wind farms to generate "clean" electricity? Should we make the investment? LO1-1

6. Who would go to college in a completely private (market) college system? How does government intervention change this FOR WHOM outcome? LO1-3

7. Why do people around the world have so much faith in free markets (World View, p. 15)? LO1-4

8. How many resources should we allocate to space exploration? How will we make this decision? LO1-4

9. What is the connection between North Korea's missile program and its hunger problem? (World View, p. 10) LO1-1

10. Why might more reliance on markets rather than government be desirable? When and how might it be undesirable? LO1-4

---

web activities to accompany this chapter can be found on the Online Learning Center:
http://www.mhhe.com/schiller13e

mobile app Visit your mobile app store and download the Schiller: Study Econ app *today!*

APPENDIX

USING GRAPHS

Economists like to draw graphs. In fact, we didn't even make it through the first chapter without a few graphs. This appendix looks more closely at the way graphs are drawn and used. The basic purpose of a graph is to illustrate a relationship between two *variables*. Consider, for example, the relationship between grades and studying. In general, we expect that additional hours of study time will lead to higher grades. Hence we should be able to see a distinct relationship between hours of study time and grade point average.

Suppose that we actually surveyed all the students taking this course with regard to their study time and grade point averages. The resulting information can be compiled in a table such as Table A.1.

According to the table, students who don't study at all can expect an F in this course. To get a C, the average student apparently spends 8 hours a week studying. All those who study 16 hours a week end up with an A in the course.

These relationships between grades and studying can also be illustrated on a graph. Indeed, the whole purpose of a graph is to summarize numerical relationships.

We begin to construct a graph by drawing horizontal and vertical boundaries, as in Figure A.1. These boundaries are called the *axes* of the graph. On the vertical axis (often called the *y*-axis) we measure one of the variables; the other variable is measured on the horizontal axis (the *x*-axis).

In this case, we shall measure the grade point average on the vertical axis. We start at the *origin* (the intersection of the two axes) and count upward, letting the distance between horizontal lines represent half (0.5) a grade point. Each horizontal line is numbered, up to the maximum grade point average of 4.0.

TABLE A.1

Hypothetical Relationship of Grades to Study Time

Study Time (Hours per Week)	Grade Point Average
16	4.0 (A)
14	3.5 (B+)
12	3.0 (B)
10	2.5 (C+)
8	2.0 (C)
6	1.5 (D+)
4	1.0 (D)
2	0.5 (F+)
0	0.0 (F)

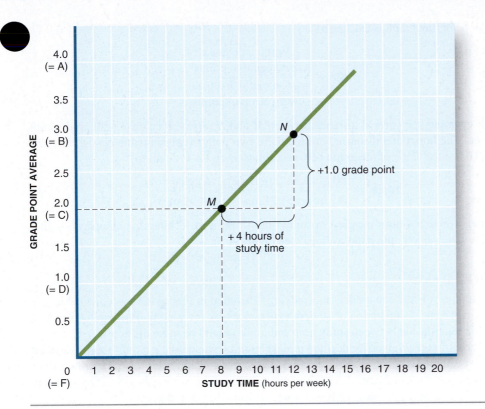

FIGURE A.1
The Relationship of Grades to Study Time

The upward (positive) slope of the curve indicates that additional studying is associated with higher grades. The average student (2.0, or C grade) studies 8 hours per week. This is indicated by point *M* on the graph.

web analysis

For online practice with graphs, visit **http://cls.syr.edu/ mathtuneup/pretest/**.

The number of hours each week spent doing homework is measured on the horizontal axis. We begin at the origin again and count to the right. The *scale* (numbering) proceeds in increments of 1 hour, up to 20 hours per week.

When both axes have been labeled and measured, we can begin illustrating the relationship between study time and grades. Consider the typical student who does 8 hours of homework per week and has a 2.0 (C) grade point average. We illustrate this relationship by first locating 8 hours on the horizontal axis. We then move up from that point a distance of 2.0 grade points, to point *M*. Point *M* tells us that 8 hours of study time per week are typically associated with a 2.0 grade point average.

The rest of the information in Table A.1 is drawn (or *plotted*) on the graph the same way. To illustrate the average grade for people who study 12 hours per week, we move upward from the number 12 on the horizontal axis until we reach the height of 3.0 on the vertical axis. At that intersection, we draw another point (point *N*).

Once we've plotted the various points describing the relationship of study time to grades, we may connect them with a line or curve. This line (curve) is our summary. In this case, the line slopes upward to the right—that is, it has a *positive* slope. This slope indicates that more hours of study time are associated with *higher* grades. Were higher grades associated with *less* study time, the curve in Figure A.1 would have a *negative* slope (downward from left to right).

Slopes

The upward slope of Figure A.1 tells us that higher grades are associated with increased amounts of study time. That same curve also tells us *by how much* grades tend to rise with study time. According to point *M* in Figure A.1, the average student studies 8 hours per week and earns a C (2.0 grade point average). To earn a B (3.0 average), students apparently need to study an average of 12 hours per week (point *N*). Hence an increase of 4 hours of study time per week is associated with a 1-point increase in grade point average. This relationship between *changes* in study time and *changes* in grade point average is expressed by the steepness, or *slope*, of the graph.

The slope of any graph is calculated as

$$\text{Slope} = \frac{\text{Vertical distance between two points}}{\text{Horizontal distance between two points}}$$

In our example, the vertical distance between M and N represents a change in grade point average. The horizontal distance between these two points represents the change in study time. Hence the slope of the graph between points M and N is equal to

$$\text{Slope} = \frac{3.0 \text{ grade} - 2.0 \text{ grade}}{12 \text{ hours} - 8 \text{ hours}} = \frac{1 \text{ grade point}}{4 \text{ hours}}$$

In other words, a 4-hour increase in study time (from 8 to 12 hours) is associated with a 1-point increase in grade point average (see Figure A.1).

Shifts

The relationship between grades and studying illustrated in Figure A.1 isn't inevitable. It's simply a graphical illustration of student experiences, as revealed in our hypothetical survey. The relationship between study time and grades could be quite different.

Suppose that the university decided to raise grading standards, making it more difficult to achieve higher grades. To achieve a C, a student now would need to study 12 hours per week, not just 8 (as in Figure A.1). Whereas students could previously get a B by studying 12 hours per week, now they'd have to study 16 hours to get that grade.

Figure A.2 illustrates the new grading standards. Notice that the new curve lies to the right of the earlier curve. We say that the curve has *shifted* to reflect a change in the relationship between study time and grades. Point R indicates that 12 hours of study time now "produce" a C, not a B (point N on the old curve). Students who now study only 4 hours per week (point S) will fail. Under the old grading policy, they could have at least

FIGURE A.2

A Shift

When a relationship between two variables changes, the entire curve *shifts*. In this case a tougher grading policy alters the relationship between study time and grades. To get a C, one must now study 12 hours per week (point *R*), not just 8 hours (point *M*).

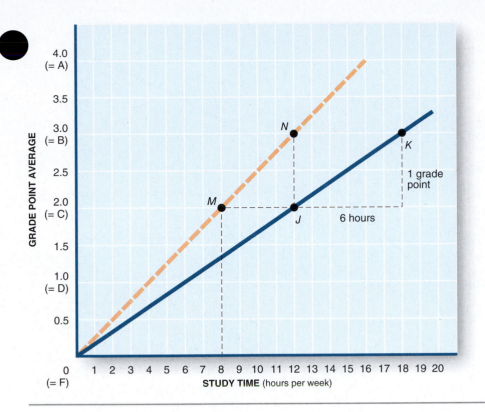

FIGURE A.3
A Change in Slope

When a curve shifts, it may change its slope as well. In this case a new grading policy makes each higher grade more difficult to reach. To raise a C to a B, for example, one must study 6 additional hours (compare points *J* and *K*). Earlier it took only 4 hours to move the grade scale up a full point. The slope of the line has declined from 0.25 (= 1 ÷ 4) to 0.17 (= 1 ÷ 6).

gotten a D. ***When a curve shifts, the underlying relationship between the two variables has changed.***

A shift may also change the slope of the curve. In Figure A.2, the new grading curve is parallel to the old one; it therefore has the same slope. Under either the new grading policy or the old one, a 4-hour increase in study time leads to a 1-point increase in grades. Therefore, the slope of both curves in Figure A.2 is

$$\text{Slope} = \frac{\text{Vertical change}}{\text{Horizontal change}} = \frac{1}{4}$$

This too may change, however. Figure A.3 illustrates such a possibility. In this case, zero study time still results in an F. But now the payoff for additional studying is reduced. Now it takes 6 hours of study time to get a D (1.0 grade point), not 4 hours as before. Likewise, another 4 hours of study time (to a total of 10) raise the grade by only two-thirds of a point. It takes 6 hours to raise the grade a full point. The slope of the new line is therefore

$$\text{Slope} = \frac{\text{Vertical change}}{\text{Horizontal change}} = \frac{1}{6}$$

The new curve in Figure A.3 has a smaller slope than the original curve and so lies below it. What all this means is that it now takes a greater effort to improve your grade.

Linear vs. Nonlinear Curves

In Figures A.1–A.3 the relationship between grades and studying is represented by a straight line—that is, a *linear curve*. A distinguishing feature of linear curves is that they have the same (constant) slope throughout. In Figure A.1 it appears that *every* 4-hour increase in study time is associated with a 1-point increase in average grades. In Figure A.3 it appears that every 6-hour increase in study time leads to a 1-point increase in grades. But the relationship between studying and grades may not be linear. Higher grades may be

FIGURE A.4
A Nonlinear Relationship

Straight lines have a constant slope, implying a constant relationship between the two variables. But the relationship (and slope) may vary. In this case, it takes 6 extra hours of study to raise a C (point *W*) to a B (point *X*) but 8 extra hours to raise a B to an A (point *Y*). The slope decreases as we move up the curve.

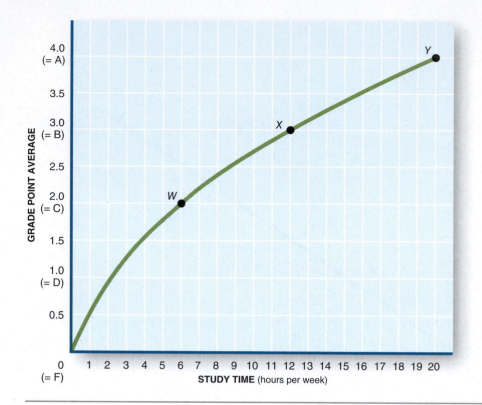

more difficult to attain. You may be able to raise a C to a B by studying 4 hours more per week. But it may be harder to raise a B to an A. According to Figure A.4, it takes an additional 8 hours of studying to raise a B to an A. Thus the relationship between study time and grades is *nonlinear* in Figure A.4; the slope of the curve changes as study time increases. In this case, the slope decreases as study time increases. Grades continue to improve, but not so fast, as more and more time is devoted to homework. You may know the feeling.

Causation

Figure A.4 doesn't by itself guarantee that your grade point average will rise if you study 4 more hours per week. In fact, the graph drawn in Figure A.4 doesn't prove that additional study ever results in higher grades. The graph is only a summary of empirical observations. It says nothing about cause and effect. It could be that students who study a lot are smarter to begin with. If so, then less able students might not get higher grades if they studied harder. In other words, the *cause* of higher grades is debatable. At best, the empirical relationship summarized in the graph may be used to support a particular theory (e.g., that it pays to study more). Graphs, like tables, charts, and other statistical media, rarely tell their own story; rather, they must be *interpreted* in terms of some underlying theory or expectation.

LO1-1 1. According to Table 1.1 (or Figure 1.1), what is the opportunity cost of the fourth truck?   _____

LO1-2 2. (*a*) Compute the opportunity cost in forgone tanks for each additional truck produced:

Truck output	0	1	2	3	4	5
Tank output	5	4.5	3.8	3.0	2.0	0
Opportunity cost	___	___	___	0.8	___	___

   (*b*) As truck output increases, are opportunity costs (A) increasing, (B) decreasing, or
   (C) remaining constant?   _____

LO1-2 3. According to Figure 1.2 (p. 9), what is the opportunity cost of North Korea moving from point *P* to
   point *N* (in terms of food output)?   _____

LO1-1 4. (*a*) What is the cost of the North Korean 2009 missile launch, according to South Korea (p. 10)?   _____
   (*b*) How many people could have been fed for an entire year at the World Bank standard of $2
   per day with that money?   _____

LO1-1 5. What is the opportunity cost (in civilian output) of a defense buildup that raises military
   spending from 4.3 to 4.7 percent of a $15 trillion economy?   _____

LO1-3 6. What are the three core economic questions societies must answer?

   _____   _____   _____

LO1-2 7. According to Figure 1.4 (reproduced below),
   (*a*) At which point(s) is this society producing some of each type of output but still producing
      inefficiently?   _____
   (*b*) At which point(s) is this society producing the most output possible with the available
      resources and technology?   _____
   (*c*) At which point(s) is the output combination currently unattainable with current available
      resources and technology?   _____
   (*d*) Show the change that would occur if the population of this society increased dramatically.
      Label this curve PPC2.
   (*e*) Show the change that would occur with a huge natural disaster that destroyed vast amounts
      of infrastructure. Label this curve PPC3.

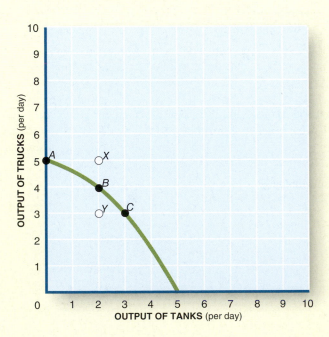

LO1-2 8. Suppose either computers or televisions can be assembled with the following labor inputs:

Units produced	1	2	3	4	5	6	7	8	9	10
Total labor used	3	7	12	15	25	33	42	54	70	90

(a) Draw the production possibilities curve for an economy with 54 units of labor. Label it P54.

(b) What is the opportunity cost of the eighth computer?   _____

(c) Suppose immigration brings in 36 more workers. Redraw the production possibilities curve to reflect this added labor. Label the new curve P90.

(d) Suppose advancing technology (e.g., the miniaturization of electronic circuits) increases the productivity of the 90-laborer workforce by 20 percent. Draw a third production possibilities curve (PT) to illustrate this change.

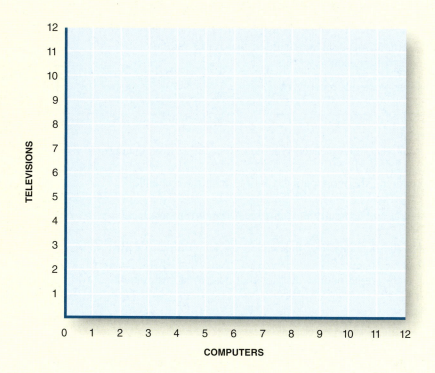

LO1-4 9. According to the World View on page 15, which nation has
(a) The highest level of faith in the market system?   _____
(b) The lowest level of faith in the market system?   _____

LO1-1 10. If a person literally had "nothing else to do,"
(a) What would be the opportunity cost of doing these problems?   _____
(b) What is the likelihood of that?   _____

LO1-2   11. Suppose there's a relationship of the following sort between study time and grades:

	(a)	(b)	(c)	(d)	(e)
Study time (hours per week)	0	2	6	12	20
Grade point average	0	1.0	2.0	3.0	4.0

If you have only 20 hours per week to use for either study time or fun time,
(a) Draw the (linear) production possibilities curve on the graph below that represents the alternative uses of your time.
(b) Indicate on the graph the point C that would get you a 2.0 grade average.
(c) What is the cost, in lost fun time, of raising your grade point average from 2.0 to 3.0? Illustrate this effort on the graph (point C to point D).   _____
(d) What is the opportunity cost of increasing your grade point average from 3.0 to 4.0? Illustrate as point D to point E.   _____

The U.S. Economy:
A Global View

All nations must confront the central economic questions of WHAT to produce, HOW to produce, and FOR WHOM to produce it. However, the nations of the world approach these issues with vastly different production possibilities. China, Canada, the United States, Russia, and Brazil have more than *3 million* square miles of land each. All that land gives them far greater production possibilities than Dominica, Tonga, Malta, or Lichtenstein, each of which has less than 300 square miles of land. The population of China totals more than 1.4 billion people, nearly five times that of the United States, and 25,000 times the population of Greenland. Obviously these nations confront very different output choices.

In addition to vastly uneven production possibilities, the nations of the world use different mechanisms for deciding WHAT, HOW, and FOR WHOM to produce. Belarus, Romania, North Korea, and Cuba still rely heavily on central planning. By contrast, Singapore, New Zealand, Ireland, and the United States permit the market mechanism to play a dominant role in shaping economic outcomes.

With different production possibilities and mechanisms of choice, you'd expect economic outcomes to vary greatly across nations. And they do. This chapter assesses how the U.S. economy stacks up. Specifically,

- **WHAT goods and services does the United States produce?**
- **HOW is that output produced?**
- **FOR WHOM is the output produced?**

In each case, we want to see not only how the United States has answered these questions but also how America's answers compare with those of other nations.

WHAT AMERICA PRODUCES

The United States has less than 5 percent of the world's population and only 12 percent of the world's arable land, yet it produces 20 percent of the world's output.

The Wealth of Nations

GDP Comparisons

The World View below shows how total U.S. production compares with that of other nations. These comparisons are based on the total market value of all the goods and services a nation produces in a year—what we call **gross domestic product (GDP)**. In effect, GDP is the "pie" of output we bake each year.

In 2010 the U.S. economy baked a huge pie—one containing nearly $15 trillion worth of output. That was far more output than any other nation produced. The second-largest economy, China, produced only two-thirds that much. Japan came in third, with about a third of U.S. output. Cuba, by contrast, produced only $1.6 *billion* of output, less than the state of South Dakota. Russia, which was once regarded as a superpower, produced only $2.7 trillion. The entire 27-member European Union produces less output than the United States.

> **gross domestic product (GDP):** The total market value of all final goods and services produced within a nation's borders in a given time period.

WORLD VIEW

Comparative Output (GDP)

The United States is by far the world's largest economy. Its annual output of goods and services is one and a half times that of China's, three times Japan's, and more than all of the European Union's. The output of Third World countries is only a tiny fraction of U.S. output.

Source: *The World Bank,* www.worldbank.org.

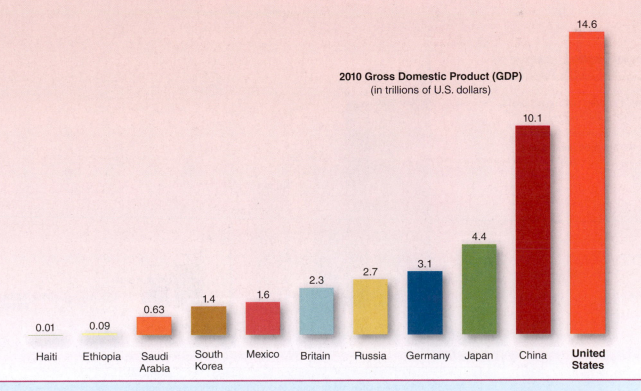

2010 Gross Domestic Product (GDP)
(in trillions of U.S. dollars)

Country	GDP
Haiti	0.01
Ethiopia	0.09
Saudi Arabia	0.63
South Korea	1.4
Mexico	1.6
Britain	2.3
Russia	2.7
Germany	3.1
Japan	4.4
China	10.1
United States	14.6

Analysis: The market value of output (GDP) is a basic measure of an economy's size. The U.S. economy is far larger than any other and accounts for over one-fifth of the entire world's output of goods and services.

Per Capita GDP. What makes the U.S. share of world output so remarkable is that we do it with so few people. The U.S. population of 310 million amounts to less than 5 percent of the world's total (6.8 billion). Yet we produce over 20 percent of the world's output. That means we're producing a lot of output *per person*. China, by contrast, has the opposite ratios: 20 percent of the world's population producing less than 13 percent of the world's output. So China is producing a lot of output but relatively less *per person*.

per capita GDP: The dollar value of GDP divided by total population; average GDP.

This people-based measure of economic performance is called **per capita GDP.** Per capita GDP is simply a nation's total output divided by its total population. It doesn't tell us how much any specific person gets. ***Per capita GDP is an indicator of how much output the average person would get if all output were divided evenly among the population.*** In effect, GDP per capita tells us how large a slice of the GDP pie the average citizen gets.

In 2010 per capita GDP in the United States was roughly $47,000. That means the average U.S. citizen could have consumed $47,000 worth of goods and services. That's a staggering amount by global standards—five times the average for the rest of the world. The following World View provides a global perspective on just how "rich" America is. Some of the country-specific comparisons are startling. China, which produces the world's

WORLD VIEW

GDP per Capita around the World

The American standard of living is nearly five times higher than the average for the rest of the world. People in the poorest nations of the world (e.g., Haiti, Ethiopia) barely survive on per capita incomes that are a tiny fraction of U.S. standards.

Source: *The World Bank,* **www.worldbank.org.**

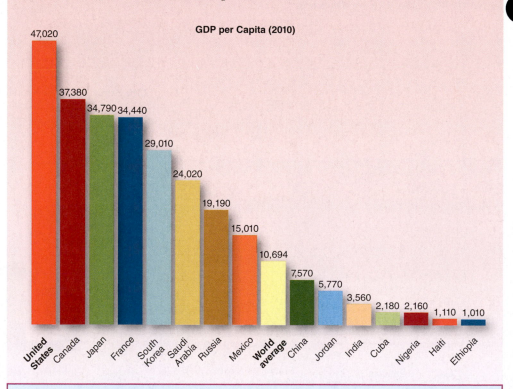

GDP per Capita (2010)

Country	GDP per Capita
United States	47,020
Canada	37,380
Japan	34,790
France	34,440
South Korea	29,010
Saudi Arabia	24,020
Russia	19,190
Mexico	15,010
World average	10,694
China	7,570
Jordan	5,770
India	3,560
Cuba	2,180
Nigeria	2,160
Haiti	1,110
Ethiopia	1,010

Analysis: Per capita GDP is a measure of output that reflects average living standards. America's exceptionally high GDP per capita implies access to far more goods and services than people in other nations have.

web analysis

To find the latest data on national economic output, access the International Monetary Fund's website at **www.imf.org,** and visit the "Country Info" tab.

second-largest GDP, has such a low *per capita* income that most of its citizens would be considered "poor" by official American standards. Yet people in other nations (e.g., Haiti, Ethiopia) don't even come close to that low standard. According to the World Bank, one-third of the people on Earth subsist on incomes of less than $2 a day—a level completely unimaginable to the average American. *Homeless* people in the United States enjoy a higher living standard than billions of poor people in other nations (see Chapter 23). In this context, it's easy to understand why the rest of the world envies (and sometimes resents) America's prosperity.

GDP Growth. What's even more startling about global comparisons is that the GDP gap between the United States and the world's poor nations keeps growing. The reason for that is **economic growth.** With few exceptions, U.S. output increases nearly every year: the pie keeps getting larger. *On average, U.S. output has grown by roughly 3 percent a year, nearly three times faster than population growth (1 percent).* So the U.S. pie is growing faster than the number of people coming to the table. Hence not only does *total* output keep rising, but *per capita* output keeps rising as well (see Figure 2.1). Even the Great Recession of 2008–2009 hardly made a dent in this pattern of ever-rising incomes.

economic growth: An increase in output (real GDP); an expansion of production possibilities.

Poor Nations. People in the world's poorest countries aren't so fortunate. China's economy has grown exceptionally fast in the last 20 years, propelling it to second place in the global GDP rankings. But in many other nations total output has actually *declined* year after year, further depressing living standards. Notice in Table 2.1, for example, what's been happening in Zimbabwe. From 2000 to 2009, Zimbabwe's output of goods and services (GDP) *declined* by an average of 7.5 percent a year. As a result, total Zimbabwean output in 2009

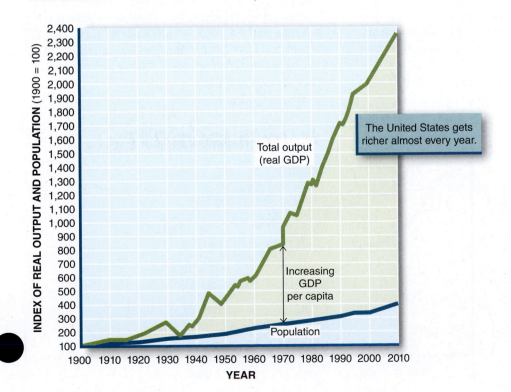

FIGURE 2.1

U.S. Output and Population Growth since 1900

Over time, the growth of output in the United States has greatly exceeded population growth. As a consequence, GDP per capita has grown tremendously. GDP per capita was five times higher in 2000 than in 1900.

Source: U.S. Department of Labor.

TABLE 2.1
GDP Growth vs. Population
Growth

The relationship between GDP
growth and population growth is
very different in rich and poor
countries. The populations of rich
countries are growing very slowly,
and gains in per capita GDP are
easily achieved. In the poorest
countries, population is still
increasing rapidly, making it difficult to raise living standards.
Notice how per capita incomes are
declining in many poor countries
(such as Zimbabwe, Haiti, and
Gaza).

	Average Growth Rate (2000–2009) of		
	GDP	**Population**	**Per Capita GDP**
High-income countries			
United States	2.0	1.1	0.9
Canada	2.1	1.0	1.1
Japan	1.1	0.2	0.9
France	1.5	0.5	1.0
Low-income countries			
China	10.9	0.8	10.1
India	7.9	1.6	6.3
Ethiopia	7.5	2.8	4.7
Burundi	2.7	2.0	0.7
Haiti	0.7	1.8	−1.1
West Bank/Gaza	−0.9	3.8	−4.7
Zimbabwe	−7.5	0.9	−8.4

Source: *The World Bank, WDR2011 Data Set,* **data.worldbank.org.**

was 90 percent *smaller* than in 2000. During those same years, the Zimbabwean population
kept growing—by 0.9 percent a year. So the Zimbabwean pie was shrinking every year even
as the number of people coming to the table was increasing. As a result, Zimbabwe's per
capita GDP fell below $400 a year. That low level of per capita GDP left two-thirds of Zim-
babwe's population undernourished.

The Mix of Output

Regardless of how much output a nation produces, the *mix* of output always includes both
goods (such as cars, big-screen TVs, and potatoes) and *services* (like this economics course,
visits to a doctor, or a professional baseball game). A century ago, about two-thirds of U.S.
output consisted of farm goods (37 percent), manufactured goods (22 percent), and mining
(9 percent). Since then, over 25 *million* people have left the farms and taken jobs in other
sectors. As a result, today's mix of output is completely reversed: ***Eighty percent of U.S.
output now consists of services, not goods*** (see Figure 2.2).

FIGURE 2.2
The Changing Mix of Output

Two hundred years ago, almost all
U.S. output came from farms. Today
80 percent of output consists of services, not farm or manufactured
goods.

Source: U.S. Department of Commerce.

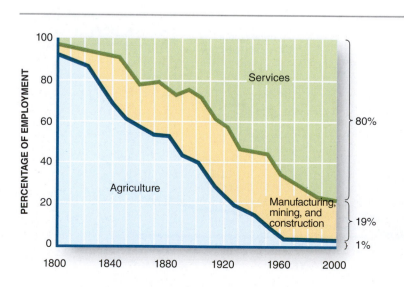

The *relative* decline in goods production (manufacturing, farming) doesn't mean that we're producing *fewer* goods today than in earlier decades. Quite the contrary. While some industries such as iron and steel have shrunk, others, such as chemicals, publishing, and telecommunications equipment, have grown tremendously. The result is that manufacturing output has increased fourfold since 1950. The same kind of thing has happened in the farm sector, where output keeps rising even though agriculture's *share* of total output has declined. It's just that our output of *services* has increased so much faster.

Development Patterns. The transformation of the United States into a service economy is a reflection of our high incomes. In Ethiopia, where the most urgent concern is to keep people from starving, over 50 percent of output still comes from the farm sector. Poor people don't have enough income to buy dental services, vacations, or even an education, so the mix of output in poor countries is weighted toward goods, not services.

HOW AMERICA PRODUCES

Regardless of how much output a nation produces, every nation ultimately depends on its resources—its **factors of production**—to produce goods and services. So *differences* in GDP must be explained in part by HOW those resources are used.

> **factors of production:** Resource inputs used to produce goods and services, such as land, labor, capital, entrepreneurship.

Human Capital

We've already observed that America's premier position in global GDP rankings isn't due to the number of humans within our borders. We have far fewer bodies than China or India, yet produce far more output than either of those nations. What counts for production purposes is not just the *number* of workers a nation has, but the *skills* of those workers—what we call **human capital.**

Over time, the United States has invested heavily in human capital. In 1940 only 1 out of 20 young Americans graduated from college; today over 30 percent of young people are college graduates. High school graduation rates have jumped from 38 percent to over 85 percent in the same period. In the poorest countries, only 1 out of 3 youth ever *attend* high school, much less graduate (see the World View on the next page). As a consequence, the United Nations estimates that 1.2 billion people—a fifth of humanity—are unable to read a book or even write their own names. Without even functional literacy, such workers are doomed to low-productivity jobs. Despite low wages, they are not likely to "steal" many jobs from America's highly educated and trained workforce.

> **human capital:** The knowledge and skills possessed by the workforce.

Capital Stock

America has also accumulated a massive stock of capital—over $50 *trillion* worth of machinery, factories, and buildings. As a result of all this prior investment, U.S. production tends to be very **capital-intensive.** The contrast with *labor-intensive* production in poorer countries is striking. A farmer in India still works mostly with his hands and crude implements, whereas a U.S. farmer works with computers, automated irrigation systems, and mechanized equipment (see the photos on page 37). Russian business managers don't have the computer networks or telecommunications systems that make U.S. business so efficient. In Haiti and Ethiopia, even telephones, indoor plumbing, and dependable sources of power are scarce.

> **capital-intensive:** Production processes that use a high ratio of capital to labor inputs.

High Productivity

When you put educated workers together with sophisticated capital equipment, you tend to get more output. This relationship largely explains why the United States has such a lead in worker **productivity**—the amount of output produced by the average worker. *American households are able to consume so much because American workers produce so much.* It's really that simple.

> **productivity:** Output per unit of input—for example, output per labor-hour.

WORLD VIEW

The Education Gap between Rich and Poor Nations

Virtually all Americans attend high school and roughly 85 percent graduate. In poor countries, relatively few workers attend high school and even fewer graduate. Half the workers in the world's poorest nations are illiterate.

Source: *The World Bank, WDI2011 Data Set*, **data.worldbank.org.**

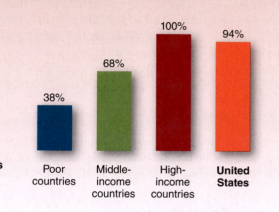

Enrollment in Secondary Schools
(percentage of school-age youth attending secondary schools)

Poor countries	Middle-income countries	High-income countries	United States
38%	68%	100%	94%

Analysis: The high productivity of the American economy is explained in part by the quality of its labor resources. Workers in poorer, less developed countries get much less education and training.

The huge output of the United States is thus explained not only by a wealth of resources but by their quality as well. ***The high productivity of the U.S. economy results from using highly educated workers in capital-intensive production processes.***

Factor Mobility. Our continuing ability to produce the goods and services that consumers demand also depends on our agility in *reallocating* resources from one industry to another. Every year, some industries expand and others contract. Thousands of new firms start up each year, and almost as many others disappear. In the process, land, labor, capital, and entrepreneurship move from one industry to another in response to changing demands and technology. In 1975 Federal Express, Dell Computer, Staples, Oracle, and Amgen didn't exist. Walmart was still a small retailer. Starbucks was selling coffee on Seattle street corners, and the founders of Google and YouTube weren't even born. Today these companies employ over a million people. These workers came from other firms and industries that weren't growing as fast.

Technological Advance. One of the forces that keeps shifting resources from one industry to another is continuing advances in technology. Advances in technology can be as sophisticated as microscopic miniaturization of electronic circuits or as simple as the reorganization of production processes. Either phenomenon increases the productivity of the workforce and potential output. ***Whenever technology advances, an economy can produce more output with existing resources;*** its **production possibilities** curve shifts outward (see Figure 1.5, page 12).

Outsourcing and Trade. The same technological advances that fuel economic growth also facilitate *global* resource use. Telecommunications has become so sophisticated and inexpensive that phone workers in India or Grenada can answer calls directed to U.S.

production possibilities:
The alternative combinations of final goods and services that could be produced in a given period with all available resources and technology.

© Santokh Kochar/Getty Images/DAL

Gene Alexander, USDA Natural Resources Conservation Service/DAL

Analysis: An abundance of capital equipment and advanced technology make American farmers and workers far more productive than workers in poor nations.

companies. Likewise, programmers in India can work online to write computer code, develop software, or perform accounting chores for U.S. corporations. Although such "outsourcing" is often viewed as a threat to U.S. jobs, it is really another source of increased U.S. output. By outsourcing routine tasks to foreign workers, U.S. workers are able to focus on higher-value jobs. U.S. computer engineers do less routine programming and more systems design. U.S. accountants do less cost tabulation and more cost analysis. By utilizing foreign resources in the production process, U.S. workers are able to pursue their *comparative advantage* in high-skill, capital-intensive jobs. In this way, both productivity and total output increase. Although some U.S. workers suffer temporary job losses in this process, the overall economy gains.

Role of Government

In assessing HOW goods are produced and economies grow, we must also take heed of the role the government plays. As we noted in Chapter 1, the amount of economic freedom varies greatly among the 200-plus nations of the world. Moreover, the Heritage Foundation has documented a positive relationship between the degree of economic freedom and economic growth. Quite simply, when entrepreneurs are unfettered by regulation or high taxes, they are more likely to design and produce better mousetraps. When the government owns the factors of production, imposes high taxes, or tightly regulates output, there is little opportunity or incentive to design better products or pursue new technology. This is one reason why more market-reliant economies grow faster than others.

Recognizing the productive value of market incentives isn't tantamount to rejecting all government intervention. No one really advocates the complete abolition of government. On the contrary, the government plays a critical role in establishing a framework in which private businesses can operate. Among its many roles are these:

- *Providing a legal framework.* One of the most basic functions of government is to establish and enforce the rules of the game. In some bygone era maybe a person's word was sufficient to guarantee delivery or payment. Businesses today, however, rely more on written contracts. The government gives legitimacy to contracts by establishing the rules for such pacts and by enforcing their provisions. In the absence of contractual rights, few companies would be willing to ship goods without prepayment (in cash). Even the incentive to write textbooks would disappear if government copyright laws didn't forbid unauthorized photocopying. By establishing ownership rights, contract rights, and other rules of the game, the government lays the foundation for market transactions.

- *Protecting the environment.* The government also intervenes in the market to protect the environment. The legal contract system is designed to protect the interests of a buyer and a seller who wish to do business. What if, however, the business they contract for harms third parties? How are the interests of persons who *aren't* party to the contract to be protected?

  Numerous examples abound of how unregulated production may harm third parties. Earlier in the century, the steel mills around Pittsburgh blocked out the sun with clouds of sulfurous gases that spewed out of their furnaces. Local residents were harmed every time they inhaled. In the absence of government intervention, such side effects would be common. Decisions on how to produce would be based on costs alone, not on how the environment is affected. However, such **externalities**—spillover costs imposed on the broader community—affect our collective well-being. To reduce the external costs of production, the government limits air, water, and noise pollution and regulates environmental use.

- *Protecting consumers.* The government also uses its power to protect the interests of consumers. One way to do this is to prevent individual business firms from becoming too powerful. In the extreme case, a single firm might have a **monopoly** on the production of a specific good. As the sole producer of that good, a monopolist could dictate the price, the quality, and the quantity of the product. In such a situation, consumers would likely end up paying too much for too little.

  To protect consumers from monopoly exploitation, the government tries to prevent individual firms from dominating specific markets. Antitrust laws prohibit mergers or acquisitions that would threaten competition. The U.S. Department of Justice and the Federal Trade Commission also regulate pricing practices, advertising claims, and other behavior that might put consumers at an unfair disadvantage in product markets.

  Government also regulates the safety of many products. Consumers don't have enough expertise to assess the safety of various medicines, for example. If they rely on trial and error to determine drug safety, they might not get a second chance. To avoid this calamity, the government requires rigorous testing of new drugs, food additives, and other products.

- *Protecting labor.* The government also regulates how labor resources are used in the production process. In most poor nations, children are forced to start working at very early ages, often for minuscule wages. They often don't get the chance to go to school or to stay healthy. In Africa, 40 percent of children under age 14 work to survive or to help support their families. In the United States, child labor laws and compulsory schooling prevent minor children from being exploited. Government regulations also set standards for workplace safety, minimum wages, fringe benefits, and overtime provisions.

externalities: Costs (or benefits) of a market activity borne by a third party.

monopoly: A firm that produces the entire market supply of a particular good or service.

Striking a Balance

All these and other government interventions are designed to change the way resources are used. Such interventions reflect the conviction that the market alone might not always select the best possible way of producing goods and services. There's no guarantee, however, that government regulation of HOW goods are produced always makes us better off. Excessive regulation may inhibit production, raise product prices, and limit consumer choices. As noted in Chapter 1, *government* failure might replace *market* failure, leaving us no better off—possibly even worse off. This possibility underscores the importance of striking the right balance between market reliance and government regulation.

FOR WHOM AMERICA PRODUCES

As we've seen, America produces a huge quantity of output, using high-quality labor and capital resources. That leaves one basic question unanswered: FOR WHOM is all this output produced?

How many goods and services one gets largely depends on how much income one has to spend. The U.S. economy uses the market mechanism to distribute most goods and services. Those who receive the most income get the most goods. This goes a long way toward explaining why millionaires live in mansions and homeless people seek shelter in abandoned cars. This is the kind of stark inequality that fueled Karl Marx's denunciation of capitalism. Even today, people wonder how some Americans can be so rich while others are so poor.

U.S. Income Distribution

Figure 2.3 illustrates the actual distribution of income in the United States. For this illustration the entire population is sorted into five groups of equal size, ranked by income. In this depiction, all the rich people are in the top **income quintile;** the poor are in the lowest quintile. To be in the top quintile in 2010, a household needed at least $102,000 of income. All the households in the lowest quintile had incomes under $20,000.

The most striking feature of Figure 2.3 is how large a slice of the income pie rich people get: *The top 20 percent (quintile) of U.S. households get half of all U.S. income.* By contrast, the poorest 20 percent (quintile) of U.S. households get only a sliver of the income pie—less than 4 percent. Those grossly unequal slices explain why nearly half of all Americans believe the nation is divided into "haves" and "have nots."

Global Inequality

As unequal as U.S. incomes are, income disparities are actually greater in many other countries. Ironically, income inequalities are often greatest in the poorest countries. The richest *tenth* of U.S. families gets 30 percent of America's income pie. The richest tenth of South Africa's families gets 45 percent of that nation's income (see the World View on the next page). Given the small size of South Africa's pie, the *bottom* tenth of South African families is left with

income quintile: One-fifth of the population, rank-ordered by income (e.g., top fifth).

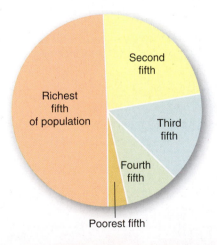

Income Quintile	2010 Income	Average Income	Share of Total Income (%)
Highest fifth	Above $102,000	$170,000	50.2
Second fifth	$63,000–102,000	$ 80,000	23.4
Third fifth	$39,000–63,000	$ 50,000	14.6
Fourth fifth	$20,000–39,000	$ 30,000	8.5
Lowest fifth	$0–20,000	$ 11,000	3.3

Source: U.S. Department of Commerce, Bureau of the Census (averages rounded to thousands of dollars; 2010 data).

web analysis

Past and present data on the U.S. income distribution are available at **www.census.gov.** In the "People and Households" category, click on the "Income" link.

FIGURE 2.3
The U.S. Distribution of Income

The richest fifth of U.S. households gets half of all the income—a huge slice of the income pie. By contrast, the poorest fifth gets only a sliver.

Analysis: The market distributes income (and, in turn, goods and services) according to the resources an individual owns and how well they are used. If the resulting inequalities are too great, some redistribution via government intervention may be desired.

mere crumbs. As we'll see in Chapter 23, 40 percent of South Africa's population lives in "severe poverty," defined by the World Bank as an income of less than $2 a day.

Comparisons across countries would manifest even greater inequality. As we saw earlier, third world GDP per capita is far below U.S. levels. As a consequence, even **poor** *people in the United States receive far more goods and services than the* **average** *household in most low-income countries.*

WORLD VIEW

Income Share of the Rich

Inequality tends to diminish as a country develops. In poor, developing nations, the richest tenth of the population typically gets 40 to 50 percent of all income. In developed countries, the richest tenth gets 20 to 30 percent of total income.

Source: *The World Bank, WDI2011 Data Set,* **data.worldbank.org.**

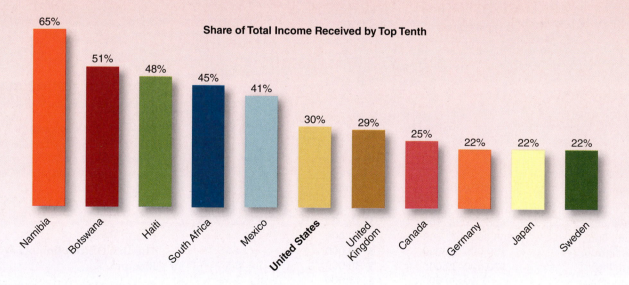

Share of Total Income Received by Top Tenth

Namibia	Botswana	Haiti	South Africa	Mexico	United States	United Kingdom	Canada	Germany	Japan	Sweden
65%	51%	48%	45%	41%	30%	29%	25%	22%	22%	22%

Analysis: The FOR WHOM question is reflected in the distribution of income. Although the U.S. distribution of income is very unequal, inequalities are even more severe in most poor nations.

THE ECONOMY TOMORROW

ENDING GLOBAL POVERTY

Global answers to the basic questions of WHAT, HOW, and FOR WHOM have been shaped by market forces and government intervention. Obviously the answers aren't yet fully satisfactory.

Millions of Americans still struggle to make ends meet. Worse yet, nearly 3 *billion* people around the world live in abject poverty—with incomes of less than $2 a day. Over a fourth of the world's population is illiterate, nearly half has no access to sanitation facilities, and a fifth is chronically malnourished.

The World Bank thinks we can do a lot better. In fact, it has set ambitious goals for the economy tomorrow. In the Millennium Declaration of October 2000, the 180 nation-members of the World Bank set specific goals for world development. By 2015, they agreed to

- Reduce extreme poverty and hunger by at least half.
- Achieve universal primary education.
- Reduce child and maternal mortality by two-thirds.
- Reduce by half the number of people without access to potable water.

Achieving these goals would obviously help billions of people. But it's obvious we're not going to succeed—certainly not by 2015. What went wrong?

The rich nations of the world have enough resources to achieve the foregoing goals. But they're not willing to give them up. People in rich nations also aspire to higher living standards in the economy tomorrow. They already enjoy more comforts than people in poor nations even dream of. But that doesn't stop them from wanting more consumer goods, better schools, improved health care, a cleaner environment, and greater economic security. So the needs of the world's poor often get lower priority.

How about the poor nations themselves? Couldn't they do a better job of mobilizing and employing their own resources to accelerate economic growth? Governments in many poor nations are notoriously self-serving and corrupt. Private property is often at risk of confiscation and contracts hard to enforce. This discourages the kind of investment poor nations desperately need. The unwillingness of rich nations to open their markets to the exports of poor nations also puts a lid on income growth. In reality, an array of domestic and international policies has perpetuated global poverty. Developing a better mix of market-based and government-directed policies is the prerequisite for ending global poverty in the economy. Chapter 23 explores some of the possibilities.

SUMMARY

- Answers to the core WHAT, HOW, and FOR WHOM questions vary greatly across nations. These differences reflect varying production possibilities, choice mechanisms, and values.   LO2-1, LO2-3, LO2-4
- Gross domestic product (GDP) is the basic measure of how much an economy produces. The United States produces roughly $15 trillion of output per year, more than one-fifth of the world's total.   LO2-1
- Per capita GDP is a nation's total output divided by its population. It indicates the average standard of living. The U.S. GDP per capita is five times the world average.   LO2-1

- The high level of U.S. per capita GDP reflects the high productivity of U.S. workers. Abundant capital, education, technology, training, and management all contribute to high productivity. The relatively high degree of U.S. economic freedom (market reliance) is also an important cause of superior economic growth.   LO2-3
- Over 75 percent of U.S. output consists of services, including government services. This is a reversal of historical ratios and reflects the relatively high incomes in the United States. Poor nations produce much higher proportions of food and manufactured goods.   LO2-2

- U.S. incomes are distributed very unequally, with households in the highest income class (quintile) receiving over 10 times more income than low-income households. Incomes are even less equally distributed in most poor nations. LO2-4

- The mix of output, production methods, and the income distribution continues to change. The WHAT, HOW, and FOR WHOM answers in tomorrow's economy will depend on the continuing interplay of (changing) market signals and (changing) government policy. LO2-2, LO2-3, LO2-4

Key Terms

gross domestic product (GDP)
per capita GDP
economic growth
factors of production

human capital
capital-intensive
productivity
production possibilities

externalities
monopoly
income quintile

Questions for Discussion

1. Americans already enjoy living standards that far exceed world averages. Do we have enough? Should we even try to produce more? LO2-1

2. Why is per capita GDP so much higher in the United States than in Mexico? LO2-3

3. Can we continue to produce more output every year? Is there a limit? LO2-3

4. The U.S. farm population has shrunk by over 25 million people since 1900. Where did all the people go? Why did they move? LO2-2

5. Is the relative decline in U.S. farming and manufacturing (Figure 2.2) a good thing or a bad thing? LO2-2

6. How many people are employed by your local or state government? What do they produce? What is the opportunity cost of that output? LO2-1

7. Where do growing companies like Google and Facebook get their employees? What were those workers doing before? LO2-2

8. Should the government try to equalize incomes more by raising taxes on the rich and giving more money to the poor? How might such redistribution affect total output and growth? LO2-4

9. Why are incomes so much more unequal in poor nations than in rich ones? LO2-4

10. How might free markets help reduce global poverty? How might they impede that goal? LO2-3

 web activities to accompany this chapter can be found on the Online Learning Center:
http://www.mhhe.com/schiller13e

 mobile app Visit your mobile app store and download the Schiller: Study Econ app *today*!

LO2-1 1. In 2010 the world's total output (real GDP) was roughly $75 trillion. What percent of this total was produced
- (a) By the three largest economies (World View, p. 31)?   _____%
- (b) By the three smallest economies in that World View?   _____%
- (c) How much larger is the U.S. economy than the Saudi economy?   _____ (times larger)

LO2-1 2. According to the World View on page 32, how does per capita GDP in the following countries stack up against America's (in percentage terms)
- (a) Mexico?   _____%
- (b) China?   _____%
- (c) Haiti?   _____%

LO2-3 3. (a) How much more output does the $15 trillion U.S. economy produce when GDP increases by 1.0 percent? $ _____
- (b) By how much does this increase the average (per capita) income if the population is 300 million? $ _____

LO2-1 4. According to Table 2.1 (p. 34), how fast does total output (GDP) have to grow in order to raise per capita GDP in
- (a) China?   _____
- (b) Ethiopia?   _____

LO2-3 5. (a) If Haiti's per capita GDP of roughly $1,150 were to DOUBLE every decade (an annual growth rate of 7.2 percent), what would Haiti's per capita GDP be in 50 years? $ _____
- (b) What is U.S. per capita GDP in 2010 (World View, p. 32)? $ _____

6. U.S. real gross domestic product increased from $10 trillion in 2000 to $15 trillion in 2010. During that same decade the share of manufactured goods (e.g., cars, appliances) fell from 16 percent to 12 percent. What was the dollar value of manufactured output
- (a) In 2000? $ _____
- (b) In 2010? $ _____
- (c) By how much did manufacturing output change?   _____%

LO2-4 7. Using the data in Figure 2.3,
- (a) Compute the average income of U.S. households. $ _____
- (b) If all incomes were equalized by government taxes and transfer payments, how much would the average household in each income quintile gain (via transfers) or lose (via taxes)?
  - (i) Highest fifth $ _____
  - (ii) Second fifth $ _____
  - (iii) Third fifth $ _____
  - (iv) Fourth fifth $ _____
  - (v) Lowest fifth $ _____
- (c) What is the implied tax rate (i.e., tax ÷ average income) on the highest quintile?   _____%

LO2-3 8. If 150 million workers produced America's GDP in 2010 (World View, p. 31), how much output did the average worker produce? $ _____

LO2-4 9. How much more output (income) per year will have to be produced in the world just to provide the 2.7 billion "severely" poor population with $1 more output per day? $ _____

LO2-1 10. Using data from Table 2.1 (p. 34), illustrate on the following graphs real GDP and population growth since 2000 (in the manner of Figure 2.1) for the nations indicated.

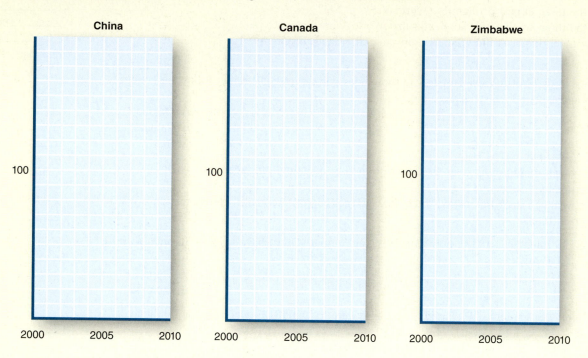

China

100

2000   2005   2010

Canada

100

2000   2005   2010

Zimbabwe

100

2000   2005   2010

LO2-1 11. Using data from the endpapers, illustrate on the graph below
(a) The federal government's share of the total output.
(b) The state/local government's share of the total output.

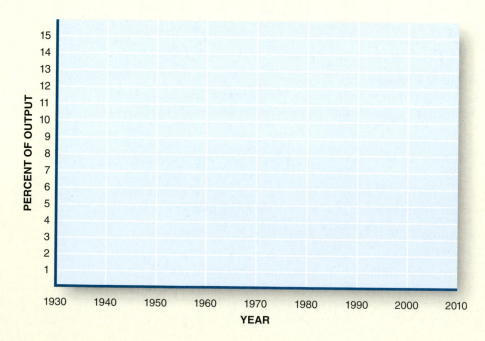

PERCENT OF OUTPUT

15
14
13
12
11
10
9
8
7
6
5
4
3
2
1

1930   1940   1950   1960   1970   1980   1990   2000   2010

YEAR

Supply and Demand

LEARNING OBJECTIVES

After reading this chapter, you should know

LO3-1. The nature and determinants of market demand.

LO3-2. The nature and determinants of market supply.

LO3-3. How market prices and quantities are established.

LO3-4. What causes market prices to change.

LO3-5. How government price controls affect market outcomes.

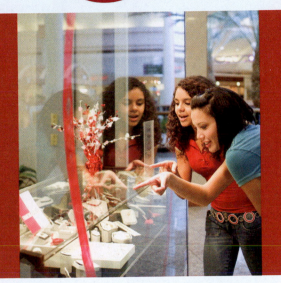

Gasoline prices surged in early 2008, rising from $2.99 a gallon in January to $4.05 in July. Consumers were angry every time they filled up their tanks. Popular opinion blamed the "Big Oil" companies and "speculators" for the sky-high prices. They demanded that the government intervene and force prices back down. Congressional hearings were conducted, government investigations were initiated, and "excess profits" taxes on oil companies were proposed.

By the end of 2008, gasoline prices had receded. In early 2009, pump prices were back to less than $2 a gallon. No oil executives or speculators had been arrested. No congressional reports had been completed. No government indictments had been issued. Economists explained this turn of events with "supply and demand." Surging demand and limited supply had caused the price spike; slowing demand and increased supply had pushed pump prices back down. Motorists weren't entirely convinced but were happy. They filled their tanks and

drove off to other economic concerns. Anxiety over high gasoline prices subsided until 2011, when pump prices surged again (see the World View on page 63).

The goal of this chapter is to explain how supply and demand really work. How do *markets* establish the price of gasoline and other products? Why do prices change so often? More broadly, how does the market mechanism decide WHAT to produce, HOW to produce, and FOR WHOM to produce? Specifically,

- **What determines the price of a good or service?**
- **How does the price of a product affect its production and consumption?**
- **Why do prices and production levels often change?**

Once we've seen how unregulated markets work, we'll observe how government intervention may alter market outcomes—for better or worse.

MARKET PARTICIPANTS

A good way to start figuring out how markets work is to see who participates in them. The answer is simple: just about every person and institution on the planet. Domestically, over 310 million consumers, about 25 million business firms, and tens of thousands of government agencies participate directly in the U.S. economy. Millions of international buyers and sellers also participate in U.S. markets.

Maximizing Behavior

All these market participants enter the marketplace to pursue specific goals. Consumers, for example, come with a limited amount of income to spend. Their objective is to buy the most desirable goods and services that their limited budgets will permit. We can't afford *everything* we want, so we must make *choices* about how to spend our scarce dollars. Our goal is to *maximize* the utility (satisfaction) we get from our available incomes.

Businesses also try to maximize in the marketplace. In their case, the quest is for maximum *profits*. Business profits are the difference between sales receipts and total costs. To maximize profits, business firms try to use resources efficiently in producing products that consumers desire.

The public sector also has maximizing goals. The economic purpose of government is to use available resources to serve public needs. The resources available for this purpose are limited too. Hence local, state, and federal governments must use scarce resources carefully, striving to maximize the general welfare of society. International consumers and producers pursue these same goals when participating in our markets.

Market participants sometimes lose sight of their respective goals. Consumers sometimes buy impulsively and later wish they'd used their income more wisely. Likewise, a producer may take a two-hour lunch, even at the sacrifice of maximum profits. And elected officials sometimes put their personal interests ahead of the public's interest. In all sectors of the economy, however, ***the basic goals of utility maximization, profit maximization, and welfare maximization explain most market activity.***

Specialization and Exchange

We are driven to buy and sell goods and services in the market by two simple facts. First, most of us are incapable of producing everything we want to consume. Second, even if we *could* produce all our own goods and services, it would still make sense to *specialize,* producing only one product and *trading* it for other desired goods and services.

Suppose you were capable of growing your own food, stitching your own clothes, building your own shelter, and even writing your own economics text. Even in this little utopia, it would still make sense to decide how *best* to expend your limited time and energy, relying on others to fill in the gaps. If you were *most* proficient at growing food, you would be best off spending your time farming. You could then *exchange* some of your food output for the clothes, shelter, and books you wanted. In the end, you'd be able to consume *more* goods than if you'd tried to make everything yourself.

Our economic interactions with others are thus necessitated by two constraints:

1. Our absolute inability as individuals to produce all the things we need or desire.
2. The limited amount of time, energy, and resources we have for producing those things we could make for ourselves.

Together these constraints lead us to specialize and interact. Most of the interactions that result take place in the market.

International Trade. The same motivations lead us to engage in international trade. The United States is *capable* of producing just about everything. But we've learned that it's cheaper to import bananas from Ecuador than to grow them in hothouses in Idaho. So we *specialize* in production, exporting tractors to Ecuador in exchange for imported bananas. Both nations end up consuming more products than they could if they had to produce everything themselves. That's why *global* markets are so vital to economic prosperity.

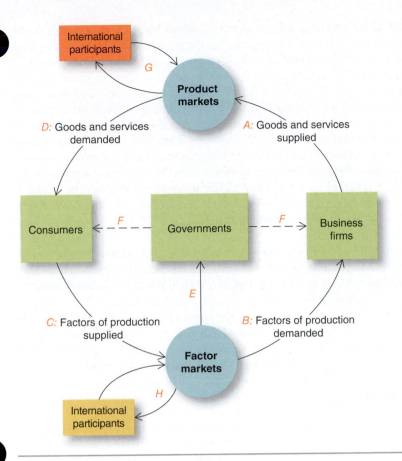

FIGURE 3.1
The Circular Flow

Business firms supply goods and services to product markets (point *A*) and purchase factors of production in factor markets (*B*). Individual consumers supply factors of production such as their own labor (*C*) and purchase final goods and services (*D*). Federal, state, and local governments acquire resources in factor markets (*E*) and provide services to both consumers and business (*F*). International participants also take part by supplying imports, purchasing exports (*G*), and buying and selling factors of production (*H*).

THE CIRCULAR FLOW

Figure 3.1 summarizes the kinds of interactions that occur among market participants. Note first that the figure identifies four separate groups of participants. Domestically, the rectangle labeled "Consumers" includes all 310 million consumers in the United States. In the "Business firms" box are grouped all the domestic business enterprises that buy and sell goods and services. The third participant, "Governments," includes the many separate agencies of the federal government, as well as state and local governments. Figure 3.1 also illustrates the role of global actors.

The Two Markets

The easiest way to keep track of all this activity is to distinguish two basic markets. Figure 3.1 makes this distinction by portraying separate circles for product markets and factor markets. In **factor markets,** factors of production are exchanged. Market participants buy or sell land, labor, or capital that can be used in the production process. When you go looking for work, for example, you're making a factor of production—your labor—available to producers. The producers will hire you—purchase your services in the factor market—if you're offering the skills they need at a price they're willing to pay.

Interactions within factor markets are only half the story. At the end of a hard day's work, consumers go to the grocery store (or to a virtual store online) to buy desired goods and services—that is, to buy *products.* In this context, consumers again interact with business firms, this time purchasing goods and services those firms have produced. These interactions occur in **product markets.** Foreigners also participate in the product market by supplying goods and services (imports) to the United States and buying some of our output (exports).

factor market: Any place where factors of production (e.g., land, labor, capital) are bought and sold.

product market: Any place where finished goods and services (products) are bought and sold.

opportunity cost: The most desired goods or services that are forgone in order to obtain something else.

The government sector also supplies services (e.g., education, national defense, high-ways). Most government services aren't explicitly sold in product markets, however. Typi-cally, they're delivered "free," without an explicit price (e.g., public elementary schools, highways). This doesn't mean government services are truly free, though. There's still an **opportunity cost** associated with every service the government provides. Consumers and businesses pay that cost indirectly through taxes rather than directly through market prices.

In Figure 3.1, the arrow connecting product markets to consumers (*D*) emphasizes the fact that consumers, by definition, don't supply products. When individuals produce goods and services, they do so within the government or business sector. For instance, a doctor, a dentist, or an economic consultant functions in two sectors. When selling services in the market, this person is regarded as a "business"; when away from the office, he or she is regarded as a "consumer." This distinction is helpful in emphasizing that *the consumer is the final recipient of all goods and services produced.*

Locating Markets. Although we refer repeatedly to two kinds of markets in this book, it would be a little foolish to go off in search of the product and factor markets. Neither mar-ket is a single, identifiable structure. The term *market* simply refers to a place or situation where an economic exchange occurs—where a buyer and seller interact. The exchange may take place on the street, in a taxicab, over the phone, by mail, or in cyberspace. In some cases, the market used may in fact be quite distinguishable, as in the case of a retail store, the Chicago Commodity Exchange, or a state employment office. But whatever it looks like, *a market exists wherever and whenever an exchange takes place.*

Dollars and Exchange

Figure 3.1 neglects one critical element of market interactions: dollars. Each arrow in the figure actually has two dimensions. Consider again the arrow (*D*) linking consumers to product markets: it's drawn in only one direction because consumers, by definition, don't provide goods and services directly to product markets. But they do provide something: dollars. If you want to obtain something from a product market, you must offer to pay for it (typically with cash, check, debit or credit card). Consumers exchange dollars for goods and services in product markets.

The same kinds of exchange occur in factor markets. When you go to work, you exchange a factor of production (your labor) for income, typically a paycheck. Here again, the path con-necting consumers to factor markets (*C*) really goes in two directions: one of real resources, the other of dollars. Consumers receive wages, rent, and interest for the labor, land, and capital they bring to the factor markets. Indeed, nearly *every market transaction involves an exchange of dollars for goods (in product markets) or resources (in factor markets).* Money is thus critical in facilitating market exchanges and the specialization the exchanges permit.

Supply and Demand

supply: The ability and willingness to sell (produce) specific quantities of a good at alternative prices in a given time period, *ceteris paribus*.

In every market transaction there must be a buyer and a seller. The seller is on the **supply** side of the market; the buyer is on the **demand** side. As noted earlier, we *supply* resources to the market when we look for a job—that is, when we offer our labor in exchange for income. We *demand* goods when we shop in a supermarket—that is, when we're prepared to offer dollars in exchange for something to eat. Business firms may *supply* goods and services in product markets at the same time they're *demanding* factors of production in fac-tor markets. Whether one is on the supply side or the demand side of any particular market transaction depends on the nature of the exchange, not on the people or institutions involved.

demand: The ability and willingness to buy specific quantities of a good at alternative prices in a given time period, *ceteris paribus*.

DEMAND

To get a sense of how the demand side of market transactions works, we'll focus first on a single consumer. Then we'll aggregate to illustrate *market* demand.

Individual Demand

We can begin to understand how market forces work by looking more closely at the behavior of a single market participant. Let us start with Tom, a senior at Clearview College. Tom has majored in everything from art history to government in his three years at Clearview. He didn't connect to any of those fields and is on the brink of academic dismissal. To make matters worse, his parents have threatened to cut him off financially unless he gets serious about his course work. By that, they mean he should enroll in courses that will lead to a job after graduation. Tom thinks he has found the perfect solution: web design. Everything associated with the Internet pays big bucks. Plus, the girls seem to think webbies are "cool." Or at least so Tom thinks. And his parents would definitely approve. So Tom has enrolled in web design courses.

Unfortunately for Tom, he never developed computer skills. Until he got to Clearview College, he thought mastering Sony's latest alien-attack video game was the pinnacle of electronic wizardry. Tom didn't have a clue about "streaming," "interfacing," "animation," or the other concepts the web design instructor outlined in the first lecture.

Given his circumstances, Tom was desperate to find someone who could tutor him in web design. But desperation is not enough to secure the services of a web architect. In a market-based economy, you must also be willing to *pay* for the things you want. Specifically, *a demand exists only if someone is willing and able to pay for the good*—that is, exchange dollars for a good or service in the marketplace. Is Tom willing and able to *pay* for the web design tutoring he so obviously needs?

Let us assume that Tom has some income and is willing to spend some of it to get a tutor. Under these assumptions, we can claim that Tom is a participant in the *market* for web design services.

But how much is Tom willing to pay? Surely Tom is not prepared to exchange *all* his income for help in mastering web design. After all, Tom could use his income to buy more desirable goods and services. If he spent all his income on a web tutor, that help would have an extremely high *opportunity cost*. He would be giving up the opportunity to spend that income on other goods and services. He'd pass his web design class but have little else. It doesn't sound like a good idea.

It seems more likely that there are *limits* to the amount Tom is willing to pay for any given quantity of web design tutoring. These limits will be determined by how much income Tom has to spend and how many other goods and services he must forsake to pay for a tutor.

Tom also knows that his grade in web design will depend in part on how much tutoring service he buys. He can pass the course with only a few hours of design help. If he wants a better grade, however, the cost is going to escalate quickly.

Naturally, Tom wants it all: an A in web design and a ticket to higher-paying jobs. But here again the distinction between *desire* and *demand* is relevant. He may *desire* to master web design, but his actual proficiency will depend on how many hours of tutoring he is willing to *pay* for.

The Demand Schedule

We assume, then, that when Tom starts looking for a web design tutor he has in mind some sort of **demand schedule,** like that described in Figure 3.2. According to row A of this schedule, Tom is willing and able to buy only 1 hour of tutoring service per semester if he must pay $50 an hour. At such an outrageous price he will learn minimal skills and just pass the course.

At lower prices, Tom would behave differently. According to Figure 3.2, Tom would purchase more tutoring services if the price per hour were less. Indeed, we see from row *I* of the demand schedule that Tom is willing to purchase 20 hours per semester—the whole bag of design tricks—if the price of tutoring got as low as $10 per hour.

Notice that the demand schedule doesn't tell us anything about *why* this consumer is willing to pay specific prices for various amounts of tutoring. Tom's expressed willingness to pay for web design tutoring may reflect a desperate need to finish a web design course, a lot of income to spend, or a relatively small desire for other goods and services. All the demand schedule tells us is what the consumer is *willing and able* to buy, for whatever reasons.

demand schedule: A table showing the quantities of a good a consumer is willing and able to buy at alternative prices in a given time period, *ceteris paribus.*

FIGURE 3.2

A Demand Schedule and Curve

A demand schedule indicates the quantities of a good a consumer is able and willing to buy at alternative prices (*ceteris paribus*). The demand schedule here indicates that Tom would buy 5 hours of web tutoring per semester if the price were $35 per hour (row *D*). If web tutoring were less expensive (rows *E–I*), Tom would purchase a larger quantity.

A demand curve is a graphical illustration of a demand schedule. Each point on the curve refers to a specific quantity that will be demanded at a given price. If, for example, the price of web tutoring were $35 per hour, this curve tells us the consumer would purchase 5 hours per semester (point *D*). If web tutoring cost $30 per hour, 7 hours per semester would be demanded (point *E*). Each point on the curve corresponds to a row in the schedule.

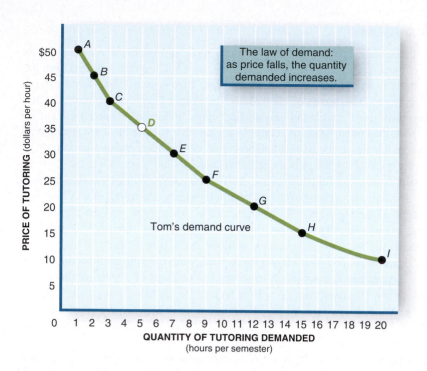

The law of demand: as price falls, the quantity demanded increases.

Tom's demand curve

web analysis

Priceline.com is an online service for purchasing airline tickets, vacation packages, and car rentals. The site allows you to specify the *highest* price you're willing to pay for air travel between two cities. In effect, you reveal your demand curve to Priceline. Try it at **www.priceline. com.**

	Tom's Demand Schedule	
	Price of Tutoring (per Hour)	Quantity of Tutoring Demanded (Hours per Semester)
A	$50	1
B	45	2
C	40	3
D	35	5
E	30	7
F	25	9
G	20	12
H	15	15
I	10	20

Also observe that the demand schedule doesn't tell us how many hours of design help the consumer will *actually* buy. Figure 3.2 simply states that Tom is *willing and able* to pay for 1 hour of tutoring per semester at $50 per hour, for 2 hours at $45 each, and so on. How much tutoring he purchases will depend on the actual price of such services in the market. Until we know that price, we cannot tell how much service will be purchased. Hence *"demand" is an expression of consumer buying intentions, of a willingness to buy, not a statement of actual purchases.*

The Demand Curve

demand curve: A curve describing the quantities of a good a consumer is willing and able to buy at alternative prices in a given time period, *ceteris paribus.*

A convenient summary of buying intentions is the **demand curve,** a graphical illustration of the demand schedule. The demand curve in Figure 3.2 tells us again that this consumer is willing to pay for only 1 hour of tutoring per semester if the price is $50 per hour (point *A*), for 2 if the price is $45 (point *B*), for 3 at $40 an hour (point *C*), and so on. Once we know what the market price of tutoring actually is, a glance at the demand curve tells us how much service this consumer will buy.

What the notion of *demand* emphasizes is that ***the amount we buy of a good depends on its price.*** We seldom if ever decide to buy only a certain quantity of a good at whatever price is charged. Instead we enter markets with a set of desires and a limited amount of money to spend. How much we actually buy of any particular good will depend on its price.

A common feature of demand curves is their downward slope. ***As the price of a good falls, people purchase more of it.*** In Figure 3.2 the quantity of web tutorial services demanded increases (moves rightward along the horizontal axis) as the price per hour decreases (moves down the vertical axis). This inverse relationship between price and quantity is so common that we refer to it as the **law of demand.** AT&T used this law to increase sales of the Apple iPhone 3GS in early 2011 (see the accompanying News).

law of demand: The quantity of a good demanded in a given time period increases as its price falls, *ceteris paribus.*

IN THE NEWS

AT&T Cuts Price on IPhone 3GS to $49

AT&T Inc. unveiled plans to sell Apple Inc.'s iPhone 3GS for $49 starting Friday. . . .

The phone is currently available on AT&T's website for $99, while the iPhone 4, released in June, sells for $299.

The latest offer is available to both new and certain existing customers and requires a two-year wireless service contract of at least $39.99 a month plus a $15 data plan.

—Tess Stynes

Source: *The Wall Street Journal,* **www.wsj.com,** January 6, 2011. Used with permission of Dow Jones & Company, Inc. via Copyright Clearance Center, Inc.

Analysis: The law of demand predicted that AT&T would sell more iPhone 3GS units (and related two-year service contracts) if it reduced its price. That is exactly what happened.

Determinants of Demand

The demand curve in Figure 3.2 has only two dimensions—quantity demanded (on the horizontal axis) and price (on the vertical axis). This seems to imply that the amount of tutoring demanded depends only on the price of that service. This is surely not the case. A consumer's willingness and ability to buy a product at various prices depend on a variety of forces. ***The determinants of market demand include***

- *Tastes* (desire for this and other goods).
- *Income* (of the consumer).
- *Other goods* (their availability and price).
- *Expectations* (for income, prices, tastes).
- *Number of buyers.*

Tom's "taste" for tutoring has nothing to do with taste buds. *Taste* is just another word for desire. In this case Tom's taste for web design services is clearly acquired. If he didn't have to pass a web design course, he would have no desire for related services, and thus no demand. If he had no income, he couldn't *demand* any web design tutoring either, no matter how much he might *desire* it.

Other goods also affect the demand for tutoring services. Their effect depends on whether they're *substitute* goods or *complementary* goods. A **substitute good** is one that might be purchased instead of tutoring services. In Tom's simple world, pizza is a substitute for tutoring. If the price of pizza fell, Tom would use his limited income to buy more pizzas and cut back on his purchases of web tutoring. When the price of a substitute good falls, the demand for tutoring services declines.

A **complementary good** is one that's typically consumed with, rather than instead of, tutoring. If textbook prices or tuition rates increase, Tom might take fewer classes and demand *less* web design assistance. In this case, a price increase for a complementary good causes the demand for tutoring to decline. When AT&T cut the price of the iPhone 3GS (see the News above), it knew that the demand for AT&T wireless service (a complementary good) would increase.

substitute goods: Goods that substitute for each other; when the price of good x rises, the demand for good y increases, *ceteris paribus.*

complementary goods: Goods frequently consumed in combination; when the price of good x rises, the demand for good y falls, *ceteris paribus.*

Expectations also play a role in consumer decisions. If Tom expected to flunk his web design course anyway, he probably wouldn't waste any money getting tutorial help; his demand for such services would disappear. On the other hand, if he expects a web tutor to determine his college fate, he might be more willing to buy such services.

Ceteris Paribus

ceteris paribus: The assumption of nothing else changing.

If demand is in fact such a multidimensional decision, how can we reduce it to only the two dimensions of price and quantity? In Chapter 1 we first encountered this *ceteris paribus* trick. To simplify their models of the world, economists focus on only one or two forces at a time and *assume* nothing else changes. We know a consumer's tastes, income, other goods, and expectations all affect the decision to hire a tutor. But we want to focus on the relationship between quantity demanded and price. That is, we want to know what *independent* influence price has on consumption decisions. To find out, we must isolate that one influence, price, and assume that the determinants of demand remain unchanged.

The *ceteris paribus* assumption is not as farfetched as it may seem. People's tastes, income, and expectations do not change quickly. Also, the prices and availability of other goods don't change all that fast. Hence a change in the *price* of a product may be the only factor that prompts an immediate change in quantity demanded.

The ability to predict consumer responses to a price change is important. What would happen, for example, to enrollment at your school if tuition doubled? Must we guess? Or can we use demand curves to predict how the quantity of applications will change as the price of college goes up? *Demand curves show us how changes in market prices alter consumer behavior.* We used the demand curve in Figure 3.2 to predict how Tom's web design ability would change at different tutorial prices.

Shifts in Demand

Although demand curves are useful in predicting consumer responses to market signals, they aren't infallible. The problem is that *the determinants of demand can and do change.* When they do, a specific demand curve may become obsolete. A *demand curve (schedule) is valid only so long as the underlying determinants of demand remain constant.* If the *ceteris paribus* assumption is violated—if tastes, income, other goods, or expectations change—the ability or willingness to buy will change. When this happens, the demand curve will **shift** to a new position.

shift in demand: A change in the quantity demanded at any (every) given price.

Suppose, for example, that Tom won $1,000 in the state lottery. This windfall would increase his ability to pay for tutoring services. Figure 3.3 shows the effect on Tom's demand. The old demand curve, D_1, is no longer relevant. Tom's lottery winnings enable him to buy *more* tutoring at any price, as illustrated by the new demand curve, D_2. According to this new curve, lucky Tom is now willing and able to buy 12 hours per semester at the price of $35 per hour (point d_2). This is a large increase in demand; previously (before winning the lottery) he demanded only 5 hours at that price (point d_1).

With his higher income, Tom can buy more tutoring services at every price. Thus *the entire demand curve shifts to the right when income goes up.* Figure 3.3 illustrates both the old (prelottery) and the new (postlottery) demand curves.

Income is only one of the basic determinants of demand. Changes in any of the other determinants of demand would also cause the demand curve to shift. Tom's taste for web tutoring might increase dramatically, for example, if his parents promised to buy him a new car for passing web design. In that case, he might be willing to forgo other goods and spend more of his income on tutors. *An increase in taste (desire) also shifts the demand curve to the right.*

Pizza and Politics. A similar demand shift occurs at the White House when a political crisis erupts. On an average day, White House staffers order about $180 worth of pizza from the nearby Domino's. When a crisis hits, however, staffers work well into the night and their demand for pizza soars. On the evening of the November 2010 midterm elections, White House staffers ordered more than $1,000 worth of pizza! Political analysts now use pizza deliveries to predict major White House announcements.

		Quantity Demanded (Hours per Semester)	
	Price (per Hour)	**Initial Demand**	**After Increase in Income**
A	$50	1	8
B	45	2	9
C	40	3	10
D	35	5	12
E	30	7	14
F	25	9	16
G	20	12	19
H	15	15	22
I	10	20	27

FIGURE 3.3
Shifts vs. Movements

A demand curve shows how a consumer responds to price changes. If the determinants of demand stay constant, the response is a *movement* along the curve to a new quantity demanded. In this case, the quantity demanded increases from 5 (point d_1), to 12 (point g_1), when price falls from $35 to $20 per hour.

If the determinants of demand *change*, the entire demand curve *shifts*. In this case, a rise in income increases demand. With more income, Tom is willing to buy 12 hours at the initial price of $35 (point d_2), not just the 5 hours he demanded before the lottery win.

Movements vs. Shifts

It's important to distinguish shifts of the demand curve from movements along the demand curve. *Movements along a demand curve are a response to price changes for that good.* Such movements assume that determinants of demand are unchanged. By contrast, *shifts of the demand curve occur when the determinants of demand change.* When tastes, income, other goods, or expectations are altered, the basic relationship between price and quantity demanded is changed (shifts).

For convenience, movements along a demand curve and shifts of the demand curve have their own labels. Specifically, take care to distinguish

- *Changes in quantity demanded:* movements along a given demand curve in response to price changes of that good.
- *Changes in demand:* shifts of the demand curve due to changes in tastes, income, other goods, or expectations.

Tom's behavior in the web tutoring market will change if either the price of tutoring changes (a movement) or the underlying determinants of his demand are altered (a shift). Notice in Figure 3.3 that he ends up buying 12 hours of web tutoring if either the price of tutoring falls (to $20 per hour) or his income increases. Demand curves help us predict those market responses.

Market Demand

Whatever we say about demand for web design tutoring on the part of one wannabe web master, we can also say about every student at Clearview College (or, for that matter, about all consumers). Some students have no interest in web design and aren't willing to pay for related services: they don't participate in the web tutoring market. Other students want such services but don't have enough income to pay for them: they too are excluded from the web tutoring market. A large number of students, however, not only have a need (or desire) for web tutoring but also are willing and able to purchase such services.

What we start with in product markets, then, is many individual demand curves. Fortunately, it's possible to combine all the individual demand curves into a single **market demand.** The aggregation process is no more difficult than simple arithmetic. Suppose you would be willing to buy 1 hour of tutoring per semester at a price of $80 per hour. George, who is also desperate to learn web design, would buy 2 at that price; and I would buy none, since my publisher (McGraw-Hill) creates a web page for me (try **www.mhhe.com/schiller13e**). What would our combined (market) demand for hours of tutoring be at that price? Collectively, we would be willing to buy a total of 3 hours of tutoring per semester if the price were $80 per hour. Our combined willingness to buy— our collective market demand—is nothing more than the sum of our individual demands. The same kind of aggregation can be performed for all consumers, leading to a summary of the total *market* demand for a specific good or service. Thus *market demand is determined by the number of potential buyers and their respective tastes, incomes, other goods, and expectations.*

> **market demand:** The total quantities of a good or service people are willing and able to buy at alternative prices in a given time period; the sum of individual demands.

The Market Demand Curve

Figure 3.4 provides the basic market demand schedule for a situation in which only three consumers participate in the market. It illustrates the same market situation with demand curves. The three individuals who participate in the market demand for web tutoring at Clearview College obviously differ greatly, as suggested by their respective demand schedules. Tom's demand schedule is portrayed in the first column of the table (and is identical to the one we examined in Figure 3.2). George is also desperate to acquire some job skills and is willing to pay relatively high prices for web design tutoring. His demand is summarized in the second column under Quantity Demanded in the table.

The third consumer in this market is Lisa. Lisa already knows the nuts and bolts of web design, so she isn't so desperate for tutorial services. She would like to upgrade her skills, however, especially in animation and e-commerce applications. But her limited budget precludes paying a lot for help. She will buy some technical support only if the price falls to $30 per hour. Should tutors cost less, she'd even buy quite a few hours of web design tutoring.

The differing circumstances of Tom, George, and Lisa are expressed in their individual demand schedules and associated curves in Figure 3.4. To determine the *market* demand for tutoring from this information, we simply add these three separate demands. The end result of this aggregation is, first, a *market* demand schedule and, second, the resultant *market* demand curve. These market summaries describe the various quantities of tutoring that Clearview College students are *willing and able* to purchase each semester at various prices.

How much web tutoring will be purchased each semester? Knowing how much help Tom, George, and Lisa are willing to buy at various prices doesn't tell you how much they're actually going to purchase. To determine the actual consumption of web tutoring, we have to know something about prices and supplies. Which of the many different prices illustrated in Figures 3.3 and 3.4 will actually prevail? How will that price be determined?

FIGURE 3.4

Construction of the Market Demand Curve

Market demand represents the combined demands of all market participants. To determine the total quantity of web tutoring demanded at any given price, we add the separate demands of the individual consumers. Row *G* of this schedule indicates that a *total* quantity of 39 hours per semester will be demanded at a price of $20 per hour. This same conclusion is reached by adding the individual demand curves, leading to point *G* on the market demand curve (see above).

| | Price (per Hour) | Quantity of Tutoring Demanded (Hours per Semester) | | | | | | |
		Tom	+	George	+	Lisa	=	Market Demand
A	$50	1		4		0		5
B	45	2		6		0		8
C	40	3		8		0		11
D	35	5		11		0		16
E	30	7		14		1		22
F	25	9		18		3		30
G	20	12		22		5		39
H	15	15		26		6		47
I	10	20		30		7		57

SUPPLY

To understand how the price of web tutoring is established, we must also look at the other side of the market: the *supply* side. We need to know how many hours of tutoring services people are willing and able to *sell* at various prices—that is, the **market supply.** As on the demand side, the *market supply* depends on the behavior of all the individuals willing and able to supply web tutoring at some price.

market supply: The total quantities of a good that sellers are willing and able to sell at alternative prices in a given time period, *ceteris paribus.*

Determinants of Supply

Let's return to the Clearview campus for a moment. What we need to know now is how much tutorial help people are willing and able to provide. Generally speaking, web design can be fun, but it can also be drudge work, especially when you're doing it for someone else. Software programs like PhotoShop, Flash, and Fireworks have made web design easier and more creative. And Wi-Fi access has made the job more convenient. But teaching someone else to design web pages is still work. So why does anyone do it? Easy answer: for the money. People offer (supply) tutoring services to earn income that they, in turn, can spend on the goods and services *they* desire.

How much money must be offered to induce web designers to do a little tutoring depends on a variety of things. The *determinants of market supply include*

- *Technology.*
- *Factor costs.*
- *Other goods.*
- *Taxes and subsidies.*
- *Expectations.*
- *Number of sellers.*

The technology of web design, for example, is always getting easier and more creative. With a program like PageOut, for example, it's very easy to create a bread-and-butter web page. A continuous stream of new software programs (e.g., Fireworks, DreamWeaver) keeps stretching the possibilities for graphics, animation, interactivity, and content. These technological advances mean that web design services can be supplied more quickly and cheaply. They also make *teaching* web design easier. As a result, they induce people to supply more tutoring services at every price.

How much web design service is offered at any given price also depends on the cost of factors of production. If the software programs needed to create web pages are cheap (or, better yet, free), web designers can afford to charge lower prices. If the required software inputs are expensive, however, they will have to charge more money per hour for their services.

Other goods can also affect the willingness to supply web design services. If you can make more income waiting tables than you can tutoring lazy students, why would you even boot up the computer? As the prices paid for other goods and services change, they will influence people's decision about whether to offer web services.

In the real world, the decision to supply goods and services is also influenced by the long arm of Uncle Sam. Federal, state, and local governments impose taxes on income earned in the marketplace. When tax rates are high, people get to keep less of the income they earn. Once taxes start biting into paychecks, some people may conclude that tutoring is no longer worth the hassle and withdraw from the market.

Expectations are also important on the supply side of the market. If web designers expect higher prices, lower costs, or reduced taxes, they may be more willing to learn new software programs. On the other hand, if they have poor expectations about the future, they may just find something else to do.

Finally, we note that the number of potential tutors will affect the quantity of service offered for sale at various prices. If there are lots of willing tutors on campus, a lot of tutorial service will be available at reasonable prices.

All these considerations—factor costs, technology, taxes, expectations—affect the decision to offer web services at various prices. In general, we assume that web architects will be willing to provide more tutoring if the per-hour price is high and less if the price is low. In other words, there is a **law of supply** that parallels the law of demand. *The law of supply says that larger quantities will be offered for sale at higher prices.* Here again, the laws rest on the *ceteris paribus* assumption: the quantity supplied increases at higher prices *if* the determinants of supply are constant. **Supply curves are upward-sloping to the right,** as shown in Figure 3.5. Note how the *quantity supplied* jumps from 39 hours (point *d*) to 130 hours (point *h*) when the price of web service doubles (from $20 to $40 per hour).

law of supply: The quantity of a good supplied in a given time period increases as its price increases, *ceteris paribus.*

Market Supply

Figure 3.5 also illustrates how *market* supply is constructed from the supply decisions of individual sellers. In this case, only three web masters are available. Ann is willing to

FIGURE 3.5
Market Supply

The market supply curve indicates the *combined* sales intentions of all market participants—that is, the total quantities they are willing and able to sell at various prices. If the price of tutoring were $45 per hour (point *i*), the *total* quantity of services supplied would be 140 hours per semester. This quantity is determined by adding the supply decisions of all individual producers. In this case, Ann supplies 93 hours, Bob supplies 33, and Cory supplies the rest.

| | Price per Hour | Quantity of Tutoring Supplied by | | | | | | |
		Ann	+	Bob	+	Cory	=	Market
j	$50	94		35		19		148
i	45	93		33		14		140
h	40	90		30		10		130
g	35	81		27		6		114
f	30	68		20		2		90
e	25	50		12		0		62
d	20	32		7		0		39
c	15	20		0		0		20
b	10	10		0		0		10

provide a lot of tutoring at low prices, whereas Bob requires at least $20 an hour. Cory won't talk to students for less than $30 an hour.

By adding the quantity each webhead is willing to offer at every price, we can construct the market supply curve. Notice in Figure 3.5 how the quantity supplied to the market at $45 (point *i*) comes from the individual efforts of Ann (93 hours), Bob (33 hours), and Cory (14 hours). *The market supply curve is just a summary of the supply intentions of all producers.*

None of the points on the market supply curve (Figure 3.5) tells us how much web tutoring is actually being sold on the Clearview campus. *Market supply is an expression of sellers' intentions—an offer to sell—not a statement of actual sales.* My next-door neighbor may be willing to sell his 2004 Honda Civic for $8,000, but most likely he'll never find a buyer at that price. Nevertheless, his *willingness* to sell his car at that price is part of the *market supply* of used cars.

Shifts of Supply

As with demand, there's nothing sacred about any given set of supply intentions. Supply curves *shift* when the underlying determinants of supply change. Thus *it is important to distinguish*

- *Changes in quantity supplied:* movements along a given supply curve.
- *Changes in supply:* shifts of the supply curve.

Our Latin friend *ceteris paribus* is once again the decisive factor. If the price of a product is the only variable changing, then we can **track changes in quantity supplied along the supply curve.** But if *ceteris paribus* is violated—if technology, factor costs, the profitability of producing other goods, tax rates, expectations, or the number of sellers changes—then **changes in supply are illustrated by shifts of the supply curve.**

The News below illustrates how a supply shift sent shrimp prices soaring in 2010. When the BP oil spill shut down fishing facilities in the Gulf of Mexico, the shrimp supply curve shifted leftward, and prices jumped.

IN THE NEWS

Seafood Prices Rise on BP Oil Spill

WASHINGTON—Diners at an upscale New Orleans–style restaurant in Washington, D.C., a thousand miles from the Gulf of Mexico, will feel the impact of the massive BP oil spill for the first time this Sunday.

Chef Jeff Tunks, whose five Washington, D.C.–area restaurants purchase 300 pounds of shrimp, 600 pounds of jumbo lump crabmeat, and 60 gallons of shucked oysters each week, will increase the raw bar surcharge by $3 at Acadiana's Sunday Brunch. . . .

The National Oceanic and Atmospheric Administration (NOAA) has closed about a third of the Gulf of Mexico to fishing, shrimping, and oystering, fearing oil contamination. As idled fishermen wait out the spill, seafood stock in the region is running out. . . .

The Gulf shrimp that is available is pricey, he says. Large, top-quality white shrimp sell for $7.50 a pound now, compared with $3.50 a pound in January.

—Donna Leinwand

Source: *USA TODAY.* June 24, 2010. Reprinted with permission.

Analysis: When factor costs or availability worsen, the supply curve *shifts* to the left. Such leftward supply-curve shifts push prices up the market demand curve.

EQUILIBRIUM

That post–BP oil spill spike in shrimp prices offers some clues to how the forces of supply and demand set—and change—market prices. For a closer look at how those forces work, we'll return to Clearview College for a moment. How did supply and demand resolve the WHAT, HOW, and FOR WHOM questions in that web tutoring market?

Figure 3.6 helps answer that question by bringing together the market supply and demand curves we've already examined (Figures 3.4 and 3.5). When we put the two curves together, we see that *only one price and quantity combination is compatible with the intentions of both buyers and sellers. This equilibrium occurs at the intersection of the supply and demand curves.* Notice in Figure 3.6 where that intersection occurs—at the price of $20 and the quantity of 39 hours. So $20 is the **equilibrium price:** campus webheads will sell a total of 39 hours of tutoring per semester—the same amount that students wish to buy at that price. Those 39 hours of tutoring service will be part of WHAT is produced in the economy.

equilibrium price: The price at which the quantity of a good demanded in a given time period equals the quantity supplied.

Market Clearing

An equilibrium doesn't imply that everyone is happy with the prevailing price or quantity. Notice in Figure 3.6, for example, that some students who want to buy web design assistance services don't get any. These would-be buyers are arrayed along the demand curve *below* the equilibrium. Because the price they're *willing* to pay is less than the equilibrium

FIGURE 3.6
Equilibrium Price

The intersection of the demand and supply curves establishes the *equilibrium* price and output. Only at equilibrium is the quantity demanded equal to the quantity supplied. In this case, the equilibrium price is $20 per hour, and 39 hours is the equilibrium quantity.

At above-equilibrium prices, a market *surplus* exists—the quantity supplied exceeds the quantity demanded. At prices below equilibrium, a market *shortage* exists.

Price (per Hour)	Quantity Supplied (Hours per Semester)		Quantity Demanded (Hours per Semester)
$50	148		5
45	140		8
40	130	Market surplus	11
35	114		16
30	90		22
25	62		30
20	39	Equilibrium	39
15	20	Market shortage	47
10	10		57

Nonequilibrium prices create surpluses or shortages.

price, they don't get any web design help. The market's FOR WHOM answer includes only those students willing and able to pay the equilibrium price.

Likewise, some would-be sellers are frustrated by this market outcome. These wannabe tutors are arrayed along the supply curve *above* the equilibrium. Because they insist on being paid *more* than the equilibrium price, they don't actually sell anything.

Although not everyone gets full satisfaction from the market equilibrium, that unique outcome is efficient. ***The equilibrium price and quantity reflect a compromise between buyers and sellers. No other compromise yields a quantity demanded that's exactly equal to the quantity supplied.***

The Invisible Hand. The equilibrium price isn't determined by any single individual. Rather, it's determined by the collective behavior of many buyers and sellers, each acting out his or her own demand or supply schedule. It's this kind of impersonal price determination that gave rise to Adam Smith's characterization of the market mechanism as "the invisible hand." In attempting to explain how the **market mechanism** works, the famed 18th-century economist noted a remarkable feature of market prices. The market behaves as if some unseen force (the invisible hand) were examining each individual's supply or demand schedule and then selecting a price that assured an equilibrium. In practice, the process of price determination isn't so mysterious: it's a simple process of trial and error.

Disequilibrium: Surplus and Shortage

Market Surplus. To appreciate the power of the market mechanism, consider interference in its operation. Suppose, for example, that campus webheads banded together and agreed to charge a minimum price of $25 per hour. By establishing a **price floor,** a minimum price for their services, the webheads hope to increase their incomes. But they won't be fully satisfied. Figure 3.6 illustrates the consequences of this *dis*equilibrium pricing. At $25 per hour, campus webheads would be offering more tutoring services (point *y*) than Tom, George, and Lisa were willing to buy (point *x*) at that price. A **market surplus** of web services would exist in the sense that more tutoring was being offered for sale (supplied) than students cared to purchase at the available price.

As Figure 3.6 indicates, at a price of $25 per hour, a market surplus of 32 hours per semester exists. Under these circumstances, campus webheads would be spending many idle hours at their keyboards waiting for customers to appear. Their waiting will be in vain because the quantity of web tutoring demanded will not increase until the price of tutoring falls. That is the clear message of the demand curve. As would-be tutors get this message, they'll reduce their prices. This is the response the market mechanism signals.

As sellers' asking prices decline, the quantity demanded will increase. This concept is illustrated in Figure 3.6 by the movement along the demand curve from point *x* to lower prices and greater quantity demanded. As we move down the market demand curve, the *desire* for web design help doesn't change, but the quantity people are *able and willing to buy* increases. When the price falls to $20 per hour, the quantity demanded will finally equal the quantity supplied. This is the *equilibrium* illustrated in Figure 3.6.

Market Shortage. A very different sequence of events would occur if a market shortage existed. Suppose someone were to spread the word that web tutoring services were available at only $15 per hour. Tom, George, and Lisa would be standing in line to get tutorial help, but campus web designers wouldn't be willing to supply the quantity demanded at that price. As Figure 3.6 confirms, at $15 per hour, the quantity demanded (47 hours per semester) greatly exceeds the quantity supplied (20 hours per semester). In this situation, we speak of a **market shortage**—that is, an excess of quantity demanded over quantity supplied. At a price of $15 an hour, the shortage amounts to 27 hours of tutoring services.

When a market shortage exists, not all consumer demands can be satisfied. Some people who are *willing* to buy web help at the going price ($15) won't be able to do so. To assure themselves of sufficient help, Tom, George, Lisa, or some other consumer may offer to pay a *higher* price, thus initiating a move up the demand curve in Figure 3.6. The higher prices

market mechanism: The use of market prices and sales to signal desired outputs (or resource allocations).

price floor: Lower limit set for the price of a good.

market surplus: The amount by which the quantity supplied exceeds the quantity demanded at a given price; excess supply.

market shortage: The amount by which the quantity demanded exceeds the quantity supplied at a given price; excess demand.

offered will in turn induce other enterprising webheads to tutor more, thus ensuring an upward movement along the market supply curve. Notice, again, that the *desire* to tutor web design hasn't changed; only the quantity supplied has responded to a change in price. As this process continues, the quantity supplied will eventually equal the quantity demanded (39 hours in Figure 3.6).

Self-Adjusting Prices. What we observe, then, is that *whenever the market price is set above or below the equilibrium price, either a market surplus or a market shortage will emerge.* To overcome a surplus or shortage, buyers and sellers will change their behavior. Sellers will have to compete for customers by reducing prices when a market surplus exists. If a shortage exists, buyers will compete for service by offering to pay higher prices. Only at the *equilibrium* price will no further adjustments be required.

Sometimes the market price is slow to adjust, and a disequilibrium persists. This is often the case with tickets to rock concerts, football games, and other one-time events. People initially adjust their behavior by standing in ticket lines for hours, or hopping on the Internet, hoping to buy a ticket at the below-equilibrium price. The tickets are typically resold ("scalped"), however, at prices closer to equilibrium. This is a common occurrence at major college sporting events such as the Final Four basketball championships (see the News below).

IN THE NEWS

Students Struggle to Find Final Four Tickets

When midnight struck Sunday, members of the Izzone had a chance to buy $25 tickets for the MSU student section of Lucas Oil Stadium in Indianapolis for MSU's Final Four matchup against Butler.

Four minutes after going on sale, most of the 660 available tickets were sold out. The rest sold out shortly after. Since then, it has been a scramble for Spartans fans to purchase a chance to see the men's basketball team make its second consecutive showing in the next-to-last stop of the NCAA championship.

Tickets still are on sale on websites such as www.stubhub.com and www.razorgator.com, ranging in price from $299 to more than $1,000. Some students said they have combed for tickets using sites such as eBay. Some have posted classified ads on sites such as allMSU.com.

—Zane McMillen

Source: *The State News*, Michigan State University, March 30, 2010. Used with permission.

Analysis: When tickets are sold initially at below-equilibrium prices, a market shortage is created. Scalpers resell tickets at prices closer to equilibrium, reaping a profit in the process.

Business firms can discover equilibrium prices by trial and error. If consumer purchases aren't keeping up with production, a firm may conclude that its price is above the equilibrium price. To get rid of accumulated inventory, the firm will have to lower its price (a grand end-of-year sale, perhaps). In the happier situation where consumer purchases are outpacing production, a firm might conclude that its price was a trifle too low and give it a nudge upward. In either case, the equilibrium price can be established after a few trials in the marketplace.

Changes in Equilibrium

No equilibrium price is permanent. The equilibrium price established in the Clearview College tutoring market, for example, was the unique outcome of specific demand and supply schedules. Those schedules themselves were based on our assumption of *ceteris paribus*. We assumed that the "taste" (desire) for web design assistance was given, as were consumers' incomes, the price and availability of other goods, and expectations. Any of these determinants of demand could change. When one does, the demand curve has to be redrawn. Such a shift of the demand curve will lead to a new equilibrium price and quantity. Indeed, *the equilibrium price will change whenever the supply or demand curve shifts.*

A Demand Shift. We can illustrate how equilibrium prices change by taking one last look at the Clearview College tutoring market. Our original supply and demand curves, together with the resulting equilibrium (point E_1), are depicted in Figure 3.7. Now suppose that all the professors at Clearview begin requiring class-specific web pages from each student. The increased need (desire) for web design ability will affect market demand. Tom, George, and Lisa will be willing to buy more web tutoring at every price than they were before. That is, the *demand* for web services has increased. We can represent this increased demand by a rightward *shift* of the market demand curve, as illustrated in Figure 3.7a.

Note that the new demand curve intersects the (unchanged) market supply curve at a new price (point E_2); the equilibrium price is now $30 per hour. This new equilibrium price will persist until either the demand curve or the supply curve shifts again.

FIGURE 3.7
Changes in Equilibrium

If demand or supply changes (shifts), market equilibrium will change as well.

Demand shift: In (*a*), the rightward shift of the demand curve illustrates an increase in demand. When demand increases, the equilibrium price rises (from E_1 to E_2).

Supply shift: In (*b*), the leftward shift of the supply curve illustrates a decrease in supply. This raises the equilibrium price to E_3.

Demand and supply curves shift only when their underlying determinants change—that is, when *ceteris paribus* is violated.

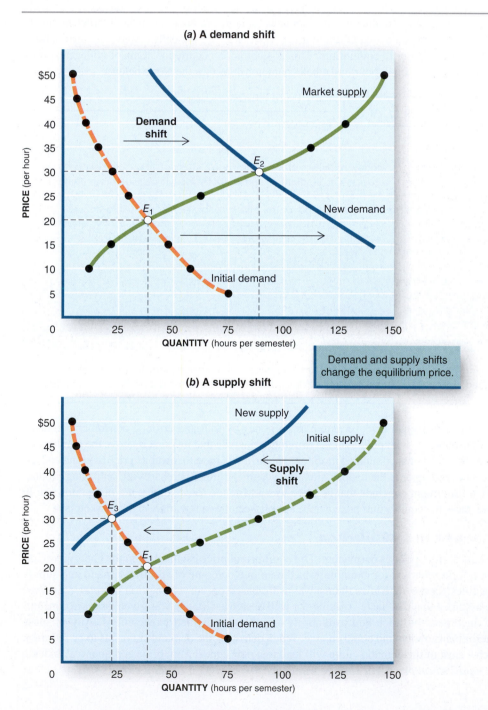

(*a*) A demand shift

(*b*) A supply shift

Demand and supply shifts change the equilibrium price.

A Supply Shift. Figure 3.7*b* illustrates a *supply* shift. The decrease (leftward shift) in supply might occur if some on-campus webheads got sick. Or approaching exams might convince would-be tutors that they have no time to spare. ***Whenever supply decreases (shifts left), price tends to rise,*** as in Figure 3.7*b*.

The rock band U2 learned about changing equilibriums the hard way. Ticket prices for the band's 1992 tour were below equilibrium, creating a *market shortage.* So U2 raised prices to as much as $52.50 a ticket for their 1997 tour—nearly double the 1992 price. By then, however, demand had shifted to the left due to a lack of U2 hits and an increased number of competing concerts. By the time they got to their second city they were playing in stadiums with lots of empty seats. The apparent *market surplus* led critics to label the 1997 "Pop Mart" tour a disaster. For their 2001 "Elevation Tour," U2 offered "festival seating" for only $35 in order to fill stadiums and concert halls. Demand shifted again in 2005. Buoyed by a spike of new hit songs (e.g., "Beautiful Day"), demand for U2's "Vertigo Tour" far outstripped available supply, sending ticket prices soaring (and scalpers celebrating). This is the kind of trial-and-error process that ultimately establishes an equilibrium price. For their ongoing 360-degree world tour, U2 cut prices again to assure filling even more concert seats.

Commodity prices are much faster to adjust than are rock bands. In the world oil market, for example, prices change daily as various forces shift market demand and supply curves. In early 2011, an increase (rightward shift) in market demand, together with a decrease (leftward shift) in market supply, pushed up the equilibrium prices of oil and gasoline, as the accompanying World View reports.

WORLD VIEW

Gas Prices High—and Might Get Higher

NEW YORK (CNNMoney)—Strong worldwide oil demand and lack of supply are to blame for steadily rising gasoline prices in the United States, an oil industry group said Friday. . . .

Felmy said worldwide oil demand in 2010 hit a record of more than 87 million barrels a day, driven largely by strong growth in India, China, and the Middle East.

Supply, meanwhile, was constricted by the drilling moratorium in the Gulf of Mexico following the BP disaster, slow production growth in non-OPEC countries, and OPEC production controls. . . .

Over the last year, prices are up 39 cents a gallon or 14 percent. Crude oil is up by a similar percentage, currently trading at just under $90 a barrel.

—Steve Hargreaves

Source: CNNMoney.com, January 21, 2011. © 2011 Time Inc. Used under license.

Analysis: Equilibrium prices change whenever market demand or supply curves shift. In this case, both curves are shifting, and the equilibrium price is rising.

MARKET OUTCOMES

Notice how the market mechanism resolves the basic economic questions of WHAT, HOW, and FOR WHOM.

WHAT

The WHAT question refers to the mix of output society produces. How much web tutorial service will be included in that mix? The answer at Clearview College was 39 hours of tutoring per semester. This decision wasn't reached in a referendum, but instead in the market equilibrium (Figure 3.6). In the same way but on a larger scale, millions of consumers and a handful of auto producers decide to include 12 million or so cars and trucks in each year's mix of output. Auto manufacturers use rebates, discounts, and variable interest rates to induce consumers to buy the same quantity that auto manufacturers are producing.

HOW

The market mechanism also determines HOW goods are produced. Profit-seeking producers will strive to produce web designs and automobiles in the most efficient way. They'll use market prices to decide not only WHAT to produce but also what resources to use in the production process. If new software simplifies web design—and is priced low enough—webheads will use it. Likewise, auto manufacturers will use robots rather than humans on the assembly line if robots reduce costs and increase profits.

FOR WHOM

Finally, the invisible hand of the market will determine who gets the goods produced. At Clearview College, who got web tutoring? Only those students who were willing and able to pay $20 per hour for that service. FOR WHOM are all those automobiles produced each year? The answer is the same: those consumers who are willing and able to pay the market price for a new car.

Optimal, Not Perfect

Not everyone is happy with these answers, of course. Tom would like to pay only $10 an hour for a tutor. And some of the Clearview students don't have enough income to buy any tutoring. They think it's unfair that they have to design their own web pages while rich students can have someone else do their design work for them. Students who can't afford cars are even less happy with the market's answer to the FOR WHOM question.

Although the outcomes of the marketplace aren't perfect, they're often optimal. Optimal outcomes are the best possible given our incomes and scarce resources. Sure, we'd like everyone to have access to tutoring and to drive a new car. But there aren't enough resources available to create such a utopia. So we have to ration available tutors and cars. The market mechanism performs this rationing function. People who want to supply tutoring or build cars are free to make that choice. And consumers are free to decide how they want to spend their income. In the process, we expect market participants to make decisions that maximize their own welfare. If they do, then we conclude that everyone is doing as well as possible, given their available resources.

THE ECONOMY TOMORROW

Organ Transplants

DEADLY SHORTAGES: THE ORGAN TRANSPLANT MARKET

As you were reading this chapter, dozens of Americans were dying from failed organs. More than 100,000 Americans are waiting for life-saving kidneys, livers, lungs, and other vital organs. They can't wait long, however. Every day at least 20 of these organ-diseased patients die. The clock is always ticking.

Modern technology can save most of these patients. Vital organs can be transplanted, extending the life of diseased patients. How many people are saved, however, depends on how well the organ "market" works.

The Supply of Organs. The only cure for liver disease and some other organ failures is a replacement organ. Over 50 years ago, doctors discovered that they could transplant an organ from one individual to another. Since then, medical technology has advanced to the point where organ transplants are exceptionally safe and successful. The constraint on this life-saving technique is the *supply* of transplantable organs.

Although over 2 million Americans die each year, most deaths do not create transplantable organs. Only 20,000 or so people die in circumstances—such as brain death after a car crash—that make them suitable donors for life-saving transplants. Additional kidneys can be "harvested" from live donors (we have two kidneys, but can function with only one; this is not true for liver, heart, or pancreas).

You don't have to die to supply an organ. Instead you become a donor by agreeing to release your organs after death. The agreement is typically certified on a driver's license and sometimes on a bracelet or "dog tag." This allows emergency doctors to identify potential organ supplies.

People become donors for many reasons. Moral principles, religious convictions, and humanitarianism all play a role in the donation decision. It's the same with blood donations: people give blood (while alive!) because they want to help save other individuals.

Market Incentives. Monetary incentives could also play a role. When blood donations are inadequate, hospitals and medical schools *buy* blood in the marketplace. People who might not donate blood come forth to *sell* blood when a price is offered. In principle, the same incentive might increase the number of *organ* donors. If offered cash now for a post-mortem organ, would the willingness to donate increase? The law of supply suggests it would. Offer $1,000 in cash for signing up, and potential donors will start lining up. Offer more, and the quantity supplied will increase further.

Zero Price Ceiling. The government doesn't permit this to happen. In 1984 Congress forbade the purchase or sale of human organs in the United States (the National Organ Transplantation Act). In part, the prohibition was rooted in moral and religious convictions. It was also motivated by equity concerns—the FOR WHOM question. If organs could be bought and sold, then the rich would have a distinct advantage in living.

The prohibition on market sales is effectively a **price ceiling** set at zero. As a consequence, the only available organs are those supplied by altruistic donors—people who are willing to supply organs at a zero price. The quantity supplied can't be increased with (illegal) price incentives. In general, *price ceilings have three predictable effects: they*

> **price ceiling:** An upper limit imposed on the price of a good.

- *Increase the quantity demanded.*
- *Decrease the quantity supplied.*
- *Create a market shortage.*

The Deadly Shortage. Figure 3.8 illustrates the consequences of this price ceiling. At a price of zero, only the quantity q_a of "altruistic" organs is available (roughly one-third of the potential supply). But the quantity q_d is demanded by all the organ-diseased individuals. The market shortage $q_d - q_a$ tells us how many patients will die.

The News on the next page argues that many of these deaths are unnecessary. Without the government-set price ceiling, more organ-diseased patients would live. Figure 3.8 shows that q_E people would get transplants in a market-driven system. In the government-regulated system, only the quantity of q_a of transplants can occur.

Why does the government impose price controls that condemn more people to die? Because it feels the market unfairly distributes available organs. Only people who can afford the price p_E end up living in the market-based system—a feature regulators say is unfair. In the absence of the market mechanism, however, the government must set other rules for who gets the even smaller quantity of organs supplied. That rationing system may be unfair as well.

web analysis

The United Network for Organ Sharing (**www.unos.org**) maintains data on organ waiting lists and transplants.

FIGURE 3.8
Organ Transplant Market

A market in human organs would deliver the quantity q_E at a price of p_E. The government-set price ceiling ($p = 0$) reduces the quantity supplied to q_a.

Study: People Would Donate Kidneys for Payment

Paying people for living kidney donations would increase the supply of the organs and would not result in a disproportionate number of poor donors, a study by researchers from the University of Pennsylvania and the Philadelphia Veterans Affairs Medical Center concludes. The study, published this month in the *Annals of Internal Medicine,* asked 342 participants whether they would donate a kidney with varying payments of $0, $10,000, and $100,000. . . .

The possibility of payments nearly doubled the number of participants in the study who said they would donate a kidney to a stranger. . . .

Last year 6,475 people died while on the waiting list for an organ transplant, and 4,476 were waiting for a kidney transplant, according to the Organ Procurement and Transplantation Network, part of the Health and Human Services Administration.

"There's no real reason why that model has to be continued," Halpern says of the current system. "There's nothing intrinsically unique about organ donation that requires it to be a truly altruistic act."

—Katharine Lackey

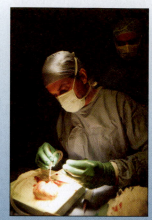
© Owen Franken/Corbis

Source: *USA TODAY.* March 31, 2010, p. 3A. Reprinted with permission.

Analysis: A prohibition against selling organs is effectively a price ceiling at zero. A positive price would increase the quantity supplied.

SUMMARY

- People participate in the marketplace by offering to buy or sell goods and services, or factors of production. Participation is motivated by the desire to maximize utility (consumers), profits (business firms), or the general welfare (government agencies) from the limited resources each participant has. LO3-1, LO3-2
- All market transactions involve the exchange of either factors of production or finished products. Although the actual exchanges can occur anywhere, they take place in product markets or factor markets, depending on what is being exchanged. LO3-1, LO3-2
- People willing and able to buy a particular good at some price are part of the market demand for that product. All those willing and able to sell that good at some price are part of the market supply. Total market demand or supply is the sum of individual demands or supplies. LO3-1, LO3-2
- Supply and demand curves illustrate how the quantity demanded or supplied changes in response to a change in the price of that good, if nothing else changes (*ceteris*

paribus). Demand curves slope downward; supply curves slope upward. LO3-1, LO3-2
- Determinants of market demand include the number of potential buyers and their respective tastes (desires), incomes, other goods, and expectations. If any of these determinants changes, the demand curve shifts. Movements along a demand curve are induced only by a change in the price of that good. LO3-4
- Determinants of market supply include factor costs, technology, profitability of other goods, expectations, tax rates, and number of sellers. Supply shifts when these underlying determinants change. LO3-4
- The quantity of goods or resources actually exchanged in each market depends on the behavior of all buyers and sellers, as summarized in market supply and demand curves. At the point where the two curves intersect, an equilibrium price—the price at which the quantity demanded equals the quantity supplied—is established. LO3-3
- A distinctive feature of the market equilibrium is that it's the only price-quantity combination acceptable to buyers

and sellers alike. At higher prices, sellers supply more than buyers are willing to purchase (a market surplus); at lower prices, the amount demanded exceeds the quantity supplied (a market shortage). Only the equilibrium price clears the market.   LO3-3

- Price ceilings are disequilibrium prices imposed on the marketplace. Such price controls create an imbalance between quantities demanded and supplied, resulting in market shortages.   LO3-5

Key Terms

factor market
product market
opportunity cost
supply
demand
demand schedule
demand curve

law of demand
substitute goods
complementary goods
ceteris paribus
shift in demand
market demand
market supply

law of supply
equilibrium price
market mechanism
price floor
market surplus
market shortage
price ceiling

Questions for Discussion

1. In our story of Tom, the student confronted with a web design assignment, we emphasized the great urgency of his desire for web tutoring. Many people would say that Tom had an "absolute need" for web help and therefore was ready to "pay anything" to get it. If this were true, what shape would his demand curve have? Why isn't this realistic?   LO3-1

2. With respect to the demand for college enrollment, which of the following would cause (1) a movement along the demand curve or (2) a shift of the demand curve?   LO3-4
   a. An increase in incomes.
   b. Lower tuition.
   c. More student loans.
   d. An increase in textbook prices.

3. What would have happened to shrimp prices and consumption if the government had prohibited price increases after the BP oil spill (see News, p. 58)?   LO3-5

4. Which determinants of pizza demand change when the White House is in crisis (p. 52)?   LO3-4

5. Why are scalpers able to resell tickets to the Final Four basketball games at such high prices?   LO3-2

6. In Figure 3.8, why is the organ demand curve downward-sloping rather than vertical?   LO3-1

7. The shortage in the organ market (Figure 3.8) requires a nonmarket rationing scheme. Who should get the available (q_a) organs? Is this fairer than the market-driven distribution?   LO3-5

8. What would happen in the apple market if the government set a *minimum* price of $5.00 per apple? What might motivate such a policy?   LO3-5

9. The World View on page 63 explains why gasoline prices rose in 2011. What will bring prices down?   LO3-4

10. Is there a shortage of on-campus parking at your school? How might the shortage be resolved?   LO3-3

 web activities to accompany this chapter can be found on the Online Learning Center: **http://www.mhhe.com/schiller13e**

 mobile app Visit your mobile app store and download the Schiller: Study Econ app *today*!

LO3-1 1. According to Figure 3.3, at what price would Tom buy 12 hours of web tutoring?

  (*a*) Without a lottery win.   _____
  (*b*) With a lottery win.   _____

LO3-3 2. According to Figures 3.5 and 3.6, what would the new equilibrium price of tutoring services be if Ann decided to stop tutoring?   _____

LO3-3 3. According to the News on page 61
  (*a*) What was the initial price of a Final Four ticket?   _____
  (*b*) At that price was there (A) an equilibrium, (B) a shortage, or (C) a surplus?   _____

LO3-3 4. Given the following data on gasoline supply and demand,
  (*a*) What is the equilibrium price?   _____
  (*b*) How large a market shortage would exist if government set a price ceiling of $2 per gallon?   _____

Price per gallon	$5.00	$4.00	$3.00	$2.00	$1.00		$5.00	$4.00	$3.00	$2.00	$1.00
Quantity demanded (gallons per day)						Quantity supplied (gallons per day)					
Al	1	2	3	4	5	Firm A	3	3	2	2	1
Betsy	0	1	1	1	2	Firm B	7	5	3	3	2
Casey	2	2	3	3	4	Firm C	6	4	3	3	1
Daisy	1	3	4	4	6	Firm D	6	5	3	2	0
Eddie	1	2	2	3	5	Firm E	4	2	2	2	1
Market total	__	__	__	__	__	Market total	__	__	__	__	__

LO3-2 5. As a result of the BP oil spill (News, p. 58), which of the following changed in the shrimp market (answer yes or no):

  (*a*) Demand?   _____
  (*b*) Quantity demanded?   _____
  (*c*) Price?   _____

LO3-4 6. Illustrate what's happening to oil prices in the World View on page 63.

Oil Market

PRICE (per barrel)

QUANTITY (barrels per day)

  (*a*) Which direction did the demand curve shift (left or right)?   _____
  (*b*) Which direction did the supply curve shift (left or right)?   _____
  (*c*) Did price (A) increase or (B) decrease?   _____

LO3-5 7. According to Figure 3.8,
  (*a*) How many people die in the market-driven economy?   _____
  (*b*) How many people die in the government-regulated economy?   _____

LO3-5 8. According to Figure 3.8,
  (*a*) How many organs are supplied at a zero price?   _____
  (*b*) If the News on page 66 is correct, how many organs would be supplied at positive prices?   _____

LO3-1 9. The goal of the price cut described in the News on page 51, was to (select one—enter letter)
  (*A*) Increase supply.   (*C*) Increase demand.   _____
  (*B*) Increase quantity supplied.   (*D*) Increase quantity demanded.

LO3-5   10. In Figure 3.8, when a price ceiling of zero is imposed on the organ market, by how much does

    (*a*) The quantity of organs demanded increase?   _____

    (*b*) The demand increase?   _____

    (*c*) The quantity of organs supplied decrease?   _____

    (*d*) The supply decrease?   _____

LO3-5   11. Use the following data to draw supply and demand curves on the accompanying graph.

Price	$ 8	7	6	5	4	3	2	1
Quantity demanded	2	3	4	5	6	7	8	9
Quantity supplied	10	9	8	7	6	5	4	3

    (*a*) What is the equilibrium price?   _____

    (*b*) If a *minimum* price (price floor) of $6 is set,

        (*i*) What kind of disequilibrium situation results?   _____

        (*ii*) How large is it?   _____

    (*c*) If a *maximum* price (price ceiling) of $3 is set,

        (*i*) What disequilibrium situation results?   _____

        (*ii*) How large is it?   _____

Illustrate these answers.

The Role of Government

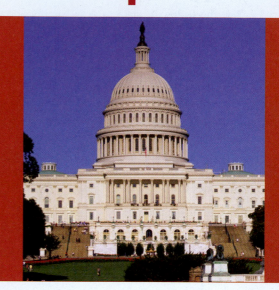

The market has a keen ear for private wants, but a deaf ear for public needs.

—Robert Heilbroner

Markets do work: the interaction of supply and demand in product markets *does* generate goods and services. Likewise, the interaction of supply and demand in labor markets *does* yield jobs, wages, and a distribution of income. As we've observed, the market is capable of determining WHAT goods to produce, HOW, and FOR WHOM.

But are the market's answers good enough? Is the mix of output produced by unregulated markets the best possible mix? Will producers choose the production process that protects the environment? Will the market-generated distribution of income be fair enough? Will there be enough jobs for everyone who wants one?

In reality, markets don't always give us the best possible outcomes. Markets dominated by a few powerful corporations may charge excessive prices, limit output, provide poor service, or even retard technological advance. In the quest for profits, producers may sacrifice the environment for cost savings. In unfettered markets, some people may not get life-saving health care, basic education, or even adequate nutrition. When markets generate such outcomes, government intervention may be needed to ensure better answers to the WHAT, HOW, and FOR WHOM questions.

This chapter identifies the circumstances under which government intervention is desirable. To this end, we answer the following questions:

- **Under what circumstances do markets fail?**
- **How can government intervention help?**
- **How much government intervention is desirable?**

As we'll see, there's substantial agreement about how and when markets fail to give us the best WHAT, HOW, and FOR WHOM answers. But there's much less agreement about whether government intervention improves the situation. Indeed, an overwhelming majority of Americans are ambivalent about government intervention. They want the government to "fix" the mix of output, protect the environment, and ensure an adequate level of income for everyone. But voters are equally quick to blame government meddling for many of our economic woes.

MARKET FAILURE

Market Failure

We can visualize the potential for government intervention by focusing on the WHAT question. Our goal here is to produce the best possible mix of output with existing resources. We illustrated this goal earlier with production possibilities curves. Figure 4.1 assumes that of all the possible combinations of output we could produce, the unique combination at point *X* represents the most desirable one. In other words, it's the **optimal mix of output,** the one that maximizes our collective social utility. We haven't yet figured out how to pinpoint that optimal mix; we're simply using the arbitrary point *X* in Figure 4.1 to represent that best possible outcome.

Ideally, the **market mechanism** would lead us to point *X*. Price signals in the marketplace are supposed to move factors of production from one industry to another in response to consumer demands. If we demand more health care—offer to buy more at a given price—more resources (labor) will be allocated to health care services. Similarly, a fall in demand will encourage health care practitioners (doctors, nurses, and the like) to find jobs in another industry. *Changes in market prices direct resources from one industry to another, moving us along the perimeter of the production possibilities curve.*

Where will the market mechanism take us? Will it move resources around until we end up at the optimal point *X*? Or will it leave us at another point on the production possibilities curve with a *sub*optimal mix of output? (If point *X* is the *optimal,* or best possible, mix, all other output mixes must be *sub*optimal.)

We use the term **market failure** to refer to situations where the market generates imperfect (suboptimal) outcomes. If the invisible hand of the marketplace produces a mix of output that's different from the one society most desires, then it has failed. *Market failure implies that the forces of supply and demand haven't led us to the best point on the production possibilities curve.* Such a failure is illustrated by point *M* in Figure 4.1. Point *M* is assumed to be the mix of output generated by market forces. Notice that the market mix (*M*) doesn't represent the optimal mix, which is assumed to be at point *X*. We get less health care and more of other goods than is optimal. The market in this case *fails;* we get the wrong answer to the WHAT question.

Market failure opens the door for government intervention. If the market can't do the job, we need some form of *nonmarket* force to get the right answers. In terms of Figure 4.1, we need something to change the mix of output—to move us from point *M* (the market mix of output) to point *X* (the optimal mix of output). Accordingly, *market failure establishes a basis for government intervention.* We look to the government to push market outcomes closer to the ideal.

Causes of Market Failure. Because market failure is the justification for government intervention, we need to know how and when market failure occurs. *The four specific sources of market failure are*

- *Public goods.*
- *Externalities.*
- *Market power.*
- *Inequity.*

We will first examine the nature of these problems, then see why government intervention is called for in each case.

optimal mix of output: The most desirable combination of output attainable with existing resources, technology, and social values.

market mechanism: The use of market prices and sales to signal desired outputs (or resource allocations).

market failure: An imperfection in the market mechanism that prevents optimal outcomes.

Production possibilities

The market fails when it produces the wrong (suboptimal) mix of output.

X (Optimal mix)

M (Market mix)

HEALTH CARE (units per time period)

ALL OTHER GOODS (units per time period)

FIGURE 4.1
Market Failure

We can produce any mix of output on the production possibilities curve. Our goal is to produce the optimal (best possible) mix of output, as represented by point *X*. Market forces, however, might produce another combination, like point *M*. In that case, the market fails—it produces a *sub*optimal mix of output.

Public Goods

The market mechanism has the unique capability to signal consumer demands for various goods and services. By offering to pay for goods, we express our preferences about WHAT to produce. However, this mode of communication works efficiently only if the benefits of consuming a particular good are available only to the individuals who purchase that product.

Consider doughnuts, for example. When you eat a doughnut, you alone get the satisfaction from its sweet, greasy taste—that is, you derive a private benefit. No one else benefits from your consumption of a doughnut: The doughnut you purchase in the market is yours alone to consume; it's a **private good.** Accordingly, your decision to purchase the doughnut will be determined only by your anticipated satisfaction, your income, and your opportunity costs.

No Exclusion. Most of the goods and services produced in the public sector are different from doughnuts—and not just because doughnuts look, taste, and smell different from "star wars" missile shields. When you buy a doughnut, you exclude others from consumption of that product. If Dunkin' Donuts sells you a particular pastry, it can't supply the same pastry to someone else. If you devour it, no one else can. In this sense, the transaction and product are completely private.

The same exclusiveness is not characteristic of national defense. If you buy a missile defense system to thwart enemy attacks, there's no way you can exclude your neighbors from the protection your system provides. Either the missile shield deters would-be attackers or it doesn't. In the former case, both you and your neighbors survive happily ever after; in the latter case, we're all blown away together. In that sense, you and your neighbors consume the benefits of a missile shield *jointly*. National defense isn't a divisible service. There's no such thing as exclusive consumption here. The consumption of nuclear defenses is a communal feat, no matter who pays for them. Accordingly, national defense is regarded as a **public good** in the sense that *consumption of a public good by one person doesn't preclude consumption of the same good by another person.* By contrast, a doughnut is a private good because if I eat it, no one else can consume it.

The Free-Rider Dilemma. The communal nature of public goods creates a dilemma. If you and I will *both* benefit from nuclear defenses, which one of us should buy the missile shield? I'd prefer that *you* buy it, thereby giving me protection at no direct cost. Hence I may profess no desire for a missile shield, secretly hoping to take a **free ride** on your market purchase. Unfortunately, you too have an incentive to conceal your desire for national defenses. As a consequence, neither one of us may step forward to demand a missile shield in the marketplace. We'll both end up defenseless.

Flood control is also a public good. No one in the valley wants to be flooded out. But each landowner knows that a flood control dam will protect *all* the landowners, regardless of who pays. Either the entire valley is protected or no one is. Accordingly, individual farmers and landowners may say they don't want a dam and aren't willing to pay for it. Everyone is waiting and hoping that someone else will pay for flood control. In other words, everyone wants a *free ride*. Thus, if we leave it to market forces, no one will *demand* flood control, and all the property in the valley will be washed away.

The difference between public goods and private goods rests on *technical considerations,* not political philosophy. The central question is whether we have the technical capability to exclude nonpayers. In the case of national defense or flood control, we simply don't have that capability. Even city streets have the characteristics of public goods. Although theoretically we could restrict the use of streets to those who paid to use them, a tollgate on every corner would be exceedingly expensive and impractical. Here again, joint or public consumption appears to be the only feasible alternative. As the following News on local firefighting emphasizes, the technical capability to exclude nonpayers is the key factor in identifying "public goods."

To the list of public goods we could add snow removal, the administration of justice (including prisons), the regulation of commerce, the conduct of foreign relations, airport security, and even Fourth of July fireworks. These services—which cost tens of *billions* of

private good: A good or service whose consumption by one person excludes consumption by others.

public good: A good or service whose consumption by one person does not exclude consumption by others.

free rider: An individual who reaps direct benefits from someone else's purchase (consumption) of a public good.

Flood control is a public good.

IN THE NEWS

Firefighters Watch as Home Burns to the Ground

OBION COUNTY, Tenn.—Imagine your home catches fire but the local fire department won't respond, then watches it burn. That's exactly what happened to a local family tonight.

A local neighborhood is furious after firefighters watched as an Obion County, Tennessee, home burned to the ground.

The homeowner, Gene Cranick, said he offered to pay whatever it would take for firefighters to put out the flames, but was told it was too late. They wouldn't do anything to stop his house from burning.

Each year, Obion County residents must pay $75 if they want fire protection from the city of South Fulton. But the Cranicks did not pay.

The mayor said if homeowners don't pay, they're out of luck.

This fire went on for hours because garden hoses just wouldn't put it out.

It was only when a neighbor's field caught fire, a neighbor who had paid the county fire service fee, that the department responded. Gene Cranick asked the fire chief to make an exception and save his home, the chief wouldn't.

—Jason Hibbs

Source: WPSD Local 6, Paducah, KY, September 30, 2010. Used with permission.

Analysis: A product is a "public good" only if nonpayers *cannot* be excluded from its consumption. Firefighters in Tennessee proved that fire protection is not inherently a public good: they let the nonpaying homeowner's house burn down!

dollars and employ thousands of workers—provide benefits to everyone, no matter who pays for them. In each instance it's technically impossible or prohibitively expensive to exclude nonpayers from the services provided.

Underproduction of Public Goods. The free riders associated with public goods upset the customary practice of paying for what you get. If I can get all the national defense, flood control, and laws I want without paying for them, I'm not about to complain. I'm perfectly happy to let you pay for the services while we all consume them. Of course, you may feel the same way. Why should you pay for these services if you can consume just as much of them when your neighbors foot the whole bill? It might seem selfish not to pay your share of the cost of providing public goods. But you'd be better off in a material sense if you spent your income on doughnuts, letting others pick up the tab for public services.

Because the familiar link between paying and consuming is broken, public goods can't be peddled in the supermarket. People are reluctant to buy what they can get free. Hence, *if public goods were marketed like private goods, everyone would wait for someone else to pay.* The end result might be a total lack of public services. This is the kind of dilemma Robert Heilbroner had in mind when he spoke of the market's "deaf ear" (see the quote at the beginning of this chapter).

The production possibilities curve in Figure 4.2 illustrates the dilemma created by public goods. Suppose that point *A* represents the optimal mix of private and public goods. It's the mix of goods and services we'd select if everyone's preferences were known and reflected in production decisions. The market mechanism won't lead us to point *A*, however, because the *demand* for public goods will be hidden. If we rely on the market, nearly everyone will withhold demand for public goods, waiting for a free ride to point *A*. As a result, we'll get a smaller quantity of public goods than we really want. The market mechanism will leave us at point *B*, with few, if any, public goods. Since point *A* is assumed to be optimal, point *B*

FIGURE 4.2

Underproduction of Public Goods

Suppose point *A* represents the optimal mix of output—that is, the mix of private and public goods that maximizes society's welfare. Because consumers won't demand purely public goods in the marketplace, the price mechanism won't allocate so many resources to their production. Instead the market will tend to produce a mix of output like point *B*, which includes fewer public goods (*0R*) than is optimal (*0S*).

must be *suboptimal* (inferior to point *A*). The market fails: we can't rely on the market mechanism to allocate enough resources to the production of public goods, no matter how much they might be desired.

Note that we're using the term "public good" in a peculiar way. To most people, "public good" refers to any good or service the government produces. In economics, however, the meaning is much more restrictive. The term "public good" refers only to those nonexcludable goods and services that must be consumed jointly, both by those who pay for them and by those who don't. Public goods can be produced by either the government or the private sector. Private goods can be produced in either sector as well. The problem is that ***the market tends to underproduce public goods and overproduce private goods.*** If we want more public goods, we need a *nonmarket* force—government intervention—to get them. The government will have to force people to pay taxes, then use the tax revenues to pay for the production of national defense, flood control, snow removal, and other public goods.

Externalities

The free-rider problem associated with public goods is one justification for government intervention. It's not the only justification, however. Further grounds for intervention arise from the tendency of costs or benefits of some market activities to "spill over" onto third parties.

Consider the case of cigarettes. The price someone is willing to pay for a pack of cigarettes reflects the amount of satisfaction a smoker anticipates from its consumption. If that price is high enough, tobacco companies will produce the cigarettes demanded. That is how market-based price signals are supposed to work. In this case, however, the price paid isn't a satisfactory signal of the product's desirability. The smoker's pleasure is offset in part by nonsmokers' *displeasure*. In this case, smoke literally spills over onto other consumers, causing them discomfort and possibly even ill health (see the World View below). Yet their loss isn't reflected in the market price: the harm caused to nonsmokers is *external* to the market price of cigarettes.

WORLD VIEW

Secondhand Smoke Kills 600,000 People a Year: Study

Secondhand smoke globally kills more than 600,000 people each year, accounting for 1 percent of all deaths worldwide, according to a new study. . . .

Researchers estimated that annually secondhand smoke causes about 379,000 deaths from heart disease, 165,000 deaths from lower respiratory disease, 36,900 deaths from asthma, and 21,400 deaths from lung cancer.

Children account for about 165,000 of the deaths, according to the researchers. . . .

The study found that 40 percent of children and 30 percent of adults regularly breathe in secondhand smoke.

Nationally, secondhand smoke causes 46,000 deaths from heart disease each year. . . .

—James Fanelli

Source: © Daily News, L.P. (New York). Used with permission.

Analysis: The health risks imposed on nonsmokers via passive smoke represent external costs. The market price of cigarettes doesn't reflect these costs borne by third parties.

externalities: Costs (or benefits) of a market activity borne by a third party; the difference between the social and private costs (benefits) of a market activity.

The term **externalities** refers to all costs or benefits of a market activity borne by a third party—that is, by someone other than the immediate producer or consumer. ***Whenever externalities are present, market prices aren't a valid measure of a good's value to society.*** As a consequence, the market will fail to produce the right mix of output. Specifically, ***the market will underproduce goods that yield external benefits and overproduce those that generate external costs.***

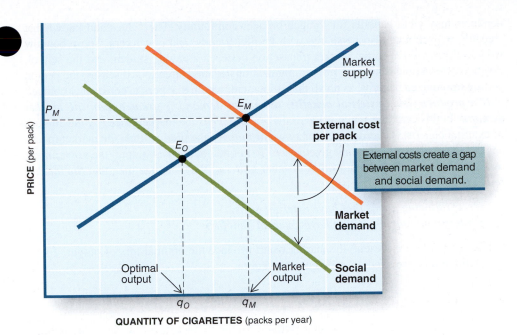

FIGURE 4.3
Externalities

The market responds to consumer demands, not externalities. Smokers demand q_M cigarettes at the equilibrium price P_M. But external costs on nonsmokers imply that the *social* demand for cigarettes is less than (below) *market* demand. The socially optimal level of output is q_O, less than the market output q_M.

External Costs. Figure 4.3 shows how external costs cause the market to overproduce cigarettes. The market demand curve includes only the wishes of smokers—that is, people who are willing and able to purchase cigarettes. The forces of market demand and supply result in an equilibrium at E_M in which q_M cigarettes are produced and consumed. The market price P_M reflects the value of those cigarettes to smokers.

The well-being of *non*smokers isn't reflected in the market equilibrium. To take the *non*smokers' interests into account, we must subtract the external costs imposed on *them* from the value that *smokers* put on cigarettes. In general,

Social demand = Market demand ± Externalities

In this case, the externality is a *cost,* so we must *subtract* the external cost from market demand to get a full accounting of social demand. The "social demand" curve in Figure 4.3 reflects this computation. To find this curve, we subtract the amount of external cost from every price on the market demand curve. Hence the social demand curve lies below the market demand curve in this case. What the social demand curve tells us is how much society would be willing and able to pay for cigarettes if the preferences of *both* smokers and nonsmokers were taken into account.

The social demand curve in Figure 4.3 creates a social equilibrium at E_O. At this juncture, we see that the socially *optimal* quantity of cigarettes is q_O, not the larger market-generated level at q_M. In this sense, the market produces too many cigarettes.

Externalities also exist in production. A power plant that burns high-sulfur coal damages the surrounding environment. Yet the damage inflicted on neighboring people, vegetation, and buildings is external to the cost calculations of the firm. Because the cost of such pollution is not reflected in the price of electricity, the firm will tend to produce more electricity (and pollution) than is socially desirable. To reduce this imbalance, the government has to step in and change market outcomes.

External Benefits. Externalities can also be beneficial. A product may generate external *benefits* rather than external *costs.* Your college is an example. The students who attend your school benefit directly from the education they receive. That's why they (and you) are willing to pay for tuition, books, and other services. The students in attendance aren't the only beneficiaries of this educational service, however. The research that a university conducts may yield benefits for a much broader community. The values and knowledge students acquire may also be shared with family, friends, and coworkers. These benefits would all be *external* to the market transaction between a paying student and the school. Positive externalities also arise from immunizations against infectious diseases: the person getting immunized benefits, as do all the people with whom that person comes into contact.

If a product yields external benefits, the social demand is greater than the market demand. In this case, the social value of the good *exceeds* the market price (by the amount of external benefit). Accordingly, society wants *more* of the product than the market mechanism alone will produce at any given price. To get that additional output, the government may have to intervene with subsidies or other policies. We conclude then that *the market fails by*

- *Overproducing goods that have external costs.*
- *Underproducing goods that have external benefits.*

If externalities are present, the market won't produce the optimal mix of output. To get that optimal mix, we need government intervention.

Market Power

In the case of both public goods and externalities, the market fails to achieve the optimal mix of output because the price signal is flawed. The price consumers are willing and able to pay for a specific good doesn't reflect all the benefits or cost of producing that good.

The market may fail, however, even when the price signals are accurate. The *response* to price signals, rather than the signals themselves, may be flawed.

monopoly: A firm that produces the entire market supply of a particular good or service.

Restricted Supply. Market power is often the cause of a flawed response. Suppose there were only one airline company in the world. This single seller of airline travel would be a **monopoly**—that is, the only producer in that industry. As a monopolist, the airline could charge extremely high prices without worrying that travelers would flock to a competing airline. At the same time, the high prices paid by consumers would express the importance of that service to society. Ideally, such prices would act as a signal to producers to build and fly more planes—to change the mix of output. But a monopolist doesn't have to cater to every consumer's whim. It can limit airline travel and obstruct our efforts to achieve an optimal mix of output.

market power: The ability to alter the market price of a good or a service.

Monopoly is the most severe form of **market power.** More generally, market power refers to any situation in which a single producer or consumer has the ability to alter the market price of a specific product. If the publisher (McGraw-Hill) charges a high price for this book, you'll have to pay the tab. McGraw-Hill has market power because there are relatively few economics textbooks and your professor has required you to use this one. You don't have power in the textbook market because your decision to buy or not won't alter the market price of this text. You're only one of the million students who are taking an introductory economics course this year.

The market power McGraw-Hill possesses is derived from the copyright on this text. No matter how profitable textbook sales might be, no one else is permitted to produce or sell this particular book. Patents are another common source of market power because they also preclude others from making or selling a specific product. Market power may also result from control of resources, restrictive production agreements, or efficiencies of large-scale production.

Whatever the source of market power, the direct consequence is that one or more producers attain discretionary power over the market's response to price signals. They may use that discretion to enrich themselves rather than to move the economy toward the optimal mix of output. In this case, the market will again fail to deliver the most desired goods and services.

antitrust: Government intervention to alter market structure or prevent abuse of market power.

The mandate for government intervention in this case is to prevent or dismantle concentrations of market power. That's the basic purpose of **antitrust** policy. Another option is to *regulate* market behavior. This was one of the goals of the antitrust case against Microsoft. The government was less interested in breaking Microsoft's near monopoly on operating systems than in changing the way Microsoft behaved.

In some cases, it may be economically efficient to have one large firm supply an entire market. Such a situation arises in **natural monopoly,** where a single firm can achieve economies of scale over the entire range of market output. Utility companies, local telephone service, subway systems, and cable all exhibit such scale (size) efficiencies. In these cases, a monopoly *structure* may be economically desirable. The government may have to regulate the *behavior* of a natural monopoly, however, to ensure that consumers get the benefits of that greater efficiency.

natural monopoly: An industry in which one firm can achieve economies of scale over the entire range of market supply.

Inequity

Public goods, externalities, and market power all cause resource misallocations. Where these phenomena exist, the market mechanism will fail to produce the optimal mix of output in the best possible way.

Beyond the questions of WHAT and HOW to produce, we're also concerned about FOR WHOM output is produced. The market answers this question by distributing a larger share of total output to those with the most income. Although this result may be efficient, it's not necessarily equitable. As we saw in Chapter 2, the market mechanism may enrich some people while leaving others to seek shelter in abandoned cars. If such outcomes violate our vision of equity, we may want the government to change the market-generated distribution of income.

Taxes and Transfers. The tax-and-transfer system is the principal mechanism for redistributing incomes. The idea here is to take some of the income away from those who have "too much" and give it to those whom the market has left with "too little." Taxes are levied to take back some of the income received from the market. Those tax revenues are then redistributed via transfer payments to those deemed needy, such as the poor, the aged, and the unemployed. **Transfer payments** are income payments for which no goods or services are exchanged. They're used to bolster the incomes of those for whom the market itself provides too little.

transfer payments: Payments to individuals for which no current goods or services are exchanged, like Social Security, welfare, and unemployment benefits.

Merit Goods. Often our vision of what is "too little" is defined in terms of specific goods and services. There is a widespread consensus in the United States that everyone is entitled to some minimum levels of shelter, food, and health care. These are regarded as **merit goods,** in the sense that everyone merits at least some minimum provision of such goods. When the market does not distribute that minimum provision, the government is called on to fill the gaps. In this case, the income transfers take the form of *in-kind* transfers (e.g., food stamps, housing vouchers, Medicaid) rather than *cash* transfers (e.g., welfare checks, Social Security benefits).

merit good: A good or service society deems everyone is entitled to some minimal quantity of.

Some people argue that we don't need the government to help the poor—that private charity alone will suffice. Unfortunately, private charity alone has never been adequate. One reason private charity doesn't suffice is the "free-rider" problem. If I contribute heavily to the poor, you benefit from safer streets (fewer muggers), a better environment (fewer slums and homeless people), and a clearer conscience (knowing that fewer people are starving). In this sense, the relief of misery is a *public* good. Were I the only taxpayer to benefit substantially from the reduction of poverty, then charity would be a private affair. As long as income support substantially benefits the public at large, then income redistribution is a *public* good, for which public funding is appropriate. This is the *economic* rationale for public income redistribution activities. To this rationale one can add such moral arguments as seem appropriate.

Macro Instability

The micro failures of the marketplace imply that we're at the wrong point on the production possibilities curve or inequitably distributing the output produced. There's another basic question we've swept under the rug, however. How do we get to the production possibilities curve in the first place? To reach the curve, we must utilize all available resources and technology. Can we be confident that the invisible hand of the marketplace will use all available resources? That confidence was shattered in 2008–2009 when total output

unemployment: The inability of labor force participants to find jobs.

contracted and **unemployment** soared. Millions of people who were willing and able to work but unable to find jobs demanded that the government intervene to increase output and create more jobs. The market had failed.

And what about prices? Price signals are a critical feature of the market mechanism. But the validity of those signals depends on some stable measure of value. What good is a doubling of salary when the price of everything you buy doubles as well? Generally, rising prices will enrich people who own property and impoverish people who rent. That's why we strive to avoid **inflation**—a situation in which the *average* price level is increasing.

inflation: An increase in the average level of prices of goods and services.

Historically, the marketplace has been wracked with bouts of both unemployment and inflation. These experiences have prompted calls for government intervention at the macro level. *The goal of macro intervention is to foster economic growth—to get us on the production possibilities curve (full employment), maintain a stable price level (price stability), and increase our capacity to produce (growth).*

GROWTH OF GOVERNMENT

The potential micro and macro failures of the marketplace provide specific justifications for government intervention. The question then turns to how well the activities of the public sector correspond to these implied mandates.

Federal Growth

Until the 1930s the federal government's role was largely limited to national defense (a public good), enforcement of a common legal system (also a public good), and provision of postal service (equity). The Great Depression of the 1930s spawned a new range of government activities, including welfare and Social Security programs (equity), minimum wage laws and workplace standards (regulation), and massive public works (public goods and externalities). In the 1950s the federal government also assumed a greater role in maintaining macroeconomic stability (macro failure), protecting the environment (externalities), and safeguarding the public's health (externalities and equity).

These increasing responsibilities have greatly increased the size of the public sector. In 1902 the federal government employed fewer than 350,000 people and spent a mere $650 *million*. Today the federal government employs nearly 4 million people and spends nearly $4 *trillion* a year.

Direct Expenditure. Figure 4.4 summarizes the growth of the public sector since 1930. World War II caused a massive increase in the size of the federal government. Federal purchases of goods and services for the war accounted for over 40 percent of total output during the 1943–1944 period. The federal share of total U.S. output fell abruptly after World War II, rose again during the Korean War (1950–1953), and has declined slightly since then.

The decline in the federal share of total output is somewhat at odds with most people's perception of government growth. This discrepancy is explained by two phenomena. First, people see the *absolute* size of the government growing every year. But we're focusing here on the *relative* size of the public sector. From 1950 until 2008 the public sector grew a bit more slowly than the private sector, slightly reducing its relative size. The trend was broken in 2008–2011, when the private sector shrank and the federal government undertook massive stimulus spending.

Income Transfers. Figure 4.4 depicts only government spending on goods and services, not *all* public spending. Direct expenditure on goods and services absorbs real resources, but income transfers don't. Hence income transfers don't directly alter the mix of output. Their effect is primarily *distributional* (the FOR WHOM question), not *allocative* (the WHAT question). Were income transfers included, the relative size and growth of the federal government would be larger than Figure 4.4 depicts. This is because *most of the growth in federal spending has come from increased income transfers, not purchases of goods and services.* Income transfers now account for over half of federal spending.

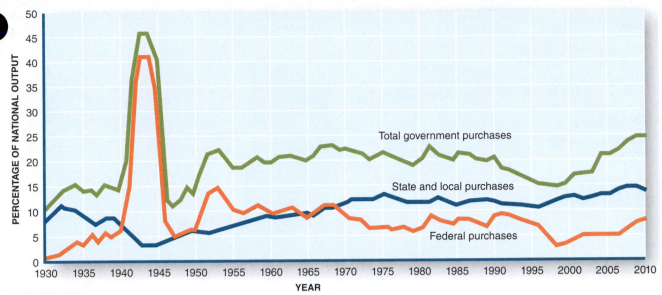

FIGURE 4.4
Government Growth

During World War II the public sector purchased nearly half of total U.S. output. Since the early 1950s the public sector share of total output has been closer to 20 percent. Within the public sector, however, there's been a major shift: state and local claims on resources have grown, while the federal share has declined significantly.

Source: U.S. Bureau of Economic Analysis.

State and Local Growth

State and local spending on goods and services has followed a very different path from federal expenditure. Prior to World War II, state and local governments dominated public sector spending. During the war, however, the share of total output going to state and local governments fell, hitting a low of 3 percent in that period (Figure 4.4).

State and local spending caught up with federal spending in the mid-1960s and has exceeded it ever since. Today *more than 80,000 state and local government entities buy much more output than Uncle Sam and employ five times as many people.* Education is a huge expenditure at lower levels of government. Most direct state spending is on colleges; most local spending is for elementary and secondary education. The fastest-growing areas for state expenditure are prisons (public safety) and welfare. At the local level, sewage and trash services are claiming an increasing share of budgets.

TAXATION

Whatever we may think of any specific government expenditure, we must recognize one basic fact of life: we pay for government spending. We pay not just in terms of tax *dollars* but in the more fundamental form of a changed mix of output. Government expenditures on goods and services absorb factors of production that could be used to produce consumer goods. The mix of output changes toward *more* public services and *fewer* private goods and services. Resources used to produce missile shields, operate elementary schools, or journey to Mars aren't available to produce cars, houses, or restaurant meals. In real terms, *the cost of government spending is measured by the private sector output sacrificed when the government employs scarce factors of production.*

The **opportunity costs** of public spending aren't always apparent. We don't directly hand over factors of production to the government. Instead we give the government part of our income in the form of taxes. Those dollars are then used to buy factors of production or goods and services in the marketplace. Thus *the primary function of taxes is to transfer*

web analysis

Information on government expenditures and national economic output for different countries can be found at **www.cia.gov.** Visit the "World Factbook" link.

opportunity costs: The most desired goods or services that are forgone in order to obtain something else.

FIGURE 4.5
Federal Taxes

Taxes transfer purchasing power from the private sector to the public sector. The largest federal tax is the individual income tax. The second-largest source of federal revenue is the Social Security payroll tax.

Source: Office of Management and Budget, FY2012 data.

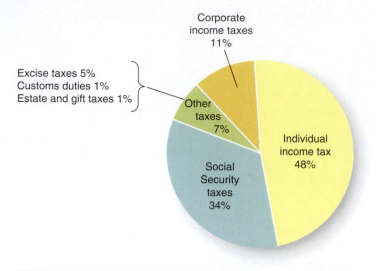

web analysis

For the most recent budget information, visit the Office of Management and Budget website (**www.whitehouse.gov/omb**), and click on the tab labeled "The Budget."

command over resources (purchasing power) from the private sector to the public sector. Although the government also borrows dollars to finance its purchases, taxes are the primary source of government revenues.

Federal Taxes

As recently as 1902, much of the revenue the federal government collected came from taxes imposed on alcoholic beverages. The federal government didn't have authority to collect income taxes. As a consequence, *total* federal revenue in 1902 was only $653 million.

Income Taxes. All that has changed. The Sixteenth Amendment to the U.S. Constitution, enacted in 1915, granted the federal government authority to collect income taxes. The government now collects well over $1 *trillion* in that form alone. Although the federal government still collects taxes on alcoholic beverages, the individual income tax has become the largest single source of government revenue (see Figure 4.5).

In theory, the federal income tax is designed to be **progressive**—that is, to take a larger *fraction* of high incomes than of low incomes. In 2010, for example, a single person with less than $8,375 of taxable income was taxed at 10 percent. People with incomes of $34,000–$82,400 confronted a 25 percent tax rate on their additional income. The marginal tax rate got as high as 35 percent for people earning more than $373,000 in income. Thus *people with high incomes not only pay more taxes but also pay a larger **fraction** of their income in taxes.*

progressive tax: A tax system in which tax rates rise as incomes rise.

Social Security Taxes. The second major source of federal revenue is the Social Security payroll tax. People working now transfer part of their earnings to retired workers by making "contributions" to Social Security. There's nothing voluntary about these "contributions"; they take the form of mandatory payroll deductions. In 2010, each worker paid 7.65 percent of his or her wages to Social Security, and employers contributed an equal amount. As a consequence, the government collected nearly $1 trillion from this tax.

At first glance, the Social Security payroll tax looks like a **proportional tax**—that is, a tax that takes the *same* fraction of every taxpayer's income. But this isn't the case. The Social Security (FICA) tax isn't levied on every payroll dollar. Incomes above a certain ceiling ($106,800 in 2011) aren't taxed. As a result, workers with *really* high salaries turn over a smaller fraction of their incomes to Social Security than do low-wage workers. This makes the Social Security payroll tax a **regressive tax**.

proportional tax: A tax that levies the same rate on every dollar of income.

regressive tax: A tax system in which tax rates fall as incomes rise.

Corporate Taxes. The federal government taxes the profits of corporations as well as the incomes of consumers. But there are far fewer corporations (less than 4 million) than consumers (310 million), and their profits are small in comparison to total consumer income. In 2011, the federal government collected less than $350 billion in corporate income taxes, despite the fact that it imposed a top tax rate of 35 percent on corporate profits.

Excise Taxes. The last major source of federal revenue is excise taxes. Like the early taxes on whiskey, excise taxes are sales taxes imposed on specific goods and services. The federal government taxes not only liquor ($13.50 per gallon) but also gasoline (18.4 cents per gallon), cigarettes ($1.01 per pack), air fares (7.5 percent), firearms (10–11 percent), gambling (0.25 percent), and a variety of other goods and services. Such taxes not only discourage production and consumption of these goods by raising their price and thereby reducing the quantity demanded; they also raise a substantial amount of revenue.

State and Local Revenues

Taxes. State and local governments also levy taxes on consumers and businesses. In general, cities depend heavily on property taxes, and state governments rely heavily on sales taxes. Although nearly all states and many cities also impose income taxes, effective tax rates are so low (averaging less than 2 percent of personal income) that income tax revenues are much less than sales and property tax revenues.

Like the Social Security payroll tax, state and local taxes tend to be *regressive*—that is, they take a larger share of income from the poor than from the rich. Consider a 4 percent sales tax, for example. It might appear that a uniform tax rate like this would affect all consumers equally. But people with lower incomes tend to spend most of their income on goods and services. Thus most of their income is subject to sales taxes. By contrast, a person with a high income can afford to save part of his or her income and thereby shelter it from sales taxes. A family that earns $40,000 and spends $30,000 of it on taxable goods and services, for example, pays $1,200 in sales taxes when the tax rate is 4 percent. In effect, then, they are handing over 3 percent of their *income* ($1,200 ÷ $40,000) to the state. By contrast, the family that makes only $12,000 and spends $11,500 of it for food, clothing, and shelter pays $460 in sales taxes in the same state. Their total tax is smaller, but it represents a much larger *share* (3.8 versus 3.0 percent) of their income.

Local property taxes are also regressive because poor people devote a larger portion of their incomes to housing costs. Hence a larger share of a poor family's income is subject to property taxes. State lotteries are also regressive for the same reason (see the following News). Low-income players spend 1.4 percent of their incomes on lottery tickets while upper-income players devote only 0.1 percent of their income to lottery purchases.

"I can't find anything wrong here, Mr. Truffle . . . you just seem to have too much left after taxes."

Analysis: Taxes are a financing mechanism that enables the government to purchase scarce resources. Higher taxes imply fewer private sector purchases.

IN THE NEWS

Perpetuating Poverty: Lotteries Prey on the Poor

A recently released Gallup survey confirms the fears of many who oppose government-promoted gambling: the poorest among us are contributing much more to lottery revenues than those with higher incomes. The poll found that people who played the lottery with an income of less than $20,000 annually spent an average of $46 per month on lottery tickets. That comes out to more than $550 per year, and it is nearly double the amount spent in any other income bracket.

The significance of this is magnified when we look deeper into the figures. Those with annual incomes ranging from $30,000 to $50,000 had the second-highest average—$24 per month, or $288 per year. A person making $20,000 spends three times as much on lottery tickets on average than does someone making $30,000. And keep in mind that these numbers represent average spending. For every one or two people who spend just a few bucks a year on lotteries, others spend thousands.

—Jordan Ballor

Source: Action Institute. March 3, 2004. From "Perpetuating Poverty: Lotteries Prey on the Poor" by Jordan Ballor, **www.action.org.** Used with permission by the author.

Analysis: Poor people spend a larger percentage of their income on lottery tickets than do rich people. This makes lotteries a regressive source of government revenue.

GOVERNMENT FAILURE

Some government intervention in the marketplace is clearly desirable. The market mechanism can fail for a variety of reasons, leaving a laissez-faire economy short of its economic goals. But how much government intervention is desirable? Communist nations once thought that complete government control of production, consumption, and distribution decisions was the surest path to utopia. They learned the hard way that *not only markets but governments as well can fail.* In this context, **government failure** means that government intervention fails to move us closer to our economic goals.

In Figure 4.6, the goal of government intervention is to move the mix of output from point M (failed market outcome) to point X (the social optimum). But government intervention might unwittingly move us to point G_1, making matters worse. Or the government might overreact, sending us to point G_2. Red tape and onerous regulation might even force us to point G_3, *inside* the production possibilities curve (with less total output than at point M). All those possibilities (G_1, G_2, G_3) represent government failure. Government intervention is desirable only to the extent that it *improves* market outcomes (e.g., G_4). Government

government failure:
Government intervention that fails to improve economic outcomes.

FIGURE 4.6
Government Failure

When the market produces a sub-optimal mix of output like point M, the goal of government is to move output to the social optimum (point X). A move to G_4 would be an improvement in the mix of output. But government intervention *may* move the economy to points G_1, G_2, or G_3—all reflecting government failure.

intervention in the FOR WHOM question is desirable only if the distribution of income gets better, not worse, as a result of taxes and transfers. Even when outcomes improve, government failure may occur if the costs of government intervention exceed the benefits of an improved output mix, cleaner production methods, or a fairer distribution of income.

Perceptions of Waste

Taxpayers seem to have strong opinions about government failure. When asked whether the government "wastes" their tax dollars or uses them well, the majority see waste in government (see the accompanying News on "Persistent Doubts"). The average taxpayer now believes that state governments waste 42 cents out of each dollar, while the federal government wastes 53 cents out of each tax dollar!

web analysis

For more public opinion on the role of government, visit the American National Election Studies website at **www.electionstudies.org**. Click on the "Tables and Graphs" tab.

IN THE NEWS

Persistent Doubts about Government Waste

Question: Do you think that people in government waste a lot of the money we pay in taxes, waste some of it, or don't waste very much of it?

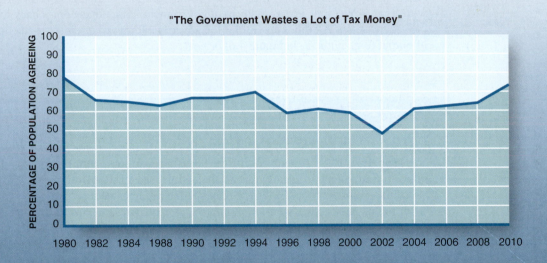

"The Government Wastes a Lot of Tax Money"

Source: American National Election Studies (**www.electionstudies.org**), with additional updates.

Analysis: If the government wastes resources, we end up inside rather than on our production possibilities curve (like point G_3 in Figure 4.6). This is a form of government failure.

Government "waste" implies that the public sector isn't producing as many services as it could with the resources at its disposal. Such inefficiency implies that we're producing somewhere *inside* our production possibilities curve rather than on it (e.g., point G_3 in Figure 4.6). If the government is wasting resources this way, we can't possibly be producing the optimal mix of output.

Opportunity Cost

Even if the government wasn't wasting resources, it might still be guilty of government failure. Notice in Figure 4.6 that points G_1 and G_2 are on the production possibilities curve.

So resources aren't being "wasted." But those points still represent suboptimal outcomes. In reality, *the issue of government failure encompasses two distinct questions:*

- *Efficiency:* Are we getting as much service as we could from the resources we allocate to government?
- *Opportunity cost:* Are we giving up too many private sector goods in order to get those services?

When assessing government's role in the economy, *we must consider not only what governments do but also what we give up to allow them to do it.* The theory of public goods tells us only what activities are appropriate for government, not the proper *level* of such activity. National defense is clearly a proper function of the public sector. Not so clear, however, is how much the government should spend on tanks, aircraft carriers, and missile shields. The same is true of environmental protection or law enforcement.

The concept of opportunity costs puts a new perspective on the whole question of government size. *Everything the government does entails an opportunity cost.* Before we can decide how big is "too big," we must decide what we're willing to give up to support the public sector. A military force of 1.4 million men and women is "too big" from an economic perspective only if we value the forgone private production and consumption more highly than we value the added strength of our defenses. The government has gone "too far" if the highway it builds is less desired than the park and homes it replaced. In these and all cases, the assessment of bigness must come back to a comparison of what is given up with what is received. The assessment of government failure thus comes back to points on the production possibilities curve. Has the government moved us closer to the optimal mix of output (e.g., point G_4 in Figure 4.6) or not?

THE ECONOMY TOMORROW

"RIGHT"-SIZING GOVERNMENT

You don't have to be a genius to find the optimal mix of output in Figure 4.6—it's clearly marked. And Figure 4.2 clearly reveals the optimal size of the government as well. In both cases, the opportunity cost principle points to the right answer.

From this perspective, *additional public sector activity is desirable only if the benefits from that activity exceed its opportunity costs.* In other words, we compare the benefits of a public project to the value of the private goods given up to produce it. By performing this calculation repeatedly along the perimeter of the production possibilities curve, we could locate the optimal mix of output—the point at which no further increase in public sector spending activity is desirable.

Valuation Problems

Although the principles of cost–benefit analysis are simple enough, they're deceptive. How are we to measure the potential benefits of improved police services, for example? Should we estimate the number of robberies and murders prevented, calculate the worth of each, and add up the benefits? And how are we supposed to calculate the worth of a saved life? By a person's earnings? Value of assets? Number of friends? And what about the increased sense of security people have when they know the police are patrolling their neighborhood? Should this be included in the benefit calculation? Some people will attach great value to this service; others will attach little. Whose values should be the standard? Should we consult liberals or conservatives on these questions?

When we're dealing with (private) market goods and services, we can gauge the benefits of a product by the amount of money consumers are willing to pay for it. This price signal isn't available for most public services, however, because of externalities and the nonexclusive nature of pure public goods (the free-rider problem). Hence *the value (benefits) of public services must be estimated because they don't have (reliable) market prices.* This opens the door to endless political squabbles about how beneficial any particular government activity is.

The same problems arise in evaluating the government's efforts to redistribute incomes. Government transfer payments now go to retired workers, disabled people, veterans, farmers, sick people, students, pregnant women, unemployed people, poor people, and a long list of other recipients. To pay for all these transfers, the government must raise tax revenues. With so many people paying taxes and receiving transfer payments, the net effects on the distribution of income aren't easy to figure out. Yet we can't determine whether this government intervention is worth it until we know how the FOR WHOM answer was changed and what the tax-and-transfer effort cost us.

Ballot Box Economics

In practice, we rely on political mechanisms, not cost–benefit calculations, to decide what to produce in the public sector and how to redistribute incomes. *Voting mechanisms substitute for the market mechanism in allocating resources to the public sector and deciding how to use them.* Some people have even suggested that the variety and volume of public goods are determined by the most votes, just as the variety and volume of private goods are determined by the most dollars. Thus governments choose the level and mix of output (and related taxation) that seem to command the most votes.

Sometimes the link between the ballot box and output decisions is very clear and direct. State and local governments, for example, are often compelled to get voter approval before building another highway, school, housing project, or sewage plant. *Bond referenda* are direct requests by a government unit for voter approval of specific public spending projects (e.g., roads, schools). In 2010, for example, governments sought voter approval for $20 billion of new borrowing to finance public expenditure; over 70 percent of those requests were approved.

Bond referenda are more the exception than the rule. Bond referenda account for less than 1 percent of state and local expenditures (and no federal expenditures). As a consequence, voter control of public spending is typically much less direct. Although federal agencies must receive authorization from Congress for all expenditures, consumers get a chance to elect new representatives only every two years. Much the same is true at state and local levels. Voters may be in a position to dictate the general level and pattern of public expenditures but have little direct influence on everyday output decisions. In this sense, the ballot box is a poor substitute for the market mechanism.

Even if the link between the ballot box and allocation decisions were stronger, the resulting mix of output might not be optimal. A democratic vote, for example, might yield a 51 percent majority for approval of new local highways. Should the highways then be built? The answer isn't obvious. After all, a large minority (49 percent) of the voters have stated that they don't want resources used this way. If we proceed to build the highways, we'll make those people worse off. Their loss may be greater than what proponents gain. Hence the basic dilemma is really twofold. *We don't know what the real demand for public services is, and votes alone don't reflect the intensity of individual demands.* Moreover, real-world decision making involves so many choices that a stable consensus is impossible.

Public Choice Theory

In the midst of all this complexity and uncertainty, another factor may be decisive— namely self-interest. In principle, government officials are supposed to serve the people. It doesn't take long, however, before officials realize that the public is indecisive about what it wants and takes little interest in government's day-to-day activities. With such latitude, government officials can set their own agendas. Those agendas may give higher priority to personal advancement than to the needs of the public. Agency directors may foster new programs that enlarge their mandate, enhance their visibility, and increase their prestige or income. Members of Congress may likewise pursue legislative favors like tax breaks for supporters more diligently than they pursue the general public interest. In such cases, the probability of attaining the socially optimal mix of output declines.

The theory of **public choice** emphasizes the role of self-interest in public decision making. Public choice theory essentially extends the analysis of market behavior to political behavior. Public officials are assumed to have specific personal goals (for example, power, recognition, wealth) that they'll pursue in office. *A central tenet of public choice theory is that bureaucrats are just as selfish (utility maximizing) as everyone else.*

Public choice theory provides a neat and simple explanation for public sector decision making. But critics argue that the theory provides a woefully narrow view of public servants. Some people do selflessly pursue larger, public goals, such critics argue, and ideas can overwhelm self-interest. Steven Kelman of Harvard, for example, argues that narrow self-interest can't explain the War on Poverty of the 1960s, the tax revolt of the 1970s, or the deregulation movement of the 1980s. These tidal changes in public policy reflect the power of ideas, not simple self-interest. Public choice theory tells us how many decisions about government are made; it doesn't tell us how they should be made. The "right" size of government in the economy tomorrow will depend less on self-interest and more on how much we trust *markets* to generate optimal outcomes or trust government intervention to *improve* on market failures.

> **public choice:** Theory of public sector behavior emphasizing rational self-interest of decision makers and voters.

SUMMARY

- Government intervention in the marketplace is justified by market failure—that is, suboptimal market outcomes.   LO4-1
- The micro failures of the market originate in public goods, externalities, market power, and an inequitable distribution of income. These flaws deter the market from achieving the optimal mix of output or distribution of income.   LO4-1
- Public goods are those that can't be consumed exclusively; they're jointly consumed regardless of who pays. Because everyone seeks a free ride, no one demands public goods in the marketplace. Hence, the market underproduces public goods.   LO4-1
- Externalities are costs (or benefits) of a market transaction borne by a third party. Externalities create a divergence between social and private costs or benefits, causing suboptimal market outcomes. The market overproduces goods with external costs and underproduces goods with external benefits.   LO4-1
- Market power enables a producer to thwart market signals and maintain a suboptimal mix of output. Antitrust policy seeks to prevent or restrict market power. The government may also regulate the behavior of powerful firms.   LO4-1

- The market-generated distribution of income may be unfair. This inequity may prompt the government to intervene with taxes and transfer payments that redistribute incomes.   LO4-1
- The macro failures of the marketplace are reflected in unemployment and inflation. Government intervention is intended to achieve full employment and price stability.   LO4-1
- The federal government expanded greatly after 1930. More recent growth has been in transfer payments, defense spending, and health programs.   LO4-2
- State and local governments purchase more output (12 percent of GDP) than the federal government (8 percent) and employ five times as many workers.   LO4-2
- Income and payroll taxes provide most federal revenues. States get most revenue from sales taxes; local governments rely on property taxes.   LO4-3
- Government failure occurs when intervention doesn't move toward the optimal mix of output (or income). Failure may result from outright waste (operational inefficiency) or from a misallocation of resources.   LO4-4
- All government activity must be evaluated in terms of its opportunity cost—that is, the *private* goods and services forgone to make resources available to the public sector.   LO4-4

Key Terms

optimal mix of output
market mechanism
market failure
private good
public good
free rider
externalities

monopoly
market power
antitrust
natural monopoly
transfer payments
merit good
unemployment

inflation
opportunity cost
progressive tax
proportional tax
regressive tax
government failure
public choice

Questions for Discussion

1. Why should taxpayers subsidize public colleges and universities? What external benefits are generated by higher education?   LO4-1

2. If everyone seeks a free ride, what mix of output will be produced in Figure 4.2? Why would anyone voluntarily contribute to the purchase of public goods like flood control or snow removal?   LO4-1

3. Should the firefighters have saved the house in the News on page 73? What was the justification for their belated intervention?   LO4-1

4. Why might Fourth of July fireworks be considered a public good? Who should pay for them? What about airport security?   LO4-1

5. What is the specific market failure justification for government spending on (*a*) public universities, (*b*) health care, (*c*) trash pickup, (*d*) highways, (*e*) police, and (*f*) solar energy? Would a purely private economy produce any of these services?   LO4-1

6. If smoking generates external costs, should smoking simply be outlawed? How about cars that pollute?   LO4-1

7. The government now spends over $700 billion a year on Social Security benefits. Why don't we leave it to individuals to save for their own retirement?   LO4-1

8. What government actions might cause failures like points G_1, G_2, and G_3 in Figure 4.6? Can you give examples?   LO4-4

9. How does XM Satellite deter nonsubscribers from listening to its transmissions? Does this make radio programming a private good or a public good?   LO4-1

10. Should the government be downsized? Which functions should be cut back? Which ones should be expanded?   LO4-2

11. Which taxes hit the poor hardest—those of local, state, or federal governments?   LO4-3

---

 web activities to accompany this chapter can be found on the Online Learning Center:
http://www.mhhe.com/schiller13e

 mobile app Visit your mobile app store and download the Schiller: Study Econ app *today!*

PROBLEMS FOR CHAPTER 4   Name: _____

LO4-1 1. In Figure 4.2 (p. 73), by how much is the market
   (a) Overproducing private goods? _____
   (b) Underproducing public goods? _____

LO4-1 2. Use Figure 4.3 (p. 75) to illustrate on the accompanying production
   possibilities curve the optimal mix of output (X).

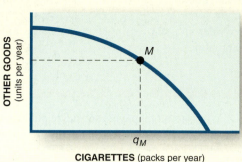

CIGARETTES (packs per year)

LO4-1 3. Assume that the product depicted below generates external costs in
   consumption of $4 per unit.
   (a) What is the market price (market value) of the product? _____
   (b) Draw the social demand curve.
   (c) What is the socially optimal output? _____
   (d) By how much does the market overproduce this good? _____

LO4-1 4. In the previous problem's
   market equilibrium, what is
   (a) The market value of
       the good? _____
   (b) The social value of
       the good? _____

LO4-1 5. If the average adult produces $90,000 of output per year, how much output is lost as a result
   of adult deaths from secondhand smoke, according to the News on page 74? $_____

LO4-3 6. (a) Assuming a 10 percent sales tax is levied on all consumption, complete the following table:

Income	Consumption	Sales Tax	Percentage of Income Paid in Taxes
$10,000	$11,000	_____	_____
20,000	20,000	_____	_____
40,000	36,000	_____	_____
80,000	60,000	_____	_____

   (b) Is the sales tax (A) progressive or (B) regressive? _____

Name: _____

LO4-4   7. If a new home can be constructed for $175,000, what is the opportunity cost of federal defense
spending, measured in terms of private housing? (Assume a defense budget of $700 billion.)   _____

LO4-1   8. Suppose the following data represent the market demand for college education:

Tuition (per year)	$1,000	$2,000	$3,000	$4,000	$5,000	$6,000	$7,000	$8,000
Enrollment demanded (in millions per year)	8	7	6	5	4	3	2	1

(a) If tuition is set at $3,000, how many students will enroll?   _____

Now suppose that society gets an external benefit of $1,000 for every enrolled student.

(b) Draw the social and market demand curves for this situation on the graph below.
(c) What is the socially optimal level of enrollment at the same tuition price of $3,000?   _____
(d) How large of a subsidy is needed to achieve this optimal outcome?   _____

College Market

LO4-1   9. Assume the market demand for cigarettes is

Price per pack	$10	$9	$8	$7	$6	$5	$4	$3
Quantity demanded (million packs per year)	2	4	6	8	10	12	14	16

(a) If cigarettes are priced at $7 a pack, how many packs will smokers buy?   _____
(b) If secondhand smoke creates $2 of harm per pack, what is the optimal rate of smoking?   _____
(c) How large a tax is needed to achieve this outcome?   _____

LO4-3   10. According to the News on page 82, what percentage of income is spent on lottery tickets by
(a) A poor family with income of $18,000 per year?   _____
(b) An affluent family with income of $40,000 per year?   _____

LO4-2   11. (a) Between 2000 and 2010, by what percent did federal spending increase
   (i) in nominal terms?   _____
   (ii) in real (inflation-adjusted terms)? Use the following values: $698.1 billion for 2000;
       $1,075.9 billion for 2010.   _____
(b) What percent of nominal total output (GDP) came from federal purchases in
   (i) 2000?   _____
   (ii) 2010?   _____

(use end covers of text or **www.bea.gov** for data)

Product Markets:
The Basics

The prices and products we see every day emerge from decisions made by millions of individual consumers and firms. A primary objective of microeconomic theory is to explain how those decisions are made. How high a price are consumers willing to pay for the products they want? Which products will consumers actually purchase—and in what quantities? We explore these dimensions of consumer *demand* in Chapters 5 and 6. We move to the *supply* side in Chapter 7, examining the costs that businesses incur in producing the products consumers demand.

Consumer Choice

LEARNING OBJECTIVES

After reading this chapter, you should know

LO5-1. Why demand curves are downward sloping.

LO5-2. The nature and source of consumer surplus.

LO5-3. The meaning and use of price discrimination.

LO5-4. How consumers maximize utility.

Steve Jobs knew he had a winner with the iPhone. Every time Apple added a feature to the iPod, sales picked up. Now Jobs had a product that combined cell phone services with wireless computing and audio and video download capabilities—all accessible on a touch screen. It was sure to be a hit. The only sticky question was *price*. What price should Apple put on its new iPhone? The company's goal was to sell 10 million iPhones in the first two years of production. If it set the price low enough, it could surely do that. But Apple didn't want to give away the iPhone—it wanted to make a nice profit. Yet if it set the price *too* high, sales would fall short of its sales target. What price should it charge? Apple's pricing committee had to know how many iPhones consumers would buy at different prices. In other words, they had to know the dimensions of *consumer demand*. After considerable deliberation, they set the initial price at $499 for the 4 GB iPhone, launched in January 2007.

Apple's iPhone pricing dilemma underscores the importance of *prices* in determining consumer behavior. Consumers "want," "need," and "just have to have" a vast array of goods and services. When decision time comes, however, product *prices* often dictate what consumers will actually buy. As we observed in Chapter 3, the quantity of a product *demanded* depends on its price.

This chapter takes a closer look at how product prices affect consumer decisions. We focus on three related questions:

- **How do we decide how much of any good to buy?**
- **Why do we feel so good about our purchases?**
- **Why do we buy certain products but not others?**

The law of demand (first encountered in Chapter 3) gives us some clues for answering these questions. But we need to look beyond that law to fashion more complete answers. We need to know what forces give demand curves their downward-sloping shape. We also need to know more about how to *use* demand curves to predict consumer behavior.

DETERMINANTS OF DEMAND

In seeking explanations for consumer behavior, we have to recognize that the field of economics doesn't have all the answers. But it does offer a unique perspective that sets it apart from other fields of study.

The Sociopsychiatric Explanation

Consider first the explanations of consumer behavior offered by other fields of study. Psychiatrists and psychologists have had a virtual field day formulating such explanations. Freud was among the first to describe us humans as bundles of subconscious (and unconscious) fears, complexes, and anxieties. From a Freudian perspective, we strive for ever higher levels of consumption to satisfy basic drives for security, sex, and ego gratifications. Like the most primitive of people, we clothe and adorn ourselves in ways that assert our identity and worth. We eat and smoke too much because we need the oral gratifications and security associated with mother's breast. Oversized homes and cars give us a source of warmth and security remembered from the womb. On the other hand, we often buy and consume some things we don't really want, just to assert our rebellious feelings against our parents (or parent substitutes). In Freud's view, it's the constant interplay of these id, ego, and superego drives that motivates us to buy, buy, buy.

Sociologists offer additional explanations for our consumption behavior. They observe our yearning to stand above the crowd, to receive recognition from the masses. For people with exceptional talents, such recognition may come easily. But for the ordinary person, recognition may depend on conspicuous consumption. A sleek car, a newer fashion, a more exotic vacation become expressions of identity that provoke recognition, even social acceptance. We strive for ever higher levels of consumption—not just to keep up with the Joneses but to surpass them.

Not *all* consumption is motivated by ego or status concerns. Some food is consumed for the sake of self-preservation, some clothing worn for warmth, and some housing built for shelter. The typical U.S. consumer has more than enough income to satisfy these basic needs, however. In today's economy, most consumers also have *discretionary* income that can be used to satisfy psychological or sociological longings. Single women are able to spend a lot of money on clothes and pets, and men spend freely on entertainment, food, and drink (see the accompanying News). Teenagers show off their affluence in purchases of electronic goods, cars, and clothes (see Figure 5.1).

IN THE NEWS

Men vs. Women: How They Spend

Are men really different from women? If spending habits are any clue, males do differ from females. That's the conclusion one would draw from the latest Bureau of Labor Statistics (BLS) survey of consumer expenditure. Here's what the BLS found out about the spending habits of young (under age 25) men and women who are living on their own:

Common Traits

- Young men have more after-tax income to spend ($14,930 per year) than do young women ($12,931). Both sexes go deep into debt, however, by spending $4,000–$6,000 more than their incomes.
- Neither sex spends much on charity, reading, or health care.

Distinctive Traits

- Men spend twice as much more on alcoholic beverages and smoking.
- Men spend almost twice as much as women do on electronic equipment.
- Young women spend twice as much money on clothing, personal care items, and their pets.

Source: U.S. Bureau of Labor Statistics, 2009, Consumer Expenditure Survey, **www.bls.gov.**

Analysis: Consumer patterns vary by gender, age, and other characteristics. Economists try to isolate the common influences on consumer behavior.

web analysis

Each year the Bureau of Labor Statistics surveys consumer expenditures. For current and historical data, visit **www.bls.gov/cex.**

FIGURE 5.1
Affluent Teenagers

Teenagers spend over $200 billion a year. Much of this spending is for cars, stereos, and other durables. The percentages of U.S. teenagers owning certain items are shown here.

Source: The TRU Study, 2011. TRU, **www.tru-insight.com**. Used with permission.

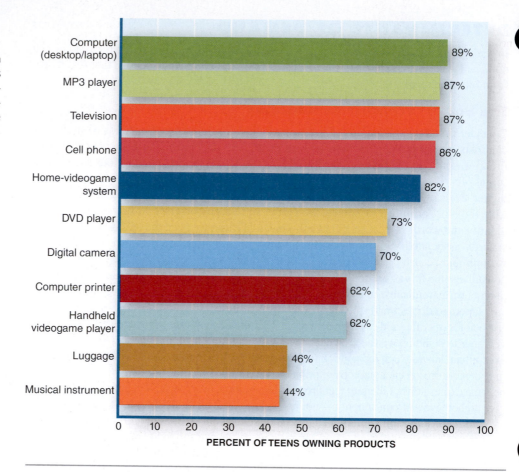

PERCENT OF TEENS OWNING PRODUCTS

The Economic Explanation

Although psychiatrists and sociologists offer intriguing explanations for our consumption patterns, their explanations fall a bit short. Sociopsychiatric theories tell us why teenagers, men, and women *desire* certain goods and services. But they don't explain which goods will actually be *purchased*. Desire is only the first step in the consumption process. To acquire goods and services, one must be willing and able to *pay* for one's wants. Producers won't give you their goods just to satisfy your Freudian desires. They want money in exchange for their goods. Hence **prices and income are just as relevant to consumption decisions as are more basic desires and preferences.**

In explaining consumer behavior, economists focus on the *demand* for goods and services. As we observed in Chapter 3, **demand** entails the *willingness and ability to pay* for goods and services. To say that someone *demands* a particular good means that he or she will offer to *buy* it at some price(s).

Determinants of Demand. What determines a person's willingness to buy a product at some price? Economists isolate four determinants of demand. We say **an individual's demand for a specific product is determined by these four factors:**

- *Tastes* (desire for this and other goods).
- *Income* (of the consumer).
- *Expectations* (for income, prices, tastes).
- *Other goods* (their availability and prices).

Freud might have been content to focus on tastes or desires originating in infancy. But economists go several steps further. Tastes alone do not guarantee you'll buy a specific product. Income, expectations, and the price and availability of other goods also come into play at the cash register. All four determinants of demand play a role in the purchase decision.

demand: The willingness and ability to buy specific quantities of a good at alternative prices in a given time period, *ceteris paribus.*

The remainder of this chapter examines these determinants of demand. The objective is not only to explain consumer behavior but also to predict how consumption patterns change in response to *changes* in the price of a good or to *changes* in underlying tastes, income, prices or availability of other goods, or expectations.

THE DEMAND CURVE

The starting point for an economic analysis of demand is quite simple. Economists accept consumer tastes as the outcome of sociopsychiatric and cultural influences. They don't look beneath the surface to see how those tastes originated. They don't care if your desires originated in the womb or in some TV ad. Economists want to know only how those tastes (desires) affect consumption decisions.

Utility Theory

The first observation economists make is that the more pleasure a product gives us—for whatever reason—the higher the price we're willing to pay for it. If the oral sensation of buttered popcorn at the movies really turns you on, you're likely to be willing to pay dearly for it. If, on the other hand, you have no great taste or desire for popcorn, the theater might have to give it away before you'd eat it.

Total vs. Marginal Utility. Economists use the term **utility** to refer to the expected pleasure, or satisfaction, obtained from goods and services. If you really like popcorn, we say you get a lot of utility (satisfaction) from consuming it. Pretty simple. But we then go a step further in explaining your satisfaction by distinguishing between the *total* utility you get from eating popcorn and your *marginal* utility. **Total utility** refers to the amount of satisfaction obtained from your *entire* consumption of a product. By contrast, **marginal utility** refers to the amount of satisfaction you get from consuming the *last* (i.e., "marginal") unit of a product. More generally, note that

$$\text{Marginal utility} = \frac{\text{Change in total utility}}{\text{Change in quantity}}$$

utility: The pleasure or satisfaction obtained from a good or service.

total utility: The amount of satisfaction obtained from entire consumption of a product.

marginal utility: The change in total utility obtained by consuming one additional (marginal) unit of a good or service.

Diminishing Marginal Utility. The concepts of total and marginal utility explain not only why we buy popcorn at the movies but also why we stop eating it at some point. Even people who love popcorn (i.e., derive great *total* utility from it) don't eat endless quantities of it. Why not? Presumably because the thrill diminishes with each mouthful. The first box of popcorn may bring sensual gratification, but the second or third box is likely to bring a stomachache. We express this change in perceptions by noting that the marginal utility of the first box of popcorn is higher than the additional or marginal utility derived from the second box.

The behavior of popcorn connoisseurs isn't abnormal. As a rule, the amount of additional utility we obtain from a product declines as we continue to consume it. The third slice of pizza isn't as desirable as the first, the sixth beer not as satisfying as the fifth, and so forth. Indeed, this phenomenon of diminishing marginal utility is so nearly universal that economists have fashioned a law around it. This **law of diminishing marginal utility** states that each successive unit of a good consumed yields less *additional* utility.

The law of diminishing marginal utility does *not* say that we won't like the second box of popcorn, the third pizza slice, or the sixth beer; it just says we won't like them as much as the ones we've already consumed. Time is also important here: if the first box of popcorn was eaten last year, the second box may now taste just as good. The law of diminishing marginal utility applies to short time periods.

law of diminishing marginal utility: The marginal utility of a good declines as more of it is consumed in a given time period.

The Popcorn Test. Let's put the law of diminishing marginal utility to a test—the popcorn test. The test measures how much popcorn you'd eat if it were absolutely free. To complete this test, we'll make up some numbers for total and marginal utility.

TABLE 5.1
The Satisfaction Meter

Marginal utility refers to the pleasure we get from one more unit of a good. Although marginal utility diminishes as we consume additional units, total utility keeps rising so long as *marginal* utility is positive.

Popcorn Consumption	Marginal Utility (in Units)	Total Utility
Sixth box	−10	40
Fifth box	1	50
Fourth box	5	49
Third box	9	44
Second box	15	35
First box	20	20
0	0	0

Let's start with the first box of popcorn. That first box is yummy. We'll assume an arbitrary number and say that first box delivers 20 units of utility. If we stopped there, at one box, our total utility would be 20 "utils" (units of utility).

But it's hard to stop munching on popcorn. So suppose we go for a *second* box (mini boxes, of course!). Will it taste good? If so, we say it has positive marginal utility; it adds to our pleasure.

But here's the tough question: Is the second box as satisfying as the first? Probably not. So we have to acknowledge that the marginal utility of the second box is less than the marginal utility of the first box (20 utils). Let's assume the second box adds only 15 units of pleasure.

Notice where we're at on the satisfaction meter in Table 5.1. Our total utility is now at 35 utils, based on the pleasures of the first (20 utils) and second boxes (15 utils).

We'll keep moving up the satisfaction meter so long as we continue to enjoy munching popcorn—so long as the marginal utility of the next box is positive. Sooner or later, however, another box of popcorn isn't going to look so appetizing. At some point, another handful of popcorn might even look repulsive—that is, deliver negative marginal utility. In Table 5.1 this threshold is reached with the sixth box. Notice that the marginal utility of the sixth box is *negative*—if you eat it, you'll feel *worse* than if you don't. That's why you move down the satisfaction meter of *total* utility from 50 to 40.

FIGURE 5.2
Total vs. Marginal Utility

The *total* utility derived from consuming a product comes from the *marginal* utilities of each successive unit. The total utility curve shows how each of the first five boxes of popcorn contributes to total utility. Note that the utility staircase is rising, but each successive step is smaller. This reflects the law of diminishing marginal utility.

The sixth box of popcorn causes the total utility steps to descend; the sixth box actually *reduces* total utility. This means that the sixth box has *negative* marginal utility.

The marginal utility curve (*b*) shows the change in total utility with each additional unit. It's derived from the total utility curve. Marginal utility here is positive but diminishing for the first five boxes.

Here's the popcorn test: Would you eat that sixth box, even if it were free? Hopefully not. Once you realize that the thrill of eating popcorn diminishes with each additional box, you will stop eating it at some point.

Figure 5.2 illustrates how we get to that point. As we consume boxes 1 thru 5, we climb the utility staircase. Each step represents the marginal utility of the next box. Because marginal utility diminishes, each successive step gets shorter. So long as we are climbing, however, total utility is increasing. *As long as marginal utility is positive, total utility must be increasing.*

The situation changes with the sixth box of popcorn. As we have already noted, the good sensations associated with popcorn consumption are completely forgotten by the time the sixth box arrives. Nausea and stomach cramps take over. Indeed, the sixth box is absolutely *distasteful,* as reflected in the downturn of *total* utility and the *negative* value for marginal utility. We were happier—in possession of more total utility—with only five boxes of popcorn. The sixth box—yielding *negative* marginal utility—reduces total satisfaction. This is the kind of sensation you'd probably experience if you ate six hamburgers (see the cartoon below).

Not every good ultimately reaches negative marginal utility. Yet the more general principle of diminishing marginal utility is experienced daily. That is, *eventually additional quantities of a good yield increasingly smaller increments of satisfaction.*

Price and Quantity

Marginal utility is essentially a measure of how much we desire particular goods, our *taste.* But which ones will we buy? Clearly, we don't always buy the products we most desire. *Price* often holds us back. All too often we have to settle for goods that yield less marginal utility simply because they are available at a lower price. This explains why most people don't drive Porsches. Our desire ("taste") for a Porsche may be great, but its price is even greater. The challenge for most of us is to somehow reconcile our tastes with our bank balances.

I ate one hamburger, and it tasted great. I ate two more, and they tasted good. The fourth one tasted okay. I wish I hadn't eated the fifth. And I'm not sure if I want to finish the sixth one.

James Eggert, *Invitation to Economics*, 2nd ed., p. 160, © 1991 The McGraw-Hill Companies, Inc. Used with permission.

Analysis: No matter how much we like a product, marginal utility is likely to diminish as we consume more of it. If marginal utility becomes *negative* (as here), total satisfaction will decrease.

ceteris paribus: The assumption of nothing else changing.

law of demand: The quantity of a good demanded in a given time period increases as its price falls, *ceteris paribus.*

demand curve: A curve describing the quantities of a good a consumer is willing and able to buy at alternative prices in a given period, *ceteris paribus.*

In deciding whether to buy something, our immediate focus is typically on a single variable, namely *price*. Assume for the moment that a person's tastes, incomes, and expectations are set in stone, and that the prices of other goods are set as well. This is the **ceteris paribus** assumption we first encountered in Chapter 1. It doesn't mean that other influences on consumer behavior are unimportant. Rather, *ceteris paribus* simply allows us to focus on one variable at a time. In this case, we are focusing on price. What we want to know is how high a price a consumer is willing to pay for another unit of a product. This is the question Steve Jobs had to confront when Apple launched the iPhone.

The concepts of marginal utility and *ceteris paribus* enable us to answer this question. *The more marginal utility a product delivers, the more a consumer will be willing to pay for it.* We also noted that marginal utility *diminishes* as increasing quantities of a product are consumed, suggesting that consumers are willing to pay progressively *less* for additional quantities of a product. The moviegoer willing to pay 50 cents for that first mouth-watering ounce of buttered popcorn may not be willing to pay so much for a second or third ounce. The same is true for a second pizza, the sixth beer, and so forth. *Because marginal utility declines, people are willing to buy additional quantities of a good only if its price falls.* In other words, as the marginal utility of a good diminishes, so does our willingness to pay. This **law of demand** is illustrated in Figure 5.3 with the downward-sloping **demand curve.**

FIGURE 5.3

An Individual's Demand Schedule and Curve

Consumers are generally willing to buy larger quantities of a good at lower prices. This demand schedule illustrates the specific quantities demanded at alternative prices. If popcorn sold for 25 cents per ounce, this consumer would buy 12 ounces per show (row *F*). At higher prices, less popcorn would be purchased.

A downward-sloping demand curve expresses the law of demand: the quantity of a good demanded increases as its price falls. Notice that points *A* through *J* on the curve correspond to the rows of the demand schedule.

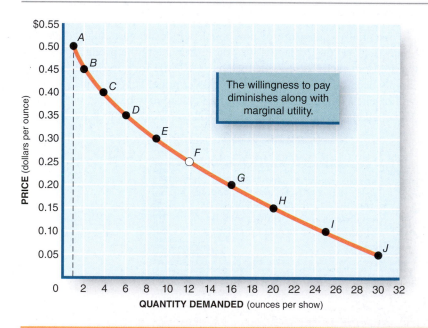

The willingness to pay diminishes along with marginal utility.

	Price (per Ounce)	Quantity Demanded (Ounces per Show)
A	$0.50	1
B	0.45	2
C	0.40	4
D	0.35	6
E	0.30	9
F	0.25	12
G	0.20	16
H	0.15	20
I	0.10	25
J	0.05	30

The law of demand and the law of diminishing marginal utility tell us nothing about why we crave popcorn or why our cravings subside. Those explanations are reserved for psychiatrists, sociologists, and physiologists. The laws of economics simply describe our market behavior.

MARKET DEMAND

Our explanation of an individual's popcorn consumption applies to all products and all consumers. As we saw in Chapter 3, the **market demand** for popcorn is just the sum of all our individual demands for that product. The market demand curve resembles an individual's demand curve but differs in two important respects. First, the units of measurement are larger: the quantities on the horizontal axis are in hundreds, thousands, or possibly millions of units, not single digits. Second, the demand curve expresses the ability and willingness to pay of thousands of consumers, not just one individual.

market demand: The total quantities of a good or service people are willing and able to buy at alternative prices in a given time period; the sum of individual demands.

CONSUMER SURPLUS

The presence of so many individuals on the market demand curve has some interesting implications for both consumers and producers. To see this, let's venture into another market—say, the new car market. Let's focus on a specific car, the Porsche 918 Spyder Hybrid, a sports car with a 500 horsepower V8 engine supplemented by two electrical engines, a top speed of 200 miles per hour, and 74 miles per gallon in all-electric mode.

Lots of people crave this car. But not everyone is willing and able to buy it at the Manufacturer's Suggested Retail Price (MSRP) of $845,500. In fact, most people who *desire* the car aren't prepared to pay anywhere near that much money. Some people are, however. Indeed, some Porsche fans would pay even a *higher* price to get their hands on a 918 Spyder. And it's not just a question of who is rich enough. Remember that there are *four* determinants of an individual's demand: tastes, income, expectations, and other goods (price and availability). So a rich person with little desire for speed might not demand a Spyder at the $845,500 price. On the other hand, a real speed freak with only a modest income might be willing to borrow money, rent out the house, and sell the kids to get behind the wheel of a 918 Spyder.

As individuals work their way through the determinants of demand, they will ultimately decide how much money they are willing to pay for a Porsche 918 Spyder. For those sorry souls who would never think of driving a Spyder, their price would be zero: they would not be part of the market demand for that car. Everyone else, however, would be deciding the *maximum* price they would be willing and able to pay for a new 918 Spyder. That decision will determine where they are positioned on the market demand curve.

Love and MU

Consider the positions depicted in Figure 5.4. Fred is positioned high up on the market demand curve because he is willing to pay as much as $1 million for a Spyder. Michel and Hua are also willing and able to shell out big bucks for the car. Blaise also wants a Spyder but can't or won't spend more than $650,000 to get one.

What we also see on the market demand curve is how many cars the Porsche dealer can sell at the MSRP of $845,500. At that price (point *A* on the graph), four Spyders will be demanded and therefore sold.

Fred will be excited with this deal. We know that Fred would pay as much as $1 million for a 918 Spyder. But he has to pay only the $845,500 price set by the dealer. In his mind, he is getting a real bargain—getting the Spyder for a lot less money than the maximum price he would be willing to pay. We call this "bargain" his **consumer surplus.** Specifically,

consumer surplus: The difference between the maximum price a person is willing to pay and the price paid.

FIGURE 5.4
Consumer Surplus

A person's position on the market demand curve expresses the maximum price he or she is willing to pay. The difference between that individualized maximum price and the price paid represents "consumer surplus." At the MSRP price of $845,500, Michel would have a consumer surplus of $104,500 (= $950,000 − $845,500).

In Fred's case, that consumer surplus amounts to $154,500 (= $1 million − $845,500).

Michel enjoys a consumer surplus as well. Notice again in Figure 5.4 where she is on the market demand curve: she is willing to pay as much as $950,000 for a Spyder. So she enjoys a consumer surplus of $104,500 (= $950,000 − $845,500). She cannot wait to tell all her friends what a "bargain" she got.

In fact, everyone who buys a Spyder thinks she or he got a bargain! That is because ***the only people who purchase a product are those whose maximum price equals or exceeds the market price***. In Figure 5.4 only the consumers at or above point *A* drive away in a new Spyder. Anyone *below* point *A* walks; John, Marty, Bob, and Blaise want a Porsche 918 Spyder but are not willing to pay $845,500 to get one.

Now you know why we love to shop. People do not buy things that are priced above their maximum price thresholds. We only buy those things priced below our maximum price threshold. So we are always getting some consumer surplus and bragging about the "bargains" we got. This collective consumer surplus is depicted in Figure 5.5.

consumer surplus is the difference between the maximum price a person is willing to pay and the price paid:

$$\text{Consumer surplus} = \text{Maximum price willing to pay} - \text{Price actually paid}$$

FIGURE 5.5
Total consumer surplus

Every consumer who buys a product must be willing and able to pay *at least* the prevailing price. Therefore, all consumers buying the good reap some consumer surplus. Their collective consumer surplus is represented by the shaded area in the graph.

PRICE DISCRIMINATION

Car dealers are well aware of this consumer surplus phenomenon and determined to profit from it. Consider their options. Figure 5.4 reveals that the dealer can sell four cars at the posted price of $845,500. That would generate **total revenue** (= price × quantity) of $3,382,000.

But he could do better than that if he priced each car separately rather than charging the *same* price for all four cars. Suppose he knew that Fred was willing and able to pay as much as $1 million for a Spyder. Instead of posting a uniform price of $845,500, the dealer could let Fred try to negotiate a price for himself. What is the *most* Fred would pay? $1 million. So the dealer could ask for $1.2 million and let Fred "bargain" his way down to $1 million. Fred would drive off in his Spyder, feeling smug about the "deal" he had struck. And the dealer would be smiling all the way to the bank.

If the dealer handled all the buyers in this way, he would bring in a lot more revenue from the sale of his four cars. He would sell the first car to Fred for $1 million, a car to Michel for $950,000, a car to Hua for $900,000, and one to Carlos for $850,000. His total revenue would be $3.7 million rather than the $3,382,000 he got with uniform pricing. Pretty nice deal.

What the dealer is doing here is practicing **price discrimination**: charging individual consumers different prices for the same good. In effect, the dealer is picking off consumers from their positions on the market demand curve and charging them the maximum price each is willing to pay. If successful, the dealer will eliminate all consumer surplus and maximize his own revenue.

There is nothing illegal about this kind of price discrimination. And no one gets harmed. No one paid more for a Spyder than she or he was willing to pay. And the buyers might even feel good about their negotiating skills.

Divide and Conquer. The key to the dealer's success is the ability to negotiate each price individually. There is no transparency here. Car dealers typically conduct negotiations in small cubicles, isolated from other consumers. That way the dealer can probe to discover what maximum price each individual is willing to pay. So long as that price is above the uniform price threshold ($845,500 in this case), the dealer extracts some of that consumer surplus (and increases total revenue).

Price discrimination is rampant in the auto industry, but common in many other markets as well. Next time you are on an airplane, ask your seatmates how much they paid for their tickets. Odds are that it is not the same price you paid. The airlines use a variety of techniques to "divide and conquer" airline passengers. People who must travel on short notice and with uncertain schedules pay high "unrestricted" fares. Travelers who are further down the market demand curve are singled out with advance ticketing, nonrefundable purchases, and minimum-stay restrictions. They end up paying a lower price for the same flight. That is price discrimination.

Even colleges engage in price discrimination. Your school may have a seemingly uniform price for tuition. But schools adjust that price on an individual basis with scholarships and grants. In so doing, they hope to "sell" the school to applicants with exceptional academic or athletic potential who otherwise are not willing and able to pay the posted price.

Price discrimination is most effective when consumers don't have perfect information about market prices and there are few sellers. Price discrimination is also easier to practice in markets where individual consumers make only occasional purchases (e.g., new cars, vacations, college).

total revenue: The price of a product multiplied by the quantity sold in a given time period: $p × q$.

price discrimination: The sale of an individual good at different prices to different consumers.

web analysis

The U.S. Department of Justice prosecutes *illegal* price discrimination. To learn more, visit **www.justice.gov/atr** and search "price discrimination."

CHOOSING AMONG PRODUCTS

Our analysis of demand thus far has focused on the decision to buy a single product at varying prices. Actual consumer behavior is multidimensional, however, and therefore more complex. When we go shopping, our concern isn't limited to how much of one good to buy. Rather, we must decide *which* of many available goods to buy at their respective prices.

The presence of so many goods complicates consumption decisions. Our basic objective remains the same, however: we want to get as much satisfaction as possible from our available income. In striving for that objective, we have to recognize that the purchase of any single good means giving up the opportunity to buy more of other goods. In other words, consuming a Porsche 918 Spyder, popcorn, or any other good entails distinct **opportunity costs.**

opportunity cost: The most desired goods or services that are forgone in order to obtain something else.

Marginal Utility vs. Price

The economic explanation for consumer choice builds on the theory of marginal utility and the law of demand. Suppose you have a $10 gift card for music and video game downloads. The first proposition of consumer choice says you'll prefer the download that gives you the most satisfaction. Hardly a revolutionary proposition.

The second postulate of consumer choice takes into account market prices. Suppose you *prefer* a video game, but music downloads are cheaper. Under these circumstances, your budget may win out over your desires. There's nothing irrational about downloading a song instead of a more desirable video game when you have only a limited amount of income to spend. On the contrary, *rational behavior requires one to compare the anticipated utility of each expenditure with its price.* The smart thing to do, then, is to choose those products that promise to provide the most pleasure for the amount of income available.

Suppose your desire for a video game is *twice* as great as your desire to hear a tune. In economic terms, this means that the marginal utility of the first video game is two times that of the first music download. Which one should you download? Before hitting buttons on the keyboard, you'd better look at relative prices. What if a game costs $3 and a song costs only $1? In this case, you must pay *three* times as much for a video game that gives only *twice* as much pleasure. This isn't a good deal. You could get more utility *per dollar* by downloading music.

The same kind of principle explains why some rich people drive a Ford rather than a shiny new Porsche 918 Spyder. The marginal utility (MU) of driving a Spyder is substantially higher than the MU of driving a Ford. A nice Spyder, however, costs about 30 times as much as a basic Ford. A rich person who drives a Ford must feel that driving a Spyder is not 30 times as satisfying as driving a Ford. For such people, a Ford yields more *marginal utility per dollar spent.*

The key to utility maximization, then, isn't simply to buy the things you like best. Instead you must compare goods on the basis of their marginal utility *and* price. *To maximize utility, the consumer should choose the good that delivers the most marginal utility per dollar.*

Utility Maximization

This basic principle of consumer choice is easily illustrated. Think about spending that $10 gift card on music or game downloads, the only available choices. Your goal, as always, is to get as much pleasure as possible from this limited income. That is, you want to maximize the *total* utility attainable from the expenditure of your income. The question is how to do it. What combination of songs and games will maximize the utility you get from $10?

We've already assumed that the marginal utility (MU) of the first game is two times higher than the MU of the first song. This is reflected in the second row of Table 5.2. The MU of the first video game has been set arbitrarily at 20 utils (units of utility). We don't need to know whether 20 utils is a real thrill or just a bit of amusement. Indeed, the concept of "utils" has little meaning by itself; it's only a useful basis for comparison. In this case, we want to compare the MU of the first game with the MU of the first song. Hence we set the MU of the first game at 20 utils and the MU of the first song at 10 utils. The first game download is twice as satisfying as the first music download:

$$\text{MU game} = 2 \text{ MU song}$$

| | Amount of Utility (in Units of Utility, or Utils) | | | |
| | From Music Downloads | | From Game Downloads | |
Quantity Consumed	Total	Marginal	Total	Marginal
0	0		0	
		> 10		> 20
1	10		20	
		> 9		> 18
2	19		38	
		> 8		> 16
3	27		54	
		> 6		> 12
4	33		66	
		> 5		> 6
5	38		72	
		> 4		> 1
6	42		73	
		> 3		
7	45			
		> 2		
8	47			
		> 1		
9	48			
		> 0		
10	48			

TABLE 5.2
Maximizing Utility

Q: How can you get the most satisfaction (utility) from $10 if you must choose between downloading songs at $1 apiece or video games at $3 apiece?

A: By playing two games and playing four songs. See the text for explanation.

The remainder of Table 5.2 indicates how marginal utility diminishes with increasing consumption of a product. Look at what happens to the sound of music. The marginal utility of the first song is 10; but the MU of the second song is only 9 utils. The third song generates even less MU (= 8). You started with your favorite song; now you're working down your hits list. By the time you get to a sixth song, music downloads aren't raising your spirits much (MU = 4). By the tenth song, you're tired of music (MU = 0).

Game downloads also conform to the law of diminishing marginal utility. You start with your favorite game (MU = 20), seeking a high score. The second game is fun, too, though not quite as much (MU = 18). As you keep playing, frustration rises and marginal utility diminishes. By the time you play a sixth game your nerves are just about shot; the sixth game gives you only 1 util of marginal utility.

With these psychological insights to guide us, we can now determine how best to spend $10. What we're looking for is the combination of songs and video games that *maximizes* the total utility attainable from an expenditure of $10. We call this combination **optimal consumption**—that is, the mix of goods that yields the most utility for the available income.

We can start looking for the optimal mix of consumer purchases by assessing the utility of spending the entire $10 on video games. At $3 per play, we could buy three games. This would give us *total* utility of 54 utils (see Table 5.2). Plus we'd have enough change to download one song (MU = 10), for a grand utility total of 64 utils.

Alternatively, you could also spend the entire gift card on music downloads. With $10 to spend, you could buy 10 songs. However, this would generate only 48 utils of total utility. Hence, if you were forced to choose between *only* downloading songs or *only* playing video games, you'd pick the games.

Fortunately, we don't have to make such extreme choices. In reality, we can buy a *combination* of songs and video games. This complicates our decision making (with more choices) but permits us to attain higher levels of total satisfaction.

To reach the peak of satisfaction, consider spending your $10 in $3 dollar increments. How should you spend the first $3? If you spend it on one game, you'll get 20 utils of satisfaction. On the other hand, $3 will buy your first three music downloads. The first song has an MU of 10 and the second song adds another 9 utils to your happiness. The third song brings in another 8 utils. Hence, by spending the $3 on songs, you reap 27 utils of total utility. This is superior to the pleasure of a first game, and it's therefore your first purchase.

optimal consumption: The mix of consumer purchases that maximizes the utility attainable from available income.

Having downloaded three songs, you now can spend the second $3. How should it be spent? Your choice now is that first game or a fourth, fifth, and sixth song. That first unplayed game still promises 20 utils of real pleasure. By constrast, the MU of a fourth song is 6 utils. And the MU of a fifth song is only 5 utils. Together, then, the fourth, fifth, and sixth songs will increase your total utility by 15 utils, whereas a first game will give you 20 utils. You should spend the second $3 on a game download.

The decision on how to spend the remaining four dollars is made the same way. The final choice is to purchase either a second game (MU = 18) or the fourth, fifth, and sixth songs (MU = 15). The second game offers more marginal utility and is thus the correct decision.

After working your way through these calculations, you'll end up downloading two games and four songs. Was it worth it? Do you end up with more total utility than you could have gotten from any other combination? The answer is yes. The *total* utility of two games (38 utils) and four songs (33 utils) is 71 units of utility. This is significantly better than the alternatives of spending your $10 on songs alone (total utility = 48) or three games and a song (total utility = 64). In fact, the combination of two games and four songs is the *best* one you can find. Because this combination maximizes the total utility of your income ($10), it represents *optimal consumption.*

Utility-Maximizing Rule

Optimal consumption refers to the mix of output that maximizes total utility for the limited amount of income you have to spend. The basic approach to utility maximization is to purchase the good next that delivers the most *marginal utility per dollar.* Marginal utility per dollar is simply the MU of the good divided by its price: MU ÷ P.

From Table 5.2 we know that a first game has an MU of 20 and a price of $3. It thus delivers a marginal utility per dollar of

$$\frac{\text{MU}_{\text{first game}}}{P_{\text{game}}} = \frac{20}{\$3} = 6.67 \text{ utils per dollar}$$

On the other hand, the first song has a marginal utility of 10 and a price of $1. It offers a marginal utility per dollar of

$$\frac{\text{MU}_{\text{first song}}}{P_{\text{song}}} = \frac{10}{\$1} = 10 \text{ utils per dollar}$$

From this perspective, the first song is a better deal than the first game and should be purchased.

Optimal consumption implies that the utility-maximizing combination of goods has been found. If this is true, you can't increase your total utility by trading one good for another. All goods included in the optimal consumption mix yield the *same* marginal utility per dollar. We know we've reached maximum utility when we've satisfied the following rule:

$$\text{Utility-maximizing rule: } \frac{\text{MU}_x}{P_x} = \frac{\text{MU}_y}{P_y}$$

where x and y represent any two goods included in our consumption.

Rational consumer choice depends on comparisons of marginal utilities and prices. If a dollar spent on product X yields more marginal utility than a dollar spent on product Y, we should buy product X. To use this principle, of course, we have to know the amounts of utility obtainable from various goods and be able to perform a little arithmetic. By doing so, however, we can get the greatest satisfaction from our limited income.

Equilibrium Outcomes

All these graphs and equations make consumer choice look dull and mechanical. Economic theory seems to suggest that consumers walk through shopping malls with marginal utility tables and handheld computers. In reality, no one does this—not even your economics instructor. Yet economic theory is pretty successful in predicting consumer decisions. Consumers don't always buy the optimal mix of goods and services with their limited income. But after some trial and error, consumers adjust their behavior. What economic theory predicts is that the final choices—the *equilibrium* outcomes—will be the predicted optimal ones.

THE ECONOMY TOMORROW

CAVEAT EMPTOR

LeBron James is paid over $35 million a year to help convince us to drink Sprite and Powerade, wear Nike shoes, eat Big Macs, chew Bubblicious gum, and purchase State Farm insurance. In 2011, LeBron started pitching ultraexpensive timepieces made by Swiss watchmaker Audemars Piguet. Do these sponsors know something economic theory doesn't? Economists *assume* consumers know what they want and will act rationally to get the most satisfaction they can. The companies that sponsor basketball star LeBron James don't accept that assumption. They think your tastes will follow LeBron's lead. Your perception of the marginal utility associated with LeBron-endorsed products will increase.

Advertisers now spend over $200 *billion* per year to change our perceptions. In the United States, this spending works out to over $400 per consumer, one of the highest per capita advertising rates in the world. Some of this advertising (including product labeling) is intended to provide information about existing products or to bring new products to our attention. A great deal of advertising, however, is also designed to exploit our senses and lack of knowledge. Recognizing that we're guilt-ridden, insecure, and sex-hungry, advertisers promise exoneration, recognition, and love; all we have to do is buy the right products.

A favorite target of advertisers is our sense of insecurity. Thousands of products are marketed in ways that appeal to our need for identity. Thousands of brand images are designed to help the consumer answer the nagging question, Who am I? The answers, of course, vary. *Playboy* magazine says, I'm a virile man of the world; Marlboro cigarettes say, I'm a rugged individualist who enjoys "man-sized flavor." Sprite says, I'll be a winner if I drink the same soda LeBron James does. And I'll be able to jump 8 feet high if I wear Zoom Soldier shoes.

Are Wants Created? Advertising can't be blamed for all of our foolish consumption. Even members of the most primitive tribes, uncontaminated by the seductions of advertising, adorned themselves with rings, bracelets, and pendants. Furthermore, advertising has grown to massive proportions only in the past 50 years, but consumption spending has been increasing throughout recorded history. Finally, a lot of advertising simply fails to change buying decisions. Accordingly, it's a mistake to attribute the growth or content of consumption entirely to the persuasions of advertisers.

This isn't to say that advertising has necessarily made us happier. The objective of all advertising is to alter the choices we make. Just as product images are used to attract us to particular products, so are pictures of hungry, ill-clothed children used to persuade us to give money to charity. In the same way, public relations gimmicks are employed to sway our votes for public servants. In the case of consumer products, advertising seeks to increase tastes for particular goods and services and therewith our willingness to pay. *A successful advertising campaign is one that increases the perceived marginal utility of a product, thereby shifting the demand curve for that product to the right* (see Figure 5.6). By influencing our choices in this way, advertising will affect the consumption choices we make in the economy tomorrow. Advertising alone is unlikely to affect the total *level* of consumption, however.

shift in demand: A change in the quantity demanded at any (every) price.

FIGURE 5.6
The Impact of Advertising on a Demand Curve

Advertising seeks to increase our taste for a particular product. If our taste (the product's perceived utility) increases, so will our willingness to buy. The resulting change in demand is reflected in a rightward shift of the demand curve, often accompanied by diminished elasticity.

SUMMARY

- Our desires for goods and services originate in the structure of personality and social dynamics and aren't explained by economic theory. Economic theory focuses on *demand*—that is, our ability and willingness to buy specific quantities of a good at various prices. LO5-1
- The determinants of demand include tastes (desires), income, other goods (price and availability), and expectations. LO5-1
- Marginal utility measures the additional satisfaction obtained from consuming one more unit of a good. The law of diminishing marginal utility says that the more of a product we consume, the smaller the increments of pleasure we tend to derive from additional units of it. This is a basis for the law of demand. LO5-1
- The determinants of demand establish the maximum price a consumer will pay for a good. That maximum price determines where an individual is positioned on the market demand curve. LO5-1

- A person will buy a product only if its price is at or below the maximum price that person is willing and able to pay. The difference between that maximum price threshold and the price paid is called "consumer surplus." LO5-2
- Producers can extract some or all consumer surplus by charging different prices to individuals, based on their willingness to pay—a practice called "price discrimination." LO5-3
- In choosing among alternative goods and services, a consumer compares the prices and anticipated satisfactions that they offer. To maximize utility with one's available income—to achieve an optimal mix of goods and services—one has to get the most utility for every dollar spent. To do so, one must choose those goods promising the most marginal utility per dollar. LO5-4
- Advertising seeks to change consumer tastes and thus the willingness to buy. If tastes do change, the demand curve for that product will shift. LO5-1

Key Terms

demand	*ceteris paribus*	total revenue
utility	law of demand	price discrimination
total utility	demand curve	opportunity cost
marginal utility	market demand	optimal consumption
law of diminishing marginal utility	consumer surplus	shift in demand

Questions for Discussion

1. What does the demand for enrollments in your college look like? What is on the axes? How do tuition, enrollment, and total revenue interact? LO5-1
2. If the marginal utility of pizza never diminished, how many pizzas would you eat? LO5-1
3. How do total and marginal utility change as you spend more time tweeting your friends? LO5-1
4. Can you think of any product that violates the law of diminishing marginal utility? LO5-1
5. If all consumers had identical demand curves, could producers price discriminate? LO5-3
6. When the producer price discriminates in Figure 5.4, what happens to unit sales? Total revenue? Total profit? LO5-3

7. Under what circumstances could a producer extract *the entire* consumer surplus in Figure 5.5? LO5-2
8. How does a car dealer determine where a buyer is on the market demand curve? LO5-3
9. Why do airlines charge different fares for the same flight? LO5-3
10. Why are per capita advertising expenditures so high in the United States and so low in Brazil? LO5-1
11. When you eat out and have $25 to spend, what information do you need to maximize your utility? LO5-4

! **web activities** to accompany this chapter can be found on the Online Learning Center:
http://www.mhhe.com/schiller13e

---

  mobile app Visit your mobile app store and download the Schiller: Study Econ app *today!*

APPENDIX

INDIFFERENCE CURVES

A consumer's demand for any specific product is an expression of many forces. As we've observed, the actual quantity of a product demanded by a consumer varies inversely with its price. The price–quantity relationship is determined by

- *Tastes* (desire for this and other goods).
- *Income* (of the consumer).
- *Expectations* (for income, prices, tastes).
- *Other goods* (their availability and price).

Economic theory attempts to show how each of these forces affects consumer demand. Thus far, we've used two-dimensional demand curves to illustrate the basic principles of demand. We saw that, in general, a change in the price of a good causes a movement along the demand curve, whereas a change in tastes, income, expectations, or other goods shifts the entire demand curve to a new position.

We haven't looked closely at the origins of demand curves, however. We assumed that a demand curve could be developed from observations of consumer behavior, such as the number of boxes of popcorn that were purchased at various prices (Figure 5.3).

It's possible, however, to derive a demand curve without actually observing consumer behavior. In theory we can identify consumer *preferences* (tastes), then use those preferences to construct a demand curve. In this case, the demand curve is developed explicitly from known preferences rather than on the basis of market observations. The end result— the demand curve—is the same, at least so long as consumers' behavior in product markets is consistent with their preferences.

Indifference curves are a mechanism for illustrating consumer tastes. We examine their construction and use in this appendix. Indifference curves provide an explicit basis for constructing a demand curve. In addition, they are another way of viewing how consumption is affected by price, tastes, and income. Indifference curves are also a useful tool for explicitly illustrating consumer *choice*—that is, the decision to purchase one good rather than another.

Constructing an Indifference Curve

Suppose you're in an arcade and want to buy some Cokes and play video games but don't have enough money to buy enough of each. The income constraint compels you to make

Combination	Cokes	Video Games
A	1	8
B	2	5
C	3	4

TABLE 5A.1
Equally Satisfying Combinations

Different combinations of two goods may be equally satisfying. In this case we assume that the combinations *A, B,* and *C* all yield equal total utility. Hence the consumer will be indifferent about which of the three combinations he or she receives.

marginal utility: The change in total utility obtained by consuming one additional (marginal) unit of a good or service.

hard decisions. You have to consider the **marginal utility** each additional Coke or video game will provide, compare their respective prices, then make a selection. With careful introspection and good arithmetic you could select the optimal mix of Cokes and video games—that is, the combination that yields the most satisfaction (utility) for the income available. This process of identifying your **optimal consumption** was illustrated in Table 5.2 with downloads of music and video games.

Computing your optimal consumption is difficult because you must assess the marginal utility of each prospective purchase. In Table 5.2 we assumed that the marginal utility of the first music download was 10 utils, while the first game download had a marginal utility of 20. Then we had to specify the marginal utility of every additional music and game download. Can we really be so specific about our tastes?

optimal consumption: The mix of consumer purchases that maximizes the utility attainable from available income.

Indifference curves require a bit less arithmetic. *Instead of trying to measure the marginal utility of each prospective purchase, we now look for combinations of goods that yield equal satisfaction.* In the arcade, this entails different combinations of Cokes and games. All we need is to determine that one particular combination of Cokes and video games is as satisfying as another. We don't have to say how many "units of pleasure" both combinations provide—it's sufficient that they're both equally satisfying.

The initial combination of 1 Coke and 8 video games is designated as combination *A* in Table 5A.1. This combination of goods yields a certain, but unspecified, level of total utility. What we want to do now is to find another combination of Cokes and games that's just as satisfying as combination *A*. Finding other combinations of equal satisfaction isn't easy, but it's at least possible. After a lot of soul searching, we decide that 2 Cokes and 5 video games would be just as satisfying as 1 Coke and 8 games.[1] This combination is designated as *B* in Table 5A.1.

Table 5A.1 also depicts a third combination of Cokes and video games that's as satisfying as the first. Combination *C* includes 3 Cokes and 4 games, a mix of consumption assumed to yield the same total utility as 1 Coke and 8 games (combination *A*).

Notice that we haven't said anything about how much pleasure combinations *A, B,* and *C* provide. We're simply asserting that these three combinations are *equally* satisfying.

Figure 5A.1 illustrates the information about tastes that we've assembled. Points *A, B,* and *C* represent the three equally satisfying combinations of Cokes and video games we've identified. By connecting these points we create an **indifference curve.** The indifference curve illustrates all combinations of two goods that are equally satisfying. A consumer would be just as happy with any combination represented on the curve, so a choice among them would be a matter of indifference.

indifference curve: A curve depicting alternative combinations of goods that yield equal satisfaction.

An Indifference Map. Not all combinations of Cokes and video games are as satisfying as combination *A,* of course. Surely 2 Cokes and 8 games would be preferred to only 1 Coke and 8 games. Indeed, *any combination that provided more of one good and no less of the other would be preferred.* Point *D* in Figure 5A.2 illustrates just one such combination.

[1]The utility computations used here aren't based on Table 5.2; a different set of tastes is assumed.

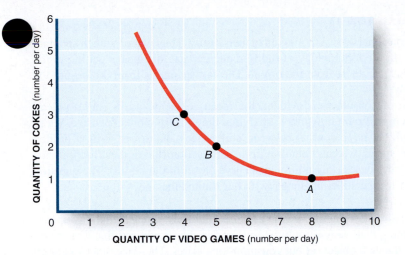

FIGURE 5A.1
An Indifference Curve

An indifference curve illustrates the various combinations of two goods that would provide equal satisfaction. The consumer is assumed to be indifferent to a choice between combinations A, B, and C (and all other points on the curve) because they all yield the same total utility.

Combination D must yield more total utility than combination A because it includes one more Coke and no fewer games. A consumer wouldn't be indifferent to a choice between A and D; on the contrary, combination D would be preferred.

Combination D is also preferred to combinations B and C. How do we know? Recall that combinations A, B, and C are all equally satisfying. Hence, if combination D is better than A, it must also be better than B and C. Given a choice, a consumer would select combination D (2 Cokes, 8 games) in preference to *any* combination depicted on indifference curve I_1.

There are also combinations that are as satisfying as D, of course. These possibilities are illustrated on indifference curve I_2. All these combinations are equally satisfying and must therefore be preferred to any points on indifference curve I_1. In general, ***the farther the indifference curve is from the origin, the more total utility it yields.***

The curve I_3 illustrates various combinations that are less satisfying. Combination F, for example, includes 3 Cokes and 3 games. This is 1 game less than the number available in combination C. Therefore, F yields less total utility than C and isn't preferred: a consumer would rather have combination C than F. By the same logic we just used, all points on indifference curve I_3 are less satisfying than combinations on curve I_2 or I_1.

Curves 1, 2, and 3 in Figure 5A.2 are the beginnings of an **indifference map.** An indifference map depicts all the combinations of goods that would yield various levels of satisfaction. A single indifference curve, in contrast, illustrates all combinations that provide a single (equal) level of total utility.

indifference map: The set of indifference curves that depicts all possible levels of utility attainable from various combinations of goods.

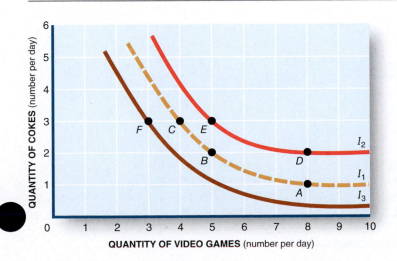

FIGURE 5A.2
An Indifference Map

All combinations of goods depicted on any given indifference curve (e.g., I_1) are equally satisfying. Other combinations are more or less satisfying, however, and thus lie on higher (I_2) or lower (I_3) indifference curves. An indifference map shows all possible levels of total utility (e.g., $I_1, I_2, I_3, \ldots, I_n$) and their respective consumption combinations.

Utility Maximization

We assume that all consumers strive to maximize their utility. They want as much satisfaction as they can get. In the terminology of indifference curves, this means getting to the indifference curve that's farthest from the origin. The farther one is from the origin, the greater the total utility.

Although the goal of consumers is evident, the means of achieving it isn't so clear. Higher indifference curves aren't only more satisfying, they're also more expensive. We're confronted again with the basic conflict between preferences and prices. With a limited amount of income to spend, we can't attain infinite satisfaction (the farthest indifference curve). We have to settle for less (an indifference curve closer to the origin). The question is, How do we maximize the utility attainable with our limited income?

The Budget Constraint. For starters, we have to determine how much we have to spend. Suppose for the moment that we have only $2 to spend in the arcade and that Cokes and video games are still the only objects of our consumption desires. The price of a Coke is 50 cents; the price of a game is 25 cents. Accordingly, the maximum number of Cokes we could buy is 4 if we didn't play any video games. On the other hand, we could play as many as 8 games if we were to forsake Coke.

Figure 5A.3 depicts the limitations placed on our consumption possibilities by a finite income. The **budget constraint** illustrates all combinations of goods affordable with a given income. In this case, the outermost budget line illustrates the combinations of Cokes and video games that can be purchased with $2.

The budget line is easily drawn. The end points of the budget constraint are found by dividing one's income by the price of the good on the corresponding axis. Thus the outermost curve begins at 4 Cokes ($2 ÷ 50 cents) and ends at 8 games ($2 ÷ 25 cents). All the other points on the budget constraint represent other combinations of Cokes and video games that could be purchased with $2.

A smaller income is also illustrated in Figure 5A.3. If we had only $1 to spend, we could afford fewer Cokes and fewer games. Hence a smaller income is represented by a budget constraint that lies closer to the origin.

Optimal Consumption. With a budget constraint looming before us, the limitation on utility maximization is evident. We want to reach the highest indifference curve possible. Our limited income, however, restricts our grasp. We can go only as far as our budget constraint allows. In this context, *the objective is to reach the highest indifference curve that is compatible with our budget constraint.*

budget constraint: A line depicting all combinations of goods that are affordable with a given income and given prices.

FIGURE 5A.3
The Budget Constraint

Consumption possibilities are limited by available income. The budget constraint illustrates this limitation. The end points of the budget constraint are equal to income divided by the price of each good. All points on the budget constraint represent affordable combinations of goods.

FIGURE 5A.4
Optimal Consumption

The optimal consumption combination—the one that maximizes the
utility of spendable income—lies at
the point where the budget line is
tangent to (just touches) an indifference curve. In this case, point *M*
represents the optimal mix of Cokes
and video games because no other
affordable combination lies on a
higher indifference curve than *I_c*.

Figure 5A.4 illustrates the process of achieving optimal consumption. We start with an indifference map depicting all utility levels and product combinations. Then we impose a budget line that reflects our income. In this case, we continue to assume that Coke costs 50 cents, video games cost 25 cents, and we have $2 to spend. Hence *we can afford only those consumption combinations that are on or inside the budget line.*

Which particular combination of Cokes and video games maximizes the utility of our $2? It must be 2 Cokes and 4 video games, as reflected in point *M*. Notice that point *M* isn't only on the budget line but also touches indifference curve *I_c*. No other point on the budget line touches *I_c* or any higher indifference curve. Accordingly, *I_c* represents the most utility we can get for $2 and is attainable only if we consume 2 Cokes and 4 video games. Any other affordable combination yields less total utility—that is, falls on a lower indifference curve. Point *G,* for example, which offers 3 Cokes and 2 video games for $2, lies on the indifference curve *I_b*. Because *I_b* lies closer to the origin than *I_c*, point *G* must be less satis-fying than point *M*. We conclude, then, that *the point of tangency between the budget constraint and an indifference curve represents optimal consumption.* It's the combina-tion we should buy if we want to maximize the utility of our limited income.

Marginal Utility and Price: A Digression. We earlier illustrated the utility-maximizing rule, which required a comparison of the ratios of marginal utilities to prices. Specifically, optimal consumption was represented as that combination of Cokes and video games that yielded

$$\frac{MU \text{ Coke}}{P \text{ Coke}} = \frac{MU \text{ games}}{P \text{ games}}$$

Does point *M* in Figure 5A.4 conform to this rule?

To answer this question, first rearrange the preceding equation as follows:

$$\frac{MU \text{ Coke}}{MU \text{ games}} = \frac{P \text{ Coke}}{P \text{ games}}$$

In this form, the equation says that the relative marginal utilities of Cokes and video games should equal their relative prices when consumption is optimal. In other words, if a Coke costs twice as much as a video game, then it must yield twice as much marginal utility if the consumer is to be in an optimal state. Otherwise, some substitution of Cokes for video games, or vice versa, would be desirable.

With this foundation, we can show that point *M* conforms to our earlier rule. Consider first the slope of the budget constraint, which is determined by the relative prices of Cokes and video games. In fact, *the (absolute) slope of the budget constraint equals the relative price of the two goods.* In Figure 5A.4 the slope equals the price of video games divided by the price of Cokes (25 cents ÷ 50 cents = ½). It tells us the rate at which video games can be exchanged for Cokes in the market. In this case, one video game is "worth" half a Coke.

The relative marginal utilities of the two goods are reflected in the slope of the indifference curve. Recall that the curve tells at what rate a consumer is willing to substitute one good for another, with no change in total utility. In fact, the slope of the indifference curve is called the **marginal rate of substitution.** It's equal to the relative marginal utilities of the two goods. Presumably one would be indifferent to a choice between 2 Cokes + 5 games and 3 Cokes + 4 games—as suggested in Table 5A.1—only if the third Coke were as satisfying as the fifth video game.

At the point of optimal consumption (*M*) in Figure 5A.4 the budget constraint is tangent to the indifference curve *I*$_c$, which means that the two curves must have the same slope at that point. In other words,

$$\frac{P \text{ games}}{P \text{ Cokes}} = \frac{MU \text{ games}}{MU \text{ Cokes}}$$

or alternatively,

$$\frac{\text{Rate of}}{\text{market exchange}} = \frac{\text{Marginal rate}}{\text{of substitution}}$$

Both indifference curves and marginal utility comparisons lead us to the same optimal mix of consumption.

Deriving the Demand Curve

We noted at the beginning of this appendix that indifference curves not only give us an alternative path to optimal consumption but also can be used to derive a demand curve. To do this, we need to consider how the optimal consumption combination changes when the price of one good is altered. We can see what happens in Figure 5A.5.

Figure 5A.5 starts with the optimal consumption attained at point *M*, with income of $2 and prices of 50 cents for a Coke and 25 cents for a video game. Now we're going to change the price of video games and observe how consumption changes.

Suppose that the price of a video game doubles, from 25 cents to 50 cents. This change will shift the budget constraint inward: our income of $2 now buys a maximum of 4 games rather than 8. Hence the lower end point of the budget constraint moves from 8 games to 4 games. *Whenever the price of a good changes, the budget constraint shifts.*

marginal rate of substitution: The rate at which a consumer is willing to exchange one good for another; the relative marginal utilities of two goods.

FIGURE 5A.5
Changing Prices

When the price of a good changes, the budget constraint shifts, and a new consumption combination must be sought. In this case, the price of video games is changing. When the price of games increases from 25 cents to 50 cents, the budget constraint shifts inward and optimal consumption moves from point *M* to point *N*.

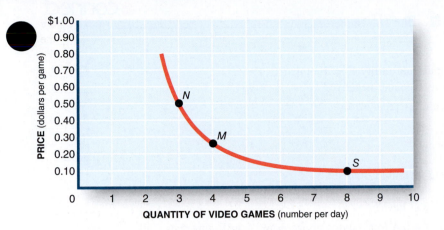

Figure 5A.5 shows how optimal consumption is altered when the price of video games changes. From that figure we can determine the quantity of video games demanded at alternative prices, *ceteris paribus*. That information is summarized here in the demand schedule (below) and the demand curve (above).

Point	Price (per Game)	Quantity Demanded (Games per Day)
N	50 cents	3
M	25	4
S	10	8

Only one end of the budget constraint is changed in Figure 5A.5. The budget line still begins at 4 Cokes because the price of Coke is unchanged. If only one price is changed, then only one end of the budget constraint is shifted.

Because the budget constraint has shifted inward, the combination *M* is no longer attainable. Two Cokes (at 50 cents each) and 4 games (at 50 cents each) now cost more than $2. We're now forced to accept a lower level of total utility. According to Figure 5A.5, optimal consumption is now located at point *N*. This is the point of tangency between the new budget constraint and a lower indifference curve. At point *N* we consume 1 Coke and 3 video games.

Consider what has happened here. The price of video games has increased (from 25 cents to 50 cents), and the quantity of games demanded has decreased. This is the kind of relationship that demand curves describe. **Demand curves** indicate how the quantity demanded of a good changes in response to a change in its price, given a fixed income and all other things held constant. Not only does Figure 5A.5 provide the same information, it also conforms to the **law of demand:** as the price of games increases, the quantity demanded falls.

Suppose the price of video games were to fall rather than increase. Specifically, assume that the price of a game fell to 10 cents. This price reduction would shift the budget constraint farther out on the horizontal axis because as many as 20 games could then be purchased with $2. As a result of the price reduction, we can now buy more goods and thus attain a higher level of satisfaction.

Point *S* in Figure 5A.5 indicates the optimal combination of Cokes and video games at the new video game price. At these prices, we consume 8 video games and 2.4 Cokes (we may have to share with a friend). The law of demand is again evident: when the price of video games declines, the quantity demanded increases.

The Demand Schedule and Curve. Figure 5A.6 summarizes the information we've acquired about the demand for video games. The demand schedule depicts the price–quantity relationships prevailing at optimal consumption points *N*, *M*, and *S* (from Figure 5A.5). The demand curve generalizes these observations to encompass other prices. What we end up with is a demand curve explicitly derived from our (assumed) knowledge of consumer tastes.

demand curve: A curve describing the quantities of a good a consumer is willing and able to buy at alternative prices in a given time period, *ceteris paribus*.

law of demand: The quantity of a good demanded in a given time period increases as its price falls, *ceteris paribus*.

Name: _____

LO5-1   1. According to Table 5.1,
  (a) With which box of popcorn does marginal utility first diminish? _____
  (b) With which box does marginal utility become negative? _____

LO5-2   2. In Figure 5.4, how much consumer surplus is received by
  (a) Hua? _____
  (b) Carlos? _____
  (c) John? _____

LO5-2   3. In Figure 5.4, if Blaise's maximum price threshold doubled,
  (a) Would she buy a Spyder? _____
  (b) How much consumer surplus would she have? _____

LO5-2   4. What is the combined consumer surplus for the four buyers above point A in Figure 5.4 if all the Spyders are sold for $845,500? _____

LO5-3   5. What is the total revenue (price × quantity) received by the car dealer in Figure 5.4 if he charges
  (a) A uniform price of $800,000? _____
  (b) Maximum individual prices to Fred, Michel, Hua, Carlos, and John? _____

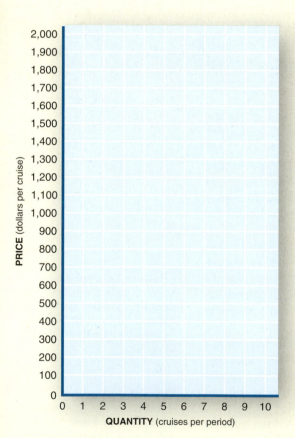

LO5-3   6. The following data reveal how much each consumer is willing to pay for an Alaskan cruise:

Amy	$ 900	Ed	$2,000
Bob	$1,100	Gigi	$1,300
Carol	$1,500	Hugo	$1,800
Eduardo	$ 400	Isabelle	$1,500

  (a) Draw the market demand for these eight consumers on the accompanying graph.
  (b) If the cruise costs $1,000, how many passengers will there be? _____
  (c) If the cruise costs $1,000, how much total revenue will be collected? _____
  (d) If the cruise costs $1,000, how much consumer surplus will those passengers enjoy? _____
  (e) If the cruise ship could perfectly price discriminate, how much more revenue could it take in? _____

LO5-4   7. Suppose movie downloads cost $2 apiece and game downloads cost $3. If the marginal utility of movie downloads at the optimal mix of consumption is 10 utils, what is the marginal utility of a game download? _____

LO5-1   8. Suppose the graph on the next page depicts the demand for football tickets at Grand University.
  (a) What is total revenue at the price of $24? $_____
  (b) If the price drops to $12, how many tickets would consumers purchase? _____
  (c) What is total revenue at that point? $_____
  (d) If the team has a winning streak and the price is still $24, at what point do we end up? _____
  (e) What is total revenue at that point? $_____

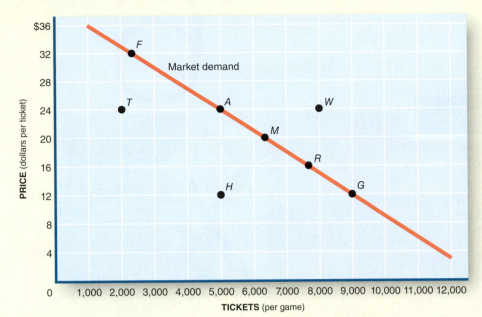

LO5-4 9. Suppose the following table reflects the total satisfaction derived from consumption of pizza slices and Pepsis. Assume that pizza costs $1 per slice and a large Pepsi costs $2. With $20 to spend, what consumption mix will maximize satisfaction?   _____ pizza slices and _____ large Pepsis

Quantity consumed	1	2	3	4	5	6	7	8	9	10	11	12	13	14
Total units of pleasure from pizza slices	47	92	132	166	196	224	251	271	288	303	313	315	312	300
Total units of pleasure from Pepsis	111	200	272	336	386	426	452	456	444	408	340	217	92	−17

LO5-1 10. Use the following data to illustrate the relevant demand curve:

Price	$ 1	2	3	4	5	6	7	8	9	10
Quantity	20	18	16	14	12	10	8	6	4	2

(a) If the price increases from $4 to $8, by how much does the quantity demanded decline?   _____

(b) If a successful advertising campaign increases the quantity demanded at every price by 4 units,
    (i) Draw the new demand curve D_2.
    (ii) How many units are now purchased at $8?   _____

115

Elasticity

LEARNING OBJECTIVES

After reading this chapter, you should know

LO6-1. How to compute price elasticity of demand.

LO6-2. The relationships between price changes, price elasticity, and total revenue.

LO6-3. What the cross-price elasticity of demand measures.

LO6-4. What the income elasticity of demand tells us.

LO6-5. What the elasticity of supply measures.

Steve Jobs made a pricing mistake when he launched the 8 GB iPhone in June 2007. He knew all about consumer demand and its many determinants. And he could draw a downward-sloping demand curve just as well as any college economics major (even though he dropped out of Reed College after just one semester). But he overestimated the dimensions of market demand. The demand curve he drew projected that the quantity of iPhones demanded at the price of $599 would be far greater than it turned out to be. This mistake created an instant dilemma. If he kept the price of $599, iPhone sales would come in below publicized projections, and the phone would be deemed a failure. Apple's image of consistent success would be tarnished. Software writers might not develop the library of iPhone apps that would make the iPhone irresistible. So Jobs knew what he had to do: reduce the iPhone's price—fast!

But he couldn't afford to make another mistake. If he reduced the price too little, iPhone sales would still fall short of projections. If he reduced the price too much, sales would soar past production rates and market shortages would frustrate would-be buyers. On the second go-round, Steve Jobs had to pick the right price—the one that would increase the quantity demanded to Apple's sales projections. The concept that could save him was the "price elasticity of demand"—a measure of how the quantity demanded *changes* in response to a *change* in price.

This chapter focuses on that *elasticity* concept. Among the questions we'll pursue are

- **How does a change in a product's price affect the quantity we purchase or the amount of money we spend on it?**
- **How do changes in the price of *other* products affect the amount of a product we buy?**
- **How do changes in income affect the quantity demanded of various goods and services?**

As we will see, the concept of "elasticity" is part of the answer to all these questions. We will also see how Steve Jobs salvaged the iPhone with the same concept.

PRICE ELASTICITY

What Steve Jobs wanted to know in September 2007 was how much phone sales would *increase* if he *reduced* its price. The same question haunts movie theater owners. They make a big chunk of profit from the sale of popcorn, candy, and soda. People are always complaining about how expensive those snacks are. But will they buy more if prices are reduced? A *lot* more, or just a *little* more?

Like Steve Jobs, theater owners know all about the **law of demand** and the downward-sloping **demand curve.** But that law isn't greatly informative; it tells them only that the quantity demanded will increase when the price is reduced. That begs the critical question of *how much.* What the theater owner wants to know is *by how much* the quantity demanded will increase if the price is reduced. Steve Jobs wanted to know the same thing about the demand for iPhones: how many *more* iPhones would be purchased if he reduced its price?

The central question in all these decisions is the response of quantity demanded to a change in price. ***The response of consumers to a change in price is measured by the price elasticity of demand.*** Specifically, the **price elasticity of demand** refers to the percentage change in quantity demanded divided by the percentage change in price:

$$\text{Price elasticity } (E) = \frac{\% \text{ change in quantity demanded}}{\% \text{ change in price}}$$

What would the value of price elasticity be if air travel didn't change at all when airfares were cut by 5 percent? In that case the price elasticity of demand would be

$$E = \frac{\% \text{ change in quantity demanded}}{\% \text{ change in price}}$$

$$= \frac{0}{5} = 0$$

But is this realistic? According to the law of demand, the quantity demanded goes up when price goes down. So we'd expect *somebody* to buy more airline tickets if fares fell by 5 percent. In a large market like air travel, we don't expect *everybody* to jump on a plane when airfares are reduced. But if *some* consumers fly more, the percentage change in quantity demanded will be larger than zero. Indeed, ***the law of demand implies that the price elasticity of demand will always be greater than zero.***

Technically, the price elasticity of demand (E) would be a negative number since quantity demanded and price always move in opposite directions (law of demand). For simplicity, however, E is typically expressed in absolute terms (without the minus sign). ***The key question, then, is how much greater than zero E actually is.***

Computing Price Elasticity

To get a feel for the dimensions of elasticity, let's return to the popcorn counter at the movies that we first encountered in Chapter 5. We observed there that at a price of 45 cents an ounce the average moviegoer demands 2 ounces of popcorn per show. This is illustrated again in Figure 6.1 at point *B*. At the lower price of 40 cents per ounce (point *C*), the quantity demanded jumps to 4 ounces per show.

Percentage Change in *q*. We can summarize this response with the price elasticity of demand. To do so, we have to calculate the *percentage* changes in quantity and price. Consider the percentage change in quantity first. In this case, the change in quantity demanded is 4 ounces − 2 ounces = 2 ounces. The *percentage* change in quantity is therefore

$$\% \text{ change in quantity} = \frac{2}{q}$$

law of demand: The quantity of a good demanded in a given time period increases as its price falls, *ceteris paribus.*

demand curve: A curve describing the quantities of a good a consumer is willing and able to buy at alternative prices in a given period, *ceteris paribus.*

price elasticity of demand: The percentage change in quantity demanded divided by the percentage change in price.

FIGURE 6.1

An Individual's Demand Schedule and Curve

Consumers are generally willing to buy larger quantities of a good at lower prices. This demand schedule illustrates the specific quantities demanded at alternative prices. If popcorn sold for 25 cents per ounce, this consumer would buy 12 ounces per show (row *F*). At higher prices, less popcorn would be purchased.

A downward-sloping demand curve expresses the law of demand: the quantity of a good demanded increases as its price falls. Notice that points *A* through *J* on the curve correspond to the rows of the demand schedule.

	Price (per Ounce)	Quantity Demanded (Ounces per Show)
A	$0.50	1
B	0.45	2
C	0.40	4
D	0.35	6
E	0.30	9
F	0.25	12
G	0.20	16
H	0.15	20
I	0.10	25
J	0.05	30

The Law of Demand

The computational problem is to transform the denominator q into a number. Should we use the quantity of popcorn purchased *before* the price reduction—that is, $q_1 = 2$? Or should we use the quantity purchased *after* the price reduction—that is, $q_2 = 4$? The choice of denominator will have a big impact on the computed percentage change. To ensure consistency, economists prefer to use the *average* quantity in the denominator:[1]

$$\% \text{ change in quantity demanded} = \frac{\text{Change in quantity}}{\text{Average quantity}}$$

Our first task is therefore to compute the ***average*** quantity: the average of the first (pre–price change) and second (post–price change) quantities. The formula for this calculation is

$$\text{Average quantity} = \frac{q_1 + q_2}{2} = \frac{2 + 4}{2} = 3 \text{ ounces}$$

(3 is the average value of 2 and 4).

---

[1]This procedure is referred to as the *arc* (midpoint) elasticity of demand. If a single quantity (price) is used in the denominator, we refer to the *point* elasticity of demand.

We can now complete the calculation of the percentage change in quantity demanded. It is

$$\begin{array}{l}\text{\% change in}\\\text{quantity demanded}\end{array} = \dfrac{\begin{array}{c}\text{Change in}\\\text{quantity}\end{array}}{\begin{array}{c}\text{Average}\\\text{quantity}\end{array}} = \dfrac{q_2 - q_1}{\dfrac{q_1 + q_2}{2}} = \dfrac{2}{3} = 0.667$$

Popcorn sales increased by an average of 67 percent when the price of popcorn was reduced from 45 cents to 40 cents per ounce.

Percentage Change in *p*. The computation of the percentage change in price is similar. We first note that the price of popcorn fell by 5 cents ($45¢ - 40¢$) when we move from point *B* to point *C* on the demand curve (Figure 6.1). We then compute the *average* price of popcorn in this range of the demand curve as

$$\begin{array}{c}\text{Average price}\\\text{of popcorn}\end{array} = \dfrac{p_1 + p_2}{2} = \dfrac{45¢ + 40¢}{2} = 42.5 \text{ cents}$$

This *average* is the denominator we use in calculating the percentage price change. Using these numbers, we see that the absolute value of the percentage change is

$$\begin{array}{c}\text{\% change}\\\text{in price}\end{array} = \dfrac{\begin{array}{c}\text{Change in}\\\text{price}\end{array}}{\begin{array}{c}\text{Average}\\\text{price}\end{array}} = \dfrac{p_2 - p_1}{\dfrac{p_1 + p_2}{2}} = \dfrac{5}{42.5} = 0.118$$

The price of popcorn fell by 11.8 percent.

These calculations are a bit cumbersome, but they give us all the information required to compute the price elasticity of demand. In this case,

$$E = \dfrac{\begin{array}{c}\text{\% change}\\\text{in quantity}\\\text{demanded}\end{array}}{\begin{array}{c}\text{\% change}\\\text{in price}\end{array}} = \dfrac{0.667}{0.118} = 5.65$$

What we get from all these calculations is a very useful number. It says that the consumer response to a price reduction will be extremely large. Specifically, the quantity of popcorn consumed will increase 5.65 times as fast as price falls. A 1 percent reduction in price brings about a 5.65 percent increase in purchases. The theater manager can therefore boost popcorn sales greatly by lowering price a little. Steve Jobs would have been thrilled if the demand for iPhones was that elastic.

Elastic vs. Inelastic Demand. We characterize the demand for various goods in one of three ways: *elastic, inelastic,* or *unitary elastic:*

- *If **E** is larger than 1, demand is elastic.* Consumer response is large relative to the change in price.
- If *E* is less than 1, we say demand is *in*elastic. *If demand is inelastic (**E** < 1), consumers aren't very responsive to price changes.*
- *If **E** is equal to 1, demand is **unitary** elastic.* In this case, the percentage change in quantity demanded is exactly equal to the percentage change in price.

Consider the case of smoking. Many smokers claim they'd "pay anything" for a cigarette after they've run out. But would they? Would they continue to smoke just as many cigarettes if prices doubled or tripled? If so, the demand curve would be vertical (as in Figure 6.2*b*) rather than downward-sloping. Research suggests this is not the case: higher cigarette prices *do* curb smoking. There is at least *some* elasticity in the demand for cigarettes. But the elasticity of demand is low; Table 6.1 indicates that the price elasticity of cigarette demand is only 0.4.

Although the average adult smoker is not very responsive to changes in cigarette prices, teen smokers apparently are. Research studies confirm that teen smoking drops by almost

(a) Completely elastic (E = ∞)

(b) Completely inelastic (E = 0)

FIGURE 6.2
Extremes of Elasticity

If demand were perfectly elastic ($E = \infty$), the demand curve would be *horizontal*. In that case, any increase in price (e.g., p_1 to p_2) would cause quantity demanded to fall to zero.

A *vertical* demand curve implies that an increase in price won't affect the quantity demanded. In this situation of perfectly *in*elastic ($E = 0$) demand, consumers are willing to pay *any* price to get the quantity q_1.

In reality, elasticities of demand for goods and services lie between these two extremes (obeying the law of demand).

7 percent when cigarette prices increase by 10 percent. Thus the price elasticity of *teen* demand for smoking is

$$E = \frac{\text{Percentage drop in quantity demanded}}{\text{Percentage increase in price}} = \frac{7\%}{10\%} = 0.7$$

Hence higher cigarette prices can be an effective policy tool for curbing teen smoking. The *tripling* of the federal excise tax on cigarettes in 2009 (see the News on the next page) was expected to deter millions of would-be smokers.

web analysis

To see price elasticity of demand estimates for a host of other goods, both in the short run and the long run, visit **www. mackinac.org** and search "price elasticity of demand."

TABLE 6.1
Elasticity Estimates

Price elasticities vary greatly. When the price of gasoline increases, consumers reduce their consumption only slightly ($E = 0.2$). When the price of fish increases, however, consumers cut back their consumption substantially ($E = 2.2$). These differences reflect the availability of immediate substitutes, the prices of the goods, and the amount of time available for changing behavior.

Product	Price Elasticity
Relatively elastic (E > 1)	
Airline travel, long run	2.4
Restaurant meals	2.3
Fresh fish	2.2
New cars, short run	1.2–1.5
Unitary elastic (E = 1)	
Private education	1.1
Radios and televisions	1.2
Shoes	0.9
Movies	0.9
Relatively inelastic (E < 1)	
Cigarettes	0.4
Coffee	0.3
Gasoline, short run	0.2
Electricity (in homes)	0.1
Long-distance phone calls	0.1

Source: Compiled from Hendrick S. Houthakker and Lester D. Taylor, *Consumer Demand in the United States, 1929–1970* (Cambridge: Harvard University Press, 1966); F. W. Bell, "The Pope and Price of Fish," *American Economic Review,* December 1968; Herbert Scarf and John Shoven, *Applied General Equilibrium Analysis* (New York: Cambridge University Press, 1984); and Michael Ward, "Product Substitutability and Competition in Long-Distance Telecommunications," *Economic Inquiry,* October 1999.

IN THE NEWS

Federal Cigarette Tax Going Up

WASHINGTION—President Barack Obama signed legislation Wednesday to more than double the federal cigarette [tax] to pay for an expansion of health insurance for poor children.

Tobacco companies hurt by declining smoking rates expect the 62-cent increase—to $1.01 per pack—to further cut cigarette sales after it takes effect April 1. . . .

Tommy Payne, spokesman for Reynolds American Inc., a tobacco company in Winston-Salem, North Carolina, said the company expects industrywide volume declines of 6 to 8 percent.

—Sean Mussenden

Source: Media General News Service, February 5, 2009. Used with permission.

PhotoAlto/PictureQuest

web analysis

For more information about smoking and its effect on youth, visit **www.cdc.gov** and search for "teen smoking."

Analysis: The demand for cigarettes is relatively inelastic. Nevertheless, higher prices still reduce the quantity demanded.

According to Table 6.1, the demand for airline travel is even more price-elastic. Whenever a fare cut is announced, the airlines get swamped with telephone inquiries. If fares are discounted by 25 percent, the number of passengers may increase by as much as 60 percent. As Table 6.1 shows, the elasticity of airline demand is 2.4, meaning that the percentage change in quantity demanded (60 percent) will be 2.4 times larger than the price cut (25 percent).

Steve Jobs was pleased to discover that the demand for iPhones was even more elastic than that. Two months after launching the 8 GB iPhone, he reduced its price from $599 to $399. Unit sales not only increased, they soared, as the accompanying News reports. Demand for the iPhone was very elastic.

IN THE NEWS

After iPhone Price Cut, Sales Are Up by 200 Percent

Piper Gene Munster, the person responsible for a survey dedicated to Apple in which he "found" out an estimated number of iPhones that were sold, has come up with yet another interesting theory.

According to Munster and the past-week Apple announcement about 1 million iPhones sold, the calculations take to the conclusion that after the price cut, the sales increased up to 200 percent. . . .

By Munster's reckoning, Apple and AT&T were selling an average of 9,000 iPhones a day before the price reduction, which would have put their quarterly sales at 594,000 as of September 5.

By the end of the quarter, he believes Apple will have sold a total of 1.28 million iPhones.

Source: Mobilewhack.com, September 11, 2007. Used with permission.

Analysis: If demand is elastic, unit sales increase by a larger percentage than price declines. The demand for iPhones was highly elastic.

Determinants of Elasticity

Why are consumers so price-sensitive ($E > 1$) with some goods and not ($E < 1$) with others? To answer that, we must go back to the demand curve itself. The elasticity of demand is computed between points on a given demand curve. Hence *the price elasticity of demand is influenced by all the determinants of demand.* Four factors are particularly worth noting.

Necessities vs. Luxuries. Some goods are so critical to our everyday life that we regard them as "necessities." A hairbrush, toothpaste, and perhaps textbooks might fall into this category. Our "taste" for such goods is so strong that we can't imagine getting along without them. As a result, we don't change our consumption of "necessities" much when the price increases; *demand for necessities is relatively inelastic.*

A "luxury" good, by contrast, is something we'd *like* to have but aren't likely to buy unless our income jumps or the price declines sharply, such as vacation travel, new cars (that Porsche 918 Spyder!), and iPhones. We want them but can get by without them. That is, *demand for luxury goods is relatively elastic.*

Availability of Substitutes. Our notion of which goods are necessities is also influenced by the availability of substitute goods. The high elasticity of demand for fish (Table 6.1) reflects the fact that consumers can eat chicken, beef, or pork if fish prices rise. On the other hand, most bleary-eyed coffee drinkers can't imagine any other product that could substitute for a cup of coffee. As a consequence, when coffee prices rise, consumers don't reduce their purchases much at all. Likewise, the low elasticity of demand for gasoline reflects the fact that most cars can't run on alternative fuels. In general, *the greater the availability of substitutes, the higher the price elasticity of demand.* That is why Sony had such a great response when it cut the price of PlayStation 3 (see the accompanying News).

IN THE NEWS

PlayStation 3 Sales More Than Double after Price Cut

LOS ANGELES, California (AP)—U.S. sales of the PlayStation 3 more than doubled in the weeks after the company slashed the video game console's price $100 and launched a low-end model, Sony Corp. CEO Howard Stringer told The Associated Press Wednesday.

Sony said it sold more than 100,000 consoles of all types in the week ending November 11.

The price cut and new model make the PS3 more competitive against Nintendo Co.'s Wii and Microsoft Corp.'s Xbox 360 as the holiday season opens, Stringer said.

"It's the breakthrough we've been anticipating," Stringer said. "We've been holding our breath."

Sony said it had been selling between 30,000 and 40,000 consoles per week before the October 18 price cut from $599 to $499 of the 80 GB model.

Analysis: When demand is elastic, unit sales increase sharply when price is reduced.

Relative Price (to Income). Another important determinant of elasticity is the price of the good in relation to a consumer's income. Airline travel and new cars are quite expensive, so even a small percentage change in their prices can have a big impact on a consumer's budget and consumption decisions. The demand for such big-ticket items tends to be elastic. By contrast, coffee is so cheap that even a large *percentage* change in price doesn't affect consumer behavior much.

Because the relative price of a good affects price elasticity, the value of E_1 *changes* along a given demand curve. At current prices the elasticity of demand for coffee is low. How would consumers behave, however, if coffee cost $5 a cup? Some people would still consume coffee. At such higher prices, however, the quantity demanded would be more sensitive to price changes. Accordingly, when we observe, as in Table 6.1, that the demand for coffee is price-inelastic, that observation applies only to the current range of prices. Were coffee prices dramatically higher, the price elasticity of demand would be higher as well. As a rule, ***the price elasticity of demand declines as price moves down the demand curve.***

Time. Finally, time affects the price elasticity of demand. Car owners can't switch to electric autos every time the price of gasoline goes up. In the short run, the elasticity of demand for gasoline is quite low. With more time to adjust, however, consumers can buy more fuel-efficient cars, relocate their homes or jobs, and even switch fuels. As a consequence, ***the long-run price elasticity of demand is higher than the short-run elasticity.*** Nobel Prize–winning economist Gary Becker used the distinction between long-run and short-run elasticities to explain why a proposed increase in cigarette excise taxes wouldn't generate nearly as much revenue as President Clinton expected (see the News below). The same elasticity error caused President Obama to overestimate the revenues his 2009 cigarette tax increase (see the News on page 121) would bring in.

IN THE NEWS

Professor Becker Corrects President's Math

President Clinton has seized upon the cigarette excise tax as an expedient and politically correct means of increasing federal revenue. In 1994 the federal government took in $12 billion from the present 24-cents-per-pack tax. If the tax were quadrupled to $1 a pack, Clinton figures tax revenues would increase by more than $50 billion over three years. Those added revenues would help finance the health care reforms the president so dearly wants.

Professor Gary Becker, a Nobel Prize–winning economist at the University of Chicago, says Clinton's math is wrong. The White House assumed that cigarette sales would drop by 4 percent for every 10 percent increase in price. Professor Becker says that reflects only the first-year response to higher prices, not the full adjustment of smokers' behavior. Over a three-year period, cigarette consumption is likely to decline by 8 percent for every 10 percent increase in price—twice as much as Clinton assumed. As a result, the $1-a-pack tax will bring in much less revenue than President Clinton projected.

Source: Gary S. Becker, "Warning: A Higher Cigarette Tax May Be Hazardous to Health Financing," *BusinessWeek,* August 15, 1994, p. 18.

Analysis: It takes time for people to adjust their behavior to changed prices. Hence the short-run price elasticity of demand is lower than the long-run elasticity.

web analysis

Gary Becker won the 1992 Nobel Prize in economics. He writes a weekly blog with Judge Richard Posner dealing with the economics of current events. Go to **www. becker-posner-blog.com.**

PRICE ELASTICITY AND TOTAL REVENUE

The concept of price elasticity refutes the popular misconception that producers charge the "highest price possible." Were that true, Steve Jobs might have initially priced the iPhone at $8,996. Except in the very rare case of completely inelastic demand, this notion makes no sense. Indeed, higher prices not only reduce unit sales, but may actually reduce total sales revenue as well.

The **total revenue** of a seller is the amount of money received from product sales. It is determined by the quantity of the product sold and the price at which it is sold:

$$\text{Total revenue} = \text{Price} \times \text{Quantity sold}$$

total revenue: The price of a product multiplied by the quantity sold in a given time period: $p \times q$.

In the movie theater example, if the price of popcorn is 40 cents per ounce and only 4 ounces are sold, total revenue equals $1.60 per show. This revenue is illustrated by the shaded rectangle in Figure 6.3. (The area of a rectangle is equal to its height [p] times its width [q].)

Now consider what happens to total revenue when the price of popcorn is increased. From the law of demand, we know that an increase in price will lead to a decrease in quantity demanded. But what about total revenue? The change in total revenue depends on *how much* quantity demanded falls when price goes up.

FIGURE 6.3

Elasticity and Total Revenue

Total revenue is equal to the price of the product times the quantity sold. It is illustrated by the area of the rectangle formed by $p \times q$.

The shaded rectangle illustrates total revenue ($1.60) at a price of 40 cents and a quantity demanded of 4 ounces. When price is increased to 45 cents (point *B*), the rectangle and total revenue shrink (see the dashed lines) because demand is relatively elastic in that price range. Price hikes increase total revenue only if demand is inelastic.

	Price	×	Quantity Demanded	=	Total Revenue
A	50¢		1		$0.50
B	45		2		0.90
C	40		4		1.60
D	35		6		2.10
E	30		8		2.40
F	25		12		3.00
G	20		16		3.20
H	15		20		3.00
I	10		25		2.50
J	5		30		1.50

Suppose we raise popcorn prices again, from 40 cents back to 45 cents. What happens to total revenue? At 40 cents per box, 4 ounces are sold (see Figure 6.3) and total revenue equals $1.60. If we increase the price to 45 cents, only 2 ounces are sold and total revenue drops to 90 cents. In this case, an *increase* in price leads to a *decrease* in total revenue. This new and smaller total revenue is illustrated by the dashed rectangle in Figure 6.3.

Price increases don't always lower total revenue. If consumer demand was relatively *inelastic* (E < 1), a price increase would lead to *higher* total revenue. Thus we conclude that

- *A price hike increases total revenue only if demand is inelastic* (**E < 1**).
- *A price hike reduces total revenue if demand is elastic* (**E > 1**).
- *A price hike does not change total revenue if demand is unitary elastic* (**E = 1**).

Table 6.2 summarizes these and other responses to price changes.

TABLE 6.2

Price Elasticity of Demand and Total Revenue

The impact of higher prices on total revenue depends on the price elasticity of demand. Higher prices result in higher total revenue only if demand is inelastic. If demand is elastic, *lower* prices result in *higher* revenues.

	Effect on Total Revenue of	
If Demand is	**Price Increase**	**Price Reduction**
Elastic (E > 1)	Decrease	Increase
Inelastic (E < 1)	Increase	Decrease
Unitary elastic (E = 1)	No change	No change

(a) The demand curve

(b) Total revenue

FIGURE 6.4

Price Elasticity Changes along a Demand Curve

The concept of price elasticity can be used to determine whether people will spend more money on cigarettes when their price rises. The answer to this question is yes and no, depending on how high the price goes.

Notice in the table and the graphs that total revenue rises when the price of cigarettes increases from $2 to $4 a pack and again to $6. At low prices, the demand for cigarettes appears relatively inelastic: price and total revenue move in the same direction.

As the price of cigarettes continues to increase, however, total revenue starts to fall. As the price is increased from $6 to $8 a pack, total revenue drops. At higher prices, the demand for cigarettes is relatively elastic: price and total revenue move in *opposite directions*. Hence the price elasticity of demand depends on where one is on the demand curve.

Price of Cigarettes	×	Quantity Demanded	=	Total Revenue	
$ 2		100		$200 ⎫	Low elasticity; *E* < 1
4		90		360 ⎬	(total revenue rises
6		70		420 ⎭	when price increases)
8		50		400 ⎫	High elasticity; *E* > 1
10		25		250 ⎬	(total revenue falls
12		10		120 ⎭	when price increases)
14		6		84	

Changing Value of *E*. Once we know the price elasticity of demand, we can predict how consumers will respond to changing prices. We can also predict what will happen to the total revenue of the seller when the price is raised or reduced. Figure 6.4 shows how elasticity and total revenue change along a given demand curve. Demand for cigarettes is *elastic* (*E* > 1) at prices above $6 per pack but *inelastic* (*E* < 1) at lower prices.

The bottom half of Figure 6.4 shows how total revenue changes along the demand curve. At very high prices (e.g., $14 a pack), few cigarettes are sold and total revenue is low. As the price is reduced, however, the quantity demanded increases so much that total revenue *increases* despite the lower price. With each price reduction from $14 down to $6, total revenue increases.

Price cuts below $6 a pack continue to increase the quantity demanded (the law of demand). The increase in unit sales is no longer large enough, however, to offset the price reductions. Total revenue starts falling after the price drops below $6 per pack. The lesson to remember here is that *the impact of a price change on total revenue depends on the (changing) price elasticity of demand.*

CROSS-PRICE ELASTICITY

The price elasticity of demand tells us how consumers will respond to a change in the price of a good under the assumption of *ceteris paribus*. But other factors do change, and consumption behavior may respond to those changes as well.

Shifts vs. Movements

We recognized this problem in Chapter 3 when we first distinguished *movements* along a demand curve from *shifts* of the demand curve. A movement along an unchanged demand curve represents consumer response to a change in the *price* of that specific good. The magnitude of that movement is expressed in the price elasticity of demand.

When the underlying determinants of demand change, the entire demand curve shifts. These shifts also alter consumer behavior. The *price* elasticity of demand is of no use in gauging these behavioral responses because it refers to price changes (movements along a constant demand curve) for that good only. Now we have to ask how consumers will respond when an underlying determinant of demand (tastes, income, other goods, or expectations) changes and the demand curve shifts.

A Change in Price of "Other Goods"

Let's sneak back into the movie theater for a moment and reconsider why we buy popcorn. Popcorn isn't the only treat at the concession stand; you can also purchase candy, soda, ice cream, and more. Thus the decision to buy popcorn depends not only on *its* price but also on the price and availability of other goods.

Suppose for the moment that the prices of these other goods were to fall. Imagine that candy bars were put on sale for a quarter, rather than the usual dollar. Would this price reduction for candy affect the consumption of popcorn?

According to Figure 6.5, the demand for popcorn might *decrease* if the price of candy fell. The leftward shift of the demand curve from D_1 to D_2 tells us that consumers now demand less popcorn at every price. At 25 cents per ounce, consumers now demand only 8 ounces of popcorn (point *R*) rather than the previous 12 ounces (point *F*). In other words, a decline in the price of *candy* has caused a reduction in the demand for *popcorn*. We conclude that candy and popcorn are **substitute goods**—when the price of one declines, demand for the other falls. That is why sales of the Palm Treo and Motorola RAZR2 declined when Apple cut the price of the iPhone (see the following News): iPhones and Treos are *substitute* goods.

Popcorn sales would follow a very different path if the price of soda fell. People like to wash down their popcorn with soda. When soda prices fall, moviegoers actually buy *more* popcorn. Here again, *a change in the price of one good affects the demand for another good.* In this case, however, we're dealing with **complementary goods,** since a decline in the price of one good causes an *increase* in the demand for the other good.

substitute goods: Goods that substitute for each other; when the price of good *X* rises, the demand for good *Y* increases, *ceteris paribus*.

complementary goods: Goods frequently consumed in combination; when the price of good *X* rises, the demand for good *Y* falls, *ceteris paribus*.

Demand for X is affected by price of Y.

FIGURE 6.5
Substitutes and Complements

The curve D_1 represents the initial demand for popcorn, given the prices of other goods. Other prices may change, however. If a reduction in the price of another good (candy) causes a *reduction* in the demand for this good (popcorn), the two goods are *substitutes*. Popcorn demand shifts to the left (to D_2) when the price of a *substitute good* falls.

If a reduction in the price of another good (e.g., Pepsi) leads to an *increase* in the demand for this good (popcorn), the two goods are *complements*. Popcorn demand shifts to the right (to D_3) when the price of a *complementary good* falls.

IN THE NEWS

iPhone Price Cut a Blow to Palm, Motorola

Apple's hefty iPhone price cut puts it in direct competition with handsets from Motorola and Palm, which are struggling to convince Wall Street they can turn around their aging brands.

With the music-playing iPhone now selling at $399 instead of $599, its price tag is much closer to other smartphones in the U.S. market, including Palm's Treo and Motorola's Razr2. . . .

Palm said in June it expected the touch-screen iPhone to temporarily slow Treo demand, and Oppenheimer analyst Lawrence Harris said Apple's price cut could exacerbate this.

"It has the potential to take away from Treo sales," Harris said.

—Sinead Carew

Analysis: Two products are substitute goods if a price decline in one causes a decline in demand (leftward shift) for the other.

The distinction between substitute goods and complementary goods is illustrated in Figure 6.5. Note that *in the case of substitute goods the price of one good and the demand for the other move in the same direction.* (A *decrease* in candy prices causes a *decrease* in popcorn demand.) The iPhone price cut increased the demand for AT&T wireless services: iPhones and wireless services are *complementary* goods. The same iPhone price cut *reduced* the demand for Treos; iPhones and Treos are *substitute* goods.

In the case of complementary goods (e.g., Pepsi and popcorn, cream and coffee), the price of one good and the demand for the other move in opposite directions. This helps explain why U.S. consumers bought more cars in 1998–1999 when gasoline prices were falling and fewer SUVs in 2011 (see the News on the next page) when gasoline prices were rising. The concept of complementary goods also explains why the demand for computer software increases when the price of computer hardware drops.

Calculating Cross-Price Elasticity.   The mathematical relationship between the price of one good and demand for another is summarized in yet another elasticity concept. The

cross-price elasticity of demand: Percentage change in the quantity demanded of *X* divided by percentage change in price of *Y*.

cross-price elasticity of demand is the *percentage* change in the quantity demanded of one good divided by the *percentage* change in the price of *another* good:

$$\text{Cross-price elasticity of demand} = \frac{\substack{\% \text{ change in quantity} \\ \text{demanded of good } X \\ (\text{at given price})}}{\substack{\% \text{ change in price} \\ \text{of good } Y}}$$

What has changed here is the denominator. Now the denominator refers to a change in the price of *another* good rather than the *same* good.

Think back to the impact of the iPhone price cut on Treo sales (see the News on the previous page). The iPhone dropped in price from $599 to $399. We compute the *percentage* decline as

$$\substack{\% \text{ change} \\ \text{in iPhone price}} = \frac{\text{Change in price}}{\text{Average price}} = \frac{\$599 - \$399}{\$499} = -0.40$$

Treo sales *declined* by 10 percent. Hence the cross-price elasticity of demand was

$$E_x = \frac{-0.10}{-0.40} = +0.25$$

Demand for Treos declined by 0.25 percent for every 1 percent decline in the iPhone price. A 40 percent iPhone price cut therefore caused a 10 percent decline in Treo demand.

Notice that the cross-price elasticity computed here is a *positive* number (+0.25). We saw earlier that the simple (same-product) price elasticity of demand is always a negative number, so we could ignore its sign. That's not the case with cross-price elasticities. In fact, the sign of the cross-price elasticity of demand is important.

If the cross-price elasticity is positive, the two goods are substitutes; if the cross-price elasticity is negative, the two goods are complements. Pepsi and popcorn are complements because a fall (−) in the price of one leads to an increase (+) in the demand for the other; in other words, the cross-price elasticity is negative. How about SUVs and gasoline (see the News below)?

IN THE NEWS

SUV Sales Drop with Gasoline Price Rise

Analysts say that with the increase in gasoline prices comes a drop in SUV sales and trade-in values at dealerships. The U.S. Department of Energy said that during the past week, U.S. gasoline prices topped $3 a gallon—the highest level since October 2008. . . .

According to Alec Gutierrez, lead analyst for vehicle evaluation at Kelley Blue Book, SUV sales have decreased about 1 percent since the last major gasoline price hike in spring 2008. He doesn't believe that SUV sales will decrease significantly unless prices reach $3.50 to $4 per gallon.

—Andrew Christian

Source: 4WheelsNews.com. Used with permission.

Analysis: Higher gasoline prices reduce the demand for SUVs. Therefore, they are complementary goods.

INCOME ELASTICITY

Changes in the price of other goods aren't the only source of demand shifts. Each of the four determinants of demand is a potential shift factor. Suppose consumer incomes were to increase. How would popcorn consumption be affected? Figure 6.6 provides an answer. Before the change in income, consumers demanded 12 ounces of popcorn at a

FIGURE 6.6
Income Elasticity

If income changes, the demand curve *shifts*. In this case, an increase in income enables consumers to buy more popcorn at every price. At a price of 25 cents, the quantity demanded increases from 12 ounces (point *F*) to 16 ounces (point *N*). The *income elasticity of demand* measures this response of demand to a change in income.

price of 25 cents per ounce. With more income to spend, the new demand curve (D_2) suggests that consumers will now purchase a greater quantity of popcorn at every price. The increase in income has caused a rightward shift in demand. If popcorn continues to sell for 25 cents per ounce, consumers will now buy 16 ounces per show (point *N*) rather than only 12 ounces (point *F*).

It appears that changes in income have a substantial impact on consumer demand for popcorn. The graph in Figure 6.6 doesn't tell us, however, how large the change in income was. Will a *small* increase in income cause such a shift, or does popcorn demand increase only when moviegoers have a *lot* more money to spend?

Figure 6.6 doesn't answer these questions. But a little math will. Specifically, the **income elasticity of demand** relates the *percentage* change in quantity demanded to the *percentage* change in income:

$$\text{Income elasticity of demand} = \frac{\begin{array}{c}\text{\% change in} \\ \text{quantity demanded} \\ \text{(at given price)}\end{array}}{\begin{array}{c}\text{\% change in} \\ \text{income}\end{array}}$$

income elasticity of demand: Percentage change in quantity demanded divided by percentage change in income.

The similarity to the price elasticity of demand is apparent. In this case, however, the denominator is *income* (a determinant of demand), not *price*.

Computing Income Elasticity. As was the case with price elasticity, we compute income elasticity with *average* values for the changes in quantity and income. Suppose that the shift in popcorn demand illustrated in Figure 6.6 occurred when income increased from $110 per week to $120 per week. We would then compute

$$\text{Income elasticity} = \frac{\dfrac{\text{Change in quantity demanded}}{\text{Average quantity}}}{\dfrac{\text{Change in income}}{\text{Average income}}}$$

$$= \frac{\dfrac{16 \text{ ounces} - 12 \text{ ounces}}{14 \text{ ounces}}}{\dfrac{\$120 - \$110}{\$115}}$$

web analysis

Learn how the latest recession affected sales of many inferior goods at **www.richmondfed. org.** Search "inferior goods."

normal good: Good for which demand increases when income rises.

inferior good: Good for which demand decreases when income rises.

$$= \frac{4}{14} \div \frac{10}{115}$$

$$= \frac{0.286}{0.087} = 3.29$$

Popcorn purchases are very sensitive to changes in income. When incomes rise by 8.7 percent, popcorn sales increase by a whopping 28.6 percent (that is, $8.7\% \times 3.29$). The computed elasticity of 3.29 summarizes this relationship.

Normal vs. Inferior Goods. Demand and income don't always move in the same direction. Popcorn is a **normal good** because consumers buy more of it when their incomes rise. People actually buy *less* of some goods, however, when they have more income. With low incomes, people buy discount clothes, used textbooks, and cheap beer, and they eat at home. With more money to spend, they switch to designer clothes, new books, premium beer, and restaurant meals. The former items are called **inferior goods** because the quantity demanded *falls* when income *rises*. Similarly, when incomes *decline,* people demand *more* spaghetti, pawnbrokers, and lottery tickets. ***For inferior goods, the income elasticity of demand is negative; for normal goods, it is positive.*** According to the accompanying News, alligator skins are a normal good.

IN THE NEWS

Recession Eats into Gator Market

NEW ORLEANS—The global economic recession is taking a bite out of an unlikely industry: the American alligator market.

A drop in world demand for designer gator-skin handbags, watch straps, and belts has caused an unprecedented decline in the American alligator industry, said Mark Shirley, coastal resources specialist at the Louisiana State University AgCenter.

Louisiana gator farmers harvest around 80 percent of the world market of American alligator skins, Shirley said. The pelts just last year were part of a $70 million annual business, used for everything from $4,000 Gucci purses to Patek Phillippe watches that fetched $60,000. As demand dropped, so did the gator skins—and farmers face the possibility of going out of business.

—Rick Jervis

Source: *USA TODAY.* October 22, 2009. Reprinted with permission.

Analysis: For "normal" goods, a decline in income causes a decline in demand. The income elasticity of demand measures that sensitivity.

ELASTICITY OF SUPPLY

law of supply: The quantity of a good supplied in a given time period increases as its price increases, *ceteris paribus.*

price elasticity of supply: The percentage change in quantity supplied divided by the percentage change in price.

Sensitivity to changing prices is not just a consumer phenomenon. Producers, too, alter their behavior when prices change. We know from the **law of supply** (Chapter 3) that businesses will produce more output at higher prices. What we want to know is how much more they'll produce as prices go up. That is what the **price elasticity of supply** tells us. Like its counterpart on the demand side, the price elasticity of supply relates *percentage* changes in the quantity supplied to *percentage* changes in price:

$$\text{Price elasticity of supply} = \frac{\text{Percentage change in quantity supplied}}{\text{Percentage change in price}}$$

A high price elasticity of supply means that producers are very responsive to price changes; a low elasticity implies a sluggish response. As the following World View reports, gold mining—even illegal mining—apparently has a high price elasticity of supply.

WORLD VIEW

High Gold Price Swells Ranks of Illegal Miners

Poor men and women in Ghana, ex-militia fighters in steamy eastern Congo, and farmers in Peru are among those joining the ranks of illegal miners and risking their lives as they seek to profit from soaring gold prices. . . .

Gold prices have trebled over the past five years. After coming off recent highs, spot gold rose to above $950 (Dh3,489) an ounce last week as tensions in the Middle East continued to encourage investors to seek a safe haven in bullion.

There are between 13 million and 20 million small-scale miners around the world, according to Communities and Small-Scale Mining (CASM), a group focusing on social and environmental problems facing artisanal mining communities.

They account for about 10 percent of the global production of metals and diamonds, and 75 percent of all gemstones. Around 100 million people are directly or indirectly dependent on small-scale mining.

"High commodity prices and declining resources around them [artisanal miners] in other areas are going to mean this is a growing phenomenon in many countries," said Jon Hobbs of the UK's Department for International Development (DFID).

—Anna Stablum

Source: Reuters.com, July 13, 2008. © Thomson Reuters 2008. All rights reserved. Used with permission.

Analysis: Higher gold prices spur additional gold mining. Apparently the price elasticity of gold supply is high.

THE ECONOMY TOMORROW

ACHIEVING ENERGY INDEPENDENCE

Every American president since Dwight Eisenhower has urged the United States to achieve energy independence. The early motivation for that goal was rooted in national security concerns. If the United States went to war again, we didn't want to depend on imported oil to fuel our airplanes, trucks, factories, or homes. In more recent decades, the quest for energy independence has had more *economic* roots. America now imports over 4 billion barrels of oil per year at a cost of roughly $400 billion. Moreover, the price of oil is heavily influenced by the oil production decisions of foreign nations, many of which are considered unfriendly to American interests. If we didn't spend so much money on imported oil, U.S. consumers would spend more on American-made products, and foreign oil-producing nations would have less political and economic power.

America has the resources to become energy independent. We have enough coal and natural gas reserves to last 100 years. We also have vast untapped reservoirs of oil and tremendous nuclear potential. Last but not least, we have virtually unlimited potential for "clean" energy from the sun and the wind.

So why don't we tap into all those domestic energy sources and wean ourselves off imported oil? The answer lies in economics—particularly the cross-price elasticity of demand. Solar and wind power are substitute goods for oil-based energy. Consumers won't demand more clean energy unless and until gasoline gets really expensive. Even though we complain every time the price of gasoline goes up a few pennies, the reality is that imported oil is cheaper than alternative energy sources. So we keep using it.

Is there a solution here? Yes, but you won't like it. Were the government to make gasoline more expensive (by raising the excise tax on gasoline), U.S. consumers and businesses would look more seriously at alternative energy sources. Raise imported oil prices high enough, and the United States will achieve energy independence in the economy tomorrow.

SUMMARY

- The price elasticity of demand (*E*) is a numerical measure of consumer response to a change in price, *ceteris paribus*. It equals the percentage change in quantity demanded divided by the percentage change in price. LO6-1
- Demand for a product is *elastic* if *E* is greater than 1.0 or *inelastic* if *E* is less than 1.0. LO6-1
- The degree of price elasticity depends on the price of a good relative to income, the availability of substitutes, and time. LO6-1
- The effect of a price change on total revenue depends on price elasticity. Total revenue and price move in the *same* direction only if demand is price-inelastic (*E* < 1). LO6-2
- The shape and position of any particular demand curve depend on a consumer's income, tastes, expectations, and the price and availability of other goods. Should

any of these factors change, the assumption of *ceteris paribus* will no longer hold, and the demand curve will *shift*. LO6-3, LO6-4
- Cross-price elasticity measures the response of demand for one good to a change in the price of another. The cross-price elasticity of demand is positive for substitute goods and negative for complementary goods. LO6-3
- The income elasticity of demand measures the response of demand to a change in income. If demand increases (shifts right) with income, the product is a normal good. If demand declines (shifts left) when income rises, it's an inferior good. LO6-4
- The price elasticity of supply is the percentage change in quantity *supplied* divided by the percentage change in price. LO6-5

Key Terms

law of demand
demand curve
price elasticity of demand
total revenue

substitute goods
complementary goods
cross-price elasticity of demand
income elasticity of demand

normal good
inferior good
law of supply
price elasticity of supply

Questions for Discussion

1. Is the demand for enrollments in your college price-elastic? How could you find out? LO6-1
2. If the price of gasoline doubled, how would consumption of (*a*) cars, (*b*) public transportation and (*c*) in-theater movies be affected? How quickly would these adjustments be made? LO6-3
3. Identify two goods each whose demand exhibits (*a*) high income elasticity, (*b*) low income elasticity, (*c*) high price elasticity, and (*d*) low price elasticity. What accounts for the differences in elasticity? LO6-4
4. Identify two pairs each of products that are (*a*) substitute goods and (*b*) complementary goods. LO6-3
5. Why does the price elasticity of demand for cigarettes differ for teenagers and adults? LO6-1
6. If you owned a movie theater, would you want the demand for movies to be elastic or inelastic? LO6-2
7. How has the Internet affected the price elasticity of demand for air travel? LO6-1
8. If the elasticity of demand for coffee is so low (Table 6.1), why doesn't Starbucks raise the price of coffee to $10 a cup? LO6-2
9. What would happen to unit sales and total revenue for this textbook if the bookstore reduced its price? LO6-2
10. Is the demand for iPhones price inelastic or elastic? Why? Is income elasticity high or low? LO6-4
11. Suppose that quantity supplied for a product falls by 10 persent. If the price elasticity of supply is 2, what should happen to the price of the product? LO6-5

 web activities to accompany this chapter can be found on the Online Learning Center: **http://www.mhhe.com/schiller13e**

 mobile app Visit your mobile app store and download the Schiller: Study Econ app *today!*

PROBLEMS FOR CHAPTER 6   Name: _____

LO6-1   1. By changing the denominator in each case, compute the percentage change in the iPhone's price (see text and News, p. 121), from
    (*a*) The initial price.   _____
    (*b*) The final price.   _____
    (*c*) The average price.   _____

LO6-1   2. What was the price elasticity of demand for iPhones in 2007 (News, p. 121)?   _____

LO6-1   3. According to Professor Becker (News, p. 123), by how much would cigarette prices have to rise to get a 20 percent reduction in smoking in
    (*a*) one year?   _____%
    (*b*) three years?   _____%

LO6-1   4. Suppose consumers buy 30 million packs of cigarettes per month at a price of $4 per pack. If a $1 tax is added to that price,
    (*a*) By what percentage does price change? (Use the midpoint formula on p. 119.)   _____%
    (*b*) By what percentage will cigarette sales decline in the short run? (See Table 6.1 for a clue.)   _____%
    (*c*) According to Gary Becker, by how much will sales decline in the long run? (News, p. 123.)   _____%

LO6-2   5. From Figure 6.1, compute (*a*) the price elasticity between each of the following points and (*b*) the total revenue at each point.

	Price Elasticity		Total Revenue
Point *D* to *E*	_____	At point *D*	_____
		E	_____
G to *H*	_____	*G*	_____
		H	_____

LO6-1   6. If the price of a pack of cigarettes (including taxes) was $4 before the 2009 tax hike (see the News, p. 121),
    (*a*) What was the price after the tax hike?   _____
    (*b*) What was the (average) percentage increase in price?   _____
    (*c*) What was the price elasticity of demand?   _____

LO6-4   7. According to the calculation on pages 129–130, by how much will popcorn sales increase if average income goes up by 10 percent?   _____%

LO6-3   8. If a gasoline price hike of 4 percent caused the SUV sales drop described in the News on page 128, what is the cross-price elasticity of demand between gasoline and SUVs?   _____

LO6-3   9. If the cross-price elasticity of demand between printed textbooks and e-books is +.20,
    (*a*) Are e-books and textbooks complementary (C) or substitute (S) goods?   _____
    (*b*) If textbook prices increase by 6 percent, by how much will e-book demand change?   _____

LO6-5   10. Suppose that in a week the price of Greek yogurt increases from $1.25/lb to $1.75/lb. At the same time, the quantity of Greek yogurt supplied increases from 100,000 lbs to 150,000 lbs. What is the price elasticity of supply for Greek yogurt?   _____

LO6-2 11. Use the following data to illustrate the (a) demand curve and (b) total revenue curve:

Price	$1	2	3	4	5	6	7	8	9	10
Quantity	20	18	16	14	12	10	8	6	4	2

(a) At what price is total revenue maximized? $_____

(b) At that price, what is the elasticity of demand?   E = _____

(c) Between what prices is demand elastic?   _____

(a) Demand curve

(b) Total revenue curve

Name: _____

LO6-3   12. On the graphs below, show the impact of the price reduction for iPhones, as described in the
    News on pages 121 and 127.

iPhone market

Treo market

The Costs of Production

Last year U.S. consumers bought more than $2 *trillion* worth of imported goods, including Japanese cars, Italian shoes, and toys from China. As you might expect, this angers domestic producers, who frequently end up with unsold goods, half-empty factories, and unemployed workers. They rage against the "unfair" competition from abroad, asserting that producers in India, Brazil, and China can undersell U.S. producers because workers in these countries are paid dirt-poor wages.

But lower wages don't necessarily imply lower costs. You could pay me $2 per hour to type and still end up paying a lot for typing. Truth is, I type only about 10 words a minute, with lots of mistakes. The cost of producing goods depends not only on the price of inputs (e.g., labor) but also on how much they produce. Paying $10 an hour to someone who types 90 words a minute is a lot cheaper than paying $2 an hour to someone who types only 10 words a minute.

In this chapter we begin looking at the costs of producing the goods and services that market participants demand. We confront the following questions:

- **How much output *can* a firm produce?**
- **How do the *costs* of production vary with the rate of output?**
- **Do larger firms have a cost advantage over smaller firms?**

The answers to these questions are important not only to producers facing foreign competition but to consumers as well. The costs of producing a good have a direct impact on the prices we pay at the grocery store, the mall, or even the campus bookstore.

THE PRODUCTION FUNCTION

No matter how large a business is or who owns it, all businesses confront one central fact: it costs something to produce goods. To produce corn, a farmer needs land, water, seeds, equipment, and labor. To produce fillings, a dentist needs a chair, a drill, some space, and labor. Even the production of educational services such as this economics class requires the use of labor (your teacher), land (on which the school is built), and capital (the building, blackboard, computers). In short, unless you're producing unrefined, unpackaged air, you need **factors of production**—that is, resources that can be used to produce a good or service. These factors of production provide the basic measure of economic cost. The costs of your economics class, for example, are measured by the amounts of land, labor, and capital it requires. These are *resource* costs of production.

To assess the costs of production, we must first determine how many resources are actually needed to produce a given product. You could use a lot of resources to produce a product or use just a few. What we really want to know is how *best* to produce. What's the *smallest* amount of resources needed to produce a specific product? Or we could ask the same question from a different perspective: what's the *maximum* amount of output attainable from a given quantity of resources?

The answers to these questions are reflected in the **production function,** which tells us the maximum amount of good *X* producible from various combinations of factor inputs. With one chair and one drill, a dentist can fill a *maximum* of 32 cavities per day. With two chairs, a drill, and an assistant, a dentist can fill up to 55 cavities per day.

A production function is a technological summary of our ability to produce a particular good.[1] Table 7.1 provides a partial glimpse of one such function. In this case, the output is designer jeans, as produced by Low-Rider Jeans Corporation. The essential inputs in the production of jeans are land, labor (garment workers), and capital (a factory and sewing machines). With these inputs, Low-Rider Jeans Corporation can produce and sell hip-hugging jeans to style-conscious consumers.

factors of production: Resource inputs used to produce goods and services, such as land, labor, capital, and entrepreneurship.

production function: A technological relationship expressing the maximum quantity of a good attainable from different combinations of factor inputs.

Varying Input Levels

As in all production endeavors, we want to know how much output we can produce with available resources. To make things easy, we'll assume that the factory is already built, with fixed space dimensions. The only inputs we can vary are labor (the number of garment workers per day) and additional capital (the number of sewing machines we lease per day).

Capital Input (Sewing Machines per Day)	Labor Input (Workers per Day)								
	0	1	2	3	4	5	6	7	8
	Jeans Output (Pairs per Day)								
0	0	0	0	0	0	0	0	0	0
1	0	15	34	44	48	50	51	51	47
2	0	20	46	64	72	78	81	82	80
3	0	21	50	73	83	92	99	103	103

TABLE 7.1

A Production Function

A production function tells us the maximum amount of output attainable from alternative combinations of factor inputs. This particular function tells us how many pairs of jeans we can produce in a day with a given factory and varying quantities of capital and labor. With one sewing machine, and one operator, we can produce a maximum of 15 pairs of jeans per day, as indicated in the second column of the second row. To produce more jeans, we need more labor or more capital.

[1]By contrast, the production possibilities curve discussed in Chapter 1 expresses our ability to produce various *combinations* of goods, given the use of *all* our resources. The production possibilities curve summarizes the output capacity of the entire economy. A production function describes the capacity of a single firm.

In these circumstances, the quantity of jeans we can produce depends on the amount of labor and capital we employ. *The purpose of a production function is to tell us just how much output we can produce with varying amounts of factor inputs.* Table 7.1 provides such information for jeans production.

Consider the simplest option—that of employing no labor or capital (the upper left corner in Table 7.1). An empty factory can't produce any jeans; maximum output is zero per day. Even though land, capital (an empty factory), and even denim are available, some essential labor and capital inputs are missing, and jeans production is impossible.

Suppose now we employ some labor (a machine operator) but don't lease any sewing machines. Will output increase? Not according to the production function. The first row in Table 7.1 illustrates the consequences of employing labor without any capital equipment. Without sewing machines (or even needles, another form of capital), the operators can't make jeans. Maximum output remains at zero no matter how much labor is employed in this case.

The dilemma of machine operators without sewing machines illustrates a general principle of production: *the* **productivity** *of any factor of production depends on the amount of other resources available to it.* Industrious, hardworking machine operators can't make designer jeans without sewing machines.

productivity: Output per unit of input—for example, output per labor-hour.

We can increase the productivity of garment workers by providing them with machines. The production function again tells us by *how much* jeans output could increase. Suppose we leased just one machine per day. Now the second row in Table 7.1 is the relevant one. It says jeans output will remain at zero if we lease one machine but employ no labor. If we employ one machine *and* one worker, however, the jeans will start rolling out the door. Maximum output under these circumstances (row 2, column 2) is 15 pairs of jeans per day. Now we're in business!

The remaining columns in row 2 tell us how many additional jeans we can produce if we hire more workers, still leasing only one sewing machine. With one machine and two workers, maximum output rises to 34 pairs per day. If a third worker is hired, output could increase to 44 pairs.

Table 7.1 also indicates how production would increase with additional sewing machines (capital). By reading down any column of the table, you can see how more machines increase potential jeans output.

Efficiency

The production function summarized in Table 7.1 underscores the essential relationship between resource *inputs* and product *outputs*. It's also a basic introduction to economic costs. To produce 15 pairs of jeans per day, we need one sewing machine, an operator, a factory, and some denim. All these inputs make up the *resource cost* of producing jeans.

Another feature of Table 7.1 is that it conveys the *maximum* output of jeans producible from particular input combinations. The standard garment worker and sewing machine, when brought together at Low-Rider Jeans Corporation, can produce *at most* 15 pairs of jeans per day. They could also produce a lot less. Indeed, a careless cutter can waste a lot of denim. A lazy or inattentive worker won't keep the sewing machines humming. As many a producer has learned, actual output can fall far short of the limits described in the production function. Jeans output will reach the levels in Table 7.1 only if the jeans factory operates with relative **efficiency.** This requires getting maximum output from the resources used in the production process. *The production function represents maximum technical efficiency—that is, the most output attainable from any given level of factor inputs.*

efficiency (technical): Maximum output of a good from the resources used in production.

We can always be inefficient, of course. This merely means getting less output than possible for the inputs we use. But this isn't a desirable situation. To a factory manager, it means less output for a given amount of input (cost). To society as a whole, inefficiency implies a waste of resources. If Low-Rider Jeans isn't producing efficiently, we're being denied some potential output. It's not only a question of having fewer jeans. We could also use the labor and capital now employed by Low-Rider Jeans to produce something else. Specifically, the **opportunity cost** of a product is measured by the most desired goods and services that could have been produced with the same resources. Hence, if jeans production isn't up to par, society is either (1) getting fewer jeans than it should for the resources

opportunity cost: The most desired goods or services that are forgone in order to obtain something else.

devoted to jeans production or (2) giving up too many other goods and services in order to get a desired quantity of jeans.

Although we can always do worse than the production function suggests, we can't do better, at least not in the short run. The production function represents the *best* we can do with our current technological know-how. For the moment, at least, there's no better way to produce a specific good. As our technological and managerial capabilities increase, however, we'll attain higher levels of future productivity. These advances in our productive capability will be represented by new production functions.

Short-Run Constraints

Let's step back from the threshold of scientific advance for a moment and return to Low-Rider Jeans. Forget about possible technological breakthroughs in jeans production (e.g., electronic sewing machines or robot operators) and concentrate on the economic realities of our modest endeavor. For the present we're stuck with existing technology. In fact, all the output figures in Table 7.1 are based on the use of a specific factory. Once we've purchased or leased that factory, we've set a limit to current jeans production. When such commitments to fixed inputs (e.g., the factory) exist, we're dealing with a **short-run** production problem. If no land or capital were in place—if we could build or lease any sized factory—we'd be dealing with a *long-run* decision.

Our short-run objective is to make the best possible use of the factory we've acquired. This entails selecting the right combination of labor and capital inputs to produce jeans. To simplify the decision, we'll limit the number of sewing machines in use. If we lease only one sewing machine, then the second row in Table 7.1 is the only one we have to consider. In this case, the single sewing machine (capital) becomes another short-run constraint on the production of jeans. With a given factory and one sewing machine, the short-run rate of output depends entirely on how many workers are hired.

Figure 7.1 illustrates the short-run production function applicable to the factory with one sewing machine. As noted before, a factory with a sewing machine but no machine

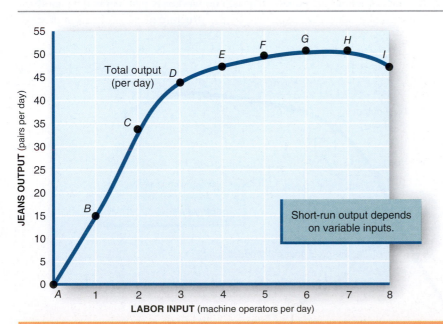

FIGURE 7.1
Short-Run Production Function

In the short run some inputs (e.g., land and capital) are fixed in quantity. Output then depends on how much of a variable input (e.g., labor) is used. The short-run production function shows how output changes when more labor is used. This figure and the table below are based on the second (one-machine) row in Table 7.1.

	A	B	C	D	E	F	G	H	I
Number of workers	0	1	2	3	4	5	6	7	8
Total output	0	15	34	44	48	50	51	51	47
Marginal physical product	—	15	19	10	4	2	1	0	−4

operators produces no jeans. This was observed in Table 7.1 (row 1, column 0) and is now illustrated by point *A* in Figure 7.1. To get any jeans output, we need to hire some labor. In this simplified example, ***labor is the variable input that determines how much output we get from our fixed inputs (land and capital).*** By placing one worker in the factory, we can produce 15 pairs of jeans per day. This possibility is represented by point *B*. The remainder of the production function shows how jeans output changes as we employ more workers in our single-machine factory.

MARGINAL PRODUCTIVITY

The short-run production function not only defines the *limit* to output but also shows how much each worker contributes to that limit. Notice again that jeans output increases from zero (point *A* in Figure 7.2) to 15 pairs (point *B*) when the first machine operator is hired. In other words, total output *increases* by 15 pairs when we employ the first worker. This increase is called the **marginal physical product (MPP)** of that first worker—that is, the *change* in total output that results from employment of one more unit of (labor) input:

> **marginal physical product (MPP):** The change in total output associated with one additional unit of input.

$$\text{Marginal physical product (MPP)} = \frac{\text{Change in total output}}{\text{Change in input quantity}}$$

With zero workers, total output was zero. When that first worker is employed, total output increases to 15 pairs of jeans per day. The MPP of the first worker is 15 pairs of jeans.

If we employ a second operator, jeans output more than doubles, to 34 pairs per day (point *C*). The 19-pair *increase* in output represents the marginal physical product of the *second* worker.

The higher MPP of the second worker raises a question about the first. Why was the first's MPP lower? Laziness? Is the second worker faster, less distracted, or harder working?

The second worker's higher MPP isn't explained by superior talents or effort. We assume, in fact, that all "units of labor" are equal—that is, one worker is just as good as another.[2] Their different marginal products are explained by the structure of the production process,

FIGURE 7.2

Marginal Physical Product (MPP)

Marginal physical product is the *change* in total output that results from employing one more unit of input. The *third* worker, for example, increases *total output* from 34 (point *C*) to 44 (point *D*). Hence the *marginal* output of the third worker is 10 pairs of jeans (point *d*). What's the MPP of the fourth worker? What happens to *total* output when this worker is hired?

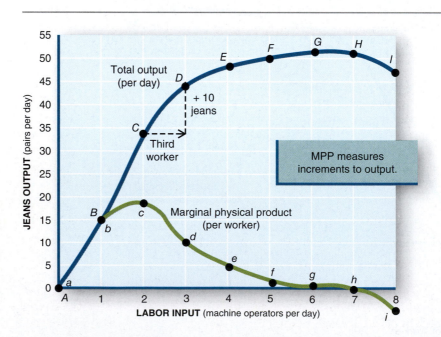

[2]In reality, garment workers do differ greatly in energy, talent, and diligence. These differences can be eliminated by measuring units of labor in *constant-quality* units. A person who works twice as hard as everyone else would count as two *quality-adjusted* units of labor.

not by their respective abilities. The first garment worker not only had to sew jeans but also had to unfold bolts of denim, measure the jeans, sketch out the patterns, and cut them to approximate size. A lot of time was spent going from one task to another. Despite the worker's best efforts, this person simply couldn't do everything at once.

A second worker alleviates this situation. With two workers, less time is spent running from one task to another. While one worker is measuring and cutting, the other can continue sewing. This improved *ratio* of labor to other factors of production results in the large jump in total output. The second worker's superior MPP isn't unique to this person: it would have occurred even if we'd hired the workers in the reverse order.

Diminishing Marginal Returns

Unfortunately, total output won't keep rising so sharply as more workers are hired. Look what happens when a third worker is hired. Total jeans production continues to increase. But the increase from point *C* to point *D* in Figure 7.2 is only 10 pairs per day. Hence the third worker's MPP (10 pairs) is *less* than that of the second (19 pairs). Marginal physical product is *diminishing*. This concept is illustrated by point *d* in Figure 7.2.

What accounts for this decline in MPP? The answer lies in the ratio of labor to other factors of production. A third worker begins to crowd our facilities. We still have only one sewing machine. Two people can't sew at the same time. As a result, some time is wasted as the operators wait for their turns at the machine. Even if they split up the various jobs, there will still be some "downtime" because measuring and cutting aren't as time-consuming as sewing. Consequently, we can't make full use of a third worker. The relative scarcity of other inputs (capital and land) constrains the third worker's marginal physical product.

Resource constraints are even more evident when a fourth worker is hired. Total output increases again, but the increase this time is very small. With three workers, we got 44 pairs of jeans per day (point *D*); with four workers, we get a maximum of 48 pairs (point *E*). Thus the fourth worker's MPP is only 4 pairs of jeans. There simply aren't enough machines to make productive use of so much labor.

If a seventh worker is hired, the operators get in one another's way, argue, and waste denim. Notice in Figure 7.1 that total output doesn't increase at all when a seventh worker is hired (point *H*). The MPP of the seventh worker is zero (point *h*). Were an eighth worker hired, total output would actually *decline,* from 51 pairs (point *H*) to 47 pairs (point *I*). The eighth worker has a *negative* MPP (point *i* in Figure 7.2).

Law of Diminishing Returns. The problems of crowded facilities apply to most production processes. In the short run, a production process is characterized by a fixed amount of available land and capital. Typically, the only factor that can be varied in the short run is labor. Yet **as more labor is hired, each unit of labor has less capital and land to work with.** This is simple division: the available facilities are being shared by more and more workers. At some point, this constraint begins to pinch. When it does, marginal physical product declines. This situation is so common that it's the basis for the **law of diminishing returns,** which says that the marginal physical product of any factor of production, such as labor, will diminish at some point as more of it is used in a given production setting. Notice in Figure 7.2 how diminishing returns set in when the third worker was hired.

law of diminishing returns: The marginal physical product of a variable input declines as more of it is employed with a given quantity of other (fixed) inputs.

RESOURCE COSTS

A production function tells us how much output a firm *can* produce with its existing plant and equipment. From Figure 7.2 we know that Low-Rider Jeans *could* produce up to 51 pairs per day, employing 6 workers. But Figure 7.2 doesn't tell us how much the firm will *want* to produce. A firm *might* want to produce at capacity if the profit picture were bright enough. On the other hand, a firm might not produce *any* output if costs always exceeded sales revenue. The most desirable rate of output is the one that maximizes total **profit**—the difference between total revenue and total costs. And **there is no reason to expect maximum profit to coincide with maximum output.**

profit: The difference between total revenue and total cost.

FIGURE 7.3
Falling MPP Implies Rising Marginal Cost

Marginal physical product (MPP) is the additional output obtained by employing one more unit of input. If MPP is falling, each additional unit of input is producing less additional output, which means the input cost of each unit of output is rising. The third worker's MPP is 10 pairs (point *d* in part *a*). Therefore, the labor cost of these additional jeans is approximately 1/10 unit of labor per pair (point 1/*d* in part *b*).

The production function therefore is just a starting point for supply decisions. To decide how much output to produce with that function, a firm must next examine the costs of production. How fast do costs rise when output increases?

The law of diminishing returns provides a clue to how fast costs rise. ***The economic cost of a product is measured by the value of the resources needed to produce it.*** What we've seen here is that those resource requirements eventually increase. Each additional sewing machine operator produces fewer and fewer jeans. In effect, then, each additional pair of jeans produced uses more and more labor.

Suppose we employ one sewing machine and one operator again, for a total output of 15 pairs of jeans per day; see point *b* in Figure 7.3*a*. Now look at production from another perspective—that of *costs*. The resource costs of producing jeans are measured by how much labor is used in the production process. How much labor cost are we using at point *b* to produce one pair of jeans? We know that one worker is producing 15 pairs of jeans, so the labor input per pair of jeans must be one-fifteenth of a worker's day—that is, 0.067 unit of labor. This resource cost is illustrated by point 1/*b* in Figure 7.3*b*. All we're doing here is translating *output* data into related *input* (cost) data.

Marginal Resource Cost

The next question is, How do input costs change when output increases? As point *c* in Figure 7.3*a* reminds us, total output increases by 19 pairs when we hire a second worker. What's the implied labor cost of those *additional* 19 pairs? By dividing one worker by 19 pairs of jeans, we observe that the labor cost of that extra output is one-nineteenth, or 0.053 of a worker's day; see point 1/*c* in Figure 7.3*b*.

When we focus on the *additional* costs incurred from increasing production, we're talking about *marginal* costs. Specifically, **marginal cost (MC)** refers to the *increase* in total costs required to get one additional unit of output. More generally,

$$\text{Marginal cost (MC)} = \frac{\text{Change in total cost}}{\text{Change in output}}$$

In this simple case—where labor is the only variable input—the marginal cost of the added jeans is

$$\text{Marginal cost} = \frac{1 \text{ additional worker}}{19 \text{ additional pairs}}$$
$$= 0.053 \text{ worker per pair}$$

The amount 0.053 of labor represents the *change* in total resource cost when we produce one *additional* pair of jeans.

Notice in Figure 7.3b that the marginal labor cost of jeans production declines when the second worker is hired. Marginal cost falls from 0.067 unit of labor (plus denim) per pair (point 1/b in Figure 7.3b) to only 0.053 unit of labor per pair (point 1/c). It costs less labor *per pair* to use two workers rather than only one. This is a reflection of the second worker's increased MPP. ***Whenever MPP is increasing, the marginal cost of producing a good must be falling.*** This is illustrated in Figure 7.3 by the upward move from *b* to *c* in part *a* and the corresponding downward move from 1/b to 1/c in part *b*.

Unfortunately, marginal physical product typically declines at some point. As it does, the marginal costs of production rise. In this sense, each additional pair of jeans becomes more expensive—we need more and more labor per pair. Figure 7.3 illustrates this inverse relationship between MPP and marginal cost. The third worker has an MPP of 10 pairs, as illustrated by point *d*. The marginal labor input of these extra 10 pairs is thus 1 ÷ 10, or 0.10 unit of labor. In other words, one-tenth of a third worker's daily effort goes into each pair of jeans. This additional labor cost *per unit* is illustrated by 1/d in part *b* of the figure.

Note in Figure 7.3 how marginal physical product declines after point *c* and how marginal costs rise after point 1/c. This is no accident. ***If marginal physical product declines, marginal cost increases.*** Thus increasing marginal cost is as common as—and the direct result of—diminishing returns. These increasing marginal costs aren't the fault of any person or factor; they simply reflect the resource constraints found in any established production setting (i.e., existing and limited plants and equipment). In the short run, the quantity and quality of land and capital are fixed, and we can vary only their intensity of use by employing more or fewer workers. It's in this short-run context that we keep running into diminishing marginal returns and rising marginal costs.

DOLLAR COSTS

This entire discussion of diminishing returns and marginal costs may seem a bit alien. After all, we're interested in the costs of production, and costs are typically measured in *dollars*, not such technical notions as MPP. Jeans producers need to know how many dollars it costs to keep jeans flowing; they don't want a lecture on marginal physical product.

Jeans manufacturers don't have to study marginal physical products, or even the production function. They can confine their attention to dollar costs. The dollar costs observed, however, are directly related to the underlying production function. To understand *why* costs rise—and how they might be reduced—some understanding of the production function is necessary. In this section we translate production functions into dollar costs.

Total Cost

The **total cost** of producing a product includes the market value of *all* the resources used in its production. To determine this cost we simply identify all the resources used in production, determine their value, and then add up everything.

marginal cost (MC): The increase in total cost associated with a one-unit increase in production.

Why Marginal Costs Rise

total cost: The market value of all resources used to produce a good or service.

TABLE 7.2

The Total Costs of Production (Total Cost of Producing 15 Pairs of Jeans per Day)

The total cost of producing a good equals the market value of all the resources used in its production. In this case, the production of 15 pairs of jeans per day requires resources worth $245.

Resource Input	×	Unit Price of Input	=	Total Cost
1 factory		$100 per day		$100
1 sewing machine		20 per day		20
1 operator		80 per day		80
1.5 bolts of denim		30 per bolt		45
Total cost				$245

In the production of jeans, these resources included land, labor, and capital. Table 7.2 identifies these resources, their unit values, and the total dollar cost associated with their use. This table is based on an assumed output of 15 pairs of jeans per day, with the use of one worker and one sewing machine (point *B* in Figure 7.2). The rent on the factory is $100 per day, a sewing machine rents for $20 per day, and the wages of a garment worker are $80 per day. We'll assume Low-Rider Jeans Corporation can purchase bolts of denim for $30 apiece, with each bolt providing enough denim for 10 pairs of jeans. In other words, one-tenth of a bolt ($3 worth of material) is required for one pair of jeans. We'll ignore any other potential expenses. With these assumptions, the total cost of producing 15 pairs of jeans per day amounts to $245, as shown in Table 7.2.

Fixed Costs. Total costs will change of course as we alter the rate of production. But not *all* costs increase. In the short run, some costs don't increase at all when output is increased. These are **fixed costs** in the sense that they don't vary with the rate of output. The factory lease is an example. Once you lease a factory, you're obligated to pay for it whether or not you use it. The person who owns the factory wants $100 per day. Even if you produce no jeans, you still have to pay that rent. That's the essence of fixed costs.

fixed costs: Costs of production that don't change when the rate of output is altered, such as the cost of basic plants and equipment.

The leased sewing machine is another fixed cost. When you rent a sewing machine, you must pay the rental charge. It doesn't matter whether you use it for a few minutes or all day long—the rental charge is fixed at $20 per day.

Variable Costs. Labor costs are another story altogether. The amount of labor employed in jeans production can be varied easily. If we decide not to open the factory tomorrow, we can just tell our only worker to take the day off (without pay, of course!). We'll still have to pay rent, but we can cut back on wages. On the other hand, if we want to increase daily output, we can also hire additional workers easily and quickly. Labor is regarded as a **variable cost** in this line of work—that is, a cost that *varies* with the rate of output.

variable costs: Costs of production that change when the rate of output is altered, such as labor and material costs.

The denim itself is another variable cost. Denim not used today can be saved for tomorrow. Hence how much we spend on denim today is directly related to how many jeans we produce. In this sense, the cost of denim input varies with the rate of jeans output.

Figure 7.4 illustrates how these various costs are affected by the rate of production. On the vertical axis are the costs of production in dollars per day. Notice that the total cost of producing 15 pairs per day is still $245, as indicated by point *B*. This cost figure consists of

DOLLAR COST OF PRODUCING 15 PAIRS

Fixed costs:

Factory rent	$100	
Sewing machine rent	20	
Subtotal		$120

Variable costs:

Wages to labor	$80	
Denim	45	
Subtotal		$125
Total costs		$245

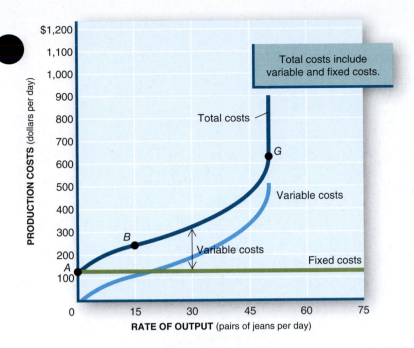

FIGURE 7.4
The Cost of Jeans Production

Total cost includes both fixed and variable costs. Fixed costs must be paid even if no output is produced (point *A*). Variable costs start at zero and increase with the rate of output. The total cost of producing 15 pairs of jeans (point *B*) includes $120 in fixed costs (rent on the factory and sewing machines) and $125 in variable costs (denim and wages). Total cost rises as output increases because additional variable costs must be incurred.

In this example, the short-run capacity is equal to 51 pairs (point *G*). If still more inputs are employed, costs will rise but not total output.

If we increase the rate of output beyond these 15 pairs, total costs will rise. *How fast total costs rise depends on variable costs only,* however, since fixed costs remain at $120 per day. (Notice the horizontal fixed cost curve in Figure 7.4.)

With one sewing machine and one factory, there's an absolute limit to daily jeans production. According to the production function in Figure 7.1, the capacity of a factory with one machine is roughly 51 pairs of jeans per day. If we try to produce more jeans than this by hiring additional workers, our total costs will rise, but our output won't. Recall that the seventh worker had a *zero* marginal physical product (Figure 7.2). In fact, we could fill the factory with garment workers and drive total costs sky-high. But the limits of space and one sewing machine don't permit output in excess of 51 pairs per day. This limit to productive capacity is represented by point *G* on the total cost curve. Further expenditure on inputs will increase production *costs* but not *output*.

Although there's no upper limit to costs, there is a lower limit. If output is reduced to zero, costs won't completely disappear. At zero output, total costs fall only to $120 per day, the level of fixed costs, as illustrated by point *A* in Figure 7.4. As before, *there's no way to avoid fixed costs in the short run.* Indeed, those fixed costs define the short run.

Average Costs

While Figure 7.4 illustrates *total* costs of production, other measures of cost are often desired. One of the most common measures of cost is average, or per-unit, cost. **Average total cost (ATC)** is simply total cost divided by the rate of output:

$$\text{Average total cost (ATC)} = \frac{\text{Total cost}}{\text{Total output}}$$

At an output of 15 pairs of jeans per day, total costs are $245. The average cost of production is thus $16.33 per pair (= 245 ÷ 15) at this rate of output.

Figure 7.5 shows how average costs change as the rate of output varies. Row *J* of the cost schedule, for example, again indicates the fixed, variable, and total costs of producing 15 pairs of jeans per day. Fixed costs are still $120; variable costs are $125. Thus the total cost of producing 15 pairs per day is $245, as we saw earlier.

The rest of row *J* shows the average costs of jeans production. These figures are obtained by dividing each dollar total (columns 2, 3, and 4) by the rate of physical output (column 1).

average total cost (ATC): Total cost divided by the quantity produced in a given time period.

FIGURE 7.5
Average Total Costs (ATC)

Average total cost (ATC) in column 7 equals total cost (column 4) divided by the rate of output (column 1). Since total cost includes both fixed (column 2) and variable (column 3) costs, ATC also equals AFC (column 5) plus AVC (column 6). This relationship is illustrated in the graph. The ATC of producing 15 pairs per day (point *J*) equals $16.33—the sum of AFC ($8) and AVC ($8.33).

Average total costs vary with the rate of output.

	(1)	(2)		(3)		(4)	(5) Average		(6) Average		(7) Average
	Rate of Output	Fixed Costs	+	Variable Costs	=	Total Cost	Fixed Cost	+	Variable Cost	=	Total Cost
H	0	$120		$ 0		$120	—		—		—
I	10	120		85		205	$12.00		$ 8.50		$20.50
J	15	120		125		245	8.00		8.33		16.33
K	20	120		150		270	6.00		7.50		13.50
L	30	120		240		360	4.00		8.00		12.00
M	40	120		350		470	3.00		8.75		11.75
N	50	120		550		670	2.40		11.00		13.40
O	51	120		633		753	2.35		12.41		14.76

average fixed cost (AFC): Total fixed cost divided by the quantity produced in a given time period.

At an output rate of 15 pairs per day, **average fixed cost (AFC)** is $8 per pair, **average variable cost (AVC)** is $8.33, and *average total cost (ATC)* is $16.33. ATC, then, is simply the sum of AFC and AVC:

$$ATC = AFC + AVC$$

Falling AFC. At this relatively low rate of output, fixed costs are a large portion of total costs. The rent paid for the factory and sewing machines works out to $8 per pair ($120 ÷ 15). This high average fixed cost accounts for nearly one-half of total average costs. This suggests that it's quite expensive to lease a factory and sewing machine to produce only 15 pairs of jeans per day. To reduce average costs, we must make fuller use of our leased plant and equipment.

average variable cost (AVC): Total variable cost divided by the quantity produced in a given time period.

Notice what happens to average costs when the rate of output is increased to 20 pairs per day (row *K* in Figure 7.5). Average fixed costs go down to only $6 per pair. This sharp decline in AFC results from the fact that total fixed costs ($120) are now spread over more output. Even though our rent hasn't dropped, the *average* fixed cost of producing jeans has.

If we produce more than 20 pairs of jeans per day, AFC will continue to fall. Recall that

$$AFC = \frac{\text{Total fixed cost}}{\text{Total output}}$$

The numerator is fixed (at $120 in this case). But the denominator increases as output expands. Hence ***any increase in output will lower average fixed cost.*** This is reflected in Figure 7.5 by the constantly declining AFC curve.

As jeans output increases from 15 to 20 pairs per day, AVC falls as well. AVC includes the price of denim used in a pair of jeans and associated labor costs. The price of denim is unchanged at $3 per pair ($30 per bolt). But per-unit *labor* costs fall when output increases from 15 to 20 pairs, from $5.33 to $4.50 per pair. Thus the reduction in AVC is completely due to the greater productivity of a second worker. To get 20 pairs of jeans, we had to employ a second worker part-time. In the process, the marginal physical product of labor rose and AVC fell.

With both AFC and AVC falling, ATC must decline as well. In this case, *average* total cost falls from $16.33 per pair to $13.50. This is reflected in row *K* in the table as well as in point *K* on the ATC curve in Figure 7.5.

Rising AVC. Although AFC continues to decline as output expands, AVC doesn't keep dropping. On the contrary, AVC tends to start rising quite early in the expansion process. Look at column 6 of the table in Figure 7.5. After an initial decline, AVC starts to increase. At an output of 20 pairs, AVC is $7.50. At 30 pairs, AVC is $8.00. By the time the rate of output reaches 51 pairs per day, AVC is $12.41.

Average variable cost rises because of diminishing returns in the production process. We discussed this concept before. As output expands, each unit of labor has less land and capital to work with. Marginal physical product falls. As it does, labor costs *per pair of jeans* rise, pushing up AVC.

U-Shaped ATC. The steady decline of AFC, when combined with the typical increase in AVC, results in a U-shaped pattern for average total costs. In the early stages of output expansion, the large declines in AFC outweigh any increases in AVC. As a result, ATC tends to fall. Notice that ATC declines from $20.50 to $11.75 as output increases from 10 to 40 pairs per day. This is also illustrated in Figure 7.5 with the downward move from point *I* to point *M*.

The battle between falling AFC and rising AVC takes an irreversible turn soon thereafter. When output is increased from 40 to 50 pairs of jeans per day, AFC continues to fall (row *N* in the table). But the decline in AFC (−60 cents) is overshadowed by the increase in AVC (+$2.25). Once rising AVC dominates, ATC starts to increase as well. ATC increases from $11.75 to $13.40 when jeans production expands from 40 to 50 pairs per day.

This and further increases in average total costs cause the ATC curve in Figure 7.5 to start rising. ***The initial dominance of falling AFC, combined with the later resurgence of rising AVC, is what gives the ATC curve its characteristic U shape.***

Minimum Average Cost. Whew! There are a lot of numbers here. It's easy to get lost in this thicket of intertwined graphs and jumble of equations. A couple of landmarks will help guide us out, however. One of those is located at the very bottom of the U-shaped average total cost curve. Point *M* in Figure 7.5 represents *minimum* average total costs. By producing exactly 40 pairs per day, we minimize the amount of land, labor, and capital used per pair of jeans. For Low-Rider Jeans Corporation, point *M* represents least-cost production—the lowest-cost jeans. For society as a whole, point *M* also represents the lowest possible opportunity cost: at point *M,* we're minimizing the amount of resources used to produce a pair of jeans and therefore maximizing the amount of resources left over for the production of other goods and services.

As attractive as point *M* is, you shouldn't conclude that it's everyone's dream. The goal of producers is to maximize *profits*. We already noted that maximum *profits* and maximum *output* don't necessarily coincide. Now we'll see that minimizing average total cost isn't necessarily the same thing as maximizing profit, either.

Marginal Cost

To get a firmer grip on profit maximization, we need to introduce one last cost concept. Indeed, this last concept is probably the most important one for production. It's *marginal cost*. We encountered this concept in our discussion of resource costs, where we noted that marginal cost refers to the value of the resources needed to produce one more unit of a good. To produce *one* more pair of jeans, we need the denim itself and a very small amount of additional labor. These are the extra or added costs of increasing output by one pair of jeans per day. To compute the *dollar* value of these marginal costs, we could determine the market price of denim and labor and then add them up. Table 7.3 provides an example. In this case, we calculate that the additional or *marginal* cost of producing a sixteenth pair of jeans is $7.24. This is how much *total* costs will increase if we decide to expand jeans output by only one pair per day (from 15 to 16).

Table 7.3 emphasizes the link between resource costs and dollar costs. However, there's a much easier way to compute marginal cost. **Marginal cost refers to the change in total costs associated with one more unit of output.** Accordingly, we can simply observe *total* dollar costs before and after the rate of output is increased. The difference between the two totals equals the *marginal cost* of increasing the rate of output. This technique is much easier for jeans manufacturers who don't know much about marginal resource utilization but have a sharp eye for dollar costs. It's also a lot easier for economics students, of course. But they have an obligation to understand the resource origins of marginal costs and what causes marginal costs to rise or fall. As we noted before, **diminishing returns in production cause marginal costs to increase as the rate of output is expanded.**

Figure 7.6 shows what the marginal costs of producing jeans look like. At each output rate, marginal cost is computed as the *change* in total cost divided by the *change* in output. When output increases from 20 jeans to 30 jeans, total cost rises by $90. Dividing this change in costs by 10 (the change in output) gives us a marginal cost of $9, as illustrated by point *s*.

Notice in Figure 7.6 how the marginal cost curve starts climbing upward after 20 units of output have been produced. This rise in marginal costs reflects the law of diminishing returns. As increases in output become more difficult to achieve, they also become more expensive. Each additional pair of jeans beyond 20 requires a bit more labor than the preceding pair and thus entails rising marginal cost. After output passes 40 pairs, marginal costs really shoot upward.

Inputs Used to Produce 16th Pair of Jeans	×	Market Value of Input	=	Marginal Cost
0.053 unit of labor		0.053 × $80 per unit of labor		
0.1 bolt of denim		0.1 × $30 per bolt		$4.24
				3.00
				$7.24

TABLE 7.3
Resource Computation of Marginal Cost

Marginal cost refers to the value of the additional inputs needed to produce one more unit of output. To increase daily jeans output from 15 to 16 pairs, we need 0.053 unit of labor and one-tenth of a bolt of denim. These extra inputs cost $7.24.

As added output is increasingly expensive to produce, MC rises.

Marginal cost

FIGURE 7.6
Marginal Costs

Marginal cost is the change in total cost that occurs when more output is produced. MC equals $\Delta TC/\Delta q$. When diminishing returns set in, MC begins rising, as it does here after the output rate of 20 pairs per day is exceeded.

	Rate of Output	Total Cost	$\dfrac{\Delta TC}{\Delta q}$ = MC
	0	$120	
p	10	205	$85/10 = $8.5
q	15	245	$40/5 = $8.0
r	20	270	$25/5 = $5.0
s	30	360	$90/10 = $9.0
t	40	470	$110/10 = $11.0
u	50	670	$200/10 = $20.0
v	51	753	$83/1 = $83.0

A Cost Summary

All these cost calculations can give you a real headache. They can also give you second thoughts about jumping into Low-Rider Jeans or any other business. There are tough choices to be made. A given firm can produce many different rates of output, each of which entails a distinct level of costs. *The output decision has to be based not only on the* **capacity** *to produce (the production function) but also on the* **costs** *of production (the cost functions).* Only those who make the right decisions will succeed in business.

The decision-making process is made a bit easier with the glossary in Table 7.4 and the generalized cost curves in Figure 7.7. As before, we're concentrating on a short-run production process, with fixed quantities of land and capital. In this case, however, we've abandoned the Low-Rider Jeans Corporation and provided hypothetical costs for an idealized production process. The purpose of these figures is to provide a more general view of how the various cost concepts relate to each other. Note that MC, ATC, AFC, and AVC can all be computed from total costs. All we need, then, are the first two columns of the table in Figure 7.7, and we can compute and graph all the rest of the cost figures.

MC–ATC Intersection. The centerpiece of Figure 7.7 is the U-shaped ATC curve (in green). Of special significance is its relationship to marginal costs. Notice that *the MC curve intersects the ATC curve at its lowest point* (point *m*). This will always be the case. So long as the marginal cost of producing one more unit is less than the previous average cost, average costs must fall. *Thus average total costs decline as long as the marginal cost curve lies below the average cost curve,* as to the left of point *m* in Figure 7.7.

FIGURE 7.7
Basic Cost Curves

With total cost and the rate of output, all other cost concepts can be computed. The resulting cost curves have several distinct features. The AFC curve always slopes downward. The MC curve typically rises, sometimes after a brief decline. The ATC curve has a U shape. And the MC curve will always intersect both the ATC and AVC curves at their lowest points (*m* and *n*, respectively).

Rate of Output	TC	MC	ATC	AFC	AVC
0	$10.00	—	—	—	—
1	13.00	$ 3.00	$13.00	$10.00	$ 3.00
2	15.00	2.00	7.50	5.00	2.50
3	19.00	4.00	6.33	3.33	3.00
4	25.00	6.00	6.25	2.50	3.75
5	34.00	9.00	6.80	2.00	4.80
6	48.00	14.00	8.00	1.67	6.33
7	68.00	20.00	9.71	1.43	8.28
8	98.00	30.00	12.25	1.25	11.00

We already observed, however, that marginal costs rise as output expands, largely because additional workers reduce the amount of land and capital available to each worker (in the short run, the size of plant and equipment is fixed). Consequently, at some point (*m* in Figure 7.7) marginal costs will rise to the level of average costs.

Total costs of production are made up of **fixed costs** and **variable costs**:

$$TC = FC + VC$$

Dividing total costs by the quantity of output yields the **average total cost**:

$$ATC = \frac{TC}{q}$$

Which also equals the sum of **average fixed cost** and **average variable cost**:

$$ATC = AFC + AVC$$

The most important measure of changes in cost is **marginal cost**, which equals the increase in total costs when an additional unit of output is produced:

$$MC = \frac{\text{Change in total cost}}{\text{Change in output}}$$

TABLE 7.4
A Guide to Costs

A quick reference to key measures of cost.

As marginal costs continue to rise beyond point *m,* they begin to pull average costs up, giving the average cost curve its U shape. ***Average total costs increase whenever marginal costs exceed average costs.*** This is the case to the right of point *m* because the marginal cost curve always lies above the average cost curve in that part of Figure 7.7.

To visualize the relationship between marginal cost and average cost, imagine computing the average height of people entering a room. If the first person who comes through the door is six feet tall, then the average height of people entering the room is six feet at that point. But what happens to average height if the second person entering the room is only three feet tall? *Average* height declines because the last (marginal) person entering the room is shorter than the previous average. Whenever the last entrant is shorter than the average, the average must fall.

The relationship between marginal costs and average costs is also similar to that between your grade in this course and your grade point average. If your grade in economics is better (higher) than your other grades, then your overall grade point average will rise. In other words, a high *marginal* grade will pull your *average* grade up. If you don't understand this, your grade point average is likely to fall.

ECONOMIC VS. ACCOUNTING COSTS

The cost curves we observed here are based on *real* production relationships. The dollar costs we compute are a direct reflection of underlying resource costs: the land, labor, and capital used in the production process. Not everyone counts this way. On the contrary, accountants and businesspeople typically count dollar costs only and ignore any resource use that doesn't result in an explicit dollar cost.

Return to Low-Rider Jeans for a moment to see the difference. When we computed the dollar cost of producing 15 pairs of jeans per day, we noted the following resource inputs:

INPUTS	COST PER DAY
1 factory rent	$100
1 machine rent	20
1 machine operator	80
1.5 bolts of denim	45
Total cost	$245

The total value of the resources used in the production of 15 pairs of jeans was thus $245 per day. But this figure needn't conform to *actual* dollar costs. Suppose the owners of Low-Rider Jeans decided to sew jeans themselves. Then they wouldn't have to hire a worker and pay $80 per day in wages. **Explicit costs**—the *dollar* payments—would drop to $165 per day. The producers and their accountant would consider this a remarkable achievement. They might assert that the cost of producing jeans had fallen.

> **explicit cost:** A payment made for the use of a resource.

Economic Cost

An economist would draw no such conclusions. ***The essential economic question is how many resources are used in production.*** This hasn't changed. One unit of labor is still being employed at the factory; now it's simply the owner, not a hired worker. In either case, one unit of labor is not available for the production of other goods and services. Hence society is still paying $245 for jeans, whether the owners of Low-Rider Jeans write checks in that amount or not. The only difference is that we now have an **implicit cost** rather than an explicit one. We really don't care who sews jeans—the essential point is that someone (i.e., a unit of labor) does.

The same would be true if Low-Rider Jeans owned its own factory rather than rented it. If the factory were owned rather than rented, the owners probably wouldn't write any rent checks. Hence, *accounting* costs would drop by $100 per day. But the factory would still be in use for jeans production and therefore unavailable for the production of other goods and services. The economic (resource) cost of producing 15 pairs of jeans would still be $245.

The distinction between an economic cost and an accounting cost is essentially one between resource and dollar costs. *Dollar cost* refers to the explicit dollar outlays made by

> **implicit cost:** The value of resources used, even when no direct payment is made.

economic cost: The value of all resources used to produce a good or service; opportunity cost.

a producer; it's the lifeblood of accountants. **Economic cost,** in contrast, refers to the *value* of *all* resources used in the production process; it's the lifeblood of economists. In other words, economists count costs as

$$\text{Economic cost} = \text{Explicit costs} + \text{Implicit costs}$$

As this formula suggests, *economic and accounting costs will diverge whenever any factor of production is not paid an explicit wage (or rent, etc.).*

The Cost of Homework. These distinctions between economic and accounting costs apply also to the "production" of homework. You can pay people to write term papers for you or buy them off the Internet. At large schools you can often buy lecture notes as well. But most students do their own homework so they'll learn something and not just turn in required assignments.

Doing homework is expensive, however, even if you don't pay someone to do it. The time you spend reading this chapter is valuable. You could be doing something else if you weren't reading right now. What would you be doing? That forgone activity—the best alternative use of your time—represents the economic cost of doing homework. Even if you don't pay yourself for reading this chapter, you'll still incur that *economic* cost.

LONG-RUN COSTS

We've confined our discussion thus far to short-run production costs. *The short run is characterized by fixed costs*—a commitment to specific plants and equipment. A factory, an office building, or some other plants and equipment have been leased or purchased: we're stuck with *fixed costs.* In the short run, our objective is to make the best use of those fixed costs by choosing the appropriate rate of production.

long run: A period of time long enough for all inputs to be varied (no fixed costs).

The long run opens up a whole new range of options. In the **long run,** we have no lease or purchase commitments. We're free to start all over again with whatever scale of plants and equipment we desire and whatever technology is available. Quite simply, *there are no fixed costs in the long run.* Nor are there any commitments to existing technology. In 2011 Ford could have built an auto plant in Kansas City of any size (see the News below). In building the plant, the company incurred a fixed cost. Once the plant is completed, Ford will focus on the short-run production decision of how many autos to manufacture.

IN THE NEWS

Ford Pumps $400 Million in Kansas City Plant

NEW YORK—Ford Motor Co. announced Tuesday that it plans to invest $400 million over the next two years in its auto manufacturing plant in Kansas City, Missouri, as it prepares to build a new vehicle there. . . .

The $400 million investment in the Kansas City plant will be used to install a new body shop, new machines, and other upgrades, Ford said.

—Peter Valdes-Dapene

Source: CNNMoney.com, January 18, 2011. © 2011 Time Inc. Used under license.

Analysis: In the long run, a firm has no fixed costs and can select any desired plant size. Once a plant is built, leased, or purchased, a firm has fixed costs and focuses on short-run output decisions.

Long-Run Average Costs

The opportunities available in the long run include building a plant of any desired size. Suppose we still wanted to go into the jeans business. In the long run, we could build or lease any size factory we wanted and could lease as many sewing machines as we desired.

FIGURE 7.8
Long-Run Costs with Three Plant Size Options

Long-run cost possibilities are determined by all possible short-run options. In this case, there are three options of varying size (ATC$_1$, ATC$_2$, and ATC$_3$). In the long run, we'd choose the plant that yielded the lowest average cost for any desired rate of output. The solid portions of the curves (LATC) represent these choices. The smallest factory (ATC$_1$) is best for output levels below *a*; the largest (ATC$_3$), output rates in excess of *b*.

Figure 7.8 illustrates three choices: a small factory (ATC$_1$), a medium-sized factory (ATC$_2$), and a large factory (ATC$_3$). As we observed earlier, it's very expensive to produce lots of jeans with a small factory. The ATC curve for a small factory (ATC$_1$) starts to head straight up at relatively low rates of output. In the long run, we'd lease or build such a factory only if we anticipated a continuing low rate of output.

The ATC$_2$ curve illustrates how costs might fall if we leased or built a medium-sized factory. With a small factory, ATC becomes prohibitive at an output of 50 to 60 pairs of jeans per day. A medium-sized factory can produce these quantities at lower cost. Moreover, ATC continues to drop as jeans production increases in the medium-sized factory—at least for a while. Even a medium-sized factory must contend with resource constraints and therefore rising average costs: its ATC curve is U-shaped also.

If we expected to sell really large quantities of jeans, we'd want to build or lease a large factory. Beyond the rate of output *b*, the largest factory offers the lowest average total cost. There's a risk in leasing such a large factory, of course. If our sales don't live up to our high expectations, we'll end up with very high fixed costs and thus very expensive jeans. Look at the high average cost of producing only 60 pairs of jeans per day with the large factory (ATC$_3$).

In choosing an appropriate factory, then, we must decide how many jeans we expect to sell. Once we know our expected output, we can select the right-sized factory. It will be the one that offers the lowest ATC for that rate of output. If we expect to sell fewer jeans than *a*, we'll choose the small factory in Figure 7.8. If we expect to sell jeans at a rate between *a* and *b*, we'll select a medium-sized factory. Beyond rate *b*, we'll want the largest factory. These choices are reflected in the solid parts of the three ATC curves. The composite "curve" created by these three segments constitutes our long-run cost possibilities. ***The long-run cost curve is just a summary of our best short-run cost possibilities, using existing technology and facilities.***

We might confront more than three choices, of course. There's really no reason we couldn't build a factory to *any* desired size. In the long run, we face an infinite number of scale choices, not just three. The effect of all these choices is to smooth out the long-run cost curve. Figure 7.9 depicts the long-run curve that results. Each rate of output is most efficiently produced by some size (scale) of plant. That sized plant indicates the minimum cost of producing a particular rate of output. Its corresponding short-run ATC curve provides one point on the long-run ATC curve.

Long-Run Marginal Costs

Like all average cost curves, the long-run (LATC) curve has its own marginal cost curve. The long-run marginal cost (LMC) curve isn't a composite of short-run marginal cost curves. Rather, it's computed on the basis of the costs reflected in the long-run ATC curve itself. We won't bother to compute those costs here. Note, however, that the long-run MC curve—like all MC curves—intersects its associated average cost curve at its lowest point.

FIGURE 7.9
Long-Run Costs with Unlimited Options

If plants of all sizes can be built, short-run options are infinite. In this case, the LATC curve becomes a smooth U-shaped curve. Each point on the curve represents lowest-cost production for a plant size best suited to one rate of output. The long-run ATC curve has its own MC curve.

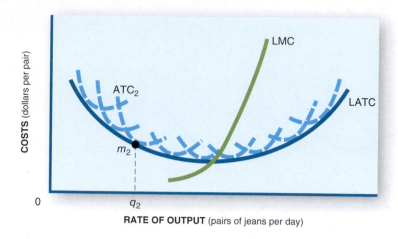

ECONOMIES OF SCALE

Figure 7.8 seems to imply that a producer must choose either a small plant or a larger one. That isn't completely true. The choice is often between one large plant or *several* small ones. Suppose the desired level of output was relatively large, as at point *c* in Figure 7.8. A single small plant (ATC_1) is clearly not up to the task. But what about using several small plants rather than one large one (ATC_3)? How would costs be affected?

Notice what happens to *minimum ATC* in Figure 7.8 when the size (scale) of the factory changes. When a medium-sized factory (ATC_2) replaces a small factory (ATC_1), minimum average cost drops (the bottom of ATC_2 is below the bottom of ATC_1). This implies that a jeans producer who wants to minimize costs should build one medium-sized factory rather than try to produce the same quantity with two small ones. **Economies of scale** exist in this situation: larger facilities reduce *minimum* average costs. Such economies of scale help explain why a single firm has come to dominate the funeral business (see the News below).

economies of scale:
Reductions in minimum average costs that come about through increases in the size (scale) of plant and equipment.

IN THE NEWS

Funeral Giant Moves In on Small Rivals

Life's two certainties are death and taxes. Some day, it could be just as certain that Service Corp. International will handle your funeral.

The Houston-based company will handle 1 in 10 funeral services in the United States this year, or about 230,000. In just 32 years, the company has grown from a single funeral home into the world's biggest death services provider with 2,631 funeral homes, 250 cemeteries, and 137 crematoria in North America, Europe, and Australia. . . .

SCI's sheer size provides big advantages over competitors. SCI is able to get cheaper prices on caskets and other products from suppliers.

Its funeral homes clustered in the same markets cut costs by sharing vehicles, personnel, services, and supplies. That helps give SCI a profit of 31 cents on every dollar it takes in for a typical funeral, versus 12 cents for the industry as a whole, SCI says.

Funeral directors "don't want to think of (death) as big business," says Betty Murray of the National Foundation of Funeral Directors. "But we're in the era of acquisitions and consolidations."

—Ron Trujillo

Source: *USA TODAY.* October 31, 1995. Reprinted with Permission.

Analysis: As the size of a firm increases, it may be able to reduce the costs of doing business. Economies of scale can give a large firm a competitive advantage over smaller firms.

FIGURE 7.10
Economies of Scale

A lot of output (Q_m) can be produced from one large plant or many small ones. Here we contrast the average total costs associated with one small plant (ATCs) and three large plants (ATC$_1$, ATC$_2$, and ATC$_3$). If a large plant attains the same *minimum* average costs (point m_1 in part *a*) as a smaller plant (point *c*), there's no advantage to large size (scale). Many small plants can produce the same output just as cheaply. However, either economies (part *b*) or diseconomies (part *c*) of scale may exist.

Larger production facilities don't always result in cost reductions. Suppose a firm has the choice of producing the quantity Q_m from several small factories or from one large, centralized facility. Centralization may have three different impacts on costs; these are illustrated in Figure 7.10. In each illustration, we see the average total cost (ATC) curve for a typical small firm or plant and the ATC curve for a much larger plant producing the same product.

Constant Returns. Figure 7.10*a* depicts a situation in which there's no economic advantage to centralization of manufacturing operations because a large plant is no more efficient than a lot of small plants. The critical focus here is on the *minimum* average costs attainable for a given rate of output. Note that the lowest point on the smaller plant's ATC curve (point *c*) is no higher or lower than the lowest point on the larger firm's ATC curve (point m_1). Hence it would be just as cheap to produce the quantity Q_m from a multitude of small plants as it would be to produce Q_m from one large plant. Thus increasing the size (or *scale*) of individual plants won't reduce minimum average costs: this is a situation of **constant returns to scale.**

Economies of Scale. Figure 7.10*b* illustrates the situation in which a larger plant can attain a lower minimum average cost than a smaller plant. That is, economies of scale (or *increasing returns to scale*) exist. This is evident from the fact that the larger firm's ATC curve falls *below* the dashed line in the graph (m_2 is less than *c*). The greater efficiency of the large factory might come from any of several sources. This is the situation of the funeral home depicted in the News feature. By centralizing core funeral services, Services Corp. International was able to reduce average costs per funeral. Larger organizations may also gain a cost advantage through specialization, by having each worker become expert in a particular skill. By contrast, a smaller establishment might have to use the same individual(s) to perform several functions, thereby reducing productivity at each task. Also, some kinds of machinery may be economical only if they're used to produce massive volumes—an opportunity only very large factories have.

Diseconomies of Scale. Even though large plants may be able to achieve greater efficiencies than smaller plants, there's no guaranty that they actually will. In fact, increasing the size (scale) of a plant may actually *reduce* operating efficiency, as depicted in Figure 7.10*c*. Workers may feel alienated in a plant of massive proportions and feel little commitment to productivity. Creativity may be stifled by rigid corporate structures and off-site management. A large plant may also foster a sense of anonymity that induces workers to underperform. When these things happen, *diseconomies of scale* result. Microsoft tries to avoid such diseconomies of scale by creating autonomous cells of no more than 35 employees ("small plants") within its larger corporate structure.

constant returns to scale: Increases in plant size do not affect minimum average cost: minimum per-unit costs are identical for small plants and large plants.

web analysis

Grocery supermarkets have pushed out small mom-and-pop neighborhood stores. Much of this is due to economies of scale. To learn more about the grocery industry visit **www.thekrogerco.com** and click the "Corporate News" tab. Then click "history."

In evaluating long-run options, then, we must be careful to recognize that *efficiency and size don't necessarily go hand in hand.* Some firms and industries may be subject to economies of scale, but others may not. Bigger isn't always better.

THE ECONOMY TOMORROW

GLOBAL COMPETITIVENESS

From 1900 to 1970, the United States regularly exported more goods and services than it imported. Since then America has had a trade deficit nearly every year. In 2010, U.S. imports exceeded exports by almost $500 billion. To many people, such trade deficits are a symptom that the United States can no longer compete effectively in world markets.

Global competitiveness ultimately depends on the costs of production. If international competitors can produce goods more cheaply, they'll be able to undersell U.S. goods in global markets.

Cheap Foreign Labor? Cheap labor keeps costs down in many countries. The average wage in Mexico, for example, ranges from $2 to $3 an hour, compared to over $18 an hour in the United States. China's manufacturing workers make only $1 to $2 an hour. Low wages are *not,* however, a reliable measure of global competitiveness. To compete in global markets, one must produce more *output* for a given quantity of *inputs.* In other words, labor is "cheap" only if it produces a lot of output in return for the wages paid.

A worker's contribution to output is measured by *marginal physical product (MPP).* What we saw in this chapter was that *a worker's productivity (MPP) depends on the quantity and quality of other resources in the production process.* In this regard, U.S. workers have a tremendous advantage: they work with vast quantities of capital and state-of-the-art technology. They also come to the workplace with more education. Their high wages reflect this greater productivity.

unit labor cost: Hourly wage rate divided by output per labor-hour.

Unit Labor Costs. A true measure of global competitiveness must take into account both factor costs (e.g., wages) and productivity. One such measure is **unit labor costs,** which indicates the labor cost of producing one unit of output. It's computed as

$$\text{Unit labor cost} = \frac{\text{Wage rate}}{\text{MPP}}$$

Suppose the MPP of a U.S. worker is 9 units per hour and the wage is $18 an hour. The unit labor cost would be

$$\begin{array}{c}\text{Unit labor cost} \\ \text{(United States)}\end{array} = \frac{\$18/\text{hour}}{9\ \text{units/hour}} = \begin{array}{c}\$2/\text{unit} \\ \text{of output}\end{array}$$

By contrast, assume the average worker in Mexico has an MPP of 1 unit per hour and a wage of $3 an hour. In this case, the unit labor cost would be

$$\begin{array}{c}\text{Unit labor cost} \\ \text{(Mexico)}\end{array} = \frac{\$3}{1} = \begin{array}{c}\$3/\text{unit} \\ \text{of output}\end{array}$$

According to these hypothetical examples, "cheap" Mexican labor is no bargain. Mexican labor is actually *more* costly in production despite the much lower wage rate.

Productivity Advance. What these calculations illustrate is how important productivity is for global competitiveness. If we want the United States to stay competitive in global markets, U.S. productivity must increase as fast as that in other nations.

The production function introduced in this chapter helps illustrate the essence of global competitiveness in the economy tomorrow. Until now, we've regarded a firm's production function as a technological fact of life—the *best* we could do, given our state of technological and managerial knowledge. In the real world, however, the best is always getting better. Science and technology are continuously advancing. So is our knowledge of how to organize and manage our resources. These advances keep *shifting* production functions upward: more can

web analysis

For current data on unit labor costs and underlying wage and productivity trends, visit the U.S. Bureau of Labor Statistics at **www.bls.gov.** Click the "Subject Areas" tab, then select "Pay & Benefits" and "Productivity."

(a) When the production function shifts up . . .

TOTAL OUTPUT (units per time period)

RESOURCE INPUTS
(units per time period)

(b) Cost curves shift down

COST (dollars per unit)

ATC_1
ATC_2
MC_1
MC_2

RATE OF OUTPUT
(units per time period)

FIGURE 7.11

Improvements in Productivity Reduce Costs

Advances in technological or managerial knowledge increase our productive capability. This is reflected in upward shifts of the production function (part *a*) and downward shifts of production cost curves (part *b*).

be produced with any given quantity of inputs. In the process, the costs of production shift downward, as illustrated in Figure 7.11 by the downward shifts of the MC and ATC curves. These downward shifts imply that we can get more of the goods and services we desire with available resources. We can also compete more effectively in global markets.

Internet-Driven Gains. The Internet has been an important source of productivity gains in the last 10 years. Although the Internet originated over 30 years ago, its commercial potential emerged with the creation of the World Wide Web around 1990. As recently as 1995 there were only 10,000 websites. Now there are over 100 *million* sites. This vastly expanded spectrum of information has helped businesses cut costs in many ways. The cost of gathering information about markets and inputs has been reduced. With the reach of the Internet, firms can engage in greater specialization. Firms can also manage their inventories and supply chains much more efficiently. Transaction and communications costs are reduced as well. All of these productivity improvements are cutting U.S. production costs

WORLD VIEW

United States Gains Cost Advantage

Productivity is increasing faster than wages in U.S. manufacturing, giving the United States an edge in the race for global competitiveness. Between 2000 and 2009, the cost of producing a widget fell by nearly 14 percent in the United States. In Canada, by contrast, unit labor costs rose by 23.7 percent.

Country	Change in Unit Labor Costs, 2000–2009
Italy	+ 45.4%
Canada	+ 23.7%
France	+ 16.8%
Korea	+ 16.0%
United Kingdom	+ 14.9%
Czech Republic	− 0.7%
Japan	− 13.3%
United States	**− 13.7%**
Taiwan	− 29.1%

Source: U.S. Bureau of Labor Statistics. **www.bls.gov.**

Analysis: Global competitiveness depends on unit labor costs. U.S. unit labor costs declined significantly in the last decade or so, increasing America's competitiveness in world markets.

by $100–250 billion a year. These kinds of cost savings helped U.S. businesses *reduce* unit labor costs by 13.7 percent between 2000 and 2009. As the previous World View confirms, those gains widened the United States' lead in the ongoing race for global competitiveness. To maintain that leading position in the economy tomorrow, U.S. productivity must continue to advance at a brisk pace.

SUMMARY

- A production function indicates the maximum amount of output that can be produced with different combinations of inputs. LO7-1
- In the short run, some inputs (e.g., land and capital) are fixed in quantity. Increases in (short-run) output result from more use of variable inputs (e.g., labor). LO7-1
- The contribution of a variable input to total output is measured by its marginal physical product (MPP). This is the amount by which *total* output increases when one more unit of the input is employed. LO7-1
- The MPP of a factor tends to decline as more of it is used in a given production facility. Diminishing marginal returns result from crowding more of a variable input (e.g., labor) into a production process, reducing the amount of fixed inputs *per unit* of variable input. LO7-2
- Marginal cost is the increase in total cost that results when output is increased by one unit. Marginal cost increases whenever marginal physical product diminishes. LO7-3
- Not all costs go up when the rate of output is increased. Fixed costs such as space and equipment leases don't vary with the rate of output. Only variable costs such as labor and material go up when output is increased. LO7-3

- Average total cost (ATC) equals total cost divided by the quantity of output produced. ATC declines when marginal cost (MC) is less than average cost and rises when MC exceeds it. The MC and ATC curves intersect at minimum ATC (the bottom of the U). That intersection represents least-cost production. LO7-3
- The economic costs of production include the value of *all* resources used. Accounting costs typically include only those dollar costs actually paid (explicit costs). LO7-4
- In the long run there are no fixed costs; the size (scale) of production can be varied. The long-run ATC curve indicates the lowest cost of producing output with facilities of appropriate size. LO7-5
- Economies of scale refer to reductions in *minimum* average cost attained with larger plant size (scale). If minimum ATC rises with plant size, diseconomies of scale exist. LO7-5
- Global competitiveness and domestic living standards depend on productivity advances. Improvements in productivity shift production functions up and push cost curves down. LO7-1

Key Terms

factors of production	profit	explicit cost
production function	marginal cost (MC)	implicit cost
productivity	total cost	economic cost
efficiency	fixed costs	long run
opportunity cost	variable costs	economies of scale
short run	average total cost (ATC)	constant returns to scale
marginal physical product (MPP)	average fixed cost (AFC)	unit labor cost
law of diminishing returns	average variable cost (AVC)	

Questions for Discussion

1. What are the production costs of your economics class? What are the fixed costs? The variable costs? What's the marginal cost of enrolling more students? LO7-3
2. Suppose all your friends offered to help wash your car. Would marginal physical product decline as more friends helped? Why or why not? LO7-2
3. How many autos will Ford want to produce in its new Kansas City plant? (See News, p. 152.) LO7-1
4. Owner/operators of small gas stations rarely pay themselves an hourly wage. How does this practice affect the economic cost of dispensing gasoline? LO7-4
5. Corporate funeral giants have replaced small family-run funeral homes in many areas, in large part because of the lower costs they achieve. (See News, p. 154.) What kind of economies of scale exist in the funeral business? Why doesn't someone build

one colossal funeral home and drive costs down further?   LO7-5

6. Are colleges subject to economies of scale or diseconomies?   LO7-5

7. Why don't more U.S. firms move to Mexico to take advantage of low wages there? Would an *identical* plant in Mexico be as productive as its U.S. counterpart?   LO7-1

8. How would your productivity in completing coursework be measured? Has your productivity changed since you began college? What caused the productivity changes? How could you increase productivity further?   LO7-1

9. What is the economic cost of doing this homework?   LO7-4

---

 web activities to accompany this chapter can be found on the Online Learning Center:
http://www.mhhe.com/schiller13e

 mobile app Visit your mobile app store and download the Schiller: Study Econ app *today*!

LO7-3   1.   (a) Complete the following cost schedule:

Rate of Output	Total Cost	Marginal Cost	Average Fixed Cost	Average Variable Cost	Average Total Cost
0	$ 800	_____	_____	_____	_____
1	1,000	_____	_____	_____	_____
2	1,250	_____	_____	_____	_____
3	1,550	_____	_____	_____	_____
4	2,000	_____	_____	_____	_____
5	2,500	_____	_____	_____	_____

(b) Use the cost data to plot the ATC and MC curves on the accompanying graph.
(c) At what output rate is ATC minimized? (Use higher rate.) _____

LO7-5   2.   Based on the News on page 154, what is the ATC per dollar of sales at
(a) The largest funeral home?   _____
(b) Smaller funeral homes (based on the industry as a whole)?   _____

LO7-4   3.   Suppose a company incurs the following costs: labor, $600; equipment, $300; and materials, $200. The company owns the building, so it doesn't have to pay the usual $900 in rent.
(a) What is the total accounting cost?   _____
(b) What is the total economic cost?   _____
(c) If the company sold the building and then leased it back, what would be the change in
(i) Accounting costs?   _____
(ii) Economic costs?   _____

LO7-2   4.   Refer to the production table for jeans (Table 7.1). Suppose a firm has two sewing machines and can vary only the amount of labor input.
(a) Graph the production function for jeans given the two sewing machines.
(b) Compute and graph the marginal physical product curve.
(c) At what amount of labor input does the law of diminishing returns first become apparent in your graph of marginal physical product?   _____
(d) Is total output still increasing when MPP begins to diminish?   _____
(e) When total output stops increasing, what is the value of MPP?   _____

LO7-3   5. The following table indicates the average total cost of producing varying quantities of output from three different plants:

Rate of output	10	20	30	40	50	60	70	80	90	100
Average total cost										
Small firm	$ 600	$500	$400	$500	$600	$700	$800	$900	$1,000	$1,100
Medium firm	800	650	500	350	200	300	400	500	600	700
Large firm	1,000	900	800	700	600	500	400	300	400	500

(a) Plot the ATC curves for all three firms on the graph.
(b) Which plant(s) should be used to produce 40 units?   _____
(c) Which plant(s) should be used to produce 100 units?   _____
(d) Are there economies of scale in these plant size choices? _____

LO7-5   6. According to the World View on page 157, (a) which nation had the biggest loss of competitive position in years 2000–2009? (b) Which nation had the biggest gain?

(a) _____
(b) _____

LO7-1   7. Suppose (A) the hourly wage rate is $18 in the United States and $2 in China, and (B) productivity is 20 units per hour in the United States and 4 units per hour in China. What are unit labor costs in

(a) The United States?   _____
(b) China?   _____

Market Structure

Market demand curves tell us what products consumers want. And production functions tell us how much it will cost producers to supply those products. What we don't yet know is how many products will actually be supplied—or at what prices. These are *behavioral decisions,* not technological facts. Chapters 8 through 12 examine these behavioral decisions. As we'll see, the *structure* of a market—the number and size of firms in it—has a profound effect on the supply of goods and services—the quantity, quality, and price of specific goods.

The Competitive Firm

LEARNING OBJECTIVES

After reading this chapter, you should know

LO8-1. How profits are computed.

LO8-2. The characteristics of perfectly competitive firms.

LO8-3. How a competitive firm maximizes profit.

LO8-4. When a firm will shut down.

LO8-5. The difference between production and investment decisions.

LO8-6. What shapes or shifts a firm's supply curve.

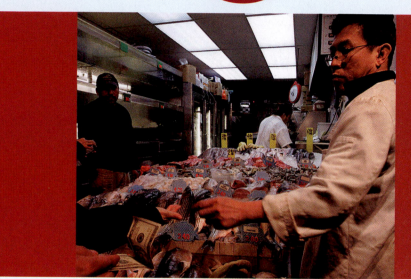

Apple computer would love to raise the price of downloading music from its iTunes store. It isn't likely to do so, however, because too many other firms also offer digital downloads. If Apple raises its prices, customers might sign up with another company.

Your campus bookstore may be in a better position to raise prices. On most college campuses there's only one bookstore. If the campus store increases the price of books or supplies, most of its customers (you) will have little choice but to pay the higher tab.

As we discover in this and the next few chapters, the degree of competition in product markets is a major determinant of product prices, quality, and availability. Although all firms are in business to make a profit, their profit opportunities are limited by the amount of competition they face.

This chapter begins an examination of how businesses make price and production decisions. We first explore the nature of profits and how they're computed. We then observe how one type of firm—a perfectly competitive one—can *maximize* its profits by selecting the right rate of output. The following questions are at the center of this discussion:

- **What are *profits?***
- **What are the unique characteristics of competitive firms?**
- **How much output will a competitive firm produce?**

The answers to these questions will shed more light on how the *supply* of goods and services is determined in a market economy.

THE PROFIT MOTIVE

The basic incentive for producing goods and services is the expectation of profit. Owning plants and equipment isn't enough. To generate a current flow of income, one must *use* the plants and equipment to produce and sell goods.

Profit is the difference between a firm's sales revenues and its total costs. It's the residual that the owners of a business receive. That profit residual may flow to the sole owner of a corner grocery store, or to the group of stockholders who collectively own a large corporation. In either case, it's the quest for profit that motivates people to own and operate a business (or a piece thereof).

> **profit:** The difference between total revenue and total cost.

Other Motivations

Profit isn't the only thing that motivates producers. Like the rest of us, producers also worry about social status and crave recognition. People who need to feel important, to control others, or to demonstrate achievement are likely candidates for running a business. Many small businesses are maintained by people who gave up 40-hour weeks, $50,000 incomes, and a sense of alienation in exchange for 80-hour weeks, $45,000 incomes, and a sense of identity and control.

In large corporations, the profit motive may lie even deeper below the surface. Stockholders of large corporations rarely visit corporate headquarters. The people who manage the corporation's day-to-day business may have little or no stock in the company. Such nonowner managers may be more interested in their own jobs, salaries, and self-preservation than in the profits that accrue to the stockholding owners. If profits suffer, however, the corporation may start looking for new managers. The cartoon on the next page notwithstanding, the "bottom line" for virtually all businesses is the level of profits.

Is the Profit Motive Bad?

If it weren't possible to make a profit, few people would choose to supply goods and services. Yet the general public remains suspicious of the profit motive. As the News below indicates, one out of four people thinks the profit motive is bad. An even higher percentage believes the profit motive results in *inferior* products at inflated prices. A 2010 Gallup poll revealed that people are particularly wary of profits received by "big businesses."

IN THE NEWS

Are Profits Bad?

The following responses to a Roper survey are typical of public opinion about profits.

Agree that the. . .

Profit motive is bad—social needs are ignored in pursuit of high profits. 27%

Profit motive is good—it causes people to invest and provide monies to build plants, industries. 42%

Both (vol.) 9%

Neither (vol.) 4%

Don't know 17%

Profit system results in better products at lower prices. 39%

Profit system results in inferior products at inflated prices. 29%

Both (vol.) 8%

Neither (vol.) 5%

Don't know 19%

Source: *The American Enterprise*, November–December 1993. Reprinted by permission of *The American Enterprise*, www.TAEmag.com.

Analysis: The profit motive is the primary incentive for supplying goods and services. Many consumers are distrustful of that motive, however.

"*You know what I think, folks? Improving technology isn't important. Increased profits aren't important. What's important is to be warm, decent human beings.*"

Analysis: The principal motivation for producing goods and services is to earn a profit. Although other goals may seem desirable, businesses that fail to earn a profit won't survive.

As we'll see, the profit motive *can* induce business firms to pollute the environment, restrict competition, or maintain unsafe working conditions. However, *the profit motive also encourages businesses to produce the goods and services consumers desire, at prices they're willing to pay.* The profit motive, in fact, moves the "invisible hand" that Adam Smith said orchestrates market outcomes.

ECONOMIC VS. ACCOUNTING PROFITS

Although profits might be a necessary inducement for producers, most consumers feel that profits are too high. And that may be so in many cases. But most consumers have no idea how much profit U.S. businesses actually make. Public *perceptions* of profit are seven or eight times higher than actual profits. The typical consumer believes that 35 cents of every sales dollar goes to profits. In reality, average profit per sales dollar is closer to 5 cents.

Faulty perceptions of profits aren't confined to the general public. As surprising as it might seem, most businesses also measure their profits incorrectly.

Economic Profits

Everyone agrees that *profit represents the difference between total revenues and total costs.* Where people part ways is over the decision of what to include in total costs. Recall from Chapter 7 how economists compute costs. **Economic cost** refers to the value of *all* resources used in production, whether or not they receive an explicit payment. By contrast, most businesses count only **explicit costs**—that is, those they actually write checks for. They typically don't take into account the **implicit costs** of the labor or land and buildings they might own. As a result, they understate costs.

If businesses (and their accountants) understate true costs, they'll overstate true profits. Part of the accounting "profit" will really be compensation to unpaid land, labor, or capital used in the production process. *Whenever economic costs exceed explicit costs, observed (accounting) profits will exceed true (economic) profits.* Indeed, what appears to be an accounting profit may actually disguise an economic loss, as illustrated by the Fujishige strawberry farm once located right next to Disneyland (see the following News). To determine

economic cost: The value of all resources used to produce a good or service; opportunity cost.

explicit cost: A payment made for the use of a resource.

implicit cost: The value of resources used, even when no direct payment is made.

IN THE NEWS

Strawberry Fields Forever?

ANAHEIM, CALIFORNIA—Hiroshi Fujishige is a successful strawberry farmer. For over 40 years he has been earning a profit growing and selling strawberries and other produce from his 58-acre farm. Fujishige could make even more money if he stopped growing strawberries. His 58-acre strawberry patch is located across the street from Disneyland. The people from Disney have offered him $32 million just to *lease* the farm; developers have offered as much as $2 million per acre to *buy* the land. But Fujishige, who lives in a tiny house on the farm he bought 45 years ago (for $2,500!) isn't selling. "I'm a farmer, and I've been farming since I got out of high school in 1941," he says. As long as he can make a profit from strawberries, he says, he'll keep growing them.

—William F. Powers

Source: "Strawberry Fields Forever?" *Washington Post*, March 9, 1994, p. D1.

Analysis: Hiroshi Fujishige thought he was making a profit because he miscalculated costs. His *implicit* costs were enormous. When Fujishige died, his family sold the strawberry farm to Disneyland for its California Adventure theme park.

the **economic profit** of a business, we must subtract all implicit factor costs from observed accounting profits:

$$\frac{\text{Economic}}{\text{profit}} = \frac{\text{Total}}{\text{revenue}} - \frac{\text{Total economic}}{\text{cost}}$$

$$\text{OR}$$

$$= \frac{\text{Accounting}}{\text{profit}} - \frac{\text{Implicit}}{\text{costs}}$$

economic profit: The difference between total revenues and total economic costs.

Suppose, for example, that Table 8.1 accurately summarizes the revenues and costs associated with a local drugstore. Monthly sales revenues amount to $27,000. Explicit costs paid by the owner–manager include the cost of merchandise bought from producers for resale to consumers ($17,000), wages to the employees of the drugstore, rent and utilities paid to the landlord, and local sales and business taxes. When all these *explicit* costs are subtracted from total revenue, we're left with an *accounting profit* of $6,000 per month.

The owner–manager of the drugstore may be quite pleased with an accounting profit of $6,000 per month. He's working hard for this income, however. To keep his store running, the owner–manager is working 10 hours per day, 7 days a week. This adds up to 300 hours of labor per month. Were he to work this hard for someone else, his labor would be compensated explicitly—with a paycheck. Although he doesn't choose to pay himself this

web analysis

For information about corporate profits, visit the Bureau of Economic Analysis at **www.bea. gov.** Search "corporate profits." What is measured here, accounting profits or economic profits?

TABLE 8.1
The Computation of Economic Profit

To calculate economic profit, we must take account of *all* costs of production. The economic costs of production include the implicit (opportunity) costs of the labor and capital a producer contributes to the production process. The accounting profits of a business take into account only explicit costs paid by the owner. Reported (accounting) profits will exceed economic profits whenever implicit costs are ignored.

Total (gross) revenues per month	$27,000
less explicit costs:	
Cost of merchandise sold	$17,000
Wages to cashier, stock, and delivery help	2,500
Rent and utilities	800
Taxes	700
Total explicit costs	$21,000
Accounting profit (revenue minus explicit costs)	$ 6,000
less implicit costs:	
Wages of owner–manager, 300 hours @ $10 per hour	$ 3,000
Return on inventory investment, 10% per year on $120,000	1,000
Total implicit costs	$ 4,000
Economic profit (revenue minus *all* costs)	$ 2,000

way, his labor still represents a real resource cost. To compute *economic* profit, we must subtract this implicit cost from the drugstore's accounting profits. Suppose the owner could earn $10 per hour in the best alternative job. Multiplying this wage rate ($10) by the number of hours he works in the drugstore (300), we see that the implicit cost of his labor is $3,000 per month.

The owner has also used his savings to purchase inventory for the store. He purchased the goods on his shelves for $120,000. If he had invested his savings in some other business, he could have earned a return of 10 percent per year. This forgone return represents a real cost. In this case, the implicit return (opportunity cost) on his capital investment amounts to $12,000 per year (10 percent × $120,000), or $1,000 per month.

To calculate the *economic* profit this drugstore generates, we count both explicit and implicit costs. Hence we must subtract all implicit factor payments (costs) from reported profits. The residual in this case amounts to $2,000 per month. That's the drugstore's *economic* profit.

Note that when we compute the drugstore's economic profit, we deduct the opportunity cost of the owner's capital. Specifically, we assumed that his funds would have reaped a 10 percent return somewhere else. In effect, we've assumed that a "normal" rate of return is 10 percent. This **normal profit** (the opportunity cost of capital) is an economic cost. Rather than investing in a drugstore, the owner could have earned a 10 percent return on his funds by investing in a fast-food franchise, a music store, a steel plant, or some other production activity. By choosing to invest in a drugstore instead, the owner was seeking a *higher* return on his funds—more than he could have obtained elsewhere. In other words, *economic profits represent something over and above "normal profits."*

Our treatment of "normal" returns as an economic cost leads to a startling conclusion: on average, economic profits are zero. Only firms that reap *above-average* returns can claim economic profits. This seemingly strange perspective on profits emphasizes the opportunity costs of all economic activities. *A productive activity reaps an economic profit only if it earns more than its opportunity cost.*

normal profit: The opportunity cost of capital; zero economic profit.

Entrepreneurship

Naturally, everyone in business wants to earn an economic profit. But relatively few people can stay ahead of the pack. To earn economic profits, a business must see opportunities that others have missed, discover new products, find new and better methods of production, or take above-average risks. In fact, economic profits are often regarded as a reward to entrepreneurship, the ability and willingness to take risks, to organize factors of production, and to produce something society desires.

Consider the local drugstore again. People in the neighborhood clearly want such a drugstore, as evidenced by its substantial sales revenue. But why should anyone go to the trouble and risk of starting and maintaining one? We noted that the owner–manager *could* earn $3,000 in wages by accepting a regular job plus $1,000 per month in returns on capital by investing in an "average" business. Why should he take on the added responsibilities and risk of owning and operating his own drugstore?

The inducement to take on the added responsibilities of owning and operating a business is the potential for economic profit, the extra income over and above normal factor payments. In the case of the drugstore owner, this extra income is the economic profit of $2,000 (Table 8.1). In the absence of such additional compensation, few people would want to make the extra effort required.

Risk

Don't forget, however, that the *potential* for profit is not a *guaranty* of profit. Quite the contrary. Substantial risks are attached to starting and operating a business. Tens of thousands of businesses fail every year, and still more suffer economic losses. From this perspective, profit also represents compensation for the risks incurred in owning or operating a business.

MARKET STRUCTURE

Not all businesses have an equal opportunity to earn an economic profit. The opportunity for profit may be limited by the *structure* of the industry in which the firm is engaged. One of the reasons Microsoft is such a profitable company is that it has long held a **monopoly** on computer operating systems. As the principal supplier of operating systems, Microsoft can raise software prices without losing many customers. T-shirt shops, by contrast, have to worry about all the other stores that sell similar products in the area (see the News below). Faced with so much competition, the owner of a T-shirt shop doesn't have the power to raise prices or accumulate economic profits.

> **monopoly:** A firm that produces the entire market supply of a particular good or service.

IN THE NEWS

T-Shirt Shop Owner's Lament: Too Many T-Shirt Shops

The small Texas beach resort of South Padre Island boasts white sand, blue skies (much of the time), the buoyant waters of the Gulf of Mexico, and, at last count, more than 40 T-shirt shops.

And that's a problem for Shy Oogav, who owns one of those shops. "Every day you have to compete with other shops," he says. "And if you invent something new, they will copy you."

Padre Island illustrates a common condition in the

© Travelshots.com/Alamy

T-shirt industry—unbridled, ill-advised growth. Many people believe T-shirts are the ticket to a permanent vacation—far too many people. "In the past years, everything that closed opened up again as a T-shirt shop," says Maria C. Hall, executive director of the South Padre Island Chamber of Commerce.

Oogav, a 29-year-old immigrant from Israel, came to South Padre Island on vacation six years ago, thought he had found paradise, and stayed on. He subsequently got a job with one of the town's T-shirt shops, which then numbered fewer than a dozen. Now that he owns his own shop, and the competition has quadrupled, his paradise is lost. "I don't sleep at night," he says, morosely.

—Mark Pawlosky

Source: *The Wall Street Journal*, July 31, 1995, p. B1. Used with permission of Dow Jones & Company, Inc. via Copyright Clearance Center, Inc.

Analysis: The ability to earn a profit depends on how many other firms offer similar products. A perfectly competitive firm, facing numerous rivals, has difficulty maintaining prices or profits.

Figure 8.1 illustrates various **market structures.** At one extreme is the monopoly structure in which only one firm produces the entire supply of the good. At the other extreme is **perfect competition.** In perfect competition a great many firms supply the same good.

There are relatively few monopolies or perfectly competitive firms in the real world. Most of the 25 million businesses in the United States fall between these extremes. They're more accurately characterized by gradations of *imperfect* competition—markets in which competition exists, but individual firms still retain some discretionary power over prices. In a *duopoly*, two firms supply the entire market. In an *oligopoly*, like credit card services, a handful of firms (Visa, MasterCard, American Express) dominate. In *monopolistic competition*, like

> **market structure:** The number and relative size of firms in an industry.

> **perfect competition:** A market in which no buyer or seller has market power.

FIGURE 8.1
Market Structures

The number and relative size of firms producing a good vary across industries. Market structures range from perfect competition (a great many firms producing the same good) to monopoly (only one firm). Most real-world firms are along the continuum of *imperfect* competition. Included in that range are duopoly (two firms), oligopoly (a few firms), and monopolistic competition (many firms).

fast-food restaurants, there are enough firms to ensure some competition, but not so many as to preclude some limited monopoly-type power. We examine all these market structures in later chapters, after we establish the nature of perfect competition.

THE NATURE OF PERFECT COMPETITION

Industries can be classified by their structure—the number and relative size of the firms producing a specific good. As we'll see, the structure of an industry has a profound effect on market outcomes.

Structure

A perfectly competitive industry has several distinguishing characteristics, including

- *Many firms*—lots of firms are competing for consumer purchases.
- *Identical products*—the products of the different firms are identical, or nearly so.
- *Low entry barriers*—it's relatively easy to get into the business.

The T-shirt business has all these traits, which is why store owners have a hard time maintaining profits (see the previous News).

Price Takers

Because they always have to contend with a lot of competition, T-shirt shops can't increase profits by raising T-shirt prices. More than 1 billion T-shirts are sold in the United States each year by tens of thousands of retail outlets. In such a competitive industry the many individual firms that make up the industry are all *price takers:* they take the price the market sets. A competitive firm can sell all its output at the prevailing market price. If it boosts its price above that level, consumers will shop elsewhere. In this sense, a perfectly competitive firm has no **market power**—no ability to control the market price for the good it sells.

At first glance, it might appear that all firms have market power. After all, who's to stop a T-shirt shop from raising prices? The important concept here, however, is *market* price—that is, the price at which goods are actually sold. If one shop raises its price to $15 and 40 other shops sell the same T-shirts for $10, it won't sell many shirts, and maybe none at all.

You may confront the same problem if you try to sell this book at the end of the semester. You might want to resell this textbook for $80. But you'll discover that the bookstore won't buy it at that price. With many other students offering to sell their books, the bookstore knows it doesn't have to pay the $80 you're asking. Because you don't have any market power, you have to accept the going price if you want to sell this book. You are a price taker in this market.

The same kind of powerlessness is characteristic of the small wheat farmer. Like any producer, the lone wheat farmer can increase or reduce his rate of output by making alternative production decisions. But his decision won't affect the market price of wheat.

market power: The ability to alter the market price of a good or service.

Even the largest U.S. wheat farmers can't change the market price of wheat. The largest wheat farm produces nearly 100,000 bushels of wheat per year. But *2 billion* bushels of wheat are brought to market every year, so another 100,000 bushels simply won't be noticed. In other words, *the output of the lone farmer is so small relative to the market supply that it has no significant effect on the total quantity or price in the market.*

A distinguishing characteristic of *powerless* firms is that, individually, they can sell all the output they produce at the prevailing market price. We call all such producers **competitive firms;** they have no independent influence on market prices. *A perfectly competitive firm is one whose output is so small in relation to market volume that its output decisions have no perceptible impact on price.*

> **competitive firm:** A firm without market power, with no ability to alter the market price of the goods it produces.

Market Demand Curves vs. Firm Demand Curves

It's important to distinguish between the market demand curve and the demand curve confronting a particular firm. T-shirt shops don't contradict the law of demand. The quantity of T-shirts purchased in the market still depends on T-shirt prices. That is, the *market* demand curve for T-shirts is still downward-sloping. A single T-shirt shop faces a *horizontal* demand curve only because its share of the market is so small that changes in its output don't disturb market equilibrium.

Collectively, though, individual firms do count. If all 40 of the T-shirt shops on South Padre Island (see the previous News) were to increase shirt production at the same time, the market equilibrium would be disturbed. That is, a competitive market composed of individually powerless producers still sees a lot of action. The power here resides in the collective action of all the producers, however, not in the individual action of any one. Were T-shirt production to increase so abruptly, the shirts could be sold only at lower prices, in accordance with the downward-sloping nature of the *market* demand curve. Figure 8.2 illustrates the distinction between the actions of a single producer and those of the market. Notice that

- *The market demand curve for a product is always downward-sloping (law of demand).*
- *The demand curve confronting a perfectly competitive firm is horizontal.*

(a) The T-shirt market   **(b) Demand facing one shop**

PRICE (dollars per shirt)

Market supply

p_e Equilibrium price

Market demand

QUANTITY (thousand shirts per day)

p_i
$\rightarrow p_e$

Demand facing single firm

QUANTITY (shirts per day)

FIGURE 8.2
Market vs. Firm Demand

Consumer demand for any product is downward-sloping. The equilibrium price (p_e) of T-shirts is established by the intersection of *market* demand and *market* supply, as in the graph on the left. This market-established price is the only one at which an individual shop can sell T-shirts. If the shop owner asks a higher price (e.g., p_i in the graph on the right), no one will buy his shirts because they can buy identical T-shirts from other shops at p_e. But he can sell all his shirts at the market-set equilibrium price. The shop owner thus confronts a horizontal demand curve for his own output. (Notice the difference in market and individual shop quantities on the horizontal axes of the two graphs.)

THE PRODUCTION DECISION

A startling implication of Figure 8.2 is that *perfectly competitive firms don't make pricing decisions;* the *market* sets the prevailing price. All competitive firms do is *respond* to that market price. As price takers, they have only one decision to make: how much to produce. Choosing a rate of output is a firm's **production decision.** Should it produce all the output it can? Or should it produce at less than capacity?

Output and Revenues

In searching for the most desirable rate of output, focus on the distinction between total *revenue* and total *profit.* **Total revenue** is the price of the good multiplied by the quantity sold:

$$\text{Total revenue} = \text{Price} \times \text{Quantity}$$

Since a competitive firm can sell all its output at the market price (p_e), total revenue is a simple multiple of p_e. The total revenue of a T-shirt shop, for example, is the price of shirts (p_e) multiplied by the quantity sold. Figure 8.3 shows the total revenue curve that results from this multiplication. Note that *the total revenue curve of a perfectly competitive firm is an upward-sloping straight line with a slope equal to p_e.*

If a competitive firm wanted to maximize its total *revenue,* its production decision would be simple: it would always produce at capacity. Life isn't that simple, however; *the firm's goal is to maximize profits, not revenues.*

Output and Costs

To maximize profits, a firm must consider how increased production will affect *costs* as well as *revenues.* How do costs vary with the rate of output?

As we observed in Chapter 7, producers are saddled with certain costs in the **short run.** A T-shirt shop has to pay the rent every month no matter how few shirts it sells. The Low-Rider Jeans Corporation in Chapter 7 had to pay the rent on its factory and lease payments on its sewing machine. These **fixed costs** are incurred even if no output is produced. Once a firm starts producing output, it incurs **variable costs** as well.

Since profits depend on the *difference* between revenues and costs, the costs of added output will determine how much profit a producer can make. Figure 8.4 illustrates a typical total cost curve. *Total costs increase as output expands. But the rate of cost increase varies.* Hence the total cost curve is *not* linear. At first total costs rise slowly (notice the gradually declining slope until point z), then they increase more quickly (the rising slope after point z). This S-shaped curve reflects the *law of diminishing returns.* As we first observed in Chapter 7,

production decision: The selection of the short-run rate of output (with existing plants and equipment).

total revenue: The price of a product multiplied by the quantity sold in a given time period: $p \times q$.

short run: The period in which the quantity (and quality) of some inputs can't be changed.

fixed costs: Costs of production that don't change when the rate of output is altered, such as the cost of basic plants and equipment.

variable costs: Costs of production that change when the rate of output is altered, such as labor and material costs.

FIGURE 8.3
Total Revenue

Because a competitive firm can sell all its output at the prevailing price, its total revenue curve is linear. In this case, the market (equilibrium) price of T-shirts is assumed to be $8. Hence a shop's total revenue is equal to $8 multiplied by quantity sold. Total revenue is maximized at capacity output.

Price × (per Shirt)	Quantity (Shirts per Day)	= Total Revenue
$8	1	$ 8
8	2	16
8	3	24
8	4	32
8	5	40
8	6	48
8	7	56
8	8	64
8	9	72

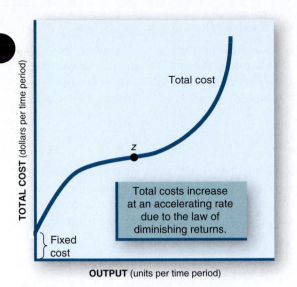

FIGURE 8.4
Total Cost

Total cost increases with output. The rate of increase isn't steady, however. Typically, the rate of cost increase slows initially, then speeds up. After point *z*, diminishing returns (rising marginal costs) cause accelerating costs. These accelerating costs limit the profit potential of increased output.

marginal costs (MC) often decline in the early stages of production and then increase as the available plants and equipment are used more intensively. These changes in marginal cost cause *total* costs to rise slowly at first, then to pick up speed as output increases.

You may suspect by now that the road to profits is not an easy one. It entails comparing ever-changing revenues with ever-changing costs. Figure 8.5 helps simplify the problem by bringing together typical total revenue and total cost curves. Notice how total costs exceed total revenues at high rates of output (beyond point *g*). As production capacity is approached, costs tend to skyrocket, offsetting any gain in sales revenue.

Total profit in Figure 8.5 is represented by the vertical distance between the two curves. Total costs in this case exceed total revenue at low rates of output (below *f*) as well as at very high rates (above *g*). The firm is profitable only at output rates between *f* and *g*.

Although all rates of output between *f* and *g* are profitable, they aren't *equally* profitable. A quick glance at Figure 8.5 confirms that the vertical distance between total revenue and total cost varies considerably within that range. ***The primary objective of the producer is to find that one particular rate of output that maximizes total profits.*** With a ruler, we could find it in Figure 8.5 by measuring the distance between the revenue and cost curves at all rates of output. In the real world, most producers need more practical guides to profit maximization.

marginal cost (MC):
The increase in total costs associated with a one-unit increase in production.

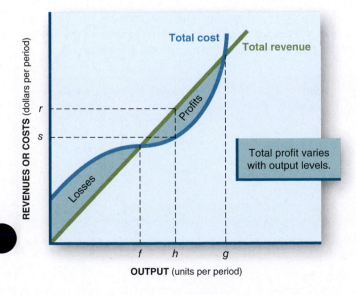

FIGURE 8.5
Total Profit

Profit is the *difference* between total revenue and total cost. It is represented as the vertical distance between the total revenue curve and the total cost curve. At output *h*, profit equals *r* minus *s*. The objective is to find the unique rate of output that *maximizes* profit.

PROFIT-MAXIMIZING RULE

The best single rule for maximizing profits in the short run is straightforward: never produce a unit of output that costs more than it brings in. By following this simple rule, a producer is likely to make the right production decision. We will see how this rule works by looking first at the revenue side of production ("what it brings in"), then at the cost side ("what it costs").

Marginal Revenue = Price

marginal revenue (MR):
The change in total revenue that results from a one-unit increase in the quantity sold.

In searching for the most profitable rate of output, we need to know what an additional unit of output will bring in—that is, how much it adds to the total revenue of the firm. In general, the contribution to total revenue of an additional unit of output is called **marginal revenue (MR)**. Marginal revenue is the *change* in total revenue that occurs when output is increased by one unit:

$$\text{Marginal revenue} = \frac{\text{Change in total revenue}}{\text{Change in output}}$$

To calculate marginal revenue, we compare the total revenues received before and after a one-unit increase in the rate of production; the *difference* between the two totals equals marginal revenue.

When the price of a product is constant, it's easy to compute marginal revenue. Suppose we're operating a catfish farm. Our product is catfish, sold at wholesale at the prevailing price of $13 per bushel. In this case, a one-unit increase in sales (one more bushel) increases total revenue by $13. As illustrated in Table 8.2, as long as the price of a product is constant, price and marginal revenue are the same. Hence, *for perfectly competitive firms, price equals marginal revenue.*

Marginal Cost

Keep in mind why we're breeding and selling catfish. It's not to maximize *revenues* but to maximize *profits*. To gauge profits, we need to know not only the price of fish but also how much each bushel costs to produce. As we saw in Chapter 7, the added cost of producing one more unit of a good is its *marginal cost*. Figure 8.6 summarizes the marginal costs associated with the production of catfish.

The production process for catfish farming is wonderfully simple. The factory is a pond; the rate of production is the number of fish harvested from the pond per day. A farmer can alter the rate of production at will, up to the breeding capacity of the pond. As Calvin Jones, a former schoolteacher now working on a Mississippi catfish farm, says, "You raise fish. You get them out of the pond and you sell them. That's pretty much all you do. There's no genius to it."[1]

Assume that the *fixed* cost of the pond is $10 per day. The fixed costs include the rental value of the pond and the cost of electricity for keeping the pond oxygenated so the fish can breathe. These fixed costs must be paid no matter how many fish the farmer harvests.

Phillip Gould/Corbis

Analysis: Fish farmers want to maximize profits.

TABLE 8.2
Total and Marginal Revenue

Marginal revenue (MR) is the *change* in total revenue associated with the sale of one more unit of output. A third bushel increases total revenue from $26 to $39; MR equals $13. If the price is constant (at $13 here), marginal revenue equals price.

Quantity Sold (Bushels per Day)	×	Price (per Bushel)	=	Total Revenue (per Day)	Marginal Revenue (per Bushel)
0	×	$13	=	$ 0	
1	×	13	=	13	$13
2	×	13	=	26	13
3	×	13	=	39	13
4	×	13	=	52	13

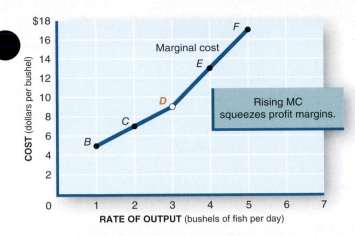

FIGURE 8.6
The Costs of Catfish Production

Marginal cost is the increase in total cost associated with a one-unit increase in production. When production expands from two to three units per day, total costs increase by $9 (from $22 to $31 per day). The marginal cost of the third bushel is therefore $9, as illustrated by point D in the graph.

	Rate of Output (Bushels per Day)	Total Cost (per Day)	Marginal Cost (per Day)	Average Cost (per Day)
A	0	$10	—	—
B	1	15	$ 5	$15.00
C	2	22	7	11.00
D	3	31	9	10.33
E	4	44	13	11.00
F	5	61	17	12.20

To harvest catfish from the pond, the farmer must incur additional costs. Labor is needed to net and sort the fish. The cost of labor is *variable,* depending on how much output the farmer decides to produce. If no fish are harvested, no variable costs are incurred.

The *marginal costs* of harvesting are the additional costs incurred to harvest *one* more basket of fish. Generally, we expect marginal costs to rise as the rate of production increases. The law of diminishing returns we encountered in Chapter 7 applies to catfish farming as well. As more labor is hired, each worker has less space (pond area) and capital (access to nets, sorting trays) to work with. Accordingly, it takes a little more labor time (marginal cost) to harvest each additional fish.

Figure 8.6 illustrates these marginal costs. Notice how the MC rises as the rate of output increases. At the output rate of 4 bushels per day (point *E*), marginal cost is $13. Hence the fourth bushel *increases* total costs by $13. The fifth bushel is even more expensive, with a marginal cost of $17.

Profit-Maximizing Rate of Output

We're now in a position to make a production decision. The rule about never producing anything that adds more to cost than it brings in can now be stated in more technical terms. Since price equals marginal revenue for competitive firms, we can base the production decision on a comparison of *price* and *marginal cost.* ***There are only three possible scenarios for MC and price:***

- **MC > p.** We don't want to produce an additional unit of output if its MC exceeds its price. If MC exceeds price, we're spending more to produce that extra unit than we're getting back: total profits will decline if we produce it.
- **p > MC.** The opposite is true when price exceeds MC. If an extra unit brings in more revenue than it costs to produce, it is *adding* to total profit. Total profits must increase in this case. Hence a competitive firm wants to expand the rate of production whenever price exceeds MC.

Profit Maximization

Price Level	Production Decision
Price > MC	Increase output
Price = MC	Maintain output (profits maximized)
Price < MC	Decrease output

TABLE 8.3
Short-Run Profit Maximization Rules for Competitive Firm

The relationship between price and marginal cost dictates short-run production decisions. For competitive firms, profits are maximized at that rate of output where price = MC.

profit maximization rule:
Produce at that rate of output where marginal revenue equals marginal cost.

- **p = MC.** Since we want to expand output when price exceeds MC and contract output if price is less than MC, the profit-maximizing rate of output is easily found. *For perfectly competitive firms, profits are maximized at the rate of output where price equals marginal cost.* The implications of this **profit maximization rule** are summarized in Table 8.3.

Figure 8.7 illustrates the application of our profit maximization rule in catfish farming. The prevailing wholesale price of catfish is $13 a bushel. At this price we can sell all the catfish we can produce, up to our short-run capacity. The catfish can't be sold at a higher price because lots of farmers raise catfish and sell them for $13 (see the News on the next page). If we try to charge a higher price, consumers will buy their fish from other vendors. Hence we confront a horizontal demand curve at the price of $13.

FIGURE 8.7
Maximization of Profits for a Competitive Firm

A competitive firm maximizes total profit at the output rate where MC = p. If MC is less than price, the firm can increase profits by producing more. If MC exceeds price, the firm should reduce output. In this case, profit maximization occurs at an output of 4 bushels per day.

	(1) Number of Bushels (per Day)	(2) Price	(3) Total Revenue	−	(4) Total Cost	=	(5) Total Profit	(6) Marginal Revenue	(7) Marginal Cost
A	0	$13	$ 0		$10		−$10	—	—
B	1	13	13		15		− 2	$13	$ 5
C	2	13	26		22		+ 4	13	7
D	3	13	39		31		+ 8	13	9
E	4	13	52		44		+ 8	13	13
F	5	13	65		61		+ 4	13	17

Southern Farmers Hooked on New Cash Crop

Catfish are replacing crops and dairy farming as a cash industry in much of the South, particularly in Mississippi's Delta region, where 80 percent of farm-bred catfish are grown.

Production has skyrocketed in the United States from 16 million pounds in 1975 to an expected 340 million pounds this year.

The business is growing among farmers in Alabama, Arkansas, and Louisiana.

Catfish farming is similar to other agriculture, experts say. One thing is the same: it takes money to get started.

"If you have a good row-crop farmer, you have a good catfish farmer," says James Hoffman of Farm Fresh Catfish Co. in Hollandale, Mississippi. "But you can't take a poor row-crop farmer and make him a good catfish farmer."

Greensboro, Alabama, catfish farmer Steve Hollingsworth says he spends $18,000 a week on feed for the 1 million catfish in his ponds.

"Each of the ponds has about 100,000 fish," he says. "You get about 60 cents per fish, so that's about $60,000."

The investment can be lost very quickly "if something's wrong in that pond," like an inadequate oxygen level, Hollingsworth says.

"You can be 15 minutes too late getting here, and all your fish are gone," he says.

—Mark Mayfield

Source: *USA TODAY.* December 5, 1989, p. 3A. Reprinted with permission.

Analysis: People go into a competitive business like catfish farming to earn a profit. Once in business, they try to maximize total profits by equating price and marginal cost.

web analysis

Go to **www.uscatfish.com** for more information about the U.S. catfish industry.

The costs of producing catfish were examined in Figure 8.6. The key concept illustrated here is marginal cost. The MC curve slopes upward in conventional fashion.

Figure 8.7 also depicts the total revenues, costs, and profits of alternative production rates. Study the table first. Notice that the firm loses $10 per day if it produces no fish (row *A*). At zero output, total revenue is zero ($p \times q = 0$). However, the firm must still contend with fixed costs of $10 per day. Total profit—total revenue minus total cost—is therefore *minus* $10; the firm incurs a loss.

Row *B* of the table shows how this loss is reduced when 1 bushel of fish is harvested per day. The production and sale of 1 bushel per day bring in $13 of total revenue (column 3). The total cost of producing 1 bushel per day is $15 (column 4). Hence the total loss at an output rate of 1 bushel per day is $2 (column 5). This may not be what we hoped for, but it's certainly better than the $10 loss incurred at zero output.

$p >$ MC: Expand. The superiority of harvesting 1 bushel per day rather than none is also evident in columns 6 and 7 of row *B*. The first bushel produced has a *marginal revenue* of $13. Its *marginal cost* is only $5. Hence it brings in more added revenue than it adds to costs. Under these circumstances—whenever price exceeds MC—output should definitely be expanded. That is one of the decision rules summarized in Table 8.3.

The excess of price over MC for the first unit of output is also illustrated by the graph in Figure 8.7. Point MR_B ($13) lies above MC_B ($5); the *difference* between these two points measures the contribution that the first bushel makes to the total profits of the firm. In this case, that contribution equals $13 - $5 = $8, and production losses are reduced by that amount when the rate of output is increased from zero to 1 bushel per day.

As long as price exceeds MC, increases in the rate of output increase total profit. Notice what happens to profits when the rate of output is increased from 1 to 2 bushels per day (row *C*). The price (MR) of the second bushel is $13; its MC is $7. Therefore it *adds* $6 to total profits. Instead of losing $2 per day, the firm is now making a profit of $4 per day.

The firm can make even more profits by expanding the rate of output further. The marginal revenue of the third bushel is $13; its marginal cost is $9 (row *D* of the table). Therefore, the third bushel makes a $4 contribution to profits.

MC = *p*: Max Profit. This firm will never make huge profits. For the fourth unit of output price and MC both equal $13. It doesn't contribute to total profits, and it doesn't subtract from them. The fourth unit of output represents the highest rate of output the firm desires. *At the rate of output where price = MC, total profits of the firm are maximized.*[2]

MC > *p*: Contract. Notice what happens if we expand output beyond 4 bushels per day. The price of the fifth bushel is still $13; its MC is $17. The fifth bushel adds more to costs than to revenue. If we produce that fifth bushel, total profit will decline by $4. In Figure 8.7 the MC curve lies above the price line at all output levels in excess of 4. The lesson here is clear: *output should not be increased if MC exceeds price.*

The correct production decision—the profit-maximizing decision—is shown in Figure 8.7 by the intersection of the price and MC curves. At this intersection, price equals MC and profits are maximized. If we produced less, we'd be giving up potential profits. If we produced more, total profits would also fall (review Table 8.3).

Adding Up Profits

To reach the right production decision, we've relied on *marginal* revenues and costs. Having found the desired rate of output, however, we may want to take a closer look at the profits we are accumulating. Figure 8.8 provides two different ways of viewing our success.

The first view focuses on *total* revenues and *total* costs. Total profits are represented in Figure 8.8*a* by the vertical distance between the total revenue and total cost curves. This is a straightforward interpretation of our definition of total profits:

$$\text{Total profits} = \text{TR} - \text{TC}$$

(a) Computing profits with total revenue and total cost

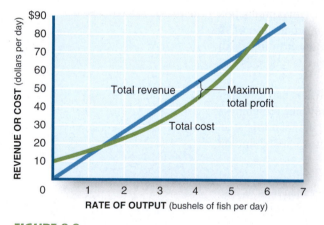

(b) Computing profits with price and average total cost

FIGURE 8.8
Alternative Views of Total Profit

Total profit can be computed as TR − TC, as in part *a*. Or it can be computed as profit *per unit* (*p* − ATC) multiplied by the quantity sold. This is illustrated in part *b* by the shaded rectangle. To find the profit-maximizing output, we could use either of these graphs or just the price and MC curves in Figure 8.7.

[2]In this case, profits are the same at output levels of 3 and 4 bushels. Given the choice between the two levels, most firms will choose the higher level. By producing the extra unit of output, the firm increases its customer base. This not only denies rival firms an additional sale but also provides some additional cushion when the economy slumps. Also, corporate size may connote both prestige and power. In any case, the higher output level defines the *limit* to maximum profit production.

The vertical distance between the TR and TC curves is maximized at the output of 4 bushels per day.

A second view of the same profits focuses on *average* costs and price. Total profit is equal to *average* profit per unit multiplied by the number of units produced. Profit *per unit*, in turn, is equal to price *minus* average total cost:

$$\text{Profit per unit} = p - \text{ATC}$$

The price of catfish is illustrated in Figure 8.8*b* by the horizontal price line at $13. The average total cost of producing catfish is shown by the ATC curve. Like the ATC curve we encountered in Chapter 7, this one has a U shape. The *difference* between price and average cost—profit per unit—is illustrated by the vertical distance between the price and ATC curves. At 4 bushels per day, for example, profit per unit equals $13 − $11 = $2.

To compute *total* profits, we note that

$$\text{Total profits} = \text{Profit per unit} \times \text{Quantity}$$
$$= (p - \text{ATC}) \times q$$

In this case, the 4 bushels generate a profit of $2 each, for a *total* profit of $8 per day. *Total* profits are illustrated in Figure 8.8*b* by the shaded rectangle. [Recall that the area of a rectangle is equal to its height (profit per unit) multiplied by its width (the quantity sold).]

Profit per unit is not only used to compute total profits but is often also of interest in its own right. Businesspeople like to cite statistics on "markups," which are a crude index to per-unit profits. However, *the profit-maximizing producer never seeks to maximize per-unit profits. What counts is* **total** *profits, not the amount of profit per unit.* This is the old $5 ice cream problem again. You might be able to maximize profit per unit if you could sell 1 cone for $5, but you would make a lot more money if you sold 100 cones at a per-unit profit of only 50 cents each.

Similarly, *the profit-maximizing producer has no desire to produce at that rate of output where ATC is at a minimum.* Minimum ATC does represent least-cost production. But additional units of output, even though they raise average costs, will increase total profits. This is evident in Figure 8.8; price exceeds MC for some output to the right of minimum ATC (the bottom of the U). Therefore, total profits are increasing as we increase the rate of output beyond the point of minimum average costs. Figure 8.9 illustrates the distinctions between these different markers.

FIGURE 8.9
Different Goals

Businesses seek to maximize total profits, not profit per unit or total revenue. Therefore, they pursue the short-run output rate q_b, not the output rates q_a or q_c.

THE SHUTDOWN DECISION

The rule established for short-run profit maximization doesn't guarantee any profits. By equating price and marginal cost, the competitive producer is only assured of achieving the *optimal* output. This is the best possible rate of output for the firm, given the existing market price and the (short-run) costs of production.

But what if the best possible rate of output generates a loss? What should the producer do in this case? Keep producing output? Or shut down the factory and find something else to do?

The first instinct may be to shut down the factory to stop the flow of red ink. But this isn't necessarily the wisest course of action. It may be smarter to keep operating a money-losing operation than to shut it down.

The rationale for this seemingly ill-advised course of action resides in the fixed costs of production. ***Fixed costs must be paid even if all output ceases.*** The firm must still pay rent on the factory and equipment even if it doesn't use these inputs. That's why we call such costs "fixed."

The persistence of fixed costs casts an entirely different light on the shutdown decision. Since fixed costs will have to be paid in any case, the question becomes: Which option creates greater losses? Does the firm lose more money by continuing to operate (and incurring a loss) or by shutting down (and incurring a loss equal to fixed costs)? In these terms, the answer becomes clear: ***A firm should shut down only if the losses from continuing production exceed fixed costs.*** This happens when total revenue is less than total *variable* cost.

Price vs. AVC

The shutdown decision can be made without explicit reference to fixed costs. Figure 8.10 shows how. The relationship to focus on is between the price of a good and its average *variable* cost.

The curves in Figure 8.10 represent the short-run costs and potential demand curves for catfish. As long as the price of catfish is $13 per bushel, the typical firm will produce

FIGURE 8.10

The Firm's Shutdown Point

A firm should cease production only if total revenue is lower than total *variable* cost. The shutdown decision may be based on a comparison of price and AVC. If the price of catfish per bushel was $13, a firm would earn a profit at point *X* in part *a*. At a price of $9 (point *Y* in part *b*), the firm is losing money (*p* is less than ATC) but is more than covering all variable costs (*p* is greater than AVC). If the price falls to $4 per bushel, as in part *c*, output should cease (*p* is less than AVC).

4 bushels a day, as determined by the intersection of the MC and MR (= price) curves (point *X* in part *a*). In this case, price ($13) exceeds average *total* cost ($11), and catfish farming is profitable.

The situation wouldn't look so good, however, if the market price of catfish fell to $9. Following the rule for profit maximization, the firm would be led to point *Y* in part *b*, where MC intersects the new demand (price) curve. At this intersection, the firm would produce 3 bushels per day. But total revenues would no longer cover total costs, as can be seen from the fact that the ATC curve now lies *above* the price line. The ATC of producing 3 bushels is $10.33 (Figure 8.6); price is $9. Hence the firm is incurring a loss of $4 per day (3 bushels at a loss of $1.33 each).

Should the firm stay in business under the circumstances? The answer is yes. Recall that the catfish farmer has already dug the pond and installed equipment at a (fixed) cost of $10 per day. The producer will have to pay these fixed costs whether or not the machinery is used. Stopping production would result in a loss amounting to $10 per day. Staying in business, even when catfish prices fall to $9 each, generates a loss of only $4 a day. In this case, *where price exceeds average variable cost but not average total cost, the profit maximization rule minimizes losses.*

The Shutdown Point

If the price of catfish falls far enough, the producer may be better off ceasing production altogether. Suppose the price of catfish fell to $4 per bushel (Figure 8.10*c*). A price this low doesn't even cover the variable cost of producing 1 bushel per day ($5). Continued production of even 1 bushel per day would imply a total loss of $11 per day ($10 of fixed costs *plus* $1 of variable costs). Higher rates of output would lead to still greater losses. Hence the firm should shut down production, even though that action implies a loss of $10 per day. In all cases *where price doesn't cover average variable costs at any rate of output, production should cease.* Thus the **shutdown point** occurs where price is equal to minimum average *variable* cost. Any lower price will result in losses larger than fixed costs. In Figure 8.10, the shutdown point occurs at a price of $5, where the MC and AVC curves intersect.

shutdown point: That rate of output where price equals minimum AVC.

THE INVESTMENT DECISION

When a firm shuts down, it doesn't necessarily leave (exit) the industry. General Motors still produces cars even though it idled 15 of its plants in 2009 (see the News on the following page). *The shutdown decision is a **short-run** response.* It's based on the fixed costs of an established plant and the variable costs of operating it.

Ideally, a producer would never get into a money-losing business in the first place. Entry was based on an **investment decision** that the producer now regrets. *Investment decisions are **long-run** decisions,* however, and the firm now must pay for its bad luck or poor judgment. The investment decision entails the assumption of fixed costs (e.g., the lease of the factory); once the investment is made, the short-run production decision is designed to make the best possible use of those fixed inputs. The short-run profit-maximizing rule we've discussed applies only to this second decision; it assumes that a production unit exists. The News on the next page shows the contrast between production and investment decisions: GM *idled* its factories; Dell permanently *closed* its factory in Texas.

The investment decision is of enormous importance to producers. The fixed costs that we've ignored in the production decision represent the producers' (or the stockholders') investment in the business. If they're going to avoid an economic loss, they have to generate at least enough revenue to recoup their investment—that is, the cost of (fixed) plants and equipment. Failure to do so will result in a net loss, despite allegiance to our profit-maximizing rule.

Whether fixed costs count, then, depends on the decision being made. For producers trying to decide how best to utilize the resources they've purchased or leased, fixed costs no

investment decision: The decision to build, buy, or lease plants and equipment; to enter or exit an industry.

long run: A period of time long enough for all inputs to be varied (no fixed costs).

GM to Close 15 Plants for 9 Weeks

DETROIT—In what appears to be a record voluntary shutdown, General Motors plans to essentially quit making cars and trucks in the United States for nine weeks from mid-May through July.

According to two sources with direct knowledge, who did not want to be identified because no official announcement had been made, the plan is to shut 15 of GM's 21 North American car and truck assembly plants, most of them in the United States.

GM will meet with United Auto Workers leaders today and Friday to spell out details.

The shutdown is aimed at cutting costs and shrinking a glut of unsold vehicles at dealers.

—Sharon Silke Carty and James R. Healey

Source: *USA TODAY.* April 23, 2009, p. 1A. Reprinted with permission.

Dell Plans to Close Plant in Texas

Dell Inc. said that it will close one of its Texas computer-manufacturing plants and is mulling options, including a possible sale, of its financial services group.

The moves, which will eliminate about 900 jobs, are the latest efforts by the Round Rock, Texas, personal computer maker to turn itself around and are part of the company's stated goal to cut $3 billion in annual expenses over three years.

—Justin Scheck

Source: "Dell to Close Texas Plant, Weighs Shutting Finance Group," *The Wall Street Journal,* April 1, 2008, p. B4. Used with permission of Dow Jones & Company, Inc. via Copyright Clearance Center, Inc.

Analysis: GM's decision to idle plants was a short-run *shutdown* decision; it is still in business. Dell, by contrast, made a long-run decision to cease operations and *exit* a specific market.

longer enter the decision-making process. For producers deciding whether to enter business, sign a lease, or replace existing machinery and plants, fixed costs count very much. Businesspeople will proceed with an investment only if the *anticipated* profits are large enough to compensate for the effort and risk undertaken.

Long-Run Costs

When businesspeople make an investment decision, they confront not one set of cost figures but many. A plant not yet built can be designed for various rates of production and alternative technologies. In making long-run decisions, a producer isn't bound to one size of plant or to a particular mix of tools and machinery. In the long run, one can be flexible. In general, *a producer will want to build, buy, or lease a plant that's the most efficient for the anticipated rate of output.* This is the (dis)economy of scale phenomenon we discussed in the previous chapter. Once the right plant size is selected, the producer may proceed with the problem of short-run profit maximization. Once production is started, she can only hope that the investment decision was a good one and that a shutdown can be avoided.

DETERMINANTS OF SUPPLY

Whether the time frame is the short run or the long run, the central force in production decisions is the quest for profits. Producers will go into production—incur fixed costs—only if they see the potential for economic profits. Once in business, they'll expand the rate of output so long as profits are increasing. They'll shut down—cease production—when revenues don't at least cover variable costs (operating loss exceeds fixed costs).

Nearly anyone could make money with these principles if given complete information on costs and revenues. What renders the road to fortune less congested is the general absence of such complete information. In the real world, production decisions involve considerably more risk. People often don't know how much profit or loss they'll incur until it's too late to alter production decisions. Consequently, businesspeople are compelled to make a reasoned guess about prices and costs, then proceed. By way of summary, we can identify the major influences that will shape their short- and long-run decisions on how much output to supply to the market.

Short-Run Determinants

A competitive firm's short-run production decisions are dominated by marginal costs. Hence the quantity of a good supplied will be affected by all forces that alter MC. Specifically, *the determinants of a firm's supply include*

- *The price of factor inputs.*
- *Technology* (the available production function).
- *Expectations* (for costs, sales, technology).
- *Taxes and subsidies.*

Each determinant affects a producer's ability and willingness to supply output at any particular price.

The price of factor inputs determines how much the producer must pay for resources used in production. Technology determines how much output the producer will get from each unit of input. Expectations are critical because they express producers' perceptions of what future costs, prices, sales, and profits are likely to be. And finally, taxes and subsidies may alter costs or the amount of profit a firm gets to keep.

The Short-Run Supply Curve. By using the familiar *ceteris paribus* assumption, we can isolate the effect of price on supply decisions. In other words, we can draw a short-run **supply curve** the same way we earlier constructed consumer demand curves. In this case, the forces we assume constant are input prices, technology, expectations, and taxes. The only variable we allow to change is the price of the product itself.

Figure 8.11 illustrates the response of quantity supplied to a change in price. Notice the critical role of marginal costs: *the marginal cost curve is the short-run supply curve for a competitive firm.* Recall our basic profit maximization rule. A competitive producer wants to supply a good only if its price exceeds its marginal cost. Hence marginal cost defines the lower limit for an "acceptable" price. A catfish farmer is willing and able to produce 4 bushels per day only if the price of a bushel is $13 (point X). If the price of catfish dropped to $9, the *quantity* supplied would fall to 3 (point Y). The marginal cost curve tells us what the quantity supplied would be at all other prices as well. As long as price exceeds minimum AVC (the shutdown point), the MC curve summarizes the response of a producer to price changes: it *is* the short-run supply curve of a perfectly competitive firm.

supply curve: A curve describing the quantities of a good a producer is willing and able to sell (produce) at alternative prices in a given time period, *ceteris paribus.*

FIGURE 8.11
A Competitive Firm's Short-Run Supply Curve

For competitive firms, marginal cost defines the lowest price a firm will accept for a given quantity of output. In this sense, the marginal cost curve *is* the supply curve; it tells us how quantity supplied will respond to price. At $p = \$13$, the quantity supplied is 4; at $p = \$9$, the quantity supplied is 3.

Recall, however, that the firm will shut down if price falls below minimum average variable cost. The supply curve does not exist below minimum AVC ($5 in this case).

The shape of the marginal cost curve provides a basic foundation for the *law of supply.* Because marginal costs tend to rise as output expands, an increase in output makes sense only if the price of that output rises. If the price does rise, it's profitable to increase the quantity supplied.

Supply Shifts

All the forces that shape the short-run supply curve are subject to change. Factor prices change; technology changes; expectations change; and tax laws get revised. ***If any determinant of supply changes, the supply curve shifts.***

An increase in wage rates, for example, would raise the marginal cost of producing catfish. This would shift the supply curve upward, making it more expensive for producers to supply larger quantities at any given price. An increase in the price of catfish feed has the same effect, as the accompanying News dramatically illustrates.

An improvement in technology would have the opposite effect. By increasing productivity, new technology lowers the marginal cost of producing a good. The supply curve shifts downward.

IN THE NEWS

As Price of Grain Rises, Catfish Farms Dry Up

LELAND, MISS.—Catfish farmers across the South, unable to cope with the soaring cost of corn and soybean feed, are draining their ponds.

"It's a dead business," said John Dillard, who pioneered the commercial farming of catfish in the late 1960s. Last year Dillard & Company raised 11 million fish. Next year it will raise none. . . .

As for his 55 employees? "Those jobs are gone."

Corn and soybeans have nearly tripled in price in the last two years for many reasons: harvest shortfalls, increasing demand by the Asian middle class, government mandates for corn to produce ethanol, and, most recently, flooding in the Midwest.

—David Streitfeld

Source: *The New York Times*, July 18, 2008. © 2008 All rights reserved. Used with permission.

Analysis: An increase in the price of factor inputs shifts the firm's MC curve upward. In this case, higher input costs forced firms to actually shut down.

Tax Effects

Changes in taxes will also alter supply behavior. But not all taxes have the same effect; some alter short-run supply behavior, whereas others affect only long-run supply decisions.

Property Taxes. Property taxes are levied by local governments on land and buildings. The tax rate is typically some small fraction (e.g., 1 percent) of total value. Hence the owner of a $10 million factory might have to pay $100,000 per year in property taxes.

Property taxes have to be paid regardless of whether the factory is used. Hence **property taxes are a fixed cost** for the firm. These additional fixed costs increase total costs and thus shift the average total cost (ATC) upward, as in Figure 8.12a.

Notice that the MC curve doesn't move when property taxes are imposed. Property taxes aren't based on the quantity of output produced. Accordingly, the production decision of the firm isn't affected by property taxes. The quantity q_1 in Figure 8.12a remains the optimal rate of output even after a property tax is introduced.

Although the optimal output remains at q_1, the profitability of the firm is reduced by the property tax. Profit per unit has been reduced by the upward shift of the ATC curve. If property taxes reduce profits too much, firms may move to a low-tax jurisdiction or another industry (investment decisions).

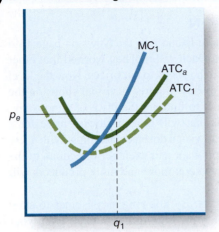

(a) Property taxes affect fixed costs but not marginal costs.

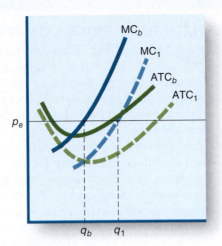

(b) Payroll taxes alter marginal costs.

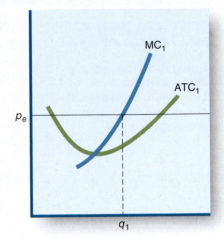

(c) Profits taxes don't change costs.

FIGURE 8.12
Impact of Taxes on Business Decisions

(a) Property taxes are a fixed cost for the firm. Since they don't affect marginal costs, they leave the optimal rate of output (q_1) unchanged. Property taxes raise average costs, however, and so reduce profits. Lower profits may alter investment decisions.

(b) Payroll taxes add directly to marginal costs and so reduce the optimal rate of output (to q_b). Payroll taxes also increase average costs and lower total and per-unit profits.

(c) Taxes on profits are neither a fixed cost nor a variable cost since they depend on the existence of profits. They don't affect marginal costs or price and so leave the optimal rate of output (q_1) unchanged. By reducing after-tax profits, however, such taxes lessen incentives to invest.

Payroll Taxes. Payroll taxes have very different effects on business decisions. Payroll taxes are levied on the wages paid by the firm. Employers must pay, for example, a 7.65 percent Social Security tax on the wages they pay (employees pay an identical amount). This tax is used to finance Social Security retirement benefits. Other payroll taxes are levied by federal and state governments to finance unemployment and disability benefits.

All payroll taxes add to the cost of hiring labor. In the absence of a tax, a worker might cost the firm $8 per hour. Once Social Security and other taxes are levied, the cost of labor increases to $8 plus the amount of tax. Hence $8-per-hour labor might end up costing the firm $9 or more. In other words, *payroll taxes increase marginal costs.* This is illustrated in Figure 8.12b by the upward shift of the MC curve.

Notice how payroll taxes change the production decision. The new MC curve (MC_b) intersects the price line at a lower rate of output (q_b). Thus payroll taxes tend to reduce output and employment.

Profits Taxes. Taxes are also levied on the profits of a business. Such taxes are very different from either property or payroll taxes since profit taxes are paid only when profits are made. Thus they are neither a fixed cost nor a variable cost! As Figure 8.12c indicates, neither the MC nor the ATC curve moves when a profits tax is imposed. The only difference is that the firm now gets to keep less of its profits, instead "sharing" its profits with the government.

Although a profits tax has no direct effect on marginal or average costs, it does reduce the take-home (after-tax) profits of a business. This may reduce investments in new businesses. For this reason, many people urge the government to reduce corporate tax rates and so encourage increased investment.

web analysis

Looking at Internet growth gives insights to e-commerce trends. Visit **www.internetworldstats. com** for detail on worldwide Internet usage.

INTERNET-BASED PRICE COMPETITION

Ten years ago the T-shirt shop owners on South Padre Island (see the News on page 169) had to worry only about the other 40 shops at that beach resort. They worried that other shops might offer T-shirts at lower prices, forcing all the shops to cut prices. Now the level of competition is much higher. Beachgoers can now buy T-shirts at virtual shops on the Internet. Indeed, consumers can click on the Internet to find out the price of almost anything. There are even electronic shopping services that will find the lowest price for a product. Want a better deal on a car? You don't have to visit a dozen dealerships. With a few clicks, you can find the lowest price for the car you want and even get directions to the appropriate dealer. In fact, you don't have to go anywhere: more and more producers will sell you their products directly over the Internet.

E-commerce intensifies competition in many ways. By allowing a consumer to shop worldwide, the Net vastly increases the number of firms in a virtual market. Even your campus bookstore now has to worry about textbook prices available at Amazon.com, Barnes and Noble, and other online booksellers.

Electronic commerce also reduces transaction costs. Retailers don't need stores or catalogs to display their products, and they can greatly reduce inventories by producing to order. This is how Dell computer supplies the $20 million of computers it sells per day online.

Electronic retailers also get a tax break. Transactions on the net aren't subject to sales taxes. Hence electronic retailers can offer products at lower prices without cutting profit margins, especially in high-tax states.

The evident advantages of e-commerce have made it the virtual mall of choice for many consumers. In 2010, consumers spent over $200 billion on electronic purchases. That was only 4 percent of total retail spending. But the trend is what counts. With Internet sales accelerating every year, e-commerce is sure to intensify price competition in the economy tomorrow.

SUMMARY

- Economic profit is the difference between total revenue and total cost. Total economic cost includes the value (opportunity cost) of *all* inputs used in production, not just those inputs for which an explicit payment is made. LO8-1

- A perfectly competitive firm is a *price taker*. It sells its output at the prevaling market price. It effectively confronts a horizontal demand for its output (even though the *market* demand for the product is downward-sloping). LO8-2

- Competitive firms don't make pricing decisions, only production decisions. LO8-2

- The short-run objective of a firm is to maximize profits from the operation of its existing facilities (fixed costs). For a competitive firm, the profit-maximizing output occurs at the point where marginal cost equals price (marginal revenue). LO8-3

- A firm may incur a loss even at the optimal rate of output. It shouldn't shut down, however, so long as price exceeds average *variable* cost. If revenues at least cover variable costs, the firm's operating loss is less than its fixed costs. LO8-4

- In the long run there are no fixed costs, and the firm may choose any-sized plant it wants. The decision to incur fixed costs (i.e., build, buy, or lease a plant) or to enter or exit an industry is an investment decision. LO8-5

- A competitive firm's supply curve is identical to its marginal cost curve (above the shutdown point at minimum average variable cost). In the short run, the quantity supplied will rise or fall with price. LO8-6

- The determinants of supply include the price of inputs, technology, taxes, and expectations. Should any of these determinants change, the firm's supply curve will shift. LO8-6

- Business taxes alter business behavior. Property taxes raise fixed costs; payroll taxes increase marginal costs. Profit taxes raise neither fixed costs nor marginal costs but diminish the take-home (after-tax) profits of a business. LO8-6

- The Internet has created virtual stores that intensify price competition. LO8-2

Key Terms

profit	perfect competition	marginal cost (MC)
economic cost	market power	marginal revenue (MR)
explicit cost	competitive firm	profit-maximization rule
implicit cost	production decision	shutdown point
economic profit	total revenue	investment decision
normal profit	short run	long run
monopoly	fixed costs	supply curve
market structure	variable costs	

Questions for Discussion

1. What economic costs will a large corporation likely overlook when computing its profits? How about the owner of a family-run business or farm? LO8-1
2. How can the demand curve facing a firm be horizontal if the market demand curve is downward-sloping? LO8-2
3. How many fish should a commercial fisher try to catch in a day? Should he catch as many as possible or return to dock before filling the boat with fish? Under what economic circumstances should he not even take the boat out? LO8-3
4. If a firm is incurring an economic loss, would society be better off if the firm shut down? Would the firm want to shut down? Explain. LO8-4
5. Why will the profit-maximizing rate of output for a profitable firm typically be larger than the rate of output that minimizes average total cost? LO8-3
6. What rate of output is appropriate for a nonprofit corporation (such as a hospital)? LO8-3
7. What costs did GM eliminate when it shut down its plants? (News, p. 182.) How about Dell? LO8-4
8. What was the opportunity cost of Hiroshi Fujishige's farm? (See News, p. 167.) Is society better off with another Disney theme park? Explain. LO8-1
9. Is Apple Computer a perfectly competitive firm? Explain your answer. LO8-2
10. If a perfectly competitive firm raises its price above the prevailing market rate, how much of its sales might it lose? Why? Can a competitive firm ever raise its prices? If so, when? LO8-2
11. Under what conditions would a firm decide to shut down in the short run but remain invested in the market in the long run? LO8-5
12. How does an employer-paid Social Security tax on wages affect a competitive firm's supply curve? LO8-6

! **web activities** to accompany this chapter can be found on the Online Learning Center:
http://www.mhhe.com/schiller13e

 mobile app Visit your mobile app store and download the Schiller: Study Econ app *today*!

PROBLEMS FOR CHAPTER 8

Name: _____

LO8-1 1. If the owner of the Table 8.1 drugstore hired a manager for $12 an hour to take his place, how much of a change would show up in

   (*a*) Accounting profits? _____
   (*b*) Economic profits? _____

LO8-1 2. If the price of catfish fell from $13 to $9 per bushel, use Figure 8.7 to determine the

   (*a*) Profit-maximizing output. _____
   (*b*) Profit or loss per bushel. _____
   (*c*) Total profit or loss. _____

LO8-2 3. (*a*) Complete the following cost and revenue schedules:

Quantity	Price	Total Revenue	Total Cost	Marginal Cost
0	$60	_____	$ 50	_____
1	60	_____	70	_____
2	60	_____	110	_____
3	60	_____	170	_____
4	60	_____	240	_____
5	60	_____	320	_____

   (*b*) Graph MC and *p*.
   (*c*) What rate of output maximizes profit? _____
   (*d*) What is MC at that rate of output? _____

LO8-2 4. Complete the following cost schedules:

Quantity	0	1	2	3	4	5	6	7
Total cost	$9	$12	$16	$21	$30	$40	$52	$66
ATC	___	___	___	___	___	___	___	___
MC	___	___	___	___	___	___	___	___

Assuming the price of this product is $10, at what output rate is

   (*a*) Total revenue maximized? _____
   (*b*) ATC minimized? _____
   (*c*) Profit per unit maximized? _____
   (*d*) Total profit maximized? _____

LO8-3 5. Assume that the price of silk ties in a perfectly competitive market is $19 and that the typical firm confronts the following costs:

Quantity (ties per day)	0	1	2	3	4	5	6	7	8	9	10
Total cost	$10	$17	$26	$37	$50	$65	$82	$101	$122	$145	$170

   (*a*) What is the profit-maximizing rate of output for the firm? _____
   (*b*) How much profit does the firm earn at that rate of output? _____
   (*c*) If the price of ties fell to $15, how many ties should the firm produce? _____
   (*d*) At what price should the firm shut down? _____

LO8-6 6. Using the data from Problem 5 (at the original price of $19), determine how many ties the producer would supply if

   (*a*) A tax of $2 per tie were collected from the producer. _____
   (*b*) A property tax of $2 were levied. _____
   (*c*) Profits were taxed at 50 percent. _____

LO8-6 7. Illustrate on the accompanying graph the News on page 184.

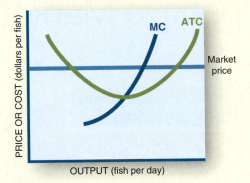

OUTPUT (fish per day)

LO8-4 8. Complete the following table:

Output	Total Cost	Marginal Cost	Average Total Cost	Average Variable Cost
0	$100	_____	_____	_____
5	110	_____	_____	_____
10	130	_____	_____	_____
15	170	_____	_____	_____
20	220	_____	_____	_____
25	290	_____	_____	_____
30	380	_____	_____	_____
35	490	_____	_____	_____

According to the table above,

(a) If the price is $8, how much output will the firm supply? _____

(b) How much profit or loss will it make? _____

(c) At what price will the firm shut down? _____

LO8-5 9. A firm has leased plant and equipment to produce video game cartridges, which can be sold in unlimited quantities at $21 each. The following figures describe the associated costs of production:

Rate of output (per day)	0	1	2	3	4	5	6	7	8
Total cost (per day)	$50	$55	$62	$75	$96	$125	$162	$203	$248

(a) How much are fixed costs? _____

(b) Draw total revenue and cost curves on the graphs here.

(c) Draw the average total cost (ATC), marginal cost (MC), and demand curves of the firm.

(d) What is the profit-maximizing rate of output? _____

(e) Should the producer stay in business? _____

(f) What is the size of the loss if production continues? _____

(g) How much is lost if the firm shuts down? _____

Competitive Markets

LEARNING OBJECTIVES

After reading this chapter, you should know

LO9-1. The market characteristics of perfect competition.

LO9-2. How prices are established in competitive markets.

LO9-3. Why long-run economic profits approach zero in competitive markets.

LO9-4. How society benefits from market competition.

Catfish farmers in the South are very upset. They invested millions of dollars converting cotton farms into breeding ponds for catfish. At its peak, the catfish industry employed over 15,000 workers and produced nearly $500 million of fish per year. But those days are long gone. First catfish farmers in the South had to contend with rising competition from Vietnamese and Chinese imports. That competition put a lid on catfish prices. Then feed prices spiked in 2009–2011, raising production costs. This combination of constrained prices and rising costs killed profits. With losses mounting, a lot of farmers got out of the catfish business, filling their ponds with dirt and planting cotton again (see the World View on the next page).

The dilemma catfish farmers find themselves in is a familiar occurrence in competitive markets. When profits look good, everybody wants to get in on the act. As more and more firms start producing the good, prices and profits tumble. This helps explain why over 200,000 new firms are formed each year and why over 50,000 others fail.

This chapter focuses on the behavior of competitive markets. We have three principal questions:

- **How are prices determined in competitive markets?**
- **How does competition affect the profits of a firm or industry?**
- **What does society gain from market competition?**

The answers to these questions will reveal how markets work when all producers are relatively small and lack market power. In subsequent chapters we emphasize how market outcomes change when markets are less competitive.

WORLD VIEW

Economy Threatens Catfish Industry

JACKSON, Miss. (AP)—Keith King never imagined his 21 years in the catfish industry would culminate in him turning his back, perhaps for good, on the work he loves so much.

Stung by sky-high feed and fuel prices and competition from cheaper imported catfish, King is draining the ponds at his Aqua Farm operation in Leland.

King, president of the Catfish Farmers of Mississippi, said he will grow corn and soybeans—much more profitable crops—in the soil once it dries.

It's becoming a common scenario as the state's farm-raised catfish industry, long one of Mississippi's most successful agriculture sectors, is seeing dozens of operations close and others drain their ponds to grow row crops. . . .

Barlow and other champions of domestically raised catfish are frustrated that Chinese imports have gained a foothold with consumers despite what they say are numerous safety concerns. . . .

But imported catfish averages $1 per pound cheaper than domestic catfish, and consumers can quickly forget any safety concerns in today's troubled economy, experts acknowledge.

Source: August 10, 2008, Alexandria 247.com. Used with permission by KALB/NBC & NALB/CBS.

Analysis: When economic profits exist in an industry, more producers try to enter. As they do, prices and economic profits decline. When losses are incurred, firms begin to exit the industry.

THE MARKET SUPPLY CURVE

In the previous chapter we examined the supply behavior of a perfectly competitive firm. The perfectly competitive firm is a price taker. It *responds* to the market price by producing that rate of output where marginal cost equals price.

But what about the *market* supply of catfish? We need a market supply curve to determine the **equilibrium price** the individual farmer will confront. In the previous chapter we simply drew a market supply curve arbitrarily to establish a market price. Now our objective is to find out where that **market supply** curve comes from.

Like the market supply curves we first encountered in Chapter 3, we can calculate the market supply of catfish by simple addition. All we have to do is add up the quantities each of America's 1,000 catfish farmers stands ready to supply at each price. Then we'll know the total quantity of fish to be supplied to the market at that price. Figure 9.1 illustrates this summation. Notice that *the market supply curve is the sum of the marginal cost curves of all the firms.* Hence whatever determines the marginal cost of a typical firm will also affect industry supply. Specifically, *the market supply of a competitive industry is determined by*

- *The price of factor inputs.*
- *Technology.*
- *Expectations.*
- *Taxes and subsidies.*
- *The number of firms in the industry.*

Entry and Exit

If more firms enter an industry, the market supply curve will shift to the right. This is the problem confronting the catfish farmers in Mississippi (see the World View above). It's fairly inexpensive to get into the catfish business: you can start with a pond, some breeding stock, and relatively little capital equipment. These **investment decisions** shift the market supply curve to the right and drive down catfish prices. This process is illustrated in Figure 9.2a. Notice how the equilibrium price slides down the market demand curve from

equilibrium price: The price at which the quantity of a good demanded in a given time period equals the quantity supplied.

market supply: The total quantities of a good that sellers are willing and able to sell at alternative prices in a given time period, *ceteris paribus.*

marginal cost (MC): The increase in total cost associated with a one-unit increase in production.

investment decision: The decision to build, buy, or lease plants and equipment; to enter or exit an industry.

FIGURE 9.1
Competitive Market Supply

A Firm's Supply. The portion of the MC curve that lies above AVC is a competitive firm's short-run supply curve. The curve MC$_A$ tells us that Farmer A will produce 40 pounds of catfish per day if the market price is $3 per pound.

Market Supply. To determine the *market* supply, we add up the quantities supplied at each price by every farmer. The total quantity supplied to the market at the price of $3 is 150 pounds per day ($a + b + c$). Market supply depends on the number of firms and their respective marginal costs.

E_1 to E_2 when more firms enter the market. The entry of Vietnamese and Chinese farmers into the catfish market caused steep declines in catfish prices.

If prices fall too far, entry will cease and some catfish farmers will drain their ponds and plant cotton again. As they leave (exit) the industry, the market supply curve will shift to the left.

Tendency toward Zero Profits

The profit motive drives these entry and exit decisions. Ten years ago catfish farming looked a whole lot more profitable than cotton farming. Farmers responded by flooding their cotton fields to create fish ponds.

FIGURE 9.2
Market Entry

If economic profits exist in an industry, more firms will want to enter it. As they do, the market supply curve will shift to the right and cause the market price to drop from p_1 to p_2 (part *a*). The

lower market price, in turn, will reduce the output and profits of the typical firm. In part *b*, the firm's output falls from q_1 to q_2.

The resulting shift of market supply caused the **economic profits** in catfish farming to disappear. (Notice in Figure 9.2b how total profits shrink when price is driven down from p_1 to p_2.) Eventually the returns in catfish farming were no better than those in cotton farming. When that happened, cotton farmers stopped building fish ponds and resumed planting cotton. ***When economic profits disappear, entry ceases, and the market stabilizes.*** At that new equilibrium, catfish farmers earn only a normal (average) rate of return.

Catfish farmers would be happier, of course, if the price of catfish didn't decline to the point where economic profits disappear. But how are they going to prevent it? Keith King evidently knows all about the laws of supply and demand (see the previous World View). He would dearly like to keep all those Vietnamese and Chinese catfish out of this country. He also wishes those farmers in Maine would keep cranberries in their ponds rather than catfish. Keith would also like to get other farmers in the South to slow production a little before all the profits disappear. But King is powerless to stop the forces of a **competitive market.** He can't even afford to reduce his *own* catfish production. Even though he has 200 acres of ponds, nobody would notice the resulting drop in market supplies, and catfish prices would continue to slide. The only one affected would be King, who'd be denying himself the opportunity to share in the (dwindling) fortunes of the catfish market while they lasted.

King's dilemma goes a long way toward explaining why catfish farming isn't highly profitable. Whenever the profit picture looks good, everybody tries to get in on the action. This kind of pressure on prices and profits is a fundamental characteristic of competitive markets. ***As long as it's easy for existing producers to expand production or for new firms to enter an industry, economic profits won't last long.*** As we'll see shortly, this is a lesson Apple Computer has learned repeatedly.

Low Barriers to Entry

New producers will be able to enter a profitable industry and help drive down prices and profits as long as they don't encounter significant barriers. Such **barriers to entry** may include patents, control of essential factors of production, control of distribution outlets, well-established brand loyalty, or even governmental regulation. All such barriers make it expensive, risky, or impossible for new firms to enter an industry. In the absence of such barriers, new firms can enter an industry more readily and at less risk. Not surprisingly, firms already entrenched in a profitable industry do their best to keep out newcomers by erecting barriers to entry. Unfortunately for Keith King, there are few barriers to entering the catfish business; all you need to get started is a pond and a few fish. Recall the Calvin Jones quote from Chapter 8 (page 174): "You raise fish. You get them out of the pond and you sell them. There's no genius to it."

Market Characteristics of Perfect Competition

This brief review of catfish economics illustrates a few general observations about the structure, behavior, and outcomes of a competitive market:

- *Many firms.* A competitive market includes a great many firms, none of which has a significant share of total output.
- *Perfect information.* All buyers and sellers have complete information on available supply, demand, and prices.
- *Identical products.* Products are homogeneous. One firm's product is the same as any other firm's product.
- *MC = p.* All competitive firms will seek to expand output until marginal cost equals price, much as price and marginal revenue are identical for such firms.
- *Low barriers.* Barriers to enter the industry are low. If economic profits are available, more firms will enter the industry.
- *Zero economic profit.* The tendency of production and market supplies to expand when profit is high puts heavy pressures on prices and profits in competitive industries. Economic profit will approach zero in the long run as prices are driven down to the level of average production costs.

economic profit: The difference between total revenues and total economic costs.

competitive market: A market in which no buyer or seller has market power.

barriers to entry: Obstacles, such as patents, that make it difficult or impossible for would-be producers to enter a particular market.

COMPETITION AT WORK: MICROCOMPUTERS

Few markets have all the characteristics just listed. That is, *few, if any, product markets are perfectly competitive.* However, many industries function much like the competitive model we sketched out. In addition to catfish farming, most other agricultural product markets are characterized by highly competitive market structures, with hundreds or even thousands of producers supplying the market. Other highly competitive, and hence not very profitable, businesses are T-shirt shops, laundromats, retail food, printing, clothing manufacturing and retailing, dry-cleaning establishments, beauty salons, and furniture. Online stockbroker services have also become highly competitive. In these markets, prices and profits are always under the threat of expanded supplies brought to market by existing or new producers.

The electronics industry offers numerous examples of how competition reduces prices and profits. Between 1972 and 1983, the price of small, handheld calculators fell from $200 to under $10. The price of digital watches fell even more dramatically, from roughly $2,000 in 1975 to under $7 in 1990. Videocassette recorders (VCRs) that sold for $2,000 in 1979 now sell for less than $30. DVD players that cost $1,500 in 1997 now sell for under $50. Cell phones that sold for $1,000 ten years ago are now given away. The same kind of competitive pressures have reduced the price of flat-screen TVs. New entrants keep bringing better TVs to market while driving prices down (see the accompanying World View).

WORLD VIEW

Flat Panels, Thin Margins

Rugged Competition from Smaller Brands Has Made the TV Sets Cheaper Than Ever

Like just about everyone else checking out the flat-panel TVs at Best Buy in Manhattan, graphic designer Roy Gantt came in coveting a Philips, Sony, or Panasonic. But after seeing the price tags, he figured a Westinghouse might be a better buy. . . .

It is just one of more than 100 flat-panel brands jamming the aisles of retailers such as Best Buy, Target, and Costco. The names on the sets range from the obscure (Sceptre, Maxent) to the recycled (Polaroid).

The free-for-all is a boon to the millions of Americans who want to trade in their bulky analog sets. . . .

For many in the industry, though, the competition is brutal. Prices for LCD sets are falling so rapidly that retailers who place orders too far in advance risk getting stuck with expensive inventory. Circuit City Stores Inc. cited plummeting prices in its February 8 announcement that it will shutter nearly 70 outlets. . . .

THE STAT

102

LCD television brands available in the United States, up from 26 in 2002

Data: Pacific Media Associates

All Outsourced

Nowadays LCD makers will sell to anyone, and the rest of the needed parts—tuners and computer chips—are available from multiple suppliers. Contract manufacturers will happily assemble all the pieces at factories in China, Mexico, or Taiwan. So the only things you need to become an instant player are strong relationships with suppliers, connections at big retailers, and a handful of engineers to design the sets.

—Pete Engardio

Analysis: Competitive pressures compel producers of flat-panel TVs to keep improving the product and reducing prices. The lure of profits encourages firms to enter this expanding market even as prices drop.

The driving force behind all these price reductions and quality improvements is *competition*. Do you really believe the price of phone calls would be falling if only one firm supplied all telephone services? Do you think thousands of software writers would be toiling away right now if popular programs didn't generate enormous profits? Would Apple, Google, and Dell Computer keep rolling out new products and services if other companies weren't always snapping at their heels?

Market Evolution

To appreciate how the process of competition works, we will examine the development of the personal computer industry. *As in other industries, the market structure of the computer industry has evolved over time. It was never a monopoly, nor was it ever perfect competition.* In its first couple of years it was dominated by only a few companies (like Apple) that were enormously successful. The high profits the early microcomputer producers obtained attracted swarms of imitators. Over 250 firms entered the microcomputer industry between 1976 and 1983 in search of high profits. The entry of so many firms transformed the industry's market structure: the industry became *more* competitive, even though not *perfectly* competitive. The increased competition pushed prices downward and improved the product. When prices and profits tumbled, scores of companies went bankrupt. They left a legacy, however, of a vastly larger market, much improved computers, and sharply lower prices.

We'll use the early experiences of the microcomputer industry to illustrate the key behavioral features of a competitive market. As we'll see, many of these competitive features are still at work in the PC market and even more visible in the markets for Internet services, content software, digital music players, smartphones, and iPads.

Initial Conditions: The Apple I

The microcomputer industry really got started in 1977. Prior to that time, microcomputers were essentially a hobby item for engineers and programmers, who bought circuits, keyboards, monitors, and tape recorders and then assembled their own basic computers. Steve Jobs, then working at Atari, and Steven Wozniak, then working at Hewlett-Packard, were among these early computer enthusiasts. They spent their days working on large systems and their nights and weekends trying to put together small computers from mail-order parts.

Courtesy of Apple Computer, Inc.

Analysis: The Apple I pictured here launched the personal computer industry in 1976. Hundreds of firms entered the industry to improve on this first preassembled microcomputer. This competition transformed the industry and the product.

Eventually, Jobs and Wozniak decided they had the capability to build commercially attractive small computers. They ordered the parts necessary for building 100 computers and set up shop in the garage of Jobs's parents. Their finished product—the Apple I—was nothing more than a circuit board with a simple, built-in operating system. This first microcomputer was packaged in a wooden box (see the previous photo). Despite primitive characteristics, the first 100 Apple I computers sold out immediately. This quick success convinced Jobs and Wozniak to package their computers more fully—which they did by enclosing them in plastic housing—and to offer more of them for sale. Shortly thereafter, in January 1977, Apple Computer Inc. was established.

Apple revolutionized the market by offering a preassembled desktop computer with attractive features and an accessible price. The impact on the marketplace was much like that of Henry Ford's early Model T: suddenly a newfangled piece of technology came into reach of the average U.S. household, and everybody, it seemed, wanted one. The first mass-produced Apple computer—called the Apple II—was just a basic keyboard with an operating system that permitted users to write their own programs. The computer had no disk drive, no monitor, and only 4K of random access memory (RAM). Consumers had to use their TV sets as screens and audiocassettes for data storage. This primitive Apple II was priced at just under $1,300 when it debuted in June 1977. Apple was producing computers at the rate of 500 per month.

Apple didn't engineer or manufacture chips or semiconductor components. Instead it simply packaged existing components purchased from outside suppliers. Hence it was easy for other companies to follow Apple's lead. Within a very brief time, other firms, such as Tandy (Radio Shack), also started to assemble computers. By the middle of 1978, the basic small computer was selling for $1,000, and industry sales were about 20,000 a month. Figure 9.3a depicts the initial (1978) equilibrium in the computer market, and

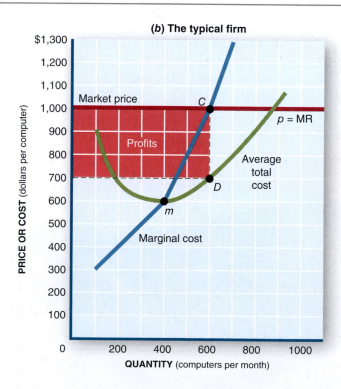

FIGURE 9.3

Initial Equilibrium in the Computer Market

(*a*) **The Industry.** In 1978 the market price of microcomputers was $1,000. This price was established by the intersection of the market supply and demand curves.

(*b*) **A Firm.** Each competitive producer in the market sought to produce computers at that rate (600 per month) where marginal cost equaled price (point *C*). Profit per computer was equal to price (point *C*) minus average total cost (point *D*). Total profits for the typical firm are indicated by the shaded rectangle.

Figure 9.3*b* illustrates the approximate costs of production for the typical computer manufacturer at that time.

The Production Decision

The short-run goal of every producer is to find the rate of output that maximizes profits. Finding this rate entails making the best possible **production decision.** In this short-run context, ***each competitive firm seeks the rate of output at which marginal cost equals price.***

   Figure 9.3*b* illustrates the cost and price curves the typical computer producer confronted in 1978. As in most lines of production, the marginal costs of computer production increased with the rate of output. Marginal costs rose in part because output could be increased in the short run (with existing plants and equipment) only by crowding additional workers onto the assembly line. In 1978 Apple had only 10,000 square feet of manufacturing space. As more workers were hired, each worker had less capital and land to work with, and marginal physical product fell. The law of diminishing returns pushed marginal costs up.

   The upward-sloping marginal cost curve intersected the price line at an output level of 600 computers per month (point *C* in Figure 9.3*b*). That was the profit-maximizing rate of output (MC = *p*) for the typical manufacturer. Manufacturing any more than 600 computers per month would raise marginal costs over price and reduce total profits. Manufacturing any fewer would be passing up an opportunity to make another buck.

> **production decision:** The selection of the short-run rate of output (with existing plants and equipment).

Profit Calculations

Table 9.1 shows how much *profit* a typical computer manufacturer was making in 1978. As the profit column indicates, the typical computer manufacturer could make a real killing in the computer market, reaping a monthly profit of $180,000 by producing and selling 600 microcomputers.

Output per Month	Price	Total Revenue	Total Cost	Total Profit	Marginal Revenue*	Marginal Cost*	Average Total Cost	Profit per Unit (Price Minus Average Cost)
0	$1,000	$ 0	$ 60,000	−$ 60,000	—	—	—	—
100	1,000	100,000	90,000	10,000	$1,000	$ 300	$ 900	$100
200	1,000	200,000	130,000	70,000	1,000	400	650	350
300	1,000	300,000	180,000	120,000	1,000	500	600	400
400	1,000	400,000	240,000	160,000	1,000	600	600	400
500	1,000	500,000	320,000	180,000	1,000	800	640	360
600	1,000	600,000	420,000	180,000	1,000	1,000	700	300
700	1,000	700,000	546,000	154,000	1,000	1,260	780	220
800	1,000	800,000	720,000	80,000	1,000	1,740	900	100
900	1,000	900,000	919,800	−19,800	1,000	1,998	1,022	−22

*Note that output levels are calibrated in hundreds in this example; that's why we have divided the *change* in total costs and revenues from one output level to another by 100 to calculate marginal revenue and marginal cost. Very few manufacturers deal in units of 1.

TABLE 9.1
Computer Revenues, Costs, and Profits

Producers seek that rate of output where total profit is maximized. This table illustrates the output choices the typical computer producer faced in 1978. The profit-maximizing rate of output occurred at 600 computers per month. At that rate of output, marginal cost was equal to price ($1,000), and profits were $180,000 per month.

We could also calculate the computer manufacturers' profits by asking how much the manufacturers make on *each* computer and then multiplying that figure by total output:

$$\text{Total profit} = \text{Profit per unit} \times \text{Quantity sold}$$

We can compute these profits by studying the first and last columns in Table 9.1 or by using a little geometry in Figure 9.3*b*. In the figure, average costs (total costs divided by the rate of output) are portrayed by the **average total cost (ATC)** curve. At the output rate of 600 (the row in white in Table 9.1), the distance between the price line ($1,000 at point *C*) and the ATC curve ($700 at point *D*) is $300, which represents the average **profit per unit.** Multiplying this figure by the number of units sold (600 per month) will give us *total* profit per month. Total profits are represented by the shaded rectangle in Figure 9.3*b* and are equal to our earlier profit figure of $180,000 per month.

The Lure of Profits

While gaping at the computer manufacturer's enormous profits, we should remind ourselves that those profits might not last long. Indeed, the more quick-witted among us already will have seen and heard enough to know they've discovered a good thing. And in fact, the kind of profits the early microcomputer manufacturers attained attracted a lot of entrepreneurial interest. *In competitive markets, economic profits attract new entrants.* This is what happened in the catfish industry and also in the computer industry. Within a very short time, a whole crowd of profit maximizers entered the microcomputer industry in hot pursuit of its fabulous profits. By the end of 1980, Apple had a lot of competition, including new entrants from IBM, Xerox, Digital Equipment, Casio, Sharp, and dozens of other start-up firms.

Low Entry Barriers

A critical feature of the microcomputer market was its lack of entry barriers. A microcomputer is little more than a box containing a microprocessor "brain," which connects to a keyboard (to enter data), a memory (to store data), and a screen (to display data). Although the microprocessors that guide the computer are extremely sophisticated, they can be purchased on the open market. Thus, to enter the computer industry, all one needs is some space, some money to buy components, and some dexterity in putting parts together. Such *low entry barriers permit new firms to enter competitive markets.* This is what facilitated competition in the flat-screen TV market (see the World View on page 194). The same low entry barriers existed in computers. According to Table 9.1, the typical producer needed only $60,000 of plant and equipment (fixed costs) to get started in the microcomputer market. Jobs and Wozniak had even less when they started making Apples in their garage.

A Shift of Market Supply

Figure 9.4 shows what happened to the computer market and the profits of the typical firm once the word got out. As more and more entrepreneurs heard how profitable computer manufacturing could be, they quickly got hold of a book on electronic circuitry, rushed to the bank, got a little financing, and set up shop. Before many months had passed, scores of new firms had started producing small computers. *The entry of new firms shifts the market supply curve to the right.* In Figure 9.4*a*, the supply curve shifted from S_1 to S_2. Almost as fast as a computer can calculate a profit (loss) statement, the willingness to supply increased abruptly.

But the new computer companies were in for a bit of disappointment. With so many new firms hawking microcomputers, it became increasingly difficult to make a fast buck. The downward-sloping market demand curve confirms that a greater quantity of microcomputers could be sold only if the price of computers dropped. And drop it did. The price slide began as computer manufacturers found their inventories growing and so offered price

---

average total cost (ATC): Total cost divided by the quantity produced in a given time period.

profit per unit: Total profit divided by the quantity produced in a given time period; price minus average total cost.

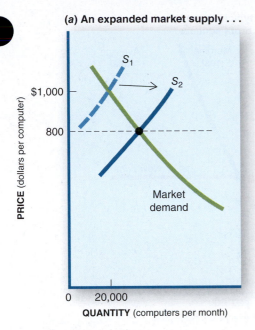

(a) An expanded market supply . . .

(b) Lowers price and profits for the typical firm.

FIGURE 9.4
The Competitive Price and Profit Squeeze

(a) The Industry. The economic profits in the computer industry encouraged new firms to enter the industry. As they did, the market supply curve shifted from S_1 to S_2. This rightward shift of the supply curve lowered the equilibrium price of computers.

(b) A Firm. The lower market price, in turn, forced the typical producer to reduce output to the point where MC and price were equal again (point G). At this reduced rate of output, the typical firm earned less total profit than it had earned before.

discounts to maintain sales volume. The price fell rapidly, from $1,000 in mid-1978 to $800 in early 1980.

The sliding market price squeezed the profits of each firm, causing the profit rectangle to shrink (compare Figure 9.3b to Figure 9.4b). The lower price also changed the production decision of the typical firm. The new price ($800) intersected the unchanged MC curve at the output rate of 500 computers per month (point G in Figure 9.4b). With average production costs of $640 (Table 9.1), the firm's total profits in 1980 were only $80,000 per month [$(p - \text{ATC}) \times 500$]. Not a paltry sum, to be sure, but nothing like the fantastic fortunes pocketed earlier.

As long as an economic profit is available, it will continue to attract new entrants. Those entrepreneurs who were a little slow in absorbing the implications of Figure 9.3 eventually woke up to what was going on and tried to get in on the action, too. Even though they were a little late, they didn't want to miss the chance to cash in on the $80,000 in monthly profits still available to the typical firm. Hence the market supply curve continued to shift, and computer prices slid further, as in Figure 9.5. This process squeezed the profits of the typical firm still more, further shrinking the profit rectangle.

As long as economic profits exist in **short-run competitive equilibrium,** that equilibrium won't last. If the rate of profit obtainable in computer production is higher than that available in other industries, new firms will enter the industry. Conversely, if the short-run equilibrium is unprofitable, firms will exit the industry. Profit-maximizing entrepreneurs have a special place in their hearts for economic profits, not computers.

Price and profit declines will cease when the price of computers equals the minimum average cost of production. At that price (point *m* in Figure 9.5b), there's no more economic profit to be squeezed out. Firms no longer have an incentive to enter the industry, and the supply curve stops shifting. This situation represents the **long-run competitive equilibrium** for the firm and for the industry. *In long-run equilibrium, entry and exit*

short-run competitive equilibrium: $p = \text{MC}$.

long-run competitive equilibrium: $p = \text{MC} = $ minimum ATC.

(a) The computer industry: continuous entry

(b) The typical firm: price and profit squeeze

FIGURE 9.5

The Competitive Squeeze Approaching Its Limit

(a) The Industry. Even at a price of $800 per computer, economic profits attracted still more entrepreneurs, shifting the market supply curve further (S_3). The next short-term equilibrium occurred at a price of $700 per computer.

(b) A Firm. At this reduced market price, the typical manufacturer wanted to supply only 430 computers per month (point *J*). Total profits were much lower than they had been earlier, with fewer producers and higher prices.

cease, and zero economic profit (that is, normal profit) prevails (see Figure 9.6). Table 9.2 summarizes the profit-maximizing rules that bring about this long-run equilibrium.

Once a long-run equilibrium is established, it will continue until market demand shifts or technological progress reduces the cost of computer production. In fact, that's just what happened in the computer market.

Home Computers vs. Personal Computers

As profit margins narrowed to the levels shown in Figure 9.5, quick-thinking entrepreneurs realized that future profits would have to come from product improvements or cost reductions. By adding features to the basic microcomputer, firms could expect to increase the demand for microcomputers and fetch higher prices. On the other hand, cost reductions would permit firms to widen their profit margins at existing prices or to reduce prices and increase sales. This second strategy wouldn't require assembling more complex computers or risking consumer rejection of an upgraded product.

TABLE 9.2

Long-Run Rules for Entry and Exit

Firms will enter an industry if economic profits exist ($p >$ ATC). They will exit if economic losses prevail ($p <$ ATC). Entry and exit cease in long-run equilibrium with zero economic profit ($p =$ ATC). (See Table 22.3 for short-run profit maximization rules.)

Price Level	Result for a Typical Firm	Market Response
$p >$ ATC	Profits	Enter industry (or expand capacity).
$p <$ ATC	Loss	Exit industry (or reduce capacity).
$p =$ ATC	Break even	Maintain existing capacity (no entry or exit).

(a) Short-run equilibrium (*p* = MC)

(b) Long-run equilibrium (*p* = MC = ATC)

FIGURE 9.6
Short- vs. Long-Run Equilibrium for the Competitive Firm

(*a*) **Short-Run.** Competitive firms strive for the rate of output at which marginal cost (MC) equals price. When they achieve that rate of output, they are in *short-run equilibrium*. Whether profitable or not, there is no incentive to alter the rate of output produced with existing (fixed) plants and equipment; it is the *best* the firm can do in the short run.

(*b*) **Long-Run.** If the short-run equilibrium (q_s) is profitable (*p* > ATC), other firms will want to enter the industry. As they do, market price will fall until it reaches the level of minimum ATC. In this *long-run equilibrium* (q_L), economic profits are zero, and nobody wants to enter or exit the industry.

In late 1979 and early 1980, both product development strategies were pursued. In the process, two distinct markets were created. Microcomputers upgraded with new features came to be known as *personal* computers, or PCs. The basic unadorned computer first introduced by Apple came to be known as a *home* computer. The limited capabilities of that basic home computer greatly restricted its usefulness to simple household record keeping, games, and elementary programming.

Apple chose the personal computer route. It started enlarging the memory of the Apple II in late 1978 (from 4K to as much as 48K). It offered a monitor (produced by Sanyo) for the first time in May 1979. Shortly thereafter, Apple ceased making the basic Apple II and instead produced only upgraded versions (the Apple IIe, the IIc, and the III). Hundreds of other companies followed Apple's lead, touting increasingly sophisticated personal computers.

While one pack of entrepreneurs was chasing PC profits, another pack was going after the profits still available in home computers. This group chose to continue producing the basic Apple II lookalike, hoping to profit from greater efficiency, lower costs, and increasing sales.

Price Competition in Home Computers

The home computer market confronted the fiercest form of price competition. With prices continually sliding, the only way to make an extra buck was to push down the cost curve.

To reduce costs, firms sought to reduce the number of microprocessor chips installed in the computer's "brain." Fewer chips not only reduce direct materials costs, but more importantly, they decrease the amount of labor required for computer assembly. The key to lower manufacturing costs was more powerful chips. More powerful chips appeared when Intel, Motorola, and Texas Instruments developed 16-bit chips, doubling the computer's "brain" capabilities.

FIGURE 9.7

FIGURE 9.7

Lower Costs Improve Profits and Stimulate Output

The quest for profits encouraged producers to discover cheaper ways to manufacture computers. The resulting improvements lower costs and encourage further increases in the rate of output. The typical computer producer increased output from point *J* (where *p* = old MC) to point *N* (where *p* = new MC).

Cost reductions promote more output.

Further Supply Shifts

The impact of the improved chips on computer production costs and profits is illustrated in Figure 9.7, which takes over where Figure 9.5 left off. Recall that the market price of computers had been driven down to $700 by the beginning of 1980. At this price the typical firm maximized profits by producing 430 computers per month, as determined by the intersection of the prevailing price and MC curves (point *J* in Figure 9.7).

The only way for the firm to improve profitability at this point was to reduce costs. The new chips made such cost reductions easy. Such *technological improvements are illustrated by a downward shift of the ATC and MC curves.* Notice in Figure 9.7 how the new technology permits 430 home computers to be produced for a lower marginal cost (about $500) than previously ($700 at point *J*).

The lower cost structure increases the profitability of computer production and stimulates a further increase in production. Note in particular that the "new MC" curve intersects the price ($700) line at an output of 600 computers per month (point *N*). By contrast, the old, higher MC curve dictated a production rate of only 430 computers per month for the typical firm (point *J*) at that price. Thus existing producers suddenly had an incentive to *expand* production, and new firms had a greater incentive to *enter* the industry. The great rush into computer production was on again.

The market implications of another entrepreneurial stampede should now be obvious. As more and more firms tried to get in on the action, the market supply curve again shifted to the right. As output increased, computer prices slid further down the market demand curve.

Figure 9.8 illustrates how steeply home computer prices fell after 1980. Texas Instruments (TI) was one of the largest firms producing home computers in 1980. The lower costs made possible by improved microprocessors enabled TI to sell its basic home computer for $650 in 1980. Despite modest improvements in the TI machine, TI had to reduce its price to $525 in early 1981 to maintain unit sales. Shortly thereafter, the additional output of new entrants and existing companies pushed market prices down still further to around $400.

Even at $400, TI and other home computer manufacturers were making handsome profits. In the fourth quarter of 1981, total industry sales were in excess of 200,000 per month—10 times the volume sold just three years earlier. Profits were good, too. A single company,

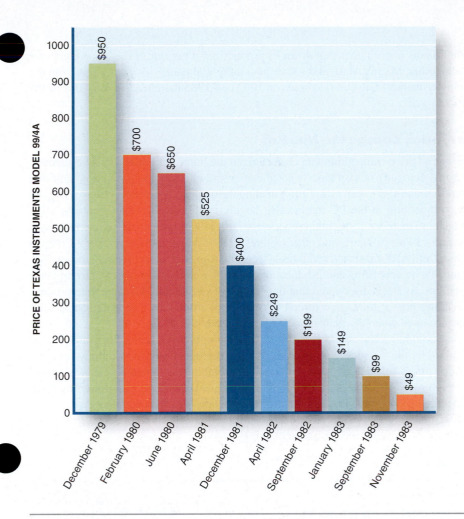

FIGURE 9.8
Plummeting Prices

Improved technology and fierce competition forced home computer prices down. In the span of only a few years, the price of a basic home computer fell from just under $1,000 to only $49. In the process, price fell below average variable cost, and many firms were forced to shut down.

Atari, recorded total profits of $137 million in the fourth quarter of 1981, far more profit than Apple Computer Inc. had made during its first five *years* of production. The profits of the home computer market appeared boundless.

The remainder of Figure 9.8 shows the consequences of the continued competition for those "boundless" profits. Between December 1981 and January 1983, the retail price of home computers fell from $400 to $149. Profit margins became razor-thin. Fourth-quarter profits at Atari, for example, fell from $137 million in 1981 to only $1.2 million in 1983.

Shutdowns

That didn't stop the competitive process, however. At Texas Instruments, minimum *variable* costs were roughly $100 per computer, so TI and other manufacturers could afford to keep producing even at lower prices. And they had little choice but to do so, since if they didn't, other companies would quickly take up the slack. Industry output kept increasing despite shrinking profit margins. The increased supply pushed computer prices ever lower.

By the time computer prices reached $99, TI was losing $300 million per year. In September 1983 the company recognized that the price would no longer even cover average variable costs. ***Once a firm is no longer able to cover variable costs, it should shut down production.*** When the price of home computers dipped below minimum average variable costs, TI had reached the **shutdown point,** and the company ceased production. At the time TI made the shutdown decision, the company had an inventory of nearly 500,000 unsold computers. To unload them, TI reduced its price to $49 (see Figure 9.8), forcing lower prices and losses on other computer firms.

shutdown point: The rate of output where price equals minimum AVC.

Exits

Shortly after Texas Instruments shut down its production, it got out of the home computer business altogether. Mattel, Atari, and scores of smaller companies also withdrew from the home computer market. The exit rate between 1983 and 1985 matched the entry rate of the period 1979 to 1982.

The Personal Computer Market

The same kind of price competition that characterized the home computer market eventually hit the personal computer market too. As noted earlier, the microcomputer industry split into two segments around 1980, with most firms pursuing the upgraded personal computer market.

At first, competition in the PC market was largely confined to product improvements. Firms added more memory, faster microprocessors, better monitors, expanded operating systems, new applications software, and other features. New entrants into the market—Compaq in 1982; then Dell, AST, Gateway, and more—were the source of most product innovations.

The stampede of new firms and products into the PC market soon led to outright price competition too. As firms discovered that they couldn't sell all the PCs they were producing at prevailing prices, they were forced to offer price discounts. These discounts soon spread, and the slide down the demand curve accelerated.

Firms that couldn't keep up with the dual pace of improving technology and falling prices soon fell by the wayside. Scores of firms ceased production and withdrew from the industry once prices fell below minimum average variable cost. Even Apple, which had taken the "high road" to avoid price competition in home computers, was slowed by price competition. And IBM, which had entered the industry late, was forced to shut down its PC division after realizing that steep price cuts would be required to sell its small PCs (the "PCjr") to household users (see the accompanying News).

IN THE NEWS

IBM to Halt PCjr Output Next Month

NEW YORK—International Business Machines Corp. ended its up-and-down struggle to revive its PCjr home computer by announcing it would stop making the product next month.

The surprise move marks IBM's most visible product failure since its enormously successful entry into the personal computer business four years ago. IBM announced the PCjr in late 1983 and began selling it early last year with an advertising campaign believed to exceed $40 million. IBM's efforts to make junior a hit ranged from technical changes to steep price cuts. . . .

At the time of its introduction, the PCjr had a list of $699 or $1,269, depending on the model. The prices later were cut to $599 and $999. . . .

—Dennis Kneale

Source: *The Wall Street Journal,* March 20, 1985, p. 1. Used with permission of Dow Jones & Company, Inc. via Copyright Clearance Center, Inc.

Analysis: Competition forces firms to improve products and reduce prices. Firms that can't keep up are forced to shut down and perhaps exit the industry.

THE COMPETITIVE PROCESS

It is now evident that consumers have reaped substantial benefits from competition in the computer market. Over 600 million home and personal computers have been sold. Along the way, technology has made personal computers a thousand times faster than the first Apple IIs, with phenomenal increases in memory. The iMac computer introduced

iMac, G3: 1998

Getty Images

Analysis: The evolution of personal computers from the Apple I (photo, page 195) to the latest iMac, iPhone, and iPad was driven by intense competition.

Courtesy of Apple

iMac, G5: 2004

AFP/Getty Images

iPhone: 2007

iPad2: 2011

by Apple in 1998 made the Apple I of 1976 look prehistoric (see the photos above). The latest iMacs make even the 1998 model look primitive. A lot of consumers have found that computers are great for doing accounting chores, keeping records, writing papers, playing games, and accessing the Internet. Perhaps it's true that an abundance of inexpensive computers would have been produced in other market (or nonmarket) situations as well. But we can't ignore the fact that *competitive market pressures were a driving force in the spectacular growth of the computer industry.* And they still are.

Allocative Efficiency: The Right Output Mix

The squeeze on prices and profits that we've observed in the computer market is a fundamental characteristic of the competitive process. The process works as well in India (see the World View on the next page) as in the United States or elsewhere. Indeed, the **market mechanism** works best under competitive pressure. The existence of economic profits is an indication that consumers place a high value on a particular product and are willing to pay a comparatively high price to get it. The high price and profits signal this information to profit-hungry entrepreneurs, who come forward to satisfy consumer demands. Thus *high profits in a particular industry indicate that consumers want a different mix of output* (more of that industry's goods). The competitive squeeze on those same profits indicates that resources are being reallocated to produce that desired

market mechanism: The use of market prices and sales to signal desired outputs (or resource allocations).

mix. In a competitive market, consumers get more of the goods they desire—and at a lower price.

The ability of competitive markets to allocate resources efficiently across industries originates in the way competitive prices are set. To attain the optimal mix of output, we must know the **opportunity cost** of producing different goods. A competitive market gives us the information necessary for making such choices. Why? Because competitive firms always strive to produce at the rate of output at which price equals marginal cost. Hence *the price signal the consumer gets in a competitive market is an accurate reflection of opportunity cost.* As such, it offers a reliable basis for making choices about the mix of output and attendant allocation of resources. In this sense, the **marginal cost pricing** characteristic of competitive markets permits society to answer the WHAT-to-produce question efficiently. The amount consumers are willing to pay for a good (its price) equals its opportunity cost (marginal cost).

opportunity cost: The most desired goods or services that are forgone in order to obtain something else.

marginal cost pricing: The offer (supply) of goods at prices equal to their marginal cost.

Production Efficiency: Minimum Average Cost

When the competitive pressure on prices is carried to the limit, we also get the right answer to the HOW-to-produce question. Competition drives costs down to their bare minimum—the hallmark of economic **efficiency.** This was illustrated by the tendency of computer prices to be driven down to the level of *minimum* average costs. Figure 9.9 summarizes this competitive process, showing how the industry moves from short-run equilibrium (point *a*) to long-run equilibrium (point *c*). Once the long-run equilibrium has been established, society is getting the most it can from its available (scarce) resources.

efficiency: Maximum output of a good from the resources used in production.

Zero Economic Profit

Competitive pressures also affect the FOR WHOM question. At the limit of long-run equilibrium, all economic profit is eliminated. This doesn't mean that producers are left empty-handed, however. The zero-profit limit is rarely, if ever, reached because new products are continually being introduced, consumer demands change, and more efficient production processes are discovered. In fact, the competitive process creates strong pressures to pursue product and technological innovation. In a competitive market, the adage about the early bird getting the worm is particularly apt. As we observed in the computer market, the first

FIGURE 9.9
Summary of Competitive Process

All competitive firms seek to produce at that output where MC = *p*. Hence a competitive *industry* will produce at that rate of output where *industry* MC (the sum of all firms' MC curves) intersects market demand (point *a*).

If economic profits exist in the industry short-run equilibrium (as they do here), more firms will enter the industry. As they do, the *industry* MC (supply) curve will shift to the right. The shifting MC curve will pull the *industry* ATC curve along with it. As the *industry* MC curve continues to shift rightward, the intersection of MC and ATC (point *b*) eventually will reach the demand curve at point *c*. At point *c*, MC still equals price, but no economic profits exist and entry (shifts) will cease. Point *c* will be the *long-run* equilibrium of the industry.

If competitive pressures reduce costs (i.e., improve technology), the supply (MC) curve will shift further to the right and *down,* reducing long-run prices even more.

Note that MC = *p* in both short- and long-run equilibrium. Notice also that equilibrium must occur on the market demand curve.

---

ones to perceive and respond to the potential profitability of computer production were the ones who made the greatest profits.

Relentless Profit Squeeze

The sequence of events common to competitive markets evolves as follows:

- High prices and profits signal consumers' demand for more output.
- Economic profit attracts new suppliers.
- The market supply curve shifts to the right.
- Prices slide down the market demand curve.
- A new equilibrium is reached at which increased quantities of the desired product are produced and its price is lower. Average costs of production are at or near a minimum, much more of the product is supplied and consumed, and economic profit approaches zero.
- Throughout the process, producers experience great pressure to keep ahead of the profit squeeze by reducing costs, a pressure that frequently results in product and technological innovation.

What is essential to remember about the competitive process is that the **potential threat of other firms expanding production or of new firms entering the industry keeps existing firms on their toes.** Even the most successful firm can't rest on its laurels for long. To stay in the game, competitive firms must continually update technology, improve their products, and reduce costs.

Competitive Pressures

THE ECONOMY TOMORROW

$99 iPADS?

Competition didn't end with computers. Steve Jobs, the guy who started the personal computer business back in 1977, knew that. He introduced another hot consumer product in November 2001—the iPod. The iPod was the first mass-produced portable digital music player. It allowed consumers to download, store, and retrieve up to 1,000 songs. Its compact size, sleek design, and simple functionality made it an instant success: Apple was selling iPods as fast as they could be produced, piling up huge profits in the process.

So what happened? Other entrepreneurs quickly got the scent of iPod's profits. Within a matter of months, competitors were designing their own digital music players. By 2003 the "attack of the iPod clones" was in full force. Major players like Sony (MusicBox), Dell (Juke-Box), Samsung (Yepp), and Creative Technology (Muvo Slim) were all bringing MP3 players to the market. Competitors were adding new features, shrinking the size, and reducing prices.

Under these circumstances, Apple could not afford to sit back and admire its profits. Steve Jobs knew he'd have to keep running to stay ahead of the MP3 player pack. He kept improving the iPod. Within 2 years Apple had three generations of iPods, each substantially better than the last. Memory capacity increased tenfold (to 10,000 songs), features were added, and the size shrank further. In less than 2.5 years, the iPod's price fell by 40 percent even while quality improved dramatically. By the time you graduate, the iPod may include a washer/dryer component, as the accompanying cartoon suggests!

The same kind of unrelenting competitive dynamic has hounded Apple's iPad. The iPad wasn't the first tablet computer, but it was a huge success: 300,000 iPads were sold on the first day and 15 million in the first year. Apple reaped enormous profits.

Those profits signaled a slew of companies to join the "tablet brigade" (see the following News), seeking to get a piece of the new profit pie. Over 100 companies entered the tablet market in 2011, putting enormous pressure on Apple's sales, price, and profits. Apple tried to stay ahead of the competitive pack by reducing price, adding new features (e.g., built-in camera, faster processor), and shrinking the tablet's size and weight (the iPad2, March 2011). With such unrelenting competitive pressure, industry analysts predicted we'd see $99 iPads in the economy tomorrow—perhaps even with washer/dryer apps!

That Genius Steve Jobs

Here Steve introduces latest iPod which incorporates a tiny washer-dryer.

DELICATES

DANZIGER
NYTS/CWS Jan 9 2007 (3087)

Jeff Danziger. New York Times Syndicate.

Analysis: New entrants and intense competition force producers to keep improving their products. Who knows how far this process can go?

IN THE NEWS

Tablet Brigade

Apple's revolutionary iPad finally has competition—lots of it. But the tablet wars are just beginning.

Tablets may have been the most talked-about new gizmos of 2010, but nearly all the talk was about one model: Apple's iPad, which instantly defined the category when Steve Jobs unveiled it nearly a year ago. By the end of the year, only one serious iPad alternative—Samsung's diminutive Galaxy Tab—had gone on sale.

That's why gadget enthusiasts were so eager to attend the big tablet coming-out party at the International Consumer Electronics Show (CES) in early January. The cavernous Las Vegas Convention Center positively bulged with the things, including newly announced contenders from Motorola, Panasonic, Toshiba, and other tech behemoths, as well as models from smaller players such as HDTV manufacturer Vizio and bargain-basement dweller Coby. Even Polaroid was showing one. . . .

Some models didn't even have names yet.

—Harry McCracken

Analysis: Economic profits attract entrepreneurs. As competition intensifies, products improve and prices fall.

SUMMARY

- A perfectly competitive firm has no power to alter the market price of the product it sells. The perfectly competitive firm confronts a horizontal demand curve for its own output even though the relevant *market* demand curve is negatively sloped. LO9-1

- Profit maximization induces the competitive firm to produce at that rate of output where marginal costs equal price (MC = p). This represents the short-run equilibrium of the firm. LO9-2

- If profits exist in short-run equilibrium, new firms will enter the market. The resulting shift of supply will drive market prices down the market demand curve. As prices fall, the profit of the industry and its constituent firms will be squeezed. LO9-3

- The limit to the competitive price and profit squeeze is reached when price is driven down to the level of minimum average total cost (MC = p = ATC). At this point (long-run equilibrium) additional output and profit will be attained only if technology is improved (lowering costs) or if market demand increases. LO9-3

- Firms will shut down production if price falls below average variable cost. Firms will exit the industry if they foresee continued economic losses. LO9-3

- The most distinctive thing about competitive markets is the persistent pressure they exert on prices and profits. The threat of competition is a tremendous incentive for producers to respond quickly to consumer demands and to seek more efficient means of production. In this sense, competitive markets do best what markets are supposed to do—efficiently allocate resources. LO9-4

Key Terms

equilibrium price	investment decision	barriers to entry
market supply	economic profit	production decision
marginal cost (MC)	competitive market	average total cost (ATC)

profit per unit   shutdown point   marginal cost pricing
short-run competitive equilibrium   market mechanism   efficiency
long-run competitive equilibrium   opportunity cost

Questions for Discussion

1. Why would anyone want to enter a profitable industry knowing that profits would eventually be eliminated by competition?   LO9-3

2. Why wouldn't producers necessarily want to produce output at the lowest average cost? Under what conditions would they end up doing so?   LO9-1

3. What industries do you regard as being highly competitive? Can you identify any barriers to entry in those industries?   LO9-1

4. Why have flat-panel TV prices fallen so much? (See World View, p. 194.)   LO9-2

5. What might cause catfish prices to rise far enough to eliminate losses in the industry? (See News, p. 191.)   LO9-2

6. As the price of computers fell, what happened to their quality? How is this possible?   LO9-4

7. How far are mobile phone prices likely to fall in India? (See World View, p. 206.)   LO9-4

8. Is "long-run" equilibrium permanent? What forces might dislodge it?   LO9-3

9. What would happen to iPad sales and profits if Apple kept price and profit margins high?   LO9-1

10. Identify two products that have either (*a*) fallen sharply in price or (*b*) gotten significantly better without price increases. How did these changes come about?   LO9-4

11. What will drive the price of an iPad down to $99? How long will it take?   LO9-2

 web activities to accompany this chapter can be found on the Online Learning Center:
http://www.mhhe.com/schiller13e

 mobile app Visit your mobile app store and download the Schiller: Study Econ app *today*!

LO9-3 1. According to the News on page 204,
   (*a*) How many years elapsed between IBM's entry and exit of the home computer market? _____
   (*b*) By what percentage did IBM cut the price of its low-end computer in a single year? _____

LO9-2 2. According to Table 9.1,
   (*a*) What were the fixed costs of production for the firm? _____
   (*b*) At what rate of output was profit per computer maximized? (Choose the highest output level.) _____
   (*c*) At what output rate was total profit maximized? _____

LO9-1 3. Suppose the following data summarize the costs of a perfectly competitive firm:

Quantity	0	1	2	3	4	5	6	7	8
Total cost	$100	101	103	106	110	115	121	128	136

   (*a*) Draw the firm's MC curve on the graph on the left here.
   (*b*) Draw the market supply curve on the right graph, assuming 8 firms identical to the one just described.
   (*c*) What is the equilibrium price in this market? _____

(a) The firm   **(b) The market**

4. Suppose the following data describe the demand for liquid-diet beverages:

Price	$11	$10	$9	$8	$7	$6	$5	$4	$3	$2
Quantity demanded	7	10	13	16	19	22	25	28	31	34

Five identical, perfectly competitive firms are producing these beverages. The cost of producing these beverages at each firm is the following:

Quantity produced	0	1	2	3	4	5	6	7	8	9	10
Total cost	$5	$8	$10	$13	$17	$22	$28	$36	$45	$55	$67

   (*a*) What price will prevail in this market? _____
   (*b*) What quantity is produced? _____
   (*c*) How much profit (loss) does each firm make? _____
   (*d*) What happens to price if two more identical firms enter the market? _____

LO9-3 5. Suppose the typical catfish farmer was incurring an economic loss at the prevailing price p_1.
   (*a*) Illustrate these losses on the firm and market graphs. (*b*) What forces would raise the price?
   (*c*) What price would prevail in long-term equilibrium? Illustrate your answers on the graphs.

(a) The market   **(b) The lone farmer**

LO9-2 6. According to Table 9.1,
(a) What was the prevailing computer price in 1978? _____
(b) How much total profit did the typical firm earn? _____
(c) At what price would profits have been zero? _____
(d) At what price would the firm have shut down? _____

LO9-2 7. According to the World View on page 194,
(a) How many brands entered the flat-panel TV market between 2002 and 2007? _____
(b) What will economic profit be in the long run? _____
(c) Will the number of firms producing TVs (A) increase, (B) decrease, or (C) stay the same between now and then? _____

LO9-4 8. Suppose that the monthly market demand schedule for Frisbees is

Price	$8	$7	$6	$5	$4	$3	$2	$1
Quantity demanded	1,000	2,000	4,000	8,000	16,000	32,000	64,000	128,000

Suppose further that the marginal and average costs of Frisbee production for every competitive firm are

Rate of output	100	200	300	400	500	600
Marginal cost	$2.00	$3.00	$4.00	$5.00	$6.00	$7.00
Average total cost	2.00	2.50	3.00	3.50	4.00	4.50

Finally, assume that the equilibrium market price is $6 per Frisbee.
(a) Draw the cost curves of the typical firm and identify its profit-maximizing rate of output and its total profits.
(b) Draw the market demand curve and identify market equilibrium.
(c) How many Frisbees are being sold? _____
(d) How many (identical) firms are initially producing Frisbees? _____
(e) How much profit is the typical firm making? _____
(f) In view of the profits being made, more firms will enter into Frisbee production, shift the market supply curve to the right, and push price down. At what equilibrium price are all profits eliminated? _____
(g) How many firms will be producing Frisbees at this long-term price? _____

(a) The firm

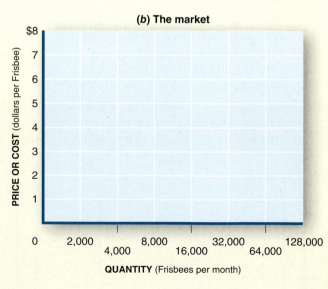

(b) The market

Monopoly

LEARNING OBJECTIVES

After reading this chapter, you should know

LO10-1. How a monopolist sets price and output.

LO10-2. How monopoly and competitive outcomes differ.

LO10-3. The pros and cons of monopoly.

In 1908 Ford produced the Model T, the car "designed for the common man." It was cheap, reliable, and as easy to drive as the horse and buggy it was replacing. Ford sold 10,000 Model Ts in its first full year of production (1909). After that, sales more than doubled every year. In 1913 nearly 200,000 Model Ts were sold; and Ford was fast changing U.S. patterns of consumption, travel, and living standards.

During this early development of the U.S. auto industry, Henry Ford dominated the field. There were other producers, but the Ford Motor Company was the only producer of an inexpensive "motorcar for the multitudes." In this situation, Henry Ford could dictate the price and the features of his cars. When he opened his new assembly line factory at Highland Park, he abruptly raised the Model T's price by $100—an increase of 12 percent—to help pay for the new plant. Then he decided to paint all Model Ts black. When told of consumer complaints about the lack of colors, Ford advised one of his executives in 1913, "Give them any color they want so long as it's black."[1]

Henry Ford had market power. He could dictate what color car Americans would buy. And he could raise the price of Model Ts without fear of losing all his customers. Such power is alien to competitive firms. Competitive firms are always under pressure to reduce costs, improve quality, and cater to consumer preferences.

In this chapter we examine how market structure influences market outcomes. Specifically, we examine how a market controlled by a single producer—a monopoly—behaves. We're particularly interested in the following questions:

- **What price will a monopolist charge?**
- **How much output will the monopolist produce?**
- **Are consumers better or worse off when only one firm controls an entire market?**

[1]Charles E. Sorensen, *My Forty Years with Ford* (New York: W. W. Norton & Co., 1956), p. 127.

MARKET POWER

market power: The ability to alter the market price of a good or service.

The essence of **market power** is the ability to alter the price of a product. The catfish farmers in Chapter 9 had no such power. Because 2,000 farms were producing and selling the same good, each catfish producer had to act as a *price taker.* Each producer could sell all it wanted at the prevailing price but would lose all its customers if it tried to charge a higher price.

The Downward-Sloping Demand Curve

Firms that have market power *can* alter the price of their output without losing all their customers. Sales volume may drop when price is increased, but the quantity demanded won't drop to zero. In other words, *firms with market power confront downward-sloping demand curves for their own output.*

The distinction between perfectly competitive (powerless) and imperfectly competitive (powerful) firms is illustrated again in Figure 10.1. Figure 10.1*a* re-creates the market situation that confronts a single catfish farmer. In Chapter 8, we assumed that the prevailing price of catfish was $13 a bushel and that a small, competitive firm could sell its entire output at this price. Hence each individual firm effectively confronted a horizontal demand curve.

We also noted earlier that catfish don't violate the law of demand. As good as catfish taste, people aren't willing to buy unlimited quantities of them at $13 a bushel. To induce consumers to buy more catfish, the market price of catfish must be reduced.

This seeming contradiction between the law of demand and the situation of the competitive firm is resolved in Figure 10.1. There are *two* relevant demand curves. The one on the left, which appears to contradict the law of demand, refers to a single competitive producer. The one on the right refers to the entire *industry,* of which the competitive producer is one very tiny part. The industry or market demand curve *does* slope downward, even though individual competitive firms are able to sell their own output at the going price.

Monopoly

monopoly: A firm that produces the entire market supply of a particular good or service.

An industry needn't be composed of many small firms. The entire output of catfish could be produced by a single large producer. Such a firm would be a **monopoly**—a single firm that produces the entire market supply of a good.

The emergence of a monopoly obliterates the distinction between industry demand and the demand curve facing the firm. A monopolistic firm *is* the industry. Hence there's only *one* demand curve to worry about, and that's the market (industry) demand curve, as illustrated in Figure 10.1*b.* This simplifies things: *in monopoly situations, the demand curve facing the firm is identical to the market demand curve for the product.*

FIGURE 10.1
Firm vs. Industry Demand

A competitive firm can sell its entire output at the prevailing market price. In this sense, the firm confronts a horizontal demand curve, as in part *a.* Nevertheless, *market* demand for the product still slopes downward. The demand curve confronting the industry is illustrated in part *b.* Note the difference in the units of measurement (single bushels vs. thousands). A monopolist confronts the *industry* (market) demand curve.

(a) The competitive firm

PRICE (dollars per bushel)

Demand facing competitive firm

$13

0

QUANTITY
(bushels of fish per day)

(b) The industry

PRICE (dollars per bushel)

Market demand

$13

In perfect competition, the **firm** is not the **industry**; in monopoly it is.

0

QUANTITY
(thousands of bushels of fish per day)

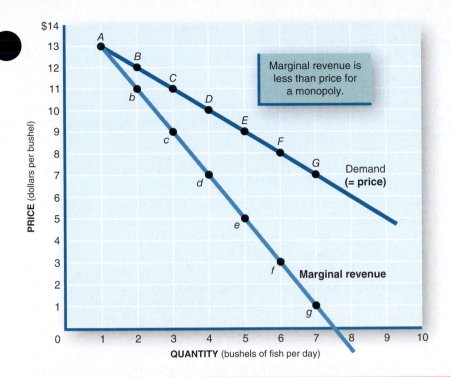

FIGURE 10.2
Price Exceeds Marginal Revenue in Monopoly

If a firm must lower its price to sell additional output, marginal revenue is less than price. If this monopoly firm wants to increase its sales from 1 to 2 bushels per day, for example, price must be reduced from $13 to $12. The marginal revenue of the second bushel is therefore only $11. This is indicated in row *B* of the table and by point *b* on the graph.

	(1) Quantity	×	(2) Price	=	(3) Total Revenue	(4) Marginal Revenue (= ΔTR ÷ Δq)
A	1		$13		$13	
						$11
B	2		12		24	
						9
C	3		11		33	
						7
D	4		10		40	
						5
E	5		9		45	

Price and Marginal Revenue

Although monopolies simplify the geometry, they complicate the arithmetic of **profit maximization.** The basic rule for maximizing profits is unchanged—that is, produce the rate of output where marginal revenue equals marginal cost. This rule applies to *all* firms. In a competitive industry, however, this general rule was simplified. For competitive firms, marginal revenue is equal to price. Hence a competitive firm can maximize profits by producing at that rate of output where marginal cost equals *price.*

This special adaptation of the profit-maximizing rule doesn't work for a monopolist. The demand curve facing a monopolist is downward-sloping. Because of this, *marginal revenue isn't equal to price for a monopolist.* On the contrary, marginal revenue is always *less* than price in a monopoly, which makes it just a bit more difficult to find the profit-maximizing rate of output.

Figure 10.2 is a simple illustration of the relationship between price and marginal revenue. The monopolist can sell 1 bushel of fish per day at a price of $13. If he wants

profit maximization rule: Produce at that rate of output where marginal revenue equals marginal cost.

to sell a larger quantity of fish, however, he has to reduce his price. According to the demand curve shown here, the price must be lowered to $12 to sell 2 bushels per day. This reduction in price is shown by a movement along the demand curve from point A to point B.

How much additional revenue does the second bushel bring in? It's tempting to say that it brings in $12, since that's its price. **Marginal revenue (MR),** however, refers to the *change* in *total* revenue that results from a one-unit increase in output. More generally, we use the formula

$$\frac{\text{Marginal}}{\text{revenue}} = \frac{\text{Change in total revenue}}{\text{Change in quantity sold}} = \frac{\Delta \text{TR}}{\Delta q}$$

where the delta symbol Δ denotes "change in." According to this formula, the marginal revenue of the second bushel is

$$\text{MR} = \frac{\$24 - \$13}{1} = \$11.$$

Hence MR ($11) is less than price ($12) for the second bushel sold.

Figure 10.2 summarizes the calculations necessary for computing MR. Row A of the table indicates that the total revenue resulting from one sale per day is $13. To increase sales, price must be reduced. Row B indicates that total revenue rises to $24 per day when fish sales double. The *increase* in total revenue resulting from the added sales is thus $11. This concept is illustrated in the last column of the table and by point b on the marginal revenue curve.

Notice that the MR of the second bushel ($11) is *less* than its price ($12) because both bushels are being sold for $12 apiece. In effect, the firm is giving up the opportunity to sell only 1 bushel per day at $13 to sell a larger quantity at a lower price. In this sense, the firm is sacrificing $1 of potential revenue on the first bushel to increase *total* revenue. Marginal revenue measures the change in total revenue that results.

So long as the demand curve is downward-sloping, MR will always be less than price. Compare columns 2 and 4 of the table in Figure 10.2. At each rate of output in excess of 1 bushel, marginal revenue is less than price. This is also evident in the graph: ***the MR curve lies below the demand (price) curve at every point but the first.***

Profit Maximization

Although the presence of market power adds a new wrinkle, the rules of profit maximization remain the same. ***Instead of looking for an intersection of marginal cost and price (as in perfect competition), we now look for the intersection of marginal cost and marginal revenue (monopoly).*** This is illustrated in Figure 10.3 by the intersection of the MR and MC curves (point d). Looking down from that intersection, we see that the associated rate of output is 4 bushels per day. Thus 4 bushels is the profit-maximizing rate of output.

How much should the monopolist charge for these 4 bushels? Naturally, the monopolist would like to charge a very high price. But the ability to charge a high price is limited by the demand curve. If the monopolist charges $13, consumers will buy only 1 bushel, leaving 3 unsold bushels of dead fish. Not a pretty picture. As the monopolist will soon learn, ***only one price is compatible with the profit-maximizing rate of output.*** In this case, the price is $10. This price is found in Figure 10.3 by moving up from the quantity 4 until reaching the demand curve at point D. Point D tells us that consumers are able and willing to buy 4 bushels of fish per day only at the price of $10 each. A monopolist who tries to charge more than $10 won't be able to sell all 4 bushels.

Figure 10.3 also illustrates the total profits of the catfish monopoly. To compute total profits we can first calculate profit per unit—that is, price minus *average* total cost. In this case, profit per unit is $2 at the profit-maximizing rate of output. Multiplying profit per unit by the quantity sold (4) gives us total profits of $8 per day, as illustrated by the shaded rectangle.

Profit Maximization (MR = MC)

The most profitable rate of output is indicated by the intersection of marginal revenue and marginal cost (point *d*). This intersection (MC = MR) establishes 4 bushels as the profit-maximizing rate of output. Point *D* indicates that consumers will pay $10 per bushel for this much output. Total profits equal price ($10) minus average total cost ($8), multiplied by the quantity sold (4).

MARKET POWER AT WORK: THE COMPUTER MARKET REVISITED

To develop a keener appreciation for the nature of market power, we can return to the computer market of Chapter 9. The computer market wasn't perfectly competitive, but it nearly behaved as though it was. We saw how the continuing entry of new firms kept competitive pressure on computer firms to reduce costs and improve quality. In this chapter, we'll make some different assumptions about market structure. In particular, assume that a single firm, Universal Electronics, acquires an exclusive patent on the production of the microprocessors that function as the computer's "brain." This one firm is now in a position to deny potential competitors access to the basic ingredient of computers. The patent thus functions as a **barrier to entry,** to be erected or set aside at the will of Universal Electronics.

Universal's management is familiar enough with the principles of economics (including W. C. Fields's advice about never giving a sucker an even break) to know when it's onto a good thing. It's not about to let every would-be Horatio Alger have a slice of the profit pie. Even the Russians understood this strategy during the heyday of communism. They made sure no one else could produce sable furs that could compete with their monopoly (see the World View on the next page). Let's assume that Universal Electronics is equally protective of its turf and will refuse to sell or give away any rights to its patent or the chips it produces. That is, Universal Electronics sets itself up as a computer monopoly.

Let's also assume that Universal has a multitude of manufacturing plants, each of which is identical to the typical competitive firm in Chapter 9. This is an unlikely situation because a monopolist would probably achieve **economies of scale** by closing at least a few plants and consolidating production in larger plants. Our fictional Universal company would maintain a multitude of small plants only if constant returns to scale or actual diseconomies of scale were rampant. Nevertheless, by assuming that multiple plants are maintained, we can compare monopoly behavior with competitive behavior on the basis of identical cost structures. In particular, if Universal continues to operate the many plants that once made up the competitive home computer industry, it will confront

barriers to entry: Obstacles, such as patents, that make it difficult or impossible for would-be producers to enter a particular market.

economies of scale: Reductions in minimum average costs that come about through increases in the size (scale) of plant and equipment.

WORLD VIEW

Foxy Soviets Pelt the West

Sable Monopoly Traps Hard Currency, Coats, Capitalists

LENINGRAD—Crown sable from the eastern Siberian region of Barguzin, star of the Soviet fur collection, went on sale just as a deep freeze gripped this former imperial city. . . .

Fur is one of the Soviet Union's best-known consumer goods exports. It is also bait for a country eager to trap hard currency: last year the Soviet Union earned $100 million in fur sales.

In the case of sable, the Soviet Union has something no one else has—in capitalist lingo, a monopoly.

Ivan the Terrible is said to have made the sale of live sables abroad a crime punishable by death. Peter the Great on his travels in the West is said to have carried along trunks of sable skins to use as currency.

In the best-selling novel *Gorky Park,* popular among fur traders, it was the Soviet sable monopoly that was the key to the tangled tale of murderous intrigue.

There is another story, origin and veracity unknown, that an American once traded a rare North American species to the Soviets in exchange for two live Russian sables—only to find when he got home that they had been sterilized.

—Celestine Bohlen

Analysis: To ward off potential competition, a monopoly must erect barriers to entry. By not letting live sables leave the country, to breed elsewhere, Russia maintained a monopoly on sable furs.

the same short-run marginal and average cost curves already encountered in Chapter 9. Later in this chapter we relax this assumption of multiplant operations to determine whether, in the long run, a monopolist may actually lower production costs below those of a competitive industry.

Figure 10.4*a* re-creates the marginal costs the typical competitive firm faced in the early stages of the microcomputer boom (from Figure 9.3 and Table 9.1). We now assume that this MC curve also expresses the costs of operating one of Universal's many (identical) plants. Thus the extension of monopoly control is assumed to have no immediate effect on production costs.

The market demand for computers is also assumed to be unchanged. There's no reason why people should be less willing to buy computers now than they were when the market was competitive. Most consumers have no notion of how many firms produce a product. Even if they knew, there's no reason why their demand for the product would change. Thus Figure 10.4*b* expresses an unchanged market demand for computers.

Our immediate concern is to determine how Universal Electronics, as a monopolist, will respond to these unchanged demand and cost curves. Will it produce exactly as many computers as the competitive industry did? Will it sell the computers at the same price that the competitive industry did? Will it improve the product as much or as fast?

The Production Decision

Like any producer, Universal Electronics will strive to produce its output at the rate that maximizes total profits. But unlike competitive firms, Universal will explicitly take account of the fact that an increase in output will put downward pressure on computer prices. This may threaten corporate profits.

FIGURE 10.4

Initial Conditions in the Monopolized Computer Market

We assume that a monopoly firm (Universal Electronics) would confront the same costs (MC and ATC) and demand as would the competitive industry in Chapter 9. In the initial short-run equilibrium, the competitive price was $1,000 (point C), and each firm (plant) was producing 600 computers (where MC = p).

A monopolist isn't bound by the competitive market price. Instead the monopolist must contend with downward-sloping demand and marginal revenue curves. If each monopoly plant produced where MC = $1,000 (point C in part a), marginal cost (point C) would exceed marginal revenue (point B). To maximize profits, the monopolist must find that rate of output where MC = MR (point M in part a). That rate of output (475) can be sold at the higher monopoly price of $1,100 (point W in part a).

Part b illustrates the market implications of the monopolist's production decision: a reduced quantity are sold at a higher price (point A).

The implications of Universal's market position for the **production decision** of its many plants can be seen in the new price and marginal revenue curves imposed on each of its manufacturing plants. Universal can't afford to let each of its plants compete with the others, expanding output and driving down prices; that's the kind of folly reserved for truly competitive firms. Instead Universal will seek to *coordinate* the production decisions of its plants, instructing all plant managers to expand or contract output simultaneously, to achieve the corporate goal of profit maximization.

A simultaneous reduction of output by each Universal plant will lead to a significant reduction in the quantity of computers supplied to the market. This reduced supply will cause a move up the market demand curve to higher prices. By the same token, an expansion of output by all Universal plants will lead to an increase in the quantity supplied to the market and a slide down the market demand curve. As a consequence, each of the monopolist's plants effectively confronts a downward-sloping demand curve. These downward-sloping demand curves are illustrated in Figure 10.4a.[2]

Notice that in Figure 10.4b the *market* demand for computers is unchanged; only the demand curve confronting each plant (firm) has changed. A competitive *industry*, like a

production decision: The selection of the short-run rate of output (with existing plants and equipment).

[2]The demand and marginal revenue curves in Figure 10.4a are illustrative; they're not derived from earlier tables. As discussed here, we're assuming that the central management of Universal determines the profit-maximizing rate of output and then instructs all individual plants to produce equal shares of that output.

monopoly, must obey the law of demand. But the individual firms that compose a competitive industry all act independently, *as if* they could sell unlimited quantities at the prevailing price. That is, they all act as if they confronted a horizontal demand curve at the market price of $1,000. A competitive firm that doesn't behave in this fashion will simply lose sales to other firms. In contrast, *a monopolist not only foresees the impact of increased production on market price but can also prevent such production increases by its separate plants.*

Marginal Revenue. The downward-sloping demand curve now confronting each Universal plant implies that marginal revenue no longer equals price. Notice that the marginal revenue curve in Figure 10.4a lies *below* the demand curve at every rate of output. Because marginal revenue is less than price for a monopoly, Universal's plants would no longer wish to produce up to the point where marginal cost equals price. *Only firms that confront a horizontal demand curve (perfect competitors) equate marginal cost and price.* Universal's plants must stick to the generic profit-maximizing rule about equating marginal revenue and marginal cost. Should the individual plant managers forget this rule, Universal's central management will fire them.

The output and price implications of Universal's monopoly position become apparent as we examine the new revenue and cost relationships. Recall that the equilibrium price of computers in the early stages of the home computer boom was $1,000. This equilibrium price is indicated in Figure 10.4b by the intersection of the *competitive* market supply curve with the market demand curve (point X). Each competitive *firm* produced up to the point where marginal cost (MC) equaled that price (point C in Figure 10.4a). At that point, each competitive firm was producing 600 computers a month.

Reduced Output. The emergence of Universal as a monopolist alters these production decisions. Now each Universal plant *does* have an impact on market price because its behavior is imitated simultaneously by all Universal plants. In fact, the marginal revenue associated with the 600th computer is only $575, as indicated by point B in Figure 10.4a. At this rate of output, the typical Universal plant would be operating with marginal costs ($1,000) far in excess of marginal revenues ($575). Such behavior is inconsistent with profit maximization.

The enlightened Universal plant manager will soon discover that the profit-maximizing rate of output is less than 600 computers per month. In Figure 10.4a we see that the marginal revenue and marginal cost curves intersect at point M. This MR = MC intersection occurs at an output level of only 475 computers per month. Accordingly, the typical Universal plant will want to produce *fewer* computers (475) than were produced by the typical competitive firm (600) in the early stages of the home computer boom. Recall that individual competitive firms had no incentive to engage in such production cutbacks. They couldn't alter the market supply curve or price on their own and weren't coordinated by a central management. Thus the first consequence of Universal's monopoly position is a reduction in the rate of industry output.

The Monopoly Price

The reduction in output at each Universal plant translates automatically into a decrease in the *quantity supplied* to the market. As consumers compete for this reduced market supply, they'll bid computer prices up. We can observe the increased prices in Figure 10.4 by looking at either the typical Universal plant or the computer market. Notice that in Figure 10.4a the price is determined by moving directly up from point M to the demand curve confronting the typical Universal plant. The demand curve always tells how much consumers are willing to pay for any given quantity. Hence, once we've determined the quantity that's going to be supplied (475 computers per month), we can look at the demand curve to determine the price ($1,100 at point *W*) that consumers will pay for these computers. That is,

- *The intersection of the marginal revenue and marginal cost curves establishes the profit-maximizing rate of output.*
- *The demand curve tells us how much consumers are willing to pay for that specific quantity of output.*

Figure 10.4*a* shows how Universal's monopoly position results in both reduced output and increased prices. This result is also evident in Figure 10.4*b*, where we see that a smaller quantity supplied to the market will force a move up the demand curve to the higher price of $1,100 per computer (point *A*).

Monopoly Profits

Universal's objective was and remains the maximization of profits. That it has succeeded in its effort can be confirmed by scrutinizing Figure 10.5. As you can see, the typical Universal plant ends up selling 475 computers a month at a price of $1,100 each (point *W*). The **average total cost (ATC)** of production at this rate of output is only $630 (point *K*), as was detailed in Table 9.1.

As always, we can compute total profit as

$$\text{Total profit} = \text{Profit per unit} \times \text{Quantity sold}$$

In this case, we see that

$$\text{Total profit} = (\$1,100 - \$630) \times 475$$
$$= \$223,250$$

This figure significantly exceeds the monthly profit of $180,000 earned by the typical competitive firm in the early stages of the computer boom (see Table 9.1).

It's apparent from these profit figures that Universal management has learned its economic principles well. By reducing the output of each plant and raising prices a little, it has managed to increase profits. This can be seen again in Figure 10.6, which is an enlarged illustration of the *market* situation for the home computer industry. The figure translates the economics of our single-plant and competitive-firm comparison into the dimensions of the whole industry.

average total cost (ATC): Total cost divided by the quantity produced in a given time period.

FIGURE 10.5
Monopoly Profits: The Typical Universal Plant

The profit-maximizing rate of output occurs where the marginal cost and marginal revenue curves intersect (point *M*). The demand curve indicates the price (point *W*) that consumers will pay for this much output. Total profit equals price (*W*) minus *average* total cost (*K*), multiplied by the quantity sold (475). Total profits are represented by the shaded rectangle.

FIGURE 10.6

Monopoly Profit: The Entire Company

Total profits of the monopolist (including all plants) are illustrated by the shaded rectangle. The monopolist's total output q_m is determined by the intersection of the (industry) MR and MC curves. The price of this output is determined by the market demand curve (point A).

In contrast, a competitive industry would produce q_c computers in the short run and sell them at a lower price (X) and profit per unit ($X - U$). Those profits would attract new entrants until long-run equilibrium (point V) was reached. (See Figure 9.9 for a summary of competitive market equilibrium.)

Figure 10.6 reaffirms that the competitive industry in Chapter 9 initially produces the quantity q_c and sells it at a price of $1,000 each. Its profits are denoted by the rectangle formed by the points *R, X, U, T*. The monopolist, on the other hand, produces the smaller q_m and charges a higher price, $1,100. The monopoly firm's profits are indicated by the larger profit rectangle shaded in the figure. We see that *a monopoly receives larger profits than a comparable competitive industry by reducing the quantity supplied and pushing prices up.* The larger profits make Universal very happy and make consumers a little sadder and wiser. Consumers are now paying more and getting less.

Barriers to Entry

The higher profits Universal Electronics attained as a result of its monopoly position aren't the end of the story. The existence of economic profit tends to bring profit-hungry entrepreneurs swarming like locusts. In the competitive computer industry of Chapter 9, the lure of high profits brought about an enormous expansion of computer output and a steep decline in computer prices. In Figure 10.6 the long-run equilibrium of a competitive industry is indicated by point *V.* What can we expect to happen in the computer market now that Universal has a monopoly position and is enjoying huge profits?

Remember that Universal is now assumed to have an exclusive patent on microprocessor chips and can use this patent as an impassable barrier to entry. Consequently, would-be competitors can swarm around Universal's profits until their wings drop off; Universal isn't about to let them in on the spoils. By locking out potential competition, Universal can prevent the surge in computer output that pushed prices down the market demand curve. As long as Universal is able to keep out the competition, only the more affluent consumers will be able to use computers. The same phenomenom explains why ticket prices for live concerts are so high. When Live Nation acquired Ticketmaster in 2009, it became a virtual monopolist for concert sites and ticket distribution. As the following News suggests, this music industry merger created a "sour note" for music fans. A monopoly has no incentive to move from point *A* in Figure 10.6, and there's no competitive pressure to force such a move. Universal may discover ways to reduce the costs of production and thus lower prices, but there's no *pressure* on it to do so, as there was in the competitive situation. Similarly, there's no *competitive pressure* on Live Nation to reduce concert prices.

IN THE NEWS

Ticketmaster–Live Nation: A Sour Note

A Merger of the Largest Ticket Seller and the Biggest Concert Promoter Could Raise Serious Antitrust Concerns

NEW YORK (CNNMoney.com)—There were plenty of stories earlier this week commemorating the 50th anniversary of the plane crash that killed Buddy Holly, Ritchie Valens, and the Big Bopper—a tragedy later dubbed "The Day the Music Died."

But if Ticketmaster and Live Nation wind up merging, that may also become an event music fans will mourn just as much.

According to several published reports, Live Nation, the country's biggest concert promoter, is in talks to combine with Ticketmaster, the largest seller of tickets for concerts, sporting events, and other live entertainment.

The two companies are reviled by many music fans because of rising ticket prices and numerous surcharges.

Ticketmaster, in particular, has been a target of both consumers and musicians alike. The rock group Pearl Jam famously canceled a concert tour in the mid-1990s because Ticketmaster would not drop some of its service fees.

But both companies have grown in clout during the past few years.

—Paul R. LaMonica

Source: CNNMoney.com, February 4, 2009. © 2009 Time Inc. Used under license.

Analysis: Control of concert sites and ticket distribution allows Live Nation Entertainment to charge monopoly prices for live concerts.

A COMPARATIVE PERSPECTIVE OF MARKET POWER

The different outcomes of the computer industry under competitive and monopoly conditions illustrate basic features of market structures. We may summarize the sequence of events that occurs in each type of market structure as follows:

COMPETITIVE INDUSTRY

- High prices and profits signal consumers' demand for more output.
- The high profits attract new suppliers.
- Production and supplies expand.
- Prices slide down the market demand curve.
- A new equilibrium is established wherein more of the desired product is produced, its price falls, average costs of production approach their minimum, and economic profits approach zero.
- Price equals marginal cost throughout the process.
- Throughout the process, there's great pressure to keep ahead of the profit squeeze by reducing costs or improving product quality.

MONOPOLY INDUSTRY

- High prices and profits signal consumers' demand for more output.
- Barriers to entry are erected to exclude potential competition.
- Production and supplies are constrained.
- Prices don't move down the market demand curve.
- No new equilibrium is established; average costs aren't necessarily at or near a minimum, and economic profits are at a maximum.
- Price exceeds marginal cost at all times.
- There's no squeeze on profits and thus no pressure to reduce costs or improve product quality.

In our discussion, we assumed that the competitive industry and the monopoly both started from the same position—an initial equilibrium in which the price of computers is $1,000. In reality, an industry may manifest concentrations of market power *before* such an equilibrium is established. That is, the sequence of events we've depicted may be altered (with step 3 occurring first, for example). Nevertheless, the basic distinctions between competitive and monopolistic behavior are evident.

Productivity Advances. To the extent that monopolies behave as we've discussed, they affect not just the price and output of a specific product but broader economic outcomes as well. Remember that competitive industries tend, in the long run, to produce at minimum average costs. Competitive industries also pursue cost reductions and product improvements relentlessly. These pressures tend to expand our production possibilities. No such forces are at work in the monopoly we've discussed here. Hence there's a basic tendency for monopolies to inhibit productivity advances and economic growth.

marginal cost pricing: The offer (supply) of goods at prices equal to their marginal cost.

The Mix of Output. Another important feature of competitive markets is their observed tendency toward **marginal cost pricing.** Marginal cost pricing is important to consumers because it permits rational choices among alternative goods and services. In particular, it informs consumers of the true opportunity costs of various goods, thereby allowing them to choose the mix of output that delivers the most utility with available resources. In our monopoly example, however, consumers end up getting fewer computers than they'd like, while the economy continues to produce other, less desired goods. Thus the mix of output shifted away from computers when Universal took over the industry.

The power to influence prices and product flows may have far-reaching consequences for our economic welfare. Changes in prices and product flows directly influence the level and composition of output, employment and resource allocation, the level and distribution of income, and, of course, the level and structure of prices. Hence firms that wield significant market power affect all dimensions of economic welfare.

Political Power. Market power isn't the only kind of power wielded in society, of course. Political power, for example, is a different kind of power and important in its own right. Indeed, the power to influence an election or to sway a Senate committee vote may ultimately be more important than the power to increase the price of laundry soap. Nevertheless, market power is a force that influences the way we live, the incomes we earn, and our relationships with other countries. Moreover, market power may be the basis for political power: the individual or firm with considerable market power is likely to have the necessary resources to influence an election or sway a vote on a congressional committee.

The Limits to Power

Even though market power enables a producer to manipulate market outcomes, there's a clear limit to the exercise of power. Even a monopolist can't get everything it wants. Universal, for example, would really like to sell q_m computers at a price of $1,500 each because that kind of price would bring it even greater profits. Yet, despite its monopoly position, Universal is constrained to sell that quantity of computers at the lower price of $1,100 each. Even monopolists have their little disappointments.

The ultimate limit to a monopolist's power is evident in Figure 10.6. Universal's attainment of a monopoly position allows it only one prerogative: the ability to alter the quantity of output *supplied* to the market. This is no small prerogative, but it's far from absolute power. Universal, and every other monopolist, must still contend with the market *demand* curve. Note again that the new equilibrium in Figure 10.6 occurs at a point on the *unchanged* market demand curve. In effect, *a monopolist has the opportunity to pick any point on the market demand curve and designate it as the new market equilibrium.* The point it selects will depend on its own perceptions of effort, profit, and risk (in this case point *A,* determined by the intersection of marginal revenue and marginal cost).

The ultimate constraint on the exercise of market power, then, resides in the market demand curve. How great a constraint the demand curve imposes depends largely on the **price elasticity of demand.** The greater the price elasticity of demand, the more a monopolist will be frustrated in attempts to establish both high prices and high volume. Consumers will simply reduce their purchases if price is increased. If, however, consumer demand is highly inelastic—if consumers need or want that product badly and few viable substitutes are available—the monopolist can reap tremendous profits from market power. That was clearly the case for the monopoly in production of a heart drug for babies (see the News below).

price elasticity of demand: The percentage change in quantity demanded divided by the percentage change in price.

IN THE NEWS

U.S. Sues over Drug's Price Hike

Ovation Pharmaceuticals violated federal law in 2006 when it bought a competitor's drug, creating a monopoly for the heart treatment used on premature babies, and then raised the price, a federal lawsuit says. The Federal Trade Commission wants Ovation to return "millions of dollars" in overcharges for the drug, used to treat a condition that afflicts 30,000 babies each year, Bureau of Competition acting Director David Wales said.

The lawsuit says the price rose from $36 a vial to nearly $500. The company said the FTC's allegations are "without merit."

—Julie Appleby

Source: *USA TODAY.* December 17, 2008, p. 3A. Reprinted with permission.

Analysis: If demand is inelastic, a monopolist can increase price without losing many sales.

web analysis

Visit **www.ftc.gov** and click on the "Competition" tab to learn more about past antitrust rulings by the Federal Trade Commission Bureau of Competition.

Price Discrimination

Even in situations where the *market* demand is relatively elastic, a monopolist may be able to extract high prices. A monopolist has the power not only to raise the market price of a good (by reducing the quantity supplied) but also to charge various prices for the same good. Recall that the market demand curve reflects the combined willingness of many individuals to buy. Some of those individuals are willing to buy the good at prices higher than the market price, just as other individuals will buy only at lower prices. A monopolist may be able to increase total profits by selling each unit of the good separately, at a price each *individual* consumer is willing to pay. This practice is called **price discrimination.**

The airline industry has practiced price discrimination for many years. Basically, there are two distinct groups of travelers: business and nonbusiness travelers. Business executives must fly from one city to another on a certain day and at a particular time. They typically make flight arrangements on short notice and may have no other way to get to their destination. Nonbusiness travelers, such as people on vacation and students going home during semester break, usually have more flexible schedules. They may plan their trips weeks or months in advance and often have the option of traveling by car, bus, or train.

The different travel needs of business and vacation travelers are reflected in their respective demand curves. Business demand for air travel tends to be less price-elastic than the demand of nonbusiness travelers. Few business executives would stop flying if airfares increased. Higher airfares would, however, discourage air travel by nonbusiness travelers.

price discrimination: The sale of an identical good at different prices to different consumers by a single seller.

What should airlines do in this case? Should they *raise* airfares to take advantage of the relative price inelasticity of business demand, or should they *lower* airfares to attract more nonbusiness travelers?

They should do both. In fact, they *have* done both. The airlines offer a full-fare ride, available at any time, and a discount-fare ride, available only by purchasing a ticket in advance and agreeing to some restrictions on time of departure. The advance purchase and other restrictions on discount fares effectively exclude most business travelers, who end up paying full fare. The higher full fare doesn't, however, discourage most nonbusiness travelers, who can fly at a discount. Consequently, the airlines are able to sell essentially identical units of the same good (an airplane ride) at substantially different prices to different customers. This price discrimination enables the airlines to capture the highest possible *average* price for the quantity supplied.

With *perfect* price discrimination, a monopolist would sell the product to each consumer on the demand curve at the maximum price that individual was willing to pay. If that happened, the monopolist would eliminate all **consumer surplus** and capture the extra revenue that a single price misses. This was the intent of the "dynamic pricing" introduced by Ticketmaster in 2011 for concert tickets (see the accompanying News). It doesn't tailor prices to each individual but facilitates much greater price discrimination. Doctors, lawyers, and car dealers commonly practice the same type of price discrimination.

> **consumer surplus:** The difference between the maximum price a person is willing to pay and the price paid.

IN THE NEWS

Ticketmaster Rolls Out "Dynamic" Pricing

LOS ANGELES—Event tickets seller Ticketmaster said Monday that it is introducing new technology to let artists and sports teams raise or lower ticket prices to reflect demand during the initial sales period—a move it said will crimp the profits of scalpers and boost revenue for performers and teams.

The technology could push up initial prices for front-row seats while reducing prices on less desirable ones that might have gone unsold otherwise. . . .

The company already is testing the system, known as "dynamic pricing," with several professional baseball, basketball, and hockey teams. Ticketmaster plans to roll it out at some North American venues in the middle of the summer concert season this year.

—Ryan Nakashima

Source: Associated Press, April 18, 2011. Used with permission of The Associated Press. Copyright © 2011. All rights reserved.

Analysis: A monopolist can increase revenue and profit by price discriminating—selling the same good to each consumer at the price she or he is willing to pay.

Entry Barriers

It's the lack of competitors that gives monopolists such pricing power. Accordingly, ***the preservation of monopoly power depends on keeping potential competitors out of the market.*** A monopolist doesn't want anyone else to produce an *identical* product or even a *close substitute.* To do that, a monopoly must erect and maintain barriers to market entry. It was the absence of significant entry barriers that permitted iPad clones to attack Apple's profits (see the News on page 209). Some of the entry barriers used to repel such attacks include:

Patents. This was the critical barrier in the mythical Universal Electronics case. A government-awarded patent gives a producer 20 years of exclusive rights to produce a particular product. The Polaroid Corporation used its patents to keep Eastman Kodak and other potential rivals out of the market for instant development cameras. In 2007 Verizon and Sprint used broad patents to curb the growth of Vonage, the leading provider of Internet phone service.

Monopoly Franchises. The government also creates and maintains monopolies by giving a single firm the exclusive right to supply a particular good or service, even though other firms could produce it. Local cable TV stations and telephone companies are examples. Congress also bestows monopoly privileges to baseball teams and the U.S. Postal Service. Your campus bookstore may have exclusive rights to sell textbooks on campus.

Control of Key Inputs. A company may lock out competition by securing exclusive access to key inputs. Airlines need landing rights and terminal gates to compete. Oil and gas producers need pipelines to supply their products. Utility companies need transmission networks to supply consumers with electricity. Software vendors need to know the features of computer operating systems. If a single company controls these critical inputs, it can lock out potential competition. Intel was accused by the Federal Trade Commission (FTC) of trying to lock out competition by enticing computer makers with hefty discounts to use Intel chips exclusively in their computers (see the News on the next page). Microsoft was accused of using similar tactics to consolidate its monopoly position in operating systems (see the Economy Tomorrow section at the end of this chapter).

Lawsuits. In the event that competitors actually surmount other entry barriers, a monopoly may sue them out of existence. Typically, start-up firms are rich in ideas but cash poor. They need to get their products to the market quickly to generate some cash. A timely lawsuit alleging patent or copyright infringement can derail such a company by absorbing critical management, cash, and time. Long before the merits of the lawsuit are adjudicated, the company may be forced to withdraw from the market. When confronted by the FTC, Intel agreed to dismantle this entry barrier as well (see the News on the next page again).

Acquisition. When all else fails, a monopolist may simply purchase a potential competitor. Live Nation's acquisition of Ticketmaster in 2009 (see the News on page 223) eliminated competition in the ticket distribution system. As the below cartoon suggests, mergers tend to raise consumer prices.

Economies of Scale. Last but far from least, a monopoly may persist because of economies of scale. If large firms have a substantial cost advantage over smaller firms, the smaller firms may not be able to compete. We look at this entry barrier again in a moment.

Analysis: Mergers and acquisitions reduce competition in an industry. The increased industry concentration may lead to higher prices.

Intel's Concessions Settle Antitrust Suit

Intel on Wednesday agreed to never again offer computer makers and retailers hefty rebates in return for exclusive agreements to use its chips.

That concession brought closure to a Federal Trade Commission antitrust lawsuit. As part of a settlement, the world's largest computer chip maker also said it would not redesign its products mainly to harm a competitor, nor retaliate against computer makers for using chips from rivals Advanced Micro Devices, Nvidia, or Via Technologies. . . .

Further, Intel agreed not to seek patent infringement claims against rival chipmakers who form joint ventures that might include pieces of Intel technology. The settlement should prevent Intel from creating "new ways to undermine competition," says FTC Chairman Jon Leibowitz. . . .

"The FTC is being much more vigorous, and this has been good for consumers and for the companies competing against each other," King says. "No one is well served by allowing one company to tilt the playing field in its favor."

—Byron Acohido

Source: *USA TODAY.* August 5, 2010. Reprinted with permission.

Analysis: Monopoly firms try to erect entry barriers to keep competitors out of their market.

PROS AND CONS OF MARKET POWER

Despite the strong case against market power, it's conceivable that monopolies could also benefit society. One argument made for concentrations of market power is that monopolies have greater ability to pursue research and development. Another argument is that the lure of market power creates a tremendous incentive for invention and innovation. A third argument in defense of monopoly is that large companies can produce goods more efficiently than smaller firms. Finally, it's argued that even monopolies have to worry about *potential* competition and will behave accordingly.

Research and Development

In principle, monopolies are well positioned to undertake valuable research and development. First, such firms are sheltered from the constant pressure of competition. Second, they have the resources (monopoly profits) with which to carry out expensive R&D functions. The manager of a perfectly competitive firm, by contrast, has to worry about day-to-day production decisions and profit margins. As a result, she is unable to take the longer view necessary for significant research and development and couldn't afford to purchase such a view even if she could see it.

The basic problem with the R&D argument is that it says nothing about *incentives*. Although monopolists have a clear financial advantage in pursuing research and development activities, they have no clear incentive to do so. Research and development aren't necessarily required for profitable survival. In fact, research and development that make existing plants and equipment technologically obsolete run counter to a monopolist's vested interest and so may actually be suppressed (see the accompanying News). In contrast, a perfectly competitive firm can't continue to make significant profits unless it stays ahead of the competition. This pressure constitutes a significant incentive to discover new products or new and cheaper ways of producing existing products.

IN THE NEWS

Jury Rules Magnetek Unit Is Liable for Keeping Technology off Market

SAN FRANCISCO—Is a company liable if it deliberately keeps a technology off the market? Apparently so, judging from an unusual ruling by a California jury.

A county superior court jury in Oakland ordered a unit of Magnetek Inc. to pay $25.8 million to two California entrepreneurs and their companies. They charged that the unit had failed to bring the pair's energy-saving fluorescent-light technology to market in a profitable manner, suppressing it in favor of an outmoded technology.

The lawsuit reads like familiar legends of big business quashing inventions that threaten its interests. . . .

In 1984 the two entrepreneurs, C. R. Stevens and William R. Alling, charged that Universal Manufacturing Corp., now a unit of Los Angeles–based Magnetek, buried a technology through which fluorescent lights use 70 percent less energy. The two said they sold Universal the technology, called a solid-state ballast, in 1981 after the company promised to market it aggressively.

Instead, they charged, Universal suppressed the technology to protect its less efficient existing ballast models. "They told us they were going to be first on the market with our tech, yet they planned otherwise," said Mr. Alling.

—Stephen Kreider Yoder

Source: *The Wall Street Journal*, January 10, 1990, p. B2. Used with permission of Dow Jones & Company, Inc. via Copyright Clearance Center, Inc.

Analysis: A monopoly has little incentive (no competitive pressure) to pursue R&D. In fact, R&D that threatens established products or processes may be suppressed.

Entrepreneurial Incentives

The second defense of market power uses a novel incentive argument. Every business is out to make a buck, and it's the quest for profits that keeps industries running. Thus, it's argued, even greater profit prizes will stimulate more entrepreneurial activity. Little Horatio Algers will work harder and longer if they can dream of one day possessing a whole monopoly.

The incentive argument for market power is enticing but not entirely convincing. After all, an innovator can make substantial profits in a competitive market before the competition catches up. Recall that the early birds did get the worm in the competitive computer industry (see Chapter 9), even though profit margins were later squeezed. It's not evident that the profit incentives available in a competitive industry are at all inadequate.

We must also recall the arguments about research and development efforts. A monopolist has little incentive to pursue R&D. Furthermore, entrepreneurs who might pursue product innovation or technological improvements may be dissuaded by their inability to penetrate a monopolized market. The barriers to entry that surround market power may not only keep out potential competitors but also lock out promising ideas.

Economies of Scale

A third defense of market power is the most plausible. A large firm, it's argued, can produce goods at a lower unit (average) cost than a small firm. If such *economies of scale* exist, we could attain greater efficiency (higher productivity) by permitting firms to grow to market-dominating size.

We sidestepped this argument in our story about the Universal Electronics monopoly. We explicitly assumed that Universal confronted the same production costs as the competitive industry. We simply converted each typical competitive firm into a separate plant owned and operated by Universal. Universal wasn't able to produce computers any more cheaply than the competitive counterpart, and we concerned ourselves only with the different production decisions made by competitive and monopolistic firms.

A monopoly *could*, however, attain greater cost savings. By centralizing various functions it might be able to eliminate some duplicative efforts. It might also shut down some plants and concentrate production in fewer facilities. If these kinds of efficiencies are attained, a monopoly would offer attractive resource savings.

There's no guarantee, however, of such economies of scale. As we observed in Chapter 7, increasing the size (scale) of a plant may actually *reduce* operating efficiency (see Figure 7.10). In evaluating the economies-of-scale argument for market power, then, we must recognize that *efficiency and size don't necessarily go hand in hand. Some firms and industries may be subject to economies of scale, but others won't.*

Even when economies of scale are present, there is no guarantee that consumers will benefit. The 2006 merger of Boeing and Lockheed cut the costs of rocket production by $100–150 million a year (see the accompanying News). But the Defense Department ended up paying higher prices. The Justice Department initially opposed the merger of the nation's only two satellite radio companies in 2007 for the same reason. Even though there were substantial short-run economies of scale in eliminating duplicate facilities, the Justice Department concluded that even a little competition (two firms) was better

The Urge to Merge

IN THE NEWS

Rocket Monopoly Approved

Boeing–Lockheed Alliance Likely to Increase Costs

U.S. antitrust authorities yesterday approved a plan by Lockheed Martin Corp. and Boeing Co. to merge their government rocket businesses, creating a monopoly in a multibillion-dollar market that the Federal Trade Commission acknowledged will probably lead to higher prices and lower quality. . . .

"Monopolies almost always lead to higher prices, lower quality, and inferior services," Michael R. Moiseyev, assistant director of the FTC's bureau of competition, said in a July letter that was made public yesterday. "Here, the competition that would be lost is significant, and the economic benefits that may materialize are unlikely to trump the transaction's harm to competition." . . .

The companies have said they expect the joint venture to generate $1.5 billion to $2 billion in revenue per year from the government and save it $100 million to $150 million a year.

Pentagon and FTC officials said the cost savings do not offset the impact of the loss of competition.

The department's "careful review of those savings leads us to conclude that the cost savings, while attractive, are not adequate to support the loss of competition," Kenneth J. Krieg, the Pentagon's acquisition chief said, in an August letter to the FTC. . . .

But "DoD has concluded that ULA would improve national security and that the unique national security benefits from the joint venture would exceed any anticompetitive harm," the FTC said in a statement yesterday.

—Renae Merle

Analysis: Mergers eliminate duplicate facilities, thereby reducing total costs. But monopoly power permits the merged entity to retain the cost savings rather than pass them along to the consumer in the form of lower prices.

than none (a monopoly) in expanding consumer choice and keeping prices low (see the accompanying News). Both the Justice Department and the Federal Communications Commission ultimately approved the XMSatellite–Sirius Radio merger, however, in return for their promise not to raise prices for at least three years.

IN THE NEWS

XM–Sirius Merger Made Simple: One Is Always Less Than Two

Sometime soon, when federal regulators decide whether to allow a merger of the nation's two satellite radio services, XM and Sirius, the government will have to take a stand: Would combining the two companies unfairly diminish consumer choice or, as the companies argue, turn losing operations into a profitable service with lower prices?

But while lawyers at the Justice Department and the Federal Communications Commission fight through a thicket of filings, the questions for listeners are different: Would a single satellite radio company produce more or less interesting and entertaining content? Would the menu of music, news, sports, comedy, and talk programming get longer or shorter—and at what price? Wouldn't reducing the satellite field to one company lead inevitably to service cuts and price increases?

Think about it: Can you name one example of a new consumer technology that was guaranteed to a single provider and still served customers well? (Don't everyone say "cable TV" at once.)

—Marc Fisher

Source: *The Washington Post*, © November 11, 2007. All rights reserved. Used with permission.

Analysis: Monopolies may enjoy economies of scale. In the long run, however, consumers may benefit more from competitive pressures to reduce costs, improve product quality, and lower prices.

---

web analysis

Information on Federal Communications Commission regulation and deregulation can be found at **www.fcc.gov**.

Natural Monopolies. Industries that exhibit economies of scale over the entire range of market output are called **natural monopolies.** In these cases, one single firm can produce the entire market supply more efficiently than any large number of (smaller) firms. As the size (scale) of the one firm increases, its minimum average costs continue to fall. These economies of scale give the one large producer a decided advantage over would-be rivals. Hence *economies of scale act as a "natural" barrier to entry.*

natural monopoly: An industry in which one firm can achieve economies of scale over the entire range of market supply.

Local telephone and utility services are classic examples of natural monopoly. A single telephone or utility company can supply the market more efficiently than a large number of competing firms.

Although natural monopolies are economically desirable, they may be abused. We must ask whether and to what extent consumers are reaping some benefit from the efficiency a natural monopoly makes possible. Do consumers end up with lower prices, expanded output, and better service? Or does the monopoly keep most of the benefits for itself, in the form of higher prices and profits? Multiplex movie theaters, for example, achieve economies of scale by sharing operating and concession facilities among as many as 30 screens. But do moviegoers get lower prices for movies or popcorn? Not often. Because megamultiplex theaters tend to drive out competition, they don't have to reduce prices when costs drop. Under such circumstances, we may need government "trustbusters" to ensure that the benefits of increased efficiency are shared with consumers. (The potential and pitfalls of government regulation are examined in Chapter 13.)

Contestable Market

Governmental regulators aren't necessarily the only force keeping monopolists in line. Even though a firm may produce the entire supply of a particular product at present, it may face *potential* competition from other firms. Potential rivals may be sitting on the sidelines,

contestable market: An imperfectly competitive industry subject to potential entry if prices or profits increase.

watching how well the monopoly fares. If it does too well, these rivals may enter the industry, undermining the monopoly structure and profits. In such **contestable markets,** monopoly behavior may be restrained by potential competition.

How "contestable" a market is depends not so much on its structure as on entry barriers. If entry barriers are insurmountable, would-be competitors are locked out of the market. But if entry barriers are modest, they'll be surmounted when the lure of monopoly profits is irresistible. When CNN's profits reached irresistible proportions, both domestic and foreign companies (e.g., CNBC, Fox News, Bloomberg News) decided to invade CNN's monopoly market. Since then, CNN hasn't been nearly as profitable.

Structure vs. Behavior. From the perspective of contestable markets, the whole case against monopoly is misconceived. Market *structure* per se isn't a problem; what counts is market *behavior*. If potential rivals force a monopolist to behave like a competitive firm, then monopoly imposes no cost on consumers or on society at large.

The experience with the Model T Ford illustrates the basic notion of contestable markets. At the time Henry Ford decided to increase the price of the Model T and paint them all black, the Ford Motor Company enjoyed a virtual monopoly on mass-produced cars. But potential rivals saw the profitability of offering additional colors and features such as a self-starter and left-hand drive. When rivals began producing cars in volume, Ford's market power was greatly reduced. In 1926 the Ford Motor Company tried to regain its dominant position by again supplying cars in colors other than black. By that time, however, consumers had more choices. Ford ceased production of the Model T in May 1927.

The experience with the Model T suggests that potential competition can force a monopoly to change its ways. Critics point out, however, that even contestable markets don't force a monopolist to act *exactly* like a competitive firm. There will always be a gap between competitive outcomes and those monopoly outcomes likely to entice new entry. That gap can cost consumers a lot. The absence of *existing* rivals is also likely to inhibit product and productivity improvements. From 1913 to 1926, all Model Ts were black, and consumers had few alternatives. Ford changed its behavior only after *potential* competition became *actual* competition. Even after 1927, when the Ford Motor Company could no longer act like a monopolist, it still didn't price its cars at marginal cost.

THE ECONOMY TOMORROW

MICROSOFT AND GOOGLE: BULLIES OR GENIUSES?

Ford Motor Company's experience is a useful reminder that monopolies rarely last forever. Potential competitors will always look for ways to enter a profitable market. Eventually they'll surmount entry barriers or develop substitute goods that supplant a monopolist's products.

Consumer advocates assert that we shouldn't have to wait for the invisible hand to dismantle a monopoly. They say the government should intervene to dismantle a monopoly or at least force it to change its behavior. Then consumers would get lower prices and better products a whole lot sooner.

Microsoft's dominant position in the computer industry highlights this issue. Microsoft produces the operating system (Windows) that powers 9 out of 10 personal computers. It also produces a huge share of applications software, including Internet browsers. Critics fear that this kind of monopoly power is a threat to consumers. They say Microsoft charges too much for its systems software, suppresses substitute technologies, and pushes potential competitors around. In short, Microsoft is a bully. In April 2000 a federal court accepted this argument (see the following News). To weaken Microsoft's grip on the computer market, courts in both the United States and Europe forced changes in both Microsoft's behavior and structure.

IN THE NEWS

Judge Says Microsoft Broke Antitrust Law

A federal judge yesterday found Microsoft Corp. guilty of violating antitrust law by waging a campaign to crush threats to its Windows monopoly, a severe verdict that opens the door for the government to seek a breakup of one of the most successful companies in history.

Saying that Microsoft put an "oppressive thumb on the scale of competitive fortune," U.S. District Judge Thomas Penfield Jackson gave the Justice Department and 19 states near-total victory in their lawsuit. His ruling puts a black mark on the reputation of a software giant that has been the starter engine of the "new economy."

"Microsoft mounted a deliberate assault upon entrepreneurial efforts that, left to rise or fall on their own merits, could well have enabled the introduction of competition into the market for Intel-compatible PC operating systems," Jackson said. . . .

In blunt language, Jackson depicted a powerful and predatory company that employed a wide array of tactics to destroy any innovation that posed a danger to the dominance of Windows. . . .

To crush the competitive threat posed by the Internet browser, Jackson ruled, Microsoft integrated its own Internet browser into its Windows operating system "to quell incipient competition," bullied computer makers into carrying Microsoft's browser by threatening to withhold price discounts, and demanded that computer makers not feature rival Netscape's browser in the PC desktop as a condition of licensing the Windows operating system.

"Only when the separate categories of conduct are viewed, as they should be, as a single, well-coordinated course of action does the full extent of the violence that Microsoft has done to the competitive process reveal itself," Jackson wrote in the 43-page ruling.

—James V. Grimaldi

Analysis: A federal court concluded that Microsoft followed the textbook script of monopoly: erecting entry barriers, suppressing innovation, and charging high prices.

web analysis

For more on Microsoft's antitrust cases in the United States and Europe, visit **www.stern.nyu.edu** and search for "economics of networks."

The AT&T Case. The federal government's authority to mend Microsoft's ways originates in the Sherman, the Clayton, and the Federal Trade Commission Acts. As noted in Table 10.1, these acts give the government broad **antitrust** authority to break up monopolies or compel them to change their behavior. The government used this authority in 1984 to dismantle American Telephone and Telegraph's (AT&T's) phone monopoly. AT&T then supplied 96 percent of all long-distance service and over 80 percent of local telephone service. AT&T kept long-distance charges high and compelled consumers to purchase hardware from its own subsidiary (Western Electric). Potential competitors claimed they could supply better and cheaper services if the government ended the AT&T monopoly. After four years of antitrust litigation, AT&T agreed to (1) separate its long-distance and local services and (2) turn over the local transmission networks to new "Baby Bell" companies. Since then there has been a competitive revolution in telephone hardware, services, and pricing.

antitrust: Government intervention to alter market structure or prevent abuse of market power.

The Microsoft Case. The U.S. Department of Justice filed a similar antitrust action against Microsoft. The first accusation leveled against Microsoft was that it thwarted competitors in operating systems by erecting entry barriers such as exclusive purchase agreements with computer manufacturers (as in the Intel case described in the News on page 228). These agreements either forbade manufacturers from installing a rival operating system or made it prohibitively expensive. The second accusation against Microsoft was that it used its monopoly position in *operating* systems to gain an unfair advantage in the *applications* market. It did this by not disclosing operating features that make applications run more efficiently or by bundling software, thereby forcing consumers to accept Microsoft applications along with the operating system. When the latter occurs, consumers have little

- **The Sherman Act (1890).** The Sherman Act prohibits "conspiracies in restraint of trade," including mergers, contracts, or acquisitions that threaten to monopolize an industry. Firms that violate the Sherman Act are subject to fines of up to $1 million, and their executives may be subject to imprisonment. In addition, consumers who are damaged—for example, via high prices—by a "conspiracy in restraint of trade" may recover treble damages. With this act as its principal "trustbusting" weapon, the U.S. Department of Justice has blocked attempted mergers and acquisitions, forced changes in price or output behavior, required large companies to sell some of their assets, and even sent corporate executives to jail for "conspiracies in restraint of trade."
- **The Clayton Act (1914).** The Clayton Act of 1914 was passed to outlaw specific antitrust behavior not covered by the Sherman Act. The principal aim of the act was to prevent the development of monopolies. To this end, the Clayton Act prohibited price discrimination, exclusive dealing agreements, certain types of mergers, and interlocking boards of directors among competing firms.

- **The Federal Trade Commission Act (1914).** The increased antitrust responsibilities of the federal government created the need for an agency that could study industry structures and behavior so as to identify anticompetitive practices. The Federal Trade Commission was created for this purpose in 1914.

Although the Sherman, Clayton, and FTC acts create a legal basis for government antitrust activity, they leave some basic implementation issues unanswered. What, for example, constitutes a "monopoly" in the real world? Must a company produce 100 percent of a particular good to be a threat to consumer welfare? How about 99 percent? Or even 75 percent?

And what specific monopolistic practices should be prohibited? Should we be looking for specific evidence of price gouging? Or should we focus on barriers to entry and unfair market practices?

These kinds of questions determine how and when antitrust laws will be enforced. The first question relates to the *structure* of markets, and the rest to their *behavior*.

TABLE 10.1
Antitrust Laws

The legal foundations for antitrust intervention are contained in three landmark antitrust laws.

---

incentive to buy a competing product. Microsoft also prohibited computer manufacturers from displaying rival product icons on the Windows desktop. Finally, Microsoft was accused of thwarting competition by simply buying out promising rivals.

Microsoft's Defense. Bill Gates, Microsoft's chairman, scoffed at the government's charges. He contends that Microsoft dominates the computer industry only because it continues to produce the best products at attractive prices. Microsoft doesn't need to lock out potential competitors, he argues, because it can and does beat the competition with superior products. Furthermore, Gates argues, the software industry is a highly *contestable* market even if not a perfectly competitive one. So Microsoft has to behave like a competitive firm even though it supplies most of the industry's output. In short, Microsoft is a genius, not a bully. Therefore, the government should leave Microsoft alone and let the market decide who best serves consumers.

The Verdict. After nine *years* of litigation, a federal court determined that Microsoft was more of a bully than a genius. The court concluded that Microsoft not only held a monopoly position in operating systems but had abused that position in a variety of anticompetitive ways. As a result, consumers were harmed. *The real economic issue, the court asserted, was not whether Microsoft was improving its products (it was) or reducing prices (it was) but instead how much faster products would have improved and prices fallen in a more competitive market.* By limiting consumer choices and stifling competition, Microsoft had denied consumers better and cheaper information technology.

The Remedy. The trial judge suggested that Microsoft might have to be broken into two companies—an operating software company and an applications software company—to ensure enough competition. Such a *structural* remedy would have resembled the court-ordered breakup of AT&T. In November 2001, however, the U.S. Department of Justice decided to seek *behavioral* remedies only. With Windows XP about to be launched, the Justice Department required Microsoft only to lower entry barriers for competing software applications (e.g., disclose middleware specifications, refrain from exclusive contracts, open desktops to competition). Although Microsoft reluctantly agreed to change its conduct in many ways, rivals complained that they still didn't have a fair chance of competing against the Microsoft monopoly. European regulators agreed, imposing still greater restrictions on Microsoft's business practices—particularly its continued bundling of Media Player in its operating system and confidential source code. Critics contend, however, that market *structure* is still the critical factor in determining market outcomes for the economy tomorrow.

Google a Bully? The same kind of anticompetitive concerns have been raised about Google. Ironically, Microsoft is one of the complainants this time (see the accompanying News). The core complaint is that Google uses its dominant search engine position to monopolize search and advertising services. It reinforces that position with entry barriers such as unique key search words, long-term exclusive advertising contracts, suppression of search results for rival firms, and outright acquisitions of potential competitors. Rivals say Google is a bully. Google contends it is a genius that welcomes online competition. U.S. and European antitrust regulators are investigating.

IN THE NEWS

Microsoft: Google Stifles Competition

BRUSSELS—Microsoft Corp. on Thursday threw its weight behind an existing probe by European Union authorities into whether rival Google Inc. is unfairly thwarting competition in the online search market.

Microsoft's General Counsel Brad Smith said the company is filing its own complaint against Google with the European Commission, citing concern over "a broadening pattern of conduct aimed at stopping anyone else from creating a competitive alternative." . . .

The commission opened a formal investigation into Google's behavior last November, following complaints from several smaller web companies that the search giant was burying them in its results and engaging in other anticompetitive practices.

—Gabriele Steinhauser

Analysis: Does Google strengthen its dominant position in search with unfair entry barriers? Rivals say it does. Google responds that it is just a better competitor.

SUMMARY

- Market power is the ability to influence the market price of goods and services. The extreme case of market power is monopoly, a situation in which only one firm produces the entire supply of a particular product. LO10-1
- The distinguishing feature of any firm with market power is the fact that the demand curve it faces is downward-sloping. In the case of monopoly, the demand curve facing the firm and the market demand curve are identical. LO10-1
- The downward-sloping demand curve facing a monopolist creates a divergence between marginal revenue and

price. To sell larger quantities of output, the monopolist must lower product prices. A firm without market power has no such problem. LO10-1
- Like other producers, a monopolist will produce at the rate of output at which marginal revenue equals marginal cost. Because marginal revenue is always less than price in monopoly, the monopolist will produce less output than a competitive industry confronting the same market demand and costs. That reduced rate of output will be sold at higher prices in accordance with the (downward-sloping) market demand curve. LO10-2

- A monopoly will attain a higher level of profit than a competitive industry because of its ability to equate industry (that is, its own) marginal revenues and costs. By contrast, a competitive industry ends up equating marginal costs and price because its individual firms have no control over market supply.   LO10-2
- Because the higher profits attained by a monopoly will attract envious entrepreneurs, barriers to entry are needed to prohibit other firms from expanding market supplies. Patents are one such barrier to entry.   LO10-2
- The defense of market power rests on (1) the alleged ability of large firms to pursue long-term research and development, (2) the incentives implicit in the chance to attain market power, (3) the efficiency that larger firms may attain, and (4) the contestability of even monopolized markets. The first two arguments are weakened by the fact that competitive firms are under much greater pressure to innovate and can stay ahead of the profit game only if they do so. The contestability defense at best concedes some amount of monopoly exploitation.   LO10-3
- A natural monopoly exists when one firm can produce the output of the entire industry more efficiently than can a number of small firms. This advantage is attained from economies of scale. Large firms aren't necessarily more efficient, however, because either constant returns to scale or diseconomies of scale may prevail.   LO10-3
- Antitrust laws restrain the acquisition and abuse of monopoly power. Where barriers to entry aren't insurmountable, market forces may ultimately overcome a monopoly.   LO10-3

Key Terms

market power
monopoly
profit maximization rule
marginal revenue (MR)
barriers to entry

economies of scale
production decision
average total cost (ATC)
marginal cost pricing
price elasticity of demand

price discrimination
consumer surplus
natural monopoly
contestable market
antitrust

Questions for Discussion

1. The objective in the game of Monopoly is to get all the property and then raise the rents. Can this power be explained with market supply and demand curves?   LO10-1
2. According to the Federal Trade Commission (News, p. 230), how often do monopolies lead to higher prices? Why, then, did the rocket merger get approved?   LO10-1
3. Why don't monopolists try to establish "the highest price possible," as many people allege? What would happen to sales? To profits?   LO10-1
4. How does Ticketmaster's "dynamic pricing" (News, p. 226) affect ticket sales, total revenue, and profit?   LO10-1
5. What are the Intel entry barriers mentioned in the News on page 228? How effective might they be?   LO10-2
6. What would have happened to iPad prices and features if Apple had not faced competition from iPad clones (Chapter 9)?   LO10-2

7. What entry barriers helped protect the following?   LO10-2
   (a) The Russian sable monopoly (World View, p. 218).
   (b) The Live Nation monopoly (News, p. 223).
   (c) The Intel monopoly (News, p. 228).
   (d) The rocket monopoly (News, p. 230).
   (e) Google's search dominance (News, p. 235).
8. What similarities exist between the AT&T, Microsoft, and Google antitrust cases?   LO10-3
9. How might consumers benefit from the merger of XM and Sirius (News, p. 231)? How might they lose?   LO10-3
10. Do price reductions and quality enhancements on Microsoft products prove that Microsoft is a perfectly competitive firm? What should be the test of competitiveness?   LO10-3

 web activities to accompany this chapter can be found on the Online Learning Center:
http://www.mhhe.com/schiller13e

 mobile app Visit your mobile app store and download the Schiller: Study Econ app *today*!

LO10-1 1. Use Figures 10.2 and 10.3 to answer the following questions:
   (a) What is the highest price the monopolist could charge and still sell fish?   _____
   (b) What is total revenue at that highest price?   _____
   (c) What rate of output maximizes total revenue?   _____
   (d) What rate of output maximizes total profit?   _____
   (e) What is MR at that rate of output?   _____
   (f) What is the price at the profit-maximizing rate of output?   _____

LO10-1 2. (a) Complete the following table:

Price	$24	$21	$18	$15	$12	$9	$6	$3
Quantity demanded	1	2	3	4	5	6	7	8
Marginal revenue	___	___	___	___	___	___	___	___

   (b) If marginal cost is constant at $6, what is the profit-maximizing rate of output?   _____
   (c) What price should be charged at that rate of output?   _____

LO10-1 3. The following table indicates the prices various buyers are willing to pay for a MiniCooper car:

Buyer	Maximum Price	Buyer	Maximum Price
Buyer A	$60,000	Buyer D	$30,000
Buyer B	50,000	Buyer E	20,000
Buyer C	40,000	Buyer F	10,000

   The cost of producing the cars includes $50,000 of fixed costs and a constant marginal cost of $10,000.
   (a) Graph below the demand, marginal revenue, and marginal cost curves.
   (b) What is the profit-maximizing rate of output and price for a monopolist? How much   Output _____
       profit does the monopolist make?   Price _____
                                            Profit _____

   (c) If the monopolist can price discriminate, how many cars will he sell?   _____
   (d) How much profit will he make?   _____

LO10-2 4. If the on-campus demand for soda is as follows:

Price (per can)	$0.25	0.50	0.75	1.00	1.25	1.50	1.75	2.00
Quantity demanded (per day)	100	90	80	70	60	50	40	30

   and the marginal cost of supplying a soda is 50 cents, what price will students end up paying in
   (a) A perfectly competitive market?   _____
   (b) A monopolized market?   _____

LO10-3 5. According to the News on page 230,
  (a) What was the annual cost saving for the rocket monopoly (in $ millions)? _____
  (b) How much of this saving did the FTC expect to be reflected in reduced rocket prices? _____
  (c) According to economic theory, which is likely to be higher, A: the merged monopoly price; or B: the 2-firm competitive price? _____

LO10-2 6. By how much did the price of the heart drug for babies increase when a monopoly was established (News, p. 225)? $ _____

LO10-2 7. The following table summarizes the weekly sales and cost situation confronting a monopolist:

Price	Quantity Demanded	Total Revenue	Marginal Revenue	Total Cost	Marginal Cost	Average Total Cost
$20	0			$ 6		
18	1			12		
16	2			20		
14	3			30		
12	4			42		
10	5			56		
8	6			72		

  (a) Complete the table.
  (b) Graph the demand, MR, and MC curves on the following graph.
  (c) At what rate of output is total revenue maximized within this range? _____
  (d) What are the values of MR and MC at the revenue-maximizing rate of output?   MR _____
                                                                                   MC _____
  (e) At what rate of output are profits maximized within this range? _____
  (f) What are the values of MR and MC at the profit-maximizing rate of output?   MR _____
                                                                                   MC _____
  (g) What are total profits at that output rate? _____
  (h) If a competitive industry confronted the same demand and costs, how much output would it produce in the short run? _____

chapter 11

●Oligopoly

LEARNING OBJECTIVES

After reading this chapter, you should know

LO11-1. The unique characteristics of oligopoly.

LO11-2. How oligopolies maximize profits.

LO11-3. How interdependence affects oligopolists' pricing decisions.

> People of the same trade seldom meet together, but the conversation ends in a conspiracy against the public, or in some diversion to raise prices.
>
> —Adam Smith, *The Wealth of Nations,* 1776

Although it's convenient to think of the economy as composed of the powerful and the powerless, market realities don't always provide such clear distinctions. There are very few perfectly competitive markets in the world, and few monopolies. Market power is an important phenomenon nonetheless; it's just that it's typically shared by several firms rather than monopolized by one. In the soft drink industry, for example, Coca-Cola and Pepsi share tremendous market power, even though neither company qualifies as a pure monopoly. The same kind of power is shared by Kellogg, General Mills, and Ralcorp in the breakfast cereals market, and by Sony, Nintendo, and Microsoft in the video game console market. Apple Computer, Inc., too, now shares power in the tablet computer market with Samsung, Sony, Amazon, Toshiba, Motorola, Google, and other firms.

These market structures fall between the extremes of perfect competition and pure monopoly; they represent *imperfect competition.* They contain some elements of competitive rivalry but also exhibit traces of monopoly. In many cases, imperfect competitors behave much like a monopoly: restricting output, charging higher prices, and reaping greater profits than firms in a competitive market. But behavior in imperfectly competitive markets is more complicated than in a monopoly because it involves a number of decision makers (firms) rather than only one.

This chapter focuses on one form of imperfect competition: *oligopoly.* We examine the nature of decision making in this market structure and the likely impacts on prices, production, and profits. What we want to know is

- **What determines how much market power a firm has?**
- **How do firms in an oligopoly set prices and output?**
- **What problems does an oligopoly have in maintaining price and profit?**

MARKET STRUCTURE

As we saw in Chapter 10, Microsoft is the dominant supplier of computer operating systems; as a near monopoly, it has tremendous market power. The corner grocery store, on the other hand, must compete with other stores and has less control over prices. But even the corner grocery isn't completely powerless. If it's the only grocery within walking distance or the only one open on Sunday, it too exerts *some* influence on prices and product flows. The amount of power it possesses depends on the availability of *substitute goods*—that is, the proximity and convenience of alternative retail outlets.

Degrees of Power

market structure: The number and relative size of firms in an industry.

Between the extremes of monopoly and perfect competition are many gradations of market power (see Figure 8.1). To sort them out, we classify firms into five specific **market structures,** based on the number and relative size of firms in an industry.

Table 11.1 summarizes the characteristics of the five major market structures. At one extreme is the structure of *perfect competition,* the subject of Chapters 8 and 9. At the other extreme of the power spectrum is perfect *monopoly.* A perfect monopoly exists when only one firm is the exclusive supplier of a particular product. Our illustration of Universal Electronics (the imaginary computer monopolist in Chapter 10) exemplifies such a firm.

oligopoly: A market in which a few firms produce all or most of the market supply of a particular good or service.

Between the two extremes of perfect competition and perfect monopoly lies most of the real world, which we call *imperfectly competitive.* ***In imperfect competition, individual firms have some power in a particular product market.*** *Oligopoly* refers to one of these imperfectly competitive market structures. **Oligopoly** is a situation in which only a *few* firms have a great deal of power in a product market. An oligopoly may exist because only a few firms produce a particular product or because a few firms account for most, although not all, of a product's output.

Determinants of Market Power

The number of firms in an industry is a key characteristic of market structure. The amount of market power the firms possess, however, depends on several factors. ***The determinants of market power include***

- ***Number of producers.***
- ***Size of each firm.***
- ***Barriers to entry.***
- ***Availability of substitute goods.***

When only one or a few producers or suppliers exist, market power is automatically conferred. In addition to the number of producers, however, the size of each firm is also important.

	Market Structure				
Characteristic	**Perfect Competition**	**Monopolistic Competition**	**Oligopoly**	**Duopoly**	**Monopoly**
Number of firms	Very large number	Many	Few	Two	One
Barriers to entry	None	Low	High	High	High
Market power (control over price)	None	Some	Substantial	Substantial	Substantial
Type of product	Standardized	Differentiated	Standardized or differentiated	Standardized or differentiated	Unique

TABLE 11.1
Characteristics of Market Structures

Market structure varies, depending on the number of producers, their size, barriers to entry, and the availability of substitute goods. An oligopoly is an imperfectly competitive structure in which a few firms dominate the market.

Over 600 firms supply long-distance telephone service in the United States. But just three of those firms (AT&T, Verizon, and Sprint Nextel) account for 82 percent of all calls. Hence it wouldn't make sense to categorize that industry on the basis of only the number of firms; relative size is also important.

A third and critical determinant of market power is the extent of barriers to entry. A highly successful monopoly or oligopoly arouses the envy of other profit maximizers. If it's a **contestable market,** potential rivals will seek to enter the market and share in the spoils. Should they succeed, the power of the former monopolist or oligopolists would be reduced. Accordingly, ease of entry into an industry limits the ability of a powerful firm to dictate prices and product flows. In Chapter 10 we saw how monopolies erect barriers to entry (e.g., patents) to maintain their power.

A fourth determinant of market power is the availability of substitute goods. If a monopolist or other power baron sets the price of a product too high, consumers may decide to switch to close substitutes. Thus, the price of Coors is kept in check by the price of Coke, and the price of sirloin steak is restrained by the price of chicken and pork. By the same token, a lack of available substitute products keeps the prices of insulin and AZT high.

Measuring Market Power

Although there are many determinants of market power, most observers use just one yardstick to measure the extent of power in an industry.

Concentration Ratio. The standard measure of market power is the **concentration ratio.** This ratio tells the share of output (or combined market share) accounted for by the largest firms in an industry. Using this ratio one can readily distinguish between an industry composed of hundreds of small, relatively powerless firms and another industry also composed of hundreds of firms but dominated by a few that are large and powerful. Thus *the concentration ratio is a measure of market power that relates the size of firms to the size of the product market.*

Table 11.2 gives the concentration ratios for selected products in the United States. The standard measure used here depicts the proportion of domestic production accounted for by the largest firms, usually the four largest. As a rule of thumb, *an industry with a concentration ratio above 60 percent is considered an oligopoly.* As is apparent from the table, the supply sides of these product markets easily qualify as *oligopolies* because most of these industries' output is produced by just three or four firms. Indeed, in some markets, one single firm is so large that an outright monopoly is nearly attained. For example, 70 percent of all canned soup is produced by Campbell. Procter & Gamble makes 62 percent of this country's disposable diapers. And Google produces 74 percent of all web search ads. All firms that have a market share of at least 40 percent are denoted by **boldface** type in Table 11.2.

Firm Size. We noted before that market power isn't necessarily associated with firm size—in other words, a small firm could possess a lot of power in a relatively small market. Table 11.2, however, should be convincing testimony that we're not talking about small product markets here. Every one of the products listed enjoys a broad-based market. Even the chewing gum market (94 percent concentration ratio) rings up annual sales of $2 billion. The three oligopolists that produce video game consoles (Sony, Nintendo, Microsoft) have 100 percent of a $14 billion market. Accordingly, for most of the firms listed in the table, market power and firm size go hand in hand. Indeed, the largest firms enjoy sales volumes that exceed the entire output of most of the *countries* in the world (see the World View on page 243). Walmart's annual revenues alone would make it the world's 25th largest country!

Measurement Problems

A high concentration ratio or large firm size isn't the only way to achieve market power. The supply and price of a product can be altered by many firms acting in unison. Even 1,000 small producers can band together to change the quantity supplied to the market, thus

---

contestable market: An imperfectly competitive industry subject to potential entry if prices or profits increase.

concentration ratio: The proportion of total industry output produced by the largest firms (usually the four largest).

web analysis

See the Federal Trade Commission website **(www.ftc.gov)** for information on industry structure. Search "concentration ratio."

Product	Largest Firms	Concentration Ratio (%)
Video game consoles	**Nintendo (Wii), Microsoft (Xbox)** Sony (PlayStation)	100%
Baby food	**Gerber Products,** Heinz, Beech-Nut	100
Instant breakfast	**Carnation,** Pillsbury, Dean Foods	100
Laser eye surgery	**VISX,** Summit Technology	100
Tennis balls	**Gen Corp (Penn),** PepsiCo **(Wilson),** Dunlop, Spalding	100
Credit cards	**Visa,** MasterCard, American Express, Discover	99
Internet browsers	**Microsoft,** Mozilla, Apple, Google	99
Disposable diapers	**Procter & Gamble,** Kimberly-Clark, Curity, Romar Tissue Mills	99
Razor blades	**Gillette,** Warner-Lambert (Schick; Wilkinson), Bic, American Safety Razor	98
Sports drinks	**PepsiCo** (Gatorade), Coca-Cola (PowerAde), Monarch (All Sport)	98
Internet search engines	**Google,** Yahoo, Microsoft (MSN), Ask.com	98
Digital music players	**Apple,** Sony, Microsoft, Real Networks	97
Scientific calculators	**Texas Instruments,** Casio, Hewlett-Packard	97
Electric razors	**Norelco,** Remington, Warner-Lambert, Sunbeam	96
Sanitary napkins	**Johnson & Johnson,** Kimberly-Clark, Procter & Gamble	96
Batteries	**Duracell,** Eveready, Ray-O-Vac, Kodak	94
Web search ads	**Google,** Yahoo, Microsoft, Aol	94
Chewing gum	**Wm. Wrigley,** Pfizer, Hershey	94
Soft drinks	**Coca-Cola,** PepsiCo, Cadbury Schweppes (7-Up, Dr. Pepper, A&W), Royal Crown	93
Breakfast cereals	Kelloggs, General Mills, Ralcorp, PepsiCo (Quaker Oats)	92
Wireless phone service	**AT&T,** Verizon, Sprint, T-Mobile	92
Computer printers	**Hewlett-Packard,** Epson, Canon, Lexmark	91
Toothpaste	Colgate-Palmolive, Procter & Gamble, Church & Dwight, Beecham	91
Local phone service	AT&T, Verizon, CenturyLink	90
Detergents	**Procter & Gamble,** Lever Bros., Dial, Colgate-Palmolive	90
Art auctions	**Sotheby's, Christie's**	90
Cigarettes	**Philip Morris,** Reynolds American, Lorillard	89
Greeting cards	**Hallmark,** American Greetings, Gibson	88
Beer	**Anheuser-Busch,** PhilipMorris (Miller, Coors), Pabst, Yuengling	85
Canned soup	**Campbell,** Progresso	85

Sources: Data from Federal Trade Commission, *The Wall Street Journal, Advertising Age, Financial World, Standard & Poor's, Fortune,* and industry sources.

Note: Individual corporations with a market share of at least 40 percent are designated in **boldface.** Market shares based on selected years, 2005–2011.

TABLE 11.2

Power in U.S. Product Markets

The domestic production of many familiar products is concentrated among a few firms. These firms have substantial control over the quantity supplied to the market and thus over market price. The concentration ratio measures the share of total output produced by the largest producers in a given market.

exercising market power. Recall how our mythical Universal Electronics (Chapter 10) exercised market power by coordinating the production decisions of its many separate plants. Those plants could have attempted such coordination on their own even if they hadn't all been owned by the same corporation. Lawyers and doctors exercise this kind of power by maintaining uniform fee schedules for members of the American Bar Association (ABA) and the American Medical Association (AMA).[1] Similarly, dairy farmers act jointly through three large cooperatives (the American Milk Producers, Mid-America Dairies, and Dairymen, Inc.), which together control 50 percent of all milk production.

[1]The courts have ruled that uniform fee schedules are illegal and that individual lawyers and doctors have the right to advertise their prices (fees). Nevertheless, a combination of inertia and self-interest has effectively maintained high fee schedules and inhibited advertising.

WORLD VIEW

Putting Size in Global Perspective

The largest firms in the United States are also the dominant forces in global markets. They export products to foreign markets and produce goods abroad for sale there or to import back into the United States. In terms of size alone, these business giants rival most of the world's nations. Walmart's gross sales, for example, would make it the 25th largest "country" in terms of national GDP.

American corporations aren't the only giants in the global markets. Toyota (Japan) and Royal Dutch Shell (The Netherlands) are among the foreign giants that contest global markets.

Rank	Country or Corporation	Sales or GDP	Rank	Country or Corporation	Sales or GDP
1	United States	$14,234	21	Poland	$468
2	Japan	4,857	22	Sweden	454
3	China	4,856	23	Saudi Arabia	437
4	Germany	3,476	24	Norway	409
5	France	2,751	25	**Walmart Stores**	408
6	United Kingdom	2,558	26	Austria	388
7	Italy	2,115	27	Iran	331
8	Brazil	1,584	28	Greece	328
9	Spain	1,476	29	Denmark	327
10	Canada	1,416	30	Venezuela	286
11	India	1,406	31	**Royal Dutch/Shell**	285
12	Russia	1,324	32	**ExxonMobil**	284
13	South Korea	967	33	South Africa	284
14	Mexico	962	34	Thailand	255
15	Australia	958	35	**British Petroleum**	246
16	The Netherlands	801	36	Finland	245
17	Turkey	652	37	Hong Kong	221
18	Switzerland	507	38	**Toyota**	204
19	Belgium	488	39	**Japan Post**	202
20	Indonesia	471	40	Ireland	197

Sources: World Bank Atlas Method, **data.worldbank.org**, and Fortune's annual ranking of the world's largest corporations, "Global 500." *Fortune* Magazine, July 26, 2010 © Time Inc. Used under license. (2009–2010 data in billions).

Analysis: Firm size is a determinant of market power. The size of the largest firms, as measured by total revenue, exceeds the value of total output in most of the world's 200-plus countries.

Finally, all the figures and corporations cited here refer to *national* markets. They don't convey the extent to which market power may be concentrated in a *local* market. In fact, many industries with low concentration ratios nationally are represented by just one or a few firms locally. Prime examples include milk, newspapers, and transportation (both public and private). For example, fewer than 60 cities in the United States have two or more independently owned daily newspapers, and nearly all those newspapers rely on only two news services (Associated Press and United Press International). Perhaps you've also noticed that most college campuses have only one bookstore. It may not be a *national* powerhouse, but it does have the power to influence what goods are available on campus and how much they cost.

OLIGOPOLY BEHAVIOR

With so much market power concentrated in so few hands, it's unrealistic to expect market outcomes to resemble those of perfect competition. As we observed in Chapter 10, *market structure affects market behavior and outcomes.* In that chapter we focused on the contrast between monopoly and perfect competition. Now we focus on the behavior of a more common market structure: oligopoly.

FIGURE 11.1

Initial Conditions in the Computer Market

As in Chapters 9 and 10, we assume that the initial equilibrium in the computer market occurs at a price of $1,000 and a quantity of 20,000 per month. How will an oligopoly alter these outcomes?

To isolate the unique character of oligopoly, we'll return to the computer market. In Chapter 9 we observed that the computer market was highly competitive in its early stages, when entry barriers were low and hundreds of firms were producing similar products. In Chapter 10 we created an impassable barrier to entry (a patent on the electronic brain of the computer) that transformed the computer industry into a monopoly of Universal Electronics. Now we'll transform the industry again. This time we'll create an oligopoly by assuming that three separate firms (Universal, World, and International) all possess patent rights. The patent rights permit each firm to produce and sell all the computers it wants and to exclude all other would-be producers from the market. With these assumptions, we create three **oligopolists,** the firms that share an *oligopoly.* Our objective is to see how market outcomes would change in such a market structure.

oligopolist: One of the dominant firms in an oligopoly.

The Initial Equilibrium

As before, we'll assume that the initial conditions in the computer market are represented by a market price of $1,000 and market sales of 20,000 computers per month, as illustrated in Figure 11.1.

We'll also assume that the **market share** of each producer is accurately depicted in Table 11.3. Thus Universal Electronics is assumed to be producing 8,000 computers per month, or 40 percent of total market supply. World Computers has a market share of 32.5 percent, while International Semiconductor has only a 27.5 percent share. The assumed concentration ratio is therefore 100.

market share: The percentage of total market output produced by a single firm.

The Battle for Market Shares

The first thing to note about this computer oligopoly is that it's likely to exhibit great internal tension. Neither World Computers nor International Semiconductor is really happy playing second or third fiddle to Universal Electronics. Each company would like to be number one in this market. On the other hand, Universal too would like a larger market share, particularly in view of the huge profits being made on computers. As we observed in Chapter 9, the initial equilibrium in the computer industry yielded an *average* profit of

TABLE 11.3

Initial Market Shares of Microcomputer Producers

The market share of a firm is the percentage of total market output it produces. These are hypothetical market shares of three fictional oligopolists.

Producer	Output (Computers per Month)	Market Share (%)
Universal Electronics	8,000	40.0%
World Computers	6,500	32.5
International Semiconductor	5,500	27.5
Total industry output	20,000	100.0%

$300 per computer, and total *industry* profits of $6 million per month (20,000 × $300). Universal would love to acquire the market shares of its rivals, thereby grabbing all this industry profit for itself.

But how does an oligopolist acquire a larger market share? In a truly competitive market, a single producer could expand production at will, with no discernible impact on market supply. That's not possible when there are only three firms in the market. *In an oligopoly, increased sales on the part of one firm will be noticed immediately by the other firms.*

How do we know that increased sales will be noticed so quickly? Because increased sales by one firm will have to take place either at the existing market price ($1,000) or at a lower price. Either of these two events will ring an alarm at the corporate headquarters of the other two firms.

Increased Sales at the Prevailing Market Price. Consider first the possibility of Universal Electronics increasing its sales at the going price of $1,000 per computer. We know from the demand curve in Figure 11.1 that consumers are willing to buy *only* 20,000 microcomputers per month at that price. Hence any increase in computer sales by Universal must be immediately reflected in *lower* sales by World or International. That is, *increases in the market share of one oligopolist necessarily reduce the shares of the remaining oligopolists.* If Universal were to increase its sales from 8,000 to 9,000 computers per month, the combined monthly sales of World and International would have to fall from 12,000 to 11,000 (see Table 11.3). The *quantity demanded* at $1,000 remains 20,000 computers per month (see Figure 11.1). Thus any increased sales at that price by Universal must be offset by reduced sales by its rivals.

This interaction among the market shares of the three oligopolists ensures that Universal's sales success will be noticed. It won't be necessary for World Computers or International Semiconductor to engage in industrial espionage. These firms can quickly figure out what Universal is doing simply by looking at their own (declining) sales figures.

Increased Sales at Reduced Prices. Universal could pursue a different strategy. Specifically, Universal could attempt to increase its sales by lowering the price of its computers. Reduced prices would expand total market sales, possibly enabling Universal to increase its sales without directly reducing the sales of either World or International.

But this outcome is most unlikely. If Universal lowered its price from $1,000 to, say, $900, consumers would flock to Universal Computers, and the sales of World and International would plummet. After all, we've always assumed that consumers are rational enough to want to pay the lowest possible price for any particular good. It's unlikely that consumers would continue to pay $1,000 for a World or International machine when they could get basically the same computer from Universal for only $900. If there were no difference, either perceived or real, among the computers of the three firms, a *pure* oligopoly would exist. In that case, Universal would capture the *entire* market if it lowered its price below that of its rivals.

More often, consumers perceive differences in the products of rival oligopolists, even when the products are essentially identical. These perceptions (or any real differences that may exist) create a *differentiated* oligopoly. In this case, Universal would gain many but not all customers if it reduced the price of its computers. That's the outcome we'll assume here. In either case, there simply isn't any way that Universal can increase its sales at reduced prices without causing alarms to go off at World and International.

Retaliation

So what if the alarms do go off at World Computers and International Semiconductor? As long as Universal Electronics is able to enlarge its share of the market and grab more profits, why should it care if World and International find out?

Universal *does* have something to worry about. World and International may not be content to stand by and watch their market shares and profits diminish. On the contrary, World and International are likely to take some action of their own once they discover what's going on.

There are two things World and International can do once they decide to act. In the first case, where Universal is expanding its market share at prevailing prices ($1,000), World and International can retaliate by

- Stepping up their own marketing efforts.
- Cutting prices on their computers.

product differentiation:
Features that make one product appear different from competing products in the same market.

To step up their marketing efforts, World and International might increase their advertising expenditures, repackage their computers, put more sales representatives on the street, or sponsor a college homecoming week. This is the kind of behavior RC Cola used to gain market share from Coke and Pepsi (see the accompanying News). Such attempts at **product differentiation** are designed to make one firm's products appear different and superior to those produced by other firms. If successful, such marketing efforts will increase RC Cola sales and market share or at least stop its rivals from grabbing larger shares.

IN THE NEWS

Pop Culture: RC Goes for the Youth Market

RC Cola, like the Brady Bunch and push-up bras, is attempting a '90s comeback. . . .

To that end, the company is spending $15 million on a new advertising campaign—the largest in RC's history—designed to cast the blue-collar drink of the Midwest and South as the hip alternative to "corporate colas," as it refers to market leaders Coke and Pepsi. Accompanying the ad blitz are new products, including a sour-tasting, Windex-colored Nehi and a long-neck brew called RC Draft, formulated specifically for younger palates.

"This company spent no money on advertising during the 1980s, and we lost an entire generation of cola drinkers who grew up in that decade," said John Carson, Royal Crown's chief executive. . . .

"Anybody in the soft drink business trying to compete with Pepsi and Coke has an uphill battle—they have huge amounts of marketing muscle, financial resources, experience and bottling agreements," said John Sicher, co-editor of Beverage Digest, an industry publication. "But RC's new tactics are smart. They are tossing out a bunch of beverages targeted toward younger drinkers. Against Coke and Pepsi, guerrilla warfare is the only thing that might work."

—Anthony Faiola

The U.S. Soda Market
Market share of soft drink makers, 2009.

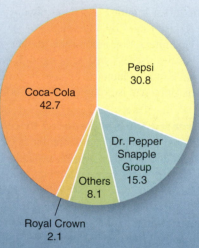

Coca-Cola 42.7
Pepsi 30.8
Dr. Pepper Snapple Group 15.3
Others 8.1
Royal Crown 2.1

Analysis: Because price competition is typically self-defeating in an oligopoly, rival firms in an oligopoly rely on advertising and product differentiation (nonprice competition) to gain market share.

web analysis

See **www.rccola.net** for more on the history of Royal Crown Cola. Click "RCCOLA Story."

An even quicker way to stop Universal from enlarging its market share is for World and International to lower the price of *their* computers. Such price reductions will destroy Universal's hopes of increasing its market share at the old price. In fact, this is the other side of a story we've already told. If the price of World and International computers drops to, say, $900, it's preposterous to assume that Universal will be able to expand its market share at a price of $1,000. Universal's market share will shrink if it maintains a price of $1,000 per computer after World and International drop their prices to $900. Hence the threat to Universal's market share grab is that the other two oligopolists will retaliate by reducing *their*

FIGURE 11.2
Rivalry for Market Shares Threatens an Oligopoly

If oligopolists start cutting prices to capture larger market shares, they'll be behaving much like truly competitive firms. The result will be a slide down the market demand curve to lower prices, increased output, and smaller profits. In this case, the market price and quantity would move from point *F* to point *G* if rival oligopolists cut prices to gain market shares.

prices. Should they carry out this threat, Universal would be forced to cut computer prices too, or accept a greatly reduced market share.

The same kind of threat exists in the second case, where we assumed that Universal Electronics expands its sales by initiating a price reduction. World and International aren't going to just sit by and applaud Universal's marketing success. They'll have to respond with price cuts of their own. Universal would then have the highest price on the market, and computer buyers would flock to cheaper substitutes. Accordingly, it's safe to conclude that *an attempt by one oligopolist to increase its market share by cutting prices will lead to a general reduction in the market price.* The three oligopolists will end up using price reductions as weapons in the battle for market shares, the kind of behavior normally associated with competitive firms. Should this behavior continue, not only will oligopoly become less fun, but it will also become less profitable as prices slide down the market demand curve (Figure 11.2). This is why *oligopolists avoid price competition and instead pursue nonprice competition* (e.g., advertising and product differentiation).

THE KINKED DEMAND CURVE

The close interdependence of oligopolists—and the limitations it imposes on individual price and output decisions—are the principal moral of this story. We can summarize the story with the aid of the kinked demand curve in Figure 11.3.

FIGURE 11.3

The Kinked Demand Curve Confronting an Oligopolist

The shape of the demand curve facing an oligopolist depends on the responses of its rivals to its price and output decisions. If rival oligopolists match price reductions but not price increases, the demand curve will be kinked.

Initially, the oligopolist is at point *A*. If it raises its price to $1,100 and its rivals don't raise their prices, it will be driven to point *B*. If its rivals match a price reduction (to $900), the oligopolist will end up at point *C*.

Recall that at the beginning of this oligopoly story Universal Electronics had a market share of 40 percent and was selling 8,000 computers per month at a price of $1,000 each. This output is represented by point A in Figure 11.3. The rest of the demand curve illustrates what would happen to Universal's unit sales if it changed its selling price. What we have to figure out is why this particular demand curve has such a strange "kinked" shape.

Rivals' Response to Price Reductions

Consider first what would happen to Universal's sales if it lowered the price of its computers to $900. In general, we expect a price reduction to increase sales. However, *the degree to which an oligopolist's sales increase when its price is reduced depends on the response of rival oligopolists.* Suppose World and International *didn't* match Universal's price reduction. In this case, Universal would have the only low-priced computer in the market. Consumers would flock to Universal, and sales would increase dramatically, from point A to point D. But point D is little more than a dream, as we've observed. World and International are sure to cut their prices to $900 to maintain their market shares. As a consequence, Universal's sales will expand only slightly, to point C rather than to point D. Universal's increased sales at point C reflect the fact that the total quantity demanded in the market has risen as the market price has fallen to $900 (see Figure 11.2). Thus, even though Universal's *market share* may not have increased, its monthly sales have.

The section of the demand curve that runs from point A to point D is unlikely to exist in an oligopolistic market. Instead *we expect rival oligopolists to match any price reductions* that Universal initiates, forcing Universal to accept the demand curve that runs from point A through point C. The News below illustrates such behavior in the airline industry, where rivals were forced to match price cuts introduced by Southwest Airlines in 2009.

IN THE NEWS

Major Airlines Match Southwest's Fare Cuts

Major airlines moved Friday to match a fare sale started by Southwest Airlines. . . .

Southwest said that through Monday it would sell seats to almost everywhere it flies starting at $49 to $99 each way. Tickets must be bought at least 14 days before flying, travel must be completed by March 11, and seats are limited, the airline said.

American Airlines, Continental Airlines, United Airlines, US Airways, JetBlue Airways, and Delta Air Lines matched the Southwest prices, officials at those carriers said. . . .

Airlines often match their rivals' fares rather than risk losing price-sensitive passengers.

Major U.S. Airlines Roll Back Latest Fare Hike

DALLAS—Major U.S. airlines are rolling back a fare increase of up to $120 per round trip on tickets favored by business travelers.

Delta Air Lines raised the fares Monday and other major airlines went along. But fare trackers say that US Airways had second thoughts and dropped the increase on Wednesday. . . .

Fare increases can fail if a major competitor refuses to go along because other airlines won't risk losing business with higher prices.

—David Koenig

Analysis: If rivals match price cuts but not price increases, the demand curve confronting an oligopolist will be kinked. Prices will increase only when all firms agree to raise them at the same time.

Rivals' Response to Price Increases

What about price increases? How will World and International respond if Universal raises the price of its computers to $1,100?

Recall that the demand for computers is assumed to be price-elastic in the neighborhood of $1,000 and that all computers are basically similar. Accordingly, if Universal raises its price and neither World nor International follows suit, Universal will be out there alone with a higher price and reduced sales. ***Rival oligopolists may choose not to match price increases.*** In terms of Figure 11.3, a price increase that isn't matched by rival oligopolists will drive Universal from point *A* to point *B*. At point *B*, Universal is selling very few computers at its price of $1,100 each.[2]

Is this a likely outcome? Suffice it to say that World Computers and International Semiconductor wouldn't be unhappy about enlarging their own market shares. Unless they see the desirability of an industrywide price increase, they're not likely to come to Universal's rescue with price increases of their own. This is why other airlines decided not to match the fare hikes announced by Delta (see the previous News).

Anything is possible, however, and World and International might match Universal's price increase. In this case, the *market price* would rise to $1,100 and the total quantity of computers demanded would diminish. Under such circumstances Universal's sales would diminish, too, in accordance with its (constant) share of a smaller market. This would lead us to point *M* in Figure 11.3.

We may draw two conclusions from Figure 11.3:

- ***The shape of the demand curve an oligopolist faces depends on the responses of its rivals to a change in the price of its own output.***
- ***That demand curve will be kinked if rival oligopolists match price reductions but not price increases.***

GAME THEORY

The central message of the kinked demand curve is that oligopolists can't make truly independent price or output decisions. Because only a few producers participate in the market, ***each oligopolist has to consider the potential responses of rivals when formulating price or output strategies.*** This *strategic interaction* is the inevitable consequence of their oligopolistic position.

Uncertainty and Risk. What makes oligopoly particularly interesting is the *uncertainty* of rivals' behavior. For example, Universal *would* want to lower its prices *if* it thought its rivals wouldn't retaliate with similar price cuts. But it can't be sure of that response. Universal must instead consider the odds of its rivals not matching a price cut. If the odds are low, Universal might decide *not* to initiate a price cut. Or maybe Universal might offer price discounts to just a few select customers, hoping World and International might not notice or react to small changes in market share.

The Payoff Matrix. Table 11.4 summarizes the strategic options each oligopolist confronts. In this case, let's assume that Universal is contemplating a price cut. Its rivals have only two options: either reduce their price also or not. Hence the payoff matrix has only four cells, each of which refers to a possible scenario. The **payoff matrix** in the table summarizes the various profit consequences of each scenario. One thing should be immediately clear: ***The payoff to an oligopolist's price cut depends on how its rivals respond.*** Indeed, the only scenario that increases Universal's profit is one in which Universal reduces its price and its

payoff matrix: A table showing the risks and rewards of alternative decision options.

[2]Notice again that we're assuming that Universal is able to sell some computers at a higher price (point *B*) than its rivals. The kinked demand curve applies primarily to differentiated oligopolies. As we'll discuss later, such differentiation may result from slight product variations, advertising, customer habits, location, friendly service, or any number of other factors. Most oligopolies exhibit some differentiation.

Universal's Options	Rivals' Actions	
	Reduce Price	**Don't Reduce Price**
Reduce price	Small loss for everyone	Huge gain for Universal; rivals lose
Don't reduce price	Huge loss for Universal; rivals gain	No change

TABLE 11.4
Oligopoly Payoff Matrix

The payoff to an oligopolist's price cut depends on its rivals' responses. Each oligopolist must assess the risks and rewards of each scenario before initiating a price change. Which option would you choose?

rivals don't. We visualized this outcome earlier as a move from point *A* to point *D* in Figure 11.3. Note again that this scenario implies losses for Universal's two rival oligopolists.

The remaining cells in the payoff matrix show how profits change with other action/response scenarios. One thing is evident: if Universal *doesn't* reduce prices, it can't increase profits. In fact, it might end up as the big loser if its rivals reduce *their* prices while Universal stands pat.

The option of reducing price doesn't guarantee a profit, but at least it won't ruin Universal's market share or profits. If rivals match a Universal price cut, all three oligopolists will suffer small losses.

So what should Universal do? The *collective* interests of the oligopoly are protected if no one cuts the market price. But an individual oligopolist could lose a lot if it holds the line on price when rivals reduce price. Hence each oligopolist might decide to play it safe by *initiating* a price cut.

Expected Gain (Loss). The decision to initiate a price cut boils down to an assessment of *risk*. If you thought the risk of a "first strike" was high, you'd be more inclined to reduce price. This kind of risk assessment is the foundation of game theory. You could in fact make that decision by *quantifying* the risks involved. Consider again the option of reducing price. As the first row of Table 11.4 shows, rivals can respond in one of only two ways. If they follow suit, a small loss is incurred by Universal. If they don't, there's a huge gain for Universal. To quantify the risk assessment, we need two pieces of information: (1) the size of each "payoff" and (2) the probability of its occurrence.

Suppose the "huge gain" is $1 million and the "small loss" is $20,000. What should Universal do? The huge gain looks enticing, but we now know it's not likely to happen. But *how* unlikely is it? What if there's only a 1 percent chance of rivals not matching a price reduction? In that case, the *expected* payoff to a Universal price cut is

$$\text{Expected payoff} = \left[\begin{array}{c} \text{Probability of} \\ \text{rivals matching} \end{array} \times \begin{array}{c} \text{Size of} \\ \text{loss from} \\ \text{price cuts} \end{array} \right] + \left[\begin{array}{c} \text{Probability} \\ \text{of rivals} \\ \text{not matching} \end{array} \times \begin{array}{c} \text{Gain} \\ \text{from lone} \\ \text{price cut} \end{array} \right]$$

$$= [(0.99) \times (-\$20,000)] + [(0.01) \times (\$1 \text{ million})]$$
$$= -\$19,800 + \$10,000$$
$$= -\$9,800$$

Hence it's not a good idea. Once potential payoffs and probabilities are taken into account, a unilateral price cut doesn't look promising. The odds say a unilateral price cut will result in a loss (−$9,800).

These kinds of computations underlay the Cold War games that the world's one-time superpowers played. Neither side was certain of the enemy's next move but knew a nuclear first strike could trigger retaliatory destruction. As a consequence, the United States and the former Soviet Union continually probed each other's responses but were quick to retreat from the brink whenever all-out retaliation was threatened. Oligopolists play the same kind of game on a much smaller scale, using price discounts and advertising rather than nuclear warheads as their principal weapons. The reward they receive for coexistence is the oligopoly profits that they continue to share. This reward, together with the threat of mutual destruction, leads oligopolists to limit their price rivalry. This explains why Coke and Pepsi quickly ended their brief price war (see the accompanying News). After finger-pointing about who started the war, the companies pulled back from the brink of mutual profit destruction. Notice in the last paragraph of the News how Coke's CEO explicitly rejects price competition as a viable strategy for oligopolists.

IN THE NEWS

Coke and Pepsi May Call Off Pricing Battle

ATLANTA—A brief but bitter pricing war within the soft drink industry might be drawing to a close—all because no one wants to be blamed for having fired the first shot.

Coca-Cola Enterprises Inc., Coca-Cola Co.'s biggest bottler, said in a recent memorandum to executives that it will "attempt to increase prices" after July 4 amid concern that heavy price discounting in most of the industry is squeezing profit margins.

The memo is a response to statements made to analysts last week by top PepsiCo Inc. executives. Pepsi, of Purchase, New York, said "irrational" pricing in much of the soft drink industry might temporarily squeeze domestic profits, and it laid the blame for the price cuts at Coke's door.

That clearly incensed executives at Coca-Cola and Coca-Cola Enterprises, which had no desire to be criticized for threatening profit margins for the entire industry. Indeed, industry analysts in the wake of Pepsi's statements expressed concern that profit margins for Pepsi and Coke bottlers may erode as a result of cutthroat pricing. . . .

In the June 5 memo, Summerfield K. Johnston Jr. and Henry A. Schimberg, the chief executive and the president of Coca-Cola Enterprises, respectively, said the bottler's plan is to "succeed based on superior marketing programs and execution rather than the short-term approach of buying share through price discounting. . . . We have absolutely no motivation to decrease prices except in response to a competitive initiative."

—Nikhil Deogun

Source: *The Wall Street Journal*, June 12, 1997, p. A3. Used with permission of Dow Jones & Company, Inc. via the Copyright Clearance Center, Inc.

Analysis: Price discounting can destroy oligopoly profits. When it occurs, rival oligopolists seek to end it as quickly as possible.

This isn't to say oligopolists won't ever cut prices or use other means to gain market share. They might, given the right circumstances and certain expectations of how rivals will behave. Indeed, there are a host of different price, output, and marketing strategies an oligopolist might want to pursue. The field of **game theory** is dedicated to the study of how decisions are made when such strategic interaction exists—for example, when the outcome of a business strategy depends on the decisions rival firms make. Just as there are dozens of different moves and countermoves in a chess game, so too are there numerous strategies oligopolists might use to gain market share.

game theory: The study of decision making in situations where strategic interaction (moves and countermoves) between rivals occurs.

OLIGOPOLY VS. COMPETITION

While contemplating strategies for maximizing their *individual* profits, oligopolists are also mindful of their common interest in maximizing *joint* (industry) profits. They want to avoid behavior that destroys the very profits that they're vying for. Indeed, they might want to coordinate their behavior in a way that maximizes *industry* profits. If they do, how will market outcomes be affected?

FIGURE 11.4
Maximizing Oligopoly Profits

An oligopoly strives to behave like a monopoly. Industry profits are maximized at the rate of output at which the *industry's* marginal cost equals marginal revenue (point *J*). In a monopoly, this profit all goes to one firm; in an oligopoly, it must be shared among a few firms.

In an oligopoly, the MC and ATC curves represent the combined production capabilities of several firms, rather than only one. The industry MC curve is derived by horizontally summing the MC curves of the individual firms.

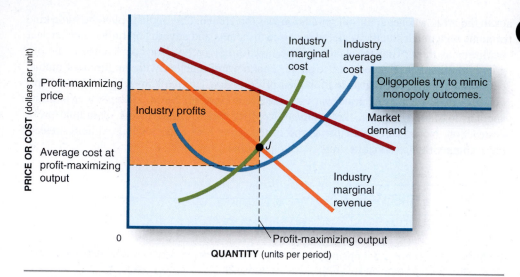

Price and Output

Thus far we've focused on a single oligopolist's decision about whether to *change* the price of its output. But how was the initial (market) price determined? In this example, we assumed that the initial price was $1,000 per computer, the price that prevailed initially in a *competitive* market. But the market is no longer competitive. As we saw in the previous chapter, a change in industry structure will affect market outcomes. A monopolist, for example, would try to maximize *industry* profits, all of which it would keep. To do this, it would select that one rate of output where marginal revenue equals marginal cost, and it would charge whatever price consumers were willing and able to pay for that rate of output (see Figure 11.4).

An oligopoly would seek similar profits. An oligopoly is really just a *shared* monopoly. Hence ***an oligopoly will want to behave like a monopoly, choosing a rate of industry output that maximizes total industry profit.***

The challenge for an oligopoly is to replicate monopoly outcomes. To do so, the firms in an oligopoly must find the monopoly price and maintain it. This is what the members of OPEC are trying to do when they meet to establish a common price for the oil they sell and agree to limit their output so as to achieve that price (see the World View below). Reaching

Pain at the Pump

WORLD VIEW

OPEC Leaves Output on Hold, Causing Oil Price Jump

VIENNA—OPEC unexpectedly left its production levels unchanged on Wednesday, causing oil prices to jump.

The news caught markets by surprise, sending oil prices sharply higher. Benchmark crude for July delivery was up $1.25 to $100.34 per barrel in morning trading.

Saudi Arabia and other influential Gulf nations had pushed to increase production ceilings to calm markets and ease concerns that crude was overpriced for consumer nations struggling with their economies. Those opposed were led by Iran, the second-strongest producer within the Organization of the Petroleum Exporting Countries.

—George Jahn

Source: Associated Press, February 17, 2011. Used with permission of The Associated Press. Copyright © 2011. All rights reserved.

Analysis: An oligopoly tries to act like a shared monopoly. To maximize industry profit, the firms in an oligopoly must concur on what the monopoly price is and agree to maintain it by limiting output and allocating market shares.

agreement requires a common view of the industry demand curve, satisfaction with respective market shares, and precise coordination.

Competitive industries would also like to reap monopoly-like profits. But competitive industries experience relentless pressure on profits as individual firms expand output, reduce costs, and lower prices. To maximize industry profits, competitive firms would have to band together and agree to restrict output and raise prices. If they did, though, the industry would no longer be competitive. The potential for maximizing industry profits is clearly greater in an oligopoly because fewer firms are involved and each is aware of its dependence on the behavior of the others.

COORDINATION PROBLEMS

A successful oligopoly will achieve monopoly-level profits by restricting industry output. As we've observed, however, this outcome depends on mutual agreement and coordination among the oligopolists. This may not come easy. *There's an inherent conflict in the joint and individual interests of oligopolists.* Their joint, or collective, interest is in maximizing industry profit. The individual interest of each oligopolist, however, is to maximize its own share of sales and profit. This conflict creates great internal tension within an oligopoly. To avoid self-destructive behavior, *oligopolists must coordinate their production decisions so that*

- Industry *output and price are maintained at profit-maximizing levels.*
- *Each oligopolistic* firm *is content with its market share.*

Price-Fixing

To bring about this happy outcome, rival oligopolists could discuss their common interests and attempt to iron out an agreement on both issues. Identifying the profit-maximizing rate of industry output would be comparatively simple, as Figure 11.4 illustrated. Once the optimal rate of output was found, the associated profit-maximizing price would be evident. The only remaining issue would be the division of industry output among the oligopolists—that is, the assignment of market shares.

The most explicit form of coordination among oligopolists is called **price-fixing.** In this case, the firms in an oligopoly explicitly agree to charge a uniform (monopoly) price. This is what the 12 OPEC member-nations do when they get together to set oil prices (see the previous World View). Some other examples of price-fixing include the following.

> **price-fixing:** Explicit agreements among producers regarding the price(s) at which a good is to be sold.

Ivy League Colleges. For more than 30 years Ivy League schools worked together to offer a uniform financial aid package for individual students, eliminating price competition. The Justice Department ordered the schools to end that practice in 1992.

Electric Generators. In 1961 General Electric and Westinghouse were convicted of fixing prices on $2 billion worth of electrical generators that they'd been selling to the Tennessee Valley Authority and commercial customers. Among the corporate executives, 7 went to prison and 23 others were put on probation. In addition, the companies were fined a total of $1.8 million and compelled to pay triple damages in excess of $500 million to their victimized customers. Nevertheless, another suit was filed against General Electric and Westinghouse in 1972, charging these same companies—still the only two U.S. manufacturers of turbine generators—with continued price-fixing.

Baby Formula. Two makers of baby formula (Bristol-Myers Squibb and American Home Products) agreed to pay $5 million in 1992 to settle Florida charges that they had fixed prices on baby formula. Three companies control 95 percent of this $1.3 billion national market.

Perfume. Thirteen companies—including Chanel, Dior, and Yves Saint Laurent—paid $55 million in penalties in 2006 for fixing prices.

Auction Commissions. Sotheby's and Christie's, who together control 90 percent of the world's art auction business, admitted in 2000 to fixing commission rates throughout the 1990s. They paid a $512 million fine when they were caught.

Laser Eye Surgery. The FTC charged the two companies that sell the lasers used for corrective eye surgery (VISX and Summit Technology) with price-fixing that inflated the retail price of surgery by $500 per eye.

Memory Chips. In 2005 the world's largest memory chip (DRAM) manufacturers (Samsung, Micron, Infineon, Hynix) admitted to fixing prices in the $16 billion-a-year DRAM market and paid nearly $700 million in criminal fines.

Elevators. In 2007 five companies were fined $1.3 billion for fixing prices on elevators and escalators in Europe for 10 years.

Candy. In 2008 major grocery stores sued Hershey, Mars, and Cadbury for allegedly fixing candy prices.

Price Leadership

Although price-fixing agreements are still a reality in many product markets, oligopolies have discovered that they don't need *explicit* agreements to arrive at uniform prices; they can achieve the same outcome in more subtle ways. **Price leadership** rather than price-fixing will suffice. If all oligopolists in a particular product market follow the lead of one firm in raising prices, the result is the same as if they had all agreed to raise prices simultaneously. Instead of conspiring in motel rooms (as in the electrical products and soft drink cases), the firms can achieve their objective simply by reading *The Wall Street Journal* or industry publications and responding appropriately. This is apparently how Coke and Pepsi communicated their desire to end their 1997 price war (see the News on page 251).

According to the U.S. Department of Justice, the major airlines developed a highly sophisticated form of price leadership. They used their shared computer reservation systems to signal *intended* price hikes. Rival oligopolists then responded with their own *intended* price changes. Only after it was clear that all the airlines would match a planned price increase was the price hike announced. The Justice Department argued that this "electronic dialogue" was equivalent to a price-fixing conspiracy that cost consumers $1.9 billion in excessive fares. In response, the major airlines agreed to stop using the reservations system to communicate *planned* fare hikes.

Allocation of Market Shares

Whenever oligopolists successfully raise the price of a product, the law of demand tells us that unit sales will decline. Even in markets with highly inelastic demand (such as those for baby formula and generic drugs), *some* decrease in sales always accompanies an increase in price. When this happens in a monopolistic industry, the monopolist simply cuts back the rate of output. In an oligopoly, however, no single firm will wish to incur the whole weight of that cutback. Some form of accommodation is required by all the oligopolists.

The adjustment to the reduced sales volume can take many forms. Members of OPEC, for example, assign explicit quotas for the oil output of each member country (see the World View on page 252). Such open and explicit production-sharing agreements transform an oligopoly into a **cartel.**

Because cartels openly violate U.S. antitrust laws, American oligopolies have to be more circumspect in divvying up shared markets. A particularly novel method of allocating market shares occurred in the price-fixing case involving General Electric and Westinghouse. Agreeing to establish high prices on electric generators wasn't particularly difficult. But how would the companies decide who was to get the restricted sales? Their solution was to designate one firm as the "low" bidder for a particular phase of the moon. The "low" bidder would charge

price leadership: An oligopolistic pricing pattern that allows one firm to establish the (market) price for all firms in the industry.

cartel: A group of firms with an explicit, formal agreement to fix prices and output shares in a particular market.

the previously agreed-upon (high) price, with the other firms offering their products at even higher prices. The "low" bidder would naturally get the sale. Each time the moon entered a new phase, the order of "low" and "high" bidders changed. Each firm got a share of the business, and the price-fixing scheme hid behind a facade of "competitive" bidding.

Such intricate systems for allocating market shares are more the exception than the rule. More often the oligopolists let the sales and output reduction be divided up according to consumer demands, intervening only when market shares are thrown markedly out of balance. At such times an oligopolist may take drastic action, such as **predatory pricing.** Predatory price cuts are temporary price reductions intended to drive out new competition or reestablish market shares. The sophisticated use of price cutting can also function as a significant barrier to entry, inhibiting potential competitors from trying to gain a foothold in the price cutter's market. The accompanying News describes how major airlines forced Independence Air out of their market with predatory pricing in 2006.

> **predatory pricing:** Temporary price reductions designed to alter market shares or drive out competition.

IN THE NEWS

Eliminating the Competition

On January 5, 2006, Independence Air ceased flying. CEO Kerry Skeen, armed with $300 million in start-up capital, had positioned Independence as a low-fare entrant at the profitable Washington, DC, Dulles airport. At its launch in June 2004, Skeen observed that the Washington, DC, area was "screaming" for low fares.

The major carriers didn't agree. United Airlines, with a hub at Dulles, slashed fares as soon as Independence took flight. The rest of the "Big Six" (Delta, American, Northwest, US Airways, Continental) did the same. The fare war kept Independence from gaining enough market share to survive. As CEO Skeen concluded, "It's a brutal industry."

The week after Independence ceased flying, the "walk-up" fare between Dulles and Atlanta jumped from $118 to $478. Other fares followed suit.

Source: "Flying Monopoly Air," McGraw-Hill News Flash, February 2006. © The McGraw-Hill Companies, Inc. Used with permission.

Analysis: To protect their prices and profits, oligopolists must be able to eliminate potential competition. Predatory pricing can serve that purpose.

BARRIERS TO ENTRY

If oligopolies succeed in establishing monopoly prices and profits, they'll attract the envy of would-be entrants. To keep potential competitors out of their industry, oligopolists must maintain **barriers to entry.** *Above-normal profits can't be maintained over the long run unless barriers to entry exist.* The entry barriers erected include those monopolists use (Chapter 10).

> **barriers to entry:** Obstacles, such as patents, that make it difficult or impossible for would-be producers to enter a particular market.

Patents

Patents are a very effective barrier to entry. Potential competitors can't set up shop until they either develop an alternative method for producing a product or receive permission from the patent holder to use the patented process. Such permission, when given, costs something, of course. In 2006 Research in Motion paid an extraordinary $612.5 million for the patent rights to produce BlackBerrys. In 2007 a federal court ordered Internet phone provider Vonage to pay $135 million and 5 percent of its future profits to its wired rivals, Verizon and Sprint.

Distribution Control

Another way of controlling the supply of a product is to take control of distribution outlets. If a firm can persuade retail outlets not to peddle anyone else's competitive wares, it will increase its market power. This control of distribution outlets can be accomplished through selective discounts, long-term supply contracts, or expensive gifts at Christmas. Recall from Chapter 10 (see the News on page 223) how Live Nation Entertainment locked up concert arenas and ticket distribution. According to the U.S. Justice Department, Visa and MasterCard prevent banks that issue their credit cards from offering rival cards. Frito-Lay elbows out competing snack companies by paying high fees to "rent" shelf space in grocery stores (see the News below). Such up-front costs create an entry barrier for potential rivals. Even if a potential rival can come up with the up-front money, the owner of an arena or grocery store chain may not wish to anger the firm that dominates the market.

IN THE NEWS

Frito-Lay Devours Snack Food Business

Once again, Frito-Lay is chewing up the competition.

The announcement Wednesday that Anheuser-Busch Cos. is selling off its Eagle Snacks business highlights the danger of trying to compete against Frito-Lay in the salty snacks game. The company owns half of the $15 billion salty snacks market.

"Frito's a fortress," says Michael Branca, an analyst at NatWest Securities. "And it continues to expand its realm. I'd tell anyone else trying to get into the business, don't try to expand, don't try to impinge on Frito's territory or you'll get crushed.". . .

In fact, competitors say that it is Frito-Lay's tactics with retailers that make it an invincible foe. Because many retailers are charging more and more for shelf space—$40,000 a foot annually in some instances—many regional companies say Frito-Lay is paying retailers to squeeze out competing brands.

"Frito can afford it," says a regional snack company executive. "But we can't. It's become a real estate business."

Frito-Lay can also afford to outpromote its competitors. In 1993 the company spent more than $60 million on advertising, while Eagle spent less than $2 million.

—Robert Frank

Snack Food Giant

Frito-Lay's market share in various snack food categories.

	Salty Snacks		Potato Chips		Tortilla Chips	
	1990	1995	1990	1995	1990	1995
Market share	43%	52%	45%	52%	63%	72%

Source: *The Wall Street Journal,* October 27, 1995, p. B1. Used with permission of Dow Jones & Company, Inc. via Copyright Clearance Center, Inc.

Analysis: Barriers to entry such as self-space rental and advertising enable a firm to maintain market dominance. Acquisitions also reduce competition.

New car warranties also serve as an entry barrier. The warranties typically require regular maintenance at authorized dealerships and the exclusive use of authorized parts. These provisions limit the ability of would-be competitors to provide cheaper auto parts and service. Frequent flier programs have similar effects in the airline industry.

Mergers and Acquisition

Large and powerful firms can also limit competition by outright *acquisition.* A *merger* between two firms amounts to the same thing, although mergers often entail the creation of new corporate identities.

Perhaps the single most dramatic case of acquisition for this purpose occurred in the breakfast cereals industry. In 1946 General Foods acquired the cereal manufacturing facilities of Campbell Cereal Company, a substantial competitor. Following this acquisition, General Foods dismantled the production facilities of Campbell Cereal and shipped them off to South Africa!

Although the General Foods acquisition was more dramatic than most, acquisitions have been the most popular route to increased market power. General Motors attained a dominant share of the auto market largely by its success in merging with and acquiring two dozen independent manufacturers. In the cigarette industry, the American Tobacco Company attained monopoly powers by absorbing 250 independent companies. Later antitrust action (1911) split up the resultant tobacco monopoly into an oligopoly consisting of four companies, which continued to dominate the cigarette market until 2004, when R. J. Reynolds bought Brown & Williamson, leaving only three firms to dominate the cigarette industry. Other companies that came to dominate their product markets through mergers and acquisitions include U.S. Steel, U.S. Rubber, General Electric, United Fruit, National Biscuit Company, International Salt, and Live Nation Entertainment. Frito-Lay's 1995 acquisitions of Eagle Snacks (see the previous News) extended its already dominant control of the chip, pretzel, and nuts markets.

Government Regulation

The government often helps companies acquire and maintain control of market supply. Patents are issued and enforced by the federal government and so represent one form of supply-restricting regulation. Barriers to international trade are another government-imposed barrier to entry. By limiting imports of everything from Chinese mushrooms to Japanese cars (see Chapter 21), the federal government reduces potential competition in U.S. product markets. Government regulation also limits *domestic* competition in many industries.

New York City also limits competition—in this case, the number of taxicabs on the streets. The maximum number of cabs was set at 11,787 in 1937 and stayed at that ceiling until 1996. The city's Taxi and Limousine Commission has since raised the ceiling to 13,237 taxis. That didn't do much to eliminate New York's perennial taxi shortage (for a population of over 8 million people), much less reduce fares. As a result, license holders continue to reap monopoly-like profits. A good measure of those profits is the price of the medallions that the city sells as taxi licenses. The market price of a New York City taxi medallion—and thus the price of entry into the industry—was over $600,000 in 2011. By contrast, a Washington, D.C., taxi license costs only $35, and fares are about half those in New York.

Nonprice Competition

Producers who control market supply can enhance their power even further by establishing some influence over market demand. The primary mechanism of control is *advertising*. To the extent that a firm can convince you that its product is essential to your well-being and happiness, it has effectively shifted your demand curve. ***Advertising not only strengthens brand loyalty but also makes it expensive for new producers to enter the market.*** A new entrant must buy both production facilities and advertising outlets.

The cigarette industry is a classic case of high concentration and product differentiation. As Table 11.2 shows, the top three cigarette companies produce 89 percent of all domestic output; small, generic firms produce the rest. Together, the three cigarette companies produce well over 100 brands. To solidify brand loyalties, the cigarette industry spent over $15 billion on advertising and promotions in 2010.

The breakfast cereal industry also uses nonprice competition to lock in consumers. Although the Federal Trade Commission has suggested that "a corn flake is a corn flake no matter who makes it," the four firms (Kellogg, General Mills, Ralcorp, and Quaker Oats) that supply more than 90 percent of all ready-to-eat breakfast cereals spend over $400 million a year—about $1 per box!—to convince consumers otherwise.

Training

In today's technology-driven markets, early market entry can create an important barrier to later competition. Customers of computer hardware and software, for example, often become familiar with a particular system or computer package. Switching to a new product may entail significant cost, including the retraining of user staff. As a consequence, would-be competitors will find it difficult to sell their products even if they offer better quality and lower prices.

Network Economies

The widespread use of a particular product may also heighten its value to consumers, thereby making potential substitutes less viable. The utility of instant messaging—or even a telephone—depends on how many of your friends have telephones. If no one else had a phone there'd be no reason to own one. In other words, the larger the network of users, the greater the value of the product. Such network economies help explain why software developers prefer to write apps for the iPhone than applications for rival smartphones.

THE ECONOMY TOMORROW

ANTITRUST ENFORCEMENT

Examples of market power at work in product markets could be extended to the closing pages of this book. The few cases cited here, however, are testimony enough to the fact that market power has some influence on our lives. Market power *does* exist; market power *is* used. Although market power may result in economies of scale, the potential for abuse is evident. Market power contributes to **market failure** when it leads to resource misallocation (restricted output) or greater inequity (monopoly profits, higher prices).

What should we do about these abuses? Should we leave it to market forces to find ways of changing industry structure and behavior? Or should the government step in to curb noncompetitive practices?

Industry Behavior. Our primary concern is the *behavior* of market participants. What ultimately counts is the quantity of goods supplied to the market, their quality, and their price. Few consumers care about the underlying *structure* of markets; what we seek are good market *outcomes*.

In principle, the government could change industry behavior without changing industry structure. We could, for example, explicitly outlaw collusive agreements and cast a wary eye on industries that regularly exhibit price leadership. We could dismantle barriers to entry and thereby promote contestable markets. We might also prohibit oligopolists from extending their market power via such mechanisms as acquisitions, excessive or deceptive advertising, and the financing of political campaigns. In fact, the existing **antitrust** laws—the Sherman Act, the Clayton Act, and the Federal Trade Commission Act (see Table 10.1)—explicitly forbid most of these practices.

There are several problems with this behavioral approach. The first limitation is scarce resources. Policing markets and penalizing noncompetitive conduct require more resources than the public sector can muster. Indeed, the firms being investigated often have more resources than the public watchdogs. The advertising expenditures of just one oligopolist, Procter & Gamble, are more than 10 times as large as the *combined* budgets of both the Justice Department's Antitrust Division and the Federal Trade Commission.

The paucity of antitrust resources is partly a reflection of public apathy. Consumers rarely think about the connection between market power and the price of the goods they buy, the wages they receive, or the way they live. As Ralph Nader discovered, "Antitrust violations are part of a phenomenon which, to the public, is too complex, too abstract, and supremely dull."[3] As a result, there's little political pressure to regulate market behavior.

The behavioral approach also suffers from the "burden-of-proof" requirement. How often will "trustbusters" catch colluding executives in the act? More often than not, the case for collusion rests on such circumstantial evidence as simultaneous price hikes, identical bids, or other market outcomes. The charge of explicit collusion is hard to prove. Even in the absence of explicit collusion, however, consumers suffer. If an oligopoly price is higher than what a competitive industry would charge, consumers get stuck with the bill whether or not the price was "rigged" by explicit collusions. The U.S.

---

market failure: An imperfection in the market mechanism that prevents optimal outcomes.

web analysis

The U.S. Department of Justice oversees antitrust enforcement. For details, go to **www.justice. gov/atr.** Click the "Antitrust Case Filings" tab to learn more.

antitrust: Government intervention to alter market structure or prevent abuse of market power.

---

[3]Mark J. Green et al., *The Closed Enterprise System: The Report on Antitrust Enforcement* (New York: Grossman, 1972), p. ix.

Supreme Court recognized that consumers may suffer from *tacit* collusion, even where no *explicit* collusion occurs.

Industry Structure. The concept of tacit collusion directs attention to the *structure* of an industry. It essentially says that oligopolists and monopolists will act in their own best interest. As former Supreme Court Chief Justice Earl Warren observed, "An industry which does not have a competitive structure will not have competitive behavior."[4] To expect an oligopolist to disavow profit opportunities or to ignore its interdependence with fellow oligopolists is naive. It also violates the basic motivations imputed to a market economy. As long as markets are highly concentrated, we must expect to observe oligopolistic behavior.

Judge Learned Hand used these arguments to dismantle the Aluminum Company of America (Alcoa) in 1945. Alcoa wasn't charged with any illegal *behavior.* Nevertheless, the company controlled over 90 percent of the aluminum supplied to the market. This monopoly structure, the Supreme Court concluded, was itself a threat to the public interest.

Corporate breakups are rarely pursued today. In 2001 the Justice Department withdrew a proposal to break up Microsoft into separate systems and applications companies. The prevalent feeling today, even among antitrust practitioners, is that the powerful firms are too big and too entrenched to make deconcentration a viable policy alternative.

Objections to Antitrust. Some people think *less* antitrust enforcement is actually a good thing. The companies challenged by the public "trustbusters" protest that they're being penalized for their success. Alcoa, for example, attained a monopoly by investing heavily in a new product before anyone else recognized its value. Other firms too have captured dominant market shares by being first, best, or most efficient. Having "won" the game fairly, why should they have to give up their prize? They contend that noncompetitive *behavior,* not industry *structure,* should be the only concern of antitrust enforcers.

Essentially the same argument is made for proposed mergers and acquisitions. The firms involved claim that the increased concentration will enhance productive efficiency (e.g., via economies of scale). They also argue that big firms are needed to maintain America's competitive position in international markets (which are themselves often dominated by foreign monopolies and oligopolies). Those same global markets, they contend, ensure that even highly concentrated domestic markets will be contested by international rivals.

Finally, critics of antitrust suggest that market forces themselves will ensure competitive behavior. Foreign firms and domestic entrepreneurs will stalk a monopolist's preserve. People will always be looking for ways to enter a profitable market. Monopoly or oligopoly power may slow entry but is unlikely to stop it forever. Eventually competitive forces will prevail.

Structural Guidelines: The Herfindahl-Hirshman Index. There are no easy answers. In theory, competition is valuable, but some mergers and acquisitions undoubtedly increase efficiency. Moreover, some international markets may require a minimum firm size not consistent with perfect competition. Finally, our regulatory resources are limited; not every acquisition or merger is worthy of public scrutiny.

Where would we draw the line? Can a firm hold a 22 percent market share, but not 30 percent? Are five firms too few, but six firms in an industry enough? Someone has to make those decisions. That is, ***the broad mandates of the antitrust laws must be transformed into specific guidelines for government intervention.***

In 1982 the Antitrust Division of the U.S. Department of Justice adopted specific guidelines for intervention based on industry *structure* alone. They're based on an index that takes into account the market share of *each* firm rather than just the *combined* market share of the top four firms. Specifically, the **Herfindahl-Hirshman Index (HHI)** of market concentration is calculated as

Herfindahl-Hirshman Index (HHI): Measure of industry concentration that accounts for number of firms and size of each.

$$HHI = \sum_{i=1}^{n} = \left(\frac{\text{Share of}}{\text{firm 1}}\right)^2 + \left(\frac{\text{Share of}}{\text{firm 2}}\right)^2 + \cdots + \left(\frac{\text{Share of}}{\text{firm } n}\right)^2$$

[4]Ibid., p. 7.

Thus a three-firm oligopoly like that described in Table 11.3 would have an HHI value of

$$\text{HHI} = (40.0)^2 + (32.5)^2 + (27.5)^2 = 3{,}412.5$$

where the numbers in parentheses indicate the market shares of the three fictional computer companies. The calculation yields an HHI value of 3,412.5.

For policy purposes, the Justice Department decided it would draw the line at 1,800. Any merger that creates an HHI value over 1,800 will be challenged by the Justice Department. If an industry has an HHI value between 1,000 and 1,800, the Justice Department will challenge any merger that *increases* the HHI by 100 points or more. Mergers and acquisitions in industries with an HHI value of less than 1,000 won't be challenged.

The HHI is an arbitrary but workable tool for deciding when the government should intervene to challenge mergers and acquisitions. The Justice Department reviews about 2,500 mergers a year but challenges fewer than 50.

The AT&T/T-Mobile Deal. The Justice Department's guidelines were put to the test in 2011. In March 2011 AT&T announced that it planned to purchase T-Mobile, the fourth largest wireless phone company (see the accompanying News). That acquisition would send the Herfindahl-Hirschmann Index through the roof. But AT&T argued that the acquisition of T-Mobile would result in economies of scale that would improve service and reduce costs. Critics said the loss of competition would raise prices and reduce phone service options. The Justice Department sided with the critics and sued in August 2011 to block the merger.

IN THE NEWS

AT&T to Buy T-Mobile Means Higher Prices, Fewer Phones

AT&T today announced that it plans to buy T-Mobile in a move that may work against consumers' interests by leading to increased prices and fewer phone selections over time.

The Dallas, Texas–based company will pay $39 billion for the fourth-largest U.S. carrier, giving it a total of 130 million subscribers, and catapulting it ahead of current frontrunner Verizon, which has 94 million customers. The two companies would control 80 percent of the U.S. cellular market, leaving Sprint in a distant third place.

The benefits for customers are more of a mixed bag. On the upside, subscribers to both companies could expect to see service improvements thanks to the increased coverage and the reduced strain on AT&T's existing network. But the loss of T-Mobile's lower-cost plans will reduce pricing pressure on the top two carriers, which could lead to more expensive service.

The acquisition would also likely reduce the handset selection in the United States, where phones are almost exclusively purchased on subsidized plans from carriers. Carriers typically try to differentiate themselves with the custom phones, so the more carriers in operation, the wider the selection of handsets, and vice versa.

For AT&T and T-Mobile, the move makes sense on several fronts. AT&T would relieve its congested network with T-Mobile's extra capacity, and the acquisition would solve T-Mobile's need for more spectrum to roll out 4G services. . . .

The acquisition is likely to result in thousands of job losses as redundant operations are shuttered. For the moment, customers of the two carriers won't see any changes. T-Mobile users cannot get iPhones yet.

—Peter Ferenczi

Source: **Mobiledia.com,** March 21, 2011.

Analysis: Mergers and acquisitions typically result in cost savings, but also more market power. Consumers don't necessarily gain.

SUMMARY

- Imperfect competition refers to markets in which individual suppliers (firms) have some independent influence on the price at which their output is sold. Examples of imperfectly competitive market structures are duopoly, oligopoly, and monopolistic competition. LO11-1
- The extent of market power (control over price) depends on the number of firms in an industry, their size, barriers to entry, and the availability of substitutes. LO11-1
- The concentration ratio is a measure of market power in a particular product market. It equals the share of total industry output accounted for by the largest firms, usually the top four. LO11-1
- An oligopoly is a market structure in which a few firms produce all or most of a particular good or service (a concentration ratio of 60 or higher); it's essentially a shared monopoly. LO11-1
- Because oligopolies involve several firms rather than only one, each firm must consider the effect of its price and output decisions on the behavior of rivals. Such firms are highly interdependent. LO11-3
- Game theory attempts to identify different strategies a firm might use, taking into account the consequences of rivals' moves and countermoves. LO11-3
- The kinked demand curve illustrates a pattern of strategic interaction in which rivals match a price cut but not a price hike. Such behavior reinforces the oligopolistic aversion to price competition. LO11-3
- A basic conflict exists between the desire of each individual oligopolist to expand its market share and the *mutual* interest of all the oligopolists in restricting total output so as to maximize industry profits. This conflict must be resolved in some way, via either collusion or some less explicit form of agreement (such as price leadership). LO11-3
- Oligopolists may use price-fixing agreements or price leadership to establish the market price. To maintain that price, the oligopolists must also agree on their respective market shares. LO11-3
- To maintain economic profits, an oligopoly must erect barriers to entry. Patents are one form of barrier. Other barriers include predatory price cutting (price wars), control of distribution outlets, government regulations, advertising (product differentiation), training, and network economies. Outright acquisition and merger may also eliminate competition. LO11-2
- Market power may cause market failure. The symptoms of that failure include increased prices, reduced output, and a transfer of income from the consuming public to a relatively few powerful corporations and the people who own them. LO11-2
- Government intervention may focus on either market structure or market behavior. In either case, difficult decisions must be made about when and how to intervene. LO11-1
- The Herfindahl-Hirshman Index is a measure of industry concentration that takes into account the number of firms and the size of each. It is used as a structural guideline to identify cases worthy of antitrust concern. LO11-1

Key Terms

market structure
oligopoly
contestable market
concentration ratio
oligopolist
market share

product differentiation
payoff matrix
game theory
price-fixing
price leadership
cartel

predatory pricing
barriers to entry
market failure
antitrust
Herfindahl-Hirshman Index (HHI)

Questions for Discussion

1. How many bookstores are on or near your campus? If there were more bookstores, how would the price of new and used books be affected? LO11-1
2. What entry barriers exist in (*a*) the fast-food industry, (*b*) cable television, (*c*) the auto industry, (*d*) illegal drug trade, (*e*) potato chips, and (*f*) beauty parlors? LO11-1
3. Why does RC Cola depend on advertising to gain market share? (See News, p. 246.) Why not offer cheaper sodas than Coke or Pepsi? LO11-3
4. Why might OPEC members have a difficult time setting and maintaining a monopoly price? (See World View, p. 252.) LO11-2
5. If an oligopolist knows rivals will match a price cut, would it ever reduce its price? LO11-3
6. How might the high concentration ratio in the credit card industry (Table 11.2) affect the annual fees and interest charges for credit card services? LO11-2

7. What evidence of economies of scale is cited in the AT&T case (News, p. 260)? Should the acquisition be approved? LO11-2

8. What reasons might rival airlines have for *not* matching Delta's fare increase? (See News, p. 248.) LO11-3

9. The Ivy League schools defended their price-fixing arrangement (see p. 253) by arguing that their coordination assured a fair distribution of scholarship aid. Who was hurt or helped by this arrangement? LO11-2

10. Using the payoff matrix in Table 11.4, decide whether Universal should cut its price. What factors will influence the decision? LO11-3

11. Domino's and Pizza Hut hold 66 percent of the delivered-pizza market. Should antitrust action be taken? LO11-1

12. Why do phone companies offer incentives to purchase two-year wireless service agreements? LO11-3

 web activities to accompany this chapter can be found on the Online Learning Center: **http://www.mhhe.com/schiller13e**

 mobile app Visit your mobile app store and download the Schiller: Study Econ app *today*!

LO11-1 1. According to Table 11.2, in how many markets do fewer than four firms produce at least 80 percent of total output?   _____

LO11-2 2. According to the News on page 246,
    (*a*) What is the concentration ratio in the U.S. soda market?   _____
    (*b*) What is the *maximum* value of the Herfindahl-Hirshman Index?   _____

LO11-3 3. Assume an oligopolist confronts *two* possible demand curves for its own output, as illustrated here. The first (*A*) prevails if other oligopolists don't match price changes. The second (*B*) prevails if rivals *do* match price changes.

    (*a*) By how much does quantity demanded increase if the price is reduced from $11 to $9 and
      (*i*) Rivals match the price cut?   _____
      (*ii*) Rivals don't match the price cut?   _____
    (*b*) By how much does quantity demanded change when the price is raised from $11 to $13 and
      (*i*) Rivals match the price hike?   _____
      (*ii*) Rivals don't match the price hike?   _____

LO11-3 4. How large would the probability of a "don't match" outcome have to be to make a Universal price cut statistically worthwhile? (See expected payoff, p. 250.)   _____

LO11-3 5. Suppose the payoff to each of four strategic interactions is as follows:

	Rival Response	
Action	**Reduce Price**	**Don't Reduce Price**
Reduce price	Loss = $400	Gain = $30,000
Don't reduce price	Loss = $5,000	No loss or gain

    (*a*) If the probability of rivals matching a price reduction is 98 percent, what is the expected payoff of a price cut?   _____
    (*b*) If the probability of rivals reducing price even though you don't is 5 percent, what is the expected payoff of *not* reducing price?   _____

LO11-2 6. Suppose that the following schedule summarizes the sales (demand) situation confronting an oligopolist:

Price (per unit)	$8	$10	$12	$14	$16	$17	$18	$19	$20
Quantity demanded (units per period)	10	9	8	7	6	5	4	3	2

Using the following graph,
(a) Draw the demand and marginal revenue curves facing the firm.
(b) Identify the profit-maximizing rate of output in a situation where marginal cost is constant at $11 per unit. _____

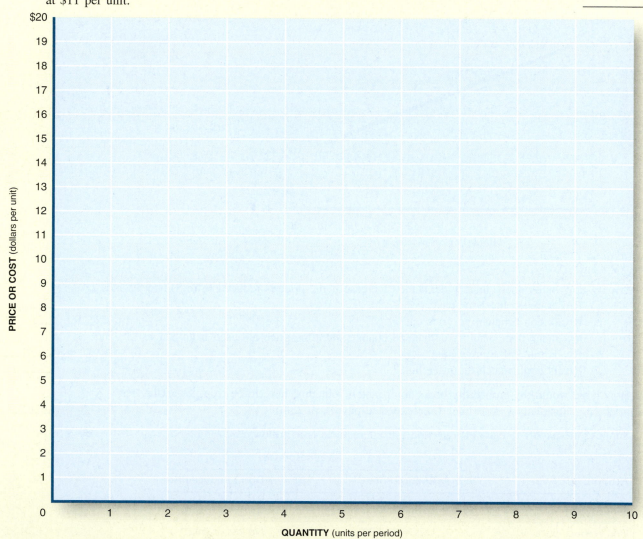

LO11-2 7. What is the price elasticity of demand between points *F* and *G* in Figure 11.2? _____

LO11-3 8. If the price elasticity of demand for oil is 0.2, by how much would oil prices have fallen in 2011 had OPEC increased output from 27 to 29 million barrels per day rather than holding output constant (World View, p. 252)? _____%

LO11-3 9. What is the maximum value of the HHI
(a) Before the AT&T/T-Mobile deal? _____
(b) If AT&T buys T-Mobile? _____
Base your answers on these 2011 cell phone market shares:
AT&T 38.3%   Verizon 31.3%   Sprint 15.9%   T-Mobile 12.2%   Other 2.3%

Monopolistic Competition

chapter

12

LEARNING OBJECTIVES

After reading this chapter, you should know

LO12-1. The unique structure of monopolistic competition.

LO12-2. The unique behavior of monopolistically competitive firms.

LO12-3. How monopolistically competitive firms maximize profits.

LO12-4. Why economic profits tend toward zero in monopolistic competition.

STARBUCKS COFFEE

Starbucks is already the biggest coffee bar chain in the country, with roughly 17,000 locations on four continents. And the company is determined to keep growing by setting up coffee bars in airports, department stores, and just about anywhere consumers congregate. Even if Starbucks achieves such meteoric growth, however, it will never have great market power. There are more than 13,000 other coffee bars in the United States, not to mention a million or so other places you can buy a cup of coffee (e.g., Dunkin' Donuts). With so many other close substitutes, the best Starbucks can hope for is a little brand loyalty. If enough consumers think of Starbucks when they get the caffeine urge, Starbucks will at least be able to charge more for coffee than a perfectly competitive firm. It won't enjoy *monopoly* profits, or even share the kind of monopoly profits *oligopolies* sometimes achieve.

It may, however, be able to maintain an economic profit for many years.

Starbucks is an example of yet another market structure—*monopolistic competition*. In this chapter we focus on how such firms make price and output decisions and the market outcomes that result. Our objective is to determine

- **The unique features of monopolistic competition.**
- **How market outcomes are affected by this market structure.**
- **The long-run consequences of different market structures.**

In this chapter we'll also see why we can't escape the relentless advertising that bombards us from every angle.

265

monopolistic competition: A market in which many firms produce similar goods or services but each maintains some independent control of its own price.

concentration ratio: The proportion of total industry output produced by the largest firms (usually the four largest).

web analysis

The North American Industrial Classification System (NAICS) defines types of industries. Go to **www.census.gov** and click "FAQ" to find out how industrial classification works.

STRUCTURE

As we first noted in Table 11.1, the distinguishing structural characteristic of **monopolistic competition** is that there are *many* firms in an industry. "Many" isn't an exact specification, of course. It's best understood as lying somewhere between the few that characterize oligopoly and the hordes that characterize perfect competition.

Low Concentration

A more precise way to distinguish monopolistic competition is to examine **concentration ratios.** Oligopolies have very high four-firm concentration ratios. As we saw in Chapter 11 (Table 11.2), concentration ratios of 70 to 100 percent are common in oligopolies. By contrast, there's much less concentration in monopolistic competition. A few firms may stand above the rest, but the combined market share of the top four firms will typically be in the range of 20 to 40 percent. Hence *low concentration ratios are common in monopolistic competition.*

Starbucks has less than 15 percent of the coffee bar business and a mere 7 percent of all coffee sales. The top four coffee bar outlets (Starbucks, Caribou, The Coffee Beanery, and Peet's) have a concentration ratio of only 28 percent (see Table 12.1). Other examples of monopolistic competition include banks, radio stations, health spas, apparel stores, convenience stores, night clubs, bars, and law firms. Notice in Table 12.1 that the personal computer market now has a monopolistically competitive structure as well. Even as large a firm as McDonald's might be regarded as a monopolistic competitor. Although "Mickey D's" has a huge share (40 percent) of the quickie *hamburger* market, its share of the much larger *fast-food* market is significantly smaller. The 13,000+ McDonald's outlets in the United States compete with over 200,000 fast-food outlets. If consumers regard pizzas, Chinese carry-outs, and delis as close substitutes for hamburgers, then the broader fast-food market is the appropriate basis for measuring market power and concentration. The same kind of

Product	Largest Firms (Market Share)	Concentration Ratio (%)
Notebook computers	Hewlett-Packard (18.8%), Dell (13.9%), Acer (12.2%), Toshiba (8.1%)	52%
Pizza delivery	Pizza Hut (20%), Domino's (10%), Papa John's (7%), Little Caesars (6%)	43
Auto tires (replacement)	Goodyear (16%), Michelin (8%), Firestone (7.5%), General (5%)	36
Bottled water	PepsiCo (Aquafina, 15.8%), Coca-Cola (Dasani, 8.7%), Perrier (Poland Spring, 6.4%), Dannon (5.3%)	36
Toys	Hasbro (15%), Mattel (11%), Tyco (5%), Fisher-Price (4%)	35
Casinos	MGM, Harrahs, Station, Mohegan Sun	33
Coffee bars	Starbucks (15%), Caribou (6%), Peet's (4%), Coffee Beanery (3%)	28
Drugs	Glaxo-Wellcome (5.8%), Hoechst-Marion Merrell Dow (4.4%), Merck (4.4%), American Home Products (3.8%)	18

Source: Industry sources and business publications (2004–2011 data).

TABLE 12.1
Monopolistic Competition

Monopolistically competitive industries are characterized by modest concentration ratios and low entry barriers. Contrast these four-firm concentration ratios with those of oligopoly (see Table 11.2).

consumer choice affects the pizza business. Three companies have 46 percent of the pizza *delivery* business. But they compete with over 65,000 pizzerias in the United States, reducing their market shares and power.

Market Power

Although concentration rates are low in monopolistic competition, the individual firms aren't powerless. There is a *monopoly* aspect to monopolistic competition. Each producer in monopolistic competition is large enough to have some **market power.** If a perfectly competitive firm increases the price of its product, it will lose all its customers. Recall that a perfectly competitive firm confronts a horizontal demand curve for its output. Competition is less intense in monopolistic competition. *A monopolistically competitive firm confronts a downward-sloping demand curve for its output.* When Starbucks increases the price of coffee, it loses some customers, but nowhere close to all of them (see the accompanying News.) Starbucks, like other monopolistically competitive firms, has some control over the price of its output. This is the *monopoly* dimension of monopolistic competition.

market power: The ability to alter the market price of a good or service.

IN THE NEWS

What's Behind Starbucks' Price Hike?

The Coffee Company Will Raise Drink Prices in October, Even as Other Chains Crowd the Market with Similar (and Cheaper) Products

Starting on October 3, the prices on lattes, cappuccinos, drip coffee, and other drinks will go up 5 cents at company-operated stores in North America. Starbucks is also jacking up the price of its coffee beans by roughly 50 cents per pound, or an average of 3.9 percent. . . .

The timing is certainly odd. For a while now, Starbucks has been struggling with labor disputes. Rivals McDonald's, Dunkin' Donuts, and Canadian restaurant chain Tim Horton's are steaming into its turf. . . .

A Confident Company

If Starbucks were really worried about any of these issues, the last thing its senior execs would consider is a price hike. In fact, Starbucks' dominant market position gives it unique pricing flexibility. Every week, the company succeeds in persuading nearly 40 million people to buy pricey espresso drinks.

"The company is selling a product that has become part of our daily lives, said Kristine Koerber, an analyst at JMP Securities. "Raising prices by a nickel is not going to meet any resistance."

Company officials say the higher prices are intended to offset higher labor and fuel costs. And while the price increases are small, they underscore just how confident Starbucks remains about its growth prospects and its ability to fend off new competitive threats. Koerber and many other analysts seem to support this optimism. "You're not going to raise prices if you have the competitive or macroeconomic environment going against you," she says.

—Stanley Holmes

Source: *BusinessWeek*, **www.businessweek.com**, September 22, 2006. Used with permission of Bloomberg L.P. Copyright © 2011. All rights reserved.

Analysis: A monopolistically competitive firm has the power to increase price unilaterally. The greater the brand loyalty, the less unit sales will decline in response.

Independent Production Decisions

In an oligopoly, a firm that increased its price would have to worry about how rivals might respond (like the airlines in the News on page 248). In monopolistic competition, however, there are many more firms. As a result, *modest changes in the output or price of any single firm will have no perceptible influence on the sales of any other firm.* This relative independence results from the fact that the effects of any one firm's behavior will be spread over many other firms (rather than only two or three other firms, as in an oligopoly).

The relative independence of monopolistic competitors means that they don't have to worry about retaliatory responses to every price or output change. As a result, they confront more traditional demand curves with no kinks. Recall that the kink in the oligopolist's curve results from the likelihood that rival oligopolists will match price reductions (to preserve market shares) but not necessarily price increases (to increase their shares). In monopolistic competition, by contrast, the market shares of rival firms aren't perceptibly altered by another firm's price changes.

Low Entry Barriers

barriers to entry: Obstacles, such as patents, that make it difficult or impossible for would-be producers to enter a particular market.

Another characteristic of monopolistic competition is the presence of *low* **barriers to entry**—it's relatively easy to get in and out of the industry. To become a coffee vendor, all you need is boiling water, some fresh beans, and cups. You can save on rent by using a pushcart to dispense the brew, which is how Starbucks itself got started on the streets of Seattle (see the photo in the left margin). Such unusually low entry barriers now keep Starbucks and other coffee bars on their toes. Low entry barriers also tend to push economic profits toward zero. In the pizza business over 4,000 firms enter and exit every year. This is the *competitive* dimension of monopolistic competition.

bobhdeering/Alamy

Low entry barriers encourage competition.

BEHAVIOR

Given the unique structural characteristics of monopolistic competition, we should anticipate some distinctive behavior.

product differentiation: Features that make one product appear different from competing products in the same market.

Product Differentiation

One of the most notable features of monopolistically competitive behavior is **product differentiation.** A monopolistically competitive firm is distinguished from a purely competitive firm by its downward-sloping demand curve. Individual firms in a perfectly competitive market confront horizontal demand curves because consumers view their respective products as interchangeable (homogeneous). As a result, an attempt by one firm to raise its price will drive its customers to other firms.

Brand Image. In monopolistic competition, each firm has a distinct identity—a *brand image.* Its output is perceived by consumers as being somewhat different from the output of all other firms in the industry. Nowhere is this more evident than in the fast-growing bottled water industry. Pepsi and Coke have become the leaders in the bottled water market as a result of effective marketing (see the News on the next page). Although Aquafina (Pepsi) and Dasani (Coke) are just filtered municipal water, clever advertising campaigns have convinced consumers that these branded waters are different—and better—than hundreds of other bottled waters. As a result of such product differentiation, Pepsi and Coke can raise the price of their bottled waters without losing all their customers to rival firms.

Brand Loyalty

At first blush, the demand curve facing a monopolistically competitive firm looks like the demand curve confronting a monopolist. There's a profound difference, however. In a monopoly, there are no other firms. In monopolistic competition, *each firm has a monopoly only on its brand image; it still competes with other firms offering close substitutes.* This implies that the extent of power a monopolistically competitive firm has depends on how successfully it can differentiate its product from those of other firms. The more brand loyalty a firm can establish, the less likely consumers are to switch brands when price is increased. In other words, *brand loyalty makes the demand curve facing the firm less price-elastic.*

IN THE NEWS

Water, Water Everywhere; Coke, Pepsi Unleash Flood of Ad Muscle

Water is water, at least until the marketers get hold of it.

Then a humble commodity that literally falls from the sky becomes something else. Something with "personality."

Not long ago, it would have been silly to think about branding water. But the big beverage companies are doing just that, and this summer marks the biggest-ever ad barrage for Dasani, Coke's water brand, and Aquafina, bottled by Pepsi-Cola Co. . . .

Branding is an important issue in a category where sales grew by nearly 26 percent in 2000, to 807 million cases—the highest growth rate in the beverage industry. The challenge is getting attention in a highly fragmented market. There are hundreds of different water brands, and some are so small that they serve just a few towns.

"Consumers are trading up. They're willing to search for a brand," said Kellam Graitcer, Dasani brand manager at Coca-Cola. "We're trying to inject a little bit of personality into the category.". . .

The two companies are likely to spend about $20 million each this year on ads.

—Scott Leith

Source: *The Atlanta Journal-Constitution* © July 12, 2001. All rights reserved. Used by permission.

Analysis: By differentiating their products, monopolistic competitors establish brand loyalty. Brand loyalty gives producers greater control over the prices of their products.

web analysis

Local gas stations are monopolistically competitive in that they differ by location. To compare prices of gas stations in your area, visit **www.gasbuddy.com.**

Brand loyalty exists even when products are virtually identical. Gasoline of a given octane rating is a very standardized product. Nevertheless, most consumers regularly buy one particular brand. Because of that brand loyalty, Exxon can raise the price of its gasoline by a penny or two a gallon without losing customers to competing companies. Brand loyalty is particularly high for cigarettes, toothpaste, and even laxatives. Consumers of those products say they'd stick with their accustomed brand even if the price of a competing brand was cut by 50 percent. In other words, ***brand loyalty implies low* cross-price elasticity of demand.** Brand loyalty is less strong (and cross-price elasticity higher) for paper towels and virtually nonexistent for tomatoes.

In the computer industry, product differentiation has been used to establish brand loyalty. Although virtually all computers use identical microprocessor "brains" and operating platforms, the particular mix of functions performed on any computer can be varied, as can its appearance (packaging). Effective advertising can convince consumers that one computer is "smarter," more efficient, or more versatile than another. Also, a single firm may differentiate itself by providing faster or more courteous customer service. If successful in any of these efforts, ***each monopolistically competitive firm will establish some consumer loyalty.*** With such loyalty a firm can alter its own price somewhat without fear of great changes in unit sales (quantity demanded). In other words, the demand curve facing each firm will slope downward, as in Figure 12.1.

cross-price elasticity of demand: Percentage change in the quantity demanded of *X* divided by the percentage change in the price of *Y*.

Repurchase Rates. One measure of brand loyalty is consumers' tendency to repurchase the same brand. Nearly 9 out of 10 Apple Macintosh users stick with Apple products when they upgrade or replace computer components. Repurchase rates are 74 percent for Dell, 72 percent for Hewlett-Packard, and 66 percent for Gateway. Starbucks also counts heavily on return customers.

To maintain such brand loyalty, monopolistically competitive firms must often expand services or product offerings. Remember that entry barriers are low. In the coffee business, it was relatively easy for fast-food companies like McDonald's and Dunkin' Donuts to enter once they saw how profitable Starbucks was. When they did, Starbucks had to expand its menu to

Steamed over Starbucks

FIGURE 12.1
Short-Run Equilibrium in Monopolistic Competition

In the short run, a monopolistically competitive firm equates marginal revenue and marginal cost (point *K*). In this case, the firm sells the resulting output at a price (point *F*) above marginal cost. Total profits are represented by the shaded rectangle.

The short-run equilibrium
for the firm (MC = MR)

maintain its market dominance. As the accompanying News relates, a "breakfast war" ensued as firms sought greater product differentiation. Although menu expansion is costly, firms often decide that increased service is more cost-effective than price competition, given the low cross-price elasticity of demand in monopolistically competitive markets. In recent years, Starbucks has continued to pursue product differentiation with a new logo, instant coffee, new cup sizes (the 31-ounce "trenta"), single-serve machines, and iPhone payments.

IN THE NEWS

Fast-Food Rivals Suit Up for Breakfast War

Competition Heats Up as Menus Expand

Hamburgers, schmamburgers. Fast food's fiery new battleground is the breakfast table.

Just about everyone—even coffee kingpin Starbucks—is entering the hot-breakfast arena in 2007 with new offerings. At stake: a piece of the $77.6 billion breakfast market that, for the fast-food giants, can mean the difference between growth and stagnation.

Marketing

Starbucks, for the first time, is rolling out five hot breakfast sandwiches. Wendy's is expanding its breakfast rollout. Burger King this week launches a breakfast value menu. McDonald's, the current breakfast behemoth, also has a breakfast value menu in testing. Next month Subway will introduce breakfast omelet sandwiches at one-third of its stores. . . .

Instead of growing by building still more restaurants, the new growth goal is to boost same-store sales—to get more dollars from each existing location, says Ron Paul, president of Technomic, a consulting firm.

—Bruce Horovitz

Source: *USA TODAY.* February 20, 2007. Reprinted with permission.

Analysis: Monopolistically competitive firms must differentiate their products to establish and maintain brand loyalty. Variations in products and services help create unique brand profiles.

Price Premiums. Another symptom of brand loyalty is the price differences between computer brands. Consumers are willing to pay more for an HP or Dell computer than a no-name computer with identical features. For the same reason, consumers are willing to pay more for Starbucks coffee, Ben and Jerry's ice cream, or Aquafina water, even when virtually identical products are available at lower prices.

Short-Run Price and Output

The monopolistically competitive firm's **production decision** is similar to that of a monopolist. Both types of firms confront downward-sloping demand and marginal revenue curves. To maximize profits, both seek the rate of output at which marginal revenue equals marginal cost. This short-run profit-maximizing outcome is illustrated by point K in Figure 12.1. That MC = MR intersection establishes q_a as the profit-maximizing rate of output. The demand curve indicates (point F) that q_a of output can be sold at the price of p_a. Hence the quantity–price combination q_a, p_a illustrates the short-run equilibrium of the monopolistically competitive firm.

production decision: The selection of the short-run rate of output (with existing plants and equipment).

Entry and Exit

Figure 12.1 indicates that this monopolistically competitive firm is earning an **economic profit:** price (p_a) exceeds average total cost (c_a) at the short-run rate of output. These profits are of course a welcome discovery for the firm. They also portend increased competition, however.

economic profit: The difference between total revenues and total economic costs.

Entry Effects. If firms in monopolistic competition are earning an economic profit, other firms will flock to the industry. Remember that *entry barriers are low in monopolistic competition, so new entrants can't be kept out of the market.* If they get wind of the short-run profits depicted in Figure 12.1, they'll come running.

As new firms enter the industry, supply increases and prices will be pushed down the market demand curve, just as in competitive markets. Figure 12.2*a* illustrates these market changes. The initial price p_1 is set by the intersection of *industry* MC and MR. Because that price generates a profit, more firms enter. This entry shifts the *industry* cost structure to the right, creating a new equilibrium price, p_2.

(a) Effect of entry on the industry

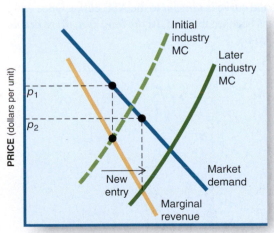

(b) Effect of entry on the monopolistically competitive firm

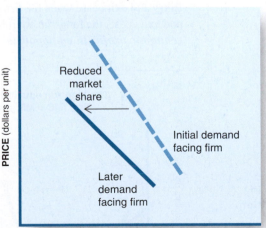

FIGURE 12.2
Market vs. Firm Effects of Entry

Barriers to entry are low in monopolistic competition. Hence new firms will enter if economic profits are available.

(*a*) **The Market.** The entry of new firms will shift the *market* cost curves to the right, as in part *a*. This pushes the average price down the *market* demand curve.

(*b*) **The Firm.** The entry of new firms also affects the demand curve facing the typical firm. The *firm's* demand curve shifts to the left and becomes more elastic because more close substitutes (other firms) are available

The impact of this entry on the firms already in the market will be different from that in competitive markets, however. As new firms enter a monopolistically competitive industry, existing firms will lose customers. This is illustrated by the leftward shift of the demand curve facing each firm, as in Figure 12.2*b*. Accordingly, we conclude that *when firms enter a monopolistically competitive industry,*

- *The industry cost curves shift to the right, pushing down price* (Figure 12.2*a*).
- *The demand curves facing individual firms shift to the left* (Figure 12.2*b*).

As the demand curve it faces shifts leftward, the monopolistically competitive firm will have to make a new production decision. It need not charge the same price as its rivals, however, or coordinate its output with theirs. Each monopolistically competitive firm has some independent power over its (shrinking numbers of) captive customers.

No Long-Run Profits

Although each firm has some control over its own pricing decisions, *entry-induced leftward shifts of the demand curve facing the firm will ultimately eliminate economic profits.*

Long-Run Equilibrium. Notice in Figure 12.3 where the firm eventually ends up. In long-run equilibrium (point G), marginal cost is again equal to marginal revenue (at the MR = MC intersection directly below G). At that rate of output (q_g), however, there are no economic profits. At that output, price (p_g) is exactly equal to average total cost. The profit-maximizing equilibrium (point G) occurs where the demand curve is tangent to the ATC curve. If the demand curve shifted any farther left, price would always be less than ATC and the firm would incur losses. If the demand curve were positioned farther to the right, price would exceed ATC at some rates of output. When the demand curve is *tangent* to the ATC curve, the firm's best possible outcome is to break even. At point G in Figure 12.3, price equals ATC and economic profit is zero.

Will a monopolistically competitive firm end up at point G? As long as other firms can enter the industry, the disappearance of economic profits is inevitable. Existing firms can postpone the day of reckoning by increasing their product differentiation and advertising. But rival firms will enter as long as the demand (price) line lies above ATC at some point. Firms will exit when the demand facing the firm lies to the left of and below the ATC curve. Entry and exit cease when the firm's demand curve is *tangent* to the ATC curve. Once entry and exit cease, the long-run equilibrium has been established. *In the long run, there are no economic profits in monopolistic competition.*

FIGURE 12.3
Long-Run Equilibrium in Monopolistic Competition

In the long run, more firms enter the industry. As they do so, the demand curve facing each firm *shifts* to the left as all market shares decline. Firms still equate MR and MC. Ultimately, however, the demand curve will be tangent to the ATC curve (point G), at which point price equals average total cost and no economic profits exist.

The long-run equilibrium for the
firm (MC = MR, *p* = ATC)

Inefficiency

The zero-profit equilibrium of firms in monopolistic competition, as illustrated in Figure 12.3, differs from the perfectly competitive equilibrium. In perfect competition, long-run profits are also zero. But at that point, a competitive industry produces at the *lowest* point on the ATC curve and thus maximizes efficiency. In monopolistic competition, however, the demand curve facing each firm slopes downward. Hence it can't be tangent to the ATC curve at its lowest point (the bottom of the U), as in perfect competition. Instead the demand curve of a monopolistically competitive firm must touch the ATC curve on the *left* side of the U. Note in Figure 12.3 how point *G* lies above and to the left of the bottom of the ATC curve. This long-run equilibrium occurs at an output rate that is less than the minimum-cost rate of production. In long-run equilibrium, the monopolistically competitive industry isn't producing at minimum average cost. As a consequence, *monopolistic competition tends to be less efficient in the long run than a perfectly competitive industry.*

Excess Capacity. One symptom of the inefficiencies associated with monopolistic competition is industrywide excess capacity (see the News below). Each firm tries to gain market share by building more outlets and advertising heavily. In equilibrium, however, the typical firm is producing at a rate of output that's less than its minimum-ATC output rate. This implies that the *same* level of *industry* output could be produced at lower cost with fewer firms. If that happened, the resources used to develop that excess capacity could be used for more desired purposes.

IN THE NEWS

Premium Coffee Shops May Be Nearing Saturation Point

ALBANY—It's easy to get a good cup of coffee on Wolf Road. And it's getting easier.

The two-mile retail strip has two Dunkin' Donuts, one Starbucks, another planned, and an independent coffee house. The McDonald's sells a premium brew, as does the Borders. And the Barnes & Noble in the mall across the street from the Starbucks sells Starbucks.

The coffee cluster is great for option-oriented commuters such as Troy Mackey, who will grab a French Vanilla at Dunkin' Donuts only if he spies a short line through his car window. "I can jump in and jump out," Mr. Mackey said as he waited in line in his business suit. But it may not be as great for Starbucks, McDonald's, and Dunkin' Donuts as they compete in crammed commercial battlegrounds such as this one in upstate New York. So many stores crowded within eyesight of each other raises a question: Is it possible to have too many places selling premium coffee? . . .

Mr. Owens compared the current coffee market to the burger boom of the 1960s and 1970s, when a number of chains opened shops near McDonald's. There was some shakeout, but he noted that chains like Burger King, Wendy's, Sonic, Carl's Jr., and Jack in the Box are still standing.

Source: *Associated Press*, January 29, 2008. Used with permission of The Associated Press. Copyright © 2011. All rights reserved.

Analysis: Continued entry will push economic profits to zero and leave the industry with excess capacity.

Flawed Price Signals. The misallocation of resources that occurs in monopolistic competition is a by-product of the flawed price signal that is transmitted in imperfectly competitive markets. Because the demand curve facing a firm in monopolistic competition slopes downward, such a firm will violate the principle of **marginal cost pricing.** Specifically, it will always price its output above the level of marginal costs, just like firms in an oligopoly or monopoly. Notice in Figures 12.1 and 12.3 that price lies above marginal cost in both the short- and long-run equilibrium. As a consequence, price always exceeds the opportunity cost. Consumers respond to these flawed signals by demanding fewer goods from monopolistically competitive industries than they would otherwise. We end up with the wrong (suboptimal) mix of output and misallocated resources.

marginal cost pricing: The offer (supply) of goods at prices equal to their marginal cost.

Thus ***monopolistic competition results in both production inefficiency (above minimum average cost) and allocative inefficiency (wrong mix of output).*** This contrasts with the model of perfect competition, which delivers both minimum average total cost and efficient (MC-based) price signals.

THE ECONOMY TOMORROW

NO CEASE-FIRE IN ADVERTISING WARS

Models of oligopoly and monopolistic competition show how industry structure affects market behavior. Of particular interest is the way different kinds of firms "compete" for sales and profits. ***In truly (perfectly) competitive industries, firms compete on the basis of price.*** Competitive firms win by achieving greater efficiency and offering their products at the lowest possible price.

Firms in imperfectly competitive markets don't "compete" in the same way. In oligopolies, the kink commonly found in the demand curve facing each firm inhibits price reductions. In monopolistic competition, there's also a reluctance to engage in price competition. Because each firm has its own captive market—consumers who prefer its particular brand over competing brands—price reductions by one firm won't induce many consumers to switch brands. As we noted earlier, the cross-price elasticity of demand is low in monopolistically competitive markets. Thus price reductions aren't a very effective way to increase sales or market share in monopolistic competition.

If imperfectly competitive firms don't compete on the basis of price, do they really compete at all? The answer is evident to anyone who listens to the radio, watches television, reads magazines or newspapers, or drives on the highway. ***Imperfectly competitive firms engage in nonprice competition.***

The most prominent form of *nonprice competition* is advertising. An imperfectly competitive firm typically uses advertising to enhance its own product's image, thereby increasing the size of its captive market (consumers who identify with a particular brand). The Coca-Cola Company hires rock stars to create the image that Coke is superior to other soft drinks (see the News below), thereby creating brand loyalty. In 2010, oligopolies and monopolistically

IN THE NEWS

The Cola Wars: It's Not All Taste

American consumers gulp nearly 40 million soft drinks per day. The Coca-Cola Company produces about 40 percent of those soft drinks, while Pepsi-Cola produces about 30 percent of the market supply. With nearly 70 percent of the market between them, Pepsi and Coke wage fierce battles for market share.

The major weapon in these "cola wars" is advertising. Coke spends $2 billion a year to convince consumers that its products are superior. Pepsi spends almost as much to win the hearts and taste buds of American consumers. The advertisements not only tout the superior taste of their respective products but also try to create a particular image for each cola.

The advertising apparently works. Half of all soft drink consumers profess loyalty to either Coke or Pepsi. In their view, there's only one "real" cola, and that's the one they'll buy every time. Few of these loyalists can be persuaded to switch cola brands, even when offered lower prices for the "other" cola.

Ironically, few people can identify their favorite cola in blind taste tests. Seventy percent of the people who swore loyalty to either Coke or Pepsi picked the wrong cola in a taste test.

The moral of the story? That in imperfectly competitive markets, product *image* and *perceptions* may be as important as product quality and price in winning market shares.

Analysis: Advertising is intended to create brand loyalty. Loyal consumers are likely to buy the same brand all the time, even if competitors offer nearly identical products.

web analysis

For further results on blind taste tests of Pepsi and Coke, visit **www.serendip.brynmawr.edu** and search for "Pepsi Challenge."

TABLE 12.2
Top 10 Advertisers

Firms with market power attempt to preserve and extend that power through advertising. A successful advertising campaign alters the demand curve facing the firm, thus increasing potential profits. Shown here are the advertising outlays of the biggest advertisers in 2010.

Company	Ad Spending in 2010 ($billion)
Procter & Gamble	$3.1 billion
General Motors	2.1
AT&T	2.1
Verizon	1.8
News Corp.	1.4
Time Warner	1.2
Pfizer	1.2
Ford	1.1
Johnson & Johnson	1.1
L'Oreal	1.1

Source: Kantar Media

competitive firms spent over $500 *billion* on advertising for such purposes. Procter & Gamble alone spent $3.1 billion (see Table 12.2). P&G hopes that these expenditures shift the demand for its products (e.g., Ivory Soap, Pampers, Jif peanut butter, Crest, Tide) to the right, while perhaps making it less price-elastic as well. By contrast, perfectly competitive firms have no incentive to advertise because they can individually sell their entire output at the current market price.

A company that runs a successful advertising campaign can create enormous *goodwill* value. That value is reflected in stronger brand loyalty—as expressed in greater demand and smaller price elasticity. Often a successful brand image can be used to sell related products as well. According to the World View on the next page, the most valuable brand name in the world is Apple, whose worldwide name recognition is worth $153 *billion*

Advertising isn't the only form of nonprice competition. Before the airline industry was deregulated (1978), individual airlines were compelled to charge the same price for any given trip; hence price competition was prohibited. But airlines did compete—not only by advertising, but also by offering "special" meals, movies, more frequent or convenient departures, and faster ticketing and baggage services.

Is there anything wrong with nonprice competition? Surely airline passengers enjoyed their "special" meals, "extra" services, and "more convenient" departure times. But these services weren't free. As always, there were opportunity costs. From an air traveler's perspective, the "special" services stimulated by nonprice competition substituted for cheaper fares. With more price competition, customers could have chosen to travel more cheaply *or* in greater comfort.

From society's perspective, the resources used in advertising and other forms of nonprice competition could be used instead to produce larger quantities of desired goods and services (including airplane trips). Unless consumers are given the chance to *choose* between "more" service and lower prices, there's a presumption that nonprice competition leads to an undesirable use of our scarce resources. For example, marketing costs absorb over a third of the price of breakfast cereal. As a result of such behavior, consumers end up with more advertising but less cereal than they would otherwise. They could, of course, save money by buying store brand or generic cereals. But they've never seen athletes or cartoon characters endorse such products. So consumers pay the higher price for branded cereals.

Models of imperfect competition imply that advertising wars between powerful corporations won't end anytime soon. As long as markets have the *structure* of oligopoly or monopolistic competition, we expect the *behavior* of nonprice competition. Advertising jingles will be as pervasive in the economy tomorrow as they are today.

WORLD VIEW

The Best Global Brands

A belief in the power of brands and brand management has spread far beyond the traditional consumer goods marketers who invented the discipline. For companies in almost every industry, brands are important in a way they never were before. Why? For one thing, customers for everything from soda pop to software now have a staggering number of choices. And the net can bring the full array to any computer screen with a click of the mouse. Without trusted brand names as touchstones, shopping for almost anything would be overwhelming. Meanwhile, in a global economy, corporations must reach customers in markets far from their home base. A strong brand acts as an ambassador when companies enter new markets or offer new products.

That's why companies that once measured their worth strictly in terms of tangibles such as factories, inventory, and cash have realized that a vibrant brand, with its implicit promise of quality, is an equally important asset. A brand has the power to command a premium price among customers and a premium stock price among investors. It can boost earnings and cushion cyclical downturns—and now a brand's value can be measured.

The World's 10 Most Valuable Brands

Rank	Brand	2010 Brand Value ($billions)
1	Apple	153
2	Google	111
3	IBM	101
4	McDonald's	81
5	Microsoft	78
6	Coca-Cola	74
7	AT&T	70
8	Marlboro	68
9	China Mobile	57
10	General Electric	50

Source: Millward Brown, BrandZ Rankings (May 2011). **www.millwardbrown.com** © Millward Brown. Reprinted with permission.

Analysis: Brand names are valuable economic assets and assist a firm in maintaining a base of loyal customers. These brands have worldwide recognition as a result of heavy advertising.

SUMMARY

- There are many (rather than few) firms in monopolistic competition. The concentration ratio in such industries tends to be low (20–40 percent).   LO12-1
- Each monopolistically competitive firm enjoys some brand loyalty. This brand loyalty, together with its relatively small market share, gives each firm a high degree of independence in price and output decisions.   LO12-1
- The amount of market share and power a monopolistically competitive firm possesses depends on how successfully it differentiates its product from similar products. Accord-

ingly, monopolistically competitive firms tend to devote more resources to advertising.   LO12-2
- The market power bestowed by brand loyalty is measured by low cross-price elasticities of demand, high repurchase rates, and price premiums.   LO12-1
- Low entry barriers permit new firms to enter a monopolistically competitive industry whenever economic profits exist. Such entry eliminates long-run economic profit and reduces (shifts leftward) the demand for the output of existing firms.   LO12-4

- Monopolistic competition results in resource misallocations (due to flawed price signals) and inefficiency (above-minimum-average cost). LO12-3
- Monopolistic competition encourages nonprice competition instead of price competition. Because the resources used in nonprice competition (advertising, packaging, service, etc.) may have more desirable uses, these industry structures lead to resource misallocation. LO12-3

Key Terms

monopolistic competition
concentration ratio
market power

barriers to entry
product differentiation
cross-price elasticity of demand

production decision
economic profit
marginal cost pricing

Questions for Discussion

1. What is the source of Starbucks' "confidence" in the News on page 267? LO12-1
2. Why do 4,000 new pizzerias open every year? Why do just as many close? LO12-4
3. Name three products each for which you have (*a*) high brand loyalty and (*b*) low brand loyalty. LO12-2
4. If one gas station reduces its prices, must other gas stations match the price reduction? Why or why not? LO12-2
5. The News article on page 274 suggests that most consumers can't identify their favorite cola in blind taste tests. Why then do people stick with one brand? What accounts for brand loyalty in bottled water (News, p. 269)? LO12-1
6. How do new product offerings like breakfast sandwiches (News, p. 270) affect Starbucks' sales and profits? What is the "saturation point" referred to in the News on page 273? LO12-4
7. Why is the mix of output produced in competitive markets more desirable than that in monopolistically competitive markets? LO12-3
8. How would our consumption of cereal change if cereal manufacturers stopped advertising? Would we be better or worse off? LO12-3
9. Why are people willing to pay more for Dreyer's ice cream when it has a Starbucks brand on it? LO12-2
10. According to the World View on page 276, what gives brand names their value? LO12-2

 web activities to accompany this chapter can be found on the Online Learning Center:
http://www.mhhe.com/schiller13e

 mobile app Visit your mobile app store and download the Schiller: Study Econ app *today!*

LO12-1 1. What is the concentration ratio in an industry with the following market shares?

| Firm A | 11.1 | Firm C | 5.2 | Firm E | 3.6 | Firm G | 1.6 |
| Firm B | 7.6 | Firm D | 4.0 | Firm F | 2.2 | Other firms | 64.7 |

_____

LO12-2 2. If Starbucks raises its price by 6 percent and McDonald's experiences a 0.4 percent increase in demand for its coffee, what is the cross-price elasticity of demand?

_____

LO12-3 3. In Figure 12.3,
    (*a*) At what output rate is economic profit equal to zero? _____
    (*b*) At what output rate(s) are positive economic profits available? _____
    (*c*) At what output rate(s) do economic losses occur? _____

LO12-3 4. (*a*) Use the accompanying graph to illustrate the short-run equilibrium of a monopolistically competitive firm.
    (*b*) At that equilibrium, what is
        (*i*) Price? _____
        (*ii*) Output? _____
        (*iii*) Total profit? _____

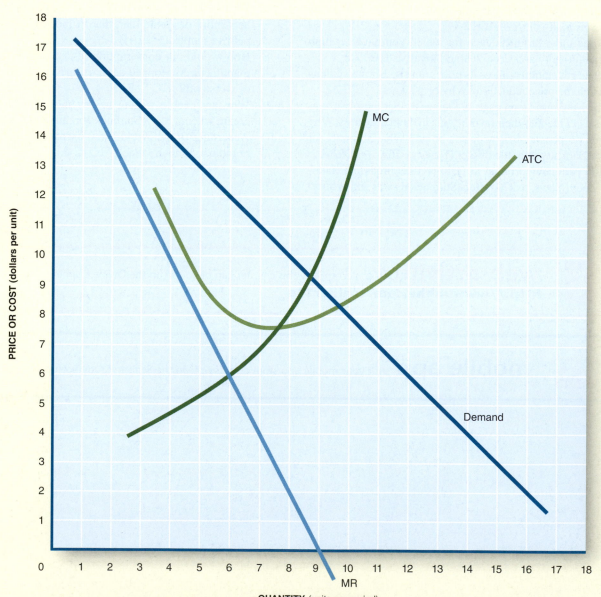

(c) Identify the long-run equilibrium of the same firm.
(d) In long-run equilibrium, what is (approximately)

	(i) Price?	_____
	(ii) Output?	_____
	(iii) Total profit?	_____

LO12-4 5. (a) In the *short*-run equilibrium of the previous problem, what is
     (i) The price of the product?   _____
     (ii) The opportunity cost of producing the last unit?   _____
  (b) In the *long*-run equilibrium of the previous problem, what is
     (i) The price of the product?   _____
     (ii) The opportunity cost of producing the last unit?   _____

LO12-1 6. According to the News on page 267,
  (a) By how much could unit sales of coffee beans at Starbucks decline after the 2006 price
    increase without reducing total revenue?   _____%
  (b) If the price elasticity of demand for Starbucks was 0.20, by how much would coffee bean
    unit sales have fallen?   _____%

LO12-4 7. On the accompanying graph, identify each of the following *market* outcomes:
  (a) Short-run equilibrium output in competition.   (c) Long-run equilibrium output in monopoly.
  (b) Long-run equilibrium output in competition.   (d) Long-run equilibrium output in monopolistic competition.

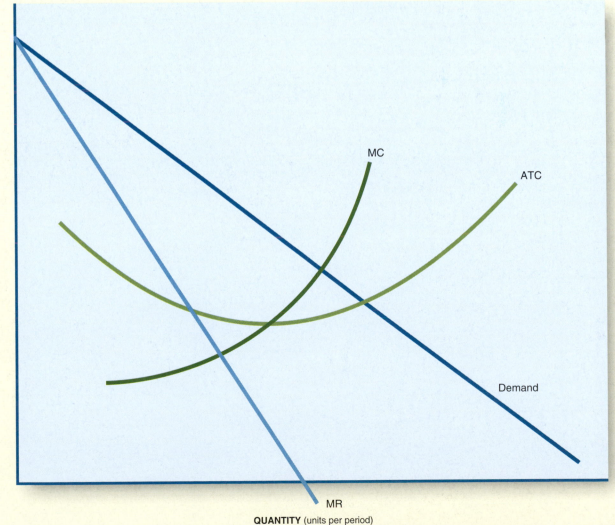

Regulatory Issues

Microeconomic theory provides insights into how prices and product flows are determined in unregulated markets. Sometimes those market outcomes are not optimal, and the government intervenes to improve them. In this section we examine government regulation of natural monopolies (Chapter 13), environmental protection (Chapter 14), and farm output and prices (Chapter 15). The goal is to determine whether and how government regulation might improve market outcomes—or possibly worsen them.

Natural Monopolies: (De)Regulation?

The lights went out in California in 2001—not just once but repeatedly. Offices went dark, air conditioners shut down, assembly lines stopped, and TV screens went blank. The state governor blamed power company "profiteers" for the rolling blackouts. He charged the companies with curtailing power supplies and hiking prices. He wanted *more* regulation of the power industry. Industry representatives responded that government regulation was itself responsible for throwing California into a new Dark Age. *Less* regulation, not more, would have kept the lights on, they claimed.

The battle over government regulation of the power industry quickly spread to other states. Some states that were deregulating power companies suspended the process. Other states also put (de)regulation plans on hold until they could better assess what went wrong in California.

Everyone agrees that markets sometimes fail—that unregulated markets may produce the wrong mix of output, undesirable methods of production, or an unfair distribution of income. But government intervention can fail as well. Hence we need to ask,

- **When is government regulation necessary?**
- **What form should that regulation take?**
- **When is it appropriate to deregulate an industry?**

In answering these questions we draw on economic principles as well as recent experience. This will permit us to contrast the theory of (de)regulation with reality.

ANTITRUST VS. REGULATION

A perfectly competitive market provides a model for economic efficiency. As we first observed in Chapter 3, the market mechanism can answer the basic economic questions of WHAT to produce, HOW to produce it, and FOR WHOM. Under ideal conditions, the market's answers may also be optimal—that is, the best possible outcomes. To achieve this **laissez-faire** ideal, all producers must be perfect competitors; people must have full information about tastes, costs, and prices; all costs and benefits must be reflected in market prices; and pervasive economies of scale must be absent.

In reality, these conditions are rarely, if ever, fully attained. Markets may be dominated by large and powerful producers. In wielding their power, these producers may restrict output, raise prices, stifle competition, and inhibit innovation. In other words, market power may cause **market failure,** leaving us with suboptimal market outcomes.

Behavioral Focus

As we observed in Chapter 11, the government has two options for intervention where market power prevails. It may focus on the *structure* of an industry or on its *behavior.* **Antitrust** laws cover both options: they prohibit mergers and acquisitions that reduce potential competition (structures) and forbid market practices (behavior) that are anticompetitive.

Government **regulation** has a different focus. Instead of worrying about industry structure, regulation focuses almost exclusively on *behavior.* In general, regulation seeks to change market outcomes directly by imposing specific limitations on the price, output, or investment decisions of private firms.

NATURAL MONOPOLY

Regulation is almost always the policy choice for dealing with natural monopolies. A **natural monopoly** exists when a single firm has such pervasive economies of scale that it will "naturally" dominate its industry. In natural monopoly, bigger *is* always better—at least in terms of production costs. The larger the firm, the lower its costs. Because of these scale economies, a natural monopoly can produce the products consumers want at the lowest possible price. A single cable company is more efficient than a horde of cable firms developing a maze of cable networks. The same is true of local telephone service and many utilities. In all of these cases, a single company can deliver products at lower cost than a bunch of smaller firms. Dismantling such a natural monopoly would destroy that cost advantage. A natural monopoly is therefore a potentially desirable market *structure*.

But what about behavior? Do we need to regulate natural monopolies? Even though a natural monopoly might enjoy economies of scale, it might not pass those savings along to consumers. In that case, the economies of scale don't do consumers any good, and the government might have to regulate the firm's behavior.

To determine whether regulation is desirable, we first have to determine how an *unregulated* natural monopoly will behave.

Declining ATC Curve

Figure 13.1 on the next page illustrates the unique characteristics of a natural monopoly. *The distinctive characteristic of a natural monopoly is its downward-sloping average total cost (ATC) curve.* Because unit costs keep falling as the rate of production increases, a single large firm can underprice any smaller firm. Ultimately, it can produce all the market supply at the lowest attainable cost. In an unregulated market, such a firm will "naturally" come to dominate the industry.

High Fixed Costs. Natural monopolies typically emerge in situations where the fixed costs of production are extremely large. To supply electricity, for example, you first need to build a power source (e.g., a coal-fired plant, hydroelectric dam, or nuclear generator), then

---

laissez faire: The doctrine of "leave it alone," or nonintervention by government in the market mechanism.

market failure: An imperfection in the market mechanism that prevents optimal outcomes.

antitrust: Government intervention to alter market structure or prevent abuse of market power.

regulation: Government intervention to alter the behavior of firms—for example, in pricing, output, or advertising.

natural monopoly: An industry in which one firm can achieve economies of scale over the entire range of market supply.

FIGURE 13.1
Declining ATC

A combination of high fixed costs
and very low marginal costs generates a unique, downward-sloping
ATC curve in natural monopoly. MC
lies below ATC at all output levels.

FIGURE 13.1
Declining ATC

A combination of high fixed costs
and very low marginal costs generates a unique, downward-sloping
ATC curve in natural monopoly. MC
lies below ATC at all output levels.

a distribution network. It's the same thing with subways and railroads: a lot of infrastructure must be constructed before anyone gets a ride. As a consequence of these high fixed
costs, the *average* total cost curve starts out very high (recall that ATC = AFC + AVC).

Low Marginal Costs. Once productive capacity is built, the focus turns to *marginal costs.*
In natural monopolies, marginal costs are typically low—*very low.* Supplying another kilowatt of electricity entails negligible marginal cost. Carrying one more passenger on a railroad or subway entails similarly negligible costs.

Even if marginal costs rise as production increases (the law of diminishing returns),
marginal cost remains less than average total cost over the entire range of output. Notice in
Figure 13.1 that *the marginal cost (MC) curve lies below the ATC curve at all rates of
output for a natural monopoly.* The ATC curve never rises into its conventional U shape
because marginal costs never exceed average costs. Hence there is no force to pull average
total costs up, as in conventional cost structures. The combination of high fixed costs and
low (negligible) marginal costs gives the ATC curve a unique shape. The ATC curve starts
out high (due to high AFC) and keeps declining as output increases (because MC < ATC
at all times). *The downward-sloping ATC curve is the hallmark of a natural monopoly.*

The declining costs of a natural monopoly are of potential benefit to society. The
economies of scale offered by a natural monopoly imply that no other market structure can
supply the good as cheaply. Hence *natural monopoly is a desirable market structure.* A
competitive market structure—with many smaller firms—would have higher average costs.

Unregulated Behavior

*Although the structure of a natural monopoly may be beneficial, its behavior may leave
something to be desired.* Natural monopolists have the same profit-maximizing motivations as other producers. Moreover, they have the monopoly power to achieve and maintain
economic profits. Hence there's no guarantee that consumers will reap the cost-saving
benefits of a natural monopoly. Critics charge that natural monopolies don't pass the cost
savings along to consumers, instead keeping most of the benefits for themselves. This has
been a recurrent criticism of cable TV operators: consumers have complained about high
prices, poor service, and a lack of programming choices from local cable monopolies.

Figure 13.2 illustrates how we expect an unregulated natural monopolist to behave. Like
all other producers, the natural monopolist will maximize profits by producing at that rate of
output where marginal revenue equals marginal cost. Point A in Figure 13.2 indicates that an
unregulated monopoly will end up producing the quantity q_A and charging the price p_A.

The natural monopolist's preferred outcome isn't the most desirable one for society. This
price–output combination violates the competitive principle of **marginal cost pricing.** The

economies of scale:
Reductions in minimum
average costs that come about
through increases in the size
(scale) of plant and equipment.

marginal cost pricing: The
offer (supply) of goods at prices
equal to their marginal cost.

FIGURE 13.2
Natural Monopoly: Price Regulation

If unregulated, a natural monopoly will produce q_A and charge p_A, as determined by the intersection of the marginal cost and marginal revenue curves (point *A*).

Regulation designed to achieve efficient prices will seek point *B*, where $p = MC$. Still lower average costs (production efficiency) are attainable at higher rates of output (capacity), however. On the other hand, a zero-profit, zero-subsidy outcome exists only at point *C*.

Which price–output combination should be sought?

monopoly price p_A greatly exceeds the marginal cost of producing q_A of output, as represented by MC_A in Figure 13.2. As a result of this gap, consumers aren't getting accurate information about the **opportunity cost** of this product. This flawed price signal is the cause of market failure. We end up consuming less of this product (and more of other goods) than we would if charged its true opportunity cost. A suboptimal mix of output results.

The natural monopolist's profit-maximizing output (q_A) also fails to minimize average total cost. In a competitive industry, ATC is driven down to its minimum by relentless competition. In this case, however, reductions in ATC cease when the monopolist achieves the profit-maximizing rate of output (q_A). Were output to increase further, average total costs would fall.

Finally, notice that the higher price (p_A) associated with the monopolist's preferred output (q_A) ensures a fat profit (= per-unit profit of $p_A - p_D$ multiplied by the quantity q_A). This **economic profit** may violate our visions of equity. In 2001 millions of Californians were convinced that this kind of "profiteering" was the root of their electricity woes.

REGULATORY OPTIONS

The suboptimal outcomes likely to emerge from a free-swinging natural monopoly prompt consumers to demand government intervention. The market alone can't overcome the natural advantage of pervasive economies of scale. (New, smaller firms would have higher average total costs and be unable to compete.) But the government could compel different outcomes. Which outcomes do we want? And how will we get them?

Price Regulation

For starters, we might consider price regulation. The natural monopolist's preferred price (p_A) is, after all, a basic cause of market failure. By regulating the firm, the government can compel a lower price. The California legislature did this in 1996 when it set a *maximum* retail price for electricity.

As is apparent from Figure 13.2, there are lots of choices in setting a regulated price. We start with the conviction that the unregulated price p_A is too high. But where on the demand

opportunity cost: The most desired goods or services that are forgone in order to obtain something else.

economic profit: The difference between total revenues and total economic costs.

curve below p_A do we want to be? A price of zero (free electricity!) sounds appealing, but we know that's not going to happen.

Price Efficiency (p = MC). A more realistic possibility might be to set the price at a level consistent with opportunity costs. As we saw earlier, a monopolist's unregulated price sends out a flawed price signal. By charging a price in excess of marginal cost, the monopolist causes a suboptimal allocation of resources (i.e., the wrong mix of output). We could improve market outcomes, therefore, by compelling the monopolist to set the price equal to marginal cost, just as perfectly competitive markets do. Such an efficient price would lead us to point B in Figure 13.2, where the demand curve and the marginal cost curve intersect. At that price (p_B), consumers would get optimal use of the good or service produced.

Subsidy. Although the price p_B will give us the right answer to the WHAT question, it will also bankrupt the producer. In a natural monopoly, MC is always less than ATC. Hence *marginal cost pricing by a natural monopolist implies a loss on every unit of output produced.* In this case, the loss per unit is equal to $B^* - B$. If confronted with the regulated price p_B, the firm will ultimately shut down and exit from the market. This was one of the many problems that plagued California. Unable to charge a price high enough to cover their costs, some of the state's utility companies were forced into bankruptcy.

If we want to require efficient pricing (p = MC), we must provide a subsidy to the natural monopoly. In Figure 13.2 the amount of the subsidy would have to equal the anticipated loss at q_B—that is, the quantity q_B multiplied by the per-unit loss ($B^* - B$). Such subsidies are provided to subway systems. With subsidies, local subway systems can charge fees below *average* cost and closer to *marginal* cost. These subsidized fares increase ridership, thus ensuring greater use of very expensive mass transportation systems.

Despite the advantages of this subsidized pricing strategy, taxpayers always complain about the cost of such subsidies. Taxpayers are particularly loath to provide subsidies for private companies. Hence political considerations typically preclude efficient (marginal cost) pricing, despite the economic benefits of this regulatory strategy.

Production Efficiency (p = min ATC). Another option is to focus on efficient *production* rather than efficient *pricing*. Production efficiency is attained at the lowest possible average total cost. At q_B we're producing a lot of output but still have some unused capacity. Since ATC falls continuously, we could achieve still lower average costs if we increased output beyond q_B. *In a natural monopoly, production efficiency is achieved at capacity production, where ATC is at a minimum.*

Increasing output beyond q_B raises the same problems we encountered at that rate of output. At production rates in excess of q_B, ATC is always higher than price. Even MC is higher than price to the right of point B. Thus *no regulated price can induce a natural monopolist to achieve minimum average cost. A subsidy would be required to offset the market losses.*

Profit Regulation

Instead of focusing on price, why don't we focus on profits instead? Simply disallow monopoly profits like those of the unregulated monopoly (at q_A and p_A in Figure 13.2). We can achieve this result by mandating a price equal to average total cost. In Figure 13.2 this regulatory objective is achieved at point C. In this case, the rate of output is q_C and the regulated price is p_C.

Profit regulation looks appealing for two reasons. First, it eliminates the need to subsidize the monopolist. Second, it allows us to focus on profits only, thus removing the need to develop demand and cost curves. In theory, all we have to do is check the firm's annual profit-and-loss statement to confirm that it's earning a normal (average) profit. If its profits are too high, we can force the firm to reduce its price; if profits are too low, we may permit a price increase.

Bloated Costs. While beautiful in principle, profit regulation can turn ugly in practice. In particular, profit regulation can lead to bloated costs and dynamic inefficiency. *If a firm is permitted a specific profit rate (or rate of return), it has no incentive to limit costs.* On the contrary, higher costs imply higher profits. If permitted to charge 10 percent over unit costs, a monopolist may be better off with average costs of $6 rather than only $5. The higher costs translate into 60 cents of profit per unit rather than only 50 cents, even though the profit *rate* is the same. Hence there's an incentive to "pad costs." If those costs actually represent improvements in the firm's wages and salaries, executive bonuses, fringe benefits, or the work environment, then cost increases are doubly attractive to the firm and its employees. Cost efficiency is as welcome as the plague under such circumstances.

Profit regulation can also motivate a firm to inflate its costs by paying above-market prices for products purchased from an unregulated subsidiary. This was the strategy AT&T used to increase its *regulated* cost base while ringing up high profits at Western Electric, its *unregulated* subsidiary (see Chapter 10). The FCC accused Nynex (the "Baby Bell" that provided phone service in New York and New England in the 1970s) of using the same strategy to pad its profits. Nynex used its *unregulated* subsidiary (Material Enterprises Co.) to sell equipment at inflated prices to its *regulated* phone company subsidiaries (New England Telephone & Telegraph and New York Telephone). Profits in all three companies increased.

Output Regulation

Given the difficulties in regulating prices and profits, regulators may choose to regulate output instead. The natural monopolist's preferred output rate is q_A, as illustrated again in Figure 13.3. We could compel this monopolist to provide a minimum level of service in excess of q_A. This regulated minimum is designated q_D in Figure 13.3. At q_D consumers get the benefit not only of more output but also of a lower price (p_D). At q_D total monopoly profit must also be less than at q_A, since q_A was the profit-maximizing rate of output.

It appears, then, that compelling any rate of output in excess of q_A can only benefit consumers. Moreover, output regulation is an easy rule to enforce.

Quality Deterioration. Unfortunately, minimum-service regulation can also cause problems. If forced to produce at the rate of q_D, the monopolist may seek to increase profits by cutting cost corners. This can be accomplished by deferring plant and equipment maintenance, reducing quality control, or otherwise lowering the quality of service. ***Regulation of***

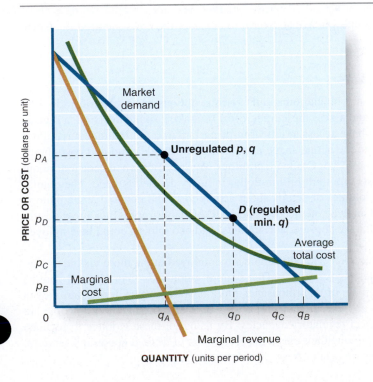

FIGURE 13.3
Minimum Service Regulation

Regulation may seek to ensure some minimal level of service. In this case, the required rate of output is arbitrarily set at q_D. Consumers are willing to pay p_D per unit for that output.

Regulated output q_D is preferable to the unregulated outcome (q_A, p_A) but may induce a decline in quality. Cost cutting is the only way to increase profits when the rate of output is fixed and price is on the demand curve.

the quantity produced may induce a decline in quality. Since a monopolist has no direct competition, consumers pretty much have to accept whatever quality the monopolist offers. This structural reality may explain why consumers complain so much about the services of local cable monopolies.

In addition to encouraging quality deterioration, output regulation at q_D also violates the principle of marginal cost pricing. Because an economic profit exists at q_D, equity goals may be jeopardized as well. Hence minimum service (output) regulation isn't a panacea for the regulatory dilemma. In fact, there is no panacea. *Goal conflicts are inescapable, and any regulatory rule may induce undesired producer responses.*

Imperfect Answers

The call for public regulation of natural monopolies is based on the recognition that the profit motive doesn't generate optimal outcomes in any monopoly environment. If unregulated, a natural monopolist will charge too much and produce too little. The regulatory remedy for these market failures isn't evident, however. Regulators can compel efficient prices or least-cost production only by offering a subsidy. Profit regulation is likely to induce cost-inflating responses. Output regulation is an incentive for quality deterioration. No matter which way we turn, regulatory problems result.

There's not much hope for transforming unregulated market failure into perfect regulated outcomes. In reality, regulators must choose a strategy that balances competing objectives (e.g., price efficiency and equity). A realistic goal for regulation is to *improve* market outcomes, not to *perfect* them. In the real world, *the choice isn't between imperfect markets and flawless government intervention but rather between imperfect markets and imperfect intervention.*

The argument for *deregulation* rests on the observation that government regulation sometimes worsens market outcomes. In some cases, **government failure** may be worse than market failure. Specifically, regulation may lead to price, cost, or production outcomes that are inferior to those of an unregulated market.

government failure:
Government intervention that fails to improve economic outcomes.

THE COSTS OF REGULATION

Let's *assume* that regulation actually improves market outcomes. Could we then claim regulatory success? Not quite yet. We also have to consider the *costs* incurred to change market outcomes.

Administrative Costs

As we've observed, industry regulation entails various options and a host of trade-offs. Someone must sit down and assess these trade-offs. To make a sound decision, a regulatory administration must have access to lots of information. At a minimum, the regulator must have some clue as to the actual shape and position of the demand and cost curves depicted in Figures 13.2 and 13.3. Crude illustrations won't suffice when decisions about the prices, output, or costs of a multibillion-dollar industry are being made. The regulatory commission needs volumes of details about actual costs and demand and a platoon of experts to collect and analyze the needed data. All this labor represents a real cost to society because the regulatory lawyers, accountants, and economists could be employed elsewhere.

As Table 13.1 illustrates, over 280,000 people are employed in the more visible regulatory agencies of the federal government. That's more employees than General Motors employs to build cars. On top of that, thousands more have regulatory responsibilities in smaller federal agencies and executive departments. Tens of thousands more people are employed by state and local regulatory agencies. By using all these workers to regulate private industry, we are forgoing their use in the production of desired goods and services. This is a significant economic cost.

Agency	Number of Employees (2011)
SOCIAL REGULATION	
Consumer Safety and Health	39,037
• Food and Drug Administration (FDA)	
• Food Safety and Inspection Service, etc.	
Homeland Security	150,201
• Transportation Security Administration (TSA)	
• Customs and Border Security	
• Immigration and Customs, etc.	
Transportation	9,863
• Federal Aviation Administration (FAA)	
• Federal Motor Carriers Safety Administration	
• Federal Railroad Administration, etc.	
Workplace	12,351
• Occupational Safety and Health Administration (OSHA)	
• Mine Safety and Health Administration	
• Employment Standards Administration, etc.	
Environment	26,900
• Environmental Protection Agency (EPA)	
• Forest and Rangeland Research	
• Fish and Wildlife Service, etc.	
Energy	4,064
• Nuclear Regulatory Agency, etc.	
ECONOMIC REGULATION	
General Business	17,517
• Patent and Trademark Office	
• Securities and Exchange Commission (SEC)	
• Federal Trade Commission (FTC), etc.	
Finance and Banking	14,985
• Federal Reserve System	
• Federal Deposit Insurance Corporation (FDIC)	
• Comptroller of the Currency, etc.	
Industry-Specific Regulation	6,914
• Agricultural Marketing Service	
• Federal Communications Commission (FCC), etc.	
Total Regulatory Employment:	**281,832**

Source: Susan Dudley and Melinda Warren, Weidenbaum Center, Washington University, May 2011.

TABLE 13.1
Employment in Federal Regulatory Agencies

The human and capital resources the bureaucracy employs represent a real opportunity cost. The 281,832 people employed in 63 federal agencies—and tens of thousands more employed in state and local bureaucracies—could be producing other goods and services. These and other costs must be compared to the benefits of regulation.

web analysis

The Weidenbaum Center on the Economy, Government, and Public Policy at Washington University tracks and analyzes regulation: **http://wc.wustl.edu.** Click the "Publications" tab to find "Regulatory Reports."

Compliance Costs

The administrative costs of regulation focus on resources used in the public sector. By its very nature, however, regulation also changes resource use in the private sector. Regulated industries must expend resources to educate themselves about the regulations, to change their production behavior, and often to file reports with the regulatory authorities. The human and capital resources used for these purposes represent the *compliance* cost of regulation.

New rules on trucking illustrate how regulation can increase production costs. In 2003 the U.S. Department of Transportation reduced the amount of driving time permitted for interstate truckers (see the News on the next page). This rule requires freight companies to use more trucks and more labor to transport goods, thereby raising economic costs. Although the resultant gain in safety is desired, the cost of achieving that gain is not inconsequential.

IN THE NEWS

Costs of Trucking Seen Rising under New Safety Rules

The first major changes in truck driver work hours since 1939 are expected to reduce highway fatalities, but also contribute to the biggest increase in trucking rates in two decades. . . .

The new rules increase the time that truck drivers must set aside to rest in each 24-hour period to 10 hours from eight hours, and the total time a driver can be on duty will fall to 14 hours from 15 hours. . . .

The government estimates the new rules could cost trucking companies about $1.3 billion a year. . . .

Because trucks haul so much commerce, accounting for more than 81 percent of the nation's $571 billion freight transportation bill last year, the effects could be far-reaching. Some users of truck transportation say higher trucking rates could lead to a broad-based increase in prices of goods from paper to chemicals, diapers to trash cans. . . .

Still, "there are about 410 fatalities a year attributed to fatigue-related truck crashes, and that's 410 very good reasons for changing the rule," says Annette Sandberg, administrator of the Transportation Department's Federal Motor Carrier Safety Administration. The agency expects the new rules to save up to 75 lives a year and prevent as many as 1,326 fatigue-related crashes a year.

—Daniel Machalaba

Source: *The Wall Street Journal,* November 12, 2003, p. A1. Used with permission of Dow Jones & Company, Inc. via Copyright Clearance Center, Inc.

Analysis: Regulations designed to improve market outcomes typically impose higher costs. The challenge is to balance benefits and costs.

Efficiency Costs

Finally, we have to consider the potential costs of changes in output. Most regulation alters the mix of output, either directly or indirectly. Ideally, regulation will always improve the mix of output. But it's possible that bad decisions, incomplete information, or faulty implementation may actually *worsen* the mix of output. If this occurs, then the loss of utility associated with an inferior mix of output imposes a further cost on society, over and above administrative and compliance costs.

Efficiency costs may increase significantly over time. Consumer tastes change, demand and marginal revenue curves shift, costs change, and new technologies emerge. Can regulatory commissions respond to these changes as fast as the market mechanism does? If not, even optimal regulations may soon become obsolete and counterproductive. Worse still, the regulatory process itself may impede new technology, new marketing approaches, or improved production processes. These losses may be the most important. As Robert Hahn of the American Enterprise Institute observed,

> [t]he measurable costs of regulation pale against the distortions that sap the economy's dynamism. The public never sees the factories that weren't built, the new products that didn't appear, or the entrepreneurial idea that drowned in a cumbersome regulatory process.[1]

These kinds of dynamic efficiency losses are a drag on economic growth, limiting outward shifts of the production possibilities curve while perpetuating an increasingly undesired mix of output.

Balancing Benefits and Costs

The economic costs of regulation are a reminder of the "no free lunch" maxim. Although regulatory intervention may improve market outcomes, that intervention isn't without cost.

[1]Cited in Louis S. Richman and John Labate, "Bringing Reason to Regulation," *Fortune,* October 19, 1992, p. 94. © 1992 Time Inc. Used under license.

The real resources used in the regulatory process could be used for other purposes. Hence, even if we could achieve perfect outcomes with enough regulation, the cost of achieving perfection might outweigh the benefits. *Regulatory intervention must balance the anticipated improvements in market outcomes against the economic cost of regulation.* In principle, the marginal benefit of regulation must exceed its marginal cost. If this isn't the case, then additional regulation isn't desirable, even if it would improve short-run market outcomes.

Price Regulation

DEREGULATION IN PRACTICE

The push to *de*regulate is prompted by two concerns. The first concern focuses on the dynamic inefficiencies that regulation imposes, stifling innovation and rendering regulated industries less productive than desired. The other push for deregulation comes from advancing technology, which often destroys the structural basis for natural monopoly. A brief review of the resulting deregulation illustrates the impact of these forces.

Railroads

The railroad industry was the federal government's first broad regulatory target. Railroads are an example of natural monopoly, with high fixed costs and negligible marginal costs. Furthermore, there were no airports or interstate highways to compete with the railroads in 1887, when Congress created the Interstate Commerce Commission (ICC). The ICC was established to limit monopolistic exploitation of this situation while assuring a fair profit to railroad owners. The ICC established rates and routes for the railroads while limiting both entry to and exit from the industry.

With the advent of buses, trucks, subways, airplanes, and pipelines as alternative modes of transportation, railroad regulation became increasingly obsolete. Regulated cargoes, routes, and prices prevented railroads from adapting their prices or services to meet changing consumer demands. With regulation-protected routes, they also had little incentive to invest in new technologies or equipment. As a result, railroad traffic and profits declined while other transportation industries flourished.

The Railroad Revitalization and Regulatory Reform Act of 1976 was a response to this crisis. Its major goal was to reduce the scope of government regulation. Reinforced by the Staggers Rail Act of 1980, railroads were granted much greater freedom to adapt their prices and service to market demands.

Railroad companies used that flexibility to increase their share of total freight traffic. Fresh fruits and vegetables, for example, were exempted from ICC rate regulation in 1979. Railroads responded by *reducing* their rates and improving service. In the first year of deregulated rates, fruits and vegetable shipments increased over 30 percent, a dramatic reversal of earlier trends. Deregulation of coal traffic (in 1980) and piggyback (trucks on railroad flatcars) traffic (in 1982) prompted similar turnarounds. The railroads prospered by reconfiguring routes and services, cutting operating costs, and offering lower rates. Between 1986 and 1993, the average cost of moving freight by rail dropped by 69 percent.

Not all rates have fallen. Indeed, one worrisome effect of deregulation is the increased concentration in the rail industry. After a series of mergers and acquisitions, the top four railroads (Burlington-Northern, Union Pacific, CSX, and Norfolk-Southern) moved nearly 80 percent of all rail freight (ton-miles). Moreover, these same firms hold monopoly positions on specific routes. Shippers in these captive markets pay rates 20 to 30 percent higher than in nonmonopoly routes.

Telephone Service

The telephone industry has long been the classic example of a natural monopoly. Although enormous fixed costs are necessary to establish a telephone network, the marginal cost of an additional telephone call approaches zero. Hence it made economic sense to have a single network of telephone lines and switches rather than a maze of competing ones. Recognizing these economies of scale, Congress permitted AT&T to maintain a monopoly on both long-distance and most local telephone service. To ensure that consumers would benefit from this natural monopoly, the Federal Communications Commission (FCC) regulated phone services and prices.

Once again, technology outpaced regulation. Communications satellites made it much easier and less costly for new firms to provide long-distance telephone service. Moreover, the rate structure that AT&T and the Federal Communications Commission had established made long-distance service highly profitable. Accordingly, start-up firms clamored to get into the industry, and consumers petitioned for lower rates.

Long Distance. In 1982 the courts put an end to AT&T's monopoly, transforming long-distance telecommunications into a more competitive industry with more firms and less regulation. Since then over 800 firms have entered the industry, and long-distance telephone rates have dropped sharply. The quality of service also improved with fiber optic cable, advanced switching systems, cell phones, and myriad new phone line services such as fax transmissions, remote access, Internet access, texting, and mobile computing. All these changes have contributed to a quadrupling of long-distance telephone use in the United States.

Local Service. The deregulation of long-distance services was so spectacularly successful that observers wondered whether *local* telephone service might be deregulated as well. As competition in *long-distance* services increased, the monopoly nature of *local* rates became painfully apparent: local rates kept increasing after 1983 while long-distance rates were tumbling.

The Baby Bells that held monopolies on local service defended their high rates based on the high costs of building and maintaining transmission networks. But new technologies permitted wireless companies to offer local service if they could gain access to the monopoly networks. Congress responded in 1996. The Telecommunications Act of 1996 required the Baby Bells to grant rivals access to their transmission networks. The Baby Bells kept rivals at bay, however, by charging excessive access fees, imposing overly complex access codes, requiring unnecessary capital equipment, and raising other entry barriers. The battle for local access continues (see the News below).

IN THE NEWS

Bell Monopolies Push to Disconnect Competition

Seven years ago, Congress set out to break up the local Bell telephone monopolies and bring competition to consumers' homes. But just as states are finally figuring out how to make that promise a reality, and some communities are seeing phone bills drop, federal regulators may unplug the competitors at the behest of the four Bell monopolies.

The Bells want to gut rules spurring competition that were enacted in the wake of the 1996 Telecommunications Act. They require the Bells to rent their networks at reasonable prices to potential rivals that may want to offer local phone service but can't afford to set up their own phone networks.

For years, the law wasn't an issue because states let the Bells charge exorbitant fees that kept competitors out of their markets. Now that several states are ordering them to cut their network fees, competition is emerging, and phone rates are decreasing. On Monday AT&T announced plans to compete in Washington, DC, after the local government cut the charges for tapping into the network operated by Verizon. Nationwide, 11 percent of local phone lines were serviced by competitors through last June, nearly double their share two years earlier.

Faced with the first real threat to their grip on local service, Verizon and the other Bells are crying to the Federal Communications Commission (FCC) that they're forced to rent their networks at a loss. They want to go back to the way it was: higher fees for rivals and less choice for consumers.

Source: *USA TODAY.* Editorial, January 14, 2003. Reprinted with permission.

Analysis: To enter local phone markets, would-be rivals (including cell phone providers) must pay an access fee to the local phone monopoly. High fees are a substantial entry barrier.

Airlines

The Civil Aeronautics Board (CAB) was created in 1938 to regulate airline routes and fares. From its inception, the primary concern of the CAB was to ensure a viable system of air transportation for both large and small communities. Such a system would be ensured, the CAB believed, only if a fair level of profits was maintained by entry and price regulations. Thus the focus of the CAB was on *profit* regulation.

Price Regulation. Initially the CAB set airline fares at roughly the levels of Pullman rates for train travel. This implied that airfares would be proportional to distance, as they were for train travel. In the late 1930s this fare structure wasn't unreasonable; most flights were relatively short, and planes were small.

As the airline industry grew, the CAB abandoned fare comparisons with trains but maintained the basic distance-based fare structure. To ensure fair profits, the CAB set fares in accordance with airline costs. This required the CAB to undertake intensive cost studies, based on accounting data provided by the airlines. Once the average cost of service and capital equipment was established, the CAB then set an average price that would ensure a fair rate of return (profit) (much like point *C* in Figure 13.2).

The CAB also wanted to ensure air service to smaller, less traveled communities. Short hauls entail higher average costs and therefore justify higher fares. To avoid high fares on such routes, the CAB permitted airlines to charge prices well in excess of average costs on longer routes as long as they maintained service on shorter, unprofitable routes. This **cross-subsidization** was similar to that of the telephone industry, in which long-distance profits helped keep local telephone charges low.

To maintain this price and profit structure, the CAB had to regulate routes and limit entry into the airline industry. Otherwise, established carriers would abandon short, unprofitable routes, and new carriers would offer service only on more profitable routes. Unregulated entry thus threatened both cross-subsidization and the CAB's vision of a fair profit.

cross-subsidization: Use of high prices and profits on one product to subsidize low prices on another product.

No Entry. The CAB was extremely effective in restricting entry into the industry. Would-be entrants had to demonstrate to the CAB that their proposed service was required by "public convenience and necessity" and was superior to that of established carriers. Established carriers could oppose a new application by demonstrating sufficient service, offering to expand their service, or claiming superior service. In view of the fact that new applicants had no airline experience, established carriers easily won the argument. From 1938 until 1977, the CAB *never* awarded a major route to a new entrant.

No Price Competition. The CAB also eliminated price competition between established carriers. The CAB fixed airfares on all routes. Airlines could reduce fares no more than 5 percent and couldn't increase them more than 10 percent without CAB approval.

Bloated Costs. Ironically, the established airlines failed to reap much profit from these high fares. Unable to compete on the basis of price, the established carriers had to engage in nonprice competition. The most costly form of nonprice competition was frequency of service. Once the CAB authorized service between any two cities, a regulated carrier could provide as many flights as desired. This enticed the regulated carriers to purchase huge fleets of planes and provide frequent departures. In the process, load factors (the percentage of seats filled with passengers) fell and average costs rose.

The regulated carriers also pursued **product differentiation** by offering special meals, first-run movies, free drinks, better service, and wider seats. This nonprice competition further inflated average costs and reduced profits.

product differentiation: Features that make one product appear different from competing products in the same market.

New Entrants. The Airline Deregulation Act of 1978 changed the structure and behavior of the airline industry. Entry regulation was effectively abandoned. With the elimination of this **barrier to entry,** the number of carriers increased greatly. Between 1978 and 1985, the number of airline companies increased from 37 to 174! The new entrants intensified competition on nearly all routes. The share of domestic markets with four or more carriers grew from 13 percent in May 1978 to 73 percent in May 1981. All those new entrants pushed airfares down sharply.

barriers to entry: Obstacles that make it difficult or impossible for would-be producers to enter a particular market, such as patents.

The CAB's authority over airfares ended January 1, 1983. Since then, airlines have been able to adapt their fares to market supply and demand. The CAB itself was eliminated in 1984.

Increasing Concentration. Although airline deregulation is hailed as one of the greatest policy achievements of the 1980s, airline industry structure and behavior remain imperfect. In the competitive fray spawned by deregulation, lots of new entrants and even some established airlines went broke. Unable to match lower fares and increased service, scores of airline companies exited the industry in the period 1985–1995. In the process, a handful of major carriers increased their market share. The combined market share of the three largest carriers (Delta, American, United) increased from 35 percent in 1985 to 60 percent in 2001. In many cases, firms gained near-monopoly power in specific hub airports; by 2005 1 out of 10 domestic routes was again monopolized. Not surprisingly, a study by the U.S. General Accounting Office found that ticket prices are 45 to 85 percent higher on monopolized routes than on routes where at least two airlines compete.

Entry Barriers. To exploit their hub dominance, major carriers must keep out rivals. One of the most effective entry barriers is their ownership of landing slots. Air traffic is limited by the number of these slots, or authorized landing permits. In 1998 United Airlines controlled 82 percent of the slots at Chicago's O'Hare; Delta controls 83 percent of the slots at New York's Kennedy Airport. Smaller airlines complain that they can't get access to these slots, even when the slots aren't being used.

Defenders of deregulation are quick to point out that despite increasing *industry* concentration, there's more competition in most airline markets. In 1979 about 22 percent of all traffic was in monopoly markets, where a single carrier supplied at least 90 percent of all traffic. By 1989 only 11 percent of all traffic was in such monopoly markets. Hence the airline industry is more of a **contestable market,** even if not a perfectly competitive one. When entry barriers (including slot access) are lowered, new competitors emerge and push down airfares (see the News on the "JetBlue effect").

contestable market:
An imperfectly competitive industry subject to potential entry if prices or profits increase.

IN THE NEWS

The JetBlue Effect

When this carrier comes to town, fares go down, traffic goes up, and the airline ends up with a big chunk of the business.

	Change in Daily Passengers	Change in Average Fare	JetBlue Local Traffic Share
New York to Miami/Fort Lauderdale	+14%	−17% to $121.50	23.1%
New York to Los Angeles Basin	+2%	−26% to $219.31	18%
New York to Buffalo	+94%	−40% to $86.09	61.2%

Figures as of second quarter, 2003.
Data: Back Aviation Solutions.

—Wendy Zellner

Source: "Is JetBlue's Flight Plan Flawed?" *BusinessWeek,* February 16, 2004, pp. 72–75. Used with permission of Bloomberg L.P. Copyright © 2011. All rights reserved.

Analysis: If entry barriers are low enough, new entrants will contest a market, keeping pressure on prices and service.

web analysis

Does your area benefit from the JetBlue effect? For a complete list of cities served by JetBlue, visit **www.jetblue.com** and click "Where we jet."

Cable TV

The cable TV industry offers examples of both deregulation and *re*regulation. Up until 1986, city and county governments had the authority to franchise (approve) local cable TV operators and regulate their rates. In almost all cases, local governments franchised only one operator, thus establishing local monopolies. The monopoly structure was justified by pervasive economies of scale and the desire to avoid the cost and disruption of laying multiple cable systems. The rationale behind local regulation of cable prices (rates) was to ensure that consumers shared in the cost advantages of natural monopoly.

Deregulation. By 1984 Congress was convinced that broadcast TV and emerging technologies (such as microwave transmissions and direct satellite broadcasts) offered sufficient competition to ensure consumers fair prices and quality service. The Cable Communications Policy Act of 1984 *de*regulated cable TV by stripping local governments of the authority to regulate prices. From 1986 to 1992, cable TV was essentially unregulated.

Soon after price regulation ended, cable companies began increasing their rates sharply. As Figure 13.4 shows, the rate of price acceleration nearly doubled after the cable industry was deregulated. Consumers also complained that local cable companies offered poor service. They demanded that Congress *re*regulate the industry.

Reregulation. In 1992 Congress responded with the Cable Television Consumer Protection and Competition Act. That act gave the Federal Communications Commission authority to reregulate cable TV rates. The FCC required cable operators to *reduce* prices by nearly 17 percent in 1993–1994. It then issued 450 pages of new rules that would limit future price increases. As Figure 13.4 illustrates, these interventions had a dramatic effect on cable prices.

While consumers applauded the new price rules, cable operators warned of unwelcome long-term effects. The rate cuts reduced cable industry revenues by nearly $4 billion between 1993 and 1995. The cable companies say they would have used that revenue to invest in improved networks and services. The cable companies also argued that increased competition from satellite transmissions and the Internet made government regulation of (wired) cable TV increasingly unnecessary.

Deregulation. Congress responded to these industry complaints by *de*regulating the cable industry again. The Telecommunications Act of 1996 mandated that rate regulation be phased out and ended completely by March 1999. Almost immediately, cable prices soared again, as Figure 13.4 shows.

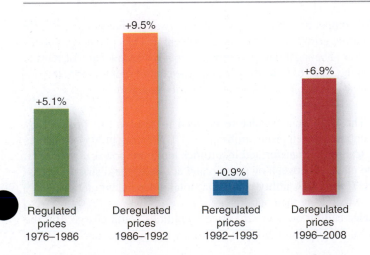

FIGURE 13.4
Annual Increase in Price of Basic Cable Service

After cable TV prices were deregulated in 1986, monthly charges moved up sharply. In 1992 Congress reregulated cable TV and prices stabilized. The Telecommunications Act of 1996 again deregulated prices and they surged, as shown in these annual averages.

Source: Industry publications.

substitute goods: Goods that substitute for each other; when the price of good *x* rises, the demand for good *y* increases, *ceteris paribus.*

Satellite Technology. The surge in cable TV prices was a boon to satellite TV providers. Satellite transmissions became a **substitute good** for cable TV—a substitute that also enjoyed pervasive economies of scale. So you suddenly had *competing* natural monopolies in a *contestable* market. Satellites Won. In 1993, when cable prices were still relatively low, cable had 93 percent of the pay TV market. By 2011 the cable market share had declined to 65 percent. The high prices and profits of the cable industry ultimately spawned effective competition, first in satellite technology, then in broadband TV services (e.g., Netflix, Hulu, Blue-ray).

Electricity

The electric utility industry is the latest target for deregulation. Here again, the industry is a natural monopoly. The enormous fixed costs of a power plant and transmission network, combined with negligible marginal costs for delivering another kilowatt of electricity, give electric utilities a downward-sloping average total cost curve. The focus of government intervention was therefore on rate regulation (behavior) rather than promoting competition (structure).

Bloated Costs, High Prices. Critics of local utility monopolies complained that local rate regulation wasn't working well enough. To get higher (retail) prices, the utility companies allowed costs to rise. They also had no incentive to pursue new technologies that would reduce the costs of power generation or distribution. Big power users like steel companies complained that high electricity prices were crippling their competitive position. The only viable option for consumers was to move from a state with a high-cost power monopoly to a state with a low-cost power monopoly.

Demise of Power Plant Monopolies. Advances in transmission technology gave consumers a new choice. High-voltage transmission lines can carry power thousands of miles with negligible power loss. Utility companies used these lines to link their power grids, thereby creating backup power sources in the event of regional blackouts. In doing so, however, they created a new entry point for potential competition. Now a Kentucky power plant with surplus capacity can supply electricity to consumers in California. There's no longer any need to rely on a regional utility monopoly. At the wholesale level, utility companies have been trading electricity across state lines since 1992.

Local Distribution Monopolies. Although technology destroyed the basis for natural monopolies in power *production,* local monopolies in power *distribution* remain. Electricity reaches consumers through the wires attached to every house and business. As with TV cables, there is a natural monopoly in electricity distribution; competing wire grids would be costly and inefficient.

To deliver the benefits of competition in power *production,* rival producers must be able to access these local distribution grids. This is the same problem that has plagued competition in local telephone service. The local power companies that own the local distribution grids aren't anxious to open the wires to new competition. The central problem for electricity deregulation has been to assure wider access to local distribution grids.

California's Mistakes. The California legislature decided to resolve this problem by stripping local utility monopolies of their production capacity. By forcing utility companies to sell their power plants, California transformed its utilities into pure power *distributors.* This seemed to resolve the conflict between ownership and access to the distribution system. However, it also made California's utility companies totally dependent on third-party power producers, many of which were then out of state.

price ceilings: An upper limit imposed on the price of a good.

California also put a **price ceiling** on the *retail* price its utilities could charge. But the state had no power to control the *wholesale* price of electricity in interstate markets. When wholesale prices rose sharply in 2000 (see the accompanying News), *California's utilities were trapped between rising costs and a fixed price ceiling.* Fearful of a political backlash, the governor refused to raise the retail price ceiling. As a result, some of the utility companies were forced into bankruptcy and power supplies were interrupted. The state itself entered the utility business by buying power plants and more out-of-state power supplies. In the end, Californians ended up with very expensive electricity.

IN THE NEWS

Financial Woes Heating Up

Pacific Gas and Electric is in financial trouble because the cost of power it purchases on the wholesale market is soaring higher than the fixed rate it charges its customers:

—Jonathan Weisman

What customers pay per kilowatt/hour: 5.4¢

What utilities pay wholesale per kilowatt/hour

40¢

1—Estimate

Source: Pacific Gas and Electric (**www.pge.com**).

Source: *USA TODAY.* January 10, 2001. Reprinted with permission.

Analysis: When wholesale prices for electricity rose above the retail price ceiling established by the California legislature, the state's utility companies lost money on every kilowatt supplied. It was a recipe for financial disaster.

web analysis

Most energy markets are broad, covering more than one state. The Federal Energy Regulatory Commission (FERC) regulates multistate energy exchanges. Learn more at **www.ferc.gov.**

THE ECONOMY TOMORROW

DEREGULATE EVERYTHING?

Deregulation of the railroad, telephone, airline, and electricity industries has yielded substantial benefits: more competition, lower prices, and improved services. Such experiences bolster the case for laissez faire. Nevertheless, we shouldn't jump to the conclusion that all regulation of business should be dismantled. All we know from experience is that the regulation of certain industries became outmoded. Changing consumer demands, new technologies, and substitute goods simply made existing regulations obsolete, even counterproductive. A combination of economic and political forces doomed them to extinction.

But were these regulations ever necessary? In the 1880s there were no viable alternatives to railroads for overland transportation. The forces of natural monopoly could easily have exploited consumers and retarded economic growth. The same was largely true for long-distance telephone service prior to the launching of communications satellites. Even the limitations on competition in trucking and banking made some sense in the depths of the

Great Depression. One shouldn't conclude that regulatory intervention never made sense just because the regulations themselves later became obsolete.

Even today, most people recognize the need for regulation of many industries. The transmission networks for local telephone service and electricity delivery are still natural monopolies. The government can force owners to permit greater access. But an unregulated network owner could still extract monopoly profits through excessive prices. Hence even a deregulated industry may still require some regulation at critical entry or supply junctures. Existing regulations may not be optimal, but they probably generate better outcomes than totally unregulated monopolies.

Likewise, few people seriously propose relying on competition and the good judgment of consumers to determine the variety or quality of drugs on the market. Regulations imposed by the Food and Drug Administration restrain competition in the drug industry, raise production costs, and inhibit new technology. But they also make drugs safer. Here, as in other industries, there's a trade-off between the virtues of competition and those of regulation. ***The basic policy issue, as always, is whether the benefits of regulation exceed their administrative, compliance, and efficiency costs.*** The challenge for public policy in the economy tomorrow is to adapt regulations—or to discard them (that is, deregulate)—as market conditions, consumer demands, or technology changes.

SUMMARY

- Antitrust and regulation are alternative options for dealing with market power. Antitrust focuses on market structure and anticompetitive practices. Regulation stipulates specific market behavior. LO13-2
- High fixed costs and negligible marginal costs create a downward-sloping ATC curve, the hallmark of natural monopoly. LO13-1
- Natural monopolies offer pervasive economies of scale. Because of this potential efficiency, a more competitive market *structure* may not be desirable. LO13-2
- Regulation of natural monopoly can focus on price, profit, or output *behavior*. Price regulation may require subsidies; profit regulation may induce cost escalation; and output regulation may lead to quality deterioration. These problems compel compromises and second-best solutions. LO13-2
- The demand for deregulation rests on the argument that the costs of regulation exceed the benefits. These costs include the opportunity costs associated with regulatory administration and compliance as well as the (dynamic) efficiency losses that result from inflexible pricing and production rules. LO13-3
- Deregulation of the railroad, telephone, and airline industries has been a success. In all these industries, regulation became outmoded by changing consumer demands, products, and technology. As regulation was relaxed, these industries became more competitive, output increased, and prices fell. LO13-4
- Recent experiences with deregulation don't imply that all regulation should end. Regulation is appropriate if market failure exists *and* if the benefits of regulation exceed the costs. As benefits and costs change, decisions about what and how to regulate must be reevaluated. LO13-3

Key Terms

laissez faire
market failure
antitrust
regulation
natural monopoly
economies of scale

marginal cost pricing
opportunity cost
economic profit
government failure
cross-subsidization

product differentiation
barriers to entry
contestable market
substitute goods
price ceiling

Questions for Discussion

1. Given the inevitable limit on airplane landings, how should available airport slots be allocated? How would market outcomes be altered? LO13-2

2. Why would a profit-regulated firm want to sell itself inputs at inflated prices? Or increase wages? LO13-3

3. Prior to 1982, AT&T kept local phone rates low by subsidizing them from long-distance profits. Was such cross-subsidization in the public interest? Explain. LO13-1

4. In most cities local taxi fares are regulated. Should such regulation end? Who would gain or lose? LO13-3

5. How would you put dollar values on the benefits and costs of truck safety regulations (News, p. 290)? Do benefits exceed costs? LO13-2

6. The Telecommunications Act of 1996 requires local phone companies to charge "reasonable" rates for transmission access (News, p. 292). What is a "reasonable" rate? LO13-4

7. How could a local phone or cable company reduce service quality if forced to accept price ceilings? LO13-2

8. Had cable TV prices stayed low, would satellite TV service have spread as fast? LO13-4

9. Do we allocate too many resources to regulatory agencies (Table 13.1)? What is the optimal size of these agencies? LO13-3

10. Why is there resistance to (*a*) local phone companies providing video and data services and (*b*) mergers of local cable and telephone companies? LO13-1

web activities to accompany this chapter can be found on the Online Learning Center:
http://www.mhhe.com/schiller13e

mobile app Visit your mobile app store and download the Schiller: Study Econ app *today*!

LO13-2 1. In Figure 13.2,
   (*a*) How much profit does an unregulated monopolist earn?   _____
   (*b*) How much profit would be earned if MC pricing were imposed?   _____

LO13-1 2. Do total profits (A) decrease, (B) increase, or (C) stay the same when new technology reduces average total costs (shifts ATC downward in Figure 13.2) in
   (*a*) An unregulated natural monopoly?   _____
   (*b*) A price-regulated natural monopoly?   _____
   (*c*) A profit-regulated natural monopoly?   _____

LO13-2 3. Suppose a natural monopolist has fixed costs of $24 and a constant marginal cost of $2. The demand for the product is as follows:

Price (per unit)	$10	$9	$8	$7	$6	$5	$4	$3	$2	$1
Quantity demanded (units per day)	0	2	4	6	8	10	12	14	16	18

Under these conditions,
   (*a*) What price and quantity will prevail if the monopolist isn't regulated?   (*a1*) Price _____
   (*a2*) Quantity _____
   (*b*) What price–output combination would exist with efficient pricing (MC = *p*)?   (*b1*) Price _____
   (*b2*) Quantity _____
   (*c*) What price–output combination would exist with profit regulation (zero economic profits)?   (*c1*) Price _____
   (*c2*) Quantity _____
   Illustrate your answers on the following graph:

LO13-3 4. According to the News on page 290, how much will annual shipping costs increase for each saved life?   _____

LO13-3 5. If the average U.S. worker produces $100,000 of output per year, what is the annual opportunity cost of the federal regulatory workforce (Table 13.1)?   _____

LO13-4 6. Suppose a corporation has two subsidiaries, one of which is unregulated and sells all of its output to the other, regulated subsidiary. Permitted profits at the regulated subsidiary are equal to 10 percent of total costs. Here is the initial profit picture for the subsidiaries:

	Unregulated Subsidiary	Regulated Subsidiary
Total revenue	$800,000	N/A
Total costs	$500,000	$1 million
Total profit	$300,000	$100,000

If the unregulated subsidiary doubles its selling price, what happens to profits at
(a) The unregulated subsidiary?   _____
(b) The regulated subsidiary?   _____

14

Environmental Protection

Progress in environmental problems is impossible without a clear understanding of how the economic system works in the environment and what alternatives are available to take away the many roadblocks to environmental quality.

—Council on Environmental Quality, First Annual Report

What good is a clean river if you've got no jobs?

—Steelworkers union official in Youngstown, Ohio

A hole in the ozone layer is allowing increased ultraviolet radiation to reach the earth's surface. The hole is the result of excessive release of chlorine gases (chlorofluorocarbons, or CFCs) from air conditioners, plastic foam manufacture, industrial solvents, and aerosol spray cans such as deodorants and insecticides. The resulting damage to the stratosphere is causing skin cancer, cataracts, and immune system disorders.

Skin cancer may turn out to be one of our less serious problems. As carbon dioxide is building up in the atmosphere, it is creating a gaseous blanket around the earth that is trapping radiation and heating the atmosphere. Scientists predict that this greenhouse effect will melt the polar ice caps, raise sea levels, flood coastal areas, and turn rich croplands into deserts within 60 years.

Everyone wants a cleaner and safer environment. So why don't we stop polluting the environment with CFCs, carbon dioxide, toxic chemicals, and other waste? If we don't do it

ourselves, why doesn't the government force people to stop polluting?

Economics is part of the answer. To reduce pollution, we have to change our patterns of production and consumption. This entails economic costs, in terms of restricted consumption choices, more expensive ways of producing goods, and higher prices. Thus we have to weigh the benefits of a cleaner, safer environment against the costs of environmental protection.

Instinctively, most people don't like the idea of measuring the value of a cleaner environment in dollars and cents. But most people might also agree that spending $2 trillion to avoid a few cataracts is awfully expensive. There has to be *some* balance between the benefits of a cleaner environment and the cost of cleaning it up.

This chapter assesses our environmental problems from this economic perspective, considering three primary concerns:

- **How do (unregulated) markets encourage pollution?**
- **What are the costs of greater environmental protection?**
- **How can government policy best ensure an *optimal* environment?**

To answer these questions, we first survey the major types and sources of pollution. Then we examine the benefits and costs of environmental protection, highlighting the economic incentives that shape market behavior.

THE ENVIRONMENTAL THREAT

The hole in the ozone layer and the earth's rising temperature are at the top of the list of environmental concerns. The list is much longer, however, and very old as well. As early as A.D. 61, the statesman and philosopher Seneca was complaining about the smoky air emitted from household chimneys in Rome. Lead emissions from ancient Greek and Roman silver refineries poisoned the air in Europe and the remote Arctic. And historians are quick to remind us that open sewers running down the street were once the principal mode of urban waste disposal. Typhoid epidemics were a recurrent penalty for water pollution. So we can't say that environmental damage is a new phenomenon or that it's now worse than ever before.

But we do know more about the sources of environmental damage than our ancestors did, and we can better afford to do something about it. Our understanding of the economics of pollution has increased as well. We've come to recognize that pollution impairs health, reduces life expectancy, and thus reduces labor force activity and output. Pollution also destroys capital (such as the effects of air pollution on steel structures) and diverts resources to undesired activities (like car washes, laundry, and cleaning). Not least of all, pollution directly reduces our social welfare by denying us access to clean air, water, and beaches.

Air Pollution

Air pollution is as familiar as a smoggy horizon. But smog is only one form of air pollution.

Acid Rain. Sulfur dioxide (SO_2) is an acrid, corrosive, and poisonous gas that's created by burning high-sulfur fuels such as coal. As a contributor to acid rain, it destroys vegetation and forests. Electric utilities and industrial plants that burn high-sulfur coal or fuel oil are the prime sources of SO_2. Coal burning alone accounts for about 60 percent of all emissions of sulfur oxides. As the World View below illustrates, SO_2 pollution is a serious problem not only in U.S. cities but all over the world: the air is much dirtier in Beijing, Calcutta, Tokyo, and Rome than in New York City—and virtually unbreathable in coal-mining areas like Guiyang, China.

WORLD VIEW

Polluted Cities

The air in New York City may be unhealthful, but it's not nearly as polluted with sulfur dioxide (SO_2) as that in some other major cities.

© Brand X Pictures/Punchstock/DAL

SO_2 Micrograms per Cubic Meter of Air

1	Havana, Cuba
25	London, England
26	New York, New York
35	Rome, Italy
69	Cairo, Egypt
74	Mexico City, Mexico
100	Yokohama, Japan
109	Moscow, Russia
120	Istanbul, Turkey
129	Rio de Janeiro, Brazil
209	Tehran, Iran
424	Guiyang, China

Source: *The World Bank, WDR2009 Data Set,* **data.worldbank.org.**

Analysis: Pollution is a worldwide phenomenon with common origins and potential remedies.

web analysis

Find out about pollution in your area from the Environmental Defense Fund's Chemical Scoreboard at **www.scorecard.org.** Just enter a zip code for results.

Smog. Nitrogen oxides (NO_x), another ingredient in the formation of acid rain, are also a principal ingredient in the formation of smog. Smog not only irritates the eyes and spoils the view, but it also damages plants, trees, and human lungs. Automobile emissions account for 40 percent of urban smog. Bakeries, dry cleaners, and production of other consumer goods account for an equal amount of smog. The rest comes from electric power plants and industrial boilers.

The Greenhouse Effect. The prime villain in the greenhouse effect is the otherwise harmless carbon dioxide (CO_2) that we exhale. Unfortunately, we and nature now release so much CO_2 that the earth's oceans and vegetation can no longer absorb it all. The excess CO_2 is creating a gaseous blanket around the earth that may warm the earth to disastrous levels. The burning of fossil fuels is a significant source of CO_2 buildup. The destruction of rain forests, which absorb CO_2, also contributes to the greenhouse effect.

Water Pollution

Water pollution is another environmental threat. Its effects are apparent in the contamination of drinking water, restrictions on swimming and boating, foul-smelling waterways, swarms of dead fish, and floating debris.

Organic Pollution. The most common form of water pollution occurs in the disposal of organic wastes from toilets and garbage disposals. The wastes that originate there are collected in sewer systems and ultimately discharged into the nearest waterway. The key question is whether the wastes are treated (separated and decomposed) before ultimate discharge. Sophisticated waste treatment plants can reduce organic pollution up to 99 percent. Unfortunately, only 70 percent of the U.S. population is served by a system of sewers and adequate (secondary) treatment plants. Inadequate treatment systems often result in the closure of waterways and beaches—even in Hawaii (see the accompanying News).

IN THE NEWS

Kaua'i Beach among Most Polluted

In a beach water quality report to be released today by the Natural Resources Defense Council, Hanama'ulu Beach County Park tied for 10th place with two mainland beaches in a list of polluted beaches in the nation that exceed national standards.

"Hanama'ulu Beach exceeded the national standard by 55 percent," Kaua'i biologist Dr. Cart Berg said. "It was found polluted 55 percent of the time it was tested in 2007."

In the NRDC report, water at American beaches last year was unsafe for swimming with the second-highest number of beach closing and advisory days ever.

"Some families can't enjoy their local beaches because they are polluted and kids are getting sick—largely because of human and animal waste in the water," Nancy Stoner, director of NRDC's clean water project, said in a statement. "What this report means for families heading to the beach is they need to be careful and do a little homework."

Though the numbers of beach closures and advisory days due to sewage spills and overflows more than tripled from 2006 to 2007, the largest known source of beach pollution continues to be contamination from stormwater.

—Rachel Gehrlein

Source: Kauaiworld.com, July 29, 2008. Used with permission by The Garden Island Newspaper.

Analysis: The pollution that closes beaches can be avoided with better sewage treatment facilities. Who should bear that cost?

In addition to household wastes, our waterways must also contend with industrial wastes. Over half the volume of industrial discharge comes from just a few industries—principally paper, organic chemicals, petroleum, and steel. Finally, there are all those farm animals: the

7.5 billion chickens and 161 million cows and hogs raised each year generate 1.4 billion tons of manure (whew!). If improperly managed, that organic waste will contaminate water supplies and trigger algae blooms that can choke waterways and kill fish. Animal wastes don't cause too great a problem in Boston or New York City, but they can wreak havoc on the water supplies of towns in California, Texas, Kansas, and Iowa.

Thermal Pollution. Thermal pollution is an increase in the temperature of waterways brought about by the discharge of steam or heated water. Heat discharges can kill fish, upset marine reproductive cycles, and accelerate biological and chemical processes in water, thereby reducing its ability to retain oxygen. Electric power plants account for over 80 percent of all thermal discharges, with primary metal, chemical, and petroleum-refining plants accounting for nearly all the rest.

Solid Waste Pollution

Solid waste is yet another environmental threat. Solid waste pollution is apparent everywhere, from the garbage can to litter on the streets and beaches, to debris in the water, to open dumps. According to EPA estimates, we generate over 5 billion tons of solid waste each year. This figure includes more than 30 billion bottles, 60 billion cans, 100 million tires, and millions of discarded automobiles and major appliances. Where do you think all this refuse goes?

   Most solid wastes originate in agriculture (slaughter wastes, orchard prunings, harvest residues) and mining (slag heaps, mill tailings). The much smaller amount of solid waste originating in residential and commercial use is considered more dangerous, however, simply because it accumulates where people live. New York City alone generates 24,000 tons of trash a day. Because it has neither the land area nor the incinerators needed for disposal, it must ship its garbage to other states. Seattle ships its trash to Oregon; Los Angeles transports its trash to the Mojave Desert; New York City sludge is dumped in west Texas; and Philadelphia ships its garbage all the way to Panama.

POLLUTION DAMAGES

Shipping garbage to Panama is an expensive answer to our waste disposal problem. But even those costs are a small fraction of the total cost of environmental damage. Much greater costs are associated with the damage to our health (labor), buildings (capital), and land. Even the little things count, like being able to enjoy a clear sunset or take a deep breath.

   Although many people don't like to put a price on the environment, some monetary measure of environmental damage is important in decision making. Unless we value the environment above everything else, we have to establish some method of ranking the importance of environmental damage. Although it's tempting to say that clean air is priceless, *we won't get clean air unless we spend resources to get it.* This economic reality suggests that we begin by determining how much cleaner air is worth to us.

Assigning Prices

In some cases, it's fairly easy to put a price on environmental damage. Scientists can measure the increase in cancer, heart attacks, and other disorders attributable to air pollution, as the EPA does for air toxins (see the News on the next page). Engineers can also measure the rate at which buildings decay or forests and lakes die. Economists can then estimate the dollar value of this damage by assessing the economic value of lives, forests, lakes, and other resources. For example, if people are willing to pay $5,000 for a cataract operation, then the avoidance of such eye damage is worth at least $5,000. Saving a tree is worth whatever the marketplace is willing to pay for the products of that tree. Using such computations, the EPA estimates that air pollution alone inflicts health, property, and vegetation damage in excess of $50 billion a year.

web analysis

The Earth Policy Institute offers data on the costs of pollution at **www.earth-policy.org.** Search "pollution."

IN THE NEWS

Dirty Air Can Shorten Your Life

The largest study ever conducted on the health effects of airborne particles from traffic and smokestacks has found that people in the nation's most polluted cities are 15 to 17 percent more likely to die prematurely than those in cities with the cleanest air.

This form of pollution is killing citizens even in areas that meet Environmental Protection Agency air quality standards, said study coauthor Douglas Dockery of the Harvard School of Public Health, who said "the impact on life and health is more pervasive than previously thought."

In Washington, where levels of airborne particles fall in the low middle range for U.S. cities, the average long-term resident loses approximately one year of life expectancy compared to the average for such relatively pristine places as Topeka, Kansas, or Madison, Wisconsin, Dockery said. In highly polluted places like Los Angeles or Salt Lake City, the toll is much greater. Compared to people in the cleanest metropolitan areas, those exposed to the highest concentrations of particles run a risk of premature death about one-sixth as great as if they had been smoking for 25 years.

—Curt Suplee

Analysis: Pollution entails real costs, as measured by impaired health, reduced life spans, and other damages.

The job of pricing environmental damage is much more difficult with intangible losses like sunsets. Nevertheless, when governmental agencies and courts are asked to assess the damages of oil spills and other accidents, they must try to inventory *all* costs, including polluted sunsets, reduced wildlife, and lost recreation opportunities. The science of computing such environmental damage is very inexact. Nevertheless, crude but reasonable procedures generate damage estimates measured in hundreds of billions of dollars per year.

Cleanup Possibilities

One of the most frustrating things about all this environmental damage is that it can be avoided. The EPA estimates that *95 percent of current air and water pollution could be eliminated by known and available technology.* Nothing very exotic is needed: just simple things like auto emission controls, smokestack cleaners, improved sewage and waste treatment facilities, and cooling towers for electric power plants. Even solid waste pollution could be reduced by comparable proportions if we used less packaging, recycled more materials, or transformed our garbage into a useful (relatively low-polluting) energy source. Why don't we do these things? Why do we continue to pollute so much?

MARKET INCENTIVES

Previous chapters emphasized how market incentives influence the behavior of individual consumers, firms, and government agencies. Incentives in the form of price reductions can be used to change consumer buying habits. Incentives in the form of high profit margins encourage production of desired goods and services. And market incentives in the form of cost differentials help allocate resources efficiently. Accordingly, we shouldn't be too surprised to learn that *market incentives play a major role in pollution behavior.*

The Production Decision

Imagine that you're the majority stockholder and manager of an electric power plant. Such plants are responsible for a significant amount of air pollution (especially sulfur dioxide

FIGURE 14.1
Profit Maximization in Electric Power Production

Production processes that control pollution may be more expensive than those that don't. If they are, the MC and ATC curves will shift upward (to MC₂ and ATC₂). At the new profit-maximizing rate of output (point *B*), output and total profit shrink. Hence a producer has an incentive to continue polluting, using cheaper technology.

---

and particulates) and nearly all thermal water pollution. Hence your position immediately puts you on the most-wanted list of pollution offenders. But suppose you're civic minded and would truly like to help eliminate pollution. Let's consider the alternatives.

As the owner–manager of an electric power plant, you'll strive to make a profit-maximizing **production decision.** That is, you'll seek the rate of output at which marginal revenue equals marginal cost. Let's assume that the electric power industry is still regulated by the state power commission so that the price of electricity is fixed, at least in the short run. The effect of this assumption is to render marginal revenue equal to price, thus giving us a horizontal price line, as in Figure 14.1*a*.

Figure 14.1*a* also depicts the marginal and average total costs (MC and ATC) associated with the production of electricity. By equating marginal cost (MC) to price (marginal revenue, MR), we observe (point *A*) that profit maximization occurs at an output of 1,000 kilowatt-hours per day. Total profits are illustrated by the shaded rectangle between the price line and the average total cost (ATC) curve.

production decision: The selection of the short-run rate of output (with existing plants and equipment).

The Efficiency Decision

The profits illustrated in Figure 14.1*a* are achieved in part by use of the cheapest available fuel under the boilers (which create the steam that rotates the generators). Recall that the construction of a marginal cost curve presumes some knowledge of alternative production processes. Recall too that the **efficiency decision** requires a producer to choose that production process (and its associated cost curve) that minimizes costs for any particular rate of output.

efficiency decision: The choice of a production process for any given rate of output.

Costs of Pollution Abatement. Unfortunately, the efficiency decision in this case leads to the use of high-sulfur coal, the prime villain in SO_2 and particulate pollution. Other fuels, such as low-sulfur coal, fuel oil, and nuclear energy, cost considerably more. Were you to switch to one of them, the ATC and MC curves would both shift upward, as in Figure 14.1*b*. Under these conditions, the most profitable rate of output would be lower than before (point *B* on the graph), and total profits would decline (note the smaller profit rectangle in Figure 14.1*b*). Thus *pollution abatement can be achieved, but only at significant cost to the plant.*

The same kind of cost considerations lead the plant to engage in thermal pollution. Cool water must be run through an electric utility plant to keep the turbines from overheating.

Once the water has run through the plant, it's too hot to recirculate. It must be either dumped back into the adjacent river or cooled off by being circulated through cooling towers. As you might expect, it's cheaper to simply dump the hot water in the river, as the Indian Point nuclear plant in New York does (see the accompanying News). The fish don't like it, but they don't have to pay the construction costs associated with cooling towers.

IN THE NEWS

Wrong Answer at Indian Point

Ever since New York State ruled in the spring that the obsolete cooling system at the Indian Point nuclear power plant in Buchanan, New York, pollutes the Hudson River and kills too many fish, the plant's owner, the Entergy Corporation, has been seeking public support for what it calls a "smarter solution" to the problem.

Finding some solution is important for Entergy, which wants to keep operating Indian Point's two nuclear reactors, whose federal licenses expire in 2013 and 2015. To renew the licenses for another 20 years, Entergy needs a water-quality certificate from the state Department of Environmental Conservation.

The agency denied the certificate in April. Indian Point's cooling system sucks up about 2.5 billion gallons of river water a day—by far the largest single industrial use of water in New York State, according to the agency. The water passes through the plant and is dumped back in the river, hotter than before. About a billion fish, larvae, and eggs are killed each year, trapped against the cooling system's intake screens or drawn through its pipes, or fatally stressed by the heated water, which holds less oxygen.

Source: *The New York Times*, August 11, 2010. © 2010 All rights reserved. Used with permission.

Analysis: When producers consider only *private* costs, they may select production processes that impose high *external* costs.

The big question here is whether you and your fellow stockholders would be willing to incur higher costs to cut down on pollution. Eliminating either the air pollution or the water pollution emanating from the electric plant will cost a lot of money. And to whose benefit? To the people who live downstream and downwind? We don't expect profit-maximizing producers to take such concerns into account. *The behavior of profit maximizers is guided by comparisons of revenues and costs, not by philanthropy, aesthetic concerns, or the welfare of fish.*

MARKET FAILURE: EXTERNAL COSTS

The moral of this story—and the critical factor in pollution behavior—is that *people tend to maximize their personal welfare, balancing private benefits against private costs.* For the electric power plant, this means making production decisions on the basis of revenues received and costs incurred. The fact that the power plant imposes costs on others, in the form of air and water pollution, is irrelevant to its profit-maximizing decisions. Those costs are *external* to the firm and don't appear on its profit-and-loss statement. Those **external costs**—or *externalities*—are no less real, but they're incurred by society at large rather than by the firm.

external cost: Cost of a market activity borne by a third party; the difference between the social and private costs of a market activity.

Externalities in Production

Whenever external costs exist, a private firm won't allocate its resources and operate its plant in such a way as to maximize social welfare. In effect, society permits the power plant the free use of valued resources—clean air and clean water. The power plant has a tremendous incentive to substitute those resources for others (such as high-priced fuel or

"Where there's smoke, there's money."

Analysis: If a firm can substitute external costs for private (internal) costs, its profits may increase.

cooling towers) in the production process. The inefficiency of such an arrangement is obvious when we recall that the function of markets is to allocate scarce resources in accordance with the consumer's expressed demands. Yet here we are, proclaiming a high value for clean air and clean water and encouraging the power plant to use up both resources by offering them at zero cost to the firm.

The inefficiency of this market arrangement can be expressed in terms of a distinction between social costs and private costs. **Social costs** are the total costs of all the resources used in a particular production activity. On the other hand, **private costs** are the resource costs incurred by the specific producer.

Ideally, a producer's private costs will encompass all the attendant social costs, and production decisions will be consistent with our social welfare. Unfortunately, this happy identity doesn't always exist, as our experience with the power plant illustrates. *When social costs differ from private costs, external costs exist. In fact, external costs are equal to the difference between the social and private costs*:

$$\text{External costs} = \text{Social costs} - \text{Private costs}$$

When external costs are present, the market mechanism won't allocate resources efficiently. This is a case of **market failure.** The price signal confronting producers is flawed. By not conveying the full (social) cost of scarce resources, the market encourages excessive pollution. We end up with a suboptimal mix of output (too much electricity, too little clean air) and the wrong production processes.

The consequences of this market failure are illustrated in Figure 14.2, which again depicts the cost situation confronting the electric power plant. Notice that we use *two* different marginal cost curves this time. The lower one, the *private* MC curve, reflects the private costs incurred by the power plant when it operates on a profit maximization basis, using high-sulfur coal and no cooling towers (described as the "wrong answer" in the News on the previous page). It's identical to the MC curve in Figure 14.1*a*. We now know, however, that such operations impose external costs on others in the form of air and water pollution. These external costs must be added to private marginal costs. When this is done, we get a *social* marginal cost curve that lies above the private MC curve.

To maximize profits, private firms seek the rate of output that equates private MC to MR (price). *To maximize social welfare, we need to equate social marginal cost to*

social costs: The full resource costs of an economic activity, including externalities.

private costs: The costs of an economic activity directly borne by the immediate producer or consumer (excluding externalities).

market failure: An imperfection in the market mechanism that prevents optimal outcomes.

FIGURE 14.2
Market Failure

Social costs exceed private costs by the amount of external costs. Production decisions based on private costs alone will lead us to point *B*, where private MC = MR. At point *B*, the rate of output is q_p.

To maximize social welfare, we equate *social* MC and MR, as at point *A*. Only q_s of output is socially desirable. The failure of the market to convey the full costs of production keeps us from attaining this outcome.

marginal revenue (price). This social optimum occurs at point *A* in Figure 14.2 and results in output of q_s. By contrast, the firm's private profit maximization occurs at point *B*, where q_p is produced. Hence the private firm ends up producing more output than socially desired, while earning more profit and causing more pollution. As a general rule, *if pollution costs are external, firms will produce too much of a polluting good.*

Externalities in Consumption

A divergence between private and social costs can also be observed in consumption. Consumers try to maximize their personal welfare. We buy and use more of those goods and services that yield the highest satisfaction (marginal utility) per dollar expended. By implication (and the law of demand), we tend to use more of a product if we can get it at a discount—that is, pay less than the full price. Unfortunately, the "discount" often takes the form of an external cost imposed on neighbors and friends.

Automobile driving illustrates the problem. The amount of driving one does is influenced by the price of a car and the marginal costs of driving it. People buy smaller cars and drive less when the attendant marginal costs (for instance, gasoline prices) increase substantially. But automobile use involves not only *private costs* but *external costs* as well. Auto emissions (carbon monoxide, hydrocarbons, and nitrogen oxides) are a principal cause of air pollution. In effect, automobile drivers have been able to use a valued resource, clean air, at no cost to themselves. Few motorists see any personal benefit in installing exhaust control devices because the quality of the air they breathe would be little affected by their efforts. Hence low private costs lead to excessive pollution when high social costs are dictating cleaner air.

A divergence between social and private costs can be observed even in the simplest of consumer activities, such as throwing an empty soda can out the window of your car. Hanging onto the can and later disposing of it in a trash barrel involve personal effort and thus private marginal costs. Throwing it out the window not only is more exciting but also effectively transfers the burden of disposal costs to someone else. The resulting externality ends up as roadside litter.

The same kind of divergence between private and social costs helps explain why people abandon old cars in the street rather than haul them to scrapyards. It also explains why people use vacant lots as open dumps. In all these cases, *the polluter benefits by substituting external costs for private costs.* In other words, market incentives encourage environmental damage.

REGULATORY OPTIONS

The failure of the market to include external costs in production and consumption decisions creates a basis for government intervention. As always, however, we confront a variety of policy options. We may define these options in terms of *two general strategies for environmental protection:*

- *Alter market incentives* in such a way that they discourage pollution.
- *Bypass market incentives* with some form of regulatory intervention.

Market-Based Options

Insofar as market incentives are concerned, the key to environmental protection is to eliminate the divergence between private costs and social costs. The opportunity to shift some costs onto others lies at the heart of the pollution problem. If we could somehow compel producers to *internalize* all costs—pay for both private and external costs—the divergence would disappear, along with the incentive to pollute.

Emission Charges. One possibility is to establish a system of **emission charges:** direct costs attached to the act of polluting. Suppose that we let you keep your power plant and permit you to operate it according to profit-maximizing principles. The only difference is that we no longer supply you with clean air and cool water at zero cost. From now on, we'll charge you for these scarce resources. We might, say, charge 2 cents for every gram of noxious emission discharged into the air. In addition we might charge 3 cents for every gallon of water you use, heat, and discharge back into the river.

Confronted with such emission charges, you'd have to alter your production decision. *An emission charge increases private marginal cost and encourages lower output and cleaner technology.* Figure 14.3 illustrates this effect. Notice how the fee raises private marginal costs and induces a lower rate of (polluting) production (q_1 rather than q_0).

Once an emission fee is in place, a producer may also reevaluate the efficiency decision. Consider again the choice of fuels to be used in our fictional power plant. We earlier chose high-sulfur coal because it was the cheapest fuel available. Now, however, there's an additional cost attached to burning such fuel, in the form of an emission charge. This added cost may encourage the firm to switch to cleaner sources of energy, which would increase private marginal costs but reduce emission fees.

An emission charge might also persuade a firm to incur higher *fixed* costs. Rather than continuing to pay emission charges, it might be more economical to install scrubbers and other smokestack controls that reduce the volume of emissions. This would entail additional

> **emission charge:** A fee imposed on polluters, based on the quantity of pollution.

PRICE OR COST (dollars per unit)

MC + fee

Private MC

Price

Fee = t →

Emission fees internalize external costs.

q_1 q_0

QUANTITY (units per time period)

FIGURE 14.3
Emission Fees

Emission charges can close the gap between marginal social costs and marginal private costs. Faced with an emission charge of t, a private producer will reduce output from q_0 to q_1. Emission charges may also induce different investment and efficiency decisions.

capital outlays for the necessary abatement equipment but might reduce variable costs (including emission charges). In this case, the fee-induced change in fixed costs might reduce pollution without any reduction in output.

The actual response of producers will depend on the relative costs involved. If emission charges are too low, it may be more profitable to continue burning and polluting with high-sulfur coal and pay a nominal fee. This is a simple pricing problem. We could set the emission price higher, prompting the behavioral responses we desire.

The same kind of relative cost considerations would apply to the thermal pollution associated with the power plant. The choice heretofore has been between building expensive cooling towers (and not polluting) or not incurring such capital costs (and simply discharging the heated water into the river). The profit-maximizing choice was obvious. Now, however, the choice is between building cooling towers or paying a steady flow of emission charges. The profit-maximizing decision is no longer evident. The decisive factor will be how high we set the emission charges. If the emission charges are set high enough, the producer will find it unprofitable to pollute.

Economic incentives can also change consumer behavior. At one time, beverage producers imposed deposits to encourage consumers to bring bottles back so they could be used again. But producers discovered that such deposits discouraged sales and yielded little cost savings. Today returnable bottles are rarely used. One result is the inclusion of over 30 billion bottles and 60 billion cans in our solid waste disposal problem. We could reverse this trend by imposing a deposit on all beverage containers. Many states do this, at least for certain cans and bottles. Such deposits internalize pollution costs for the consumer and render the throwing of a soda can out the window equivalent to throwing away money.

Some communities have also tried to reduce solid waste processing by charging a fee for each container of garbage collected. In Charlotte, Virginia, a fee of 80 cents per 32-gallon bag of garbage had a noticeable impact on consumer behavior. Economists Don Fullerton and Thomas Kinnaman observed that households reduced the weight of their garbage by 14 percent and the volume by 37 percent. As they noted, "Households somehow stomped their garbage to get more in a container and trim their garbage bill." Here again, the use of the market mechanism (higher prices) brought about the desired environmental protection.

Recycling Materials. An important bonus that emission charges offer is an increased incentive for the recycling of materials. The glass and metal in used bottles and cans can be recycled to produce new bottles and cans. Such recycling not only eliminates a lot of unsightly litter but also diminishes the need to mine new resources from the earth, a process that often involves its own environmental problems. The critical issues are once again relative costs and market incentives. *A container producer has no incentive to use recycled materials unless they offer superior cost efficiency and thus greater profits.* The largest component in the costs of recycled materials is usually the associated costs of collection and transportation. In this regard, an emission charge such as the 5-cent container deposit lowers collection costs because it motivates consumers to return all their bottles and cans to a central location.

Higher User Fees. Another market alternative is to raise the price consumers pay for scarce resources. If people used less water, we wouldn't have to build so many sewage treatment plants. In most communities, however, the price of water is so low that people use it indiscriminately. Higher water fees would encourage water conservation.

A similar logic applies to auto pollution. The cheapest way to cut down on auto pollution is to drive less. Higher gasoline prices would encourage people to use alternative transportation and drive more fuel-efficient cars. Consumers would complain, of course, about higher taxes on gasoline, but at least they'd be able to breathe cleaner air.

"Green" Taxes. Automakers don't want gasoline prices to go up; neither do consumers. So the government may have to impose *green taxes* to get the desired response. A green tax on gasoline, for example, raises the price of gasoline. The taxes not only curb auto emissions (less driving) but also create a revenue source for other pollution abatement efforts. Other nations impose far more green taxes than does the United States.

Pollution Fines. Not far removed from the concept of emission and user charges is the imposition of fines or liability for cleanup costs. In some situations, such as the April 2010 BP oil spill in the Gulf of Mexico, the pollution is so sudden and concentrated that society has little choice but to clean it up quickly. The costs for such cleanup can be imposed on the polluter, however, through appropriate fines. Such fines place the cost burden where it belongs.

Although pollution fines are inevitably imposed after the damage is done, the *expectation* of a fine can encourage more environmentally conscious behavior. To avoid a potential fine, oil companies may invest in double-hulled oil tankers and more efficient safety mechanisms on offshore oil wells. When Royal Caribbean Cruises was fined $9 million in 1998 for dumping garbage and oil from its cruise ships, the firm decided to monitor waste disposal practices more closely. In the absence of such fines, firms have little incentive to invest in environmental protection.

Tradable Pollution Permits ("Cap and Trade")

Another environmental policy option makes even greater use of market incentives. Rather than penalize firms that have already polluted, let firms *purchase* the right to continue polluting. As crazy as this policy might sound, it can be effective in limiting environmental damage.

The key to the success of pollution permits is that they're bought and sold among private firms. The system starts with a government-set standard for pollution reduction. Firms that reduce pollution by more than the standard earn pollution credits. They may then sell these credits to other firms, who are thereby relieved of cleanup chores. ***The principal advantage of pollution permits is their incentive to minimize the cost of pollution control.***

To see how the permits work, suppose the policy objective is to reduce sulfur dioxide emissions by two tons. There are only two major polluters in the community: a copper smelter and an electric utility. Should each company be required to reduce its SO_2 emissions by one ton? Or can the same SO_2 reduction be achieved more cheaply with marketable pollution rights?

Focus on Marginal Abatement Costs. Table 14.1 depicts the assumed cost of pollution abatement at each plant. The copper smelter would have to spend $200 to achieve a one-ton reduction in SO_2 emissions. The utility can do it for only $100. Table 14.1 also indicates that the utility can attain a *second* ton of SO_2 abatement for $150. Even though its marginal cost of pollution control is increasing, the utility still has lower abatement costs than the smelter. This cost advantage creates an interesting economic opportunity.

Recall that the policy goal is to reduce emissions by two tons. The copper smelter would have to spend $200 to achieve its one-ton share of the policy target. But the utility can abate a *second* ton for $150. Accordingly, the smelter would save money by *paying* the utility for additional pollution abatement.

How much would the smelter have to pay? The utility would want at least $150 to cover its own marginal costs of additional pollution abatement. The smelter would save money at any price below $200. Accordingly, the price of this transaction would be somewhere between $150 (the utility's marginal cost of a second ton) and $200 (the smelter's marginal cost of the first ton). If they do the deal—trade pollution rights—the smelter would continue to pollute, but total SO_2 emissions would still drop by two tons (all at the electric utility). Both firms would be better off (the smelter with lower costs, the utility with more revenue).

TABLE 14.1
Pricing Pollution Permits

If both firms reduce emissions by one ton each, the cost is $300. If the utility instead reduces emissions by two tons, the cost is only $250. A permit system allows the smelter to pay the utility for assuming the added abatement responsibility.

Reduction in Emissions (in Tons)	Marginal Cost of Pollution Abatement	
	Copper Smelter	**Electric Utility**
1	$200	$100
2	250	150
3	300	200

Society also benefits from this cap-and-trade system: the social goal of pollution abatement is achieved at lower cost. Without tradable permits, the resource cost of a two-ton reduction was $300. With the cap-and-trade option, the resource cost falls to $250. So society ends up with $50 of "extra" resources to produce other desired goods and services.

At the first real auction of pollution credits, the average price paid was $156. For this price a firm could pay someone else to reduce SO_2 emissions by one ton rather than curb its own emissions. The Carolina Power and Light Company spent $11.5 *million* buying such permits.

Since they first became available in 1992, tradable pollution permits ("allowances") have become a popular mechanism for pollution control. Millions of allowances are now traded in the open market every year. Moreover, the permit market has gotten increasingly efficient, with visible bid and ask prices, broker specialists, and low transaction costs. In 2000, 12.7 *million* sulfur dioxide allowances were traded, each covering one ton of emission reduction. The price of a permit has also steadily declined, indicating that companies are discovering cheaper methods of pollution control.

Environmental Innovation. Pollution permits also encourage innovation in abatement technology. Entrepreneurs now have an incentive to discover cheaper methods for pollution abatement. They don't have to own a smelter or utility; they can now *sell* their pollution control expertise to the highest bidder. As the market for permits has expanded, the profit opportunities for environmental engineering firms have increased. This has accelerated productivity and reduced the cost of pollution abatement by 25 to 34 percent. In view of these results, the EPA extended the pollution permit trading system to *water* pollution in 2003, and the European Union extended it to carbon dioxide emissions in 2005 (see the World View below).

WORLD VIEW

Paying to Pollute

System Would Limit Emission, Allow Trading of Credits

It costs nothing to pump greenhouse gases into the air. . . .

That is starting to change.

Driven by fears of global warming, countries and states are trying to place a price tag on emissions of carbon dioxide, the gas considered most responsible for rising temperatures.

They are turning to a system called "cap and trade," which limits the overall amount of carbon dioxide an area or industry can emit and then lets individual companies buy and sell credits to release specific amounts of the gas.

The cap-and-trade concept is considered an alternative to strict government mandates. It tries to use market dynamics to cut pollution, allowing flexibility on emission levels—for a price. Emissions that were free in the past, regardless of their environmental cost, now would cost an amount set by the market.

In theory at least, it allows businesses that emit carbon dioxide to choose the most cost-effective way to cut their emissions. And it gives them leeway in the speed of their cuts. . . .

Europe has a carbon dioxide market up and running, with release of a ton of gas now trading at 27 euros, about $32. New York and six other Eastern states plan to open one in 2009. California energy regulators last week took the first step toward such a system.

—David R. Baker

Source: *San Francisco Chronicle*, February 19, 2006, p. J1. Used with permission via Copyright Clearance Center, Inc.

Analysis: Marketable pollution permits encourage firms with more efficient pollution control technologies to overachieve, thereby earning pollution permits that can be sold to firms with more expensive pollution control technologies. Such trades reduce the *average* cost of pollution control.

Command-and-Control Options

Public policy needn't rely on tradable permits or other market incentives to achieve desired pollution abatement. The government could instead simply *require* firms to reduce pollutants by specific amounts and even specify which abatement technology must be used. This approach is often referred to as the "command-and-control" option. The government *commands* firms to reduce pollution and then *controls* the process for doing so.

The potential inefficiency of the command-and-control strategy was already revealed in Table 14.1. Had the government required *each* firm to reduce pollution by one ton, the total cost would have been $300. By allowing firms to use tradable permits, the cost of obtaining the same level of pollution abatement was only $250. The cost saving of $50 represents valuable resources that could be used to produce other desired goods and services.

Despite the superior efficiency of market-based environmental policies, the government often relies on the command-and-control approach. The Clean Air Acts of 1970 and 1990, for example, mandated not only fewer auto emissions but also specific processes such as catalytic converters and lead-free gasoline for attaining them. Specific processes and technologies are also required for toxic waste disposal and water treatment. Laws requiring the sorting and recycling of trash are other examples of process regulation.

Although such command-and-control regulation can be effective, this policy option also entails risks. By requiring all market participants to follow specific rules, the regulations may impose excessive costs on some activities and too low a constraint on others. Some communities may not need the level of sewage treatment the federal government prescribes. Individual households may not generate enough trash to make sorting and separate pickups economically sound. Some producers may have better or cheaper ways of attaining environmental standards. ***Excessive process regulation may raise the costs of environmental protection and discourage cost-saving innovation.*** There's also the risk of regulated processes becoming entrenched long after they are obsolete. When that happens we may end up with worse outcomes than a less regulated market would have generated—that is, **government failure.**

web analysis

Environmental policy is a big part of the Obama administration's vision. To learn more, see the 2011 Economic Report of the President at **www.gpoaccess.gov/eop.** Of special interest is Chapter 6, "Transitioning to a Clean Energy Future."

government failure: Government intervention that fails to improve economic outcomes.

BALANCING BENEFITS AND COSTS

Protecting the environment entails costs as well as benefits. Installing smokestack scrubbers on factory chimneys and catalytic converters on cars requires the use of scarce resources. Taking the lead out of gasoline wears out engines faster and requires expensive changes in technology. Switching to clean fuels requires enormous investments in technology, plants, and equipment. The EPA estimates that a 10-year program to achieve national air and water standards would cost more than $1 trillion. President Obama's proposals for developing alternative, "clean energy" sources (e.g., solar, wind) would more than double that outlay. Restoring the ozone layer, removing hazardous wastes, and cleaning up the rest of the environment would cost trillions more.

Opportunity Costs

Although cleaning up the environment is a worthwhile goal, we must remind ourselves that those resources could be used to fulfill other goals as well. The multitrillion-dollar tab would buy a lot of subways and parks or build decent homes for the poor. If we choose to devote those resources instead to pollution abatement efforts, we'll have to forgo some other goods and services. This isn't to say that environmental goals don't deserve that kind of priority but simply to remind us that any use of our scarce resources involves an **opportunity cost.**

Fortunately, the amount of additional resources required to clean up the environment is relatively modest in comparison to our productive capacity. Over a 10-year period we'll produce close to $200 trillion of goods and services (GDP). On this basis, the environmental expenditures contemplated by present environmental policies and goals represent only 1 to 3 percent of total output.

opportunity cost: The most desired goods or services that are forgone in order to obtain something else.

The Optimal Rate of Pollution

optimal rate of pollution:
The rate of pollution that occurs when the marginal social benefit of pollution control equals its marginal social cost.

Spending even a small percentage of GDP on environmental protection nevertheless entails value judgments. The **optimal rate of pollution** occurs at the point at which the opportunity costs of further pollution control equal the benefits of further reductions in pollution. *To determine the optimal rate of pollution, we need to compare the marginal social benefits of additional pollution abatement with the marginal social costs of additional pollution control expenditure.* The optimal rate of pollution is achieved when we've satisfied the following equality:

$$\begin{array}{ccc} \text{Optimal} & \text{Marginal benefit} & \text{Marginal cost} \\ \text{rate of} \;\; : & \text{of pollution} & = \;\; \text{of pollution} \\ \text{pollution} & \text{abatement} & \text{abatement} \end{array}$$

An Inconvenient Truth

This formulation is analogous to the utility-maximizing rule in consumption. If another dollar spent on pollution control yields less than a dollar of social benefits, then additional pollution control expenditure isn't desirable. In such a situation, the goods and services that would be forsaken for additional pollution control are more valued than the environmental improvements that would result.

A 2003 White House study concluded that past efforts to clean up the air have yielded far more benefits than costs. As the accompanying News reports, the benefits of a 10-year (1992–2002) air pollution abatement program were five to seven times greater than its cost.

IN THE NEWS

Study Finds Net Gain from Pollution Rules

A new White House study concludes that environmental regulations are well worth the costs they impose on industry and consumers, resulting in significant public health improvements and other benefits to society. . . .

The report, issued this month by the Office of Management and Budget, concludes that the health and social benefits of enforcing tough new clean air regulations during the past decade were five to seven times greater in economic terms than were the costs of complying with the rules. The value of reductions in hospitalization and emergency room visits, premature deaths, and lost workdays resulting from improved air quality were estimated between $120 billion and $193 billion from October 1992 to September 2002.

By comparison, industry, states, and municipalities spent an estimated $23 billion to $26 billion to retrofit plants and facilities and make other changes to comply with new clean air standards, which are designed to sharply reduce sulfur dioxide, fine particle emissions, and other health-threatening pollutants.

—Eric Pianin

Source: *The Washington Post,* © September 27, 2003. All rights reserved. Used with permission.

Analysis: The benefits of pollution abatement have generally exceeded its costs. However, *marginal* benefits and costs are critical in setting policy goals.

Although pollution abatement has been an economic success, that doesn't mean *all* pollution controls are desirable. The focus must still be on *marginal* benefits and costs. In that context, a surprising conclusion emerges: *a totally clean environment isn't economically desirable.* The marginal benefit of achieving zero pollution is infinitesimally small. But the marginal cost of eliminating that last particle of pollution will be very high. As we weigh the marginal benefits and costs, we'll inevitably conclude that *some* pollution is cost-effective.

Cost–Benefit Analysis

Although marginal analysis tells us that a zero-pollution goal isn't economically desirable, it doesn't really pinpoint the optimal level of pollution. To apply those guidelines we need to identify and evaluate the marginal benefits of any intervention and its marginal costs. Sometimes such calculations yield extraordinarily high cost–benefit ratios. According to researchers at the Harvard Center for Risk Analysis, the *median* cost per life-year saved by EPA regulations is $7.6 million. One of the highest cost–benefit ratios is attached to chloroform emission controls at pulp mills: the cost per life-year saved exceeds $99 *billion!* A human life may in fact be too precious to value in dollars and cents. But in a world of limited resources, the opportunity costs of every intervention need to be assessed. How many lives would be saved if we spent $99 billion on cancer or AIDS research?

Mayor Bloomberg performed the same kind of analysis for New York City's recycling program. Sure, everyone thinks recycling is a good idea. But Mayor Bloomberg started looking at the cost of the recycling program and decided it didn't make economic sense (see the News below). He figured the city could use the $57 million cost of recycling for higher-priority programs, yielding greater (marginal) benefits to NYC residents.

IN THE NEWS

Forced Recycling Is a Waste

As New York City faces the possibility of painful cuts to its police and fire department budgets, environmentalists are bellyaching over garbage. Mayor Michael Bloomberg's proposed budget for 2003 would temporarily suspend the city's recycling of metal, glass, and plastic, saving New Yorkers $57 million.

The city's recycling program—like many others around the country—has long hemorrhaged tax dollars. . . .

The city spends about $240 per ton to "recycle" plastic, glass, and metal, while the cost of simply sending waste to landfills is about $130 per ton.

You don't need a degree in economics to see that something is wrong here. Isn't recycling supposed to save money and resources? Some recycling does—when driven by market forces. Private parties don't voluntarily recycle unless they know it will save money and resources. But forced recycling can be a waste of both because recycling itself entails using energy, water, and labor to collect, sort, clean, and process the materials. There are also air emissions, traffic, and wear on streets from the second set of trucks prowling for recyclables. The bottom line is that most mandated recycling hurts, not helps, the environment. . . .

"You could do a lot better things in the world with $57 million," says Mayor Bloomberg.

—Angela Logomasini

Source: *The Wall Street Journal*, March 19, 2002, p. A22. Used with permission of Dow Jones & Company, Inc. via Copyright Clearance Center, Inc.

Analysis: Recycling uses scarce resources that could be employed elsewhere. The benefits of recycling may not exceed its (opportunity) costs.

Who Will Pay?

The costs of pollution control aren't distributed equally. In New York City, the cost of the recycling program is borne by those who end up with fewer city services and amenities (opportunity costs). A national pollution abatement program would target the relatively small number of economic activities that account for the bulk of emissions and effluents. These activities will have to bear a disproportionate share of the cleanup burden.

Higher Costs. To ascertain how the burden of environmental protection will be distributed, consider first the electric power plant discussed earlier. As we observed (Figure 14.2), the plant's output will decrease if production decisions are based on social rather than private marginal costs—that is, if environmental consequences are considered. If the plant itself is compelled to pay full social costs, in the form of either compulsory investment or emission charges, its profits will be reduced. Were no other changes to take place, the burden of environmental improvements would be borne primarily by the producer.

Higher Prices. Such a scenario is unlikely, however. Rather than absorb all the costs of pollution controls themselves, producers will pass some of this burden on to their customers in the form of higher prices. Their ability to do so will depend on the extent of competition in their industry, their relative cost position in it, and the price elasticity of consumer demand. In reality, the electric power industry isn't very competitive, and its prices are still subject to government regulation. In addition, consumer demand is relatively price-inelastic. Accordingly, the profit-maximizing producer will appeal to the state or local power commission for an increase in electricity prices based on the costs of pollution control. Electric power consumers are likely to end up footing the environmental bill.

Job Losses. Workers in the impacted industry are likely to suffer as well. All of the policy options we have looked at end up reducing the production and consumption of the polluting good. That implies job losses for the affected workers. According to the government itself, environmental regulations proposed in 2011 for the mining industry would eliminate thousands of mining jobs across the country (see the accompanying News). Those workers are sure to argue that the economic costs outweigh the environmental benefits.

IN THE NEWS

New Rules Would Cut Thousands of Coal Jobs

CHARLESTON, W.Va.—The Obama administration's own experts estimate their proposal for protecting streams from coal mining would eliminate thousands of jobs and slash production across much of the country, according to a government document obtained by the Associated Press.

The Office of Surface Mining Reclamation and Enforcement document says the agency's preferred rules would impose standards for water quality and restrictions on mining methods that would affect the quality or quantity of streams near coal mines. . . .

The office, a branch of the Interior Department, estimated that the protections would trim coal production to the point that an estimated 7,000 of the nation's 80,600 coal-mining jobs would be lost. . . . The agency maintains in the document that its proposal "attempts to balance the protection of natural resources with imposing a reasonable administrative and economic burden on the coal mining industry."

The National Mining Association blasted the proposal, saying OSM is vastly underestimating the economic impact.

"OSM's preferred alternative will destroy tens of thousands of coal-related jobs across the country from Appalachia to Alaska and Illinois to Texas with no demonstrated benefit to the environment," the trade group said.

Analysis: Reducing the production of polluting products implies job losses in the affected industry. Displaced workers argue that this is an unfair burden.

THE ECONOMY TOMORROW

THE GREENHOUSE THREAT

Forget about littered beaches, smelly landfills, eye-stinging smog, and contaminated water. The really scary problem for the economy tomorrow is much more serious: some scientists say that the carbon emissions we're now spewing into the air are warming the earth's atmosphere. If the earth's temperature rises only a few degrees, they contend, polar caps will melt, continents will flood, and weather patterns will go haywire (see the accompanying World View). If things get bad enough, there may not be any economy tomorrow.

WORLD VIEW

Evidence Is Now "Unequivocal" That Humans Are Causing Global Warming

Changes in the atmosphere, the oceans, and glaciers and ice caps now show unequivocally that the world is warming due to human activities, the United Nations Intergovernmental Panel on Climate Change (IPCC) said in a new report released today in Paris. . . .

The IPCC, which brings together the world's leading climate scientists and experts, concluded that major advances in climate modelling and the collection and analysis of data now give scientists "very high confidence"—at least a 9 out of 10 chance of being correct—in their understanding of how human activities are causing the world to warm. This level of confidence is much greater than the IPCC indicated in their last report in 2001.

Today's report . . . confirms that it is "very likely" that humanity's emissions of carbon dioxide, methane, nitrous oxide, and other greenhouse gases have caused most of the global temperature rise observed since the mid-20th century. The report says that it is likely that the effect of human activities since 1750 is five times greater than the effect of fluctuations in the sun's output.

Susan Soloman, co-chair of the IPCC working group that produced the report, said records from ice cores, going back 10,000 years, show a dramatic rise in greenhouse gases from the onset of the industrial era. "There can be no question that the increase in these greenhouse gases are dominated by human activity." . . .

The report describes an accelerating transition to a warmer world—an increase of 3°C is expected this century—marked by more extreme temperatures including heat waves, new wind patterns, worsening drought in some regions, heavier precipitation in others, melting glaciers and Arctic ice, and rising global average sea levels.

Source: Excerpt from UN News Service article, February 2, 2007. Reprinted with permission. For the latest information on related developments, visit the UN's climate change gateway at **www.un.org/climatechange.**

Analysis: The external costs of consumption and production activities contribute to global environmental problems. What should be done to curb these global external costs?

web analysis

You can review federal government research on climate change at **www.globalchange.gov.** Click the "News" tab.

The Greenhouse Effect. The earth's climate is driven by solar radiation. The energy the sun absorbs must be balanced by outgoing radiation from the earth and the atmosphere. Scientists fear that a flow imbalance is developing. Of particular concern is a buildup of carbon dioxide (CO_2) that might trap heat in the earth's atmosphere, warming the planet.

The natural release of CO_2 dwarfs the emissions from human activities. But there's a concern that the steady increase in man-made CO_2 emissions—principally from burning fossil fuels like gasoline and coal—is tipping the balance.

The Skeptics. Other scientists are skeptical about both the temperature change and its causes. A 1988 National Oceanic and Atmospheric Administration study concluded that there's been no ocean warming in this past century. Furthermore, they say, the amount of CO_2 emitted into the atmosphere by human activity (about 7 billion tons per year) is only a tiny fraction of natural emissions from volcanoes, fires, and lightning (200 billion tons per year). Skeptics also point out that the same computer models predicting global warming in the next generation predicted a much larger increase in temperature for the previous century than actually occurred.

In mid-2001, the National Academy of Sciences resolved one of those issues. The Academy confirmed that the earth is warming, largely due to the increased buildup of greenhouse gas concentrations. A 2004 analysis by the National Center for Atmospheric Research concluded that natural climate changes were responsible for the earth's warming from 1900 to 1950, but could not explain the continuing rise in the earth's temperature since then. Human activity seemed to be the only possible culprit. In 2007 the United Nations concluded with 90 percent certainty that this was the case (see the previous World View).

Global Externalities. The U.N. conclusion implies that we must reduce CO_2 emissions. But how should this be done? We have to recognize that ***CO_2 emissions are a global externality*** of industrial production and fuel consumption. Without some form of government intervention, there's little likelihood that market participants will voluntarily reduce CO_2 emissions.

Kyoto Treaty. In December 1997, 141 nations pledged to reduce CO_2 emissions. The Kyoto treaty they initialed in 1997 expressed an international commitment to reduce greenhouse emissions during the period 2008–2012. The world's industrialized nations promised to cut their emissions below 1990 levels. That would require some industries (e.g., autos, steel, paper, and electric power) to substantially alter production methods and possibly output. For their part, the developing nations of the world promised to curb their *growth* of emissions.

The United States, Australia, and other nations refused to ratify the treaty. President Bush argued that the implied curbs on production would cost the United States 5 million jobs and $400 billion of output annually. It would also put the United States and other industrial nations at a competitive disadvantage in global markets relative to China, India, and other developing nations without CO_2 limits. The implied costs of mandatory CO_2 reductions, President Bush asserted, exceed the promised and uncertain benefits.

The Kyoto treaty expired in 2012 without meeting its CO_2 reduction targets. It did spawn a vast increase in global trading of pollution permits, however, especially between Europe and China. In 2006, for example, China sold roughly 200 million metric tons of CO_2 credits for $6–8 a ton per year. This allowed the European utilities and manufacturers who bought the credits to maintain CO_2 emission levels while financing CO_2 controls in China. In the process, the *growth* of CO_2 emissions slowed, even if an outright emission *reduction* didn't occur.

The Copenhagen Accord. 192 nations reconvened in December 2009 to hammer out a new agreement on greenhouse emissions. Prior to the Copenhagen Climate Change Conference, President Obama suggested that the United States would reduce its CO_2 emissions by 17 percent by 2020 and by an incredible 83 percent by 2050. He hoped other nations would make similar commitments. But the world economy was in a recession, and nations were unwilling to risk the job losses that CO_2 reductions would cause. In addition, China—which by then was the world's biggest CO_2 polluter, owing to rapid GDP growth, intensive use of coal-fired electricity, and weak environmental safeguards—wasn't willing to make any such pledge. Neither, it turned out, was the U.S. Congress. So the only agreement that came out of the conference was the "Copenhagen Accord," a nonbinding and vague commitment by 117 nations to reduce global emissions. Specific targets, timetables, mechanisms, and commitments were deferred to later conferences. Sponsors of the Accord were hopeful that more progress toward curbing greenhouse emissions would be made in the economy tomorrow.

SUMMARY

- Air, water, and solid waste pollution impose social and economic costs. The costs of pollution include the direct damages inflicted on our health and resources, the expense of cleaning up, and the general aesthetic deterioration of the environment.   LO14-1
- Pollution is an external cost, a cost of a market activity imposed on someone (a third party) other than the immediate producer or consumer.   LO14-1
- Producers and consumers generally operate on the basis of private benefits and costs. A private producer or consumer has an incentive to minimize his own costs by transforming private costs into external costs. One way of making such a substitution is to pollute—to use "free" air and water rather than install pollution control equipment, or to leave the job of waste disposal to others.   LO14-1
- Social costs are the total amount of resources used in a production or consumption process. When social costs are greater than private costs, the market's price signals are flawed. This market failure will induce people to harm the environment by using suboptimal processes and products.   LO14-1
- One way to correct the market inefficiency created by externalities is to compel producers and consumers to internalize all (social) costs. This can be done by imposing emission charges and higher user fees. Such charges create an incentive to invest in pollution abatement

equipment, recycle reusable materials, and conserve scarce elements of the environment.   LO14-2
- Tradable pollution permits help minimize the cost of pollution control by (a) promoting low-cost controls to substitute for high-cost controls and (b) encouraging innovation in pollution control technology.   LO14-2
- An alternative approach to cleaning up the environment is to require specific pollution controls or to prohibit specific kinds of activities. Direct regulation runs the risk of higher cost and discouraging innovations in environmental protection.   LO14-2
- The opportunity costs of pollution abatement are the most desired goods and services given up when factors of production are used to control pollution. The optimal rate of pollution is reached when the marginal social benefits of further pollution control equal associated marginal social costs.   LO14-3
- In addition to diverting resources, pollution control efforts alter relative prices, change the mix of output, and redistribute incomes. These outcomes cause losses for particular groups and may thus require special economic or political attention.   LO14-3
- The greenhouse effect represents a global externality. Reducing global emissions requires consensus on optimal pollution levels (i.e., the optimal balance of pollution abatement costs and benefits) and the distribution of attendant costs.   LO14-2

Key Terms

production decision	private costs	government failure
efficiency decision	market failure	opportunity cost
external cost	emission charge	optimal rate of pollution
social costs		

Questions for Discussion

1. What are the *economic* costs of the externalities caused by air toxins (News, p. 306)? Or beach closings (News, p. 304)? Or thermal pollution (News, p. 308)? How would you measure their value?   LO14-1
2. Should we try to eliminate *all* pollution? What economic considerations might favor permitting some pollution?   LO14-3
3. Why would auto manufacturers resist higher fuel efficiency standards? How would their costs, sales, and profits be affected?   LO14-1
4. Does anyone have an incentive to maintain auto exhaust control devices in good working order? How can we

ensure that they will be maintained? Are there any costs associated with this policy?   LO14-1
5. Suppose we established a $100,000 fine for water pollution. Would some companies still find that polluting was economical? Under what conditions?   LO14-2
6. What economic costs are imposed by mandatory sorting of trash (News, p. 317)?   LO14-2
7. "The issuance of a pollution permit is just a license to destroy the environment." Do you agree? Explain.   LO14-2
8. If a high per-bag fee were charged for garbage collection, how would consumers respond?   LO14-2

9. Why couldn't nations agree on a more binding and specific Copenhagen Accord?   LO14-2

10. Might the exemption of China from the Kyoto Treaty CO_2 limits give it an incentive to *increase* CO_2 emissions, whose later reduction it could sell (tradable permits)?   LO14-1

11. Why do consumers complain about pollution, then resist fees and taxes (e.g., on containers, gasoline) that would help reduce pollution?   LO14-2

 web activities to accompany this chapter can be found on the Online Learning Center:
http://www.mhhe.com/schiller13e

 mobile app Visit your mobile app store and download the Schiller: Study Econ app *today*!

PROBLEMS FOR CHAPTER 14   Name: _____

LO14-2 1. How high would its pollution control costs have to be before a firm would "pay to pollute" a
ton of carbon dioxide (World View, p. 314)? $ _____

LO14-3 2. In some states, mining for coal leaves large mounds of rubble, which pose flooding problems,
cause land damage, and are unsightly. The following table shows the estimated annual social
benefits and costs of restoring various amounts of such land:

Land restored (in acres)	0	100	200	300	400	500
Social benefits of restoring land	0	$70	$120	$160	$190	$220
Social costs of restoring land	0	$10	$40	$80	$140	$230

(a) Compute the marginal social benefits and the marginal social costs for each restoration level.

Land restored (in acres)	0	100	200	300	400	500
Marginal benefit (per 100 acres)	____	____	____	____	____	____
Marginal cost (per 100 acres)	____	____	____	____	____	____

(b) What is the optimal rate of restoration?   _____

LO14-1 3. Most people pay nothing for each extra pound of garbage they create. Yet the garbage imposes
external costs on a community. In view of this factor, what's an appropriate price for garbage
collection? Answer the questions based on the following graph.
(a) What is the quantity of (free) garbage collection now demanded?   _____
(b) How much would be demanded if a fee of $3 per pound were charged?   _____
(c) Draw the social demand curve when an external benefit of $2 per pound exists.
(d) If the marginal cost of collecting garbage were constant at $6 per pound, what would be the
optimal level of garbage collection?   _____

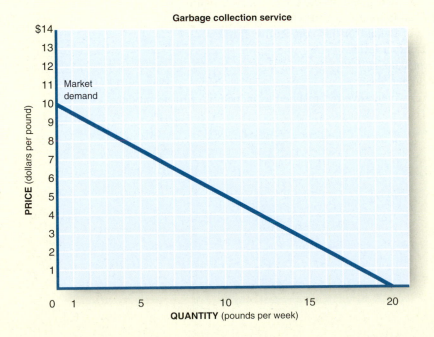

LO14-3 4. Using the *high* estimate of costs and *low* estimate of benefits for pollution controls (News, p. 316),
what is the average benefit per dollar spent?   _____

LO14-3 5. How much more per ton is New York City paying to recycle rather than just dump its garbage
(News, p. 317)?   _____

LO14-2 6. Suppose three firms confront the following costs for pollution control:

	Total Costs of Control		
Emissions Reduction (Tons per Year)	Firm A	Firm B	Firm C
1	$ 40	$ 50	$ 60
2	90	130	130
3	145	220	280
4	280	340	500

(a) If each firm must reduce emissions by one ton, how much will be spent? _____

(b) If the firms can trade pollution rights, what would be the cheapest way of attaining a net three-ton reduction? _____

(c) How much would a pollution permit trade for (price range)? _____

Now suppose the goal is to reduce pollution by six tons.

(d) What is the marginal cost of a second abatement ton at
    (i) Firm A? _____
    (ii) Firm B? _____
    (iii) Firm C? _____

(e) If each firm must reduce emissions by two tons, how much will be spent? _____

(f) If the firms can trade permits, what is the cheapest way of attaining a six-ton reduction? _____

(g) How much will a permit cost (price change)? _____

LO14-1 7. The following cost schedule depicts the private and social costs associated with the daily production of apacum, a highly toxic fertilizer. The sales price of apacum is $22 per ton.

Output (in tons)	0	1	2	3	4	5	6	7	8
Total private cost	$ 5	7	13	23	37	55	77	103	133
Total social cost	$45	63	85	111	141	175	213	255	301

Answer the questions using this schedule, and graph on the accompanying figure.

(a) Graph the private and social marginal costs associated with apacum production.

(b) What is the profit-maximizing rate of output for this competitive firm? _____

(c) How much profit is earned at that output level? _____

(d) What is the socially optimal rate of output? _____

(e) How much profit is there at that output level? _____

(f) How much of a "green tax" per ton would have to be levied to induce the firm to produce the socially optimal rate of output? _____

The Farm Problem

LEARNING OBJECTIVES

After reading this chapter, you should know

LO15-1. What makes the farm business different from others.

LO15-2. Some mechanisms used to prop up farm prices and incomes.

LO15-3. How subsidies affect farm prices, output, and incomes.

In 1996 the U.S. Congress charted a new future for U.S. farmers. No longer would they look to Washington, DC, for decisions on what crops to plant or how much farmland to leave fallow. The Freedom to Farm Act would get the government out of the farm business and let "laissez faire" dictate farm outcomes. Farmers would lose their federal subsidies but could earn as much as they wanted in the marketplace. Taxpayers loved the idea. So did most farmers, who were enjoying unusually high prices and bumper profits in 1996.

The Asian crisis that began in mid-1997 dealt farmers a severe blow. U.S. farms export 25–50 percent of all the wheat, corn, soybeans, and cotton they grow. When Asia's economies plunged into recession, those export sales plummeted. With sales, prices, and profits all declining, farmers lost their enthusiasm for the "freedom to farm"; they wanted Uncle Sam to jump back into the farm business with price and income guarantees. The U.S. Congress obliged by passing the Farm Security Act of 2001. That act not only increased farm subsidies, but also extended them to peanut farmers, hog farmers, and horse breeders. The Farm Act of 2007 spread federal subsidies to still more farmers, abandoning any notion of "free-market" agriculture.

This chapter examines the rationale for continuing farm subsidies and their effects on farm production, prices, and exports. In particular, we confront these questions:

- **Why do farmers need any subsidies?**
- **How do government subsidies affect farm production, prices, and incomes?**
- **Who pays for farm subsidies?**

DESTABILIZING FORCES

market power: The ability to alter the market price of a good or service.

The agriculture industry is one of the most competitive of all U.S. industries. First, there are 2 million farms in the United States. Although some of these farms are immense—with tens of thousands of acres—no single farm has the power to affect the market supply or price of farm products. That is, individual farmers have no **market power.**

Competition in Agriculture

barriers to entry: Obstacles, such as patents, that make it difficult or impossible for would-be producers to enter a particular market.

Competition in agriculture is maintained by low **barriers to entry.** Although farmers need large acreages, expensive farm equipment, substantial credit, hard work, and hired labor, all these resources become affordable when farming is generating **economic profits.** When farming is profitable, existing farmers expand their farms and farmers' children are able to start new farms. It would be much harder to enter the automobile industry, the airline business, or even the farm machinery market than it would be to enter farming. Because of these low barriers to entry, economic profits don't last long in agriculture.

economic profit: The difference between total revenues and total economic costs.

Given the competitive structure of U.S. agriculture, *individual farmers tend to behave like perfect competitors.* Individual farmers seek to expand their rate of output until marginal cost equals price. By following this rule, each farmer makes as much profit as possible from existing resources, prices, and technology.

Like other competitive firms, U.S. farmers can maintain economic profits only if they achieve continuing cost reductions. Above-normal profits obtained from current production techniques and prices aren't likely to last. Such economic profits will entice more people into agriculture and will stimulate greater output from existing farmers. That is exactly the kind of dilemma that confronted catfish farmers in the South and the early producers of microcomputers (Chapter 9). To stay ahead, individual farms must continue to improve their productivity.

Technological Advance

The rate of technological advance in agriculture has, in fact, been spectacular. Since 1929, the farm labor force has shrunk by two-thirds, yet farm output has increased by 80 percent. Between the early 1950s and today,

- Annual egg production has jumped from 183 to 260 eggs per laying chicken.
- Milk output has increased from 5,400 to 21,149 pounds per cow annually.
- Wheat output has increased from 17 to 46 bushels per acre.
- Corn output has jumped from 39 to 164 bushels per acre.

Farm output per labor-hour has grown even faster, having increased 10 times over in the same period. Such spectacular rates of productivity advance rival those of our most high-tech industries. These technological advances resulted from the development of higher-yielding seeds (the "green revolution"), advanced machinery (mechanical feeders and milkers), improved animal breeding (crossbreeding), improved plants (rust-resistant wheat), better land use practices (crop rotation and fertilizers), and computer-based management systems.

Inelastic Demand

In most industries, continuous increases in technology and output would be most welcome. The agricultural industry, however, confronts a long-term problem. Simply put, there's a limit to the amount of food people want to eat.

price elasticity of demand: The percentage change in quantity demanded divided by the percentage change in price.

This constraint on the demand for agricultural output is reflected in the relatively inelastic demand for food. Consumers don't increase their food purchases very much when farm prices fall. The **price elasticity** of food demand is low. As a consequence, when harvests are good, farmers must reduce prices a lot to sell all that extra food. Recall the formula for the price elasticity of demand:

$$E = \frac{\text{Percentage change in quantity demanded}}{\text{Percentage change in price}}$$

FIGURE 15.1
Short-Term Instability

Changes in weather cause abrupt shifts of the food supply curve. When combined with the relatively inelastic demand for food, these supply shifts result in wide price swings. Notice how the price of grain jumps from p_1 to p_2 when bad weather reduces the harvest. If good weather follows, prices may fall to p_3.

Rearranging this formula gives us a guide to how far prices must fall for farmers to unload a bumper crop:

$$\text{Required percentage change in price} = \frac{\text{Percentage change in quantity (harvest)}}{\text{Price elasticity of demand}}$$

Even if the price elasticity of demand were as high as 0.2, the percentage change in price would have to be five times as large as the percentage change in quantity produced. Hence prices would have to fall 25 percent to sell a bumper crop that was 5 percent larger than normal:

$$\% \Delta p = \frac{0.05}{0.20} = 0.25$$

In 2007 the corn crop was 24 percent *larger* than the year before. In 2008 the corn crop *decreased* by 7 percent. As Figure 15.1 illustrates, **with low price elasticity of demand, abrupt changes in farm output have a magnified effect on market prices.** Between 2005 and 2008, corn prices ranged from a low of $1.96 a bushel to a high of $4.78 (see Figure 15.2). That's a *lot* of price instability.

FIGURE 15.2
Unstable Corn Prices

Most agricultural prices are subject to abrupt short-term changes. Notice how corn prices rose dramatically during World Wars I and II, then fell sharply. Poor harvests in the rest of the world increased demand for U.S. food in 1973–1974. Since then prices have moved sharply in both directions.

Source: U.S. Department of Agriculture.

income elasticity of demand: Percentage change in quantity demanded divided by percentage change in income.

The **income elasticity** of food demand is also low. The income elasticity of demand for food refers to the responsiveness of food demand to changes in income. Specifically,

$$\text{Income elasticity of demand} = \frac{\text{\% change in quantity demanded (at constant price)}}{\text{\% change in income}}$$

Since 1929, per capita income has quadrupled. But per capita food consumption has increased only 85 percent. Hence *neither lower prices nor higher incomes significantly increase the quantity of food demanded.*

In the long run, then, the increasing ability of U.S. agriculture to produce food must be reconciled with very slow growth of U.S. demand for food. Over time, this implies that farm prices will fall, relative to nonfarm prices. And they have. Between the years 1910–1914 and 2009, the ratio of farm prices to nonfarm prices fell 60 percent. In the absence of government price support programs and foreign demand for U.S. farm products, farm prices would have fallen still further.

Abrupt Shifts of Supply

The long-term downtrend in (relative) farm prices is only one of the major problems confronting U.S. agriculture. The second major problem is short-run. Prices of farm products are subject to abrupt short-term swings. If the weather is good, harvests are abundant. Normally, this might be a good thing. In farming, however, abundant harvests imply a severe drop in prices. On the other hand, a late or early freeze, a drought, or an infestation by disease or insect pests can reduce harvests and push prices sharply higher (see Figure 15.1).

Response Lags. Time lags between the production decision and the resultant harvest also contribute to price instability. If prices are high one year, farmers have an incentive to increase their rate of output. In this sense, prices serve the same signaling function in agriculture as they do in nonfarm industries. What distinguishes the farmers' response is the lack of inventories and the fixed duration of the production process. In the computer industry, a larger quantity of output can be supplied to the market fairly quickly by drawing down inventories or stepping up the rate of production. In farming, supply can't respond so quickly. In the short run, the farmer can only till more land, plant additional seed, or breed more livestock. No additional food supplies will be available until a new crop or herd grows. Hence the agricultural supply response to a change in prices is always one harvest (or breeding period) later.

This lagged supply response intensifies short-term price swings. Suppose corn prices are exceptionally high at the end of a year because of a reduced harvest. High prices will make corn farming appear unusually profitable. Farmers will want to expand their rate of output— plant more corn acreage—to share in these high profits. But the corn won't appear on the market until the following year. By that time, there's likely to be an abundance of corn on the market, as a result of both better weather and increased corn acreage. Hence corn prices are likely to plummet. This is what happened again in 2006–2008.

No single farmer can avoid these boom-or-bust movements of prices. Even a corn farmer who has mastered the principles of economics has little choice but to plant more corn when prices are high. If he doesn't plant additional corn, prices will fall anyway because his own production decisions don't affect market prices. By not planting additional corn, he only denies himself a share of corn market sales. *In a highly competitive market, each producer acts independently.*

Corn prices spiked to $4.20 per bushel after President Bush proposed expanded use of corn-based ethanol as an alternative fuel source. Farmers rushed to plant additional acreage (see the News on the next page). The 24 percent increase in production that followed pushed prices back down (see Figure 15.2).

IN THE NEWS

Corn Acres Expected to Soar in 2007; USDA Says Ethanol, Export Demand Lead to Largest Planted Area in 63 Years

WASHINGTON, Mar. 30, 2007—Driven by growing ethanol demand, U.S. farmers intend to plant 15 percent more corn acres in 2007, according to the *Prospective Plantings* report released today by the U.S. Department of Agriculture's National Agricultural Statistics Service (NASS). Producers plan to plant 90.5 million acres of corn, the largest area since 1944 and 12.1 million acres more than in 2006.

Expected corn acreage is up in nearly all states due to favorable prices fueled by increased demand from ethanol producers as well as strong export sales.

The increase in intended corn acres is partially offset by a decrease in soybean acres in the Corn Belt and Great Plains, as well as fewer expected acres of cotton and rice in the Delta and Southeast.

Source: U.S. Department of Agriculture, National Agricultural Statistics Service.

Analysis: Price swings motivate farmers to alter their production. The abrupt change in production may reverse the price movement in the next harvest, however.

THE FIRST FARM DEPRESSION, 1920–1940

The U.S. agricultural industry operated without substantial government intervention until the 1930s. In earlier decades, an expanding population, recurrent wars, and less advanced technology had helped maintain a favorable supply–demand relationship for farm products. There were frequent short-term swings in farm prices, but these were absorbed by a generally healthy farm sector. The period 1910–1919 was particularly prosperous for farmers, largely because of the expanded foreign demand for U.S. farm products by countries engaged in World War I.

The two basic problems of U.S. agriculture grew to crisis proportions after 1920. In 1919 most farm prices were at historical highs (see Figures 15.2 and 15.3). After World War I ended, however, European countries no longer demanded as much American food. U.S. exports of farm products fell from nearly $4 billion in 1919 to $1.9 billion in 1921. Farm exports were further reduced in the following years by increasing restrictions on

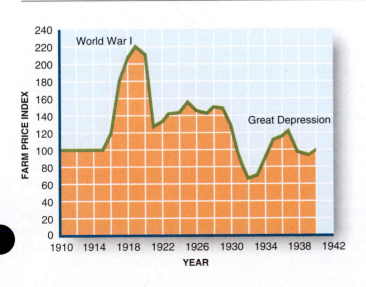

YEAR

web analysis

Annual prices for farm products are compiled by the National Agricultural Statistics Service at the U.S. Department of Agriculture. Visit **www.nass.usda.gov** and click on "Economics" for more information.

FIGURE 15.3
Farm Prices, 1910–1940
(1910–1914 = 100)

Farm prices are less stable than nonfarm prices. During the 1930s, relative farm prices fell 50 percent. This experience was the catalyst for government price supports and other agricultural assistance programs.

TABLE 15.1
Size Distribution of U.S. Farms, 1910 and 2002

Inelastic food demand, combined with increasing agricultural productivity, implies a declining number of farmers. Small farmers are particularly vulnerable because they don't have the resources to maintain a high rate of technological improvement. As a result, the number of small farms has declined dramatically while the number of large farms has grown.

Size of Farm	Number, 1910	Percent	Number, 2002	Percent
Under 100 acres	3,691,611	58.0%	943,118	44.3%
100–499 acres	2,494,461	39.2	847,322	39.8
500–999 acres	125,295	2.0	161,552	7.6
1,000 acres and over	50,135	0.8	176,990	8.3
Total	6,361,502	100.0%	2,128,982	100.0%

Source: U.S. Department of Agriculture.

international trade. At home, the end of the war implied an increased availability of factors of production and continuing improvement in farm technology.

The impact of reduced demand and increasing supply is evident in Figure 15.3. In 1919 farm prices were more than double their levels of the period 1910–1914. Prices then fell abruptly. In 1921 alone, farm prices fell nearly 40 percent.

Farm prices stabilized in the mid-1920s but resumed a steep decline in 1930. In 1932 average farm prices were 75 percent lower than they had been in 1919. At the same time, the average income per farmer from farming fell from $2,651 in 1919 to $855 in 1932.

The Great Depression hit small farmers particularly hard. They had fewer resources to withstand consecutive years of declining prices and income. Even in good times, small farmers must continually expand output and reduce costs just to maintain their incomes. Hence the Great Depression accelerated an exodus of small farmers from agriculture, a trend that continues today.

Table 15.1 shows that the number of small farms has declined dramatically. In 1910 there were 3.7 million farms under 100 acres in size. Today there are fewer than 1 million small farms. During the same period, the number of huge farms (1,000 acres or more) has more than tripled. This loss of small farmers, together with the increased mechanization of larger farms, has reduced the farm population by 23 million people since 1910.

U.S. FARM POLICY

The U.S. Congress has responded to these agricultural problems with a variety of programs. Most seek to raise and stabilize the price of farm products. Other programs seek to reduce the costs of production. When all else fails, the federal government also provides direct income support to farmers.

Price Supports

Price supports have always been the primary focus of U.S. farm policy. As early as 1926, Congress decreed that farm products should sell at a fair price. By "fair," Congress meant a price higher than the market equilibrium. The consequences of this policy are evident in Figure 15.4: *a price floor creates a* **market surplus.**

Once it set an above-equilibrium price for food, Congress had to find some way of disposing of the resultant food surplus. Initially, Congress proposed to get rid of this surplus by selling it abroad at world market prices. President Calvin Coolidge, a staunch opponent of government intervention, vetoed this legislation both times Congress passed it.

The notion of fair prices resurfaced in the Agricultural Adjustment Act of 1933. During the Great Depression farmers were going bankrupt in droves. To help them, Congress sought to restore the purchasing power of farm products to the 1909–1914 level (see Figure 15.3). The farm–nonfarm price relationships of 1909–1914 were regarded by Congress as fair and came to be known as **parity** prices. If parity prices could be restored, Congress reasoned, farm incomes would improve.

market surplus: The amount by which the quantity supplied exceeds the quantity demanded at a given price; excess supply.

parity: The relative price of farm products in the period 1910–1914.

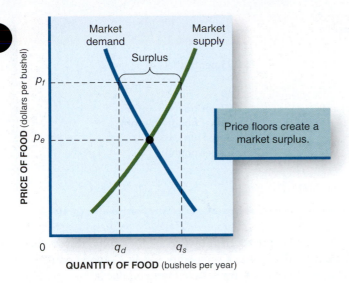

FIGURE 15.4
Fair Prices and Market Surplus

The interaction of market supply and demand establishes an equilibrium price (p_e) for any product, including food. If a higher price (p_f) is set, the quantity of food supplied (q_s) will be larger than the quantity demanded (q_d). Hence attempts to establish a "fair" (higher) price for farm products must cope with resultant market surpluses.

Supply Restrictions

The goal of parity pricing couldn't be attained without altering market supply and demand in some way.

Set-Asides. The easiest way to increase farm prices without creating a surplus is to reduce the production of food. Congress does this by paying farmers for voluntary reductions in crop acreage. These **acreage set-asides** shift the food supply curve to the left. In 2007 nearly 40 *million* acres of farmland—one-sixth of the nation's wheat, corn, sorghum, rice, and cotton acreage—were idled by government set-asides. If farmers don't agree to these set-asides, they can't participate in the price support programs.

acreage set-aside: Land withdrawn from production as part of policy to increase crop prices.

Dairy Termination Program. To prop up dairy prices, the federal government also started a Dairy Termination Program in 1985. This is analogous to a set-aside program. In this case, however, the government pays dairy farmers to slaughter or export dairy cattle. Between 1985 and 1987 the government paid dairy farmers over $1 billion to "terminate" 1.6 million cows. The reduction in dairy herds boosted prices for milk and other dairy products.

Marketing Orders. The federal government also permits industry groups to limit the quantity of output brought to market. By themselves, individual farmers can't raise the market price by withholding output. If they act collectively, however, they can. If a quantity greater than authorized is actually grown, the "surplus" is disposed of by individual farmers. In the 1980s these *marketing orders* forced farmers to waste each year roughly 500 million lemons, 1 billion oranges, 70 million pounds of raisins, 70 million pounds of almonds, and millions of plums, nectarines, and other fruits. This wholesale destruction of crops gave growers market power and kept farm prices artificially high.

Import Quotas. The market supply of farm products is also limited by import restrictions. Imports of sugar, dairy products, cotton, and peanuts are severely limited by import quotas. Imports of beef are limited by "voluntary" export limits in foreign countries. Import taxes (duties) limit the foreign supply of other farm products.

Demand Distortions

While trying to limit the *supply* of farm products, the government also inflates the *demand* for selected farm products.

TABLE 15.2
2010–2012 Loan Rates

The Commodity Credit Corporation lends money to farmers at fixed "loan rates" that are implicit price floors. If the market price falls below the CCC loan rate, the government keeps the crop as full payment of the loan or *pays* farmers a "loan deficiency payment."

Commodity	Loan Rate
Corn	$1.95 per bushel
Wheat	2.94
Soybeans	5.00
Cotton (upland)	0.52 per pound
Rice	6.50 per hundredweight
Peanuts	355 per ton
Honey	0.69 per pound

Source: U.S. Department of Agriculture (2011).

loan rate: The implicit price paid by the government for surplus crops taken as collateral for loans to farmers.

Government Stockpiles. An executive order signed by President Franklin Roosevelt in 1933 altered the demand for farm products. The Commodity Credit Corporation (CCC) created at that time became a buyer of last resort for selected farm products.

The CCC becomes a buyer of last resort through its loan programs. Farmers can borrow money from the CCC at **loan rates** set by Congress (see Table 15.2). In 2012, for example, a wheat farmer could borrow $2.94 in cash for every bushel of wheat he relinquished to the CCC. If the market price of wheat goes above $2.94, the farmer can sell the wheat in the open market, repay the CCC, and pocket the difference. If, instead, the price falls below the loan rate, the farmer can simply let the CCC keep the wheat and repay nothing. Hence, *whenever market prices are below CCC loan rates, the government ends up buying surplus crops.*

Figure 15.5 illustrates the effect of CCC price supports on individual farmers and the agricultural market. In the absence of price supports, competitive farmers would confront

(a) Impact of price supports on the individual farmer

(b) Impact of price supports on the agricultural market

FIGURE 15.5
The Impact of Price Supports

In the absence of price supports, the price of farm products would be determined by the intersection of market supply and demand. In this case, the equilibrium price would be p_e, as shown in part b. All individual farmers would confront this price and produce up to the point where MC = p_e, as in part a.

Government price supports raise the price to p_2. By offering to buy (or "loan") unlimited quantities at this price, the government shifts the demand curve facing each farmer upward. Individual farmers respond by increasing their output from q_1 to q_2. As farmers increase their output, a market surplus develops (part b).

a horizontal demand curve at price p_e, itself determined by the intersection of market supply and demand (in part *b*). The CCC's offer to buy ("loan") unlimited quantities at a higher price shifts the demand curve facing each farmer upward to the guaranteed price p_2. This higher price induces individual farmers to increase their rate of output from q_1 to q_2.

As farmers respond to price supports, the agriculture market is pushed out of equilibrium. At the support level p_2, more output is supplied than demanded. The market surplus created by government price supports creates an additional policy dilemma. ***The market surplus induced by price supports must be eliminated in one of three ways:***

- ***Government purchases*** and stockpiling of surplus food.
- ***Export sales.***
- ***Restrictions on supply.***

Government purchases of surplus crops have led to massive stockpiles of wheat, cotton, corn, and dairy products. At one time, the excess wheat was stored in old ammunition bunkers in Nebraska and scrubbed-out oil tanks in Texas. More than 130 million pounds of surplus nonfat dry milk is now stored in limestone caverns under Kansas City, and surplus cotton filled warehouses in the South for many years. Even today about one-fourth of U.S. farm output is destroyed or stored.

Deficiency Payments. To keep these stockpiles from growing further, Congress amended the CCC loan program in 2001. When market prices fall below CCC loan rates (Table 15.2), farmers don't have to turn over their crops to the government. Instead the government pays them a *loan deficiency payment* equal to the *difference* between the loan rate and the market price. The farmer can then sell his crop on the open market. By dumping excess supply on the market rather than stockpiling it, this policy tends to aggravate downward price swings.

Because farm prices are artificially high in the United States, export sales are sometimes difficult. As a result, the federal government must give away lots of food to poor nations and even subsidize exports to developed nations. The United States isn't alone in this regard: the European Union maintains even higher prices and subsidies (see the World View below).

WORLD VIEW

EU Farm Subsidies

In Europe, believe it or not, the subsidy for every cow is greater than the personal income of half the people in the world.

—Former British Prime Minister Margaret Thatcher

United States farm policy isn't unique. Most industrialized countries go to even greater lengths to protect domestic agriculture. For example, France, Germany, and Switzerland all shield their farmers from international competition while subsidizing their exports. Japan protects its inefficient rice producers, while the Netherlands subsidizes greenhouse vegetable farmers.

The motivations for farm subsidies are pretty much the same in every country in the world. Every country wants a secure source of food in the event of war. Most nations also want to maintain a viable farm sector, which is viewed as a source of social stability. Finally, politicians in every country must be responsive to a well-established and vocal political constituency.

The European Union (EU) imposes high tariffs on imported food, keeping domestic prices high. The member governments also agree to purchase any surplus production. To get rid of the surplus, the governments then subsidize exports. In 2000 direct EU farm subsidies exceeded $45 billion, triple the size of U.S. farm subsidies. All this protection costs the average EU consumer over $200 a year.

Analysis: Farm subsidies are common around the world. Such subsidies alter not only domestic output decisions but international trade patterns as well.

FIGURE 15.6
The Impact of Cost Subsidies

Cost subsidies lower the marginal cost of producing at any given rate of output, thereby shifting the marginal cost curve downward. The lower marginal costs make higher rates of output more profitable and thus increase output. At price p_2, lower marginal costs increase the farmer's profit-maximizing rate of output from q_2 to q_3.

Cost Subsidies

The market surplus induced by price supports is exacerbated by cost subsidies. Irrigation water, for example, is delivered to many farmers by federally funded reclamation projects. The price farmers pay for the water is substantially below the cost of delivering it; the difference amounts to a subsidy. This water subsidy costs taxpayers over $500 million a year. The Department of Agriculture also distributes an additional $150 million to $200 million a year to farmers to help defray the costs of fertilizer, drainage, and other production costs.

The federal government also provides basic research, insurance, marketing, grading, and inspection services to farmers at subsidized prices. All these subsidies serve to lower fixed or variable costs. Their net impact is to stimulate additional output, as illustrated in Figure 15.6.

Direct Income Support

Price supports, cost subsidies, and supply restrictions are designed to stabilize agricultural markets and ensure farmers an adequate income. As we've seen, however, they entail significant distortions of market outcomes. The Congressional Budget Office estimates that the milk price supports alone have increased retail dairy prices 3 to 6 percent, reduced consumption 1 to 5 percent, and encouraged excessive dairy production. Because of such distortions, direct income supports were authorized by the Agriculture and Consumer Protection Act of 1973. ***The advantage of direct income supports is that they achieve the goal of income security without distortions of market prices and output.***

countercyclical payment:
Income transfer paid to farmers for difference between target and market prices.

The principal form of direct income support is so-called **countercyclical payments.** Congress identifies specific "target prices" for selected crops. In 2012, the target price for wheat was $4.17 a bushel (see Table 15.3). If market prices fall below these targets, the government makes up the difference. Target prices are another form of price floor. Unlike the case of CCC loan rates, however, target prices don't trigger government purchases of surplus crops. The target price is used only to compute the amount of the "countercyclical" payment paid directly to farmers.

TABLE 15.3
2010–2012 Target Prices

Congress sets target prices for selected commodities. If the market price falls below the target price, a *deficiency payment* is made directly to the farmer.

Commodity	Target Price
Corn	$ 2.63 per bushel
Oats	1.79
Wheat	4.17
Soybeans	6.00
Cotton (upland)	0.7125 per pound
Rice	10.50 per hundredweight

Source: U.S. Department of Agriculture (2011).

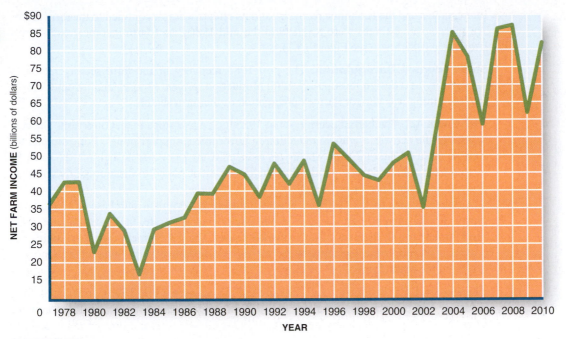

FIGURE 15.7
Net Farm Income, 1977–2010

Between 1979 and 1983 net farm income fell 64 percent. This decline was steeper than the income slide that occurred during the Great Depression (when net farm income fell 45 percent between 1929 and 1933). Farm incomes rose sharply from 1983 to 1989 but were unstable for the subsequent decade.

Source: *Economic Report of the President, 2011.*

THE SECOND FARM DEPRESSION, 1980–1986

With so many price supports, supply restrictions, cost subsidies, and income transfers, one would think that farming is a riskless and profitable business. But this hasn't been the case. Incomes remain low and unstable, especially for small farmers. In fact, the entire agricultural sector experienced another setback in the 1980s. In 1980 the net income of U.S. farmers fell 42 percent. As Figure 15.7 shows, farm incomes recovered somewhat in 1981 but then resumed their steep decline in 1982. In 1983 farmers' net income was only one-third the level of 1979. This income loss was steeper than that of the Great Depression. Real farm income was actually lower in 1983 than in 1933. This second depression of farm incomes accelerated the exodus of small farmers from agriculture, severely weakened rural economies, and bankrupted many farm banks and manufacturers of farm equipment and supplies.

The Cost Squeeze

This second depression of farm incomes was not caused by abrupt price declines. Prices for farm products increased slightly between 1979 and 1983. But production costs rose much faster, led by higher fuel, fertilizer, and interest rate costs. Average farm production costs rose 30 percent between 1979 and 1983 while the average price of farm products increased only 1.5 percent. As a result, the **profit** (net income) of farmers fell abruptly.

web analysis

For the latest information on farm income in the United States, visit **www.ers.usda.gov.** Click "Farm Economy."

profit: The difference between total revenue and total cost.

THE ECONOMY TOMORROW

FARMERS ON THE DOLE

To a large extent, the farm crisis of the 1980s had nothing to do with federal farm policy. The increase in oil prices was initiated by OPEC. Higher interest rates were a reflection of macroeconomic conditions. Likewise, the high value of the dollar was a response to U.S.

interest rates and the economic recovery, and its effects weren't confined to the farm sector. All these adverse forces were reversed in the mid-1980s, and farm incomes rose sharply from their 1983 lows (see Figure 15.7).

Steps toward Deregulation. The post-1983 recovery of the farm sector created an opportunity to redesign farm policy. With production, prices, exports, and incomes all rising, the timing was perfect for the deregulation of the farm sector.

1985 Farm Act. The Farm Security Act of 1985 took a few steps in that direction. The core feature of the act was a gradual reduction in government support prices. For example, the support price ("loan rate") for wheat was reduced from $3.30 per bushel in 1986 to $1.95 in 1990. By reducing the support price, the government hoped to discourage overproduction and recurrent market surpluses.

Another feature of the 1985 act was to limit the government purchase of market surpluses. Rather than buying surpluses at the guaranteed loan rate, the government encouraged farmers to sell their surpluses at market prices. The government then used deficiency payments to reimburse the farmers for the difference between the guaranteed (support) price and the market price.

The 1990 Act. By the time the authority of the 1985 act expired (in 1990), crop prices, farm incomes, and the price of farmland had all risen significantly, thanks to the continued expansion of the U.S. economy, declining oil and fertilizer costs, and strong foreign demand for U.S. farm products.

Despite the increased prosperity of farming during the 1985–1990 period, the basic structure of farm subsidies was continued in the 1990 Farm Act. Indeed, loan rates were *increased,* effectively raising the price floor for farm products. At the same time, however, Congress reduced the amount of set-aside acreage by 15 percent. It also gave farmers more discretion to farm on unsubsidized acreage. Target prices were reduced and frozen for five years.

The net effect of the 1990 legislation was to move farming another small step closer to market realities. A bit more acreage was freed from government regulation, target prices were set closer to market prices, and more market surpluses were sold rather than stored in government warehouses.

The 1996 Freedom to Farm Act. In 1996 Congress moved farmers considerably further down the road toward deregulation with two radical changes in farm policy. The first change was the phaseout of deficiency payments. Target prices (Table 15.3) and their associated deficiency payments were terminated. In their place, farmers were offered "market transition payments." The size of the transition payments wasn't dependent on commodity prices but instead was fixed by Congress for a period of seven years. In this way, Congress focused on stabilizing farm *incomes* rather than farm *prices.* In 2002 all such income support was scheduled to end, leaving farmers the "freedom to farm" (off the dole).

The 1996 act also eliminated many restrictions on acreage set-asides. Up to 36.4 million acres were still eligible for "production flexibility contract payments" (set-asides). But farmers no longer had to keep set-aside acreage completely idle or grow only specific commodities. Markets, not politicians, would decide what farmers should grow.

Back from the Brink. At first farmers loved the 1996 policy reforms. In the 1996–1997 crop year, commodity prices were up and farm incomes were at an all-time high (Figure 15.7). Yet farmers were still getting billions of dollars in taxpayer subsidies. What a great deal!

The Asian Crisis. Then the farm economy turned sour again. The Asian crisis that began in July 1997 was the principal cause. When the currencies of Thailand, Korea, Indonesia, Malaysia, and other Asian nations fell in value, the foreign price of U.S. farm output soared. When the economies of these Asian nations stumbled into recession, their ability to buy American farm products was further diminished. As a result, U.S. farm exports fell sharply during 1997 and 1998, and farm prices tumbled.

Renewed Subsidies. When farm prices and incomes plunged, farmers again demanded federal aid. Just prior to the November 1998 elections, Congress increased market transition payments by 50 percent. Congress also authorized the early payment of $5 billion in

web analysis

See the latest U.S. House of Representatives Agriculture Committee legislation at **www.house.gov/agriculture.**

farm aid not due until 1999. Finally, Congress approved $500 million in "disaster payments"—a new form of aid—to offset falling prices and exports.

The 2002 Farm Act. The intent of the 1996 Farm Act ostensibly had been to wean farmers off the dole, making them more reliant on market forces. That isn't how it worked out, however. When the market for farm products went bad, farmers expected more federal aid, not more freedom to farm. They got that help in the 2002 Farm Act. Congress not only increased existing farm subsidies but also created new ones for sugar growers, peanut farmers, hog operators, and even horse breeders.

The 2007 Farm Act. Rising commodity prices in 2006–2007 created another opportunity to wean farmers off the dole. As alternatives to so many subsidies, critics suggested that farmers make greater use of crop insurance and futures markets to stabilize their incomes. But those proposals never got much of a hearing. With the 2008 presidential elections on the horizon, no politician wanted to offend the farm bloc, least of all the farmers in Iowa, where the first presidential primary vote is held. There was little enthusiasm for reducing, much less eliminating, farm subsidies. In fact, the 2007 Farm Act increased farm subsidies and extended them to specialty crops.

The 2012 Farm Act. The 2007 Farm Act was set to expire in 2012. The timing seemed particularly bad for farm subsidies. Lawmakers in Washington were desperately looking for ways to cut outsized budget deficits. President Obama had already pledged to end subsidies to millionaire farmers. Farm prices and profits were at near-record levels. And critics were questioning the economic basis for any subsidies (see the accompanying News). But the political reality was not so conducive to reform: farm subsidies are received in 364 of the nation's 435 congressional districts and are significant in a dozen politically important states. With the 2012 presidential elections on the horizon, the odds were good that farmers would still be on the dole in the economy tomorrow.

Moo . . .

web analysis

To learn more about the 2007 Farm Act visit **www.usda.gov/ farmbill.**

IN THE NEWS

Farm Subsidies Ripe for Reform

Lawmakers seeking to rein in the spending spree that has produced a staggering $1.4 trillion budget deficit are ignoring one of the ripest sources of potential savings: farm subsidies. . . .

Farm subsidies are supposed to protect farmers against poverty and instability. This Norman Rockwell image aside, farm subsidies are actually America's largest corporate welfare program.

The average farmer earns more than $83,000 annually (nearly 20 percent above the national average), according to the Department of Agriculture. Commercial farmers, who receive the majority of subsidies, report an average net income of $170,000, and a net worth close to $1 million. . . .

Farm subsidy advocates often respond that farms could not survive without large subsidies. Nonsense. Producers of just five crops—wheat, cotton, corn, soybeans, and rice—receive nearly all farm subsidies. In fact, only one-third of the $390 billion in annual agricultural production is directly subsidized. All other farmers—including growers of fruits, vegetables, livestock, and poultry—receive nearly nothing.

This begs the question: If farm subsidies are necessary to produce an adequate food supply with stable prices and thriving farmers, why haven't the growers of nonsubsidized crops experienced these problems? . . .

Yet the prices and supplies of these products are relatively stable, and the farmers' incomes are just as high as those of subsidized farmers. The free market already works for all other farm production. Surely it can work for producers of wheat, cotton, corn, soybeans, and rice.

—Brian Riedl

Source: Editorial, "Riedl: Farm Subsidies Ripe for Reform," *The Washington Times*, March 29, 2011. Used with permission via icopyright.

Analysis: Critics of farm subsidies point out that nonsubsidized crops are subject to the same weather and market forces as subsidized crops, but seem to fare at least as well.

SUMMARY

- The agricultural sector has a highly competitive structure, with approximately 2 million farms. Many crops are regulated, however, by government restrictions and subsidies.   LO15-1
- Most farm output is produced by the small percentage of large farms that enjoy economies of scale. Most small farmers rely on nonfarm employment for their income.   LO15-1
- In a free market, farm prices tend to decline over time because of increasing productivity and low income elasticity of demand. Variations in harvests, combined with a low price elasticity of demand, make farm prices unstable.   LO15-1
- Most of today's farm policies originated during the Great Depression in response to low farm prices and incomes.   LO15-3
- The government uses price supports and cost subsidies to raise farm prices and profits. These policies cause resource

- misallocations and create market surpluses of specific commodities.   LO15-2
- Direct income support in the form of countercyclical payments also generates excess supply but can be targeted more to income needs.   LO15-2
- Farm incomes declined sharply between 1979 and 1983, causing a second depression in the farm sector. The drop was caused by sharp increases in fuel, fertilizer, and interest costs. The Asian crisis that began in 1997 caused another U.S. farm crisis.   LO15-1
- The 1996 Farm Act called for a phaseout of farm subsidies. Falling prices and incomes during 1997–2001 stalled and eventually reversed that process, as reflected in the 2007 Farm Act.   LO15-2
- Government regulation not only risks design flaws but creates moral hazards that may reduce efficiency.   LO15-3

Key Terms

market power
barriers to entry
economic profit
price elasticity of demand

income elasticity of demand
market surplus
parity
acreage set-aside

loan rate
countercyclical payment
profit

Questions for Discussion

1. Would the U.S. economy be better off without government intervention in agriculture? Who would benefit? Who would lose?   LO15-3
2. Are large price movements inevitable in agricultural markets? What other mechanisms might be used to limit such movement?   LO15-1
3. Why doesn't the United States just give its crop surpluses to poor countries? What problems might such an approach create?   LO15-3
4. Farmers can eliminate the uncertainties of fluctuating crop prices by selling their crops in futures markets (agreeing to a fixed price for crops to be delivered in the future). Who gains or loses from this practice?   LO15-2

5. Why do farmers prefer price supports to direct payments?   LO15-2
6. How do farmers of unsubsidized crops survive and thrive (News, p. 337)?   LO15-2
7. You need a government permit (allotment) to grow tobacco. Who gains or loses from such regulation?   LO15-2
8. Why are the price and income elasticities for food so low?   LO15-1
9. How have farmers increased milk production per cow so much (p. 326)? How does this affect milk prices?   LO15-1
10. What changes to farm subsidies were included in the 2012 Farm Act (Google the news)? Did they move farmers closer to free markets or not?   LO15-2

 web activities to accompany this chapter can be found on the Online Learning Center: http://www.mhhe.com/schiller13e

 mobile app Visit your mobile app store and download the Schiller: Study Econ app *today*!

LO15-2 1. Suppose the market price of corn is $1.50 per bushel.
   (a) Would a farmer sell corn to the market or to the government (CCC)? (See Table 15.2.)   _____
   (b) How much of a countercyclical payment per bushel would the farmer receive? (See Table 15.3.)   _____
   (c) If the market price rose to $2, what would the farmer do with his corn?   _____

LO15-1 2. Suppose that consumers' incomes increase 15 percent, which results in a 0.5 percent increase in consumption of farm goods at current prices. What is the income elasticity of demand for farm goods?   _____

LO15-3 3. Assume that the unregulated supply schedule for milk is the following:

Price (per pound)	5¢	7¢	9¢	11¢	13¢
Quantity supplied (billions of pounds per year)	43	53	63	73	83

   (a) Draw the supply and demand curves for milk, assuming that the demand for milk is perfectly inelastic and consumers will buy 53 billion pounds of it. What is the equilibrium price?   _____
   (b) Suppose that the farmers' response to the government's offer to pay them for not producing milk results in the following supply schedule:

Price (per pound)	5¢	7¢	9¢	11¢	13¢
Quantity supplied (billions of pounds per year)	23	33	43	53	63

   (c) Draw this new supply curve on the same set of axes as the supply curve prior to the government's action. What is the equilibrium price following the government's action?   _____
   (d) How much more money would consumers pay for the 53 billion pounds of milk because of the higher equilibrium price?   _____
   (e) Shade the area in your diagram that represents how much more consumers will pay because of the government-sponsored cutbacks.

LO15-3 4. Suppose there are 100 grain farmers, each with identical cost structures as shown in the following tables:

Production Costs (per Farm)		Demand	
Output (Bushels per Day)	Total Cost (per Day)	Price (per Bushel)	Quantity Demanded (Bushels per Day)
0	$ 5	$1	600
1	7	2	500
2	10	3	400
3	14	4	300
4	19	5	200
5	25	6	100
6	33	7	50

Under these circumstances, graph the market supply and demand.
(a) What is the equilibrium price for grain?   _____
(b) How much grain will be produced at the equilibrium price?   _____
(c) How much total profit will each farmer earn at that price?   _____
(d) If the government gives farmers a cost subsidy equal to $1 a bushel, what will happen to
                                                          (i) Output?   _____
                                                           (ii) Price?   _____
                                                          (iii) Profit?   _____
(e) What will happen to total output if the government additionally guarantees a price of
$5 per bushel?   _____
(f) What price is required to sell this output?   _____
(g) What is the cost to the government in d?   _____
(h) Show your answers on the accompanying graph.

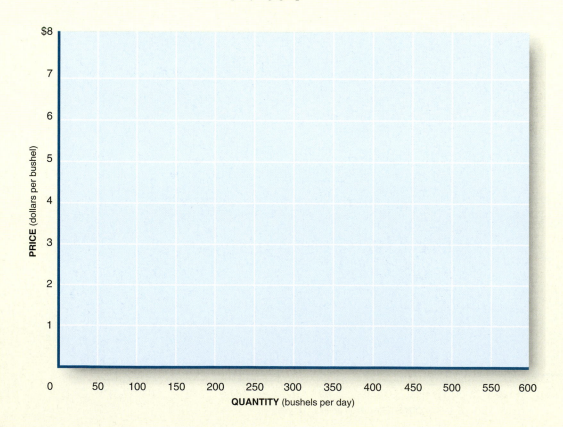

Factor Markets: Basic Theory

Factor markets operate like product markets, with supply and demand interacting to determine prices and quantities. In factor markets, however, resource inputs rather than products are exchanged. Those exchanges determine the wages paid to workers and the rent, interest, and profits paid to other inputs. The micro theories presented in Chapters 16 through 18 explain how those factor payments are determined.

The Labor Market

LEARNING OBJECTIVES

After reading this chapter, you should know

LO16-1. What factors shape labor supply and demand.

LO16-2. How market wage rates are established.

LO16-3. How wage floors alter labor market outcomes.

In 2010, **Larry Ellison**, the CEO of Oracle, was paid $84 million for his services. Reese Witherspoon was fetching $20 million per movie. And LeBron James had endorsement contracts worth more than $150 million (see Chapter 5). Yet the president of the United States was paid only $400,000. And the secretary who typed the manuscript of this book was paid just $19,000. What accounts for these tremendous disparities in earnings?

Why does the average college graduate earn over $50,000 while the average high school graduate earns just $27,000? Are such disparities simply a reward for enduring four years of college, or do they reflect real differences in talent?

Surely we can't hope to explain these earnings disparities on the basis of the willingness to work. After all, my secretary would be more than willing to work day and night for

$84 million per year. For that matter, so would I. Accordingly, the earnings disparities can't be attributed to differences in the quantity of labor supplied. If we're going to explain why some people earn a great deal of income while others earn very little, we must consider both the *supply* and the *demand* for labor. In this regard, the following questions arise:

- **How do people decide how much time to spend working?**
- **What determines the wage rate an employer is willing to pay?**
- **Why are some workers paid so much and others so little?**

To answer these questions, we must examine the behavior of labor *markets*.

LABOR SUPPLY

The following two ads recently appeared in the campus newspaper of a well-known university:

> Will do ANYTHING for money: able-bodied liberal-minded male needs money, will work to get it. Have car. Call Josh 765-3210.

> Web architect. Experienced website designer. Looking for part-time or consulting position on or off campus. Please call Danielle, ext. 0872, 9–5.

Although placed by individuals of very different talents, the ads clearly expressed Josh's and Danielle's willingness to work. Although we don't know how much money they were asking for their respective talents or whether they ever found jobs, we can be sure that they were prepared to take a job at some wage rate. Otherwise they wouldn't have paid for the ads in the "Jobs Wanted" column of their campus newspaper.

The advertised willingness to work represents a **supply of labor.** These individuals are offering to sell their time and talents to anyone who's willing to pay the right price. Their explicit offers are similar to those of anyone who looks for a job. Job seekers who check the current job openings at the student employment office, tap into Monster.com, or e-mail résumés to potential employers are demonstrating a willingness to accept employment—that is, to *supply* labor. The 3,700 people who applied for jobs at a New York City job fair (see the accompanying News) were also offering to supply labor.

> **labor supply:** The willingness and ability to work specific amounts of time at alternative wage rates in a given time period, *ceteris paribus.*

IN THE NEWS

Job Fairs: Long Lines and a Ray of Hope

More Than 3,700 People Descended upon 92 Employers at a New York Job Fair. Some Were Happy Just to Talk to a Recruiter Face-to-Face.

NEW YORK (CNNMoney.com)—Howard La waited 90 minutes in line for the chance to spend three minutes with a recruiter from Charles Schwab.

La, who lost his human resources job at Wall Street firm Goldman Sachs in November, had prepared his spiel. The Hoboken, New Jersey, resident told the recruiter how he could help reevaluate the brokerage's call centers to be more efficient. He walked away upbeat, with the promise that his résumé would be reviewed.

"It was worth the hour-and-a-half wait to speak with him," said La, 26. "He said he'll pass my résumé to his manager and he sounded genuine."

La was among the 3,700 people who packed a midtown Manhattan hotel ballroom Thursday for a chance to meet with representatives from more than 90 companies at a job fair put on by Monster.com.

— Tami Luhby

Source: CNNMoney.com, March 6, 2009. © 2009 Time Inc. Used under license.

Analysis: The quantity of labor supplied at any given wage rate depends on the value of leisure and the desire for income. These New Yorkers were all willing to supply labor.

Our first concern in this chapter is to explain these labor supply decisions. How do people decide how many hours to supply at any given wage rate? Do people try to maximize their total wages? If they did, we'd all be holding three jobs and sleeping on the commuter bus. Since most of us don't behave this way, other motives must be present.

Income vs. Leisure

The reward for working comes in two forms: (1) the intrinsic satisfaction of working and (2) a paycheck. MBA grads say they care more about the intrinsic satisfaction than the pay (see the News on the next page). They also get huge paychecks, however. Those big paychecks are explained in part by the quantity of labor supplied: MBA grads often end up

IN THE NEWS

Challenging Work and Corporate Responsibility Will Lure MBA Grads

STANFORD GRADUATE SCHOOL OF BUSINESS—A survey of 759 graduating MBAs at 11 top business schools reveals that the future business leaders rank corporate social responsibility high on their list of values, and they are willing to sacrifice a significant part of their salaries to find an employer whose thinking is in sync with their own.

The study by David Montgomery and Catherine Ramus of UC Santa Barbara examines the trade-offs students are willing to make when selecting a potential employer. They found that intellectual challenge ranked number one in desirable job attributes, while money and location were essentially tied for second, each roughly 80 percent as important as the most important factor.

The researchers found that the students expected to earn an average of $103,650 a year at their first job. Nearly all (97.3 percent) said they would be willing to make a financial sacrifice to work for a company that exhibited all four characteristics of social responsibility. They said they would sacrifice an average of $14,902 a year, or 14.4 percent of their expected salary.

What MBAs at Some Top Schools Earn

School	Starting Salaries in 2010
Harvard	$161,887
Stanford	164,863
University of Pennsylvania	160,848
Columbia	160,679
MIT	154,058
Dartmouth	152,802
Chicago	151,758
University of California, Berkley	140,478

Global MBA Rankings 2010, *Financial Times*, www.ft.com. © The Financial Times Ltd. 2010. All rights reserved.

Source: Stanford Graduate School of Business. Used with permission.

Analysis: The quantity of labor supplied depends on the intrinsic satisfaction of working and the wages paid. MBA grads apparently work long hours for both high wages and job satisfaction. Would they work just as hard for *less* pay?

working 60 or more hours a week. The reason people are willing to work so many hours is that they want more income.

Not working obviously has some value, too. In part, we need some nonwork time just to recuperate from working. We also want some leisure time to watch television, go to a soccer game, or enjoy other goods and services we've purchased.

Since both working and *not* working are rewarding, we have a dilemma: the more time we spend working, the more income we have but also less time to enjoy it. Working, like all activities, involves an opportunity cost: *the opportunity cost of working is the amount of leisure time that must be given up in the process.*

This inevitable trade-off between labor and leisure explains the shape of individual labor supply curves. As we work more hours, our leisure time becomes more scarce—and thus more valuable. Hence **higher wage rates are required to compensate for the increasing opportunity cost of labor** (forgone leisure). We'll work more—supply a larger quantity of labor—only if offered a higher wage rate. This is reflected in the upward slope of the labor supply curve in Figure 16.1.

The upward slope of the labor supply curve is reinforced with the changing value of income. Those first few dollars earned on the job are really precious, especially if you have bills to pay. As you work and earn more, however, your most urgent needs will be satisfied. You may still want more things, but the urgency of your consumption desires is likely to diminish. Another dollar of wages doesn't mean as much. In other words, **the marginal utility of income may decline as you earn more.** If this happens, you may not be willing to work more hours unless offered a still higher wage rate.

FIGURE 16.1
The Supply of Labor

The quantity of any good or service offered for sale typically increases as its price rises. Labor supply responds in the same way. At the wage rate w_1, the quantity of labor supplied is q_1 (point *A*). At the higher wage w_2, workers are willing to work more hours per week—that is, to supply a larger quantity of labor (q_2).

The upward slope of an individual's labor supply curve is therefore explained by the fact that as hours worked increase,

- The value of leisure time increases.
- The marginal utility of income decreases.

Money isn't necessarily the only thing that motivates people to work. People *do* turn down higher-paying jobs in favor of lower-wage jobs that they like. Many parents forgo high-wage "career" jobs to have more flexible hours and time at home. Volunteers offer their services just for the sense of contributing to their communities; they don't need a paycheck. Even MBA graduates say they're motivated more by the challenge of high-paying jobs than the money (see the previous News). But money almost always makes a difference: *People do supply more labor when offered higher wages.*

A Backward Bend?

The force that drives people up the labor supply curve is the lust for more income. Higher wages enable people to buy more goods and services. To achieve higher levels of consumption, people decide to *substitute* labor for leisure. This is the **substitution effect of higher wages.**

At some point, however, higher wages may not be so persuasive. Working added hours just to accumulate a few more toys may not seem so compelling. In fact, higher wages might create the opportunity to work *less*—without giving up any toys. Muhammad Ali once announced that he wouldn't spend an hour in the ring for less than $1 million and would box *less,* not more, as the pay for his fights exceeded $3 million. For him, the added income from one championship fight was so great that he felt he didn't have to fight more to satisfy his income and consumption desires.

A low-wage worker might also respond to higher wage rates by working *less,* not more. People receiving very low wages (such as migrant workers, household help, and babysitters) have to work really long hours just to pay the rent. The increased income made possible by higher wage rates might permit them to work *fewer* hours. These *negative* labor supply responses to increased wage rates are referred to as the **income effect of higher wages.**

The conflict between income and substitution effects shapes an individual's labor supply curve. The *substitution effect* of higher wages encourages people to work more hours. The *income effect,* on the other hand, allows them to reduce work hours without losing income. If substitution effects dominate, the labor supply curve will be upward-sloping. *If income effects outweigh substitution effects, an individual will supply **less** labor at higher wages.* This kind of reaction is illustrated by the backward-bending portion of the supply curve in Figure 16.2.

substitution effect of higher wages: An increased wage rate encourages people to work more hours (to substitute labor for leisure).

income effect of higher wages: An increased wage rate allows a person to reduce hours worked without losing income.

FIGURE 16.2

The Backward-Bending Supply Curve

Increases in wage rates make additional hours of work more valuable but also less necessary. Higher wage rates increase the quantity of labor supplied as long as substitution effects outweigh income effects. At the point where income effects begin to outweigh substitution effects, the labor supply curve starts to bend backward.

Backward-bending labor supply curves are more the exception than the rule. Most Americans do want more leisure. But given the choice between more leisure or more income, Americans choose added income (see the World View below). In other words, substitution effects outweigh income effects in the U.S. labor force. This explains why Americans work such long hours despite their comparatively high incomes. Workers in Mexico and India, by contrast, appear to covet more leisure rather than more income.

WORLD VIEW

Your Money or Your Life

Would you rather have more time or more money? Here's how people in six countries answered.

Analysis: Despite already high incomes, Americans are still willing to sacrifice leisure for more income; *substitution effects* outweigh *income effects.*

MARKET SUPPLY

market supply of labor:
The total quantity of labor that workers are willing and able to supply at alternative wage rates in a given time period, *ceteris paribus.*

The **market supply of labor** represents the sum of all individual labor supply decisions. Although some individuals have backward-bending supply curves, these negative responses to higher wages are swamped by positive responses from the 160 million individuals who participate in the U.S. labor market. As a result, the *market* supply curve is upward-sloping.

The upward slope of the labor supply curve doesn't imply that we'll all be working longer hours in the future. As time passes, the labor supply curve can *shift.* And it will whenever one of the underlying determinants of supply changes. *The determinants of labor supply include*

- *Tastes* (for leisure, income, and work).
- *Income and wealth.*
- *Expectations* (for income or consumption).
- *Prices* of consumer goods.
- *Taxes.*

These shift factors determine the position and slope of the labor supply curve at any point in time. As time passes, however, these underlying determinants change, causing the labor supply curve to shift. This has evidently happened. In 1890 the average U.S. worker was employed 60 hours a week at a wage rate of 20 cents an hour. In 2011 the average worker worked fewer than 34 hours per week at a wage rate of $18 an hour. Contributing to this long-run leftward shift has been (1) the spectacular rise in living standards (a change in income and wealth), (2) the growth of income transfer programs that provide economic security when one isn't working (a change in income and expectations), and (3) the increased diversity and attractiveness of leisure activities (a change in tastes and other goods).

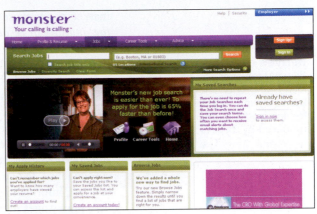

Courtesy of Monster.com

Analysis: Monster.com brings together the supply and demand for labor.

Elasticity of Labor Supply

Despite the evident *long*-run shifts of the labor supply curve, workers still respond positively to higher wage rates in the *short* run. To measure the resulting movements along the labor supply curve, we use the familiar concept of elasticity. Specifically, the **elasticity of labor supply** is the percentage change in the quantity of labor supplied divided by the percentage change in the wage rate:

$$\text{Elasticity of labor supply} = \frac{\%\ \text{change in quantity of labor supplied}}{\%\ \text{change in wage rate}}$$

The elasticity of labor tells us how much *more* labor will be available if a higher wage is offered. If the elasticity of labor is 0.2, a 10 percent increase in wage rates will induce a 2 percent increase in the quantity of labor supplied.

The actual responsiveness of workers to a change in wage rates depends on the determinants of labor supply. Time is also important for labor supply elasticity because individuals can't always adjust their schedules or change jobs instantaneously.

> **elasticity of labor supply:** The percentage change in the quantity of labor supplied divided by the percentage change in wage rate.

Institutional Constraints

The labor supply curve and its related elasticities tell us how much time people would like to allocate to work. We must recognize, however, that people seldom have the opportunity to adjust their hours of employment at will. True, a Bill Gates or a Lady Gaga can easily choose to work more or fewer hours. Most workers, however, face more rigid choices. They must usually choose to work at a regular job for eight hours a day, five days a week, or not to work at all. Very few firms are flexible enough to accommodate a desire to work only between the hours of 11 a.m. and 3 p.m. on alternate Thursdays. Adjustments in work hours are more commonly confined to choices about overtime work or secondary jobs (moonlighting) and vacation and retirement. Families may also alter the labor supply by varying the number of family members sent into the labor force at any given time. Students, too, can often adjust their work hours. The flow of immigrants into the U.S. labor market also increases when U.S. wages rise.

LABOR DEMAND

Regardless of how many people are *willing* to work, it's up to employers to decide how many people will *actually* work. That is, there must be a **demand for labor.** What determines the number of workers employers are willing to hire at various wage rates?

> **demand for labor:** The quantities of labor employers are willing and able to hire at alternative wage rates in a given time period, *ceteris paribus*.

Derived Demand

In earlier chapters we emphasized that employers are profit maximizers. In their quest for maximum profits, firms seek the rate of output at which marginal revenue equals marginal cost. Once they've identified the profit-maximizing rate of output, firms enter factor markets to purchase the required amounts of labor, equipment, and other resources. Thus *the quantity of resources purchased by a business depends on the firm's expected sales and output.* In this sense, the demand for factors of production, including labor, is a derived demand; it's derived from the demand for goods and services.

Consider the plight of strawberry pickers. Strawberry pickers are paid very low wages and are employed only part of the year. But their plight can't be blamed on the greed of the strawberry growers. Strawberry growers, like most producers, would love to sell more strawberries at higher prices. If they did, the growers would hire more pickers and might even pay them higher wages. But the growers must contend with the market demand for strawberries: consumers aren't willing to buy more strawberries at higher prices. As a consequence, the growers can't afford to hire more pickers or pay them higher wages. In contrast, information technology (IT) firms are always looking for more workers and offer very high wages to get them. This helps explain why college students who major in engineering, math, or computer science get paid a lot more than philosophy majors. IT specialists benefit from the growing demand for Internet services, while philosophy majors suffer because the search for the meaning of life is not a growth industry.

The principle of derived demand suggests that if consumers really want to improve the lot of strawberry pickers, they should eat more strawberries. An increase in the demand for strawberries will motivate growers to plant more berries and hire more labor to pick them. Until then, the plight of the pickers isn't likely to improve.

The Labor Demand Curve

The number of strawberry pickers hired by the growers isn't completely determined by the demand for strawberries. The number of pickers hired will also depend on the wage rate. That is, *the quantity of labor demanded depends on its price (the wage rate).* In general, we expect that strawberry growers will be *willing to hire* more pickers at low wages than at higher wages. Hence the demand for labor looks very much like the demand for any good or service (see Figure 16.3).

Marginal Physical Product

The fact that the demand curve for labor slopes downward doesn't tell us what quantity of labor will be hired. Nor does it tell us what wage rate will be paid. To answer such questions, we need to know what determines the particular shape and position of the labor demand curve.

A strawberry grower will be willing to hire another picker only if that picker contributes more to output than he or she costs. Growers, as rational businesspeople, recognize that *every* sale and *every* expenditure have some impact on total profits. Hence the truly profit-maximizing grower will evaluate each picker's job application in terms of the applicant's potential contribution to profits.

derived demand: The demand for labor and other factors of production results from (depends on) the demand for final goods and services produced by these factors.

FIGURE 16.3
The Demand for Labor

The higher the wage rate, the smaller the quantity of labor demanded (*ceteris paribus*). At the wage rate W_1, only L_1 of labor is demanded. If the wage rate falls to W_2, a larger quantity of labor (L_2) will be demanded. The labor demand curve obeys the law of demand.

Demand for labor

More workers are sought at lower wages.

W_1 ... A

W_2 ... B

WAGE RATE (dollars per hour)

L_1 L_2

QUANTITY OF LABOR (hours per month)

Fortunately, a strawberry picker's contribution to output is easy to measure; it's the number of boxes of strawberries he or she picks. Suppose for the moment that Marvin, a college dropout with three summers of experience as a canoe instructor, is able to pick five boxes per hour. These five boxes represent Marvin's **marginal physical product (MPP).** In other words, Marvin's MPP is the *addition* to total output that occurs when the grower hires him for an hour:

marginal physical product (MPP): The change in total output associated with one additional unit of input.

$$\frac{\text{Marginal}}{\text{physical product}} = \frac{\text{Change in total output}}{\text{Change in quantity of labor}}$$

Marginal physical product establishes an *upper* limit to the grower's willingness to pay. Clearly the grower can't afford to pay Marvin more than five boxes of strawberries for an hour's work; the grower won't pay Marvin more than he produces.

Marginal Revenue Product

Most strawberry pickers don't want to be paid in strawberries. At the end of a day in the fields, the last thing a picker wants to see is another strawberry. Marvin, like the rest of the pickers, wants to be paid in cash. To find out how much cash he might be paid, we need to know what a box of strawberries is worth. This is easy to determine. The market value of a box of strawberries is simply the price at which the grower can sell it. Thus Marvin's contribution to output can be measured by either marginal physical product (five boxes per hour) or the dollar value of that product.

The dollar value of a worker's contribution to output is called **marginal revenue product (MRP).** Marginal revenue product is the *change* in total revenue that occurs when more labor is hired:

marginal revenue product (MRP): The change in total revenue associated with one additional unit of input.

$$\frac{\text{Marginal}}{\text{revenue product}} = \frac{\text{Change in total revenue}}{\text{Change in quantity of labor}}$$

In Marvin's case, the "change in quantity of labor" is one extra hour of picking strawberries. The "change in total revenue" is the *value* of the extra five boxes of berries Marvin picks in that hour. If the grower can sell strawberries for $2 a box, Marvin's marginal revenue product is simply 5 boxes per hour × $2 per box, or $10 per hour. We could have come to the same conclusion by multiplying marginal *physical* product times *price:*

$$\text{MRP} = \text{MPP} \times p$$

or

$$\text{\$10 per hour} = \text{5 boxes per hour} \times \text{\$2 per box}$$

In compliance with the rule about not paying anybody more than he or she contributes, the profit-maximizing grower should be willing to pay Marvin *up to* $10 an hour. In other words, *marginal revenue product sets an upper limit to the wage rate an employer will pay.*

But what about a lower limit? Suppose the pickers aren't organized and Marvin is desperate for money. Under such circumstances, he might be willing to work—to supply labor—for only $4 an hour.

Should the grower hire Marvin for such a low wage? The profit-maximizing answer is obvious. If Marvin's marginal revenue product is $10 an hour and his wages are only $4 an hour, the grower will be eager to hire him. The difference between Marvin's marginal revenue product ($10) and his wage ($4) implies additional profits of $6 an hour. In fact, the grower will be so elated by the economics of this situation that he'll want to hire everybody he can find who's willing to work for $4 an hour. After all, if the grower can make $6 an hour by hiring Marvin, why not hire 1,000 pickers and accumulate profits at an even faster rate?

The Law of Diminishing Returns

The exploitative possibilities suggested by Marvin's picking are too good to be true. It isn't at all clear, for example, how the grower could squeeze 1,000 workers onto one acre of land and have any room left over for strawberry plants. There must be some limit to the profit-making potential of this situation.

A few moments' reflection on the absurdity of trying to employ 1,000 people to pick one acre of strawberries should be ample warning of the limits to profits here. You don't need two years of business school to recognize this. But some grasp of economics may help explain exactly why the grower's eagerness to hire additional pickers will begin to fade long before 1,000 are hired. The operative concept here is *marginal productivity*.

Diminishing MPP. The decision to hire Marvin originated in his marginal physical product—that is, the five boxes of strawberries he can pick in an hour's time. To assess the wisdom of hiring still more pickers, we have to **consider how total output will change if additional labor is employed.** To do so, we need to keep track of marginal physical product.

Figure 16.4 shows how strawberry output changes as additional pickers are hired. Marvin picks five boxes of strawberries per hour. Total output and his marginal physical

FIGURE 16.4
Diminishing Marginal Physical Product

The marginal physical product (MPP) of labor is the *increase* in total production that results when one additional worker is hired. MPP tends to fall as additional workers are hired in any given production process. This decline occurs because each worker has increasingly less of other factors (e.g., land) with which to work.

When the second worker (George) is hired, total output increases from 5 to 10 boxes per hour. Hence the second worker's MPP equals 5 boxes per hour. Thereafter, capital and land constraints diminish marginal physical product.

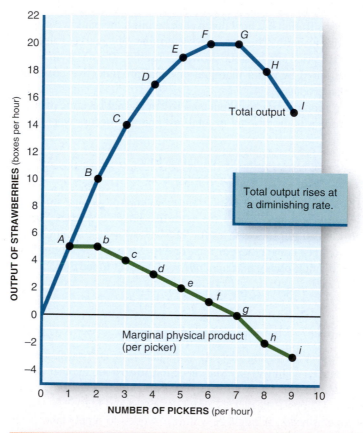

	Number of Pickers (per Hour)	Total Strawberry Output (Boxes per Hour)	Marginal Physical Product (Boxes per Hour)
A	1 (Marvin)	5	5
B	2 (George)	10	5
C	3	14	4
D	4	17	3
E	5	19	2
F	6	20	1
G	7	20	0
H	8	18	−2
I	9	15	−3

product are identical because he's initially the only picker employed. When the grower hires George, Marvin's old college roommate, we observe that the total output increases to 10 boxes per hour (point *B* in Figure 16.4). This figure represents another increase of five boxes per hour. Accordingly, we may conclude that George's *marginal physical product* is five boxes per hour, the same as Marvin's. Given such productivity, the grower will want to hire George and continue looking for more pickers.

As more workers are hired, total strawberry output continues to increase but not nearly as fast. Although the later hires work just as hard, the limited availability of land and capital constrain their marginal physical product. One problem is the number of boxes. There are only a dozen boxes, and the additional pickers often have to wait for an empty box. The time spent waiting depresses marginal physical product. The worst problem is space: as additional workers are crowded onto the one-acre patch, they begin to get in one another's way. The picking process is slowed, and marginal physical product is further depressed. Note that the MPP of the fifth picker is two boxes per hour, while the MPP of the sixth picker is only one box per hour. By the time we get to the seventh picker, marginal physical product actually falls to zero because no further increases in total strawberry output take place.

Things get even worse if the grower hires still more pickers. If eight pickers are employed, total output actually *declines*. The pickers can no longer work efficiently under such crowded conditions. The MPP of the eighth worker is *negative,* no matter how ambitious or hardworking this person may be. Figure 16.4 illustrates this decline in marginal physical product, beyond point *G* on the total output curve and beyond point *g* on the MPP curve.

Our observations on strawberry production are similar to those made in most industries. In the short run, the availability of land and capital is limited by prior investment decisions. Hence additional workers must share existing facilities. As a result, **the marginal physical product of labor eventually declines as the quantity of labor employed increases.** This is the **law of diminishing returns** we first encountered in Chapter 7. It's based on the simple observation that an increasing number of workers leaves each worker with less land and capital to work with. At some point, this "crowding" causes MPP to decline.

law of diminishing returns: The marginal physical product of a variable factor declines as more of it is employed with a given quantity of other (fixed) inputs.

Diminishing MRP. As marginal *physical* product diminishes, so does marginal *revenue* product (MRP). As noted earlier, marginal revenue product is the increase in the *value* of total output associated with an added unit of labor (or other input). In our example, it refers to the increase in strawberry revenues associated with one additional picker and is calculated as MPP $\times$ *p*.

The decline in marginal revenue product mirrors the drop in marginal physical product. Recall that a box of strawberries sells for $2. With this price and the output statistics in Figure 16.4, we can readily calculate marginal revenue product, as summarized in Table 16.1. As the growth of output diminishes, so does marginal revenue product. Marvin's marginal

Number of Pickers (per Hour)	Total Strawberry Output (in Boxes per Hour)	$\times$	Price of Strawberries (per Box)	$=$	Total Strawberry Revenue (per Hour)	Marginal Revenue Product
0	0		$2		0	—
1 (Marvin)	5		2		$10	$10
2 (George)	10		2		20	10
3	14		2		28	8
4	17		2		34	6
5	19		2		38	4
6	20		2		40	2
7	20		2		40	0
8	18		2		36	−4
9	15		2		30	−6

TABLE 16.1
Diminishing Marginal Revenue Product

Marginal revenue product (MRP) measures the change in total revenue that occurs when one additional worker is hired. At constant product prices, MRP equals MPP $\times$ price. Hence MRP declines along with MPP.

revenue product of $10 an hour has fallen to $6 by the time four pickers are employed and reaches zero when seven pickers are employed.[1]

A FIRM'S HIRING DECISION

The tendency of marginal revenue product to diminish will cool the strawberry grower's eagerness to hire 1,000 pickers. We still don't know, however, how many pickers will be hired.

The Firm's Labor Supply

Our earlier discussion of labor supply indicated that more workers are available only at higher wage rates. But that's true only for the *market* supply. A single producer may be able to hire an unlimited number of workers at the prevailing wage rate—if the firm is perfectly competitive in the labor market. This happens when the single firm (or farm) is just a bit player in a much larger labor market. Like small firms in big product markets, it has no market power. In other words, *a firm that's a perfect competitor in the labor market can hire all the labor it wants at the prevailing market wage.*

Let's assume that the strawberry grower is so small that his hiring decisions have no effect on local wages. As far as he's concerned, there's an unlimited supply of strawberry pickers willing to work for $4 an hour. His only decision is how many of these willing pickers to hire at that wage rate.

MRP = Firm's Labor Demand

Figure 16.5 provides the answer. We already know that the grower is eager to hire pickers whose marginal revenue product exceeds their wage. He'll therefore hire at least one worker at that wage because the MRP of the first picker is $10 an hour (point *A* in Figure 16.5). A second worker will be hired as well because that picker's MRP (point *B* in Figure 16.5) also exceeds the going wage rate. In fact, *the grower will continue hiring pickers until the MRP has declined to the level of the market wage rate.* Figure 16.5 indicates that this intersection (point *C*) occurs when five pickers are employed. Accordingly the grower will be willing to hire—will *demand*—five pickers if wages are $4 an hour.

FIGURE 16.5
The Marginal Revenue Product Curve Is the Labor Demand Curve

An employer is willing to pay a worker no more than the marginal revenue product. In this case, a grower would gladly hire a second worker because that worker's MRP (point *B*) exceeds the wage rate ($4). The sixth worker won't be hired at that wage rate, however, since the MRP (at point *D*) is less than $4. The MRP curve is the labor demand curve.

[1]Marginal revenue product would fall even faster if the price of strawberries declined as increasing quantities were supplied. We're assuming that the grower's output doesn't influence the market price of strawberries and hence that the grower is a *competitive* producer.

The folly of hiring more than five pickers is also apparent in Figure 16.5. The marginal revenue product of the sixth worker is only $2 an hour (point *D*). Hiring a sixth picker will cost more in wages ($4) than the picker brings in as revenue ($2). That makes no sense. The *maximum* number of pickers the grower will employ at prevailing wages is five (point *C*).

Equal Pay. The law of diminishing returns also implies that all five pickers will be paid the same wage. Once five pickers are employed, we can't say that any single picker is responsible for the observed decline in marginal revenue product. Marginal revenue product of labor diminishes because each worker has less capital and land to work with, not because the last worker hired is less able than the others. Accordingly, the "fifth" picker can't be identified as any particular individual. Once five pickers are hired, Marvin's MRP is no higher than any other picker's. *Each (identical) worker is worth no more than the marginal revenue product of the last worker hired, and all workers are paid the same wage rate.*

IN THE NEWS

Mauer, Twins Agree to Eight-Year, $184 Million Extension

Minneapolis (AP)—Joe Mauer is staying home.

The ALMVP agreed to an eight-year, $184 million contract extension with Minnesota on Sunday that includes a full no-trade clause, a massive deal that shows the Twins are no longer a frugal small-market club.

The deal covers the 2011–2018 seasons and is the fourth largest—both in its total value and average salary—in major league history. Starting next season, the all-star catcher will make an average of $23 million per season. . . .

The 26-year old Mauer. . . won three AL hitting titles and is considered one of the best defensive catchers in the game. . . .

Last year, after missing the first month of the season with a back injury, Mauer hit .365 with 28 home runs and 96 RBIs to help the Twins win the AL.

—Jon Krawczynski

Analysis: Marginal revenue product measures what a worker is worth to an employer. The Minnesota Twins expected a high MRP from Mauer.

The principles of marginal revenue product apply to baseball players as well as strawberry pickers. When the Minnesota Twins agreed to pay Joe Mauer $184 million (see the News above), they had his MRP in mind. Not only had he helped the Twins get to the American League Championships in 2010 (which boosted ticket sales, TV revenues, and advertising sales, and convinced the team's owners to build a new and larger stadium), but he also caused a spike in sales of souvenirs. The Twins decided Mauer's MRP justified his high salary.

Whatever the explanation for the disparity between the incomes of baseball players and strawberry pickers, the enormous gap between them seems awfully unfair. An obvious question then arises: Can't the number of pickers or their wages be increased?

Changes in Wage Rates

Suppose the government were to set a minimum wage for strawberry pickers at $6 an hour. At first glance this action would appear to boost the wages of pickers, who have been earning only $4 an hour. This isn't all good news for the strawberry pickers, however. *There's*

(a) Lower wages spur more hires.

(b) Higher productivity also spurs more hires.

FIGURE 16.6
Incentives to Hire

(a) Lower wage   If the wage rate drops, an employer will be willing to hire more workers, *ceteris paribus*. At $4 an hour, only five pickers per hour would be demanded (point *C*). If the wage rate dropped to $2 an hour, six pickers per hour would be demanded (point *D*).

(b) Higher productivity   If the marginal revenue product of labor improves, the employer will hire a greater quantity of labor at any given wage rate. The labor demand curve will shift up (from D_1 to D_2). In this case, an increase in MRP leads the employer to hire six workers (point *E*) rather than only five workers (point *C*) at $4 per hour.

a trade-off between wage rates and the number of workers demanded. If wage rates go up, growers will hire fewer pickers.

Figure 16.6*a* illustrates this trade-off. The grower's earlier decision to hire five pickers was based on a wage of $4 an hour (point *C*). If the wage jumps to $6 an hour, it no longer makes economic sense to keep five pickers employed. The MRP of the fifth worker is only $4 an hour. The grower will respond to higher wage rates by moving up the labor demand curve to point *G*. At point *G*, only four pickers are hired, and MRP again equals the wage rate. If more workers are to be hired, the wage rate must drop.

Changes in Productivity

The downward slope of the labor demand curve doesn't doom strawberry pickers to low wages. It does emphasize, however, the inevitable link between workers' productivity and wages. *To get higher wages without sacrificing jobs, productivity (MRP) must increase.*

Suppose Marvin and his friends all enroll in a local agricultural extension course and learn new methods of strawberry picking. With these new methods, the marginal physical product of each picker increases by one box per hour. With the price of strawberries still at $2 a box, this productivity improvement implies an increase in marginal *revenue* product of $2 per worker. This change causes an upward *shift* of the labor demand (MRP) curve, as in Figure 16.6*b*.

Notice how the improvement in productivity has altered the value of strawberry pickers. The MRP of the fifth picker is now $6 an hour (point *F*) rather than $4 (point *C*). Hence the grower can now afford to pay higher wages. Or the grower could employ more pickers than before, moving from point *C* to point *E*. *Increased productivity implies that workers can get higher wages without sacrificing jobs or more employment without lowering wages.* Historically, increased productivity has been the most important source of rising wages and living standards.

Changes in Price

An increase in the price of strawberries would also help the pickers. Marginal revenue product reflects the interaction of productivity and product prices. If strawberry prices were to double, strawberry pickers would become twice as valuable, even without an increase in physical productivity. Such a change in product prices depends, however, on changes in the market supply and demand for strawberries.

MARKET EQUILIBRIUM

The principles that guide the hiring decisions of a single strawberry grower can be extended to the entire labor market. This suggests that *the market demand for labor depends on*

- *The number of employers.*
- *The marginal revenue product of labor in each firm and industry.*

Increases in either the demand for final products or the productivity of labor will tend to increase marginal revenue productivity and therewith the demand for labor.

On the supply side of the labor market we have already observed that *the market supply of labor depends on*

- *The number of available workers.*
- *Each worker's willingness to work at alternative wage rates.*

The supply decisions of workers are in turn a reflection of tastes, income, wealth, expectations, other prices, and taxes.

Equilibrium Wage

Figure 16.7 brings these market forces together. *The intersection of the market supply and demand curves establishes the **equilibrium wage.*** This is the only wage rate at which the quantity of labor supplied equals the quantity of labor demanded. Everyone who's willing and able to work for this wage will find a job.

If the labor market is perfectly competitive, all employers will be able to hire as many workers as they want at the equilibrium wage. Like our strawberry grower, every competitive

equilibrium wage: The wage rate at which the quantity of labor supplied in a given time period equals the quantity of labor demanded.

(a) The labor market

(b) A competitive firm

FIGURE 16.7
Equilibrium Wage

The intersection of *market* supply and demand determines the equilibrium wage in a competitive labor market. All the firms in the industry can then hire as much labor as they want at that

equilibrium wage. In this case, the firm can hire all the workers it wants at the equilibrium wage, w_e. It chooses to hire q_0 workers, as determined by their marginal revenue product within the firm.

TABLE 16.2
Minimum Wage History

The federal minimum wage has been increased periodically since first set in 1938. In 2007 Congress raised the minimum to $7.25, effective July 2009.

Oct. 1938	$0.25	Jan. 1978	$2.65
Oct. 1939	0.30	Jan. 1979	2.90
Oct. 1945	0.40	Jan. 1980	3.10
Jan. 1950	0.75	Jan. 1981	3.35
Mar. 1956	1.00	Apr. 1990	3.80
Sept. 1961	1.15	Apr. 1991	4.25
Sept. 1963	1.25	Oct. 1996	4.75
Feb. 1967	1.40	Sept. 1997	5.15
Feb. 1968	1.60	July 2007	5.85
May 1974	2.00	July 2008	6.55
Jan. 1975	2.10	July 2009	7.25
Jan. 1976	2.30		

firm is assumed to have no discernible effect on market wages. *Competitive employers act like price takers with respect to wages as well as prices.* This phenomenon is also portrayed in Figure 16.7.

Minimum Wages

Some people will be unhappy with the equilibrium wage. Employers may grumble that wages are too high. Workers may complain that wages are too low. They may seek government intervention to change market outcomes. This is the goal of Congress when it establishes a legal *minimum* wage (see Table 16.2).

Figure 16.8 illustrates the effects of such government intervention. The market-determined equilibrium wage is W_e, and q_e workers are employed. A government-imposed minimum wage of W_M is then set, above the market equilibrium. The wage W_M encourages more low-skilled workers to seek employment; the quantity supplied *increases* from q_e to q_s. At the same time, however, the number of available jobs *declines* from q_e to q_d. This leaves a **market surplus** at the wage W_M. As a result of the increased wage, some workers have lost jobs ($q_e - q_d$) and some new entrants fail to find employment ($q_s - q_e$). Only those workers who remain employed (q_d) benefit from the higher wage.

Government-imposed wage floors thus have two distinct effects: *A legal minimum wage*

- *Reduces the quantity of labor demanded, and*
- *Increases the quantity of labor supplied, thereby*
- *Creating a market surplus.*

The extent of job loss resulting from a minimum wage hike is hotly debated. How many jobs are lost obviously depends on how far the minimum wage is raised above the market

market surplus: The amount by which the quantity supplied exceeds the quantity demanded at a given price; excess supply.

FIGURE 16.8
Minimum Wage Effects

If the minimum wage exceeds the equilibrium wage, a labor surplus will result: more workers will be willing to work at that wage rate than employers will be willing to hire. Some workers will end up with higher wages, but others will end up unemployed.

equilibrium. The elasticity of labor demand is also important. Democrats argue that labor demand is inelastic, so few jobs will be lost. Republicans assert that labor demand is elastic, so more jobs will be lost. In the early 1980s the elasticity of labor demand was found to be 0.10. Hence a 10 percent increase in the minimum wage would cause a 1 percent reduction in employment. Between 1981 and 1990, however, the minimum was stuck at $3.35 an hour while average wages increased 30 percent. By 1989 the federal minimum may have actually been *below* the equilibrium wage for low-skilled labor. When the minimum wage is below the equilibrium wage, an increase in the minimum may have little or no adverse employment effects. This appeared to be the case again in 1996. Because the federal minimum hadn't been raised for five years (see Table 16.2), the 50-cent-per-hour hike in October 1996 caused few job losses. According to Federal Reserve estimates, the 1997 wage hike may have reduced employment growth by only 100,000 to 200,000 jobs.

The same situation existed again in 2007. By then, the federal minimum of $5.15 hadn't been lifted for 10 years (Table 16.2) and had fallen below equilibrium levels (McDonald's and other fast-food outlets were paying entry wages of $6.50 and more in 2007). When Congress raised the minimum to $5.85, the legislated floor still lagged behind market wages. Further hikes, to $7.25 an hour, did cause some job losses, however. In general, *the further the minimum wage rises above the market's equilibrium wage, the greater the job loss.* That was a major source of concern when President Obama proposed raising the minimum wage again, to $9.50 an hour in 2011 (see the News below).

The Minimum Wage Debate

IN THE NEWS

Obama Wants $9.50 Minimum Wage

(Crains)—When Barack Obama and his fellow Democrats take power in Washington, DC, restaurant operators are expecting them to push a minimum wage hike. . . .

Obama wants to boost the federal minimum wage to $9.50 an hour by 2011, up from $7.25 an hour in 2009. . . .

Minimum Wage

The National Restaurant Association opposes raising the minimum wage, which has gone to $6.55 this year from $5.15 in 2006, and is scheduled to rise to $7.25 in July.

The association in June conducted a survey of 1,300 members in 18 states that found that 58 percent raised menu prices and 41 percent reduced employee hours because of the higher minimum wages.

Joe Sabia, an assistant professor of public policy at American University in Washington, D.C., says that a 10 percent increase in minimum wage reduces retail employment by 1 percent and reduces employment among young workers by 3.4 percent.

"Obama's proposal would raise the federal minimum wage by over 30 percent, causing even greater job loss at a time when our economy can least afford it," Mr. Sabia contends.

—David Sterrett

Source: Reprinted with permission, Crain's Chicago Business, November 11, 2008. © Crain Communications, Inc.

Analysis: A higher minimum wage encourages firms to hire fewer workers. How many jobs are lost depends on the size of the wage hike and the price elasticity of labor demand.

web analysis

Go to **www.dol.gov** for information on the federal minimum wage. Search "minimum wage history."

CHOOSING AMONG INPUTS

One of the options employers have when wage rates rise is to utilize more machinery in place of labor. In most production processes there are possibilities for substituting capital inputs for labor inputs. In the long run, there are still more possibilities for redesigning the whole production process. Given these options, how should the choice of inputs be made?

Suppose a mechanical strawberry picker can pick berries twice as fast as Marvin. Which will the grower hire, Marvin or the mechanical picker? At first it would seem that the grower would choose the mechanical picker. But the choice isn't so obvious. So far, all we know is that the mechanical picker's MPP is twice as large as Marvin's. But we haven't said anything about the *cost* of the mechanical picker.

Cost Efficiency

Suppose that a mechanical picker can be rented for $10 an hour, while Marvin is still willing to work for $4 an hour. Will this difference in hourly cost change the grower's input choice?

To determine the relative desirability of hiring Marvin or renting the mechanical picker, the grower must compare the ratio of their marginal physical products to their cost. This ratio of marginal product to cost expresses the **cost efficiency** of an input:

cost efficiency: The amount of output associated with an additional dollar spent on input; the MPP of an input divided by its price (cost).

$$\text{Cost efficiency} = \frac{\text{Marginal physical product of an input}}{\text{Cost of an input}}$$

Marvin's MPP is five boxes of strawberries per hour and his cost (wage) is $4. Thus the return on each dollar of wages paid to Marvin is

$$\begin{array}{c}\text{Cost} \\ \text{efficiency} \\ \text{of labor}\end{array} = \frac{\text{MPP}_{\text{labor}}}{\text{Cost}_{\text{labor}}} = \frac{5 \text{ boxes}}{\$4} = 1.25 \text{ boxes per } \$1 \text{ of cost}$$

By contrast, the mechanical picker has an MPP of 10 boxes per hour and costs $10 per hour:

$$\begin{array}{c}\text{Cost} \\ \text{efficiency of} \\ \text{mechanical} \\ \text{picker}\end{array} = \frac{\begin{array}{c}\text{MPP of} \\ \text{mechanical} \\ \text{picker}\end{array}}{\begin{array}{c}\text{Cost of} \\ \text{mechanical} \\ \text{picker}\end{array}} = \frac{10 \text{ boxes}}{\$10} = 1 \text{ box per } \$1 \text{ of cost}$$

These calculations indicate that Marvin is more cost-effective than the mechanical picker. From this perspective, the grower is better off hiring Marvin than renting a mechanical picker.

From the perspective of cost efficiency, the cheapness of a productive input is measured not by its price but by the amount of output it delivers for that price. Thus *the most cost-efficient factor of production is the one that produces the most output per dollar.*

The concept of cost efficiency helps explain why American firms don't move en masse to Haiti, where peasants are willing to work for as little as 80 cents an hour. Although this wage rate is far below the minimum wage in the United States, the marginal physical product of Haitian peasants is even further below American standards. American workers remain more cost-efficient than the "cheap" labor available in Haiti, making it unprofitable to **outsource** U.S. jobs. So long as U.S. workers deliver more output per dollar of wages, they will remain cost-effective in global markets.

outsourcing: The relocation of production to foreign countries.

Alternative Production Processes

Typically a producer doesn't choose between individual inputs but rather between alternative production processes. General Motors, for example, can't afford to compare the cost efficiency of each job applicant with the cost efficiency of mechanical tire mounters. Instead GM compares the relative desirability of a **production process** that is labor-intensive (uses a lot of labor) with others that are less labor-intensive. GM ignores individual differences in marginal revenue product. Nevertheless, the same principles of cost efficiency guide the decision.

production process: A specific combination of resources used to produce a good or service.

The Efficiency Decision

Let's return to the strawberry patch to see how the choice of an entire production process is made. We again assume that strawberries can be picked by either human or mechanical

	Alternative Processes for Producing One Ton of Strawberries		
Input	Process A	Process B	Process C
Labor (hours)	400	270	220
Machinery (hours)	13	15	18
Land (acres)	1	1	1

TABLE 16.3
Alternative Production Processes

One ton of strawberries can be produced with varying input combinations. Which process is most efficient? What information is missing?

hands. Now, however, we assume that one ton of strawberries can be produced by only one of the three production processes described in Table 16.3. Process A is most *labor-intensive;* it uses the most labor and thus keeps more human pickers employed. By contrast, process C is *capital-intensive;* it uses the most mechanical pickers and provides the least employment to human pickers. Process B falls between these two extremes.

Which of these three production processes should the grower use? If he used labor-intensive process A, he'd be doing the pickers a real favor. But his goal is to maximize profits, so we assume he'll choose the production process that best serves this objective. That is, he'll choose the *least-cost* process to produce one ton of strawberries.

But which of the production processes in Table 16.3 is least expensive? We really can't tell on the basis of the information provided. To determine the relative cost of each process—and thus to understand the producer's choice—we must know something more about input costs. In particular, we have to know how much an hour of mechanical picking costs and how much an hour of human picking (labor) costs. Then we can determine which combination of inputs is least expensive in producing one ton of strawberries—that is, which is most *cost-efficient.* Note that we don't have to know how much the land costs because the same amount of land is used in all three production processes. Thus land costs won't affect our efficiency decision.

Suppose that strawberry pickers are still paid $4 an hour and that mechanical pickers can be rented for $10 an hour. The acre of land rents for $500 per year. With this information we can now calculate the total dollar cost of each production process and quickly determine the most cost-efficient. Table 16.4 summarizes the required calculations.

The calculations performed in Table 16.4 clearly identify process C as the least expensive way of producing one ton of strawberries. Process A entails a total cost of $2,230, whereas the capital-intensive process C costs only $1,560 to produce the same quantity of

Input	Cost Calculation
Process A (labor-intensive)	
Labor	400 hours at $4 per hour = $1,600
Machinery	13 hours at $10 per hour = 130
Land	1 acre at $500 = 500
	Total cost $2,230
Process B (intermediate)	
Labor	270 hours at $4 per hour = $1,080
Machinery	15 hours at $10 per hour = 150
Land	1 acre at $500 = 500
	Total cost $1,730
Process C (capital-intensive)	
Labor	220 hours at $4 per hour = $ 880
Machinery	18 hours at $10 per hour = 180
Land	1 acre at $500 = 500
	Total cost $1,560

TABLE 16.4
The Least-Cost Combination

A producer wants to produce a given rate of output for the least cost. Choosing the least expensive production process is the efficiency decision. In this case, process C represents the most cost-efficient production process for producing one ton of strawberries.

output. As a profit maximizer, the grower will choose process C, even though it implies less employment for strawberry pickers.

The choice of an appropriate production process—the decision about *how* to produce—is called the **efficiency decision.** As we've seen, a producer seeks to use the combination of resources that produces a given rate of output for the least cost. The efficiency decision requires the producer to find that particular least-cost combination.

efficiency decision: The choice of a production process for any given rate of output.

THE ECONOMY TOMORROW

CAPPING CEO PAY

At the beginning of this chapter we noted that Larry Ellison, the CEO of Oracle, was paid $84 million for his services in 2010. He thinks he earned it. In that year, Oracle's sales increased by more than $3.5 *billion.*

Critics of CEO pay don't accept Ellison's explanation. They contend that Oracle revenues would have risen even without Ellison's leadership. Sales growth is a product of general economic growth, not just company management. They also assert that $84 million was more than enough to secure Ellison's services; he probably would have worked just as hard for a mere $50 million.

Critics conclude that many CEO paychecks are out of line with realities of supply and demand (see the cartoon below). They want corporations to reduce CEO pay and revise the process used for setting CEO pay levels. President Obama moved in this direction by setting a pay cap of $500,000 for executives of corporations receiving government aid (see the News on the next page).

Unmeasured MRP. One of the difficulties in determining the appropriate level of CEO pay is the elusiveness of marginal revenue product. It's easy to measure the MRP of a strawberry picker or even a salesclerk. But a corporate CEO's contributions are less well defined. A CEO is supposed to provide strategic leadership and a sense of mission. These are critical to a corporation's success but hard to quantify.

Congress confronts the same problem in setting the president's pay. We noted earlier that the president of the United States is paid $400,000 a year. Can we argue that this

"O.K. guys, now lets go and __earn__ that four hundred times our workers' salaries."

© William Hamilton/The New Yorker Collection/www.cartoonbank.com.

Analysis: The wages of top corporate officers may not be fully justified by their marginal revenue product.

IN THE NEWS

Obama Talks Tough on CEO Pay

The President Outlined New Rules Limiting Executive Pay for Firms Receiving Government Aid

NEW YORK (Fortune)—President Obama is having his say on soaring executive pay.

New rules unveiled Wednesday morning will cap annual cash compensation for executives at firms receiving future government aid at $500,000. . . .

Current rules bar such companies from taking a tax deduction for compensation above half a million dollars but don't restrict how much executives can receive in salary and bonuses. In addition, the new rules will increase the bans on so-called golden parachute severance packages available for executives. . . .

The pay rules come amid a fury in Washington over the huge bonuses handed out by Wall Street firms that were on life support before the government stepped in last fall. . . .

Executives on Wall Street made mind-bending sums in the boom years earlier this decade. Goldman Sachs, which received $10 billion from the government in October, paid chief Lloyd Blankfein $68 million in cash and stock in 2007. JPMorgan Chase, recipient of $25 billion, paid CEO Jamie Dimon $30 million that year.

—Colin Barr

Source: *Fortune*, February 4, 2009. © 2009 Time Inc. Used under license.

Analysis: Sky-high paychecks cause resentment. Pay caps, however, may discourage retention, innovation, and risk taking.

web analysis

Read more about top CEO salaries at **www.aflcio.org**. Click the "Corporate Watch" tab.

salary represents the president's marginal revenue product? It has been estimated that the president's pay would be in the range of $38–58 million if he were paid on performance (MRP). The wage we actually pay a president is less a reflection of contribution to total output than a matter of custom. The salary also reflects the price voters believe is required to induce competent individuals to forsake private sector jobs and assume the responsibilities of the presidency. In this sense, the wage paid to the president and other public officials is set by their **opportunity wage**—that is, the wage they could earn in private industry.

The same kinds of considerations influence the wages of college professors. The marginal revenue product of a college professor isn't easy to measure. Is it the number of students she teaches, the amount of knowledge conveyed, or something else? Confronted with such problems, most universities tend to pay college professors according to their opportunity wage—that is, the amount the professors could earn elsewhere.

Opportunity wages also help explain the difference between the wage of the CEO of Oracle and the workers who produce its products. The lower wage of systems engineers reflects not only their marginal revenue product but also the fact that they're not trained for many other jobs. That is, their opportunity wages are low. By contrast, Oracle's CEO has impressive managerial skills that are in demand by many corporations; his opportunity wages are high.

Opportunity wages help explain CEO pay but don't fully justify such high pay levels. If Oracle's CEO pay is justified by opportunity wages, that means another company would be willing to pay him that much. But what would justify such high pay at another company? Would his MRP be any easier to measure? Maybe *all* CEO paychecks have been inflated.

Critics of CEO pay conclude that the process of setting CEO pay levels should be changed. All too often, executive pay scales are set by self-serving committees composed of executives of the same or similar corporations. Critics want a more independent assessment of pay scales, with nonaffiliated experts and stockholder representatives. Some critics want to go a step further and set mandatory "caps" on CEO pay. President Clinton rejected

opportunity wage: The highest wage an individual would earn in his or her best alternative job.

legislated caps but convinced Congress to limit the tax deductibility of CEO pay. Any "unjustified" CEO pay in excess of $1 million a year can't be treated as a business expense but instead must be paid out of after-tax profits. This change put more pressure on corporations to examine the rationale for multimillion-dollar paychecks. President Obama wanted even stricter limits on CEO pay, especially for banks and other companies getting government "bailout" money (see the previous News).

If markets work efficiently, such government intervention shouldn't be necessary. Corporations that pay their CEOs excessively will end up with smaller profits than companies that pay market-based wages. Over time, "lean" companies will be more competitive than "fat" companies, and excessive pay packages will be eliminated. Legislated CEO pay caps imply that CEO labor markets aren't efficient or that the adjustment process is too slow. To forestall more government intervention in pay decisions, companies may tie executive pay more explicitly to performance (marginal revenue product) in the economy tomorrow.

SUMMARY

- The motivation to work arises from social, psychological, and economic forces. People need income to pay their bills, but they also need a sense of achievement. As a consequence, people are willing to work—to supply labor. LO16-1
- There's an opportunity cost involved in working—namely, the amount of leisure time one sacrifices. By the same token, the opportunity cost of not working (leisure) is the income and related consumption possibilities thereby forgone. Everyone confronts a trade-off between leisure and income. LO16-1
- Higher wage rates induce people to work more—that is, to substitute labor for leisure. But this substitution effect may be offset by an income effect. Higher wages also enable a person to work fewer hours with no loss of income. When income effects outweigh substitution effects, the labor supply curve bends backward. LO16-2
- A firm's demand for labor reflects labor's marginal revenue product. A profit-maximizing employer won't pay a worker more than the worker produces. LO16-2

- The marginal revenue product of labor diminishes as additional workers are employed on a particular job (the law of diminishing returns). This decline occurs because additional workers have to share existing land and capital, leaving each worker with less land and capital to work with. LO16-2
- A producer seeks to get the most output for every dollar spent on inputs. This means getting the highest ratio of marginal product to input price. A profit-maximizing producer will choose the most cost-efficient input (not necessarily the one with the cheapest price). LO16-1
- The efficiency decision involves the choice of the least-cost productive process and is also made on the basis of cost efficiency. A producer seeks the least expensive process to produce a given rate of output. LO16-3
- Differences in marginal revenue product are an important explanation of wage inequalities. But the difficulty of measuring MRP in some jobs leaves many wage rates to be determined by opportunity wages or other mechanisms. LO16-3

Key Terms

labor supply	derived demand	cost efficiency
substitution effect of higher wages	marginal physical product (MPP)	outsourcing
income effect of higher wages	marginal revenue product (MRP)	production process
market supply of labor	law of diminishing returns	efficiency decision
elasticity of labor supply	equilibrium wage	opportunity wage
demand for labor	market surplus	

Questions for Discussion

1. Why are you doing this homework? What are you giving up? What utility do you expect to gain?   LO16-1
2. Would you continue to work after winning a lottery prize of $50,000 a year for life? Would you change schools, jobs, or career objectives? What factors besides income influence work decisions?   LO16-1
3. According to the World View on page 346 does the substitution effect or the income effect dominate in India? In Russia? Why might this be the case?   LO16-1
4. Explain why marginal physical product would diminish as
    (*a*) More secretaries are hired in an office.
    (*b*) More professors are hired in the economics department.
    (*c*) More construction workers are hired to build a school.   LO16-2
5. Is this course increasing your marginal productivity? If so, in what way?   LO16-2
6. How might you measure the marginal revenue product of (*a*) a quarterback and (*b*) the team's coach?   LO16-2
7. Who is hurt and who is helped by an increase in the legal minimum wage? Under what circumstances might a higher minimum *not* reduce employment?   LO16-3
8. In 2007 the president of the University of Southern California was paid $900,000 and the football coach was paid $4 million. Does this make any sense?   LO16-2
9. Is it possible that the president of the United States is overpaid? How should his MRP be measured?   LO16-2
10. The minimum wage in Mexico is less than $1 an hour. Does this make Mexican workers more cost-effective than U.S. workers? Explain.   LO16-3
11. Why didn't President Obama set pay limits on baseball players who play in publicly funded stadiums (News, p. 353)? Why did he single out bank executives (News, p. 361)?   LO16-2

---

 web activities to accompany this chapter can be found on the Online Learning Center:
http://www.mhhe.com/schiller13e

 mobile app Visit your mobile app store and download the Schiller: Study Econ app *today!*

LO16-1   1. (*a*) How many runs did Joe Mauer score (home runs + RBIs) in 2010? (See News, p. 353).   _____
        (*b*) If his annual salary were based on runs alone, how much would each run be worth?   _____

LO16-2   2. By what percentage did
        (*a*) The federal minimum wage increase between July 1990 and July 2010? (See Table 16.2.)   _____
        (*b*) If using *The Micro Economy Today,* use the following question: Compensation per hour
             increase between 1990 and 2009? (See the tables at the end of the text.)   _____
            If using *The Economy Today,* use the following question: Average consumer prices
             increase between 1990 and 2010? (See the tables at the end of the text.)   _____

LO16-1   3. According to the News on page 343, what was the situation in the 2009 NYC labor market?
        A: Labor surplus   B: Labor shortage   C: Equilibrium   _____

LO16-3   4. According to the News on page 357, what percentage of retail jobs would be lost if the
        minimum wage were increased to $9.50?   _____

LO16-3   5. (*a*) According to Figure 16.8, how many workers are unemployed at the equilibrium wage?   _____
        (*b*) How many workers are unemployed at the minimum wage?   _____

LO16-1   6. Suppose a wage increase from $11 to $13 an hour increases the number of job applicants
        from 42 to 56. What is the price elasticity of labor supply?   _____

LO16-1   7. If the price of strawberries doubled, how many pickers would be hired at $4 an hour,
        according to Table 16.1?   _____

LO16-3   8. Apples can be harvested by hand or machine. Handpicking yields 80 pounds per hour;
        mechanical pickers yield 120 pounds per hour.
        (*a*) If the wage rate of human pickers is $8 an hour and the rental on a mechanical picker is
             $15 an hour, which is more cost-effective?   _____
        (*b*) If the wage rate increased to $12 an hour, which would be more cost-effective?   _____

LO16-3   9. Assume that the following data describe labor market conditions:

Wage rate (per hour)	$3	$4	$5	$6	$7	$8	$9	$10
Labor demanded	50	45	40	35	30	25	20	15
Labor supplied	20	30	40	50	60	70	80	90

On the graph below, illustrate
(*a*) The equilibrium wage.
(*b*) A government-set minimum wage of $6 per hour when the minimum wage is implemented.
(*c*) How many workers lose jobs?   _____
(*d*) How many additional workers seek jobs?   _____
(*e*) How many workers end up unemployed?   _____

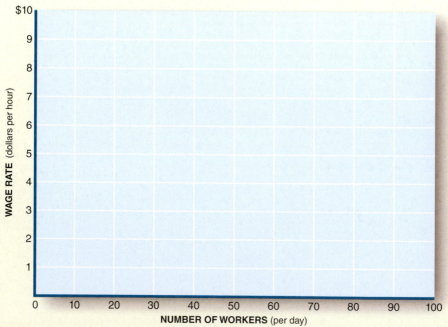

LO16-2 10. The following table depicts the number of grapes that can be picked in an hour with varying amounts of labor:

Number of pickers (per hour)	1	2	3	4	5	6	7	8
Output of grapes (in flats)	20	38	53	64	71	74	74	70

(a) Illustrate the supply and demand of labor for a single farmer, assuming that the local wage rate is $6 an hour and a flat of grapes sells for $2.

(b) How many pickers will be hired?   _____

(c) If the wage rate doubles, how many pickers will be hired?   _____

(d) If the productivity of all workers doubles, how many pickers will be hired at a wage of $12 an hour?   _____

(e) Illustrate your answers on the following graph.

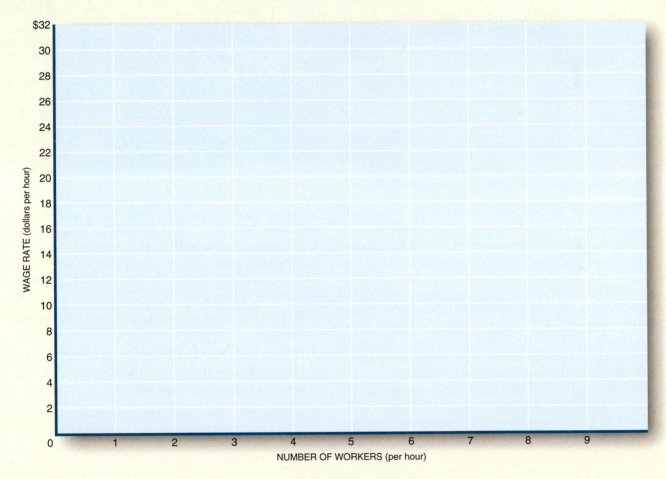

LO16-3 11. By how much would the quantity of labor demanded have decreased as the result of the 2009 hike in the minimum wage (Table 16.2) if the elasticity of labor demand were 0.10?   _____%

Labor Unions

chapter

17

LEARNING OBJECTIVES

After reading this chapter, you should know

LO17-1. How unions secure higher wages.

LO17-2. The factors that affect collective bargaining outcomes.

LO17-3. How unions affect nonunion wages.

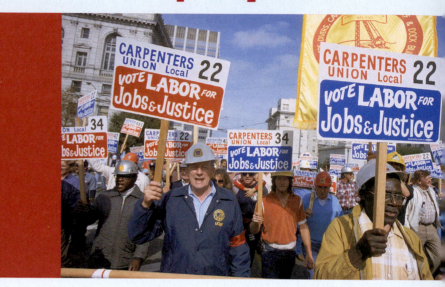

The **United Auto Workers Union** (UAW) launched a strike against Caterpillar, Inc., in November 1991. The union wanted the manufacturer of construction machinery to increase pay, benefits, and job security. *Four years* later, Caterpillar hadn't budged; it continued to operate with replacement workers, management crews, and union members who crossed the picket line. The union finally capitulated in December 1995, sending its 8,700 members back to work with neither higher pay nor even a new contract. The union struck again in 1996 but relented after 17 months. Seven years after their first strike, the Caterpillar workers still had no contract.

To many observers, the failed UAW strike at Caterpillar climaxed a steady decline in the power of labor unions. This impression was reinforced by the failure of *public* unions in Illinois and Ohio to safeguard benefits in early 2011. But the union movement is far from dead. Labor unions are even expanding in some sectors (especially government employment). Many unions still have considerable influence on employment, wages, and working conditions. This chapter focuses on how unions acquire and use such influence. We address the following questions:

- **How do large and powerful employers affect market wages?**
- **How do labor unions alter wages and employment?**
- **What outcomes are possible from collective bargaining between management and unions?**

In the process of answering these questions, we look at the nation's most powerful unions and their actual behavior.

THE LABOR MARKET

To gauge the impact of labor market power, we must first observe how a competitive labor market sets wages and employment. On the supply side, we have all those individuals who are willing to work—to supply labor—at various wage rates. By counting the number of individuals willing to work at each and every wage rate, we can construct a *market* **labor supply** curve, as in Figure 17.1.

The willingness of producers (firms) to hire labor is reflected in the market labor demand curve. The curve itself is constructed by counting the number of workers each firm says it is willing and able to hire at each and every wage rate. The curve illustrates the market **demand for labor.**

Competitive Equilibrium

The intersection of the labor supply and labor demand curves (point *C* in Figure 17.1) reveals the **equilibrium wage** rate (w_e): the wage rate at which the quantity of labor supplied equals the quantity demanded. At this wage rate, every job seeker who's willing and able to work for the wage w_e is employed. In addition, firms are able to acquire all the labor they're willing and able to hire at that wage.

Not everyone is employed in equilibrium. Workers who demand wages in excess of w_e are unable to find jobs. By the same token, employers who refuse to pay a wage as high as w_e are unable to attract workers.

Local Labor Markets

Figure 17.1 appears to suggest that there's only *one* labor market and thus only one equilibrium wage. This is a gross oversimplification. If you were looking for a job in Tulsa, you'd have little interest in employment prospects or power configurations in New York City. You'd be more concerned about the available jobs and wages in Tulsa—that is, the condition of the *local* labor market.

Even within a particular geographical area, interest usually focuses on particular occupations and workers rather than on all the people supplying or demanding labor. If you were looking for work as a dancer, you'd have little interest in the employment situation for carpenters or dentists. Rather, you'd want to know how many nightclubs or dance troupes had job vacancies, and what wages and working conditions they offered.

The distinction among various geographical, occupational, and industrial labor markets provides a more meaningful basis for analyzing labor market power. The tremendous size of the national labor market, with over 150 million workers, precludes anyone from acquiring control of the entire market. The largest employer in the United States (Walmart)

labor supply: The willingness and ability to work specific amounts of time at alternative wage rates in a given time period, *ceteris paribus.*

demand for labor: The quantities of labor employers are willing and able to hire at alternative wages in a given time period, *ceteris paribus.*

equilibrium wage: The wage rate at which the quantity of labor supplied in a given time period equals the quantity of labor demanded.

FIGURE 17.1
Competitive Equilibrium in the Labor Market

The market labor supply curve includes all persons willing to work at various wage rates. The labor demand curve tells us how many workers employers are willing to hire. In a competitive market, the intersection of the labor supply and labor demand curves (point *C*) determines the equilibrium wage (w_e) and employment (q_e) levels.

market power: The ability to alter the market price of a good or service.

employs less than 1 percent of the labor force. General Motors employs far fewer than that, and the top 500 industrial corporations employ less than 20 percent of all workers. The situation on the supply side is similar. The largest labor union (Service Employees International Union) represents just 1 percent of all workers in the country. All unions together represent only one out of every nine U.S. workers. This doesn't mean that particular employers or unions have no influence on our economic welfare. It does suggest, however, that **market power** *in labor markets is likely to be more effective in specific areas, occupations, and industries.*

LABOR UNIONS

The immediate objective of labor unions is to alter the equilibrium wage and employment conditions in specific labor markets. *To be successful, unions must be able to exert control over the market supply curve.*

Types of Unions

That's why workers have organized themselves along either industry or occupational craft lines. *Industrial unions* include workers in a particular industry (the United Auto Workers, for example). *Craft unions* represent workers with a particular skill (like the International Brotherhood of Electrical Workers), regardless of the industry in which they work.

The purpose of both types of labor unions is to coordinate the actions of thousands of individual workers, thereby achieving control of market supply. If a union is able to control the supply of workers in a particular industry or occupation, the union acquires a *monopoly* in that market. Like most monopolies, unions attempt to use their market power to increase their incomes.

Union Objectives

A primary objective of unions is to raise the wages of union members. In the 2005 dispute between pro hockey team owners and players, money was the sole issue. The players, who were already getting an average paycheck of $1.8 million per season, were resisting a salary cap that would restrain wages. The team owners wanted to limit total player salaries to 53–55 percent of league revenues.

An exclusive focus on wages is somewhat unusual. Union objectives also include improved working conditions, job security, and other nonwage forms of compensation, such as retirement (pension) benefits, vacation time, and health insurance. The Players Association and the National Football League have bargained about the use of artificial turf, early retirement, player fines, television revenues, game rules, the use of team doctors, drug tests, pensions, and the number of players permitted on a team. A recurring concern of the United Auto Workers is job security. Consequently, they focus on work rules that may eliminate jobs and unemployment benefits for laid-off workers.

Although union objectives tend to be as broad as the concerns of union members, we focus here on just one objective: wage rates. This isn't too great a simplification because most nonwage issues can be translated into their effective impact on wage rates. In 2007, for example, the UAW and GM agreed to over a dozen different job provisions, ranging from job security to drug prescriptions (see the following News). It was possible, however, to figure out the cost of these many provisions ($3,264 per worker per year). Hence the "bottom line" of the compensation package could be expressed in terms of wage costs.

The 2011 negotiations between the National Football League and the player's union had a similar array of provisions. In contention were the number of games to be played in a season; a new and lower rookie pay scale; year-round health benefits; and a retirement fund. But the central issue was money: the team owners wanted a bigger piece of the $9 billion a year revenue stream than the players would agree to. All of these provisions could be expressed in terms of average wage per player. What we seek to determine is whether and how unions can raise effective wage rates in a specific labor market by altering the competitive equilibrium depicted in Figure 17.1.

IN THE NEWS

The GM–UAW Deal

After months of negotiations and a 41-hour strike, GM and the UAW signed a new four-year contract in September 2007. Terms of the deal included the following:

For GM

- **Termination of health plan.** The UAW agreed to assume responsibility for funding and managing the employee/retiree health plan, with an initial $30 billion payment from GM.
- **Two-tier wages.** GM got the right to hire new workers at half the base wage ($14/hour) of existing workers ($28/hour).
- **Reduced pension.** New hires get 40l(k) contributions rather than guaranteed pensions.

For UAW

- **Guaranteed jobs.** GM agreed to maintain production levels at 16 U.S plants for four years.
- **Back-to-work bonus.** GM agreed to pay each worker a $3,000 bonus.
- **Wage hikes.** GM agreed to make two lump-sum payments equal to 3–4 percent of each employee's wages.
- **Job security.** GM agreed to a moratorium on outsourcing; 3,000 part-time jobs became full-time.

Analysis: Labor unions bargain with management over a variety of employment conditions. Most issues, however, can be expressed in terms of their impact on wage costs.

web analysis

For an overview and update on UAW activity, visit the organization's website at **www.uaw.org.**

THE POTENTIAL USE OF POWER

In a competitive labor market, each worker makes a labor supply decision on the basis of his or her own perceptions of the relative values of labor and leisure (Chapter 16). Whatever decision is made won't alter the market wage. One worker simply isn't that significant in a market composed of thousands. Once a market is unionized, however, these conditions no longer hold. A *union evaluates job offers on the basis of the collective interests of its members.* In particular, it must be concerned with the effects of increased employment on the wage rate paid to its members.

The Marginal Wage

Like all monopolists, unions have to worry about the downward slope of the demand curve. In the case of labor markets, a larger quantity of labor can be "sold" only at lower wage rates. Suppose the workers in a particular labor market confront the market labor demand schedule depicted in Figure 17.2. This schedule tells us that employers aren't willing to hire any workers at a wage rate of $6 per hour (row *S*) but will hire one worker per hour if the wage rate is $5 (row *T*). At still lower rates, the quantity of labor demanded increases; five workers per hour are demanded at a wage of $1 per hour.

An individual worker offered a wage of $1 an hour would have to decide whether such wages merited the sacrifice of an hour's leisure. But a union would evaluate the offer differently. A union must consider how the hiring of one more worker will affect the wages of all the workers.

Total Wages Paid. Notice that when four workers are hired at a wage rate of $2 an hour (row *W*), *total* wages are $8 per hour. In order for a fifth worker to be employed, the wage rate must drop to $1 an hour (row *X*). At wages of $1 per hour, the *total* wages paid to the five workers amount to only $5 per hour. Thus total wages paid to the workers actually *fall* when a fifth worker is employed. Collectively the workers would be better off sending only four people to work at the higher wage of $2 an hour and paying the fifth worker $1 an hour to stay home!

FIGURE 17.2
The Marginal Wage

The *marginal wage* is the change in *total wages* (paid to all workers) associated with the employment of an additional worker. If the wage rate is $4 per hour, only two workers will be hired (point *U*). The wage rate must fall to $3 per hour if three workers are to be hired (point *V*). In the process, *total* wages paid rise from $8 ($4 × 2 workers) to $9 ($3 × 3 workers). The *marginal* wage of the third worker is only $1 (point *v*).

The graph illustrates the relationship of the marginal wage to labor demand. The marginal wage curve lies below the labor demand curve because the marginal wage is less than the nominal wage. Compare the marginal wage (point *v*) and the nominal wage (point *V*) of the third worker.

The marginal wage is critical to union demands.

	Wage Rate (per Hour)	×	Number of Workers Demanded (per Hour)	=	Total Wages Paid (per Hour)		Marginal Wage (per Labor-Hour)
S	$6		0		$0		
T	5		1		5	>	$5
U	4		2		8	>	3
V	3		3		9	>	1
W	2		4		8	>	−1
X	1		5		5	>	−3

The basic mandate of a labor union is to evaluate wage and employment offers from this *collective* perspective. To do so, *a union must distinguish the marginal wage from the market wage.* The market wage is simply the current wage rate paid by the employer; it's the wage received by individual workers. The **marginal wage,** on the other hand, is the change in *total* wages paid (to all workers) when an additional worker is hired:

$$\frac{\text{Marginal}}{\text{wage}} = \frac{\text{Change in total wages paid}}{\text{Change in quantity of labor employed}}$$

The distinction between marginal wages and market wages arises from the downward slope of the labor demand curve. It's analogous to the distinction we made between marginal revenue and price for monopolists in product markets. The distinction simply reflects the law of demand: if more workers are to be hired, wage rates must fall.

The impact of increased employment on marginal wages is also illustrated in Figure 17.2. According to the labor demand curve, one worker will be hired at a wage rate of $5 an hour (point *T*); two workers will be hired only if the market wage falls to $4 an hour (point *U*), at which point the first and second workers will each be getting $4 an hour. Thus the increased wages of the second worker (from zero to $4) will be partially offset by the reduction in the wage rate paid to the first worker (from $5 to $4). *Total* wages paid will increase by only $3; this is the *marginal* wage (point *u*). The marginal wage actually becomes negative at some point, when the implied wage loss to workers already on the job begins to exceed the wage of a new hired worker.

marginal wage: The change in total wages paid associated with a one-unit increase in the quantity of labor employed.

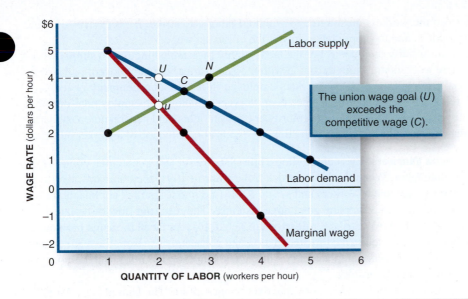

FIGURE 17.3
The Union Wage Objective

The intersection of the marginal wage and labor supply curves (point *u*) determines the union's desired employment. Employers are willing to pay a wage rate of $4 per hour for that many workers, as revealed by point *U* on the labor demand curve.

More workers (*N*) are willing to work at $4 per hour than employers demand (*U*). To maintain that wage rate, the union must exclude some workers from the market. In the absence of such power, wages would fall to the competitive equilibrium (point *C*).

The Union Wage Goal

A union never wants to accept a negative marginal wage, of course. At such a point, union members would be better off paying someone to stay home. *The central question for the union is what level of (positive) marginal wage to accept.*

We can answer this question by looking at the labor supply curve. The labor supply curve tells us how much labor workers are *willing to supply* at various wage rates. Hence the labor supply curve depicts the lowest wage *individual* union members would accept. If the union adopts a *collective* perspective on the welfare of its members, however, it will view the wage offer differently. From their collective perspective, the wage that union members are getting for additional labor is the *marginal* wage, not the nominal (market) wage. Hence the marginal wage curve, not the labor demand curve, is decisive in the union's assessment of wage offers.

If the union wants to maximize the *total* welfare of its members, it will seek the level of employment that equates the marginal wage with the supply preferences of union members. In Figure 17.3, *the intersection of the marginal wage curve with the labor supply curve identifies the desired level of employment for the union.* This intersection occurs at point *u*, yielding total employment of two workers per hour.

The marginal wage at point *u* is $3. However, the union members will get paid an actual wage higher than that. Look up from point *u* on the marginal wage curve to point *U* on the employer's labor demand curve. Point *U* tells us that the employer is *willing to pay* a wage rate of $4 an hour to employ two workers. The union knows it can demand and get $4 an hour if it supplies only two workers to the firm.

What the union is doing here is choosing a point on the labor demand curve that the union regards as the optimal combination of wages and employment. In a competitive market, point *C* would represent the equilibrium combination of wages and employment. But the union forces employers to point *U*, thereby attaining a higher wage rate and reducing employment.

Exclusion

The union's ability to maintain a wage rate of $4 an hour depends on its ability to exclude some workers from the market. Figure 17.3 reveals that three workers are willing and able to work at the union wage of $4 an hour (point *N*), whereas only two are hired (point *U*). If the additional worker were to offer his services, the wage rate would be pushed down the labor demand curve (to $3 per hour). Hence, *to maintain a noncompetitive wage, the union must be able to exercise some control over the labor supply decisions of individual workers.* The essential force here is union solidarity. Once unionized, the individual workers must agree not to compete among themselves by offering their labor at nonunion wage

union shop: An employment setting in which all workers must join the union within 30 days after being employed.

Controlling Labor Supply

rates. Instead the workers must agree to withhold labor—to strike, if necessary—if wage rates are too low, and to supply labor only at the union-set wage.

Unions can solidify their control of the labor supply by establishing **union shops:** workplaces where workers must join the union within 30 days after being employed. In this way, the unions gain control of all the workers employed in a particular company or industry, thereby reducing the number of replacement workers available for employment during a strike. Stiff penalties (such as loss of seniority or pension rights) and general union solidarity ensure that only nonunion workers will "fink" or "scab"—take the job of a worker on strike.

Replacement Workers. Even union shops, however, are subject to potential competition from substitute labor. When the UAW struck Caterpillar in 1991, the company advertised nationally for replacement workers and set up a toll-free phone line for applicants. In the midst of a recession, the company got a huge response. The resulting flow of replacement workers crippled the UAW strike. Professional baseball players faced the same problem in 1995. When the continued strike threatened a second consecutive season, the team owners started hiring new players to replace the regulars. The huge supply of aspiring ball players forced the strikers to reconsider.

Replacement workers are even more abundant in agriculture. The United Farm Workers has been trying for decades to organize California's 20,000 strawberry pickers. But the workers know that thousands of additional workers will flock to California from Mexico if they protest wages and working conditions.

THE EXTENT OF UNION POWER

The first labor unions in America were organized in the 1780s, and the first worker protests as early as 1636. Union power wasn't a significant force in labor markets, however, until the 1900s, when heavily populated commercial centers and large-scale manufacturing became common. Only then did large numbers of workers begin to view their employment situations from a common perspective.

Early Growth

The period 1916–1920 was one of particularly fast growth for labor unions, largely because of the high demand for labor resulting from World War I. All these membership gains were lost, however, when the Great Depression threw millions of people out of work. By 1933 union membership had dwindled to the levels of 1915.

As the Depression lingered on, public attitudes and government policy changed. Too many people had learned the meaning of layoffs, wage cuts, and prolonged unemployment. In 1933 the National Industrial Recovery Act (NIRA) established the right of employees to bargain collectively with their employers. When the NIRA was declared unconstitutional by the Supreme Court in 1935, its labor provisions were incorporated into a new law, the Wagner Act. With this legislative encouragement, union membership doubled between 1933 and 1937. Unions continued to gain in strength as the production needs of World War II increased the demand for labor. Figure 17.4 reflects the tremendous spurt of union activity between the depths of the Depression and the height of World War II.

FIGURE 17.4
Changing Unionization Rates

Unions grew most rapidly during the decade 1935–1945. Since that time, the growth of unions hasn't kept pace with the growth of the U.S. labor force. Most employment growth has occurred in service industries that have traditionally been nonunion.

Source: U.S. Department of Labor.

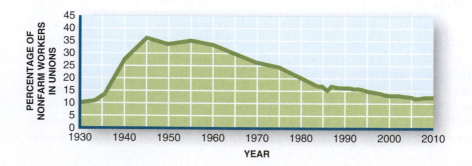

Union Power Today

Union membership stopped increasing in the 1950s, even though the labor force kept growing. As a result, the unionized percentage of the labor force—the **unionization rate**—has been in steady decline for more than 40 years. The current unionization rate of 11.9 percent is less than a third of its post–World War II peak and far below unionization rates in other industrialized nations (see the World View below).

unionization rate: The percentage of the labor force belonging to a union.

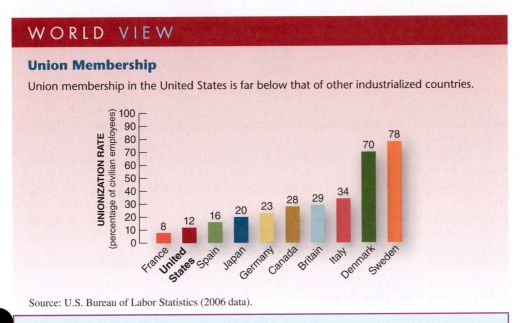

WORLD VIEW

Union Membership

Union membership in the United States is far below that of other industrialized countries.

Source: U.S. Bureau of Labor Statistics (2006 data).

Analysis: Unionization rates are comparatively low and declining in the United States.

web analysis

What kind of work is most unionized in the United States? To find out, go to **www.aflcio.org/aboutus/unions**.

Private vs. Public Sector Trends. The decline in the *national* unionization rate conceals two very different trends. Union representation of *private* sector workers has plunged even more sharply than Figure 17.4 suggests. In the last 10 years, the unionization rate in the private sector has fallen from 11.5 percent to only 6.9 percent. At the same time, union membership has increased sharply among teachers, government workers, and nonprofit employees. As of 2010, over 36 percent of workers on government payrolls were union members. This concentration of unions in the public sector is evident in Figure 17.5. The trend is clear: *the old industrial unions are being supplanted by unions of service workers, especially those employed in the public sector.* Unionization is highest among public schoolteachers, including college professors.

Although industrial unions have been in general decline, they still possess significant pockets of market power. The Teamsters, the UAW, the United Mine Workers, the Union of Needletrades and Textile Employees, and the Food Workers all have substantial representation in their respective markets. Their strength in those specific markets, not national averages, determines their ability to alter market outcomes.

The AFL-CIO. One labor organization with a decidedly national focus is the AFL-CIO (the American Federation of Labor–Congress of Industrial Organizations). The AFL-CIO is not a separate union but a representational body of more than 50 national unions, representing 9 million workers. It doesn't represent or negotiate for any particular group of workers but focuses instead on issues of general labor interest. The AFL-CIO acts as an advocate for the labor movement and represents labor's interest in legislative areas. It's the primary vehicle for political action. In addition, the AFL-CIO may render economic assistance to member unions or to groups of workers who wish to organize.

FIGURE 17.5
Private vs. Public Unions

Unionization rates have declined sharply in private industry but risen in the public sector. Public sector union membership now exceeds private sector union membership.

Source: U.S. Bureau of Labor Statistics (2010 data).

Change to Win Coalition. The AFL-CIO's political activity upset member unions who favored more focus on traditional union interests, particularly union organizing. In September 2005 some of these unions (including teamsters, garment workers, food workers, service workers) quit the AFL-CIO and formed a new multiunion organization, the Change to Win Coalition. By 2011 the coalition included seven of the largest unions, representing more than 5 million workers.

EMPLOYER POWER

The power possessed by labor unions in various occupations and industries seldom exists in a power vacuum. Power exists on the demand side of labor markets, too. The United Auto Workers confront GM, Ford, and Chrysler; the Steelworkers confront U.S. Steel, International Steel Group, and AK Steel; the Teamsters confront the Truckers' Association; the Communications Workers confront AT&T; and so on. An imbalance of power often exists on one side of the market or the other (as with, say, the Carpenters versus individual construction contractors). However, *labor markets with significant power on both sides are common.* To understand how wage rates and employment are determined in such markets, we have to assess the market power possessed by employers.

Monopsony

Power on the demand side of a market belongs to a *buyer* who can influence the market price of a good. With respect to labor markets, market power on the demand side implies the ability of a single employer to alter the market wage rate. The extreme case of such power is a **monopsony,** a situation in which one employer is the only buyer in a particular market. The classic example of a monopsony is a company town—that is, a town that depends for its livelihood on the decisions of a single employer.

monopsony: A market in which there's only one buyer.

Graduate teaching assistants have complained that the universities that employ them are much like company towns. Once they've started taking graduate classes at one university, it's difficult to transfer to another. As they see it, there is only one local labor market for graduate students. They complain that their monopsony employer compels them to work long hours at low wages. In 1998 University of California graduate students went out on strike to protest those conditions. In 1999 over 10,000 of those graduate students affiliated with the United Auto Workers to gain more power. In November 2000 the National Labor Relations Board decreed that graduate research and teaching assistants are employees with the right to organize and strike (see the News on the next page).

IN THE NEWS

A Win for the Graduate(s)

Finally, Teaching Assistants Can Unionize

For years, New York University and other private institutions have argued successfully that graduate students who work as research and teaching assistants shouldn't be treated as employees under federal labor law. The money that grad students earn is financial aid, not compensation, universities say. And while critics complain that grad students are exploited as cheap labor, administrators respond that aspiring PhD's gain vital career training by teaching undergraduate discussion sections and conducting research.

Last week, however, in a case involving NYU graduate assistants, the National Labor Relations Board gave a decisive thumbs down to these claims. Overturning nearly a quarter century of precedent, the federal panel said that graduate research and teaching assistants at private universities are employees who have the right to form unions and bargain collectively. "We will not deprive workers . . . of their fundamental statutory rights to organize and bargain with their employer, simply because they also are students," the ruling said, upholding a decision issued last spring by a regional NLRB director. Grad student unions have already been recognized at a growing number of public universities, which are governed by state labor laws.

—Ben Wildavsky

Source: *U.S. News & World Report*, November 13, 2000, Vol. 129, Issue 19, p. 40. Used with permission.

Analysis: Universities have monopsony power in setting wage and workloads for graduate assistants. To counterbalance that power, grad assistants may organize and bargain collectively.

Before 1976 professional sports teams also had monopsony power. Sports contracts prohibited pro players from moving from one team (employer) to another without permission. This gave team owners a lot of power to set wages and working conditions. That power was diluted when players got the right to be "free agents" and bargain with more than one team (see the accompanying News).

IN THE NEWS

Free Agents in Sports: A Threat to Monopsony

Before 1976 the owners of professional baseball, football, and basketball teams enjoyed monopsonistic power. This power was bestowed by the "reserve clause" included in player contracts. Individual players were permitted to negotiate with only one team. Once signed, they couldn't move to another team without their owner's permission. The player's only option was to "take it or leave"—that is, to accept his team's wage offer or quit playing altogether for at least one season. Team owners used the reserve clause to hold down player salaries far below their marginal revenue product.

In 1976 baseball players won the right to become free agents—to negotiate and play for any team—after six years of major league experience. In 1977 pro football players also won the right to become free agents, but under more restrictive conditions (the team losing a free agent had to be "compensated" with draft choices). Pro basketball players became true free agents in 1980.

The weakening of monopsonistic power led to dramatically higher player salaries. The average baseball salary soared from about $51,000 in 1976 to $900,000 in 1992 and surpassed $3 million in 2010.

Analysis: Because "reserve clauses" limited competing wage offers, they conferred monopsony power on team owners. This kept athletes' wages below competitive equilibrium. Free agency changed that.

web analysis

A history of the Major League Baseball Players Association can be found at **www.mlbplayers. com.** Click the "MLBPA INFO" tab.

There are many degrees of market power, and they can be defined in terms of *buyer concentration*. When buyers are many and of limited market power, the demand for resources is likely to be competitive. When only one buyer has access to a particular resource market, a monopsony exists. Between the two extremes lie the various degrees of imperfect competition, including the awkward-sounding but empirically important case of *oligopsony*. In an oligopsony (e.g., the auto industry), only a few firms account for most of the industry's employment.

The Potential Use of Power

Firms with power in labor markets generally have the same objective as all other firms—to maximize profits. What distinguishes them from competitive (powerless) firms is their ability to attain and keep economic profits. In labor markets, this means using fewer workers and paying them lower wages.

The distinguishing characteristic of labor market monopsonies is that their hiring decisions influence the market wage rate. In a competitive labor market, no single employer has any direct influence on the market wage rate; each firm can hire as much labor as it needs at the prevailing wage. But a monopsonist confronts the *market* labor supply curve. As a result, any increase in the quantity of labor demanded will force the monopsonist to climb up the labor supply curve in search of additional workers. In other words, *a monopsonist can hire additional workers only if it offers a higher wage rate.*

Marginal Factor Cost. Any time the price of a resource (or product) changes as a result of a firm's purchases, a distinction between marginal cost and price must be made. Making this distinction is one of the little headaches—and potential sources of profit—of a monopsonist. For labor, we distinguish between the **marginal factor cost (MFC)** of labor and its wage rate.

Suppose that Figure 17.6 accurately describes the labor supply schedule confronting a monopsonist. It's evident that the monopsonist will have to pay a wage of at least $2 an hour if it wants any labor. But even at that wage rate (row *F* of the supply schedule), only one worker will be willing to work. If the firm wants more labor, it will have to offer higher wages.

Two things happen when the firm raises its wage offer to $3 an hour (row *G*). First, the quantity of labor supplied increases (to two workers per hour). Second, the total wages paid rise by $4. This *marginal* cost of labor is attributable to the fact that the first worker's wages also rise when the wage rate is increased to attract additional workers. If all the workers perform the same job, the first worker will demand to be paid the new (higher) wage rate. Thus *the marginal factor cost exceeds the wage rate because additional workers can be hired only if the wage rate for all workers is increased.*

The Monopsony Firm's Goal. The marginal factor cost curve confronting this monopsonist is shown in the upper half of Figure 17.6. It starts at the bottom of the labor supply curve and rises above it. The monopsonist must now decide how many workers to hire, given the impact of its hiring decision on the market wage rate.

Remember from Chapter 16 that the labor demand curve is a reflection of labor's **marginal revenue product**—that is, the increase in total revenue attributable to the employment of one additional worker.

As we've emphasized, the profit-maximizing producer always seeks to equalize marginal revenue and marginal cost. Accordingly, the monopsonistic employer will seek to hire the amount of labor at which the marginal revenue product of labor equals its marginal factor cost:

$$\text{Profit-maximizing level of input use} : \frac{\text{Marginal revenue}}{\text{product of input}} = \frac{\text{Marginal factor}}{\text{cost of input}}$$
$$\text{(MRP)} \qquad \text{(MFC)}$$

In Figure 17.6, this objective is illustrated by the intersection of the marginal factor cost and labor demand curves at point *U*.

marginal factor cost (MFC): The change in total costs that results from a one-unit increase in the quantity of a factor employed.

marginal revenue product (MRP): The change in total revenue associated with one additional unit of input.

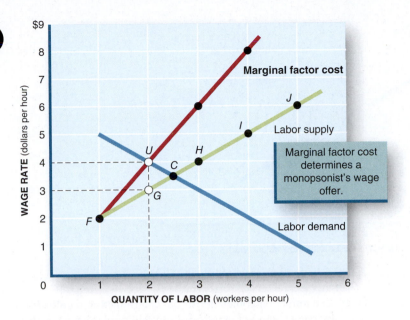

FIGURE 17.6
Marginal Factor Cost

More workers can be attracted only if the wage rate is increased. As it rises, all workers must be paid the higher wage. Consequently, the change in *total* wage costs exceeds the actual wage paid to the last worker. In the table, notice that in row *I*, for example, the marginal factor cost of the fourth worker ($8) exceeds the wage actually paid to that worker ($5). Thus the marginal factor cost curve lies above the labor supply curve.

In the graph, the intersection of the marginal factor cost and labor demand curves (point *U*) indicates the quantity of labor a monopsonist will want to hire. The labor supply curve (at point *G*) indicates the wage rate that must be paid to attract the desired number of workers. This is the monopsonist's desired wage ($3). In the absence of market power, an employer would end up at point *C* (the competitive equilibrium), paying a higher wage and employing more workers.

	Wage Rate (per Hour)	×	Quantity of Labor Supplied (Workers per Hour)	=	Total Wage Cost (per Hour)		Marginal Factor Cost (per Labor-Hour)
D	$0		0		$ 0		
E	1		0		0		
F	2		1		2	>	2
G	3		2		6	>	4
H	4		3		12	>	6
I	5		4		20	>	8
J	6		5		30	>	10

At point *U* the monopsonist is *willing to hire* two workers per hour at a wage rate of $4. But the firm doesn't have to pay this much. The labor supply curve informs us that two workers are *willing to work* for only $3 an hour. Hence the firm first decides how many workers it wants to hire (at point *U*) and then looks at the labor supply curve (point *G*) to see what it has to pay them. As we suspected, *a monopsonistic employer ends up hiring fewer workers at a lower wage rate than would prevail in a competitive market* (point *C*).

COLLECTIVE BARGAINING

The potential for conflict between a powerful employer and a labor union should be evident:

- *The objective of a labor union is to establish a wage rate that's **higher** than the competitive wage* (Figure 17.3).
- *A monopsonist employer seeks to establish a wage rate that's **lower** than competitive standards* (Figure 17.6).

The resultant clash generates intense bargaining that often spills over into politics, the courts, and open conflict.

The confrontation of power on both sides of the labor market is a situation referred to as **bilateral monopoly.** In such a market, wages and employment aren't determined simply by

bilateral monopoly: A market with only one buyer (a monopsonist) and one seller (a monopolist).

FIGURE 17.7

The Boundaries of Collective Bargaining

Firms with power in the labor market seek to establish wages and employment levels corresponding to point *G* (from Figure 17.6). Unions, on the other hand, seek to establish an equilibrium at point *U* (from Figure 17.3). The competitive equilibrium is at point *C*. The function of collective bargaining is to identify a compromise between these points—that is, to locate an equilibrium somewhere in the shaded area.

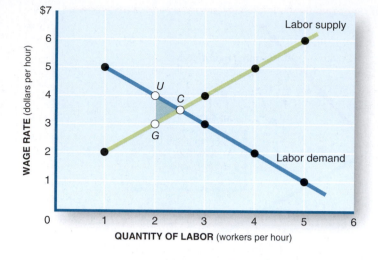

collective bargaining: Direct negotiations between employers and unions to determine labor market outcomes.

supply and demand. Rather, economic outcomes must be determined by **collective bargaining**—that is, direct negotiations between employers and labor unions for the purpose of determining wages, employment, working conditions, and related issues.

Possible Agreements

In a typical labor–business confrontation, the two sides begin by stating their preferences for equilibrium wages and employment. The *demands* laid down by the union are likely to revolve around point *U* in Figure 17.7; the *offer* enunciated by management is likely to be at point *G*.[1] Thus the boundaries of a potential settlement—a negotiated final equilibrium—are usually established at the outset of collective bargaining. The accompanying News summarizes the points of contention in the 1991–1998 dispute between Caterpillar and the UAW.

IN THE NEWS

Caterpillar vs. the UAW

What Separates the Two Sides

	Company Proposal	Union Proposal
Wages	One 3% wage hike for 12,800 of Cat's 16,500 union workers.	One 3% wage hike for all workers, plus two one-time payments of 3% each.
	Lower pay for new hires at parts distribution centers.	Same wage scales for all union workers.
Benefits	Medical co-payments and a preferred provider plan.	A traditional plan with no co-payments.
Job security	Employment levels can fall by attrition.	Guaranteed number of union jobs.

—Kevin Kelly

Source: "This Brawl Could Cost Cat a Couple of Its Lives," *BusinessWeek,* March 23, 1992, pp. 82–84. Used with permission of Bloomberg L.P. Copyright © 2011. All rights reserved.

Analysis: Collective bargaining begins with a set of union demands and management offers. The outcome depends on the relative strength and tactics of the two parties.

[1]Even though points *U* and *G* may not be identical to the initial bargaining positions, they represent the positions of maximum attainable benefit for both sides. Points outside the demand or supply curve will be rejected out of hand by one side or the other.

The interesting part of collective bargaining isn't the initial bargaining positions but the negotiation of the final settlement. The speed with which a settlement is reached and the terms of the resulting compromise depend on the patience, tactics, and resources of the negotiating parties. ***The fundamental source of negotiating power for either side is its ability to withhold labor or jobs.*** The union can threaten to strike, thereby cutting off the flow of union labor to the employer. The employer can impose a lockout, thereby cutting off jobs and paychecks. The effectiveness of those threats depends on the availability of substitute workers or jobs.

The Pressure to Settle

Labor and management both suffer from either a strike or a lockout, no matter who initiates the work stoppage. The strike benefits paid to workers are rarely comparable to wages they would otherwise have received, and the payment of those benefits depletes the union treasury. By the same token, the reduction in labor costs and other expenses rarely compensates the employer for lost profits.

When the UAW was unable to attain its bargaining goals with Caterpillar, it instructed its 12,600 workers to go out on strike. The Caterpillar company, however, held a strong bargaining position. As a result of the 1990–1991 recession, it had a huge inventory of unsold farm equipment and was in no hurry to settle. When inventories got low, Caterpillar found a willing supply of replacement workers. This substitute labor put pressure on the union to settle. In 1994 the company actually attained record profits, despite the continuing strike.

In 1996 a strike by UAW workers at a GM brake plant caused shutdowns at all of GM's 29 U.S. assembly plants. More than 175,000 workers were idled. GM's 1,600 parts suppliers also had to lay off workers. With heavy inventories of unsold cars, GM had a relatively strong bargaining position. The UAW caved in quickly (17 days later). In 1998 the balance of power was reversed. Car sales were brisk, and inventories were lean. So when the UAW struck a key parts plant in June 1998, GM was under greater pressure to settle. Rather than continuing to lose over $100 million a day, GM relented after 54 days, accepting little more than a UAW promise not to strike again for a year and a half.

The bargaining situation was very different in 2007. GM had been losing money and market share for years, largely due to its high labor costs (roughly $25–30 an hour higher than nonunionized U.S-based foreign automakers like Toyota). GM also had ample inventories of unsold cars and lots of cash ($23 billion) in the bank. Last but far from least, GM had the threat of moving more production to overseas GM plants. The UAW was in a much weaker position. The first nationwide UAW strike since 1976 ended in a mere 41 hours, and GM got much of what it wanted (see the News on page 369).

The 2004–2005 National Hockey League bargaining ended up even worse for the union. Unable to compromise on the level of salary caps (team budgets for player pay), the NHL *canceled* the entire 2004–2005 hockey season. That cancellation cost the players $1 *billion* in lost pay and the team owners more than $200 million.

In March 2011 the owners of National Football League teams locked out their players after months of unresolved negotiations. The owners were hoping that the financial squeeze on the players would make them more amenable to settlement. Walmart used an extreme version of that tactic to fend off union power: it simply shuttered its Canadian store and eliminated all the jobs (see the World View on the next page).

Because potential income losses are usually high, both labor and management try to avoid a strike or lockout if they can. In fact, ***over 90 percent of the 20,000 collective bargaining agreements negotiated each year are concluded without recourse to a strike*** and often without even the explicit threat of one.

The Final Settlement

The built-in pressures for settlement help resolve collective bargaining. They don't tell us, however, what the dimensions of that final settlement will be. All we know is that the settlement will be located within the boundaries established in Figure 17.7. The relative pressures on each side will determine whether the final equilibrium is closer to the union or the management position.

Analysis: The power to lock out workers is the ultimate source of employer power in collective bargaining. Walmart chose an extreme use of that power.

The final settlement almost always necessitates hard choices on both sides. The union usually has to choose between an increase in job security or higher pay. A union must also consider how management will react in the long run to higher wages, perhaps by introducing new technology that reduces its dependence on labor. The employer has to worry whether productivity will suffer if workers are dissatisfied with their pay package.

THE IMPACT OF UNIONS

We know that unions tend to raise wage rates in individual companies, industries, and occupations. But can we be equally sure that unions have raised wages in general? If the UAW is successful in raising wages in the automobile industry, what, if anything, happens to car prices? If car prices rise in step with UAW wage rates, labor and management in the auto industry will get proportionally larger slices of the economic pie. At the same time, workers in other industries will be burdened with higher car prices.

Relative Wages

One measure of union impact is *relative* wages—the wages of union members in comparison with those of nonunion workers. As we've noted, unions seek to control the supply of labor in a particular industry or occupation. This forces the excluded workers to seek work elsewhere. As a result of this labor supply imbalance, wages tend to be higher in unionized industries than in nonunionized industries. Figure 17.8 illustrates this displacement effect.

Although the theoretical impact of union exclusionism on relative wages is clear, empirical estimates of that impact are fairly rare. We do know that union wages in general are significantly higher than nonunion wages ($917 versus $717 per week in 2010). But part of this differential is due to the fact that unions are more common in industries that have always been more capital-intensive and paid relatively high wages. When comparisons are made within particular industries or sectors, the differential narrows considerably. Nevertheless, there's a general consensus that unions have managed to increase their relative wages by 15 to 20 percent.

Labor's Share of Total Income

Even though unions have been successful in redistributing some income from nonunion to union workers, the question still remains whether they've increased labor's share of *total* income. The *labor share* of total income is the proportion of income received by all

(a) Unionized labor market

(b) Nonunionized labor market

FIGURE 17.8
The Effect of Unions on Relative Wages

In the absence of unions, the average wage rate would be equal to w_1. As unions take control of the market, however, they seek to raise wage rates to w_2, in the process reducing the amount of employment in that market from l_1 to l_2. The workers displaced from the unionized market will seek work in the nonunionized market, thereby shifting the nonunion supply curve to the right. The result will be a reduction of wage rates (to w_3) in the nonunionized market. Thus union wages end up higher than nonunion wages.

workers, in contrast to the share of income received by owners of capital (the *capital share*). The labor share of total income will rise only if the gains to union workers exceed the losses to the (excluded) nonunion workers.

Evidence of unions' impact on labor's share is almost as difficult to assemble as evidence on relative wages, and for much the same reasons. Labor's share of national income has risen dramatically, from only 56 percent in 1919 to 75 percent today. But there have been tremendous changes in the mix of output during that same period. The proportion of output composed of personal services (accountants, teachers, electricians) is much larger now than it was in 1919. The labor share of income derived from personal services is and always was close to 100 percent. Accordingly, ***most of the rise in labor's share of total income is due to changes in the structure of the economy rather than to unionization.***

Prices

One way firms can protect their profits in the face of rising union wages is to raise product prices. If firms raise prices along with union wages, consumers end up footing the bill. In that case, profits and the capital share of total income might not be reduced.

The ability of firms to pass along increased union wages depends on the structure of product markets as well as labor markets. If a firm has power in both markets, it's better able to protect itself in this way. There's little evidence, however, that unions have contributed significantly to general cost-push inflation.

Productivity

Unions also affect prices indirectly via changes in **productivity.** Unions bargain not only for wages but also for work rules that specify how goods should be produced. Work rules may limit the pace of production, restrict the type of jobs a particular individual can perform, or require a minimum number of workers to accomplish a certain task. A factory carpenter, for example, may not be permitted to change a lightbulb that burns out in his shop area. And the electrician who is summoned may be required to have an apprentice on all work assignments. Such restrictive work rules would make it very costly to change a burned-out lightbulb.

Not all work rules are so restrictive. In general, however, work rules are designed to protect jobs and maximize the level of employment at any given rate of output. From this perspective, work rules directly restrain productivity and thus inflate costs and prices.

productivity: Output per unit of input—for example, output per labor-hour.

Work rules may also have some beneficial effects. The added job security provided by work rules and seniority provisions tends to reduce labor turnover (quitting) and thus saves recruitment and training costs. Protective rules may also make workers more willing to learn new tasks and to train others in specific skills. Richard Freeman of Harvard asserts that unions have actually accelerated advances in productivity and economic growth.

Political Impact

Perhaps more important than any of these specific union effects is the general impact the union movement has had on our economic, social, and political institutions. Unions are a major political force in the United States. They've not only provided critical electoral and financial support for selected political candidates (including President Obama), but they've also fought hard for important legislation. Unions have succeeded in establishing minimum wage laws, work and safety rules, and retirement benefits. They've also actively lobbied for civil rights legislation and health and education programs. Whatever one may think of any particular union or specific union action, it's clear that our institutions and national welfare would be very different in their absence.

THE ECONOMY TOMORROW

MERGING TO SURVIVE

Unions have been in retreat for nearly a generation. As shown in Figure 17.4, the unionized share of the labor force has fallen from 35 percent in 1950 to less than 12 percent today. Even that modest share has been maintained only by the spread of unionism among public schoolteachers and other government employees. In the private sector, the unionization rate is less than 7 percent and still declining. The Teamsters, the Auto Workers, and the Steelworkers have lost over 1 million members in the last 15 years.

The decline in unionization is explained by three phenomena. Most important is the relative decline in manufacturing, coupled with rapid growth in high-tech service industries (like computer software, accounting, and medical technology). The second force is the downsizing of major corporations and the relatively faster growth of smaller companies. These structural changes have combined to shrink the traditional employment base of labor unions.

The third cause of shrinking unionization is increased global competition. The decline of worldwide trade and investment barriers has made it easier for firms to import products from low-wage nations and even to relocate production plants. With more options, firms can more easily resist increased wage demands.

The labor union movement is fully aware of these forces and determined to resist them. To increase their power, unions are merging across craft and industry lines. In 1995 the Rubber Workers merged with the Steelworkers, the two major textile unions combined forces, and the Food Workers and Retail Clerks formed a new union. In 1999 the Grain Millers merged with the Paperworkers Union. By merging, the unions hope to increase representation, gain financial strength, and enhance their political clout. They're also seeking to broaden their appeal by organizing low-wage workers in the service industries. These efforts, together with their political strength, will help unions to play a continuing role in the economy tomorrow, even if their share of total employment continues to shrink.

web analysis

For information about recent union contracts and strikes, see the U.S. Bureau of Labor Statistics at **www.bls.gov** and search for "collective bargaining."

SUMMARY

- Power in labor markets is the ability to alter market wage rates. Such power is most evident in local labor markets defined by geographical, occupational, or industrial boundaries. LO17-1

- Power on the supply side of labor markets is manifested by unions, organized along industry or craft lines. The basic function of a union is to evaluate employment offers in terms of the *collective* interest of its members. LO17-1

- The downward slope of the labor demand curve creates a distinction between the marginal wage and the market wage. The marginal wage is the change in *total* wages occasioned by employment of one additional worker and is less than the market wage. LO17-1

- Unions seek to establish that rate of employment at which the marginal wage curve intersects the labor supply curve. The desired union wage is then found on the labor demand curve at that level of employment. LO17-1

- Power on the demand side of labor markets is manifested in buyer concentrations such as monopsony and oligopsony. Such power is usually found among the same firms that exercise market power in product markets. LO17-2

- By definition, power on the demand side implies some direct influence on market wage rates; additional hiring by a monopsonist will force up the market wage rate. Hence a monopsonist must recognize a distinction between the marginal factor cost of labor and its (lower) market wage rate. LO17-2

- The goal of a monopsonistic employer is to hire the number of workers at which the marginal factor cost of labor equals its marginal revenue product. The employer then looks at the labor supply curve to determine the wage rate that must be paid for that number of workers. LO17-2

- The desire of unions to establish a wage rate that's higher than competitive wages directly opposes the desire of powerful employers to establish lower wage rates. In bilateral monopolies unions and employers engage in collective bargaining to negotiate a final settlement. LO17-2

- The impact of unions on the economy is difficult to measure. It appears, however, that they've increased their own relative wages and contributed to rising prices. They've also had substantial political impact. LO17-3

Key Terms

labor supply	union shop	bilateral monopoly
demand for labor	unionization rate	collective bargaining
equilibrium wage	monopsony	productivity
market power	marginal factor cost (MFC)	
marginal wage	marginal revenue product (MRP)	

Questions for Discussion

1. Collective bargaining sessions often start with unreasonable demands and categorical rejections. Why do unions and employers tend to begin bargaining from extreme positions? LO17-2

2. Does a strike for a raise of 5 cents an hour make any sense? What kinds of long-term benefits might a union gain from such a strike? LO17-1

3. Why do some college professors join a union? What are the advantages or disadvantages of campus unionization? LO17-1

4. Are large and powerful firms easier targets for union organization than small firms? Why or why not? LO17-1

5. Nonunionized firms tend to offer wage rates that are close to rates paid by unionized firms in the same industry. How do you explain this? LO17-3

6. Why are farmworkers much less successful than airplane machinists in securing higher wages? LO17-2

7. In 1998 teaching assistants at the University of California struck for higher wages and union recognition, something they had sought for 14 years. How might the availability of replacement workers have affected their power? LO17-2

8. Why was the 2007 UAW strike (News, p. 369, and text, p. 379) so short? LO17-2

9. Why did Walmart choose to close its store rather than hire 30 more workers (World View, p. 380)? LO17-2

10. How will union mergers affect the market power of unions? LO17-2

 web activities to accompany this chapter can be found on the Online Learning Center: **http://www.mhhe.com/schiller13e**

 mobile app Visit your mobile app store and download the Schiller: Study Econ app *today!*

LO17-1 1. Complete the following table:

Wage rate	$14	$13	$12	$11	$10	$9	$8	$7
Quantity of labor demanded	0	5	20	50	75	95	110	120
Marginal wage	___	___	___	___	___	___	___	___

(a) What is the marginal wage when the nominal wage is $11?

(b) At what wage rate does the marginal wage first become negative?

LO17-1 2. Complete the following table:

Wage rate	$6	$7	$8	$9	$10	$11	$12
Quantity of labor supplied	80	120	155	180	200	210	215
Marginal factor cost	___	___	___	___	___	___	___

LO17-2 3. Based on the data in Problems 1 and 2 above,

(a) What is the competitive wage rate?

(b) Approximately what wage will the union seek?

(c) How many workers will the union have to exclude in order to get that wage?

LO17-2 4. At the time of the National Football League strike in 1987, the football owners made available the following data:

	Total Team Revenues and Costs	
Source of Revenue	Before the Strike	During the Strike
Television	$973,000	$973,000
Stadium gate	526,000	126,000
Luxury box seats	255,000	200,000
Concessions	60,000	12,000
Radio	40,000	40,000
Players' salaries and costs	854,000	230,000
Nonplayer costs (coaches' salaries)	200,000	200,000

(a) Compute total revenues, total expenses, and profits both before and during the strike.

	Before Strike	During Strike
Total revenue	_____	_____
Total expense	_____	_____
Total profit	_____	_____

(b) Who was better positioned to endure the strike?   A: NFL owners   B: players

LO17-3 5. Suppose the following supply and demand schedules apply in a particular labor market:

Wage rate (per hour)	$4	$5	$6	$7	$8	$9	$10
Quantity of labor supplied (workers per hour)	2	3	4	5	6	7	8
Quantity of labor demanded (workers per hour)	6	5	4	3	2	1	0

Graph the relevant curves and identify the

(a) Competitive wage rate. _____

(b) Union wage rate. _____

(c) Monopsonist's wage rate. _____

Financial Markets

Christopher Columbus had a crazy entrepreneurial idea. He was certain he could find a new route to the Indies by sailing not east from Europe but west—around the world. Such a route, he surmised, would give Europe quicker access to the riches of the East Indies. Whoever discovered that western route could become very, very rich.

To find that route, Columbus needed ships, sailors, and tons of provisions. He couldn't afford to supply these resources himself. He needed financial backers who would put up the money. For several years he tried to convince King Ferdinand of Spain to provide the necessary funds. But the king didn't want to risk so much wealth on a single venture. Twice he turned Columbus down.

Fortunately, Genoese merchant bankers in Seville came to Columbus's rescue. Convinced that Columbus's "enterprise of the Indies" might bring back "pearls, precious stones, gold, silver, spiceries," and other valuable merchandise, they guaranteed repayment of any funds lent to Columbus. With that guarantee in hand, the Duke of Medina Sidonia, in April 1492, offered to lend 1,000 maravedis (about $5,000 in today's dollars) to Queen Isabella for the purpose of funding Columbus's expedition. With no personal financial risk, King Ferdinand then granted Columbus the funds and authority for a royal expedition.

Columbus's experience in raising funds for his expedition illustrates a critical function of financial markets—namely, the management of *risk*. This chapter examines how financial markets facilitate economic activities (like Columbus's expedition) by managing the risks of failure. Three central questions guide the discussion:

- **What is traded in financial markets?**
- **How do the financial markets affect the economic outcomes of WHAT, HOW, and FOR WHOM?**
- **Why do financial markets fluctuate so much?**

THE ROLE OF FINANCIAL MARKETS

A central question for every economy is WHAT to produce. In 1492 all available resources were employed in farming, fishing, food distribution, metalworking, and other basic services. For Columbus to pursue his quest, he needed some of those resources. To get them, he needed money to bid scarce resources from other pursuits and employ them on his expedition.

Financial Intermediaries

Entrepreneurs who don't have great personal wealth must get start-up funds from other people. There are two possibilities: either *borrow* the money, or invite other people to *invest* in the new venture.

How might you pursue these options? You could ask your relatives for a loan or go door-to-door in your neighborhood seeking investors. But such direct fund-raising is costly, inefficient, and often unproductive. Columbus went hat in hand to the Spanish royal court twice, but each time he came back empty-handed.

The task of raising start-up funds is made much easier by the existence of **financial intermediaries**—institutions that steer the flow of savings to cash-strapped entrepreneurs and other investors. Funds flow into banks, pension funds, bond markets, stock markets, and other financial intermediaries from businesses, households, and government entities that have some unspent income. This pool of national savings is then passed on to entrepreneurs, expanding businesses, and other borrowers by these same institutions (see Figure 18.1).

Financial intermediaries provide several important services. They greatly reduce the cost of locating loanable funds. Their pool of savings offers a clear economy of scale compared to the alternative of door-to-door solicitations. They also reduce the cost to savers of finding suitable lending or investment opportunities. Few individuals have the time, resources, or interest to do the searching on their own. With huge pools of amassed savings, however, financial intermediaries have the incentive to acquire and analyze information about lending and investment opportunities. Hence *financial intermediaries reduce search and information costs* in the financial markets. In so doing, they make the allocation of resources more efficient.

Although financial intermediaries make the job of acquiring start-up funds a lot easier, there's no guarantee that the funds needed will be acquired. First, there must be an adequate supply of funds available. Second, financial intermediaries must be convinced that they should allocate some of those funds to a project.

> **financial intermediary:**
> Institution (e.g., bank or the stock market) that makes savings available to dissavers (e.g., investors).

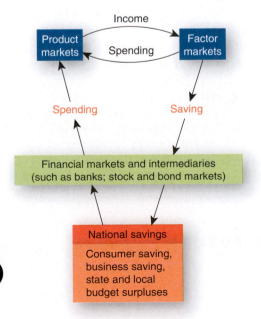

FIGURE 18.1
Mobilizing Savings

The central economic function of financial markets is to channel national savings into new investment and other desired expenditure. Financial intermediaries such as banks, insurance companies, and stockbrokers help transfer purchasing power from savers to spenders.

The Supply of Loanable Funds

As noted, the supply of loanable funds originates in the decisions of market participants to not spend all their current income. Those saving decisions are influenced by time preferences and interest rates.

Time Preferences. In deciding to *save* rather than *spend,* people effectively reallocate their spending over time. That is, people save *now* in order to spend more *later.* How much to save, then, depends partly on *time preference.* If a person doesn't give any thought to the future, she's likely to save little. If, by contrast, a person wants to buy a car, a vacation, or a house in the future, she's more inclined to save some income now.

Interest Rates. Interest rates also affect saving decisions. If interest rates are high, the future payoff to every dollar saved is greater. A higher return on savings translates into more future income for every dollar of current income saved. Hence **higher interest rates increase the quantity of available savings (loanable funds).**

Risk. In early 2009 banks in Zimbabwe were offering interest rates on savings accounts of more than 100,000 percent a year. Yet few people rushed to deposit their savings in Zimbabwean banks. Inflation was running at a rate of 230 *million* percent a year, making a 100,000 percent return look pitifully small. Further, people worried that political instability in Zimbabwe might cause the banks to fail, wiping out their savings in the process. In other words, there was a high *risk* attached to those phenomenal interest rates.

Anyone who contemplated lending funds to Columbus confronted a similar risk: the potential payoff was huge but so was the risk. That was the dilemma King Ferdinand confronted. He had enough funds to finance Columbus's expedition, but he didn't want to risk losing so much on a single venture.

Risk Management. This is why the Genoese bankers were so critical: these financial intermediaries could spread the risk of failure among many individuals. Each investor could put up just a fraction of the needed funds. No one had to put all his eggs in one basket. Once the consortium of bankers agreed to share the risks of Columbus's expedition, the venture had wings. The Genoese merchant bankers could afford to take portions of the expedition's risks because they also financed many less risky projects. By diversifying their portfolios, they could attain whatever degree of *average* risk they preferred. That is the essence of risk management.

risk premium: The difference in rates of return on risky (uncertain) and safe (certain) investments.

Risk Premiums. Even though diversification permits greater risk management, lenders will want to be compensated for any above-average risks they take. Money lent to local merchants must have seemed a lot less risky than lending funds to Columbus. Thus no one would have stepped forward to finance Columbus unless promised an *above-average* return upon the expedition's success. The difference between the rates of return on a safe (certain) investment and a risky (uncertain) one is called the **risk premium.** Risk premiums compensate people who finance risky ventures that succeed. Because these ventures are risky, however, investors often lose their money in such ventures too.

Risk premiums help explain why blue-chip corporations such as Microsoft can borrow money from a bank at the low "prime" rate while ordinary consumers have to pay much higher interest rates on personal loans. Corporate loans are less risky because corporations typically have plenty of revenue and assets to cover their debts. Consumers often get overextended, however, and can't pay all their bills. As a result, there's a greater risk that consumers' loans won't be paid back. Banks charge higher interest rates on consumer loans to compensate for this risk.

THE PRESENT VALUE OF FUTURE PROFITS

In deciding whether to assume the *risk* of supplying funds to a new venture, financial intermediaries assess the potential *rewards.* In Columbus's case, the rewards were the fabled treasures of the East Indies. Even if he found those treasures, however, the rewards would only come long after the expedition was financed. When Columbus proposed his East Indies expedition, he envisioned a round trip that would last at least six months. If he located the treasures he sought, he planned subsequent trips to acquire and transport his precious cargoes back home. Although King Ferdinand granted Columbus only one-tenth of any profits from the first expedition, Columbus had a claim on one-eighth of the profits of any subsequent voyages. Hence, even if Columbus succeeded in finding a shortcut to the East, he wouldn't generate any substantial profit for perhaps two years or more. That's a long time to wait.

Suppose for the moment that Columbus expected no profit from the first expedition but a profit of $1,000 at the end of two years from a second voyage. How much was that future profit worth to Columbus in 1492?

Time Value of Money

To assess the present value of *future* receipts, we have to consider the *time value* of money. A dollar received today is worth more than a dollar received two years from today. Why? Because a dollar received today can earn *interest*. If you have a dollar today and put it in an interest-bearing account, in two years you'll have your original dollar *plus* accumulated interest. *As long as interest-earning opportunities exist, present dollars are worth more than future dollars.*

In 1492 there were plenty of opportunities to earn interest. Indeed, the Genoese bankers were charging high interest rates on their loans and guarantees. If Columbus had had the cash, he too could have lent money to others and earned interest on his funds.

To calculate the present value of future dollars, this forgone interest must be taken into account. This computation is essentially interest accrual in reverse. *We "discount" future dollars by the opportunity cost of money*—that is, the market rate of interest.

Suppose the market rate of interest in 1492 was 10 percent. To compute the **present discounted value (PDV)** of future payment, we discount as follows:

present discounted value (PDV): The value today of future payments, adjusted for interest accrual.

$$PDV = \frac{\text{Future payment}_N}{(1 + \text{Interest rate})^N}$$

where N refers to the number of years into the future when a payment is to be made. If the future payment is to be made in one year, the N in the equation equals 1, and we have

$$PDV = \frac{\$1,000}{1.10}$$
$$= \$909.09$$

Hence the present discounted value of $1,000 to be paid one year from today is $909.09. If $909.09 were received today, it could earn interest. In a year's time, the $909.09 would grow to $1,000 with interest accrued at the rate of 10 percent per year.

Suppose it would have taken Columbus two years to complete his expeditions and collect his profits, rather than one year. In that case, the present value of the $1,000 payment would be lower. The N in the formula would be 2, and the present value would be

$$PDV = \frac{\$1,000}{(1.10)^2} = \frac{\$1,000}{1.21} = \$826.45$$

Hence *the longer one has to wait for a future payment, the less present value it has.*

Lottery winners often have to choose between present and future values. In July 2004, for example, Geraldine Williams, a 68-year-old housekeeper in Lowell, Massachusetts, won a $294 million MegaMillions lottery. The $294 million was payable in 26 annual installments of $11.3 million. If the lucky winner wanted to get her prize sooner, she could accept an immediate but smaller payout rather than 25 future installments.

Table 18.1 shows how the lottery officials figured the present value of the $294 million prize. The first installment of $11.3 million would be paid immediately. Mrs. Williams would have had to wait one year for the second check, however. At the then-prevailing interest rate of 4.47 percent, the *present* value of that second $11.3 million check was only $10.82 million. The *last* payoff check had even less present value since it wasn't due to be

TABLE 18.1
Computing Present Value

The present value of a future payment declines the longer one must wait for a payment. At an interest rate of 4.47 percent, $11.3 million payable in one year is worth only $10.82 million today. A payout of $11.3 million 25 years from now has a present value of only $3.79 million. A string of $11.3 million payments spread out over 25 years has a present value of $168 million (at 4.47 percent interest).

Years in the Future	Future Payment ($ millions)	Present Value ($ millions)
0	$ 11.3	$ 11.30
1	11.3	10.82
2	11.3	10.35
3	11.3	9.91
4	11.3	9.49
5	11.3	8.04
*	*	*
*	*	*
*	*	*
25	11.3	3.79
	$294.0	$168.0

Note: The general formula for computing present values is $PDV = \Sigma \dfrac{\text{Payment in year } N}{(1 + r)^N}$, where r is the prevailing rate.

web analysis

To make quick present value calculations, visit **www. moneychimp.com.** Click the "Calculator" tab.

paid for 25 years. With so much time for interest to accrue, that final $11.3 million payment had a present value of only $3.79 million. The calculations in Table 18.1 convinced lottery officials to offer an immediate (present) payout of only $168 million on the $294 million (future) prize. Mrs. Williams wasn't too disappointed.

Interest Rate Effects

The winner would have received even *less* money had interest rates been higher. At the time Mrs. Williams won the lottery, the interest rate on bonds was 4.47 percent. Had the interest rate been higher, the discount for immediate payment would have been higher as well. Table 18.2 indicates that Mrs. Williams would have received only $107 million had the prevailing interest rate been 10 percent. What Tables 18.1 and 18.2 illustrate, then, is that *the present discounted value of a future payment declines with*

- *Higher interest rates.*
- *Longer delays in future payment.*

Uncertainty

The valuation of future payments must also consider the possibility of *non*payment. State governments are virtually certain to make promised lottery payouts, so there's little risk in accepting a promised payout of 25 annual installments. But what about the booty from Columbus's expeditions? There was great uncertainty that Columbus would ever return from his expeditions, much less bring back the "pearls, precious stones, gold, silver, and

The success of Columbus's voyage was highly uncertain.

TABLE 18.2
Higher Interest Rates Reduce Present Values

Higher interest rates raise the *future* value of current dollars. The rates therefore reduce the *present* value of future payments. Shown here is the present discounted value of the July 2004 MegaMillions lottery prize of $294 million at different interest rates.

Interest Rate (%)	Present Discounted Value of $294 Million Lottery Prize ($ millions)
5.0%	$166.3
6.0	150.8
7.0	137.5
8.0	126.0
9.0	115.9
10.0	107.1

spiceries" that people coveted. Investing in those expeditions was far riskier than deferring a lottery payment.

Expected Value. Whenever an anticipated future payment is uncertain, a risk factor should be included in present value computations. This is done by calculating the **expected value** of a future payment. Suppose there was only a 50:50 chance that Columbus would bring back the goods. In that event, the expected payoff would be

Expected value = (1 − Risk factor) × Present discounted value

With a 50:50 chance of failure, the expected value of Columbus's first-year profits would have been

$$\text{Expected value} = (1 - 0.5) \times \$909.09$$
$$= \$454.55$$

Expected values also explain why people buy more lottery tickets when the prize is larger. The odds of winning the multistate Powerball lottery are 80 *million*:1. That's about the same odds as getting struck by lightning *14 times* in the same year! So it makes almost no sense to buy a ticket. With a $16 million prize, the *undiscounted* expected value of a $1 lottery ticket is only 20 cents. When the lottery prize increases, however, the expected value of a ticket grows as well (there are still only 80 million possible combinations of numbers). When the grand prize reached $250 million in July 1998, the undiscounted expected value of a lone winning ticket jumped to over $3. Millions of people decided that the expected value was high enough to justify buying a $1 lottery ticket. People took off from work, skipped classes, and drove across state lines to queue up for lottery tickets. So many people bought tickets on the last day that the lottery grand prize swelled to $295 million. (Thirteen machinists from Ohio had the winning ticket and chose the present discounted value of $165.6 million.) When the prize is only $10 million, far fewer people buy tickets.

The Demand for Loanable Funds

People rarely borrow money to buy lottery tickets. But entrepreneurs and other market participants often use other people's funds to finance their ventures. *How much loanable funds are demanded depends on*

- *The expected rate of return.*
- *The cost of funds.*

The higher the expected return, or the lower the cost of funds, the greater will be the amount of loanable funds demanded.

Figure 18.2 offers a general view of the loanable funds market that emerges from these considerations. From the entrepreneur's perspective, the prevailing interest rate represents

expected value: The probable value of a future payment, including the risk of nonpayment.

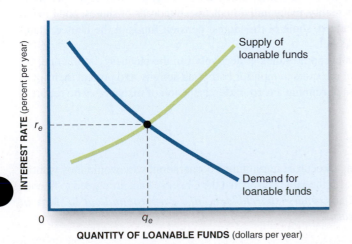

FIGURE 18.2
The Loanable Funds Market

The market rate of interest (r_e) is determined by the intersection of the curves representing supply of and demand for loanable funds. The rate of interest represents the price paid for the use of money.

the cost of funds. From the perspective of savers, the interest rate represents the payoff to savings. When interest rates rise, the quantity of funds supplied goes up and the quantity demanded goes down. The prevailing (equilibrium) interest rate is set by the intersection of these supply and demand curves.

THE STOCK MARKET

The concept of a loanable funds market sounds a bit alien. But the same principles of supply, demand, and risk management go a long way in explaining the action in stock markets. Suppose you had $1,000 to invest. Should you invest it all in lottery tickets that offer a multimillion-dollar payoff? Put it in a savings account that pays next to nothing? Or how about the stock market? The stock market can reward you handsomely, or it can wipe out your savings if the stocks you own tumble. Hence *stocks offer a higher average return than bank accounts but also entail greater average risk.* People who bought Amazon.com stock in May 1997 got a 1,000 percent profit on their stock in only two years. But people who bought Amazon.com stock in December 1999 lost 90 percent of their investment in even less time.

Corporate Stock

When people buy a share of stock, they're buying partial ownership of a corporation. The three legal forms of business entities are

- Corporations.
- Partnerships.
- Proprietorships.

corporation: A business organization having a continuous existence independent of its members (owners) and power and liabilities distinct from those of its members.

Limited Liability. Proprietorships are businesses owned by a single individual. The owner–proprietor is entirely responsible for the business, including repayment of any debts. Members of a partnership are typically liable for all business debts and activities as well. By contrast, a **corporation** is a limited liability form of business. The corporation itself, not its individual shareholders, is responsible for all business activity and debts. As a result of this limited liability, you can own a piece of a corporation without worrying about being sued for business mishaps (like environmental damage) or nonpayment of debt. This feature significantly reduces the risk of owning corporate stock.

corporate stock: Shares of ownership in a corporation.

Shared Ownership. The ownership of a corporation is defined in terms of stock shares. Each share of **corporate stock** represents partial ownership of the business. Chipmaker Intel, for example, has nearly 6 *billion* shares of stock outstanding (that is, shares held by the public). Hence each share of Intel stock represents less than one-sixth of one-billionth ownership of the corporation. Potentially, this means that as many as 6 billion people could own the Intel Corporation. In reality, many individuals own hundreds of shares, and institutions may own thousands. Indeed, some of the largest pension funds in the United States own over a million shares of Intel.

In principle, the owners of corporate stock collectively run the business. In practice, the shareholders select a board of directors to monitor corporate activity and protect their interests. The day-to-day business of running a corporation is the job of managers who report to the board of directors.

Stock Returns

If shareholders don't have any direct role in running a corporation, why would they want to own a piece of it? Essentially, for the same reason that the Genoese bankers agreed to finance Columbus's expedition: profits. *Owners (shareholders) of a corporation hope to share in the profits the corporation earns.*

Dividends. Shareholders rarely receive their full share of the company's profits in cash. Corporations typically use some of the profits for investment in new plants or equipment. They may also want to retain some of the profits for operational needs or unforeseen contingencies. *Corporations may choose to retain earnings or pay them out to shareholders as* **dividends.** Any profits *not* paid to shareholders are referred to as **retained earnings.** Thus

$$\text{Dividends} = \text{Corporate profits} - \text{Retained earnings}$$

In 2010 Intel paid quarterly dividends amounting to 72 cents per share for the year. But the company earned profits equal to $2.01 per share. Thus shareholders received only 36 percent of their accrued profits in dividend checks; Intel retained the remaining $1.29 per-share profit earned in 2010 for future investments.

dividend: Amount of corporate profits paid out for each share of stock.

Capital Gains. If Intel invests its retained earnings wisely, the corporation may reap even larger profits in the future. As a company grows and prospers, each share of ownership may become more valuable. This increase in value would be reflected in higher market prices for shares of Intel stock. Any increase in the value of a stock represents a **capital gain** for shareholders. Capital gains directly increase shareholder wealth.

retained earnings: Amount of corporate profits not paid out in dividends.

Total Return. People who own stocks can thus get two distinct payoffs: dividends and capital gains. Together these payoffs represent the total return on stock investments. Hence *the higher the expected total return (future dividends and capital gains), the greater the desire to buy and hold stocks.* If a stock paid no dividends and had no prospects for price appreciation (capital gain), you'd probably hold your savings in a different form (such as another stock or maybe an interest-earning bank account).

capital gain: An increase in the market value of an asset.

Initial Public Offering

When a corporation is formed, its future sales and profits are most uncertain. When shares are first offered to the public, the seller of stock is the company itself. By *going public,* the corporation seeks to raise funds for investment and growth. A true *start-up* company may have nothing more than a good idea, a couple of dedicated employees, and big plans. To fund these plans, it sells shares of itself in an **initial public offering (IPO).** People who buy the newly issued stock are putting their savings directly into the corporation's accounts.[1] As new owners, they stand to profit from the corporation's business or take their lumps if the corporation fails.

initial public offering (IPO): The first issuance (sale) to the general public of stock in a corporation.

In 2004 Google was still a relatively new company. Although the company had been in operation since 1999, search engine capacities were limited. To expand, it needed more computers, more employees, and more technology. To finance this expansion, Google needed more money. The company could have borrowed money from a bank or other financial institution, but that would have saddled the company with debt and forced it to make regular interest payments.

Rather than borrow money, Google's directors elected to sell ownership shares in the company. In August 2004 the company raised $1.7 *billion* in cash by selling 19.6 million shares for $85 per share in its initial public offering.

Secondary Trading

Why were people eager to buy shares in Google? They certainly weren't buying the stock with expectations of high dividends. The company hadn't earned much profit in its first five years and didn't expect substantial profits for at least another few years.

---

[1] In reality, some of the initial proceeds will go to stockbrokers and investment bankers as compensation for their services as financial intermediaries. The entrepreneur who starts the company, other company employees, and any venture capitalists who help fund the company before the public offering may also get some of the IPO receipts by selling shares they acquired before the company went public.

price/earnings (P/E) ratio: The price of a stock share divided by earnings (profit) per share.

P/E Ratio. In 2003 Google had earned only 41 cents of profit per share. In 2004 it would earn 1.46 per share. So people who were buying Google stock for $85 per share in August 2004 were paying a comparatively high price for relatively little profit. This can be seen by computing the **price/earnings (P/E) ratio**:

$$\text{P/E ratio} = \frac{\text{Price of stock share}}{\text{Earnings (profit) per share}}$$

For Google in 2004,

$$\text{P/E ratio} = \frac{\$85}{\$1.46} = 58.2$$

In other words, investors were paying $58.20 for every $1 of profits. That implies a rate of return of $1 \div \$58.20$, or only 1.7 percent. Compared to the interest rates banks were paying on deposit balances, Google shares didn't look like a very good buy.

Profit Expectation. People weren't buying Google stock just to get a piece of *current* profits. What made Google attractive was its *growth* potential. The company projected that revenues and profits would grow rapidly as its search capabilities expanded, more people used its services, and, most important, more advertisers clamored to get premium spots on the company's web pages. Given these expectations, investors projected that Google's profits would jump from $1.46 per share in 2004 to roughly $10 in four years. From that perspective, the *projected* P/E ratio looked cheap.

Investors who wanted a piece of those future profits rushed to buy Google stock after its IPO. On the first day of trading, the share price rose from the IPO price of $85 to $100. Within a month the price rose to $120. Two years later Google's stock sold for more than $450 a share! A lot of investors racked up huge capital gains.

That post-IPO rise in Google's stock price had no direct effect on the company. A corporation reaps the proceeds of stock sales only when it sells shares to the public (the initial public offering). After the IPO, the company's stock is traded among individuals in the "after market." Virtually all the trading activity on major stock exchanges consists of such after-market sales. Mr. Dow sells his Google shares to Ms. Jones, who may later sell them to Mr. Pitt. Such *secondary* trades may take place at the New York Stock Exchange (NYSE) on Wall Street or in the computerized over-the-counter market (e.g., NASDAQ).

Market Fluctuations

The price of a stock at any moment is the outcome of supply-and-demand interactions. I wouldn't mind owning a piece of Google. But since I think the current share price is too high, I'll buy the stock only if the price falls substantially. Even though I'm not buying any Google stock now, I'm part of the *market demand*. That is, all the people who are willing and able to buy Google stock at *some* price are included in the demand curve in Figure 18.3. The cheaper the stock, the more people will want to buy it, *ceteris paribus*. The opposite is true on the supply side of the market: ever-higher prices are necessary to induce more shareholders to part with their shares.

Changing Expectations. In early 2006 investors reevaluated the profit prospects for Google and other Internet companies. Several years of experience had shown that earning profits in e-commerce wasn't so easy. Projections of advertising sales growth and future profits were sharply reduced. In two months' time Google's stock price fell from $470 to $340. Figure 18.3 illustrates how this happened. Higher perceived risk reduced the demand for Google stock and increased the willingness of existing shareholders to sell. Such ***changes in expectations imply shifts in supply and demand for a company's stock.*** As Figure 18.3 illustrates, these combined shifts sent Google stock plummeting.

PRICE (dollars per share)

Initial supply of stock

New supply of stock

A

Expectations drive stock prices.

Initial demand for stock

B

New demand for stock

QUANTITY OF STOCK (shares per day)

FIGURE 18.3
Worsened Expectations

The supply and demand for stocks is fueled by expectations of future profits. When investors concluded that Google's future profit potential wasn't so great (see the News on the next page), demand for the stock decreased, supply increased, and the share price fell from point *A* to point *B*.

web analysis

You can retrieve the latest news about a company and its stock from various online brokerage and investment advice services. You can also retrieve charts showing how a stock price has fluctuated during the day or over longer periods. Free charts on individual stocks are available at **www. bigcharts.com.**

Table 18.3 summarizes the action in Google stock on a single day. On that day 2 million shares of Google were bought and sold. At the end of the trading day (4 p.m. in New York City) Google shares were selling for $529.55 apiece (see "Close" in Table 18.3). Along the path to that closing equilibrium, the price had fluctuated between $529.05 ("Lo") and $535.92 ("Hi"). The stock price fluctuated even more over the preceding year: the "52-week Hi" was $642.96, while the "52-week Lo" was only $433.63. This huge range in the price of Google shares reflects the changing performance and market expectations for the company.

| 52 Weeks | | | | | | | Vol | | | | Net |
Hi	Lo	Stock	Sym	Div	Yld%	P/E	100s	Hi	Lo	Close	Chg
23.86	17.60	Intel	INTC	0.72	3.10	10.91	531049	23.80	23.36	23.41	−0.30
642.96	433.63	Google	GOOG	0	0	20.57	21076	535.92	529.05	529.55	−5.50

The information provided by this quotation includes the following:
52-Weeks Hi and Lo: The highest and lowest prices paid for a share of stock in the previous year.
Stock: The name of the corporation whose shares are being traded.
Sym: The symbol used as a shorthand description for the stock.
Div: A dividend is the amount of profit paid out by the corporation in the preceding year for each share of stock.
Yld%: The yield is the dividend paid per share divided by the price of a share.
P/E: The price of the stock (P) divided by the earnings (profit) per share (E). This indicates how much a purchaser is effectively paying for each dollar of profits.
Vol 100s: The number of shares traded in hundreds.
Hi: The highest price paid for a share of stock on the previous day.
Lo: The lowest price paid for a share of stock on the previous day.
Close: The price paid in the last trade of the day as the market was closing.
Net Chg: The change in the closing price yesterday vs. the previous day's closing price.

Source: E-Trade (May 13, 2011).

TABLE 18.3
Reading Stock Quotes

The financial pages of the daily newspaper summarize the trading activity in corporate stocks. The quotation here summarizes trading in Intel and Google shares on May 13, 2011.

The Value of Information. The wide fluctuations in the price of Google stock illustrate the value of *information* in financial markets. People who paid high prices for Google shares in 2011 had optimistic expectations for the company's continued growth and share appreciation. Those who *sold* shares at high prices weren't so sure. No one *knew* what future profits would be; everyone was acting on the basis of expectations. The news that Yahoo and Microsoft were gaining market share in the search business (see the accompanying News) worsened expectations and drove Google's stock price down by $5.50 (Table 18.3).

IN THE NEWS

Yahoo, Microsoft Gain Slim Search Share from Google—ComScore

Yahoo Inc. (YHOO) and Microsoft Corp. (MSFT) sites gained Internet search market share last month from leader Google Inc. (GOOG), which still dominates the realm by a wide margin, according to researcher comScore Inc. (SCOR).

ComScore said Google's share of the explicit search market dropped three-tenths of a percentage point to 65.4 percent in April. Both Yahoo and Microsoft sites gained two-tenths of a point in share, rising to 15.9 percent and 14.1 percent, respectively.

Market share for the fourth- and fifth-largest search engines, IAC/InterActiveCorp. (IACI) and AOL Inc. (AOL), each fell a tenth of a percentage point.

Overall, users made fewer searches on all these companies' sites in April compared with March. Google, the volume leader, saw its total search number fall 4 percent to 10.7 billion.

—Joan E. Solsman

Source: *Dow Jones Newswires*, www.DowJonesNews.com, May 11, 2011. Used with permission of Dow Jones & Company, Inc. via Copyright Clearance Center, Inc.

Analysis: People who buy a company's stock are betting on *future* sales and profits. If expectations change, the price of the stock will change as well.

The evident value of information raises a question of access. Do some people have better information than others? Do they get their information fairly? Or do they have "inside" sources (such as company technicians, managers, directors) who give them preferential access to information? If so, these insiders would have an unfair advantage in the marketplace and could alter the distribution of income and wealth in their favor.

The value of information also explains the demand for information services. People pay hundreds and even thousands of dollars for newsletters, wire services, and online computer services that provide up-to-date information on companies and markets. They also pay for the services of investment bankers, advisers, and brokers to help keep them informed. These services help disseminate information quickly, thereby helping financial markets operate efficiently.

Booms and Busts. If stock markets are so efficient at computing the present value of future profits, why does the entire market make abrupt moves every so often? Fundamentally, the same factors that determine the price of a single stock influence the broader stock market averages as well. An increase in interest rates, for example, raises the opportunity cost of holding stocks. Hence higher interest rates should cause stock prices to fall, *ceteris paribus*. Stocks might decline even further if higher interest rates are expected to curtail investment and consumption, thus reducing future sales and profits. Such a double whammy could cause the whole stock market to tumble.

Other factors also affect the relative desirability of holding stock. Congressional budget and deficit decisions, monetary policy, consumer confidence, business investment plans, international trade patterns, and new inventions are just a few of the factors that may alter present and future profits. These *broad changes in the economic outlook tend to push all stock prices up or down at the same time.*

Managing Risk

Broad changes in the economic outlook, however, seldom occur overnight. Moreover, these changes are rarely of a magnitude that could precipitate a stock market boom or bust. In reality, the stock market often changes more abruptly than the economic outlook. These *exaggerated movements in the stock market are caused by sudden and widespread changes in expectations.* Keep in mind that the value of the stock depends on anticipated *future* profits and expectations for interest rates and the economic outlook. No elements of the future are certain. Instead people use present clues to try to discern the likely course of future events. In other words, *all information must be filtered through people's expectations.*

The central role of expectations implies that the economy can change more gradually than the stock market. If, for example, interest rates rise, market participants may regard the increase as temporary or inconsequential: their expectations for the future may not change. If interest rates keep rising, however, investors may have greater doubts. At some point, the market participants may revise their expectations. Stock prices may falter, triggering an adjustment in expectations. A herding instinct may surface, sending expectations for stock prices abruptly lower (see the cartoon below).

Resource Allocations

Although it's fascinating and sometimes fun to watch stock market gyrations, we shouldn't lose sight of the *economic* role of financial markets. Columbus needed *real* resources—ships, men, equipment—for his expeditions. Five centuries later, Google also needed real resources—computers, labor, technology—to expand. To find the necessary economic resources, both Columbus and Google had to convince society to reallocate resources from other activities to their new ventures.

Financial markets facilitate resource reallocations. In Columbus's case, the Genoese bankers lent the funds that Columbus used to buy scarce resources. The funds obtained from

Just a normal day at the nation's most important financial institution . . .

© 1989 Baltimore Sun Company. Used with permission of Baltimore Sun Company via Copyright Clearance Center, Inc.

Analysis: Sudden changes in expectations can substantially alter stock prices.

TABLE 18.4
Stock Market Averages

Over 1,600 stocks are listed (traded) on the New York Stock Exchange, and many times that number are traded in other stock markets. To gauge changes in so many stocks, people refer to various indexes, such as the Dow Jones Industrial Average. The Dow and similar indexes help us keep track of the market's ups and downs. Some of the most frequently quoted indexes are

Dow Jones

Industrial Average: An arithmetic average of the prices of 30 blue-chip industrial stocks traded on the New York Stock Exchange (NYSE) and by computers of the National Association of Securities Dealers (NASD).

Transportation Average: An average of 20 transportation stocks traded on the NYSE.

Utilities Average: An average of 15 utility stocks traded on the NYSE.

S&P 500: An index compiled by Standard and Poor of 500 stocks drawn from major stock exchanges as well as over-the-counter stocks. The S&P 500 is made up of 400 industrial companies, 40 utilities, 20 transportation companies, and 40 financial institutions.

NASDAQ Composite: Index of stocks traded in the over-the-counter market among securities dealers.

New York Stock Exchange composite index: The "Big Board" index, which includes all 1,600-plus stocks traded on the NYSE.

Nikkei index: An index of 225 stocks traded on the Tokyo stock market.

Google's 2004 initial public offering served the same purpose. In both cases, the funds obtained in the financial markets helped change the mix of output. If the financial markets hadn't supplied the necessary funding, neither Columbus nor Google would have been able to go forth. The available resources would have been used to produce other goods.

THE BOND MARKET

The bond market is another financial mechanism for transferring the pool of national savings into the hands of would-be spenders. It operates much like the stock market. The major difference is the kind of paper traded. *In the stock market, people buy and sell shares of corporate ownership. In the bond market, people buy and sell promissory notes (IOUs).* A **bond** is simply an IOU, a written promise to repay a loan. The bond itself specifies the terms of repayment, noting both the amount of interest to be paid each year and the maturity date (the date on which the borrower is to repay the entire debt). The borrower may be a corporation (corporate bonds), a local government (municipal bonds), the federal government (Treasury bonds), or some other institution.

bond: A certificate acknowledging a debt and the amount of interest to be paid each year until repayment; an IOU.

Bond Issuance

A bond is first issued when an institution wants to borrow money. Recall the situation Google faced in 2004. The company needed additional funds to expand its Internet operations. Rather than sell equity shares in itself, Google could have *borrowed* funds. The advantage of borrowing funds rather than issuing stock is that the owners can keep control of their company. *Lenders aren't owners, but shareholders are.* The disadvantage of borrowing funds is that the company gets saddled with a repayment schedule. Lenders want to be paid back—with interest. For a new company like Google, the burden of interest payments may be too great.

Ignoring these problems momentarily, let's assume that Google decided in 2004 to borrow funds rather than sell stock in itself. To do so, it would have *issued* bonds. This simply means that it would have printed formal IOUs called bonds. Typically, each bond certificate would have a **par value** (face value) of $1,000. The bond certificate would also specify the rate of interest to be paid and the promised date of repayment. A Google bond issued in

par value: The face value of a bond; the amount to be repaid when the bond is due.

2004, for example, might specify repayment in 10 years, with annual interest payments of $100. The individual who bought the bond from Google would lend $1,000 for 10 years and receive annual interest payments of $100. Thus *the initial bond purchaser lends funds directly to the bond issuer.* The borrower (such as Google, General Motors, or the U.S. Treasury) can then use those funds to acquire real resources. Thus the bond market also functions as a financial intermediary, transferring available savings (wealth) to those who want to acquire more resources (invest).

As in the case of IPOs of stock, the critical issue here is the *price* of the bond. How many people are willing and able to lend funds to the company? What rate of interest will they charge?

As we observed in Figure 18.2, the quantity of loanable funds supplied depends on the interest rate. At low interest rates no one is willing to lend funds to the company. Why lend your savings to a risky venture like Google when more secure bonds and even banks pay higher interest rates? Google might not succeed and later **default** on (not pay) its obligations. Potential lenders would want to be compensated for this extra risk with above-average interest rates—that is, a risk premium. Remember that lenders don't share in any profits Google might earn; they get only interest payments. Hence they'd want a hefty premium to compensate them for the risk of default.

default: Failure to make scheduled payments of interest or principal on a bond.

Suppose that market participants will lend the desired amount of money to Google only at 16 percent interest. In this case, Google may agree to pay an interest rate—the so-called **coupon rate**—of 16 percent to secure start-up funding of $50 million. That means Google agrees to pay $160 of interest each year for every $1,000 borrowed and to repay the entire $50 million at the end of 10 years.

coupon rate: Interest rate set for a bond at time of issuance.

Bond Trading

Once a bond has been issued, the initial lenders don't have to wait 10 years to get their money back. They can't go back to the company and demand early repayment, but they can sell their bonds to someone else. This **liquidity** is an important consideration for prospective bondholders. If a person had no choice but to wait 10 years for repayment, he or she might be less willing to buy a bond (lend funds). *By facilitating resales, the bond market increases the availability of funds to new ventures and other borrowers.* As is the case with stocks, most of the action in the bond markets consists of such after-market trades—that is, the buying and selling of bonds issued at some earlier time. The company that first issued the bonds doesn't participate in these trades.

liquidity: The ability of an asset to be converted into cash.

The portfolio decision in the bond market is motivated by the same factors that influence stock purchases. The *opportunity cost* of buying and selling bonds is the best alternative rate of return—for example, the interest rate on other bonds or money market mutual funds. *Expectations* also play a role in gauging both likely changes in opportunity costs and the ability of the borrower to redeem (pay off) the bond when it's due. *Changes in expectations or opportunity costs shift the bond supply and demand curves,* thereby altering market interest rates.

Current Yields

We've assumed that Google would have had to offer 16 percent interest to induce enough people to lend the company (buy bonds worth) $50 million for its initial operations. This was far higher than the 6 percent the U.S. Treasury was paying on its bonds (borrowed funds). This large risk premium reflected the fear that Google might not succeed and end up defaulting on it loans.

Suppose that Google actually took off. The risk of a bond default would diminish, and people would be more willing to lend it funds. This change in the availability of loanable funds is illustrated in the rightward shift of the supply curve in Figure 18.4.

According to the new supply curve in Figure 18.4, Google could now borrow $50 million at 10 percent interest (point *B*) rather than paying 16 percent (point *A*). Unfortunately, Google already borrowed the funds and is obliged to continue paying $160 per year in interest on each bond. Hence the company doesn't benefit directly from the supply shift.

web analysis

Ten-year Treasury Bonds give a good look at bond markets. To see long-run activity in this market, go to the St. Louis Fed at **www.stlouisfed.org.** Click the "Research & Data" tab, then click "FRED."

FIGURE 18.4
Shifts in Funds Supply

If lenders decide that a company's future is less risky, they will be more willing to lend it money or hold its bonds. The resulting shift of the loanable funds supply curve reduces the current yield on a bond by raising its price.

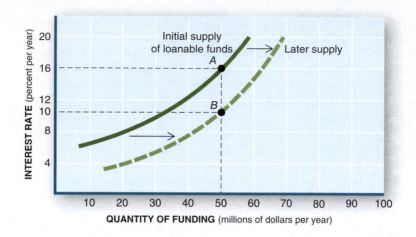

current yield: The rate of return on a bond; the annual interest payment divided by the bond's price.

The change in the equilibrium value of Google bonds must show up somewhere, however. People who hold Google bonds continue to get $160 per year in interest (16 percent of $1,000). Now there are lots of people who would be willing to lend funds to Google at that rate. These people want to hold Google bonds themselves. To get them, they'll have to buy the bonds in the market from existing bondholders. Thus the *increased willingness to lend funds is reflected in an increased demand for bonds.* This increased demand will push up the price of Google bonds. As bond prices rise, their implied effective interest rate **(current yield)** falls. Table 18.5 illustrates this relationship. Notice the phenomenal yield (50.5 percent) on GM bonds in February 2009. GM was teetering on bankruptcy back then, raising the prospect of a bond default. So prospective GM bondholders wanted a huge risk

Price of Bond	Coupon Rate (Annual Interest Payment)	Current Yield
$ 600	$150	25.0%
800	150	18.8
1,000	150	15.0
1,200	150	12.5

The annual interest payment on a bond—the "coupon rate"—is fixed at the time of issuance. Accordingly, only the market (resale) price of the bond itself can change. An increase in the price of the bond lowers its *effective* interest rate, or yield. The formula for computing the current yield on a bond is

$$\text{Current yield} = \frac{\text{Annual interest payment}}{\text{Market (resale) price of bond}}$$

Thus higher bond prices imply lower yields (effective interest rates), as confirmed in the table above. Bond prices and yields vary with changes in expectations and opportunity costs.

The newspaper quotation below shows how changing bond prices and yields are reported. This General Motors (GM) bond was issued with a coupon rate (nominal interest rate) of 8⅜ percent. Hence GM promised to pay $83.75 in interest each year until it redeemed (paid off) the $1,000 bond in the year 2033. In February 2009, however, the market price of the bond was only $160.50 ("16.50"). This created a phenomenal yield of 50.5 percent!

Bond	Current Yield	Volume	Close
GM 8⅜ 33	50.5	142	16.50

TABLE 18.5
Bond Price and Yields Move in Opposite Directions

premium for buying GM bonds (they ended up losing when GM declared bankruptcy in June 2009).

Changing bond prices and yields are important market signals for resource allocation. In our example, the rising price of Google's bonds reflects increased optimism for the company's sales prospects. The collective assessment of the marketplace is that web search engines will be profitable. The increase in the price of Google bonds will make it easier and less costly for the company to borrow additional funds. The reverse scenario unfolded in 2008–2009. When investors concluded that the recession was sapping corporate finances, the supply of funds to dot-coms dried up. That supply shift raised interest rates and made it more difficult for firms to borrow money for new investments.

THE ECONOMY TOMORROW

VENTURE CAPITALISTS—FINANCING TOMORROW'S PRODUCTS

One of the proven paths to high incomes and wealth is entrepreneurship. Most of the great American fortunes originated in entrepreneurial ventures, such as building railroads, mass-producing automobiles, introducing new computers, perfecting mass-merchandising techniques, or pioneering social networking sites (e.g., Facebook). These successful ventures all required more than just a great idea. To convert the original idea into actual output requires the investment of real resources.

Recall that Apple Computer started in a garage with a minimum of resources (Chapter 9). The idea of packaging a personal computer was novel, and few resources were required to demonstrate that it could be done. But Steven Jobs couldn't have become a multimillionaire by building just a few dozen computers a month. To reap huge economic profits from his idea, he needed much greater production capacity. He also needed resources for marketing the new Apples to a broader customer base. In other words, Steven Jobs needed lots of economic resources—land, labor, and capital—to convert his entrepreneurial dream into a profit-making reality.

Steven Jobs and his partner, Steve Wozniak, had few resources of their own. In fact, they'd sold Jobs's Volkswagen and Wozniak's scientific calculator to raise the finances for the first computer. To go any further, they needed financial support from others. Loans were hard to obtain since the company had no assets, no financial history, and no certainty of success. Jobs needed people who were willing to share the *risks* associated with a new venture. He found one such person in A. C. Markkula, who put up $250,000 and became a partner in the new venture. Shortly thereafter, other venture capitalists provided additional financing. With this start-up financing, Jobs was able to acquire more resources and make the Apple Computer Company a reality.

Facebook. Facebook grew from equally modest origins (Mark Zuckerberg's Harvard dorm room) back in 2004. It went from a small start-up to a national phenomenon only with the help of venture capitalists. Three venture capitalists invested $40 million, giving Facebook the resources to buy its own domain name ($200,000) and build the infrastructure that allowed it to become the premier social networking site. These are classic case studies in venture capitalism. As the News on the next page documents, most business start-ups are created with shoestring budgets, averaging $10,000 (Apple and Facebook started with even less). The initial seed money typically comes from an entrepreneur's own assets or credit, with a little help from family and friends. If the idea pans out, entrepreneurs need a lot more money to develop their product. This is where venture capitalists come in. Venture capitalists provide initial funding for entrepreneurial ventures. In return for their financial backing, the venture capitalists are entitled to a share of any profits that result. If the venture fails, however, they get nothing. Thus *venture capitalists provide financial support for entrepreneurial ideas and share in the risks and rewards.*

IN THE NEWS

Where Do Start-Ups Get Their Money?

SAN FRANCISCO—YouTube landed millions in venture capital money in its first year to expand so fast that its founders were able to sell the video-sharing company to Google last week for $1.7 billion.

For most entrepreneurs, however, venture capital isn't an option. Venture capitalists, investing for institutions and rich individuals, likely will invest in fewer than 3,400 of the more than 20 million small U.S. firms this year.

Instead a majority of founders reach into their own pockets or turn to family members, who provide nearly $60 billion a year in start-up and expansion funding. Today's typical new business sells a service, such as bookkeeping, and so requires little more than an inexpensive computer, a fax machine, and a home office. Even trendy start-ups such as YouTube get going with a handful of computers lashed together in a garage.

Banking giant Wells Fargo found in a recent survey of owners that their start-up costs averaged just $10,000.

—Jim Hopkins

Source: *USA TODAY.* October 18, 2006, p. 3B. Reprinted with permission.

Financing start-ups

Major sources of funding:

Personal/family savings — **57%**

Bank business loan — **12%**

Personal/business credit card — **9%**

Personal/family assets, such as second mortgage — **9%**

Outside investors — **3%**

Government-guaranteed bank loan — **1%**

Business loan from government — **1%**

Source: Small Business Administration.

Source: Alejandro Gonzalez, *USA TODAY.* October 18, 2006, p. 3B. Reprinted with permission.

Analysis: Business start-ups need outside financing to transform hot new ideas into market reality. Venture capitalists provide speculative funding to acquire needed resources.

Even Christopher Columbus needed venture capitalists to fund his risky expeditions to the New World.

Venture capital is as important to the economy tomorrow as it was to Columbus. For technology and entrepreneurship to continue growing, market conditions and tax provisions must be amenable to venture capitalists.

SUMMARY

- The primary economic function of financial markets is to help allocate scarce resources to desired uses. They do this by providing access to the pool of national savings for entrepreneurs, investors, and other would-be spenders. LO18-4

- Financial markets enable individuals to manage risk by holding different kinds of assets. Financial intermediaries also reduce the costs of information and search, thereby increasing market efficiency. LO18-4

- Future returns on investments must be discounted to present value. The present discounted value (PDV) of a future payment adjusts for forgone interest accrual. LO18-1

- Future returns are also uncertain. The *expected* value of future payments must also reflect the risk of nonpayment. LO18-1

- Shares of stock represent ownership in a corporation. The shares are initially issued to raise funds and are then traded on the stock exchanges. LO18-2

- Changes in the value of a corporation's stock reflect changing expectations and opportunity costs. Share price changes, in turn, act as market signals to direct more or fewer resources to a company. LO18-4
- Bonds are IOUs issued when a company (or government agency) borrows funds. After issuance, bonds are traded in the after (secondary) market. LO18-2
- The interest (coupon) rate on a bond is fixed at the time of issuance. The price of the bond itself, however, varies with changes in expectations (perceived risk) and opportunity cost. Yields vary inversely with bond prices. LO18-3

Key Terms

financial intermediary
risk premium
present discounted value (PDV)
expected value
corporation
corporate stock

dividend
retained earnings
capital gain
initial public offering (IPO)
price/earnings (P/E) ratio
bond

par value
default
coupon rate
liquidity
current yield

Questions for Discussion

1. If there were no organized financial markets, how would an entrepreneur acquire resources to develop and produce a new product? LO18-2
2. Why would anyone buy shares of a corporation that had no profits and paid no dividends? What's the highest price a person would pay for such a stock? LO18-3
3. Why would anyone sell a bond for less than its face (par) value? LO18-3
4. If you could finance a new venture with either a stock issue or bonds, which option would you choose? What are their respective (dis)advantages? LO18-2
5. Why is it considered riskier to own stock in a software company than to hold U.S. Treasury savings bonds? Which asset will generate a higher return? LO18-4

6. How does a successful IPO affect WHAT, HOW, and FOR WHOM the economy produces? LO18-2
7. What considerations might have created the difference between the coupon rate and current yield on GM bonds (Table 18.5)? LO18-3
8. What is the price of Google stock now? What caused the change in the price of Google stock from its IPO price of $85 a share to its May 2011 price (Table 18.3)? LO18-4
9. Could Facebook have become a premier social networking site without venture capitalists? How? LO18-2
10. Why do people say "a dollar today is worth more than a dollar tomorrow"? LO18-1

---

 web activities to accompany this chapter can be found on the Online Learning Center:
http://www.mhhe.com/schiller13e

---

 mobile app Visit your mobile app store and download the Schiller: Study Econ app *today*!

LO18-3 1. If a $60 stock pays a quarterly dividend of $1, what is the implied annual rate of return?   _____%

LO18-3 2. If a $24 per share stock has a P/E ratio of 20 and pays out 40 percent of its profits in dividends,
    (*a*) How large is its dividend? $_____
    (*b*) What is the implied rate of return?   _____%

LO18-3 3. According to the data in Table 18.3,
    (*a*) How much profit per share did Google earn? $_____
    (*b*) How much of that profit did it pay out in dividends? $_____

LO18-3 4. According to the data in Table 18.3,
    (*a*) How much profit per share did Intel earn? $_____
    (*b*) How much of that profit did it pay out in dividends? $_____

LO18-1 5. If the market rate of interest is 5 percent, what is the present discounted value of $1,000 that will be paid in
    (*a*) 1 year?   _____
    (*b*) 5 years?   _____
    (*c*) 10 years?   _____

LO18-1 6. What is the present discounted value of $10,000 that is to be received in 4 years if the market rate of interest is
    (*a*) 0 percent?   _____
    (*b*) 5 percent?   _____
    (*c*) 10 percent?   _____

LO18-4 7. What was the expected return on Columbus's expedition, assuming that he had a 50 percent chance of discovering valuables worth $1 million, a 25 percent chance of bringing home only $10,000, and a 25 percent chance of sinking?   _____

LO18-3 8. Compute the market price of the GM bonds described in Table 18.5 if the yield falls to 20 percent.   _____

LO18-3 9. What is the current yield on a $1,000 bond with a 4 percent coupon if its market price is
    (*a*) $900?   _____
    (*b*) $1,000?   _____
    (*c*) $1,100?   _____

LO18-4 10. How much interest accrued each day on the immediate cash payoff of the MegaMillions jackpot? (See Table 18.1.)   _____

LO18-4 11. Illustrate with demand and supply shifts the impact of the following events on stock prices:
    (*a*) A federal court finds Microsoft guilty of antitrust violations. Which way (right or left) did
        (*i*) Demand shift?   _____
        (*ii*) Supply shift?   _____

Microsoft stock

PRICE (dollars per share)

QUANTITY (shares per day)

(b) Intel announces a new and faster processor. Which way did

Intel stock

PRICE (dollars per share)

QUANTITY (shares per day)

(i) Demand shift? _____

(ii) Supply shift? _____

(c) Corporate executives announce that they intend to sell a large block of stock. Which way did

Company stock

PRICE (dollars per share)

QUANTITY (shares per day)

(i) Demand shift? _____

(ii) Supply shift? _____

(d) Google enhances its search capabilities. Which way did

Google stock

PRICE (dollars per share)

QUANTITY (shares per day)

(i) Demand shift? _____

(ii) Supply shift? _____

LO18-2 12. Which investment has a higher rate of annual cash return? Investment A: $1,000 bond with a coupon rate of 4 percent selling for $1,200 or Investment B: $1,000 stock with a P/E ratio of 10 that pays out half its profits in dividends. _____

Distributional Issues

Of the three core questions in economics, the FOR WHOM issue is often the most contentious. Should the market decide who gets the most output? Or should the government intervene and redistribute market incomes to achieve greater equity?

Tax and transfer systems are designed to redistribute market incomes. The next two chapters survey these systems. In the process, we assess not only how effective they are in achieving greater *equity,* but also what impacts they have on *efficiency.* High taxes and generous transfer payments may blunt work incentives and so reduce the size of the pie being resliced. This creates a fundamental conflict between the goals of equity and efficiency. Chapters 19 and 20 examine this conflict.

Taxes: Equity versus Efficiency

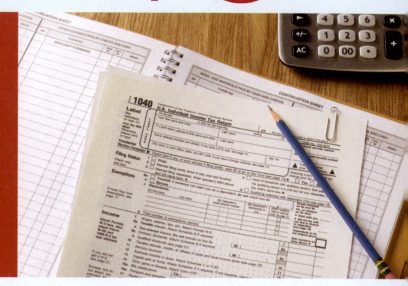

chapter 19

LEARNING OBJECTIVES

After reading this chapter, you should know

LO19-1. How the U.S. tax system is structured.

LO19-2. What makes taxes more or less progressive.

LO19-3. The nature of the equity–efficiency trade-off.

Insistence on carving the pie into equal slices would shrink the size of the pie. That fact poses the trade-off between economic equality and economic efficiency.

—Arthur M. Okun

Eric Schmidt was rewarded handsomely for his effort in cofounding Google in 2001. When he stepped down as CEO in 2011, Schmidt had amassed 9.2 million shares of Google stock, worth nearly $6 billion. As a parting gift, Google gave him an additional $100 million bonus when he turned the CEO job over to fellow cofounder Larry Page in January 2011. That would have been enough income to lift more than 2 million poor persons out of poverty. But Schmidt didn't share his good fortune with those people, and they remained poor.

The market mechanism generated both Schmidt's extraordinary income and that of so many poor families. Is this the way we want the basic FOR WHOM question to be settled? Should some people own vast fortunes while others seek shelter in abandoned cars? Or do the inequalities that emerge in product and factor markets violate our notions of equity? If

the market's answer to the FOR WHOM question isn't right, some form of government intervention to redistribute incomes may be desired.

The tax system is the government's primary lever for redistributing income. But taxing Peter to pay Paul may affect more than just income shares. If taxed too heavily, Peter may stop producing so much. Paul, too, may work less if assured of government support. The end result may be *less* total income to share. In other words, ***taxes affect production as well as distribution. This creates a potential trade-off between the goal of equity and the goal of efficiency.***

This chapter examines this equity–efficiency trade-off, with the following questions as a guide:

- **How are incomes distributed in the United States?**
- **How do taxes alter that distribution?**
- **How do taxes affect the rate and mix of output?**

After addressing these questions, we examine some proposed tax changes.

408

WHAT IS *INCOME*?

Before examining the distribution of income in the United States, let's decide what to count as *income*. There are several possibilities.

Personal Income

The most obvious choice is **personal income (PI)**—the flow of annual income received by households before payment of personal income taxes. Personal income includes wages and salaries, corporate dividends, rent, interest, Social Security benefits, welfare payments, and any other form of money income.

Personal income isn't a complete measure of income, however. Many goods and services are distributed directly as **in-kind income** rather than through market purchases. Many poor people, for example, live in public housing and pay little or no rent. As a consequence, they receive a larger share of total output than their money incomes imply. People with low incomes also receive food stamps (now called Supplemental Nutrition Assistance Program [SNAP] vouchers) that allow them to purchase more food than their money incomes would allow. In this sense, food stamp recipients are better off than the distribution of personal income (which omits food stamps) implies.

In-kind benefits aren't limited to low-income households. Students who attend public schools and colleges consume more goods and services than they directly pay for: public education is subsidized by all taxpayers. People over age 65 also get medical services through Medicare that they don't directly pay for. Middle-class workers get noncash fringe benefits (like health insurance, paid vacations, pension contributions) that don't show up in their paychecks or on their tax returns. Even the president of the United States gets substantial in-kind benefits. President Obama doesn't pay rent at the White House and gets free food, health care, transportation, and security services. Hence his real income greatly exceeds his $400,000-a-year paycheck.

So long as some goods and services needn't be purchased in the marketplace, *the distribution of money income isn't synonymous with the distribution of goods and services.* This measurement problem is particularly important when comparisons are made over time. For example, the federal government officially classifies people as "poor" if their money income is below a certain threshold. By this standard, we've made no progress against poverty. The Census Bureau counted 46 million Americans as "poor" in 2010, more than it counted in 1965. In both years the Census Bureau counted only money incomes. In 1965 that approach was acceptable because little income was transferred in-kind. In 2010, however, the federal government spent $70 billion on food stamps, $35 billion on housing subsidies, and $374 billion on Medicaid. Had all this in-kind income been counted, 10 million fewer Americans would have been counted as poor in 2010. Although that would still leave a lot of people in poverty, at least more progress in eliminating poverty would be evident.

Wealth

If our ultimate concern is access to goods and services, the distribution of wealth is also important. **Wealth** refers to the market value of assets (such as houses and bank accounts) people own. Hence *wealth represents a stock of potential purchasing power; income statistics tell us only how this year's flow of purchasing power (income) is being distributed.* Accordingly, to provide a complete answer to the FOR WHOM question, we have to know how wealth, as well as income, is distributed. In general, wealth tends to be distributed much less equally than income. The Internal Revenue Service estimates that 3 percent of the adult population own 30 percent of all personal wealth in the United States but get less than 20 percent of total income.

THE SIZE DISTRIBUTION OF INCOME

Although incomes aren't a perfect measure of access to goods and services (much less happiness), they're the best single indicator of the FOR WHOM outcomes. The **size distribution of income** tells us how large a share of total personal income is received by various households, grouped by income class. Imagine for the moment that the entire population is

---

personal income (PI): Income received by households before payment of personal taxes.

in-kind income: Goods and services received directly, without payment in a market transaction.

web analysis

The U.S. Census Bureau compiles data on poverty from each year's March household survey. For the most recent data, visit **www. census.gov/hhes/www/ poverty.html.**

wealth: The market value of assets.

size distribution of income: The way total personal income is divided up among households or income classes.

lined up in order of income, with lowest-income recipients in front and highest-income recipients at the end of the line. We want to know how much income the people in front get in comparison with those at the back.

We first examined the size distribution of income in Chapter 2. Figure 2.3 showed that households in the lowest quintile received less than $20,000 apiece in 2010. As a group, this class received only 3.3 percent of total income, despite the fact that it included 20 percent of all households (the lowest fifth). Thus the **income share** of the people in the lowest group (3.3 percent) was much smaller than their proportion in the total population (20 percent).

Moving back to the end of the line, we observed that a household needed $100,000 to make it into the highest income class in 2010. Many families in that class made much more than $100,000—some even millions of dollars. But $100,000 was at least enough to get into the top fifth (quintile).

The top quintile ended up with half of total U.S. income and, by implication, that much of total output.

The Lorenz Curve

The size distribution of income provides the kind of information we need to determine how total income (and output) is distributed. The **Lorenz curve** is a convenient summary of that information; it is a graphical illustration of the size distribution.

Figure 19.1 is a Lorenz curve for the United States. Our lineup of individuals is on the horizontal axis, with the lowest-income earners on the left. On the vertical axis we depict the cumulative share of income received by people in our income line. Consider the lowest quintile of the distribution again. They're represented on the horizontal axis at 20 percent. If their share of income was identical to their share of population, they'd get 20 percent of total income. This would be represented by point *C* in the figure. In fact, the lowest quintile gets only 3.3 percent, as indicated by point *A*. Point *B* tells us that the *cumulative* share of income received by the lowest *three*-fifths of the population was 26.6 percent.

The really handy feature of the Lorenz curve is the way it contrasts the actual distribution of income with an absolutely equal one. If incomes were distributed equally, the first 20 percent of the people in line would be getting exactly 20 percent of all income. In that case, the Lorenz curve would run through point *C*. Indeed, the Lorenz "curve" would be a straight line along the diagonal. The actual Lorenz curve lies below the diagonal because

income share: The proportion of total income received by a particular group.

Lorenz curve: A graphic illustration of the cumulative size distribution of income; contrasts complete equality with the actual distribution of income.

FIGURE 19.1
The Lorenz Curve

The Lorenz curve illustrates the extent of income inequality. If all incomes were equal, each fifth of the population would receive one-fifth of total income.

In this case, the diagonal line through point *C* would represent the cumulative size distribution of income. In reality, incomes aren't distributed equally. Point *A*, for example, indicates that the 20 percent of the population with the lowest income receive only 3.3 percent of total income.

Source: Figure 2.3.

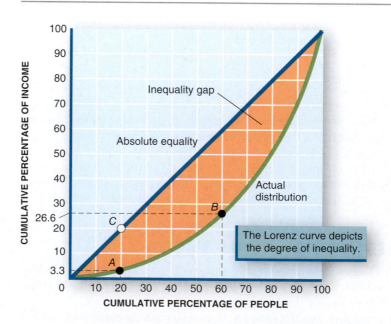

Analysis: An increase in the size of the economic pie doesn't ensure everyone a larger slice. A goal of the tax system is to attain a fairer distribution of the economic pie.

our national income isn't distributed equally. In fact, the area between the diagonal and the actual Lorenz curve (the shaded area in Figure 19.1) is a convenient measure of the degree of inequality. *The greater the area between the Lorenz curve and the diagonal, the more inequality exists.*

The visual summary of inequality the Lorenz curve provides is also expressed in a mathematical relationship. The ratio of the shaded area in Figure 19.1 to the area of the triangle formed by the diagonal is called the **Gini coefficient.** The higher the Gini coefficient, the greater the degree of inequality. Between 1980 and 2010, the Gini coefficient rose from 0.403 to 0.469. In other words, the shaded area in Figure 19.1 expanded by about 16 percent, indicating *increased* inequality. Although the size of the economic pie (real GDP) more than *doubled* between 1980 and 2010, some people's slices got a lot bigger while other people saw little improvement, or even less (see the cartoon above).

> **Gini coefficient:** A mathematical summary of inequality based on the Lorenz curve.

The Call for Intervention

To many people, large and increasing inequality represents a form of **market failure:** the market is generating a suboptimal (unfair) answer to the FOR WHOM question. As in other instances of market failure, the government is called on to intervene. The policy lever in this case is taxes. **By levying taxes on the rich and providing transfer payments to the poor, the government *redistributes* market incomes.**

> **market failure:** An imperfection in the market mechanism that prevents optimal outcomes.

THE FEDERAL INCOME TAX

The federal income tax is designed for this redistributional purpose. Specifically, the federal income tax is designed to be **progressive**—that is, to impose higher tax *rates* on high incomes than on low ones. Progressivity is achieved by imposing increasing **marginal tax rates** on higher incomes. The *marginal* tax rate refers to the tax rate imposed on the last (marginal) dollar of income.

> **progressive tax:** A tax system in which tax rates rise as incomes rise.

Tax Brackets and Rates

In 2010, the tax code specified the six tax brackets shown in Table 19.1. For an individual with less than $8,375 of taxable income, the tax rate was 10 percent. Any income in excess of $8,375 was taxed at a *higher* rate of 15 percent. If an individual's income rose above $82,400, the amount between $82,400 and $171,850 was taxed at 28 percent. Any income greater than $373,650 was taxed at 35 percent.

To understand the efficiency and equity effects of taxes, we must distinguish between the *marginal* tax rate and the *average* tax rate. A person who earned $380,000 in 2010 paid the 35 percent tax only on the income in excess of $373,650—that is, the last (marginal) $6,350. The first $8,375 was taxed at a marginal rate of only 10 percent.

> **marginal tax rate:** The tax rate imposed on the last (marginal) dollar of income.

TABLE 19.1
Progressive Taxes

The federal income tax is progressive because it levies higher tax rates on higher incomes. The 2010 marginal tax rate started out at 10 percent for incomes below $8,375 and rose to 35 percent for incomes above $373,650.

Tax Bracket	Marginal Tax Rate
$0–8,375	10%
$8,375–34,000	15
$34,000–82,400	25
$82,400–171,850	28
$171,850–373,650	33
Over $373,650	35

Source: Internal Revenue Service (2010 tax rates for single individuals).

web analysis

Visit **www.irs.gov** and search for "tax rate schedules" for the latest tax tables for individuals. Use these tables to calculate tax rates at different income levels.

Here is how taxes are computed on $380,000 of income:

Marginal Tax Rate	Income		Tax
10% of	$ 8,375	=	$ 837.50
15% of	25,625	=	3,843.75
25% of	48,400	=	12,100.00
28% of	89,450	=	25,046.00
33% of	201,800	=	66,594.00
35% of	6,350	=	2,222.50
	$380,000		$110,643.75

Notice that the various marginal tax rates apply only to the income in that specific bracket. By adding up the taxes in each bracket, we get a total tax of $110,643.75. This represents only 29.1 percent of this individual's income. Hence this person had a

- *Marginal* tax rate of 35 percent.
- *Average* tax rate of 29.1 percent.

By contrast, a person with only $20,000 of income would pay a *marginal* tax of only 15 percent and an *average* tax of 13 percent. The rationale behind this progressive system is to tax ever-larger percentages of higher incomes, thereby reducing income inequalities. This makes the *after-tax* distribution of income more equal than the *before-tax* distribution. This is how ***progressive taxes reduce inequality.***

Efficiency Concerns

Although the redistributive intent of a progressive tax system is evident, it raises concerns about efficiency. As noted in the chapter-opening quote, attempts to reslice the pie may end up reducing the size of the pie. The central issue here is incentives. Chapter 16 emphasized that the supply of labor is motivated by the pursuit of income. If Uncle Sam takes away ever-larger chunks of income, won't that dampen the desire to work? If so, ***the incentive to work more, produce more, or invest more is reduced by higher marginal tax rates.*** This suggests that as marginal tax rates increase, total output shrinks, creating a basic conflict between the goals of equity (more progressive taxes) and efficiency (more output).

Tax Elasticity of Supply. How great the conflict is between the equity and efficiency depends on how responsive market participants are to higher tax rates. The Rolling Stones left Great Britain off their 1998–1999 world tour because the British marginal tax rate was so high. The band U2 went a step further—moving their home base from Ireland to the Netherlands to avoid paying Irish income taxes (see the World View on the next page). Many other businesses relocate to low-tax nations for the same reason. For the typical household, however, the response to higher tax rates is limited to reducing hours worked. In all cases we can summarize the response with the **tax elasticity of supply:**

tax elasticity of supply:
The percentage change in quantity supplied divided by the percentage change in tax rate.

$$\text{Tax elasticity} \atop \text{of supply} = \frac{\text{\% change in quantity supplied}}{\text{\% change in tax rate}}$$

WORLD VIEW

U2 Avoids Taxes, Raising Ire in Ireland

DUBLIN, Ireland—U2 Ltd., the Irish band's music publishing company, raked in $30 million-plus last year—and $25.8 million of it went to five unidentified "employees," according to documents obtained Friday by The Associated Press.

Those "employees" are suspected to be the band members and their longtime manager, Paul McGuinness. But U2's public relations firms in Dublin and London refused to confirm that.

While Bono has won accolades worldwide for raising awareness of Third World poverty, he has been criticized for moving U2's corporate offices out of Ireland to avoid paying taxes. . . .

U2 Ltd. said it paid nearly $1.1 million in 2006 tax to Ireland, compared to just $46,500 in 2005.

The increased tax bill in 2006 reflects U2's sudden exposure to taxes on royalty income in Ireland. Last year the government—stung by criticism that its traditional tax-free status for artists was not intended to support multimillionaires like U2—capped the tax-free benefit at $360,000 annually.

Within months, U2 relocated its corporate base to Amsterdam.

Source: Associated Press, October 29, 2007. Used with permission of The Associated Press. Copyright © 2011. All rights reserved.

Analysis: High tax rates deter people from supplying resources. In this case, high taxes motivated U2 to move to another country.

If the tax elasticity of supply were zero, there'd be no conflict between equity and efficiency. But a zero tax elasticity would also imply that people would continue to work, produce, and invest even if Uncle Sam took *all* their income in taxes. In today's range of taxes, the average household's tax elasticity of labor supply is between 0.15 and 0.30. Hence, if tax *rates* go up by 20 percent, the quantity of labor supplied would decline by 3 to 6 percent. In other words, the size of the pie being resliced would shrink by 3–6 percent. Figure 19.2 confirms that the top marginal tax rate has changed by

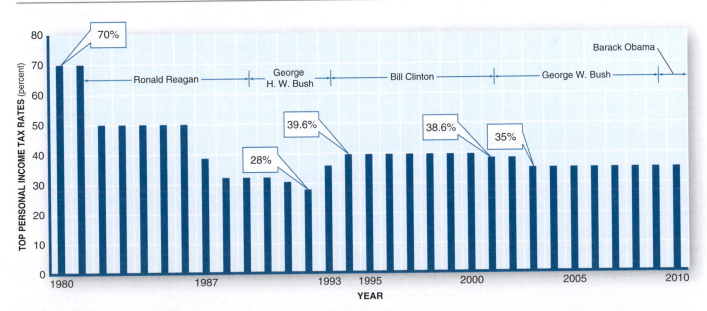

FIGURE 19.2
Changes in Marginal Tax Rates

During the past 30 years, Congress revised the federal income tax system many times. The top marginal tax rates were steadily reduced from 70 percent in 1980 to 28 percent in 1992. They were raised in 1993–1995. The Bush tax cuts of 2001–2004 reduced marginal tax rates again. President Obama vowed to increase the top marginal tax rate to 39.6 again in 2011.

Source: Internal Revenue Service.

much more than 20 percent in the past, thereby significantly altering the size of the economic pie.

Equity Concerns

As if the concern about efficiency weren't enough, critics also raise questions about how well the federal income tax promotes equity. What appears to be a fairly progressive tax in theory turns out to be a lot less progressive in practice. Hundreds of people with $1 million incomes pay no taxes. They aren't necessarily breaking any laws, just taking advantage of loopholes in the tax system.

Loopholes. The progressive *tax rates described in the tax code apply to "taxable" income, not to all income.* The so-called loopholes in the system arise from the way Congress defines taxable income. The tax laws permit one to subtract certain exemptions and deductions from gross income in computing taxable income:

$$\frac{\text{Taxable}}{\text{income}} = \frac{\text{Gross}}{\text{income}} - \text{Exemptions and deductions}$$

Exemptions are permitted for dependent children, spouses, old age, and disabilities. Deductions are permitted for an array of expenses, including home mortgage interest, work-related expenses, child care, depreciation of investments, interest payments, union dues, medical expenses, charitable contributions, and many other items.

The purpose of these many *itemized deductions* is to encourage specific economic activities and reduce potential hardship. The deduction for mortgage interest payments, for example, encourages people to buy their own homes. The deduction for medical expenses helps relieve the financial burden of illness.

Whatever the merits of specific exemptions and deductions, they create potential inequities. *People with high incomes can avoid high taxes by claiming large exemptions and deductions.* Each year the Internal Revenue Service discovers individuals earning million-dollar incomes and paying little or no taxes. They aren't doing anything illegal, just taking advantage of the many deductions Congress permits. Nevertheless, this means that some people with high incomes could end up paying *less* tax than people with lower incomes. This violates the principle of **vertical equity,** the progressive intent of taxing people on the basis of their ability to pay.

Table 19.2 illustrates vertical *in*equity. Mr. Jones has an income ($90,000) three times larger than Ms. Smith's ($30,000). However, Mr. Jones also has huge deductions ($70,000) that reduce his *taxable* income dramatically. In fact, Mr. Jones ends up with less *taxable* income ($20,000) than Ms. Smith ($25,000). As a result, he also ends up paying lower taxes ($4,000 vs. $5,500). How is this possible? Simply because Mr. Jones has huge itemized deductions for things like mortgage interest, charitable contributions, and the like, and Ms. Smith has nothing comparable.

The deductions that create the vertical inequity between Mr. Jones and Ms. Smith could also violate the principle of **horizontal equity**—as people with the *same* incomes end up paying different amounts of income tax. These horizontal *in*equities also contradict basic notions of fairness.

vertical equity: Principle that people with higher incomes should pay more taxes.

horizontal equity: Principle that people with equal incomes should pay equal taxes.

TABLE 19.2
Vertical Inequity

Tax exemptions and deductions create a gap between total income and *taxable* income. In this case, Mr. Jones has both a higher income and extensive deductions. He ends up with less *taxable* income than Ms. Smith and so pays less taxes. This vertical inequity is reflected in the lower effective tax rate paid by Mr. Jones (4.4 percent) than Ms. Smith (18.3 percent).

		Mr. Jones	Ms. Smith
1.	Total income	$90,000	$30,000
2.	Less exemptions and deductions	−$70,000	−$ 5,000
3.	Taxable income	$20,000	$25,000
4.	Tax	$ 4,000	$ 5,500
5.	Nominal tax rate (= row 4 ÷ row 3)	20%	22%
6.	Effective tax rate (= row 4 ÷ row 1)	4.4%	18.3%

Nominal vs. Effective Tax Rates. The "loopholes" created by exemptions, deductions, and tax credits cause a distinction between gross economic income and taxable income. That distinction, in turn, requires us to distinguish between *nominal* tax rates and *effective* tax rates. The term **nominal tax rate** refers to the taxes actually paid as a percentage of *taxable* income. By contrast, the **effective tax rate** is the tax paid divided by *total* economic income without regard to exemptions, deductions, or other intricacies of the tax laws.

As Table 19.2 illustrates, someone with a gross income of $90,000 might end up with a much lower *taxable* income, thanks to various tax deductions and exemptions. Mr. Jones ended up with a taxable income of only $20,000 and a tax bill of merely $4,000. As a result, we can characterize Mr. Jones's tax burden in two ways:

$$\frac{\text{Nominal}}{\text{tax rate}} = \frac{\text{Tax paid}}{\text{Taxable income}}$$

$$= \frac{\$4,000}{\$20,000} = 20 \text{ percent}$$

or alternatively,

$$\frac{\text{Effective}}{\text{tax rate}} = \frac{\text{Tax paid}}{\text{Total economic income}}$$

$$= \frac{\$4,000}{\$90,000} = 4.4 \text{ percent}$$

This huge gap between the nominal tax rate (20 percent) and the effective tax rate (4.4 percent) is a reflection of loopholes in the tax code. It's also the source of the vertical and horizontal inequities discussed earlier. Notice that Ms. Smith, with much less gross income, ends up with an effective tax rate (18.3 percent) that's more than four times higher than Mr. Jones's (4.4 percent).

The accompanying News reveals how the Obamas used tax "loopholes" (adjustments, deductions, exemptions) to reduce their effective tax rate in 2010. Instead of paying taxes on their *gross* income of $1,728,096, they had to pay taxes only on their *taxable* income of $1,340,207. This reduced their tax bill by over $200,000.

> **nominal tax rate:** Taxes paid divided by taxable income.

> **effective tax rate:** Taxes paid divided by total income.

IN THE NEWS

The Obamas' Taxes

Gross Income		Deductions	
Wages	$ 395,188	State/local taxes	$ 52,527
Interest	8,066	Property taxes	25,742
Dividends	9,997	Mortgage interest	49,945
Tax refunds	1,151	Charity	245,075
Book royalties	1,382,889	Total allowed	$ 373,289
Capital loss	(3,000)		
Trust income	1,323		
Total income	$1,795,614		
Adjustments		**Exemptions**	$ 14,600
Self-employment tax	$ 18,518	**Taxable Income**	$1,340,207
Pension contribution	49,000	**Tax**	$ 438,949
	$ 67,518		
Adjusted Gross Income	$1,728,096		

Source: The White House (2010 returns).

Analysis: Taxes are levied on *taxable* income, not total income. Various deductions and exemptions reduce taxable income and *effective* tax rates.

web analysis

To view tax returns of U.S. presidents visit **www. taxhistory.org.** Click on "Presidential Tax Returns."

Tax-Induced Misallocations. Tax loopholes not only foster inequity but encourage inefficiency as well. The optimal mix of output is the one that balances consumer preferences and opportunity costs. Tax loopholes, however, encourage a different mix of output. By offering preferential treatment for some activities, the tax code reduces their relative accounting cost. In so doing, ***tax preferences induce resource shifts into tax-preferred activities.*** The deduction for mortgage interest, for example, encourages people to purchase homes, thereby changing the mix of output.

These resource allocations are the explicit goal of tax preferences. The accumulation of exemptions, deductions, and credits has become so unwieldy and complex, however, that tax considerations often overwhelm economic considerations in many investment and consumption decisions. The resulting mix of output, many observers feel, is decidedly inferior to a *pure* market outcome. From this viewpoint, the federal income tax promotes both inequity and inefficiency.

> **tax base:** The amount of income or property directly subject to nominal tax rates.

A Shrinking Tax Base. Loopholes in the tax code create yet another problem. As the **tax base** gets smaller and smaller, it becomes increasingly difficult to sustain, much less increase, tax revenues. The tax arithmetic is simple:

$$\text{Tax revenue} = \frac{\text{Average}}{\text{tax rate}} \times \frac{\text{Tax}}{\text{base}}$$

As deductions, exemptions, and credits accumulate, the tax base (taxable income) keeps shrinking. To keep tax rates low—or to reduce them further—Congress has to stop this erosion of the tax base.

The Bush Tax Cuts (2001–2010)

Tax reforms in 1986 and 1993 broadened the tax base but also raised tax rates (to a top rate of 39.6 percent). President Bush worried that those higher marginal tax rates would slow economic growth. He also felt that low-income households would gain more from faster economic growth than from progressive tax and transfer policies. After his 2000 election, he made tax *cuts* one of his highest priorities.

Reduced Marginal Rates. Initially President Bush wanted the top marginal tax rate of 39.6 percent reduced to 33 percent. Compromises with Congress achieved a smaller rate reduction, however, phased in over several years. As Figure 19.2 illustrated, the 2001 Tax Relief Act reduced the highest marginal tax rate in three steps, to 35 percent. That act also reduced the marginal tax rate for the *lowest* income class to only 10 percent (from 15 percent). The goal of this rate cut was to increase the disposable income of low-wage workers (equity) while giving them more incentive to work (efficiency).

New "Loopholes." Aside from encouraging more *work,* President Bush also sought to encourage more *education.* The biggest incentive was a tuition tax deduction of $3,000 per year. This allows students, or their parents, to reduce their taxable income by the amount of tuition payments. In effect, Uncle Sam ends up paying part of the first $3,000 in tuition. In addition, the 2001 legislation allows people to save more money for college in tax-free accounts.

As welcome as these "loopholes" are to college students, they raise the same kind of efficiency and equity concerns as other tax preferences. If most of the students who take the tax deduction would have gone to college anyway, the deduction isn't very *efficient* in promoting education. Furthermore, most of the deductions go to middle-class families who itemize deductions. Hence the tuition deduction introduces new vertical *inequities.* Few students have protested this particular loophole, however.

The creation of this and other tax preferences raises all the same issues about equity and efficiency. ***The greater the number of loopholes, the wider the distinction between gross incomes and taxable incomes.*** President Obama used some of these same loopholes to reduce his effective tax rate, as the previous News reveals.

Tax "Loopholes"

The Obama Tax Hikes

Despite his personal exposure to the highest tax rates, President Obama vowed to reverse the "Bush tax cuts for the rich." Within a month of his inauguration, Obama proposed to raise the highest marginal tax rate from 35 percent to its former 39.6 percent, beginning in 2011. The tax rate for the second-highest bracket (see Table 19.1) would also increase, from 33 percent to 36 percent. New limits on deductions would raise *effective* tax rates even more. So anyone with at least $165,000 in taxable income would end up paying more. He also proposed raising taxes on capital gains, dividends, and estates. Critics objected that the resultant gains in *equity* (Obama's avowed goal) would be more than offset by the loss of *efficiency*. In other words, the pie would shrink when Obama resliced it. When the economy fell into the 2008–2009 recession, President Obama agreed to table the proposed tax hikes. In 2011 he again pressed for higher marginal tax rates, however (see the News below), and made it a pledge of his reelection campaign.

IN THE NEWS

Obama Pitches Tax Hike on the Rich

WASHINGTON—President Barack Obama on Wednesday proposed raising taxes on the wealthiest Americans during a major speech Wednesday outlining his long-term plan to bring the federal budget closer to balance.

"At a time when the tax burden on the wealthy is at its lowest level in half a century, the most fortunate among us can afford to pay a little more," Obama told an audience at George Washington University. . . .

Republicans denounced the proposed tax hikes as a sure way to slow economic growth in the United States.

"It's very ironic that a few days before tax day in this country that the president would be coming out asking people to pay more taxes," said Representative Eric Cantor, the Republican majority leader in the House of Representatives.

"I don't think many Americans believe that that's the answer to fix this economy and grow jobs."

—Sheldon Alberts

Source: April 13, 2011. Material reprinted with the express permission of: Postmedia News, a division of Postmedia Network Inc.

Analysis: President Obama proposed ending the "tax break for the rich" by increasing the top marginal tax rate from 35 percent to 39.6 percent.

PAYROLL, STATE, AND LOCAL TAXES

The federal income tax is only one of many taxes the average taxpayer must pay. For many families, in fact, the federal income tax is the smallest of many tax bills. Other tax bills come from the Social Security Administration and from state and local governments. These taxes also affect both efficiency and equity.

Sales and Property Taxes

Sales taxes are the major source of revenue for state governments. Many local governments also impose sales taxes, but most cities rely on *property taxes* for the bulk of their tax receipts. Both taxes are **regressive:** they impose higher tax rates on lower incomes.

At first glance, a 5 percent sales tax doesn't look very regressive. After all, the same 5 percent tax is imposed on virtually all goods. But we're interested in *people,* not goods and services, so **we gauge tax burdens in relation to people's incomes.** A tax is regressive if it imposes a proportionally *larger* burden on *lower* incomes.

This is exactly what a uniform sales tax does. To understand this concept, we have to look not only at how much tax is levied on each dollar of consumption but also at *what percentage of income* is spent on consumer goods.

regressive tax: A tax system in which tax rates fall as incomes rise.

	High-Income Family	Low-Income Family
Income	$70,000	$20,000
Consumption	$40,000	$19,000
Saving	$30,000	$ 1,000
Sales tax paid (5% of consumption)	$ 2,000	$ 950
Effective tax rate (sales tax ÷ income)	2.86%	4.75%

tax incidence: Distribution of the real burden of a tax.

Low-income families spend everything they've got (and sometimes more) on basic consumption. As a result, most of their income ends up subject to sales tax. By contrast, higher-income families save more. As a result, a smaller proportion of their income is subject to a sales tax. Table 19.3 illustrates this regressive feature of a sales tax. Notice that the low-income family ends up paying a larger fraction of its income (4.75 percent) than does the high-income family (2.86 percent).

Property taxes are regressive also and for the same reason. Low-income families spend a higher percentage of their incomes for shelter. A uniform property tax thus ends up taking a larger fraction of their income than it does of the incomes of high-income families.

Tax Incidence. It may sound strange to suggest that low-income families bear the brunt of property taxes. After all, the tax is imposed on the landlords who *own* property, not on people who *rent* apartments and houses. However, here again we have to distinguish between the apparent payee and the individual whose income is actually reduced by the tax. **Tax incidence** refers to the actual burden of a tax—that is, who really ends up paying it.

In general, people who rent apartments pay higher rents as a result of property taxes. In other words, landlords pass along to tenants any property taxes they must pay. Thus to a large extent ***the burden of property taxes is reflected in higher rents.*** Tenants pay property taxes *indirectly* via these higher rents. The incidence of the property tax thus falls on renters in the form of higher rents, rather than on the landlords who write checks to the local tax authority.

Payroll Taxes

Payroll taxes also impose effective tax burdens quite different from their nominal appearance. Consider, for example, the Social Security payroll tax, the second-largest source of federal tax revenue (see Figure 4.5). Every worker sees a Social Security (FICA) tax taken out of his or her paycheck. The nominal tax rate on workers is 7.65 percent. But there's a catch: only wages below a legislated ceiling are taxable. In 2011, the taxable wage ceiling was $106,800. Hence a worker earning $200,000 paid no more tax than a worker earning $106,800. As a result, the effective tax *rate* (tax paid ÷ total wages) is lower for high-income workers than low- and middle-income workers. That's a *regressive* tax.

There is another problem in gauging the impact of the Social Security payroll tax. Nominally, the Social Security payroll tax consists of two parts: half paid by employees and half by employers. But do employers really pay their half? Or do they end up paying lower wages to compensate for their tax share? If so, employees end up paying *both* halves of the Social Security payroll tax.

Figure 19.3 illustrates how the tax incidence of the payroll tax is distributed. The supply of labor reflects the ability and willingness of people to work for various wage rates. Labor demand reflects the **marginal revenue product (MRP)** of labor; it sets a *limit* to the wage an employer is willing to pay.

marginal revenue product (MRP): The change in total revenue associated with one additional unit of input.

Cost of Labor. The employer's half of the payroll tax increases the nominal cost of labor. Thus the S + tax curve lies *above* the labor supply curve. It incorporates the wages that must be paid to workers *plus* the payroll tax that must be paid to the Social Security Administration.

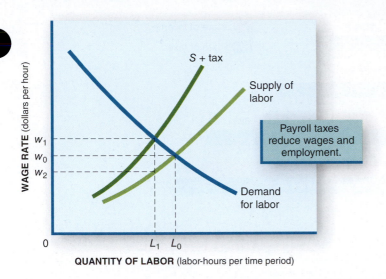

FIGURE 19.3
The Incidence of a Payroll Tax

Some portion of a payroll tax imposed on employers may actually be borne by workers. The tax raises the cost of labor and so imposes a tax-burdened supply curve (S + tax) on employers. The intersection of this tax-burdened supply curve with the labor demand curve determines a new equilibrium of employment (L_1). At that level, employers pay w_1 in wages and taxes, but workers get only w_2 in wages. The wage reduction from w_0 to w_2 is a real burden of the payroll tax, and it is borne by workers.

This total labor cost is the one that will determine how many workers are hired. Specifically, the intersection of the S + tax curve and the labor demand curve determines the equilibrium level of employment (L_1). The employer will pay the amount w_1 for this much labor. But part of that outlay ($w_1 - w_2$) will go to the public treasury in the form of payroll taxes. Workers will receive only w_2 in wages. This is less than they'd get in the absence of the payroll tax (compare w_0 and w_2). Thus *fewer workers are employed, and the net wage is reduced when a payroll tax is imposed.*

Tax Incidence. What Figure 19.3 reveals is how the true incidence of payroll taxes is distributed. The employer share of the Social Security tax is $w_1 - w_2$. This is the amount sent to the Social Security Administration for every hour of labor. Of this amount, the employer incurs higher labor costs ($w_1 - w_0$) and workers lose ($w_0 - w_2$) in the wage rate. Hence workers end up paying *their* share (7.65 percent) of the Social Security tax *plus* a sizable part ($w_0 - w_2$) of the employer's share ($w_1 - w_2$).

These reflections on tax incidence don't imply that payroll taxes are necessarily bad. They do emphasize, however, that *the apparent taxpayer isn't necessarily the individual who bears the real burden of a tax.*

TAXES AND INEQUALITY

The regressivity of the Social Security payroll tax and of many state and local taxes offsets most of the progressivity of the federal income tax. The top 1 percent of income recipients gets 22 percent of total income and pays 40 percent of federal income tax (see Figure 19.4). Hence the federal income tax is still progressive, despite rampant loopholes. Other federal taxes (Social Security, excise), however, reduce the tax share of the rich to only 21 percent. State and local tax incidence reduces their tax share still further.

A Proportional System

The final result is that *the tax system as a whole ends up being nearly proportional.* High-income families end up paying roughly the same percentage of their income in taxes as do low-income families. The tax system does reduce inequality somewhat, but the redistributive impact is quite small.

The Impact of Transfers

The tax system tells only half the redistribution story. It tells whose income was taken away. Equally important is who gets the income the government collects. The government completes the redistribution process by *transferring* income to consumers. The **income transfers**

income transfers: Payments to individuals for which no current goods or services are exchanged, such as Social Security, welfare, and unemployment benefits.

FIGURE 19.4
Income Tax Shares

Despite loopholes, the federal income tax remains progressive. The richest 1 percent of households pay 40 percent of all federal income taxes, though they receive only 22 percent of all income.

Source: Internal Revenue Service (2006 data).

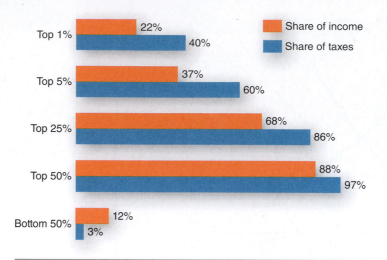

may be explicit, as in the case of welfare benefits, Social Security payments, and unemployment insurance. Or the transfers may be indirect, as in the case of public schools, farm subsidies, and student loans. We'll look more closely at how income transfers alter the distribution of income in the next chapter.

WHAT IS *FAIR*?

To many people, the apparent ineffectiveness of the tax system in redistributing income is a mark of **government failure.** They want a much more decisive reslicing of the pie—one in which the top quintile gets a *lot* less than half the pie and the poor get more than 3.4 percent (Figure 2.3). But how much redistribution should we attempt? Rich people can rattle off as many good reasons for preserving income inequalities as poor people can recite for eliminating them.

Economists aren't uniquely qualified to overcome self-interest, much less to divine what a fair distribution of income might look like. But economists can assess some of the costs and benefits of altering the distribution of income.

The Costs of Greater Equality

The greatest potential cost of a move toward greater equality is the reduced incentives it might leave in its wake. People *are* motivated by income. In factor markets, higher wages call forth more workers and induce them to work longer hours. In fields where earnings are very high, as in the medical and legal professions, people are willing to spend many years and thousands of dollars acquiring the skills such earnings require. Could we really expect people to make such sacrifices in a market that paid everyone the same wage?

The same problem exists in product markets. The willingness of producers to supply goods and services depends on their expectation of profits. Why should they work hard and take risks to produce goods and services if their efforts won't make them any better off? If incomes were distributed equally, producers might just as well sit back and enjoy the fruits of someone else's labor.

The essential economic problem absolute income equality poses is that it breaks the market link between effort and reward. If all incomes were equal, it would no longer pay to make an above-average effort. If people stopped making such efforts, total output would decline, and we'd have less income to share (a smaller pie). Not that all high incomes are attributable to great skill or effort. Such factors as luck, market power, and family connections also influence incomes. It remains true, however, that the promise of higher income encourages work effort. Absolute income equality threatens those conditions.

government failure: Government intervention that fails to improve economic outcomes.

"I suppose one could say it favors the rich, but, on the other hand, it's a great incentive for everyone to make two hundred grand a year."

Analysis: Inequalities are an incentive for individuals to work and invest more.

The argument for preserving income inequalities is thus anchored in a concern for productivity. From this perspective, income inequalities are the driving force behind much of our production. By preserving inequalities, we not only enrich the fortunate few, but also provide incentives to take risks, invest more, and work harder (see the cartoon above). In so doing, we enlarge the economic pie, including the slices available to lower-income groups. Thus everyone is potentially better off, even if only a few end up rich. This is the rationale that keeps the top marginal tax rate in the United States below those in most other countries (see the accompanying World View).

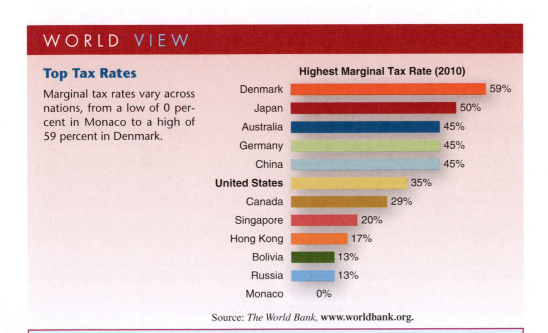

WORLD VIEW

Top Tax Rates

Marginal tax rates vary across nations, from a low of 0 percent in Monaco to a high of 59 percent in Denmark.

Highest Marginal Tax Rate (2010)

Country	Rate
Denmark	59%
Japan	50%
Australia	45%
Germany	45%
China	45%
United States	35%
Canada	29%
Singapore	20%
Hong Kong	17%
Bolivia	13%
Russia	13%
Monaco	0%

Source: *The World Bank,* **www.worldbank.org.**

Analysis: The highest marginal tax rate in the United States is lower than in most industrial nations. Some nations offer even lower tax rates, however.

The Benefits of Greater Equality

Although the potential benefits of inequality are impressive, **there's a trade-off between efficiency and equality.** Moreover, many people are convinced that the terms of the trade-off are exaggerated and the benefits of greater equality are ignored. These rebuttals take the form of economic and noneconomic arguments.

The economic arguments for greater equality also focus on incentives. The first argument is that the present degree of inequality is more than necessary to maintain work incentives. Upper-class incomes needn't be 14 times as large as those of the lowest-income classes; perhaps 4 times as large would do as well.

The second argument is that low-income earners might actually work harder if incomes were distributed more fairly. As matters now stand, the low-income worker sees little chance of making it big. Extremely low income can also inhibit workers' ability to work by subjecting them to poor health, malnutrition, or inadequate educational opportunities. Accordingly, some redistribution of income to the poor might improve the productivity of low-income workers and compensate for reduced productivity among the rich.

Finally, we noted that the maze of loopholes that preserves inequality also distorts economic incentives. Labor and investment decisions are influenced by tax considerations, not just economic benefits and costs. If greater equality were achieved via tax simplification, a more efficient allocation of resources might result.

THE ECONOMY TOMORROW

A FLAT TAX?

Widespread dissatisfaction with the present tax system has spawned numerous reform proposals. One of the most debated proposals is to replace the current federal income tax with a **flat tax.** First proposed by Nobel Prize–winner Milton Friedman in the early 1960s, the flat tax was championed in Congress by former majority leader (and former economics professor) Dick Armey. The concept resurfaced as a political issue in the 2012 presidential election.

flat tax: A single-rate tax system.

The key features of a flat tax include

- Replacing the current system of multiple tax brackets and rates with a single (flat) tax rate that would apply to all taxable income.
- Eliminating all deductions, credits, and most exemptions.

Simplicity. A major attraction of the flat tax is its simplicity. The current 1,600-page tax code that details all the provisions of the present system would be scrapped. The 437 different IRS tax forms now in use would be replaced by a single, postcard-sized form.

Fairness. Flat tax advocates also emphasize its fairness. They point to the rampant vertical and horizontal inequities created by the current tangle of tax loopholes. By scrapping all those deductions, the flat tax would treat everyone equally.

Some progressivity could also be preserved with a flat tax. In the version proposed by Dick Armey, the flat tax rate would be 17 percent, but one personal exemption would be maintained. Every adult would get a personal exemption of $13,100 and each child an exemption of $5,300. Accordingly, a family of four would have personal exemptions of $36,800. Hence a family earning less than that amount would pay no income tax. *Effective* tax rates would increase along with rising incomes above that threshold.

Efficiency. Proponents of a flat tax claim it enhances efficiency as well as equity. Taxpayers now spend over a billion hours a year preparing tax returns. Legions of lobbyists, accountants, and lawyers devote their energy to tax analysis and avoidance. With a simplified flat tax, all those labor resources could be put to more productive use.

A flat tax would also change the mix of output. Consumption and investment decisions would be made on the basis of economic considerations, not tax consequences.

The Critique. As alluring as a flat tax appears, it has aroused substantial opposition. As proposed by Dick Armey, the flat tax would not apply to all income. Income on savings and investments (such as interest and dividends, capital gains) wouldn't be taxed. The purpose of that exemption would be to encourage greater saving, investment, and economic growth. At the same time, however, such a broad exemption creates a whole new set of horizontal and vertical inequities. Someone receiving $1 million in interest and dividends could escape all income taxes, while a family earning $50,000 would have to pay.

Critics also object to the wholesale elimination of all deductions and credits. Many of those loopholes are expressly designed to encourage desired economic activity. The Bush tax cuts were explicitly designed to encourage education, family stability, and savings. By discarding all tax preferences, the flat tax significantly reduces the government's ability to alter the mix of output. Even if the current maze of loopholes exceeds the threshold of government failure, complete reliance on the market mechanism isn't necessarily appropriate. A careful pruning of the tax code rather than a complete uprooting might yield better results.

Finally, critics point out that the transition to a flat tax would entail a wholesale reshuffling of wealth and income. Home values would fall precipitously if the tax preference for homeownership were eliminated. That would hit the middle class particularly hard. State and local governments would have greater difficulty raising their own revenues if the federal deduction for state and local taxes were eliminated. Confronted with such consequences, many people begin to have second thoughts about the desirability of adopting a flat tax in the economy tomorrow. Taxpayers seem to like the *principle* of a flat tax more than its actual provisions.

SUMMARY

- The distribution of income largely determines access to the goods and services we produce. Wealth distribution is important for the same reason. LO19-3
- The size distribution of income tells us how incomes are divided up among individuals. The Lorenz curve is a graphic summary of the cumulative size distribution of income. The Gini coefficient is a mathematical summary. LO19-3
- Personal incomes are distributed quite unevenly in the United States. At present, the highest quintile (the top 20 percent) gets half of all cash income, and the bottom quintile gets less than 4 percent. LO19-3
- The trade-off between equity and efficiency is rooted in supply incentives. The tax elasticity of supply measures how the quantity of available resources (labor and capital) declines when tax rates rise. LO19-3
- The progressivity of the federal income tax is weakened by various loopholes (exemptions, deductions, and credits) that create a distinction between nominal and effective tax rates and cause vertical and horizontal inequities. LO19-2

- Marginal tax rates were reduced greatly in the 1980s and have alternately risen and fallen since. LO19-1
- Mildly progressive federal income taxes are offset by regressive payroll, state, and local taxes. Overall, the tax system redistributes little income; most redistribution occurs through transfer payments. LO19-2
- Tax incidence refers to the real burden of a tax. In many cases, reductions in wages, increases in rent, or other real income changes represent the true burden of a tax. LO19-2
- There is a trade-off between efficiency and equality. If all incomes are equal, there's no economic reward for superior productivity. On the other hand, a more equal distribution of incomes might increase the productivity of lower-income groups and serve important noneconomic goals as well. LO19-3
- A flat tax is a nominally proportional tax system. A personal exemption and the exclusion of capital income can render a flat tax progressive or regressive, however. A flat tax reduces the government's role in resource allocation (the WHAT and HOW questions). LO19-1

Key Terms

personal income (PI)	progressive tax	regressive tax
in-kind income	marginal tax rate	tax incidence
wealth	tax elasticity of supply	marginal revenue product (MRP)
size distribution of income	vertical equity	income transfers
income share	horizontal equity	government failure
Lorenz curve	nominal tax rate	flat tax
Gini coefficient	effective tax rate	
market failure	tax base	

Questions for Discussion

1. What goods or services do you and your family receive without directly paying for them? How do these goods affect the distribution of economic welfare? LO19-2

2. Why are incomes distributed so unevenly? Identify and explain three major causes of inequality. LO19-3

3. Do inequalities stimulate productivity? In what ways? Provide two specific examples. LO19-3

4. What loopholes reduced President Obama's 2010 tax bill (see News, p. 415)? What's the purpose of those loopholes? LO19-1

5. How might a flat tax affect efficiency? Fairness? LO19-3

6. If a new tax system encouraged more output but also created greater inequality, would it be desirable? LO19-3

7. If the tax elasticity of supply were zero, how high could the tax rate go before people reduced their work effort? How do families vary the quantity of labor supplied when tax rates change? LO19-3

8. Is a tax deduction for tuition likely to increase college enrollments? How will it affect horizontal and vertical equities? LO19-3

9. How are the equity and efficiency arguments used in the News on page 417? LO19-3

10. What share of taxes *should* the rich pay (see Figure 19.4)? Should the poor pay *any* taxes? LO19-3

11. If U2's tax bill falls by $1 million when the band relocates to the Netherlands (World View, p. 413), who really pays for the band's charitable contributions? LO19-3

---

 web activities to accompany this chapter can be found on the Online Learning Center:
http://www.mhhe.com/schiller13e

 mobile app Visit your mobile app store and download the Schiller: Study Econ app *today!*

LO19-2 1. How much more income tax would President Obama have paid in 2010 (News, p. 415) if he had used no "loopholes"? (Use the tax rates in Table 19.1.) $ _____

LO19-2 2. Had Obama succeeded in raising the top marginal tax rate (News, p. 417), how much more tax would he have paid in 2010? (Use the tax rates in Table 19.1 and the News on p. 415.) $ _____

LO19-2 3. In 2010 what was the Obamas'
  (a) Nominal tax rate?   _____%
  (b) Effective tax rate?   _____%

LO19-1 4. Use Table 19.1 to compute the taxes on a taxable income of $175,000.
  (a) What is the marginal tax rate?   _____%
  (b) What is the average tax rate?   _____%

LO19-1 5. Using Table 19.1, compute the taxable income and taxes for the following taxpayers:

Taxpayer	Gross Income	Exemptions and Deductions	Taxable Income	Tax
A	$ 20,000	$ 6,000	_____	_____
B	40,000	28,000	_____	_____
C	80,000	34,000	_____	_____
D	200,000	110,000	_____	_____

  Which taxpayer has
  (a) The highest nominal tax rate?   _____
  (b) The highest effective tax rate?   _____
  (c) The highest marginal tax rate?   _____

LO19-2 6. If the tax elasticity of supply is 0.15, by how much will the quantity supplied decrease when the marginal tax rate increases from 35 to 45 percent?   _____%

LO19-2 7. By how much might the quantity of labor supplied decrease if the tax elasticity of supply were 0.20 and the marginal tax rate increased from 35 to 39 percent?   _____%

LO19-2 8. If the tax elasticity of labor supply were 0.16, by how much would the quantity of labor supplied increase among people in the top U.S. tax bracket if the highest marginal tax rate in the United States were reduced to the level of Hong Kong's (World View, p. 421)?   _____%

LO19-2 9. What percentage of income is paid in Social Security taxes by a worker earning
  (a) $40,000?   _____%
  (b) $80,000?   _____%
  (c) $200,000?   _____%
  (d) What kind of tax is this? (A: progressive; B: regressive; C: proportional)   _____

LO19-3 10. What is the effective tax rate with Dick Armey's proposed flat tax (p. 422) for a family of four with earnings of
  (a) $35,000?   _____%
  (b) $60,000?   _____%
  (c) $100,000?   _____%

LO19-1 11. Following are hypothetical data on the size distribution of income and wealth for each quintile (one-fifth) of a population:

Quintile	Lowest	Second	Third	Fourth	Highest
Income	5%	10%	15%	25%	45%
Wealth	2%	8%	12%	20%	58%

  (a) On the graph on the next page, draw the line of absolute equity; then draw a Lorenz curve for income, and shade the area between the two curves.
  (b) In the same diagram, draw a Lorenz curve for wealth. Is the distribution of wealth more equal ("A") or less equal ("B") than the distribution of income?   _____

LO19-2 12. If Obama's proposed marginal tax rates (News, p. 417) were enacted, by how much would the total tax increase for the example on page 412? $ _____

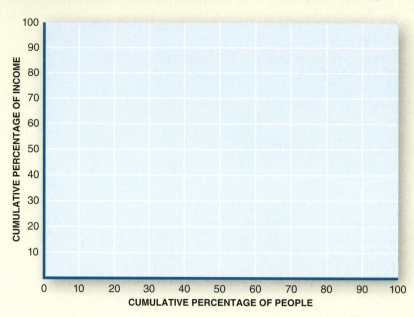

LO19-3 13. (*a*) On the graph shown below, draw the supply and demand for labor represented by the following data:

Wage	$1	2	3	4	5	6	7	8	9	10	11	12
Quantity of labor												
Supplied	1	2	3	4	5	6	8	10	12	14	17	20
Demanded	20	18	16	14	12	10	8	6	5	4	3	2

(*b*) How many workers are employed in equilibrium? _____

(*c*) What wage are they paid? _____

(*d*) Now suppose a payroll tax of $2 per worker is imposed on the employer. Draw the "supply + tax" graph that results.

(*e*) How many workers are now employed? _____

(*f*) How much is the employer paying for each worker? _____

(*g*) How much is each worker receiving? _____

For the incidence of this tax,

(*h*) What is the increase in unit labor cost to the employer? _____

(*i*) What is the reduction in the wage paid to labor? _____

426

Transfer Payments:
Welfare and Social Security

Americans are compassionate. Public opinion polls reveal that an overwhelming majority of the public wants to "help the needy." Most Americans say they're even willing to pay more taxes to help fund aid to the poor. But their compassion is tempered by caution: taxpayers don't want to be ripped off. They want to be sure their money is helping the "truly needy," not being squandered by deadbeats, drug addicts, shirkers, and "welfare queens."

The conflict between compassion and resentment affects not only welfare programs for the poor but also Social Security for the aged, unemployment insurance benefits for the jobless, and even disability benefits for injured workers. In every one of these programs, people are getting money without working. In effect, they're getting a "free ride."

The risk of providing a free ride is that some of the people who take it could have gotten by without it. As the humorist Dave Barry observed, if the government offers $1 million to people with six toes, a lot of people will try to grow a sixth toe or claim they have one. Income transfers create similar incentives: they encourage people to change their behavior in order to get a free ride.

This chapter focuses on how income transfer programs change not only the distribution of income but also work incentives and behavior. We address the following central questions:

- **How much income do income transfer programs redistribute?**
- **How are transfer benefits computed?**
- **How do transfer payments alter market behavior?**

income transfers: Payments to individuals for which no current goods or services are exchanged, such as Social Security, welfare, and unemployment benefits.

MAJOR TRANSFER PROGRAMS

More than half of every dollar the federal government spends goes to **income transfers** (see Figure 4.5). That amounts to *$2 trillion* a year in transfer payments. Who gets all this money?

The easy answer to this question is that almost every household gets some of the transfer money. There are over 100 federal income transfer programs. Students get tuition grants and subsidized loans. Farmers get crop assistance. Home owners get disaster relief when their homes are destroyed. Veterans get benefit checks and subsidized health care. People over age 65 get Social Security benefits and subsidized health care. And poor people get welfare checks, food stamps, and subsidized housing.

Although income transfers are widely distributed, not everyone shares equally in the tax-paid bounty. As Figure 20.1 shows, just three of the myriad transfer programs account for 85 percent of total outlays. Social Security, the largest program, alone accounts for 41 percent of the transfer budget. Medicare and Medicaid benefits absorb another 43 percent. By contrast, welfare checks account for only 4 percent of all income transfers.

Cash versus In-Kind Benefits

Income transfer doesn't always entail cash payments. The Medicare program, for example, is a health insurance subsidy program that pays hospital and doctor bills for people over age 65. The 48 million people who receive Medicare benefits don't get checks from Uncle Sam; instead Uncle Sam pays the bills for the medical *services* they receive. The same is true for the 60 million people who get Medicaid. Poor people get free health care from the Medicaid program; their benefits are paid *in-kind,* not in cash. Such programs provide **in-kind transfers**— that is, direct transfers of goods and services rather than cash. Food stamps, rent subsidies, legal aid, and subsidized school lunches are all in-kind transfer programs. By contrast, Social Security is a **cash transfer** because it mails benefit checks, not services, to recipients.

The provision of in-kind benefits rather than cash is intended to promote specific objectives. Few taxpayers object to feeding the hungry. But they bristle at the thought that welfare recipients might spend the income they receive on something potentially harmful like liquor or drugs or on nonessentials like cars or fancy clothes. To minimize that risk, taxpayers offer electronic food stamps (now called Supplemental Nutrition Assistance Program [SNAP] vouchers), not cash, thereby limiting the recipient's consumption choices. This helps reassure taxpayers that their assistance is being well spent.

in-kind transfers: Direct transfers of goods and services rather than cash, such as food stamps, Medicaid benefits, and housing subsidies.

cash transfers: Income transfers that entail direct cash payments to recipients, such as Social Security, welfare, and unemployment benefits.

web analysis

For more information on the three major income transfer programs, visit **www.omb.gov** and search for them by name.

FIGURE 20.1
Income Transfer Programs

There are nearly 100 different federal income transfer programs. However, just three programs—Social Security, Medicare, and Medicaid—account for nearly 80 percent of all transfers. Cash welfare benefits (TANF, SSI) absorb only 5 percent of all income transfers.

Source: U.S. Office of Management and Budget (FY 2008 data).

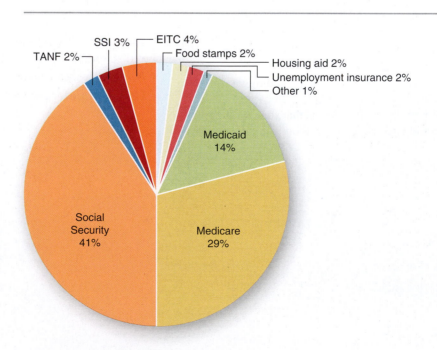

TANF 2%
SSI 3%
EITC 4%
Food stamps 2%
Housing aid 2%
Unemployment insurance 2%
Other 1%
Medicaid 14%
Medicare 29%
Social Security 41%

Similar considerations shape the Medicare program. Taxpayers could "cash out" Medicare by simply mailing older people the $600 billion now spent on the program every year. But then some healthy older Americans would get cash they didn't need. Some sick people might not get as much money as *they* needed. Or they might choose to spend their new-found income on something other than health care. The end result would be a smaller health care gain than in-kind transfers facilitate.

The **target efficiency** of a transfer program refers to how well income transfers attain their intended purpose. In-kind medical transfers are more target-efficient than cash transfers because recipients can spend cash transfers for other purposes. Food stamps are more target-efficient than cash in reducing hunger for the same reason. If given cash rather than food stamps, recipients would spend less than 70 cents of each dollar on food.

Social Insurance versus Welfare

You may have noted by now that not all income transfers go to the poor. A lot of student loans go to middle-class college students. And disaster relief helps rebuild both mansions and trailer parks. Such income transfers are triggered by specific *events,* not the recipient's income. By contrast, welfare checks are *means-tested:* they go only to families with little income and few assets.

Welfare programs always entail some kind of income eligibility test. To receive welfare payments, a family must prove that it has too little income to fend for itself. Medicaid is an in-kind **welfare program** because only poor people are eligible for the health care benefits of that program. To get food stamps, another in-kind welfare program, a family must also pass an income test.

Social Security and Medicare aren't *welfare* programs because recipients don't have to be poor. To get Social Security or Medicare benefits you just have to be old enough. The *event* of reaching age 62 makes people eligible for Social Security retirement benefits. At age 65 everyone—whether rich or poor—gets Medicare benefits. These event-conditioned benefits are the hallmark of **social insurance programs:** they insure people against the costs of old age, illness, disability, unemployment, and other specific problems. As Figure 20.2 illustrates, *most income transfers are for social insurance programs, not welfare.*

Transfer Goals

If the market sliced up the economic pie in a manner that society deemed fair, there would be no need for all these government-provided income transfers. Hence the mere existence of such programs implies a **market failure**—an unfair market-generated distribution of income. When the market alone slices up the pie, some people get too much and others get too little. To redress this inequity, we ask the government to play Robin Hood—taking income from the rich and giving it to the poor. Thus *the basic goal of income transfer programs is to reduce income inequalities*—to change the market's answer to the FOR WHOM question.

target efficiency: The percentage of income transfers that go to the intended recipients and purposes.

welfare programs: Means-tested income transfer programs, such as welfare and food stamps.

social insurance programs: Event-conditioned income transfers intended to reduce the costs of specific problems, such as Social Security and unemployment insurance.

market failure: An imperfection in the market mechanism that prevents optimal outcomes.

WELFARE
Food stamps
TANF
SSI
Housing aid
Child nutrition
Medicaid

SOCIAL INSURANCE
Social Security
Medicare
Unemployment insurance

FIGURE 20.2
Social Insurance versus Welfare

Social insurance programs provide *event*-based transfers—for example, upon reaching age 65 or becoming unemployed or disabled. Welfare programs offer benefits only to those in need; they're *means-tested.* Social insurance transfers greatly outnumber welfare transfers.

Source: U.S. Office of Management and Budget.

FIGURE 20.3
Reduced Labor Supply and Output

Transfer payments may induce people to supply less labor. If this happens, the supply of labor shifts to the left and the economy's production possibilities shrink. We end up with less total output.

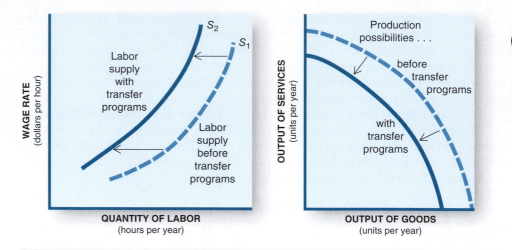

labor supply: The willingness and ability to work specific amounts of time at alternative wage rates in a given time period, *ceteris paribus*.

Unintended Consequences

Although income transfers try to change the distribution of income in desired ways, they are not costless interventions. The Law of Unintended Consequences rears its ugly head here: *income transfers often change market behavior and outcomes in unintended (and undesired) ways.*

Reduced Output. Work incentives are a potential problem. If you can get paid for *not* working (via a transfer payment), why would you go to work? Why endure 40 hours of toil for a paycheck when you can stay home and collect a welfare check, an unemployment check, or Social Security? If the income transfers are large enough, I'll stay home too. When people reduce their **labor supply** in response to income transfers, total output will shrink. Figure 20.3 shows that *attempts to redistribute income may reduce total income.* In other words, the pie shrinks when we try to reslice it.

Undesirable Behavior. A reduction in labor supply isn't the only unintended consequence of income transfer programs. People may also change their *nonwork* behavior. Welfare benefits give a (small) incentive to women to have more children and to teen moms to establish their own households. Medicare and Medicaid encourage people to overuse health care services and neglect the associated costs. Unemployment benefits encourage workers to stay jobless longer. And as Dave Barry noted at the beginning of the chapter, disability payments encourage people to grow a sixth toe. Although the actual response to these incentives is hotly debated, the existence of the undesired incentives is unambiguous.

WELFARE PROGRAMS

To understand how income transfer programs change market behavior and outcomes, let's look closely at how welfare programs operate. The largest federal cash welfare program is called Temporary Aid to Needy Families (TANF). The TANF program was created by congressional welfare reforms in 1996 and replaced an earlier program (AFDC) that had operated since 1935. The new program offers states more discretion to decide who gets welfare, under what conditions, and for how long.

Benefit Determination

The first task of the TANF program is to identify potential recipients. In principle, this task is easy: find out who is poor. To do this, the federal government has established a poverty line that specifies how much cash income families of different sizes need just to buy basic necessities.

Number of Family Members	Family Income
1	$11,000
2	14,000
3	17,100
4	22,000
5	26,000
6	29,500
7	33,400
8	37,300

Source: U.S. Bureau of the Census (rounded to 100s) (2010).

TABLE 20.1
Poverty Lines

The official definition of poverty relates current income to the minimal needs of a family. Poverty thresholds vary with family size. In 2010, a family of four was considered poor if it had less than $22,000 of income.

web analysis

Current statistics on poverty are available from the U.S. Census Bureau at **www.census.gov.** Click on "Poverty."

poverty gap: The shortfall between actual income and the poverty threshold.

In 2010, the federal government estimated that a family of four was poor if its income was less than $22,000. Table 20.1 shows how this poverty threshold varies by family size.

According to Table 20.1, a four-person family with $18,000 of income in 2010 would have had a **poverty gap**—the shortfall between actual income and the poverty threshold—of $4,000. The Jones family needed at least that much additional income to purchase what the government deems a "minimally adequate" standard of living.

So how much welfare should the government give this family? Should it give $4,000 to this family, thereby closing its poverty gap? As simple as that proposition sounds, it creates some unintended problems.

The Work Incentive Problem

Suppose we guaranteed all families enough income to reach their respective poverty line. Any family earning less than the poverty line would receive a welfare check in the amount of their poverty gap. No one would be poor.

This sounds like a simple solution to the poverty problem, but it isn't. First, people who *weren't* poor would have a strong incentive to become poor. Why try to support a family of four with a paycheck of $25,000 when you can quit and get $22,000 in welfare checks? Recall from Chapter 16 that the decision to work is a response to both the financial and psychological rewards associated with employment. People in dull, dirty, low-paying jobs get little of either. By quitting their jobs, declaring themselves poor, and accepting a guaranteed income transfer, they would gain much more leisure at little financial or psychological cost. In the process, total output would shrink (Figure 20.3).

The second potential problem affects the work behavior of people who were poor to begin with. We assumed that the Jones family was earning $18,000 before they got a welfare check. The question now is whether the welfare check will change their work behavior.

Suppose that family gets an opportunity to earn an extra $2,000 a year by working overtime. Should they seize that opportunity? Consider the effect of the higher *wages* on the family's *income*. Before working overtime, the Jones family earned

INCOME WITHOUT OVERTIME WAGES

Wages	$18,000
Welfare benefits	4,000
Total income	$22,000

If they now work overtime, their income is

INCOME WITH OVERTIME WAGES

Wages	$20,000
Welfare benefits	2,000
Total income	$22,000

Something is wrong here: although *wages* have gone up, the family's *income* hasn't. How would you like to be in this position? How would you react?

Implicit Marginal Tax Rates. The failure of income to rise with wages is the by-product of how welfare benefits were computed. *If welfare benefits are set equal to the poverty gap, every additional dollar of wages reduces welfare benefits by the same amount.* In effect, the Jones family confronts a **marginal tax rate** of 100 percent: every dollar of wages results in a lost dollar of benefits. Uncle Sam isn't literally raising the family's taxes by a dollar. By reducing benefits dollar for dollar, however, the end result is the same.

marginal tax rate: The tax rate imposed on the last (marginal) dollar of income.

With a 100 percent marginal tax rate, a family can't improve its income by working more. In fact, this family might as well work *less*. As wages decline, welfare benefits increase by the same amount. Thus we end up with a conflict between compassion and work incentives. By guaranteeing a poverty-level income, we destroy the economic incentive of low-income workers to support themselves. This creates a **moral hazard** for welfare recipients; that is, we encourage undesirable behavior. The moral hazard here is the temptation not to support oneself by working—choosing welfare checks instead.

moral hazard: An incentive to engage in undesirable behavior.

Less Compassion

To reduce this moral hazard, Congress and the states changed the way benefits are computed. First, they set a much lower ceiling on welfare benefits. States don't offer to close the poverty gap; instead they set a maximum benefit far below the poverty line. Hence we have this amended benefit formula:

$$\text{Welfare benefit} = \text{Maximum benefit} - \text{Wages}$$

In 2010, the typical state set a maximum benefit of about $8,000 for a family of four. Hence a family without any other income couldn't get enough money from welfare to stay out of poverty. As a result, *a family totally dependent on welfare is unquestionably poor.* Although the lower benefit ceiling is less compassionate, it reduces the risk of people climbing on the welfare wagon for a free ride.

More Incentives

To encourage welfare recipients to lift their own incomes above the poverty line, welfare departments made another change in the benefit formula. As we just saw, *the rate at which benefits are reduced as wages increase is the marginal tax rate.* The dollar-for-dollar benefit cuts illustrated destroyed the financial incentive to work. To give recipients more incentive to work, the marginal tax rate was cut from 100 to 67 percent. So we now have a new benefit formula:

$$\text{Welfare benefit} = \text{Maximum benefit} - \frac{2}{3}[\text{Wages}]$$

Figure 20.4 illustrates how this lower marginal tax rate alters the relationship of total income to wages. The black line in the figure shows the total wages Mrs. Jones could earn at $8 per hour. She could earn nothing by not working or as much as $16,000 per year by working full-time (2,000 hours per year, as depicted by point *F* in the figure).

The blue lines in the figure show what happens to her welfare benefits and total income when a 100 percent marginal tax rate is imposed. At point *A* she gets $8,000 in welfare benefits because she's not working at all. That $8,000 is also her total income because she has no wages.

Now consider what happens to the family's total income if Mrs. Jones goes to work. If she works 1,000 hours per year (essentially half-time), she could earn $8,000 (point *B*). But what would happen to her income? If the welfare department cuts her benefit by $1 for every dollar she earns, her benefit check slides down the blue "welfare benefits" line to point *C*,

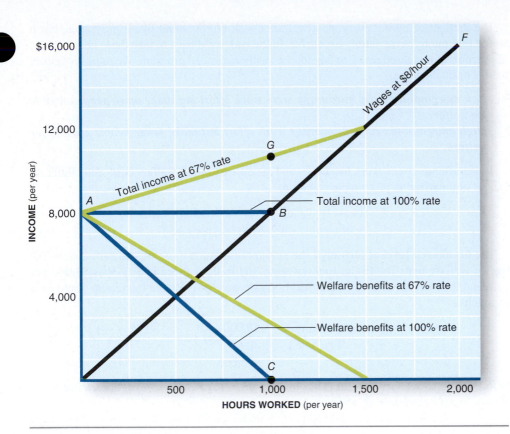

FIGURE 20.4
Work (Dis)Incentives

If welfare benefits are reduced dollar for dollar as wages increase, the implied marginal tax rate is 100 percent. In that case, total income remains at the benefit limit of $8,000 (point *A*) as work effort increases from 0 to 1,000 hours (point *B*). There is no incentive to work in this range.

When the marginal tax rate is reduced to 67 percent, total income starts increasing as soon as the welfare recipient starts working. At 1,000 hours of work, total income is $10,226 (point *G*).

where she gets nothing from welfare. By working 1,000 hours per year, all Mrs. Jones has done is replace her welfare check with a paycheck. That might make taxpayers smile, but Mrs. Jones will wonder why she bothered to go to work. With a 100 percent tax rate, her total income doesn't rise above $8,000 until she works more than 1,000 hours.

The green lines in Figure 20.4 show how work incentives improve with a lower marginal tax rate. Now welfare benefits are reduced by only 67 cents for every $1 of wages earned. As a result, total income starts rising as soon as Mrs. Jones goes to work. If she works 1,000 hours, her total income will include

Wages	$ 8,000	
Welfare benefit	2,667	= $8,000 − 2/3 ($8,000)
Total income	$10,667	

Point *G* on the graph illustrates this outcome.

Incentives versus Costs

It may be comforting to know that the Jones family can now increase its income from $8,000 when not working to $10,667 by working 1,000 hours per year. But they still face a higher marginal tax rate (67 percent) than rich people (the top marginal tax rate on federal income taxes is 35 percent). Why not lower their marginal tax rate even further, thus increasing both their work incentives and their total income?

Unfortunately, a reduction in the marginal tax rate would also increase welfare costs. Suppose we eliminated the marginal tax rate altogether. Then the Jones family could earn $8,000 *and* keep welfare benefits of $8,000. That would boost their total income to $16,000. Sounds great, doesn't it? But should we still be providing $8,000 in welfare payments to someone who earns $8,000 on her own? How about someone earning $20,000 or $30,000? Where should we draw the line? Clearly, *if we don't impose a marginal tax rate at some point, everyone will be eligible for welfare benefits.*

The thought of giving everyone a welfare check might sound like a great idea, but it would turn out to be incredibly expensive. In the end, we'd have to take those checks back, in the form of increased taxes, to pay for the vastly expanded program. We must recognize, then, a basic dilemma:

- *Low marginal tax rates encourage more work effort but make more people eligible for welfare.*
- *High marginal tax rates discourage work effort but make fewer people eligible for welfare.*

The conflict between work incentives and the desire to limit welfare costs and eligibility can be summarized in this simple equation:

$$\text{Breakeven level of income} = \frac{\text{Basic benefits}}{\text{Marginal tax rate}}$$

breakeven level of income: The income level at which welfare eligibility ceases.

The **breakeven level of income** is the amount of income a person can earn before losing all welfare benefits. In the Joneses' case, the basic welfare benefit was $8,000 per year and the benefit reduction (marginal tax) rate was 0.67. Hence the family could earn as much as

$$\begin{aligned}\text{Breakeven level of income} &= \frac{\$8,000}{0.67}\text{ per year} \\ &= \$12,000\end{aligned}$$

before losing all welfare benefits. Thus *low marginal tax rates encourage work but make it hard to get completely off welfare.*

If the marginal tax rate were 100 percent, as under the old welfare system, the breakeven point would be $8,000 divided by 1.00. In that case, people who earned $8,000 on their own would get no assistance from welfare. Fewer people would be eligible for welfare, but those who drew benefits would have no incentive to work. If the marginal tax rate were lowered to 0, the breakeven point would rise to infinity ($8,000 divided by 0)—and we'd all be on welfare.

As this arithmetic shows, *there's a basic conflict between work incentives (low marginal tax rates) and welfare containment (smaller welfare rolls and outlays).* We can achieve a lower breakeven level of income (less welfare eligibility) only by sacrificing low marginal tax rates or higher income floors (basic benefits). Hence welfare costs can be minimized only if we sacrifice income provision or work incentives.

Tax Elasticity of Labor Supply. The terms of the trade-off between more welfare and less work depend on how responsive people are to marginal tax rates. As we first noted in Chapter 19, the **tax elasticity of labor supply** measures the response to changes in tax rates:

tax elasticity of labor supply: The percentage change in quantity of labor supplied divided by the percentage change in tax rates.

$$\text{Tax elasticity of labor supply} = \frac{\%\text{ change in quantity of labor supplied}}{\%\text{ change in tax rate}}$$

If the tax elasticity of labor supply were zero, it wouldn't matter how high the marginal tax rate was: people would work for nothing (100 percent tax rate). In reality, the tax elasticity of labor supply among low-wage workers is more in the range of 0.2 to 0.3, so marginal tax rates *do* affect work effort. *So long as the tax elasticity of labor supply is greater than zero, there is a conflict between equity (more welfare) and efficiency (more work).*

Time Limits. The 1996 welfare reforms partially sidestepped this dilemma by setting time limits on welfare eligibility. TANF recipients *must* engage in some sort of employment-related activity (e.g., a job, job search, or training) within two years of first receiving benefits. There is also a five-year *lifetime* limit on welfare eligibility. States, however, can still use their own (nonfederal) funds to extend welfare benefits beyond those time limits.

SOCIAL SECURITY

Like welfare programs, the Social Security program was developed to redistribute incomes. In the case of Social Security, however, *age,* not low income, is the primary determinant of eligibility. The program seeks to provide a financial prop under retirement incomes. Although Social Security is a *social insurance* program rather than a *welfare* program, it has the same kind of conflict between equity and efficiency. Here again we have to confront policy conflicts among the goals of compassion, work incentives, and program costs.

Program Features

The Social Security program is actually a mix of three separate income transfers. The main program is for retired workers, the second for survivors of deceased workers, and the third for disabled workers. Created in 1935, this combined Old Age Survivors and Disability Insurance (OASDI) program is now so large that it accounts for over 40 percent of all federal income transfers. The monthly benefit checks distributed to 50 million recipients are financed with a payroll tax on workers and employers.

Retirement Age. As Figure 20.5 confirms, the retirement program is by far the largest component of OASDI. Individuals become eligible for Social Security retirement benefits when they reach certain ages. People can choose either "early" retirement (at age 62 to 64) or "normal" retirement (at age 65 to 67). Those who choose early retirement receive a smaller monthly benefit because they're expected to live longer in retirement.

For people born after 1940, the age threshold for "normal" retirement is increasing each year. By the year 2022, the age threshold for normal retirement will be age 67. This delay in benefit eligibility is intended to keep aging baby boomers working longer, thereby curtailing a surge in benefit outlays.

Progressive Benefits. Retirement benefits are based on an individual's wages. In 2010, the median Social Security retirement benefit for an individual was about $14,000. But high-wage workers could get nearly $30,000 and low-wage workers as little as $8,000 a year.

Although high-wage workers receive larger benefit checks than low-wage workers, the *ratio* of benefits to prior wages isn't constant. Instead the ***Social Security benefits formula is progressive*** because the ratio of benefits to prior wages declines as wages increase. Social Security replaces 90 percent of the first $749 of prior average monthly earnings but only 15 percent of monthly wages above $4,517 (see Table 20.2). The declining **wage replacement rate** ensures that low-wage workers receive *proportionately* greater benefits.

wage replacement rate: The percentage of base wages paid out in benefits.

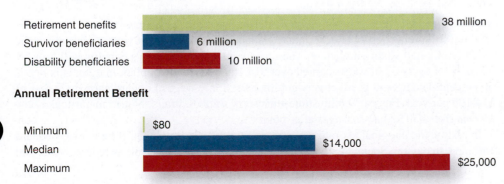

Who Pays Social Security Taxes

Payroll taxes
    7.65% paid by workers
    7.65% paid by employers

Who Gets Social Security Checks

Retirement benefits — 38 million
Survivor beneficiaries — 6 million
Disability beneficiaries — 10 million

Annual Retirement Benefit

Minimum — $80
Median — $14,000
Maximum — $25,000

FIGURE 20.5
Social Security Finances

The Social Security retirement, survivor, and disability programs are financed with payroll taxes. Most benefits go to retired workers, who get a median transfer of $14,000 per year.

Source: U.S. Social Security Administration (2011 data).

TABLE 20.2
Progressive Benefits

Social Security redistributes income progressively by replacing a larger share of low wages than high wages. Shown here are the wage replacement rates for 2011 (adjusted annually for inflation).

Wage Replacement Rate (%)	For Average Monthly Wages of
90%	$1–749
32	$749–4,517
15	over $4,517

Source: U.S. Social Security Administration (2011).

Suppose two workers are retiring. One had prior wages averaging $9,000 per month; the other had $3,000. These workers will get Social Security benefits of

High-wage worker = .90($749) + .32($3,768) + .15($4,483) = $2,552.31

Low-wage worker = .90($749) + .32($2,251) = $1,394.42

Notice how their relative incomes change. While working, the high-wage worker had three times more income than the low-wage worker. In retirement, however, the high-wage worker's benefits are not even two times the low-wage worker's benefits. Thus ***retirement benefits end up more equally distributed than wages.*** In this sense, Social Security is a *progressive* mechanism of income distribution.

The Earnings Test

In reality, a worker doesn't have to *retire* to receive Social Security benefits. But the government imposes an *earnings test* to determine how much retirement benefits an older person can collect while still working. The earnings test is similar to the formula used to compute welfare benefits. The formula establishes a maximum benefit amount and a marginal tax rate that reduces benefits as wages increase:

$$\frac{\text{Benefit}}{\text{amount}} = \frac{\text{Maximum}}{\text{award}} - 0.5 \text{ (Wages in excess of ceiling)}$$

Consider the case of Leonard, a 62-year-old worker contemplating retirement. Suppose Leonard's wage history entitles him to a maximum award of $12,000 per year. But he wants to keep working to supplement Social Security benefits with wages. What happens to his benefits if he continues to work?

In 2011, the wage "ceiling" for workers 62 to 64 was $14,160. Hence the benefit formula was

$$\frac{\text{Benefit}}{\text{amount}} = \$12,000 - 0.5 \text{ (Wage} > \$14,160)$$

As a result, a person could earn as much as $14,160 and still get maximum retirement benefits ($12,000) since there would be no wage-related deduction. This would put Leonard's total income at $26,160.

The Work Disincentive

Suppose Leonard wants a bit more income than that. Can he increase his total income by working still more? Yes, but not by much. He faces the same kind of work disincentives the Jones family had when on welfare. The formula just described says benefits will drop by 50 cents for every $1 of wages earned over $14,160. Hence the implicit marginal tax rate is 50 percent. Uncle Sam is effectively getting half of any wages Leonard earns in excess of $14,160 per year. Figure 20.6 illustrates this sorry state of affairs. Notice in particular how *income* rises half as fast as *wages* after point *C*.

In reality, the marginal tax rate on Leonard's wages is even higher. If he works, Leonard will have to pay the Social Security payroll tax (7.65 percent) as well as federal, state, and

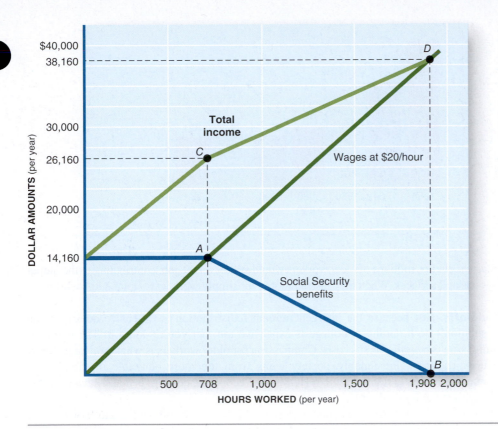

FIGURE 20.6
**The Social Security
Earnings Test**

A worker aged 62–64 can earn up to $14,160 (point *A*) without losing any Social Security benefits. At point *C,* income includes $12,000 in benefits and $14,160 in wages.

If wages increase beyond $14,160, however, Social Security benefits decline by 50 cents for every $1 earned. After point *C,* income rises only half as fast as wages. At the breakeven point *D,* earnings and income are $38,160, and there are no Social Security benefits (point *B*).

local income taxes (say, another 15 percent). Hence the full burden of taxes and benefit losses includes

ITEM	MARGINAL TAX RATE
Social Security benefit loss	50.00%
Payroll tax	7.65
Income taxes	15.00
Total explicit and implicit tax rate	72.65%

As a consequence, Leonard's income goes up by only 27.35 cents with every $1 he earns. The remaining 72.65 cents of every wage dollar is lost to taxes or reduced Social Security benefits.

Declining Labor Supply

Like welfare recipients, older people are quick to realize that work no longer pays. Not surprisingly, they've exited the labor market in droves. The **labor force participation rate** measures the percentage of the population that is either employed or actively seeking a job (unemployed). Figure 20.7 shows how precipitously the labor force participation rate has declined among older Americans. This problem isn't unique to the United States. The relative size of the over-65 population is growing everywhere, and more older people are retiring earlier.

Prior to the creation of the Social Security system, most older people had to continue working until advanced age. Many "died with their boots on" because they had no other means of support. Just a generation ago, over 75 percent of men 62 to 64 were working. Today less than 50 percent of that group is working.

Compassion, Incentives, and Cost

The primary economic cost of the Social Security program isn't the benefits it pays but the reduction in total output that occurs when workers retire early. In the absence of Social

labor force participation rate: The percentage of the working-age population working or seeking employment.

web analysis

The U.S. Census Bureau calculates labor force participation rates and also makes projections. Visit **www.census. gov** and search "labor force participation" for more information.

FIGURE 20.7

Declining Labor Force Participation

In the 1960s and 1970s, the eligibility age for Social Security was lowered for men and benefits were increased. This convinced an increased percentage of older men to leave the labor force and retire. In a single generation the labor force participation rate of men over age 65 was halved.

Source: U.S. Bureau of Labor Statistics.

Work Incentives

Security benefits, millions of older workers would still be on the job, contributing to the output of goods and services. When they instead retire—or simply work less—total output shrinks.

Trade-offs. Just because the intergenerational redistribution is expensive doesn't mean we shouldn't do it. Going to college is expensive too, but you're doing it. The real economic issue is benefits versus costs. Compassion for older workers is what motivates Social Security transfers. Presumably, society gains from the more equitable distribution of income that results (a revised FOR WHOM). The economic concern is that we *balance* this gain against the implied costs.

One way of reducing the economic cost of the Social Security program would be to eliminate the earnings test. The American Association of Retired Persons (AARP) has advocated this option for many years. If the earnings test were eliminated, the marginal tax rate on the wages of older workers would drop from 50 percent to 0. In a flash, the work disincentive would vanish, and older workers would produce more goods and services.

There's a downside to this reform, however. If the earnings test were eliminated, all older individuals would get their full retirement benefit, even if they continued to work. This would raise the budgetary cost of the program substantially. To cover that cost, payroll taxes would have to increase. Higher payroll taxes would in turn reduce supply and demand for *younger* workers. Hence the financial burden of eliminating the earnings test might actually *increase* the economic cost of Social Security.

There's also an equity issue here. Should we increase payroll taxes on younger low-income workers to give higher Social Security benefits to older workers who still command higher salaries? In 2000 Congress gave a very qualified "yes" to this question. The earnings test was eliminated for workers over age 70 and for workers who retired at "normal" age (65–67 depending on year of birth). The marginal tax rate for workers who "retire" early but continue working at ages 65–69 was also reduced to 33.3 percent. The lower earnings test and 50 percent marginal tax rate were left intact, however, for people aged 62–64, the ones for whom the retirement decision is most pressing. The *budget* cost of greater work incentives for "early retirees" (ages 62–64) was regarded as too high.

THE ECONOMY TOMORROW

PRIVATIZE SOCIAL SECURITY?

All income transfer programs entail a redistribution of income. In the case of Social Security, the redistribution is largely intergenerational: payroll taxes levied on younger workers finance retirement benefits for older workers. The system is financed on a pay-as-you-go basis; future benefits depend on future taxes. This is very different from private pension plans, whereby you salt away some wages while working to finance your own eventual benefits. Such private plans are *advance-funded*.

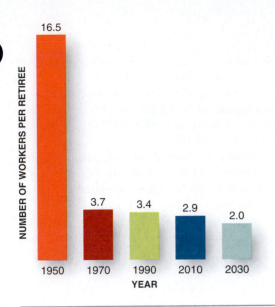

FIGURE 20.8
A Declining Tax Base

Because Social Security benefits are financed by payroll taxes, the ratio of workers to retirees is a basic measure of the program's fiscal health. That ratio has declined dramatically, and it will decline even more as the baby boomers are retiring.

Source: U.S. Social Security Administration.

Many people say we should run the Social Security system the same way. They want to "privatize" Social Security by permitting workers to establish their own retirement plans. Instead of paying payroll taxes to fund someone else's benefits, you'd make a contribution to your *own* pension fund.

The case for privatizing Social Security is based on both efficiency and equity. The efficiency argument reflects the core laissez-faire argument that markets know best. In a privatized system, individuals would have the freedom to tailor their consumption and saving choices. The elimination of mandatory payroll taxes and the earnings test would also lessen work disincentives. People would work harder and longer, maximizing total output.

Advocates of privatization also note how inequitable the existing program is for younger workers. The people now retired are getting a great deal: they paid relatively low payroll taxes when young and now receive substantial benefits. In part this high payoff is due to demographics. Thirty years ago there were four workers for every retired person. As the post–World War II baby boomers retire, the ratio of workers to retirees will decline dramatically. By the year 2030, there will be only two workers for every retiree (see Figure 20.8). As a result, the tax burden on tomorrow's workers will have to be a lot higher, or the baby boomers will have to accept much lower Social Security benefits. Either way, some generation of workers will get a lot less than everyone else. If Social Security is privatized, tomorrow's workers won't have to bear such a demographic tax burden.

As alluring as these suggestions sound, the privatization of Social Security would foster other inequities. The primary goal of Social Security is to fend off poverty among the aged. Social Security does this in two ways: by (1) transferring income from workers to retirees and (2) redistributing income from high-wage workers to low-wage workers in retirement with progressive wage replacement rates. By contrast, a privatized system would let the market alone determine FOR WHOM goods are produced. Low-income workers and other people who saved little while working would end up poor in their golden years. In a privatized system, even some high earners and savers might end up poor if their investments turned sour. Would we turn our collective backs on these people? If not, then the government would have to intervene with *some* kind of transfer program. The real issue, therefore, may not be whether a privatized Social Security system would work but what kind of *public* transfer program we'd have to create to supplement it. Then the choice would be either (1) Social Security or (2) a privatized retirement system plus a public welfare program for the aged poor. Framed in this context, the choice for the economy tomorrow is a lot more complex.

web analysis

Read about the future of Social Security at **www.ssa.gov.** Click the "Budget & Performance" link.

SUMMARY

- Income transfers are payments for which no current goods or services are exchanged. They include both cash payments such as welfare checks and in-kind transfers such as food stamps and Medicare. LO20-1

- Most transfer payments come from social insurance programs that cushion the income effects of specific events, such as aging, illness, or unemployment. Welfare programs are means-tested; they pay benefits only to the poor. LO20-1

- The basic goal of transfer programs is to alter the market's FOR WHOM outcome. Attempts to redistribute income may, however, have the unintended effect of reducing total income. This is the core equity versus efficiency dilemma. LO20-2

- Welfare programs reduce work incentives in two ways. They offer some income to people who don't work at all,

and they also tax the wages of recipients who do work via offsetting benefit reductions. LO20-2

- The benefit reduction that occurs when wages increase is an implicit marginal tax. The higher the marginal tax rate, (1) the less the incentive to work but (2) the smaller the welfare caseload. LO20-3

- The Social Security retirement program creates similar work disincentives. It provides an income floor for people who don't work and imposes a high marginal tax rate on workers aged 62–64. LO20-2

- The core policy dilemma is to find an optimal balance between compassion (transferring more income) and incentives (keeping people at work contributing to total output). LO20-3

Key Terms

income transfers	social insurance programs	moral hazard
in-kind transfers	market failure	breakeven level of income
cash transfers	labor supply	tax elasticity of labor supply
target efficiency	poverty gap	wage replacement rate
welfare programs	marginal tax rate	labor force participation rate

Questions for Discussion

1. If we have to choose between compassion and incentives, which should we choose? Do the terms of the trade-off matter? LO20-3

2. What's so hard about guaranteeing everyone a minimal level of income support? What problems arise? LO20-2

3. If poor people don't want to work, should they get welfare? What about their children? LO20-3

4. Once someone has received TANF welfare benefits for a total of five years, he or she is permanently ineligible for more TANF benefits. Should this person receive any further assistance? How will work incentives be affected? LO20-2

5. In what ways do younger workers pay for Social Security benefits received by retired workers? LO20-2

6. Should the Social Security earnings test be eliminated? What are the benefits and costs of doing so? LO20-2

7. How would the distribution of income change if Social Security were privatized? LO20-1

8. Who pays the economic cost of Social Security? In what ways? LO20-2

9. Why don't we give poor people more cash welfare instead of in-kind transfers like food stamps, housing assistance, and Medicaid? LO20-3

 web activities to accompany this chapter can be found on the Online Learning Center:
http://www.mhhe.com/schiller13e

 mobile app Visit your mobile app store and download the Schiller: Study Econ app *today*!

PROBLEMS FOR CHAPTER 20   Name: _____

LO20-2 1. Suppose the welfare benefit formula is

$$\text{Benefit} = \$4,800 - 0.67\,(\text{Wages} > \$6,000)$$

(a) What is the marginal tax rate on

  (i) The first $6,000 of wages?   _____
  (ii) Wages above $6,000?   _____

(b) How large is the benefit if wages equal

  (i) $0?   _____
  (ii) $4,000?   _____
  (iii) $9,000? _____

(c) What is the breakeven level of income in this case?   _____

LO20-2 2. A welfare recipient can receive food stamps as well as cash welfare benefits. If the food stamp allotment is set as follows,

$$\text{Food stamps} = \$5,000 - 0.30\,(\text{Wages})$$

(a) How high can wages rise before all food stamps are eliminated?   _____
(b) If the welfare benefit formula in Problem 1 applies, what is the *combined* marginal tax rate of both welfare and food stamps for wages above $6,000?   _____

LO20-3 3. Draw a graph showing how benefits, total income, and wages change under the following conditions:

$$\text{Wage rate} = \$10 \text{ per hour}$$

$$\text{Welfare benefit} = \$5,000 - 0.5\,(\text{Wages} > \$3,000)$$

Identify here and label on the graph the following points:
  A—welfare benefit when wages = 0
  B—welfare benefit when wages = $10,000
  C—breakeven level of income

(a) How much is that benefit?   _____
(b) How much is that benefit?   _____
(c) What is that income level?   _____

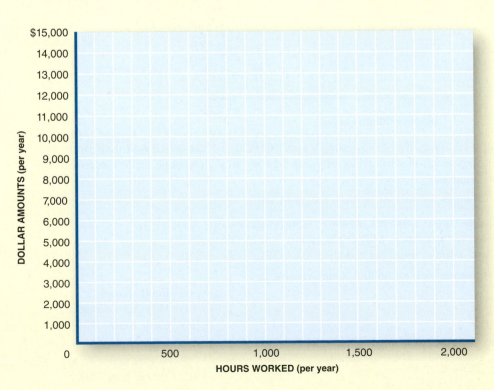

LO20-3 4. What is the breakeven level of income for Social Security as depicted in Figure 20.6? _____

LO20-3 5. According to the benefit formula in Table 20.2, how large will the Social Security benefit be for a worker who had prior earnings of

(a) $24,000 a year? _____

(b) $60,000 a year? _____

What is the marginal wage replacement rate for

(c) The $24,000 per year worker? _____

(d) The $60,000 per year worker? _____

LO20-3 6. How large a monthly Social Security check will a retiree get if her maximum benefit is $1,600 per month and she continues working for wages of $2,000 per month? (See Table 20.2.) _____

LO20-3 7. (a) On the following graph, depict the wages, income, and Social Security benefits at different hours of work for a worker aged 62–64 who earns $15 per hour and is eligible for $15,000 in Social Security benefits.

(b) What is the total income if the person works 1,000 hours per year? _____

(c) What is the breakeven level of income? _____

LO20-3 8. If older workers have a tax elasticity of labor supply equal to 0.20, by how much will their work activity decline when they reach the Social Security earnings test limit? (Assume *explicit* taxes of 30 percent below that limit.) _____%

LO20-1 9. Suppose the benefit formulas for various welfare programs are

Food stamps: $400 per month − 0.30 (Wages)
Housing assistance: $1,000 per month − 0.25 (Wages)
Cash welfare: $400 per month − 0.67 (Wages above $500)

(a) How much will someone earning $600 a month receive in

(i) Food stamps? _____

(ii) Housing assistance? _____

(iii) Cash welfare? _____

(b) What is the cumulative marginal tax rate at

(i) Wages under $500? _____

(ii) Wages over $500? _____

International Economics

Our interactions with the rest of the world have a profound impact on the mix of output (WHAT), the methods of production (HOW), and the distribution of income (FOR WHOM). Trade and global money flows can also affect the stability of the macro economy. Chapters 21 and 22 explore the motives, the nature, and the effects of international trade and finance.

Chapter 23 examines one of the world's most urgent problems—the deprivation that afflicts nearly 3 billion people worldwide. In this last chapter, the dimensions, causes, and potential cures for global poverty are discussed.

International Trade

LEARNING OBJECTIVES

After reading this chapter, you should know

LO21-1. What comparative advantage is.

LO21-2. What the gains from trade are.

LO21-3. How trade barriers affect prices, output, and incomes.

The 2010 World Series between the San Francisco Giants and the Texas Rangers was played with Japanese gloves, baseballs made in Costa Rica, and Mexican bats. Most of the players were wearing shoes made in Korea or China. And during the regular season, many of the games throughout the major leagues were played on artificial grass made in Taiwan. Baseball, it seems, has become something less than the "all-American" game.

Imported goods have made inroads into other activities as well. All DVDs, smartphones, and video game consoles are imported, as are most televisions, fax machines, personal computers, and iPads. Most of these imported goods could have been produced in the United States. Why did we purchase them from other countries? For that matter, why does the rest of the world buy computers, tractors, chemicals, airplanes, and wheat from us rather than produce such products for themselves? Wouldn't we all be better off relying on ourselves for the goods we consume (and the jobs we need)

rather than buying and selling products in international markets? Or is there some advantage to be gained from international trade?

This chapter begins with a survey of international trade patterns—what goods and services we trade, and with whom. Then we address basic issues related to such trade:

- **What benefit, if any, do we get from international trade?**
- **How much harm do imports cause, and to whom?**
- **Should we protect ourselves from "unfair" trade by limiting imports?**

After examining the arguments for and against international trade, we draw some general conclusions about trade policy. As we'll see, international trade tends to increase *average* incomes, although it may diminish the job and income opportunities for specific industries and workers.

U.S. TRADE PATTERNS

The United States is by far the largest player in global product and resource markets. In 2010 we purchased 20 percent of the world's exports and sold 15 percent of the same total.

Imports

In dollar terms, our imports in 2010 exceeded $2.3 trillion. These **imports** included the consumer items mentioned earlier as well as capital equipment, raw materials, and food. Table 21.1 represents the goods and services we purchase from foreign suppliers.

Although imports represent only 18 percent of total GDP, they account for larger shares of specific product markets. Coffee is a familiar example. Since virtually all coffee is imported (except for a tiny amount produced in Hawaii), Americans would have a harder time staying awake without imports. Likewise, there'd be no aluminum if we didn't import bauxite, no chrome bumpers if we didn't import chromium, no tin cans without imported tin, and a lot fewer computers without imported components. We couldn't even play the all-American game of baseball without imports because baseballs are no longer made in the United States.

We import *services* as well as *goods*. If you fly to Europe on Virgin Airways, you're importing transportation services. If you stay in a London hotel, you're importing lodging services. When you go to Barclay's Bank to cash traveler's checks, you're importing foreign financial services. These and other services now account for one-sixth of U.S. imports.

imports: Goods and services purchased from international sources.

Country	Imports from	Exports to
Australia	Beef Alumina Autos	Airplanes Computers Auto parts
Belgium	Jewelry Cars Optical glass	Cigarettes Airplanes Diamonds
Canada	Cars Trucks Paper	Auto parts Cars Computers
China	Computers Clothes Toys	Scrap and trash Electrical generators Oil seeds
Germany	Cars Engines Auto parts	Airplanes Computers Cars
Japan	Cars Computers Telephones	Airplanes Computers Timber
Russia	Oil Platinum Artworks	Corn Wheat Oil seeds
South Korea	Shoes Cars Computers	Airplanes Leather Iron ingots and oxides

Source: U.S. Department of Commerce.

web analysis

After long-standing trade sanctions, the United States has restored limited trade with Cuba in recent years. For information on trade with Cuba, see **www.cubatrade.org**.

TABLE 21.1
A U.S. Trade Sampler

The United States imports and exports a staggering array of goods and services. Shown here are the top exports and imports with various countries. Notice that we export many of the same goods we import (such as cars and computers). What's the purpose of trading goods we produce ourselves?

Exports

While we're buying goods (merchandise) and services from the rest of the world, global consumers are buying our **exports.** In 2010 we exported $1.8 trillion of *goods,* including farm products (wheat, corn, soybeans), tobacco, machinery (computers), aircraft, automobiles and auto parts, raw materials (lumber, iron ore), and chemicals (see Table 21.1 for a sample of U.S. merchandise exports). We also exported $545 billion of services (movies, software licenses, tourism, engineering, financial services, etc.).

Although the United States is the world's largest exporter of goods and services, exports represent a relatively modest fraction of our total output. As the World View below illustrates, other nations export much larger proportions of their GDP. Belgium is one of the most export-oriented countries, with tourist services and diamond exports pushing its export ratio to an incredible 73 percent. By contrast, Myanmar (Burma) is basically a closed economy with few exports (other than opium and other drugs traded in the black market).

WORLD VIEW

Export Ratios

Very poor countries often have little to export and thus low export ratios. Saudi Arabia, by contrast, depends heavily on its oil exports. Fast-developing countries in Asia also rely on exports to enlarge their markets and raise incomes. The U.S. export ratio is low by international standards.

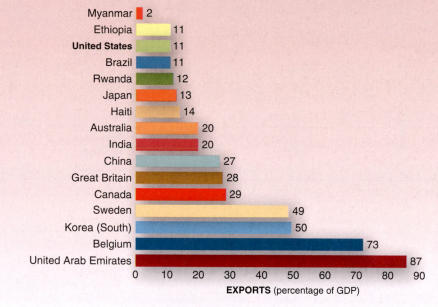

EXPORTS (percentage of GDP)

Source: *The World Bank, WDI2011 Data Set,* **data.worldbank.org.**

Analysis: The relatively low U.S. export ratio reflects the vast size of our domestic market and our relative self-sufficiency in food and resources. European nations are smaller and highly interdependent.

The low U.S. export ratio (11 percent) disguises our heavy dependence on exports in specific industries. We export 25 to 50 percent of our rice, corn, and wheat production each year, and still more of our soybeans. Clearly a decision by international consumers to stop eating U.S. agricultural products could devastate a lot of American farmers. Such companies as Boeing (planes), Caterpillar Tractor (construction and farm machinery), Weyerhaeuser (logs, lumber), Dow (chemicals), and Sun Microsystems (computer workstations) sell over one-fourth of their output in foreign markets. McDonald's sells hamburgers to nearly 60 million people a day in 128 countries around the world; to do so, the company exports management and marketing services (as well as frozen food) from the United States. The Walt Disney

Product Category	Exports ($ billions)	Imports ($ billions)	Surplus (Deficit) ($ billions)
Merchandise	$1,289	$1,936	$(647)
Services	545	394	151
Total trade	$1,834	$2,330	$(496)

Source: U.S. Department of Commerce.

TABLE 21.2
Trade Balances

Both merchandise (goods) and services are traded between countries. The United States typically has a merchandise deficit and a services surplus. When combined, an overall trade deficit remained in 2010.

Company produces the most popular TV shows in Russia and Germany, publishes Italy's best-selling weekly magazine, and has the most popular tourist attraction in Japan (Tokyo Disneyland). The 500,000 foreign students attending U.S. universities are purchasing $5 billion of American educational services. All these activities are part of America's service exports.

Trade Balances

Although we export a lot of products, we usually have an imbalance in our trade flows. The trade balance is the difference between the value of exports and imports:

$$\text{Trade balance} = \text{Exports} - \text{Imports}$$

During 2010 we imported much more than we exported and so had a *negative* trade balance. A negative trade balance is called a **trade deficit.**

Although the overall trade balance includes both goods and services, these flows are usually reported separately, with the *merchandise* trade balance distinguished from the *services* trade balance. As Table 21.2 shows, the United States had a merchandise (goods) trade deficit of $647 billion in 2010 and a *services* trade *surplus* of $151 billion, leaving the overall trade balance in the red.

When the United States has a trade deficit with the rest of the world, other countries must have an offsetting **trade surplus.** On a global scale, imports must equal exports because every good exported by one country must be imported by another. Hence *any imbalance in America's trade must be offset by reverse imbalances elsewhere.*

Whatever the overall balance in our trade accounts, bilateral balances vary greatly. Table 21.3 shows, for example, that our 2010 aggregate trade deficit ($496 billion) incorporated huge bilateral trade deficits with China, Mexico, and Japan. In the same year, however, we had trade surpluses with Brazil, the Netherlands, Belgium, Australia, and Hong Kong.

trade deficit: The amount by which the value of imports exceeds the value of exports in a given time period.

trade surplus: The amount by which the value of exports exceeds the value of imports in a given time period.

Country	Exports to ($ billions)	Imports from ($ billions)	Trade Balance ($ billions)
Top Deficit Countries			
China	$113	$376	−$263
Mexico	186	247	−61
Japan	108	149	−41
Germany	74	114	−40
Canada	299	306	−7
Top Surplus Countries			
Brazil	$51	$29	+$21
Hong Kong	33	12	+21
The Netherlands	48	28	+20
Australia	35	15	+20
Belgium	29	20	+9

Source: U.S. Department of Commerce, International Trade Administration.

TABLE 21.3
Bilateral Trade Balances

The U.S. trade deficit is the net result of bilateral deficits and surpluses. We had huge trade deficits with China, Mexico, and Japan in 2010, for example, but small trade surpluses with Brazil, the Netherlands, Belgium, Australia, and Hong Kong. International trade is *multi*national, with surpluses in some countries being offset by trade deficits elsewhere.

MOTIVATION TO TRADE

Many people wonder why we trade so much, particularly since (1) we import many of the things we also export (like computers, airplanes, clothes), (2) we *could* produce many of the other things we import, and (3) we worry so much about trade imbalances. Why not just import those few things that we can't produce ourselves, and export just enough to balance that trade?

Specialization

Trade Deficits

Although it might seem strange to be importing goods we could produce ourselves, such trade is entirely rational. Our decision to trade with other countries arises from the same considerations that motivate individuals to specialize in production: satisfying their remaining needs in the marketplace. Why don't you become self-sufficient—growing all your own food, building your own shelter, and recording your own songs? Presumably because you've found that you can enjoy a much higher standard of living (and better music) by working at just one job and then buying other goods in the marketplace. When you do so, you're no longer self-sufficient. Instead you are *specializing* in production, relying on others to produce the array of goods and services you want. When countries trade goods and services, they are doing the same thing—*specializing* in production and then *trading* for other desired goods. Why do they do this? Because **specialization increases total output.**

To see how nations benefit from trade, we'll examine the production possibilities of two countries. We want to demonstrate that two countries that trade can together produce more output than they could in the absence of trade. If they can, **the gain from trade is increased world output and a higher standard of living in all trading countries.** This is the essential message of the *theory of comparative advantage.*

Production and Consumption without Trade

production possibilities: The alternative combinations of final goods and services that could be produced in a given time period with all available resources and technology.

Consider the production and consumption possibilities of just two countries—say, the United States and France. For the sake of illustration, assume that both countries produce only two goods: bread and wine. Let's also set aside worries about the law of diminishing returns and the substitutability of resources, thus transforming the familiar **production possibilities** curve into a straight line, as in Figure 21.1.

The "curves" in Figure 21.1 suggest that the United States is capable of producing much more bread than France. With our greater abundance of labor, land, and other resources, we assume that the United States is capable of producing up to 100 zillion loaves of bread per year. To do so, we'd have to devote all our resources to that purpose. This capability is indicated by point A in Figure 21.1a and in row A of the accompanying production possibilities schedule. France (Figure 21.1b), on the other hand, confronts a *maximum* bread production of only 15 zillion loaves per year (point G) because it has little available land, less fuel, and fewer potential workers.

The capacities of the two countries for wine production are 50 zillion barrels for us (point F) and 60 zillion for France (point L), largely reflecting France's greater experience in tending vines. Both countries are also capable of producing alternative *combinations* of bread and wine, as evidenced by their respective production possibilities curves (points A–F for the United States and G–L for France).

closed economy: A nation that doesn't engage in international trade.

A nation that doesn't trade with other countries is called a **closed economy.** In the absence of contact with the outside world, the production possibilities curve for a closed economy also defines its **consumption possibilities.** Without imports, a country cannot consume more than it produces. Thus the only immediate issue in a closed economy is which mix of output to choose—*what* to produce and consume—out of the domestic choices available.

consumption possibilities: The alternative combinations of goods and services that a country could consume in a given time period.

Assume that Americans choose point D on their production possibilities curve, producing and consuming 40 zillion loaves of bread and 30 zillion barrels of wine. The French, on the other hand, prefer the mix of output represented by point I on their production possibilities curve. At that point they produce and consume 9 zillion loaves of bread and 24 zillion barrels of wine.

(a) U.S. production possibilities

(b) French production possibilities

In a closed economy, production possibilities and consumption possibilities are identical.

U.S. Production Possibilities		
Bread (Zillions of Loaves)	+	Wine (Zillions of Barrels)
A 100	+	0
B 80	+	10
C 60	+	20
D 40	+	30
E 20	+	40
F 0	+	50

French Production Possibilities		
Bread (Zillions of Loaves)	+	Wine (Zillions of Barrels)
G 15	+	0
H 12	+	12
I 9	+	24
J 6	+	36
K 3	+	48
L 0	+	60

FIGURE 21.1
Consumption Possibilities without Trade

In the absence of trade, a country's consumption possibilities are identical to its production possibilities. The assumed production possibilities of the United States and France are illustrated in the graphs and the corresponding schedules. Before entering into trade, the United States chose to produce and consume at point *D*, with 40 zillion loaves of bread and 30 zillion barrels of wine. France chose point *I* on its own production possibilities curve. By trading, each country hopes to increase its consumption beyond these levels.

To assess the potential gain from trade, we must focus the *combined* output of the United States and France. In this case, total world output (points *D* and *I*) comes to 49 zillion loaves of bread and 54 zillion barrels of wine. What we want to know is whether world output would increase if France and the United States abandoned their isolation and started trading. Could either country, or both, consume more output by engaging in a little trade?

Production and Consumption with Trade

Because both countries are saddled with limited production possibilities, trying to eke out a little extra wine and bread from this situation might not appear very promising. Such a conclusion is unwarranted, however. Take another look at the production possibilities confronting the United States, as reproduced in Figure 21.2. Suppose the United States were to produce at point *C* rather than point *D*. At point *C* we could produce 60 zillion loaves of bread

FIGURE 21.2
Consumption Possibilities with Trade

A country can increase its consumption possibilities through international trade. Each country alters its mix of domestic output to produce more of the good it produces best. As it does so, total world output increases, and each country enjoys more consumption. In this case, trade allows U.S. consumption to move from point D to point N. France moves from point I to point M.

and 20 zillion barrels of wine. That combination is clearly *possible*, since it lies on the production possibilities curve. We didn't choose that point earlier because we assumed the mix of output at point *D* was preferable. The mix of output at point *C* could be produced, however.

We could also change the mix of output in France. Assume that France moved from point *I* to point *K*, producing 48 zillion barrels of wine and only 3 zillion loaves of bread.

Two observations are now called for. The first is simply that output mixes have changed in each country. The second, and more interesting, is that total world output has *increased*. Notice how this works. When the United States and France were at points *D* and *I*, their *combined* output consisted of

	Bread (Zillions of Loaves)	Wine (Zillions of Barrels)
United States (at point D)	40	30
France (at point I)	9	24
Total pre-trade output	49	54

After they moved along their respective production possibilities curves to points *C* and *K*, the combined world output became

	Bread (Zillions of Loaves)	Wine (Zillions of Barrels)
United States (at point C)	60	20
France (at point K)	3	48
Total output with trade	63	68

Total world output has increased by 14 zillion loaves of bread and 14 zillion barrels of wine. **Just by changing the mix of output in each country, we've increased total world output.** This additional output creates the potential for making both countries better off than they were in the absence of trade.

The United States and France weren't producing at points *C* and *K* before because they simply didn't want to *consume* those particular output combinations. Nevertheless, our discovery that points *C* and *K* allow us to produce *more* output suggests that everybody can consume more goods and services if we change the mix of output in each country. This is our first clue as to how specialization and trade can benefit an **open economy**—a nation that engages in international trade.

Suppose we Americans are the first to discover the potential benefits from trade. Using Figure 21.2 as our guide, we suggest to the French that they move their mix of output from point *I* to point *K*. As an incentive for making such a move, we promise to give them 6 zillion loaves of bread in exchange for 20 zillion barrels of wine. This would leave them at point *M*, with as much bread to consume as they used to have, plus an extra 4 zillion barrels of wine. At point *I* they had 9 zillion loaves of bread and 24 zillion barrels of wine. At point *M* they can have 9 zillion loaves of bread and 28 zillion barrels of wine. Thus by altering their mix of output (from point *I* to point *K*) and then trading (point *K* to point *M*), the French end up with more goods and services than they had in the beginning. Notice in particular that this new consumption possibility (point *M*) lies *outside* France's domestic production possibilities curve.

The French will be quite pleased with the extra output they get from trading. But where does this leave us? Does France's gain imply a loss for us? Or do we gain from trade as well?

Mutual Gains

As it turns out, *both* the United States and France gain by trading. The United States, too, ends up consuming a mix of output that lies outside our production possibilities curve.

Note that at point *C* we produce 60 zillion loaves of bread per year and 20 zillion barrels of wine. We then export 6 zillion loaves to France. This leaves us with 54 zillion loaves of bread to consume.

In return for our exported bread, the French give us 20 zillion barrels of wine. These imports, plus our domestic production, permit us to *consume* 40 zillion barrels of wine. Hence we end up consuming at point *N*, enjoying 54 zillion loaves of bread and 40 zillion barrels of wine. Thus by first changing our mix of output (from point *D* to point *C*), then trading (point *C* to point *N*), we end up with 14 zillion more loaves of bread and 10 zillion more barrels of wine than we started with. International trade has made us better off, too.

Table 21.4 recaps the gains from trade for both countries. Notice that U.S. imports match French exports and vice versa. Also notice how the trade-facilitated consumption in each country exceeds no-trade levels.

	Production and Consumption with Trade						Production and Consumption with No Trade
	Production	+	Imports	−	Exports	= Consumption	
United States at . . .	Point *C*					Point *N*	Point *D*
Bread	60	+	0	−	6	= 54	40
Wine	20	+	20	−	0	= 40	30
France at . . .	Point *K*					Point *M*	Point *I*
Bread	3	+	6	−	0	= 9	9
Wine	48	+	0	−	20	= 28	24

TABLE 21.4
Gains from Trade

When nations specialize in production, they can export one good and import another and end up with *more* total goods to consume than they had without trade. In this case, the United States specializes in bread production. Notice how U.S. *consumption* of both goods increases (compare total U.S. consumption of bread and wine at point *N* [with trade] to consumption at point *D* [no trade]).

All these numbers look like some kind of magic trick, but there's no sleight of hand going on here; the gains from trade are due to specialization in production. When each country goes it alone, it's a prisoner of its own production possibilities curve; it must make production decisions on the basis of its own consumption desires. When international trade is permitted, however, each country can concentrate on the exploitation of its production capabilities. *Each country produces those goods it makes best and then trades with other countries to acquire the goods it desires to consume.*

The resultant specialization increases total world output. In the process, each country is able to escape the confines of its own production possibilities curve, to reach beyond it for a larger basket of consumption goods. *When a country engages in international trade, its consumption possibilities always exceed its production possibilities.* These enhanced consumption possibilities are emphasized by the positions of points N and M outside the production possibilities curves (Figure 21.2). If it weren't possible for countries to increase their consumption by trading, there'd be no incentive for trading, and thus no trade.

PURSUIT OF COMPARATIVE ADVANTAGE

Although international trade can make everyone better off, it's not so obvious which goods should be traded, or on what terms. In our previous illustration, the United States ended up trading bread for wine in terms that were decidedly favorable to us. Why did we export bread rather than wine, and how did we end up getting such a good deal?

Opportunity Costs

comparative advantage: The ability of a country to produce a specific good at a lower opportunity cost than its trading partners.

The decision to export bread is based on **comparative advantage**—that is, the *relative* cost of producing different goods. Recall that we can produce a maximum of 100 zillion loaves of bread per year or 50 zillion barrels of wine. Thus the domestic **opportunity cost** of producing 100 zillion loaves of bread is the 50 zillion barrels of wine we forsake in order to devote our resources to bread production. In fact, at every point on the U.S. production possibilities curve (Figure 21.2a), the opportunity cost of a loaf of bread is ½ barrel of wine. We're effectively paying half a barrel of wine to get a loaf of bread.

opportunity cost: The most desired goods or services that are forgone in order to obtain something else.

Although the cost of bread production in the United States might appear outrageous, even higher opportunity costs prevail in France. According to Figure 21.2b, the opportunity cost of producing a loaf of bread in France is a staggering 4 barrels of wine. To produce a loaf of bread, the French must use factors of production that could otherwise be used to produce 4 barrels of wine.

Comparative Advantage. A comparison of the opportunity costs prevailing in each country exposes the nature of comparative advantage. The United States has a comparative advantage in bread production because less wine has to be given up to produce bread in the United States than in France. In other words, the opportunity costs of bread production are lower in the United States than in France. *Comparative advantage refers to the relative (opportunity) costs of producing particular goods.*

A country should specialize in what it's *relatively* efficient at producing—that is, goods for which it has the lowest opportunity costs. In this case, the United States should produce bread because its opportunity cost (½ barrel of wine) is less than France's (4 barrels of wine). Were you the production manager for the whole world, you'd certainly want each country to exploit its relative abilities, thus maximizing world output. Each country can arrive at that same decision itself by comparing its own opportunity costs to those prevailing elsewhere. *World output, and thus the potential gains from trade, will be maximized when each country pursues its comparative advantage. To do so, each country*

- *Exports goods with relatively low opportunity costs.*
- *Imports goods with relatively high opportunity costs.*

That's the kind of situation depicted in Table 21.4.

Absolute Costs Don't Count

In assessing the nature of comparative advantage, notice that we needn't know anything about the actual costs involved in production. Have you seen any data suggesting how much labor, land, or capital is required to produce a loaf of bread in either France or the United States? For all you and I know, the French may be able to produce both a loaf of bread and a barrel of wine with fewer resources than we're using. Such an **absolute advantage** in production might exist because of their much longer experience in cultivating both grapes and wheat or simply because they have more talent.

We can envy such productivity, and even try to emulate it, but it shouldn't alter our production or trade decisions. All we really care about are *opportunity costs*—what *we* have to give up in order to get more of a desired good. If we can get a barrel of wine for less bread in trade than in production, we have a comparative advantage in producing bread. As long as we have a *comparative* advantage in bread production, we should exploit it. It doesn't matter to us whether France could produce either good with fewer resources. For that matter, even if France had an absolute advantage in *both* goods, we'd still have a *comparative* advantage in bread production, as we've already confirmed. The absolute costs of production were omitted from the previous illustration because they were irrelevant.

To clarify the distinction between absolute advantage and comparative advantage, consider this example. When Charlie Osgood joined the Willamette Warriors football team, he was the fastest runner ever to play football in Willamette. He could also throw the ball farther than most people could see. In other words, he had an *absolute advantage* in both throwing and running. Charlie would have made the greatest quarterback or the greatest end ever to play football. *Would have.* The problem was that he could play only one position at a time. Thus the Willamette coach had to play Charlie either as a quarterback or as an end. He reasoned that Charlie could throw only a bit farther than some of the other top quarterbacks but could far outdistance all the other ends. In other words, Charlie had a *comparative advantage* in running and was assigned to play as an end.

TERMS OF TRADE

It definitely pays to pursue one's comparative advantage by specializing in production. It may not yet be clear, however, how we got such a good deal with France. We're clever traders; but beyond that, is there any way to determine the **terms of trade**—the quantity of good A that must be given up in exchange for good B? In our previous illustration, the terms of trade were very favorable to us; we exchanged only 6 zillion loaves of bread for 20 zillion barrels of wine (Table 21.4). The terms of trade were thus 6 loaves = 20 barrels.

Limits to the Terms of Trade

The terms of trade with France were determined by our offer and France's ready acceptance. But why did France accept those terms? France was willing to accept our offer because the terms of trade permitted France to increase its wine consumption without giving up any bread consumption. Our offer of 6 loaves for 20 barrels was an improvement over France's domestic opportunity costs. France's domestic possibilities required it to give up 24 barrels of wine in order to produce 6 loaves of bread (see Figure 21.2b). Getting bread via trade was simply cheaper for France than producing bread at home. France ended up with an extra 4 zillion barrels of wine (take another look at the last two columns in Table 21.4).

Our first clue to the terms of trade, then, lies in each country's domestic opportunity costs. *A country won't trade unless the terms of trade are superior to domestic opportunities.* In our example, the opportunity cost of 1 barrel of wine in the United States is 2 loaves of bread. Accordingly, we won't *export* bread unless we get at least 1 barrel of wine in exchange for every 2 loaves of bread we ship overseas.

All countries want to gain from trade. Hence we can predict that *the terms of trade between any two countries will lie somewhere between their respective opportunity costs in production.* That is, a loaf of bread in international trade will be worth at least ½ barrel

absolute advantage: The ability of a country to produce a specific good with fewer resources (per unit of output) than other countries.

terms of trade: The rate at which goods are exchanged; the amount of good A given up for good B in trade.

web analysis

Find out more about trade patterns and policy from the International Trade Commission at **dataweb.usitc.gov.**

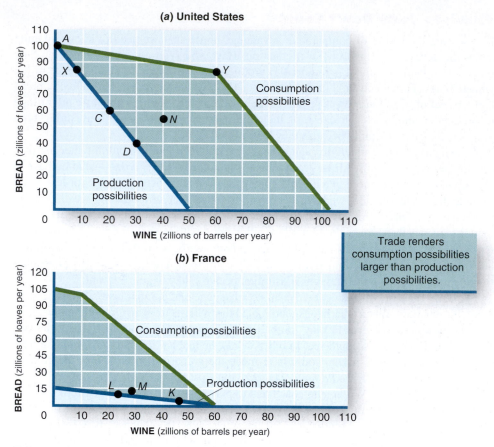

> Trade renders consumption possibilities larger than production possibilities.

FIGURE 21.3
Searching for the Terms of Trade

Assume the United States can produce 100 zillion loaves of bread per year (point *A*). If we reduce output to only 85 zillion loaves, we could move to point *X*. At point *X* we have 7.5 zillion barrels of wine and 85 zillion loaves of bread.

Trade increases consumption possibilities. If we continued to produce 100 zillion loaves of bread, we could trade 15 zillion loaves to France in exchange for as much as 60 zillion barrels of wine. This would leave us *producing* at point *A* but *consuming* at point *Y*. At point *Y* we have more wine and no less bread than we had at point *X*. This is our motivation to trade.

A country will end up on its consumption possibilities curve only if it gets *all* the gains from trade. It will remain on its production possibilities curve only if it gets *none* of the gains from trade. The terms of trade determine how the gains from trade are distributed, and thus at what point in the shaded area each country ends up.

Note: The kink in the consumption possibilities curve at point *Y* occurs because France is unable to produce more than 60 zillion barrels of wine.

___

of wine (the U.S. opportunity cost), but no more than 4 barrels (the French opportunity cost). In our example, the terms of trade ended up at 1 loaf = 3.33 barrels (that is, at 6 loaves = 20 barrels). This represented a very large gain for the United States and a small gain for France. Figure 21.3 illustrates this outcome and several other possibilities.

The Role of Markets and Prices

Relatively little trade is subject to such direct negotiations between countries. More often than not, the decision to import or export a particular good is left up to the market decisions of individual consumers and producers.

Individual consumers and producers aren't much impressed by such abstractions as comparative advantage. Market participants tend to focus on prices, always trying to allocate their resources in order to maximize profits or personal satisfaction. Consumers tend to buy the products that deliver the most utility per dollar of expenditure, while producers try to get the most output per dollar of cost. Everybody's looking for a bargain.

So what does this have to do with international trade? Well, suppose that Henri, an enterprising Frenchman, visited the United States before the advent of international trade. He observed that bread was relatively cheap while wine was relatively expensive—the opposite of the price relationship prevailing in France. These price comparisons brought to his mind the opportunity for making a fast euro. All he had to do was bring over some French wine and trade it in the United States for a large quantity of bread. Then he could return to France and exchange the bread for a greater quantity of wine. *Alors!* Were he to do this a few times, he'd amass substantial profits.

Henri's entrepreneurial exploits will not only enrich him but will also move each country toward its comparative advantage. The United States ends up exporting bread to France, and France ends up exporting wine to the United States, exactly as the theory of comparative advantage suggests. The activating agent isn't the Ministry of Trade and its 620 trained economists but simply one enterprising French trader. He's aided and encouraged, of course, by consumers and producers in each country. American consumers are happy to trade their bread for his wines. They thereby end up paying less for wine (in terms of bread) than they'd otherwise have to. In other words, the terms of trade Henri offers are more attractive than the prevailing (domestic) relative prices. On the other side of the Atlantic, Henri's welcome is equally warm. French consumers are able to get a better deal by trading their wine for his imported bread than by trading with the local bakers.

Even some producers are happy. The wheat farmers and bakers in the United States are eager to deal with Henri. He's willing to buy a lot of bread and even to pay a premium price for it. Indeed, bread production has become so profitable in the United States that a lot of people who used to grow and mash grapes are now growing wheat and kneading dough. This alters the mix of U.S. output in the direction of more bread, exactly as suggested in Figure 21.2*a*.

In France the opposite kind of production shift is taking place. French wheat farmers are planting more grape vines so they can take advantage of Henri's generous purchases. Thus Henri is able to lead each country in the direction of its comparative advantage while raking in a substantial profit for himself along the way.

Where the terms of trade and the volume of exports and imports end up depends partly on how good a trader Henri is. It will also depend on the behavior of the thousands of individual consumers and producers who participate in the market exchanges. In other words, trade flows depend on both the supply and the demand for bread and wine in each country. *The terms of trade, like the price of any good, depend on the willingness of market participants to buy or sell at various prices.* All we know for sure is that the terms of trade will end up somewhere between the limits set by each country's opportunity costs.

PROTECTIONIST PRESSURES

Although the potential gains from world trade are impressive, not everyone will be cheering at the Franco–American trade celebration. On the contrary, some people will be upset about the trade routes that Henri has established. They'll not only boycott the celebration but actively seek to discourage us from continuing to trade with France.

Microeconomic Pressures

Consider, for example, the winegrowers in western New York. Do you think they're going to be happy about Henri's entrepreneurship? Americans can now buy wine more cheaply from France than they can from New York. Before long we may hear talk about unfair foreign competition or about the greater nutritional value of American grapes (see the News on the next page). The New York winegrowers may also emphasize the importance of maintaining an adequate grape supply and a strong wine industry at home, just in case of terrorist attacks.

IN THE NEWS

California Grape Growers Protest Mixing Foreign Wine

California wine grape growers are growing increasingly frustrated and angry at each market percentage point gain of foreign wine in the U.S. wine market.

By the end of the year, burgeoning wine imports are expected to account for 30 percent of the U.S. market.

As the overall wine market in the United States grows at a healthy 2 percent to 5 percent annual clip, California grape growers continue to rip out vineyards. More than 100,000 acres in the Central Valley have been destroyed in the past five years. Growers are beyond weary of prices offered at less than production costs. . . .

Rubbing salt into the open economic sore this season includes record bulk, inexpensive wine imports that are being blended with California wines and sold by California wineries as "American" appellation wine. . . .

"California grape growers made a significant investment in wine grape vineyards on the signals from wineries that there was a bright future in California wine." Those same growers are seeing at least some of that bright future being taken by imports.

—Harry Cline

Source: **WesternFarmPress.com**, December 6, 2006. Used with permission of Penton Media, Inc.

Analysis: Although trade increases consumption possibilities, imports typically compete with a domestic industry. The affected industries will try to restrict imports in order to preserve their own jobs and incomes.

Import-Competing Industries. Joining with the growers will be the farmworkers and the other merchants whose livelihood depends on the New York wine industry. If they're clever enough, the growers will also get the governor of the state to join their demonstration. After all, the governor must recognize the needs of his people, and his people definitely don't include the wheat farmers in Kansas who are making a bundle from international trade, much less French vintners. New York consumers are of course benefiting from lower wine prices, but they're unlikely to demonstrate over a few cents a bottle. On the other hand, those few extra pennies translate into millions of dollars for domestic wine producers.

The wheat farmers in France are no happier about international trade than are the wine-growers in the United States. They'd dearly love to sink all those boats bringing cheap wheat from America, thereby protecting their own market position.

If we're to make sense of trade policies, then, we must recognize one central fact of life: Some producers have a vested interest in restricting international trade. In particular, ***workers and producers who compete with imported products—who work in import-competing industries—have an economic interest in restricting trade.*** This helps explain why GM, Ford, and Chrysler are unhappy about auto imports and why shoe workers in Massachusetts want to end the importation of Italian shoes. It also explains why textile producers in South Carolina think China is behaving irresponsibly when it sells cotton shirts and dresses in the United States.

Export Industries. Although imports typically mean fewer jobs and less income for some domestic industries, exports represent increased jobs and income for other industries. Producers and workers in export industries gain from trade. Thus on a microeconomic level there are identifiable gainers and losers from international trade. ***Trade not only alters the mix of output but also redistributes income from import-competing industries to export industries.*** This potential redistribution is the source of political and economic friction.

Net Gain. We must be careful to note, however, that the microeconomic gains from trade are greater than the microeconomic losses. It's not simply a question of robbing Peter to enrich Paul. We must remind ourselves that consumers enjoy a higher standard of living as a result of international trade. As we saw earlier, trade increases world efficiency and total output. Accordingly, we end up slicing up a larger pie rather than just reslicing the same old smaller pie.

The gains from trade will mean little to workers who end up with a smaller slice of the (larger) pie. It's important to remember, however, that the gains from trade are large enough to make everybody better off. Whether we actually choose to distribute the gains from trade in this way is a separate question, to which we shall return shortly. Note here, however, that *trade restrictions designed to protect specific microeconomic interests reduce the total gains from trade.* Trade restrictions leave us with a smaller pie to split up.

Additional Pressures

Import-competing industries are the principal obstacle to expanded international trade. Selfish micro interests aren't the only source of trade restrictions, however. Other arguments are also used to restrict trade.

National Security. The national security argument for trade restrictions is twofold. We can't depend on foreign suppliers to provide us with essential defense-related goods, it is said, because that would leave us vulnerable in time of war. The machine tool industry used this argument to protect itself from imports. In 1991 the Pentagon again sided with the toolmakers, citing the need for the United States to "gear up military production quickly in case of war," a contingency that couldn't be assured if weapons manufacturers relied on imported lathes, milling machines, and other tools. After the September 11, 2001, terrorist attacks on the World Trade Center and Pentagon, U.S. farmers convinced Congress to safeguard the nation's food supply with additional subsidies (see Chapter 15). The steel industry emphasized the importance of not depending on foreign suppliers.

Dumping. Another argument against free trade arises from the practice of **dumping.** Foreign producers "dump" their goods when they sell them in the United States at prices lower than those prevailing in their own country, perhaps even below the costs of production.

> **dumping:** The sale of goods in export markets at prices below domestic prices.

Dumping may be unfair to import-competing producers, but it isn't necessarily unwelcome to the rest of us. As long as foreign producers continue dumping, we're getting foreign products at low prices. How bad can that be? There's a legitimate worry, however. Foreign producers might hold prices down only until domestic producers are driven out of business. Then we might be compelled to pay the foreign producers higher prices for their products. In that case, dumping could consolidate market power and lead to monopoly-type pricing. The fear of dumping, then, is analogous to the fear of predatory pricing.

The potential costs of dumping are serious. It's not always easy to determine when dumping occurs, however. Those who compete with imports have an uncanny ability to associate any and all low prices with predatory dumping. The United States has used dumping *charges* to restrict imports of Chinese shrimp, furniture, lingerie, and other products in which China has an evident comparative advantage. The Chinese have retaliated with dozens of their own dumping investigations, including the fiber optic cable case. As the World View on the next page explains, such actions slow imports and protect domestic producers.

Infant Industries. Actual dumping threatens to damage already established domestic industries. Even normal import prices, however, may make it difficult or impossible for a new domestic industry to develop. Infant industries are often burdened with abnormally high start-up costs. These high costs may arise from the need to train a whole workforce and the expenses of establishing new marketing channels. With time to grow, however, an infant industry might experience substantial cost reductions and establish a comparative advantage. When this is the case, trade restrictions might help nurture an industry in its infancy. Trade restrictions are justified, however, only if there's tangible evidence that the industry can develop a comparative advantage reasonably quickly.

WORLD VIEW

China Accuses Corning of "Dumping"

Corning Inc., the big U.S. fiber optic and glass maker, said the Chinese government has charged it with selling optical fiber products in China at an unfairly low price that damaged Chinese producers, a practice known as dumping.

Corning denied the charge, which followed a nearly yearlong investigation by China's Ministry of Commerce after two Chinese companies alleged that optical fiber imports were priced below what market conditions justified. . . .

Since it joined the WTO, China has brought about 25 dumping cases against foreign companies, according to a King & Spalding estimate. In that same period, U.S. companies have brought 24 dumping cases against China, according to the International Trade Commission. . . .

Recent U.S. trade actions against China, most notably an antidumping case launched in October against $1 billion worth of Chinese wood and bedroom furniture imports, have likely played a role, too, according to trade experts.

The high-profile U.S. furniture case against China and China's charge against fiber makers such as Corning also exemplify the chief economic concerns in each economy: the United States is preoccupied with protecting workers in its hard-hit manufacturing sector, while China is interested in nurturing its technology industry. . . .

With the filing of the Chinese charges, Corning customers in China will have to pay a 16 percent deposit on the purchase price of the company's products, starting immediately. That money will be held in an escrow account until the matter is resolved.

Source: *The Wall Street Journal*, June 17, 2004, p. B2. Used with permission of Dow Jones & Company, Inc. via Copyright Clearance Center, Inc.

Analysis: *Dumping* means that a foreign producer is selling exports at prices below cost or below prices in the home market, putting import-competing industries at a competitive disadvantage. *Accusations* of dumping are an effective trade barrier.

Improving the Terms of Trade. A final argument for restricting trade rests on how the gains from trade are distributed. As we observed, the distribution of the gains from trade depends on the terms of trade. If we were to buy fewer imports, foreign producers might lower their prices. If that happened, the terms of trade would move in our favor, and we'd end up with a larger share of the gains from trade.

One way to bring about this sequence of events is to put restrictions on imports, making it more difficult or expensive for Americans to buy foreign products. Such restrictions will reduce the volume of imports, thereby inducing foreign producers to lower their prices. Unfortunately, this strategy can easily backfire. Retaliatory restrictions on imports, each designed to improve the terms of trade, will ultimately eliminate all trade and therewith all the gains people were competing for in the first place.

BARRIERS TO TRADE

The microeconomic losses associated with imports give rise to a constant clamor for trade restrictions. People whose jobs and incomes are threatened by international trade tend to organize quickly and air their grievances. The World View on the next page depicts the efforts of farmers in the Czech Republic to limit imports of Austrian pork. They wanted their government to impose restrictions on imports. More often than not, governments grant the wishes of these well-organized and well-financed special interests.

Embargoes

embargo: A prohibition on exports or imports.

The surefire way to restrict trade is simply to eliminate it. To do so, a country need only impose an embargo on exports or imports, or both. An **embargo** is nothing more than a prohibition against trading particular goods.

Meat Imports "Threaten" Farmers

Around 200 Czech farmers held a protest action March 26 on the Czech–Austrian border crossing in Dolni Dvořiště, South Bohemia, against meat imports. The protest was to draw attention to the situation of Czech pig breeders who claim they are threatened by growing pork imports to Czech retail chains and low purchasing prices.

Representatives of the Agricultural Chamber (AK) said it was a token protest, but didn't rule out further actions.

"We will . . . send an appeal to the Ministry of Agriculture, the Chamber of Deputies, and the Senate, asking them for public support of Czech farmers and Czech food," said Jan Veleba, president of the AK. . . .

Minister of Agriculture Petr Gandalovič said blockades won't resolve the situation and would probably only worsen relations between the Czech Republic and Austria.

Source: *Czech Business Weekly*, April 2, 2007. Used with permission.

Analysis: Import-competing industries cite lots of reasons for restricting trade. Their primary concern, however, is to protect their own jobs and profits.

In 1951 Senator Joseph McCarthy convinced the U.S. Senate to impose an embargo on Soviet mink, fox, and five other furs. He argued that such imports helped finance world communism. Senator McCarthy also represented the state of Wisconsin, where most U.S. minks are raised. The Reagan administration tried to end the fur embargo in 1987 but met with stiff congressional opposition. By then U.S. mink ranchers had developed a $120 million per year industry.

The United States has also maintained an embargo on Cuban goods since 1959, when Fidel Castro took power there. This embargo severely damaged Cuba's sugar industry and deprived American smokers of the famed Havana cigars. It also fostered the development of U.S. sugar beet and tobacco farmers, who now have a vested interest in maintaining the embargo.

Tariffs

A more frequent trade restriction is a **tariff,** a special tax imposed on imported goods. Tariffs, also called *customs duties,* were once the principal source of revenue for governments. In the 18th century, tariffs on tea, glass, wine, lead, and paper were imposed on the American colonies to provide extra revenue for the British government. The tariff on tea led to the Boston Tea Party in 1773 and gave added momentum to the American independence movement. In modern times, tariffs have been used primarily as a means to protect specific industries from import competition. The current U.S. tariff code specifies tariffs on over 9,000 different products—nearly 50 percent of all U.S. imports. Although the average tariff is less than 5 percent, individual tariffs vary widely. The tariff on cars, for example, is only 2.5 percent, while cotton sweaters confront a 17.8 percent tariff.

The attraction of tariffs to import-competing industries should be obvious. *A tariff on imported goods makes them more expensive to domestic consumers and thus less competitive with domestically produced goods.* Among familiar tariffs in effect in 2011 were 50 cents per gallon on Scotch whiskey and 76 cents per gallon on imported champagne. These tariffs made American-produced spirits look relatively cheap and thus contributed to higher sales and profits for domestic distillers and grape growers. In the same manner, imported baby food is taxed at 34.6 percent, maple sugar at 9.4 percent, golf shoes at 8.5 percent, and imported sailboats at 1.5 percent. In 2009 President Obama imposed a 35 percent tariff on imported Chinese tires (see the World View on the next page). In each case, domestic producers in import-competing industries gain. The losers are domestic consumers, who end up paying higher prices. The tariff on orange juice, for example, raises the price

tariff: A tax (duty) imposed on imported goods.

WORLD VIEW

U.S. to Impose Tariff on Tires from China

In one of his first major decisions on trade policy, President Obama opted Friday to impose a tariff on tires from China, a move that fulfills his campaign promise to "crack down" on imports that unfairly undermine American workers but risks angering the nation's second-largest trading partner.

The decision is intended to bolster the ailing U.S. tire industry, in which more than 5,000 jobs have been lost over the past five years as the volume of Chinese tires in the market has tripled.

The tire tariff will amount to 35 percent the first year, 30 percent the second, and 25 percent the third.

Marguerite Trossevin, who represents a coalition of U.S. tire companies that import Chinese tires, said the tariff decision is "very disappointing." She predicted price increases for U.S. consumers and losses for U.S. tire importers.

"For the U.S. tire distributors and consumers, there's going to be a heavy burden to bear," she said. "It sends the message that special interests will get protection if they ask for it—regardless of what that means for broader trade policy."

—Peter Whoriskey and Anne Kornblut

Analysis: By raising the price of imported goods, tariffs reduce imports and protect import-compelling industries. But consumers lose.

---

of drinking orange juice by $525 million a year. Tariffs also hurt foreign producers, who lose business, and world efficiency, as trade is reduced.

"Beggar Thy Neighbor." Microeconomic interests aren't the only source of pressure for tariff protection. Imports represent leakage from the domestic circular flow and a potential loss of jobs at home. From this perspective, reducing imports looks like an easy solution to the problem of domestic unemployment. Just get people to "buy American" instead of buying imported products, so the argument goes, and domestic output and employment will surely expand. President Obama used this argument to include "buy American" rules in his 2009 stimulus package.

Congressman Willis Hawley used this same argument in 1930. He assured his colleagues that higher tariffs would "bring about the growth and development in this country that has followed every other tariff bill, bringing as it does a new prosperity in which all people, in all sections, will increase their comforts, their enjoyment, and their happiness."[1] Congress responded by passing the Smoot-Hawley Tariff Act of 1930, which raised tariffs to an average of nearly 60 percent, effectively cutting off most imports.

Tariffs designed to expand domestic employment are more likely to fail than to succeed. If a tariff wall does stem the flow of imports, it effectively transfers the unemployment problem to other countries, a phenomenon often referred to as "beggar thy neighbor." The resultant loss of business in other countries leaves them less able to purchase our exports. The imported unemployment also creates intense political pressures for retaliatory action. That's exactly what happened in the 1930s. Other countries erected trade barriers to compensate for the effects of the Smoot-Hawley tariff. World trade subsequently fell from $60 billion in 1928 to a mere $25 billion in 1938. This trade contraction increased the severity of the Great Depression (see the World View on the next page).

The same kind of macroeconomic threat surfaced in 2009. The "buy American" provisions introduced by the Obama administration angered foreign nations that would lose export sales. When they threatened to retaliate with trade barriers of their own, President Obama had to offer reassurances about America's commitment to "free trade."

---

[1]*The New York Times,* June 15, 1930, p. 25.

WORLD VIEW

"Beggar-Thy-Neighbor" Policies in the 1930s

President Herbert Hoover, ignoring the pleas of 1,028 economists to veto it, signed the Smoot-Hawley Tariff Act on June 17, 1930. It was a hollow celebration. The day before, anticipating the signing, the stock market suffered its worst collapse since November 1929, and the law quickly helped push the Great Depression deeper.

The new tariffs, which by 1932 rose to an all-time high of 59 percent of the average value of imports (today it's 5 percent), were designed to save American jobs by restricting foreign competition. Economists warned that angry nations would retaliate, and they did.

- Spain passed the Wais tariff in July in reaction to U.S. tariffs on grapes, oranges, cork, and onions.
- Switzerland, objecting to new U.S. tariffs on watches, embroideries, and shoes, boycotted American exports.
- Italy retaliated against tariffs on hats and olive oil with high tariffs on U.S. and French automobiles in June 1930.
- Canada reacted to high duties on many food products, logs, and timber by raising tariffs threefold in August 1932.
- Australia, Cuba, France, Mexico, and New Zealand also joined in the tariff wars.

From 1930 to 1931 U.S. imports dropped 29 percent, but U.S. exports fell even more, 33 percent, and continued their collapse to a modern-day low of $2.4 billion in 1933. World trade contracted by similar proportions, spreading unemployment around the globe.

In 1934 the U.S. Congress passed the Reciprocal Trade Agreements Act to empower the president to reduce tariffs by half the 1930 rates in return for like cuts in foreign duties on U.S. goods. The "beggar-thy-neighbor" policy was dead. Since then, the nations of the world have been reducing tariffs and other trade barriers.

Source: "Economists Are Right for a Change, 1930," *The Wall Street Journal,* April 28, 1989, p. 1. Used with permission of Dow Jones & Company, Inc. via Copyright Clearance Center, Inc.; and The World Bank, "'Beggar-Thy-Neighbor' Policies in the 1930s," *World Development Report 1987,* p. 139, Box 8.4. Used with permission.

Analysis: Tariffs inflict harm on foreign producers. If foreign countries retaliate with tariffs of their own, world trade will shrink and unemployment will increase in all countries.

web analysis

The tariff schedule for imported products is available online from the U.S. International Trade Commission. Go to **www.usitc.gov** and click the "Tariff Affairs" tab, and then "Harmonized Tariff Schedule."

Quotas

Tariffs reduce the flow of imports by raising import prices. The same outcome can be attained more directly by imposing import **quotas,** numerical restrictions on the quantity of a particular good that may be imported. The United States limits the quantity of ice cream imported from Jamaica to 950 gallons a year. Only 1.4 million kilograms of Australian cheddar cheese and no more than 7,730 tons of Haitian sugar can be imported. Textile quotas are imposed on every country that wants to ship textiles to the U.S. market. According to the U.S. Department of State, approximately 12 percent of our imports are subject to import quotas.

quota: A limit on the quantity of a good that may be imported in a given time period.

Comparative Effects

Quotas, like all barriers to trade, reduce world efficiency and invite retaliatory action. Moreover, their impact can be even more damaging than tariffs. To see this, we may compare market outcomes in four different contexts: no trade, free trade, tariff-restricted trade, and quota-restricted trade.

No-Trade Equilibrium. Figure 21.4a depicts the supply-and-demand relationships that would prevail in an economy that imposed a trade *embargo* on foreign textiles. In this situation, the **equilibrium price** of textiles is completely determined by domestic demand and supply curves. The no-trade equilibrium price is p_1, and the quantity of textiles consumed is q_1.

equilibrium price: The price at which the quantity of a good demanded in a given time period equals the quantity supplied.

FIGURE 21.4
The Impact of Trade Restrictions

In the *absence of trade*, the domestic price and sales of a good will be determined by domestic supply and demand curves (point *A* in part *a*). Once trade is permitted, the market supply curve will be altered by the availability of imports. With *free trade* and unlimited availability of imports at price p_2, a new market equilibrium will be established at world prices (point *B*).

Tariffs raise domestic prices and reduce the quantity sold (point *C*). *Quotas* put an absolute limit on imported sales and thus give domestic producers a great opportunity to raise the market price (point *D*).

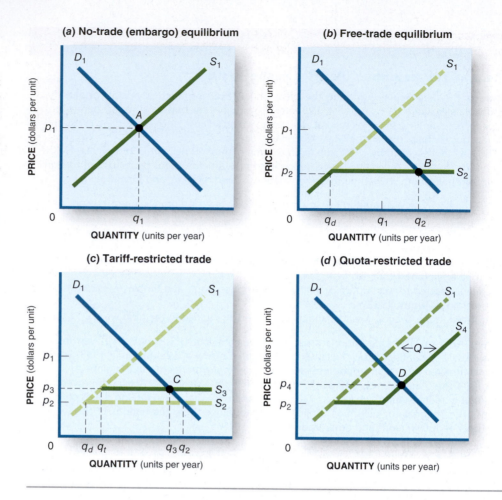

(a) No-trade (embargo) equilibrium

(b) Free-trade equilibrium

(c) Tariff-restricted trade

(d) Quota-restricted trade

"TELL ME AGAIN HOW THE QUOTAS ON JAPANESE CARS HAVE PROTECTED US"

A 1987 Herblock Cartoon © The Herb Block Foundation.

Analysis: Trade restrictions that protect import-competing industries also raise consumer prices.

* Reprinted by permission of SLL/Sterling Lord Literistic, Inc. Copyright by Herbert Block.

Free-Trade Equilibrium. Suppose now that the embargo is lifted. The immediate effect of this decision will be a rightward shift of the market supply curve, as foreign supplies are added to domestic supplies (Figure 21.4b). If an unlimited quantity of textiles can be bought in world markets at a price of p_2, the new supply curve will look like S_2 (infinitely elastic at p_2). The new supply curve (S_2) intersects the old demand curve (D_1) at a new equilibrium price of p_2 and an expanded consumption of q_2. At this new equilibrium, domestic producers are supplying the quantity q_d while foreign producers are supplying the rest ($q_2 - q_d$). Comparing the new equilibrium to the old one, we see that *free trade results in reduced prices and increased consumption.*

Domestic textile producers are unhappy, of course, with their foreign competition. In the absence of trade, the domestic producers would sell more output (q_1) and get higher prices (p_1). Once trade is opened up, the willingness of foreign producers to sell unlimited quantities of textiles at the price p_2 puts a lid on domestic prices. Domestic producers hate this.

Tariff-Restricted Trade. Figure 21.4c illustrates what would happen to prices and sales if the United Textile Producers were successful in persuading the government to impose a tariff. Assume that the tariff raises imported textile prices from p_2 to p_3, making it more difficult for foreign producers to undersell domestic producers. Domestic production expands from q_d to q_t, imports are reduced from $q_2 - q_d$ to $q_3 - q_t$, and the market price of textiles rises. Domestic textile producers are clearly better off. So is the U.S. Treasury, which will collect increased tariff revenues. Unfortunately, domestic consumers are worse off (higher prices), as are foreign producers (reduced sales).

Quota-Restricted Trade. Now consider the impact of a textile *quota*. Suppose we eliminate tariffs but decree that imports can't exceed the quantity Q. Because the quantity of imports can never exceed Q, the supply curve is effectively shifted to the right by that amount. The new curve S_4 (Figure 21.4d) indicates that no imports will occur below the world price p_2 and above that price the quantity Q will be imported. Thus the *domestic* demand curve determines subsequent prices. Foreign producers are precluded from selling greater quantities as prices rise further. This outcome is in marked contrast to that of tariff-restricted trade (Figure 21.4c), which at least permits foreign producers to respond to rising prices. Accordingly, *quotas are a greater threat to competition than tariffs because quotas preclude additional imports at any price.* The actual quotas on textile imports raise the prices of shirts, towels, and other textile products by 58 percent. As a result, a $10 shirt ends up costing consumers $15.80. All told, U.S. consumers end up paying an extra $25 billion a year for textile products.

The sugar industry is one of the greatest beneficiaries of quota restrictions. By limiting imports to 15 percent of domestic consumption, sugar quotas keep U.S. prices artificially high (see the News below). This costs consumers nearly $3 billion a year in higher prices. Candy and soda producers lose sales and profits. According to the U.S. Department of Commerce, over 6,000 jobs have been lost in sugar-using industries (e.g., candy manufacturing) due to high sugar costs. Hershey alone closed plants in Pennsylvania, Colorado, and California and moved candy production to Canada. Foreign sugar producers (mainly in poor nations) also lose sales, profits, and jobs. Who gains? Domestic sugar producers—who, coincidently, are highly concentrated in key electoral states like Florida.

IN THE NEWS

End the Import Quotas on Sugar

For years, domestic sugar producers have profited from quotas limiting sugar imports, boosting prices to American users.

Such protectionism takes from American consumers for politically powerful sugar producers. And it is an issue now that the difference between American prices (35.02 cents per pound) and world prices (19.67 cents per pound) has reached its highest level in over a decade. . . .

Quotas effectively impose a steep sugar tax on consumers, with the proceeds paid to domestic producers. One result? The makers of Life Savers, Red Hots, Jaw Breakers, and other candies have shifted production elsewhere in response. . . .

America's sugar protectionism has never been anything but a concentrated interest group—sugar producers. . . —using government power to keep out lower-cost foreign producers and rip off American consumers on their behalf. It is a sweet deal for them only because it is such a sour deal for the rest of us.

—Gary M. Galles

Source: Editorial, "End the Import Quotas on Sugar," *St. Petersburg Times*, March 23, 2010. Used with permission via icopyright.

Analysis: Import quotas preclude increased foreign competition when domestic prices rise. Protected domestic producers enjoy higher prices and profits while consumers pay higher prices.

Voluntary Restraint Agreements

A slight variant of quotas has been used in recent years. Rather than impose quotas on imports, the U.S. government asks foreign producers to "voluntarily" limit their exports. These so-called **voluntary restraint agreements** have been negotiated with producers in Japan, South Korea, Taiwan, China, the European Union, and other countries. Korea, for example, agreed to reduce its annual shoe exports to the United States from 44 million pairs to 33 million pairs. Taiwan reduced its shoe exports from 156 million pairs to 122 million pairs per year. In 2005 China agreed to slow its exports of clothing, limiting its sales growth to 8–17 percent a year. For their part, the Japanese agreed to reduce sales of color TV sets in the United States from 2.8 million to 1.75 million per year. In 2006 Mexico agreed to limit its cement exports to the United States to 3 million tons a year.

voluntary restraint agreement (VRA): An agreement to reduce the volume of trade in a specific good; a voluntary quota.

All these voluntary export restraints, as they're often called, represent an informal type of quota. The only difference is that they're negotiated rather than imposed. But these differences are lost on consumers, who end up paying higher prices for these goods. The voluntary limit on Japanese auto exports to the United States alone cost consumers $15.7 billion in only four years.

Nontariff Barriers

Tariffs and quotas are the most visible barriers to trade, but they're only the tip of the iceberg. Indeed, the variety of protectionist measures that have been devised is testimony to the ingenuity of the human mind. At the turn of the century, the Germans were committed to a most-favored-nation policy: a policy of extending equal treatment to all trading partners. The Germans, however, wanted to lower the tariff on cattle imports from Denmark without extending the same break to Switzerland. Such a preferential tariff would have violated the most-favored-nation policy. Accordingly, the Germans created a new and higher tariff on "brown and dappled cows reared at a level of at least 300 meters above sea level and passing at least one month in every summer at an altitude of at least 800 meters." The new tariff was, of course, applied equally to all countries. But Danish cows never climb that high, so they weren't burdened with the new tariff.

With the decline in tariffs over the last 20 years, nontariff barriers have increased. The United States uses product standards, licensing restrictions, restrictive procurement practices, and other nontariff barriers to restrict roughly 15 percent of imports. In 1999–2000 the European Union banned imports of U.S. beef, arguing that the use of hormones on U.S. ranches created a health hazard for European consumers. Although both the U.S. government and the World Trade Organization disputed that claim, the ban was a highly effective nontariff trade barrier. The United States responded by slapping 100 percent tariffs on dozens of European products.

Mexican Trucks. One of the more flagrant examples of nontariff barriers is the use of safety regulations to block Mexican trucking companies from using U.S. roads to deliver goods. The resulting trade barrier forces Mexican trucks to unload their cargoes at the U.S. border, and then reload them into U.S. (Teamster-driven) trucks for shipment to U.S. destinations. The U.S. agreed to lift that restriction in 1995, but didn't. In 2009 President Obama actually solidified the Mexican roadblock, despite the fact that Mexican trucks passed all 22 safety (nontariff) regulations the U.S. Department of Transportation had imposed. In so doing, President Obama secured more jobs for Teamster-union drivers, but raised costs for U.S. shippers and consumers and drove down sales and employment for Mexican trucking companies. Fed up with U.S. protectionism, Mexico retaliated by slapping tariffs on 90 U.S. export products (see the World View below). By early 2011, U.S. exports to Mexico of those products had declined by 81 percent. This prompted President Obama to offer Mexico a new round of negotiations for a "reciprocal, phase-in program" that would ease trade barriers.

WORLD VIEW

Mexico Retaliates for Loss of Truck Program

Mexico announced Monday it will increase tariffs on 90 U.S. industrial and agricultural goods in reprisal for the United States canceling a test program that gave Mexican trucks access to U.S. highways. Mexican Economy Minister Gerardo Ruiz said around $2.4 billion worth of U.S. exports would be affected and that the government would soon publish a list. U.S. labor, highway safety, and consumer groups have opposed the truck access permitted under the North American Free Trade Agreement.

Source: *USA TODAY*, March 17, 2009, p. B1. Reprinted with permission.

Analysis: Nontariff barriers like extraordinary safety requirements on Mexican trucks limit import competition and invite retaliation.

POLICING WORLD TRADE

Proponents of free trade and import-competing industries are in constant conflict. Most of the time the trade policy deck seems stacked in favor of the special interests. Because import-competing firms and workers are highly concentrated, they're quick to mobilize politically. By contrast, the benefits of freer trade are less direct and spread over millions of consumers. As a consequence, the beneficiaries of freer trade are less likely to monitor trade policy—much less lobby actively to change it. Hence the political odds favor the spread of trade barriers.

Multilateral Trade Pacts. Despite these odds, the long-term trend is toward *lowering* trade barriers, thereby increasing global competition. Two forces encourage this trend. ***The principal barrier to protectionist policies is worldwide recognition of the gains from freer trade.*** Since world nations now understand that trade barriers are ultimately self-defeating, they're more willing to rise above the din of protectionist cries and dismantle trade barriers. They diffuse political opposition by creating across-the-board trade pacts that seem to spread the pain (and gain) from freer trade across a broad swath of industries. Such pacts also incorporate multiyear timetables that give affected industries time to adjust.

Trade liberalization has also been encouraged by firms that *export* products or use imported inputs in their own production. Tariffs on imported steel raise product costs for U.S.-based auto producers and construction companies. In 2007 the European Union eliminated a tariff on frozen Chinese strawberries, largely due to complaints from EU yogurt and jam producers who were incurring higher costs.

Global Pacts: GATT and WTO. The granddaddy of the multilateral, multiyear free-trade pacts was the 1947 *General Agreement on Tariffs and Trade (GATT)*. Twenty-three nations pledged to reduce trade barriers and give all GATT nations equal access to their domestic markets.

Since the first GATT pact, seven more "rounds" of negotiations have expanded the scope of GATT; 117 nations signed the 1994 pact. As a result of these GATT pacts, average tariff rates in developed countries have fallen from 40 percent in 1948 to less than 4 percent today.

WTO. The 1994 GATT pact also created the *World Trade Organization (WTO)* to enforce free-trade rules. If a nation feels its exports are being unfairly excluded from another country's market, it can file a complaint with the WTO. This is exactly what the United States did when the EU banned U.S. beef imports. The WTO ruled in favor of the United States. When the EU failed to lift its import ban, the WTO authorized the United States to impose retaliatory tariffs on European exports.

The EU turned the tables on the United States in 2003. It complained to the WTO that U.S. tariffs on imported steel violated trade rules. The WTO agreed and gave the EU permission to impose retaliatory tariffs on $2.2 billion of U.S. exports. That prompted the Bush administration to scale back the tariffs in December 2003.

In effect, the WTO is now the world's trade police force. It is empowered to cite nations that violate trade agreements and even to impose remedial action when violations persist. Why do sovereign nations give the WTO such power? Because they are all convinced that free trade is the surest route to GDP growth.

Regional Pacts. Because worldwide trade pacts are so complex, many nations have also pursued *regional* free-trade agreements.

NAFTA. In December 1992 the United States, Canada, and Mexico signed the *North American Free Trade Agreement (NAFTA),* a 1,000-page document covering more than 9,000 products. The ultimate goal of NAFTA is to eliminate all trade barriers between these three countries. At the time of signing, intraregional tariffs averaged 11 percent in Mexico, 5 percent in Canada, and 4 percent in the United States. NAFTA requires that all tariffs among the three countries be eliminated. The pact also requires the elimination of specific nontariff barriers.

The NAFTA-initiated reduction in trade barriers substantially increased trade flows between Mexico, Canada, and the United States. It also prompted a wave of foreign investment in Mexico, where both cheap labor and NAFTA access were available. Overall, NAFTA accelerated economic growth and reduced inflationary pressures in all three nations. Some industries (like construction and apparel) suffered from the freer trade, but others (like trucking, farming, and finance) reaped huge gains (see the News below).

IN THE NEWS

NAFTA Reallocates Labor: Comparative Advantage at Work

More Jobs in These Industries		but . . .	Fewer Jobs in These Industries	
Agriculture	+10,600		Construction	−12,800
Metal products	+6,100		Medicine	−6,000
Electrical appliances	+5,200		Apparel	−5,900
Business services	+5,000		Lumber	−1,200
Motor vehicles	+5,000		Furniture	−400

Source: Congressional Budget Office.

The lowering of trade barriers between Mexico and the United States is changing the mix of output in both countries. New export opportunities create jobs in some industries while increased imports eliminate jobs in other industries. (Estimated gains and losses are during the first five years of NAFTA.)

Analysis: The specialization encouraged by free trade creates new jobs in export but reduces employment in import-competing industries. In the process, total world output increases.

CAFTA. The success of NAFTA prompted a similar 2005 agreement between the United States and Central American nations. The Central American Free Trade Agreement (CAFTA) aims to standardize trade and investment policies in CAFTA nations, while eliminating tariffs on thousands of products.

As trade barriers continue to fall around the world, the global marketplace is likely to become more open. The resulting increase in competition should spur efficiency and growth in the economy tomorrow.

SUMMARY

- International trade permits each country to specialize in areas of relative efficiency, increasing world output. For each country, the gains from trade are reflected in consumption possibilities that exceed production possibilities. LO21-2

- One way to determine where comparative advantage lies is to compare the quantity of good A that must be given up in order to get a given quantity of good B from domestic production. If the same quantity of B can be obtained for less A by engaging in world trade, we have a comparative advantage in the production of good A. Comparative advantage rests on a comparison of relative opportunity costs. LO21-1

- The terms of trade—the rate at which goods are exchanged—are subject to the forces of international supply and demand. The terms of trade will lie somewhere between the opportunity costs of the trading partners. The terms of trade determine how the gains from trade are shared. LO21-2

- Resistance to trade emanates from workers and firms that must compete with imports. Even though the country as a whole stands to benefit from trade, these individuals and companies may lose jobs and incomes in the process. LO21-3

- Trade barriers take many forms. Embargoes are outright prohibitions against import or export of particular goods. Quotas limit the quantity of a good imported or exported.

Tariffs discourage imports by making them more expensive. Other nontariff barriers make trade too costly or time-consuming. LO21-3

- The World Trade Organization (WTO) seeks to reduce worldwide trade barriers and enforce trade rules. Regional accords such as the North American Free Trade Agreement (NAFTA) and the Central American Free Trade Agreement (CAFTA) pursue similar objectives among fewer countries. LO21-3

Key Terms

imports	consumption possibilities	dumping
exports	open economy	embargo
trade deficit	comparative advantage	tariff
trade surplus	opportunity cost	quota
production possibilities	absolute advantage	equilibrium price
closed economy	terms of trade	voluntary restraint agreement (VRA)

Questions for Discussion

1. Suppose a lawyer can type faster than any secretary. Should the lawyer do her own typing? Can you demonstrate the validity of your answer? LO21-1
2. What would be the effects of a law requiring bilateral trade balances? LO21-2
3. If a nation exported much of its output but imported little, would it be better or worse off? How about the reverse—that is, exporting little but importing a lot? LO21-2
4. How does international trade restrain the price behavior of domestic firms? LO21-3
5. Suppose we refused to sell goods to any country that reduced or halted its exports to us. Who would benefit and who would lose from such retaliation? Can you suggest alternative ways to ensure import supplies? LO21-2
6. Domestic producers often base their demands for import protection on the fact that workers in country X are paid substandard wages. Is this a valid argument for protection? LO21-1
7. On the basis of the News on page 466, how do U.S. furniture manufacturers feel about NAFTA? How about farmers? LO21-3
8. Why did President Obama pursue "Buy American" rules if they actually hurt the economy? LO21-3
9. Who gains and who loses from nontariff barriers to Mexican trucks (World View, p. 464)? What made President Obama offer renewed negotiations? LO21-3
10. Has the tariff on Chinese tires (World View, p. 460) affected you or your family? Who has been affected? LO21-3

 web activities to accompany this chapter can be found on the Online Learning Center:
http://www.mhhe.com/schiller13e

 mobile app Visit your mobile app store and download the Schiller: Study Econ app *today!*

LO21-2 1. Which countries are the two largest export markets for the United States? (See Table 21.3.) (1) _____

(2) _____

LO21-1 2. Suppose a country can produce a maximum of 20,000 jumbo airliners or 2,000 aircraft carriers.
(a) What is the opportunity cost of an aircraft carrier? _____
(b) If another country offers to trade six planes for one aircraft carrier, should the offer be accepted? _____
(c) What is the implied price of the carrier in trade? _____

LO21-1 3. If it takes 24 farmworkers to harvest 1 ton of strawberries and 8 farmworkers to harvest 1 ton of wheat, what is the opportunity cost of 5 tons of strawberries? _____

LO21-2 4. Alpha and Beta, two tiny islands off the east coast of Tricoli, produce pearls and pineapples. The following production possibilities schedules describe their potential output in tons per year:

Alpha		Beta	
Pearls	Pineapples	Pearls	Pineapples
0	30	0	20
2	25	10	16
4	20	20	12
6	15	30	8
8	10	40	4
10	5	45	2
12	0	50	0

(a) Graph the production possibilities confronting each island.
(b) What is the opportunity cost of pineapples on each island (before trade)?   Alpha: _____

Beta: _____

(c) Which island has a comparative advantage in pearl production? _____
(d) Graph the consumption possibilities of each island with free trade.
(e) If Beta produced only pearls,
    (i) How many could it produce? _____
    (ii) How many pearls would it have to export to get 20 pineapples in return? _____
    (iii) What is the net gain to Beta in this case? _____

LO21-3 5. (a) How much more are U.S. consumers paying for the 20 billion pounds of sugar they consume each year as a result of the quotas on sugar imports? (See News, p. 463.) _____
(b) How much sales revenue are foreign sugar producers losing as a result of those same quotas? _____

LO21-2 6. Suppose the two islands in Problem 4 agree that the terms of trade will be one for one and exchange 10 pearls for 10 pineapples.

(a) If Alpha produced 6 pearls and 15 pineapples while Beta produced 30 pearls and   Alpha: _____
8 pineapples before they decided to trade, how many pearls would each be producing   Beta: _____
after trade? Assume that the two countries specialize according to their comparative
advantage.

(b) How much would the combined production of pineapples increase for the two islands
due to specialization?   _____

(c) How much would the combined production of pearls increase?   _____

LO21-3 7. Suppose the following table reflects the domestic supply and demand for compact discs (CDs):

Price ($)	18	16	14	12	10	8	6	4
Quantity supplied	8	7	6	5	4	3	2	1
Quantity demanded	2	4	6	8	10	12	14	16

(a) Graph these market conditions and identify
  (i) The equilibrium price.   _____
  (ii) The equilibrium quantity.   _____
(b) Now suppose that foreigners enter the market, offering to sell an unlimited supply of CDs
for $6 apiece. Illustrate and identify
  (i) The new market price.   _____
  (ii) Domestic consumption.   _____
  (iii) Domestic production.   _____
(c) If a tariff of $2 per CD is imposed, what will be
  (i) The market price?   _____
  (ii) Domestic consumption?   _____
  (iii) Domestic production?   _____
Graph your answers.

International Finance

Textile, furniture, and shrimp producers in the United States want China to increase the value of the yuan. They say China's undervalued currency makes Chinese exports too cheap, undercutting American firms. On the other hand, Walmart thinks a cheap yuan is a good thing because it keeps prices low for the *$16 billion* of toys, tools, linens, and other goods it buys from China each year. Those low import prices help Walmart keep its own prices low and its sales volume high.

This chapter examines how currency values affect trade patterns and ultimately the core questions of WHAT, HOW, and FOR WHOM to produce. We focus on the following questions:

- **What determines the value of one country's money compared to the value of another's?**
- **What causes the international value of currencies to change?**
- **Should governments intervene to limit currency fluctuations?**

EXCHANGE RATES: THE GLOBAL LINK

As we saw in Chapter 21, the United States exports and imports a staggering volume of goods and services. Although we trade with nearly 200 nations around the world, we seldom give much thought to where imports come from and how we acquire them. Most of the time, all we want to know is which products are available and at what price.

Suppose you want to buy an Apple iPad. You don't have to know that iPads are manufactured in China. And you certainly don't have to fly to China to pick it up. All you have to do is drive to the nearest electronics store; or you can just "click and buy" at the Internet's virtual mall.

But you may wonder how the purchase of an imported product was so simple. Chinese companies sell their products in yuan, the currency of China. But you purchase the iPad in dollars. How is this possible?

There's a chain of distribution between your dollar purchase in the United States and the yuan-denominated sale in China. Somewhere along that chain someone has to convert your dollars into yuan. The critical question for everybody concerned is how many yuan we can get for our dollars—that is, what the **exchange rate** is. If we can get eight yuan for every dollar, the exchange rate is 8 yuan = 1 dollar. Alternatively, we could note that the price of a yuan is 12.5 U.S. cents when the exchange rate is 8 to 1. Thus *an exchange rate is the price of one currency in terms of another.*

> **exchange rate:** The price of one country's currency expressed in terms of another's; the domestic price of a foreign currency.

FOREIGN EXCHANGE MARKETS

Most exchange rates are determined in foreign exchange markets. Stop thinking of money as some sort of magical substance, and instead view it as a useful commodity that facilitates market exchanges. From that perspective, an exchange rate—the price of money—is subject to the same influences that determine all market prices: demand and supply.

The Demand for Dollars

When the Japanese Toshiba Corporation bought Westinghouse Electric Co. in 2006, it paid $5.4 billion. When Belgian beer maker InBev bought Anheuser-Busch (Budweiser, etc.) in 2008, it also needed dollars—over 50 billion of them. When Fiat acquired control of Chrysler in 2011, it also needed U.S. dollars. In all three cases, the objective of the foreign investor was to acquire an American business. To attain their objectives, however, the buyers first had to buy *dollars.* The Japanese, Belgian, and Italian buyers had to exchange their own currency for American dollars.

Canadian tourists also need American dollars. Few American restaurants or hotels accept Canadian currency as payment for goods and services; they want to be paid in U.S. dollars. Accordingly, Canadian tourists must buy American dollars if they want to warm up in Florida.

Some foreign investors also buy U.S. dollars for speculative purposes. When the ruble collapsed, Russians feared that the value of the ruble would drop further and preferred to hold U.S. dollars. Barclay's Bank also speculates in dollars on occasions when it fears that the value of the British pound will drop.

All these motivations give rise to a demand for U.S. dollars. Specifically, *the market demand for U.S. dollars originates in*

- *Foreign demand for American exports* (including tourism).
- *Foreign demand for American investments.*
- *Speculation.*

Governments also create a demand for dollars when they operate embassies, undertake cultural exchanges, or engage in intergovernment financial transactions.

The Supply of Dollars

The *supply* of dollars arises from similar sources. On the supply side, however, it's Americans who initiate most of the exchanges. Suppose you take a trip to Mexico. You'll need to buy Mexican pesos at some point. When you do, you'll be offering to *buy* pesos by offering to *sell* dollars. In other words, *the* **demand** *for foreign currency represents a* **supply of U.S. dollars.**

When Americans buy BMW cars, they also supply U.S. dollars. American consumers pay for their BMWs in dollars. Somewhere down the road, however, those dollars will be exchanged for European euros. At that exchange, dollars are being *supplied* and euros *demanded.*

American corporations demand foreign exchange too. General Motors builds cars in Germany, Coca-Cola produces Coke in China, and Exxon produces and refines oil all over the world. In nearly every such case, the U.S. firm must first build or buy some plants and equipment, using another country's factors of production. This activity requires foreign currency and thus becomes another component of our demand for foreign currency.

We may summarize these market activities by noting that *the supply of dollars originates in*

- *American demand for imports* (including tourism).
- *American investments in foreign countries.*
- *Speculation.*

As on the demand side, government intervention can also contribute to the supply of dollars.

The Value of the Dollar

web analysis

The Federal Reserve Bank of New York carries out foreign exchange–related activities for the Fed. To learn more, visit **www.newyorkfed.org,** and click the "Markets" tab.

Whether American consumers will choose to buy an imported BMW depends partly on what the car costs. The price tag isn't always apparent in international transactions. Remember that the German BMW producer and workers want to be paid in their own currency. Hence the *dollar* price of an imported BMW depends on two factors: (1) the German price of a BMW and (2) the *exchange rate* between U.S. dollars and euros. Specifically, the U.S. price of a BMW is

$$\text{Dollar price of BMW} = \text{Euro price of BMW} \times \text{Dollar price of euro}$$

Suppose the BMW company is prepared to sell a German-built BMW for 100,000 euros and that the current exchange rate is 2 euros = \$1. At these rates, a BMW will cost you

$$\text{Dollar price of BMW} = 100{,}000 \text{ euros} \times \frac{\$1}{2 \text{ euros}}$$
$$= \$50{,}000$$

If you're willing to pay this much for a shiny new German-built BMW, you may do so at current exchange rates.

Now suppose the exchange rate changes from 2 euros = \$1 to 1 euro = \$1. Now you're getting only 1 euro for your dollar rather than 2 euros. In other words, euros have become more expensive. *A higher dollar price for euros will raise the dollar costs of European goods.* In this case, the dollar price of a euro increases from \$0.50 to \$1. At this new exchange rate, the BMW plant in Germany is still willing to sell BMWs at 100,000 euros apiece. And German consumers continue to buy BMWs at that price. But this constant euro price now translates into a higher *dollar* price. That same BMW that you previously could buy for \$50,000 now costs you \$100,000—not because the cost of manufacturing the car in Germany went up, but simply because the exchange rate changed.

As the dollar price of a BMW rises, the number of BMWs sold in the United States will decline. As BMW sales decline, the quantity of euros demanded may decline as well. Thus the quantity of foreign currency demanded declines when the exchange rate rises because foreign goods become more expensive and imports decline. When the dollar price of European currencies actually increased in 1992, BMW decided to start producing cars in South Carolina. A year later Mercedes-Benz decided to produce cars in the United

FIGURE 22.1
The Foreign Exchange Market

The foreign exchange market operates like other markets. In this case, the "good" bought and sold is dollars (foreign exchange). The price and quantity of dollars actually exchanged are determined by the intersection of market supply and demand.

States as well. Sales of American-made BMWs and Mercedes no longer depend on the exchange rate of the U.S. dollars.

The Supply Curve. These market responses suggest that the supply of dollars is upward-sloping. If the value of the dollar rises, Americans will be able to buy more euros. As a result, the dollar price of imported BMWs will decline. American consumers will respond by demanding more imports, thereby supplying a larger quantity of dollars. The supply curve in Figure 22.1 shows how the quantity of dollars supplied rises as the value of the dollar increases.

The Demand Curve. The demand for dollars can be explained in similar terms. Remember that the demand for dollars arises from the foreign demand for U.S. exports and investments. If the exchange rate moves from 2 euros = $1 to 1 euro = $1, the euro price of dollars falls. As dollars become cheaper for Germans, all American exports effectively fall in price. Germans will buy more American products (including trips to Disney World) and therefore demand a greater quantity of dollars. In addition, foreign investors will perceive in a cheaper dollar the opportunity to buy U.S. stocks, businesses, and property at fire-sale prices. Accordingly, they join foreign consumers in demanding more dollars. Not all these behavioral responses will occur overnight, but they're reasonably predictable over a brief period of time.

Equilibrium

Given market demand and supply curves, we can predict the **equilibrium price** of any commodity—that is, the price at which the quantity demanded will equal the quantity supplied. This occurs in Figure 22.1 where the two curves cross. At that equilibrium, the value of the dollar (the exchange rate) is established. In this case, the euro price of the dollar turns out to be 0.90.

The value of the dollar can also be expressed in terms of other currencies. The World View on the next page displays a sampling of dollar exchange rates in March 2011. Notice how many Indonesian rupiah you could buy for $1: a dollar was worth 8,590 rupiah. By contrast, a U.S. dollar was worth only 0.71 euro. The *average* value of the dollar is a weighted mean of the exchange rates between the U.S. dollar and all these currencies. The value of the dollar is "high" when its foreign exchange price is above recent levels, and it is "low" when it is below recent averages.

equilibrium price: The price at which the quantity of a good demanded in a given time period equals the quantity supplied.

The Balance of Payments

The equilibrium depicted in Figure 22.1 determines not only the *price* of the dollar but also a specific *quantity* of international transactions. Those transactions include the exports, imports, international investments, and other sources of dollar supply and demand. A

WORLD VIEW

Foreign Exchange Rates

The foreign exchange midrange rates here show (a) how many U.S. dollars are needed to buy one unit of foreign currency and (b) how many units of foreign currency are needed to buy one U.S. dollar.

Country	(a) U.S. Dollar per Unit (Dollar Price of Foreign Currency)	(b) Currency per U.S. Dollar (Foreign Price of U.S. Dollar)
Brazil (real)	0.612	1.6345
Britain (pound)	1.612	0.6205
Canada (dollar)	1.025	0.9760
China (yuan)	0.154	6.5058
Indonesia (rupiah)	0.001	8590.9860
Japan (yen)	0.012	81.8620
Mexico (peso)	0.085	11.7280
Russia (ruble)	0.022	28.4974
Euroland (euro)	1.402	0.7132

Source: May 23, 2011, data from Federal Reserve Board of Governors.

Analysis: The exchange rates between currencies are determined by supply and demand in foreign exchange markets. The rates reported here represent the equilibrium exchange rates on a particular day.

balance of payments: A summary record of a country's international economic transactions in a given period of time.

summary of all those international money flows is contained in the **balance of payments**—an accounting statement of all international money flows in a given period of time.

Trade Balance. Table 22.1 depicts the U.S. balance of payments for 2010. Notice first how the millions of separate transactions are classified into a few summary measures. The trade balance is the difference between exports and imports of goods (merchandise) and services. In 2010 the United States imported over $2.3 trillion of goods and services but

web analysis

The latest statistics on the balance of payments are available from the Bureau of Economic Analysis at **www.bea.gov.**

TABLE 22.1
The U.S. Balance of Payments

The balance of payments is a summary statement of a country's international transactions. The major components of that activity are the trade balance (merchandise exports minus merchandise imports), the current account balance (trade, services, and transfers), and the capital account balance. The net total of these balances must equal zero because the quantity of dollars paid must equal the quantity received.

Item	Amount ($ billions)
1. Merchandise exports	$1,289
2. Merchandise imports	(1,936)
3. Service exports	546
4. Service imports	(394)
Trade balance (items 1–4)	−495
5. Income from U.S. overseas investments	662
6. Income outflow for foreign-owned U.S. investments	(488)
7. Net U.S. government grants	(55)
8. Net private transfers and pensions	(82)
Current account balance (items 1–8)	−458
9. U.S. capital inflow	947
10. U.S. capital outflow	−1,030
11. Increase in U.S. official reserves	(2)
12. Increase in foreign official assets in U.S.	298
Capital account balance (items 9–12)	213
13. Statistical discrepancy	245
Net balance (items 1–13)	0

Source: U.S. Department of Commerce (2010 data).

exported only $1.8 trillion. This created a **trade deficit** of $495 billion. That trade deficit represents a net outflow of dollars to the rest of the world.

$$\text{Trade balance} = \text{Exports} - \text{Imports}$$

The excess supply of dollars created by the trade gap widened further by other net outflows. U.S. government grants to foreign nations (line 7 in Table 22.1) contributed $55 billion to the net *supply* of dollars.

Current Account Balance. The current account balance is a subtotal in Table 22.1. It includes the merchandise, services, and investment balances as well as government grants and private transfers such as wages sent home by foreign citizens working in the United States.

$$\frac{\text{Current account}}{\text{balance}} = \frac{\text{Trade}}{\text{balance}} + \frac{\text{Unilateral}}{\text{transfers}}$$

The current account balance is the most comprehensive summary of our trade relations. As indicated in Table 22.1, the United States had a current account deficit of $458 billion in 2010.

Capital Account Balance. The current account deficit is offset by the capital account surplus. The capital account balance takes into consideration assets bought and sold across international borders:

$$\frac{\text{Capital account}}{\text{balance}} = \frac{\text{Foreign purchase}}{\text{of U.S. assets}} - \frac{\text{U.S. purchases}}{\text{of foreign assets}}$$

As Table 22.1 shows, foreign consumers demanded $947 billion in 2010 to buy farms and factories as well as U.S. bonds, stocks, and other investments (item 9). This exceeded the flow of U.S. dollars going overseas to purchase foreign assets (item 10). In addition, the United States and foreign governments bought and sold dollars, creating an additional inflow of dollars (items 11 and 12).

The net capital inflows were essential in financing the U.S. trade deficit (negative trade balance). As in any market, the number of dollars demanded must equal the number of dollars supplied. Thus *the capital account surplus must equal the current account deficit.* In other words, there can't be any dollars left lying around unaccounted for. Item 13 in Table 22.1 reminds us that our accounting system isn't perfect—we can't identify every transaction. Nevertheless, all the accounts must eventually "balance out":

$$\frac{\text{Net balance}}{\text{of payments}} = \frac{\text{Current account}}{\text{balance}} + \frac{\text{Capital account}}{\text{balance}} = 0$$

That's the character of a market *equilibrium:* the quantity of dollars demanded equals the quantity of dollars supplied.

MARKET DYNAMICS

The interesting thing about markets isn't their character in equilibrium but the fact that prices and quantities are always changing in response to shifts in demand and supply. The U.S. demand for BMWs shifted overnight when Japan introduced a new line of sleek, competitively priced cars (e.g., Lexus). The reduced demand for BMWs shifted the supply of dollars leftward. That supply shift raised the value of the dollar vis-à-vis the euro, as illustrated in Figure 22.2. (It also increased the demand for Japanese yen, causing the yen value of the dollar to *fall.*)

Depreciation and Appreciation

Exchange rate changes have their own terminology. **Depreciation** of a currency occurs when one currency becomes cheaper in terms of another currency. In our earlier discussion of exchange rates, for example, we assumed that the exchange rate between euros and dollars

trade deficit: The amount by which the value of imports exceeds the value of exports in a given time period.

depreciation (currency): A fall in the price of one currency relative to another.

(a) Dollar–euro market

(b) Dollar–yen market

FIGURE 22.2
Shifts in Foreign Exchange Markets

When the Japanese introduced luxury autos into the United States, the American demand for German cars fell. As a consequence, the supply of dollars in the dollar–euro market (part *a*) shifted to the left and the euro value of the dollar rose. At the same time, the increased American demand for Japanese cars shifted the dollar supply curve in the yen market (part *b*) to the right, reducing the yen price of the dollar.

---

changed from 2 euros = $1 to 1 euro = $1, making the euro price of a dollar cheaper. In this case, the dollar *depreciated* with respect to the euro.

The other side of depreciation is **appreciation,** an increase in value of one currency as expressed in another country's currency. ***Whenever one currency depreciates, another currency must appreciate.*** When the exchange rate changed from 2 euros = $1 to 1 euro = $1, not only did the euro price of a dollar fall, but also the dollar price of a euro rose. Hence the euro appreciated as the dollar depreciated.

Figure 22.3 illustrates actual changes in the exchange rate of the U.S. dollar since 1980. The trade-adjusted value of the U.S. dollar is the (weighted) average of all exchange rates for the dollar. Between 1980 and 1985, the U.S. dollar appreciated over 80 percent. This appreciation greatly reduced the price of imports and thus increased their quantity. At the same time, the dollar appreciation raised the foreign price of U.S. exports and so reduced their volume. U.S. farmers, aircraft manufacturers, and tourist services suffered huge sales losses. The trade deficit ballooned.

The value of the dollar briefy reversed course after 1985 but started appreciating again, slowing export growth and increasing imports throughout the 1990s. After a long steep appreciation, the dollar started losing value in 2003. Between 2003 and 2011, the U.S. dollar depreciated by 25 percent. This was good for U.S. exporters but bad for U.S. tourists and foreign producers (see the World View on the next page).

appreciation: A rise in the price of one currency relative to another.

Market Forces

Exchange rates change for the same reasons that any market price changes: the underlying supply or demand (or both) has shifted. Among the more important sources of such shifts are

The Cheap Dollar

- *Relative income changes.* If incomes are increasing faster in country A than in country B, consumers in A will tend to spend more, thus increasing the demand for B's exports and currency. B's currency will appreciate.
- *Relative price changes.* If domestic prices are rising rapidly in country A, consumers will seek out lower-priced imports. The demand for B's exports and currency will increase. B's currency will appreciate.

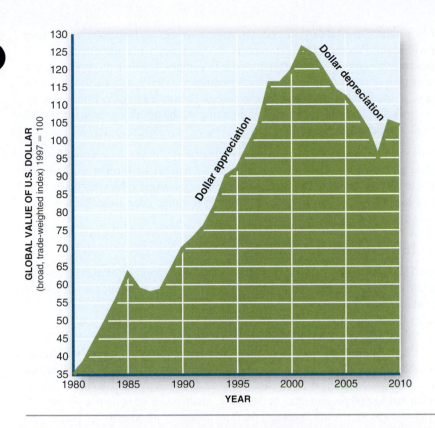

FIGURE 22.3
Changing Values of U.S. Dollar

Since 1973, exchange rates have been flexible. As a result, the value of the U.S. dollar has fluctuated with international differences in inflation, interest rates, and economic growth. U.S. economic stability has given the U.S. dollar increasing value over time.

Source: Federal Reserve Board of Governers.

web analysis

How much are 100 Japanese yen worth in U.S. dollars? Find out by using the currency converter at **www.xe.com/ucc.**

WORLD VIEW

Weak Dollar Helps U.S. Firms

The dollar's precipitous decline against European currencies has brought overseas customers to Al Lubrano's small Rhode Island manufacturing firm that he hasn't heard from in five years.

Gerry Letendre's manufacturing plant in New Hampshire just hired five employees to keep up with growing European demand, two and a half years after Letendre laid off a quarter of his workforce. . . .

The dollar's slide has made U.S. goods far cheaper for European consumers, and European exports considerably more expensive here. Letendre's Diamond Casting and Machine Company in Hollis, New Hampshire, has already boosted shipments of its circuit board printing equipment and industrial valves to Europe by 30 percent. Lubrano, president of Technical Materials Incorporated in Lincoln, Rhode Island, said his export business should jump as much as 25 percent this year.

"On balance, the weak dollar has been tremendous for us," Lubrano said.

—Jonathan Weisman

Dollar's Fall Puts Big Crimp in European Tourism

ROME—As the euro continues to strengthen against the battered U.S. dollar, tourists, businesses, and Americans living abroad complain that Europe is pricing itself out of the market.

"It has become so expensive it almost makes me ill," says Nancy Oliveira, 55, an American living in Rome on what she says was once a "comfortable fixed income.". . .

The Italian National Tourist office reports a 15 percent decline in the number of Americans visiting from 2000 to 2002. . . .

Companies that rely on tourists and visitors estimate business is down 20 percent to 30 percent. . . .

Sales at Florence Moon, a leather store in Rome that caters primarily to Americans, are down 50 percent, says Farshad Shahabadi, whose family owns the store. "If it's bad for us, then it must be bad for everyone else, too," Shahabadi says.

—Ellen Hale

Analysis: Depreciation of a nation's currency is good for that nation's exporters but bad for that nation's importers (including its tourists).

- *Changes in product availability.* If country A experiences a disastrous wheat crop failure, it will have to increase its food imports. B's currency will appreciate.
- *Relative interest rate changes.* If interest rates rise in country A, people in country B will want to move their deposits to A. Demand for A's currency will rise and it will appreciate.
- *Speculation.* If speculators anticipate an increase in the price of A's currency, for the preceding reasons or any other, they'll begin buying it, thus pushing its price up. A's currency will appreciate.

foreign exchange markets: Places where foreign currencies are bought and sold.

All these various changes are taking place every minute of every day, thus keeping **foreign exchange markets** active. On an average day, over *$4 trillion* of foreign exchange is bought and sold in the market. Significant changes occur in currency values, however, only when several of these forces move in the same direction at the same time. This is what caused the Asian crisis of 1997–1998.

The Asian Crisis of 1997–1998

In July 1997 the Thai government decided the baht was overvalued and let market forces find a new equilibrium. Within days, the dollar price of the baht plunged 25 percent. This sharp decline in the value of the Thai baht simultaneously increased the Thai price of the U.S. dollar. As a consequence, Thais could no longer afford to buy as many American products.

The devaluation of the baht had a domino effect on other Asian currencies. The plunge in the baht shook confidence in the Malaysian ringget, the Indonesian rupiah, and even the Korean won. People wanted to hold "hard" currencies like the U.S. dollar. As people rushed to buy U.S. dollars with their local currencies, the value of those currencies plunged. At one point the Indonesian rupiah had lost 80 percent of its dollar value, making U.S. exports five times more expensive for Indonesians. As a result, Indonesians could no longer afford to buy imported rice, machinery, cars, or pork. Indonesian students attending U.S. colleges could no longer afford to pay tuition. The sudden surge in prices and scarcity of goods led to street demonstrations and a change in government. Similar problems erupted throughout Southeast Asia.

The "Asian contagion" unfortunately wasn't confined to that area of the world. Hog farmers in the United States saw foreign demand for their pork evaporate. Koreans stopped taking vacations in Hawaii. Thai Airways canceled orders for Boeing jets. Japanese consumers bought fewer Washington State apples and California oranges. This loss of export markets slowed economic growth in the United States, Europe, Japan, and other nations.

RESISTANCE TO EXCHANGE RATE CHANGES

Given the scope and depth of the Asian crisis of 1997–1998, it's easy to understand why people crave *stable* exchange rates. The resistance to exchange rate fluctuations originates in various micro- and macroeconomic interests.

Micro Interests

The microeconomic resistance to changes in the value of the dollar arises from two concerns. First, people who trade or invest in world markets want a solid basis for forecasting future costs, prices, and profits. Forecasts are always uncertain, but they're even less dependable when the value of money is subject to change. An American firm that invests $2 million in a ski factory in Sweden expects not only to make a profit on the production there but also to return that profit to the United States. If the Swedish krona depreciates sharply in the interim, however, the profits amassed in Sweden may dwindle to a mere trickle, or even a loss, when the kronor are exchanged back into dollars. Even the Nobel Prize loses a bit of its luster when the krona depreciates (see the World View on the next page). From this view, the uncertainty associated with fluctuating exchange rates is an unwanted burden.

Even when the direction of an exchange rate move is certain, those who stand to lose from the change are prone to resist. *A change in the price of a country's money automatically alters the price of all its exports and imports.* When the Russian ruble and Japanese yen depreciated in 2000–2001, for example, the dollar price of Russian and Japanese steel

WORLD VIEW

Nobel Prize Was Nobler in October

STOCKHOLM—Winners of the four Nobel science awards said yesterday that the honor is more important than the money, so it does not matter much that each award has lost $242,000 in value since October.

"If we had been more intelligent, we would have done some hedging," said Gary S. Becker, 61, a University of Chicago professor and a Nobel economics laureate. Sweden's decision last month to let the krona float caused the prizes' value to drop from $1.2 million each when announced in October to $958,000 when King Carl XVI Gustaf presents them Thursday.

The recipients are Becker; American Rudolph A. Marcus, the chemistry laureate; Frenchman Georges Charpak, the physics laureate; and medicine prize winners Edmond Fischer and Edwin Krebs of the University of Washington in Seattle.

Analysis: Currency depreciation reduces the external value of domestic income and assets. The dollar value of the Nobel Prize fell when the Swedish krona depreciated.

declined as well. This prompted U.S. steelmakers to accuse Russia and Japan of "dumping" steel. Steel companies and unions appealed to Washington to protect their sales and jobs.

Even in the country whose currency becomes cheaper, there will be opposition to exchange rate movements. When the U.S. dollar appreciates, Americans buy more foreign products. This increased U.S. demand for imports may drive up prices in other countries. In addition, foreign firms may take advantage of the reduced American competition by raising their prices. In either case, some inflation will result. The consumer's insistence that the government "do something" about rising prices may turn into a political force for "correcting" foreign exchange rates.

Macro Interests

Any microeconomic problem that becomes widespread enough can turn into a macroeconomic problem. The huge U.S. trade deficits of the 1980s effectively exported jobs to foreign nations. Although the U.S. economy expanded rapidly in 1983–1985, the unemployment rate stayed high, partly because American consumers were spending more of their income on imports. Yet fear of renewed inflation precluded more stimulative fiscal and monetary policies.

The U.S. trade deficits of the 1980s were offset by huge capital account surpluses. Foreign investors sought to participate in the U.S. economic expansion by buying land, plants, and equipment and by lending money in U.S. financial markets. These capital inflows complicated monetary policy, however, and greatly increased U.S. foreign debt and interest costs.

U.S. a Net Debtor

The inflow of foreign investment also raised anxieties about "selling off" America. As Japanese and other foreign investors increased their purchases of farmland, factories, and real estate (e.g., Rockefeller Center), many Americans worried that foreign investors were taking control of the U.S. economy.

Fueling these fears was the dramatic change in America's international financial position. From 1914 to 1984, the United States had been a net creditor in the world economy. We owned more assets abroad than foreign investors owned in the United States. Our financial position changed in 1985. Continuing trade deficits and offsetting capital inflows transformed the United States into a net debtor in that year. Since then foreigners have owned more U.S. assets than Americans own of foreign assets.

America's new debtor status can complicate domestic policy. A sudden flight from U.S. assets could severely weaken the dollar and disrupt the domestic economy. To prevent that from occurring, policymakers must consider the impact of their decisions on foreign investors. This may necessitate difficult policy choices.

There's a silver lining to this cloud, however. The inflow of foreign investment is a reflection of confidence in the U.S. economy. Foreign investors want to share in our growth and profitability. In the process, their investments (like BMW's auto plant) expand America's production possibilities and stimulate still more economic growth.

Foreign investors actually assume substantial risk when they invest in the United States. If the dollar falls, the foreign value of *their* U.S. investments will decline. Hence foreigners who've already invested in the United States have no incentive to start a flight from the dollar. On the contrary, a strong dollar protects the value of their U.S. holdings.

EXCHANGE RATE INTERVENTION

Given the potential opposition to exchange rate movements, governments often feel compelled to intervene in foreign exchange markets. The intervention is usually intended to achieve greater exchange rate stability. But such stability may itself give rise to undesirable micro- and macroeconomic effects.

Fixed Exchange Rates

One way to eliminate fluctuations in exchange rates is to fix a currency's value. The easiest way to do this is for each country to define the worth of its currency in terms of some common standard. Under a **gold standard,** each country declares that its currency is worth so much gold. In so doing, it implicitly defines the worth of its currency in terms of all other currencies that also have a fixed gold value. In 1944 the major trading nations met at Bretton Woods, New Hampshire, and agreed that each currency was worth so much gold. The value of the U.S. dollar was defined as being equal to 0.0294 ounce of gold, while the British pound was defined as being worth 0.0823 ounce of gold. Thus the exchange rate between British pounds and U.S. dollars was effectively fixed at $1 = 0.357 pound, or 1 pound = $2.80 (or $2.80/0.0823 = $1/0.0294).

gold standard: An agreement by countries to fix the price of their currencies in terms of gold; a mechanism for fixing exchange rates.

Balance-of-Payments Problems. It's one thing to proclaim the worth of a country's currency; it's quite another to *maintain* the fixed rate of exchange. As we've observed, foreign exchange rates are subject to continual and often unpredictable changes in supply and demand. Hence two countries that seek to stabilize their exchange rate at some fixed value will have to somehow neutralize such foreign exchange market pressures.

Suppose the exchange rate officially established by the United States and Great Britain is equal to e_1, as illustrated in Figure 22.4. As is apparent, that particular exchange rate is consistent with the then-prevailing demand and supply conditions in the foreign exchange market (as indicated by curves D_1 and S_1).

FIGURE 22.4
Fixed Rates and Market Imbalance

If exchange rates are fixed, they can't adjust to changes in market supply and demand. Suppose the exchange rate is initially fixed at e_1. When the demand for British pounds increases (shifts to the right), an excess demand for pounds emerges. More pounds are demanded (q_D) at the rate e_1 than are supplied (q_S). This causes a balance-of-payments deficit for the United States.

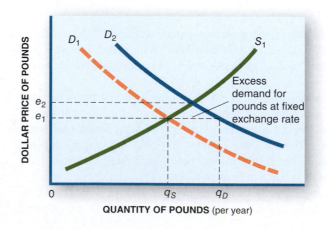

Now suppose that Americans suddenly acquire a greater taste for British cars and start spending more income on Jaguars, Bentleys, and Mini Coopers. This increased desire for British goods will *shift* the demand for British currency from D_1 to D_2 in Figure 22.4. Were exchange rates allowed to respond to market influences, the dollar price of a British pound would rise, in this case to the rate e_2. But we've assumed that government intervention has *fixed* the exchange rate at e_1. Unfortunately, at e_1, American consumers want to buy more pounds (q_D) than the British are willing to supply (q_S). The difference between the quantity demanded and the quantity supplied in the market at the rate e_1 represents a **market shortage** of British pounds.

The excess demand for pounds implies a **balance-of-payments deficit** for the United States: more dollars are flowing out of the country than into it. The same disequilibrium represents a **balance-of-payments surplus** for Britain because its outward flow of pounds is less than its incoming flow.

Basically, there are only two solutions to balance-of-payments problems brought about by the attempt to fix exchange rates:

- Allow exchange rates to rise to e_2 (Figure 22.4), thereby eliminating the excess demand for pounds.
- Alter market supply or demand so they intersect at the fixed rate e_1.

Since fixed exchange rates were the initial objective of this intervention, only the second alternative is of immediate interest.

The Need for Reserves. One way to alter market conditions would be for someone simply to supply British pounds to American consumers. The U.S. Treasury could have accumulated a reserve of foreign currency in earlier periods. By selling some of those **foreign exchange reserves** now, the Treasury would be *supplying* British pounds, helping to offset excess demand. The rightward shift of the pound supply curve in Figure 22.5 illustrates the sale of accumulated British pounds—and related purchase of U.S. dollars—by the U.S. Treasury. (In 2010 the U.S. Treasury reduced foreign exchange reserves by $2 billion; see item 11 in Table 22.1.)

Although foreign exchange reserves can be used to fix exchange rates, such reserves may not be adequate. Indeed, Figure 22.6 should be testimony enough to the fact that today's deficit isn't always offset by tomorrow's surplus. A principal reason that fixed exchange rates didn't live up to their expectations is that the United States had balance-of-payments deficits for 22 consecutive years. This long-term deficit overwhelmed the government's stock of foreign exchange reserves.

The Role of Gold. Gold reserves are a potential substitute for foreign exchange reserves. As long as each country's money has a value defined in terms of gold, we can use gold to buy British pounds, thereby restocking our foreign exchange reserves. Or we can simply

web analysis

Gold has traded widely for centuries. To see recent data on gold prices and exchanges, visit **http://finance.yahoo.com.** Search "gold."

QUANTITY OF POUNDS (per year)

FIGURE 22.5
The Impact of Monetary Intervention

If the U.S. Treasury holds reserves of British pounds, it can use them to buy U.S. dollars in foreign exchange markets. As it does so, the supply of pounds will shift to the right, to S_2, thereby maintaining the desired exchange rate, e_1. The Bank of England could bring about the same result by offering to buy U.S. dollars with pounds (i.e., *supplying* pounds).

FIGURE 22.6
The U.S. Balance of Payments,
1950–1973

The United States had a balance-of-payments deficit for 22 consecutive years. During this period, the foreign exchange reserves of the U.S. Treasury were sharply reduced. Fixed exchange rates were maintained by the willingness of foreign countries to accumulate large reserves of U.S. dollars. However, neither the Treasury's reserves nor the willingness of foreigners to accumulate dollars was unlimited. In 1973 fixed exchange rates were abandoned.

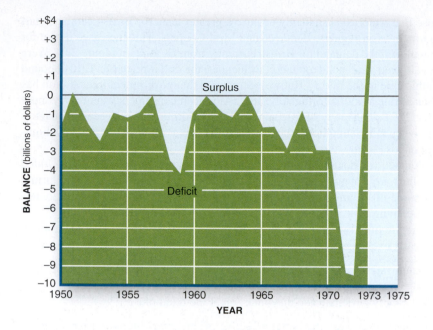

gold reserves: Stocks of gold held by a government to purchase foreign exchange.

use the gold to purchase U.S. dollars in foreign exchange markets. In either case, the exchange value of the dollar will tend to rise. However, we must have **gold reserves** available for this purpose. Unfortunately, the continuing U.S. balance-of-payments deficits recorded in Figure 22.6 exceeded even the hoards of gold buried under Fort Knox. As a consequence, our gold reserves lost their credibility as a guarantor of fixed exchange rates. When it appeared that foreigners would demand more gold than the U.S. government possessed, President Nixon simply ended the link between the U.S. dollar and gold. As of August 15, 1971, the U.S. dollar had no guaranteed value.

Domestic Adjustments. Government can also use fiscal, monetary, and trade policies to achieve a desired exchange rate. With respect to trade policy, *trade protection can be used to prop up fixed exchange rates.* We could eliminate the excess demand for pounds (Figure 22.4), for example, by imposing quotas and tariffs on British goods. Such trade restrictions would reduce British imports to the United States and thus the demand for British pounds. In August 1971 President Nixon imposed an emergency 10 percent surcharge on all imported goods to help reduce the payments deficit that fixed exchange rates had spawned. Such restrictions on international trade, however, violate the principle of comparative advantage and thus reduce total world output. Trade protection also invites retaliatory trade restrictions (see the World View on Mexico's 2009 retaliation against U.S. trade barriers on page 464).

Fiscal policy is another way out of the imbalance. An increase in U.S. income tax rates will reduce disposable income and have a negative effect on the demand for all goods, including imports. A reduction in government spending will have similar effects. In general, *deflationary (or restrictive) policies help correct a balance-of-payments deficit by lowering domestic incomes and thus the demand for imports.*

Monetary policies in a deficit country could follow the same restrictive course. A reduction in the money supply raises interest rates. The balance of payments will benefit in two ways. The resultant slowdown in spending will reduce import demand. In addition, higher interest rates may induce international investors to move more of their funds into the deficit country. Such moves will provide immediate relief to the payments imbalance.[1] Russia

[1]Before 1930, not only were foreign exchange rates fixed, but domestic monetary supplies were tied to gold stocks as well. Countries experiencing a balance-of-payments deficit were thus forced to contract their money supply, and countries experiencing a payments surplus were forced to expand their money supply by a set amount. Monetary authorities were powerless to control domestic money supplies except by erecting barriers to trade. The system was abandoned when the world economy collapsed into the Great Depression.

tried this strategy in 1998, tripling key interest rates (to as much as 150 percent). But even that wasn't enough to restore confidence in the ruble, which kept depreciating. Within three months of the monetary policy tightening, the ruble lost half its value.

A surplus country could help solve the balance-of-payments problem. By pursuing expansionary—even inflationary—fiscal and monetary policies, a surplus country could stimulate the demand for imports. Moreover, any inflation at home will reduce the competitiveness of exports, thereby helping to restrain the inflow of foreign demand. Taken together, such efforts would help reverse an international payments imbalance.

Even under the best of circumstances, domestic economic adjustments entail significant costs. In effect, ***domestic adjustments to payments imbalances require a deficit country to forsake full employment and a surplus country to forsake price stability***. China has had to grapple with these domestic consequences of fixing the value of its currency. The artificially low value of the yuan promoted Chinese exports and accelerated China's GDP growth. But it also created serious macro problems. To keep the value of the yuan low, the Chinese had to keep buying dollars. By 2011 China had over $3 trillion of foreign currency reserves (see the accompanying World View). It paid for those dollars with yuan, adding to China's money supply. All that money stoked inflation in China. Ultimately, the Chinese government had to adopt restrictive monetary and fiscal policies to keep inflation in check. The Chinese government also had to be willing to keep accumulating U.S. dollars and other currencies.

There's no easy way out of this impasse. Market imbalances caused by fixed exchange rates can be corrected only with abundant supplies of foreign exchange reserves or deliberate changes in fiscal, monetary, or trade policies. At some point, it may become easier to let a currency adjust to market equilibrium.

WORLD VIEW

Analysis: China's $3 Trillion in Reserves More Bane Than Boon

BEIJING (Reuters)—China's foreign exchange reserves have topped $3 trillion and counting, stoking inflation, knocking the economy off kilter, and leaving the country's money managers with an impossible assignment.

At first glance, the eye-watering stockpile appears to be a symbol of China's fast-growing wealth. But on deeper inspection, the vast cash holdings are an unflattering testament to much that is wrong in the world's second-largest economy.

They reveal how undervalued the yuan is, how inflation could soar in the future, and how much more the government could be investing at home to engender sustainable growth, analysts say. . . .

In the last decade, China's gaping trade surpluses and its incessant buying of dollars to suppress the yuan's value have led the reserves to balloon 17-fold.

For every dollar that goes into reserves, China prints about 6.5 yuan, adding even more cash to its economy. This is worrying since China is already at pains to drain excess money, with inflation running near its fastest in three years.

"Every new dollar of foreign exchange reserves is every new dollar of base money. And that drives up inflation," Green said. . . .

"The government is moving too slowly toward a more flexible yuan exchange rate. They should definitely quicken the pace of appreciation," said Zhang Bin, an economist at the Chinese Academy of Social Sciences.

—Koh Gui Qing and Aileen Wang

Source: Reuters.com, April 14, 2011. © Thomson Reuters 2011. All rights reserved. Used with permission.

Analysis: When a currency is deliberately undervalued, strong export demand may kindle inflation. The trade surplus that results also increases foreign exchange reserves.

The Euro Fix. The original 12 nations of the European Monetary Union (EMU) fixed their exchange rates in 1999. They went far beyond the kind of exchange rate fix we're discussing here. Members of the EMU *eliminated* their national currencies, making the euro the common currency of Euroland. They don't have to worry about reserve balances or domestic adjustments. However, they do have to reconcile their varied national interests to a single monetary authority, which may prove to be difficult politically in times of economic stress.

Flexible Exchange Rates

flexible exchange rates: A system in which exchange rates are permitted to vary with market supply-and-demand conditions; floating exchange rates.

Balance-of-payments problems wouldn't arise in the first place if exchange rates were allowed to respond to market forces. Under a system of **flexible exchange rates** (often called floating exchange rates), the exchange rate moves up or down to choke off any excess supply of or demand for foreign exchange. Notice again in Figure 22.4 that the exchange rate move from e_1 to e_2 prevents any excess demand from emerging. *With flexible exchange rates, the quantity of foreign exchange demanded always equals the quantity supplied,* and there's no imbalance. For the same reason, there's no need for foreign exchange reserves.

Although flexible exchange rates eliminate balance-of-payments and foreign exchange reserves problems, they don't solve all of a country's international trade problems. *Exchange rate movements associated with flexible rates alter relative prices and may disrupt import and export flows.* As noted before, depreciation of the dollar raises the price of all imported goods, contributing to domestic cost-push inflation. Also, domestic businesses that sell imported goods or use them as production inputs may suffer sales losses. On the other hand, appreciation of the dollar raises the foreign price of U.S. goods and reduces the sales of American exporters. Hence *someone is always hurt, and others are helped, by exchange rate movements.* The resistance to flexible exchange rates originates in these potential losses. Such resistance creates pressure for official intervention in foreign exchange markets or increased trade barriers.

The United States and its major trading partners abandoned fixed exchange rates in 1973. Although exchange rates are now able to fluctuate freely, it shouldn't be assumed that they necessarily undergo wild gyrations. On the contrary, experience with flexible rates since 1973 suggests that some semblance of stability is possible even when exchange rates are free to change in response to market forces.

Speculation. One force that often helps maintain stability in a flexible exchange rate system is—surprisingly—speculation. Speculators often counteract short-term changes in foreign exchange supply and demand. If a currency temporarily rises above its long-term

"Damn it! How can I relax, knowing that out there, somewhere, somehow, someone's attacking the dollar?"

Analysis: A "weak" dollar reduces the buying power of American tourists.

equilibrium, speculators will move in to sell it. By selling at high prices and later buying at lower prices, speculators hope to make a profit. In the process, they also help stabilize foreign exchange rates.

Speculation isn't always stabilizing, however. Speculators may not correctly gauge the long-term equilibrium. Instead they may move "with the market" and help push exchange rates far out of kilter. This kind of destabilizing speculation sharply lowered the international value of the U.S. dollar in 1987, forcing the Reagan administration to intervene in foreign exchange markets, borrowing foreign currencies to buy U.S. dollars. In 1997 the Clinton administration intervened for the opposite purpose: stemming the rise in the U.S. dollar. The Bush administration was more willing to stay on the sidelines, letting global markets set the exchange rates for the U.S. dollar. The Obama administration was accused of keeping the value of the U.S. dollar deliberately low to boost exports and create more jobs.

These kinds of interventions are intended to *narrow* rather than *eliminate* exchange rate movements. Such limited intervention in foreign exchange markets is often referred to as **managed exchange rates,** or, popularly, "dirty floats."

managed exchange rates: A system in which governments intervene in foreign exchange markets to limit but not eliminate exchange rate fluctuations; "dirty floats."

Although managed exchange rates would seem to be an ideal compromise between fixed rates and flexible rates, they can work only when some acceptable "rules of the game" and mutual trust have been established. As Sherman Maisel, a former governor of the Federal Reserve Board, put it, "Monetary systems are based on credit and faith: If these are lacking, a . . . crisis occurs."[2]

THE ECONOMY TOMORROW

CURRENCY BAILOUTS

The world has witnessed a string of currency crises, including the one in Asia during 1997–1998, the Brazilian crisis of 1999, the Argentine crisis of 2001–2002, recurrent ruble crises in Russia, and periodic panics in Mexico and South America. In every instance, the country in trouble pleads for external help. In most cases, a currency "bailout" is arranged, whereby global monetary authorities lend the troubled nation enough reserves (such as U.S. dollars) to defend its currency. Typically the International Monetary Fund (IMF) heads the rescue party, joined by the central banks of the strongest economies.

The Case for Bailouts. The argument for currency bailouts typically rests on the domino theory. Weakness in one currency can undermine another. This seemed to be the case during the 1997–1998 Asian crisis. After the **devaluation** of the Thai baht, global investors began worrying about currency values in other Asian nations. Choosing to be safe rather than sorry, they moved funds out of Korea, Malaysia, and the Philippines and invested in U.S. and European markets (notice in Figure 22.3 the 1997–1998 appreciation of the U.S. dollar).

devaluation: An abrupt depreciation of a currency whose value was fixed or managed by the government.

The initial baht devaluation also weakened the competitive trade position of these same economies. Thai exports became cheaper, diverting export demand from other Asian nations. To prevent loss of export markets, Thailand's neighbors felt they had to devalue as well. Speculators who foresaw these effects accelerated the domino effect by selling the region's currencies.

When Brazil devalued its currency (the *real*) in January 1999, global investors worried that a "samba effect" might sweep across Latin America. The domino effect could reach across the ocean and damage U.S. and European exports as well. Hence the industrial countries often offer a currency bailout as a form of self-defense.

The Case against Bailouts. Critics of bailouts argue that such interventions are ultimately self-defeating. They say that once a country knows for sure that currency bailouts are in the wings, it doesn't have to pursue the domestic policy adjustments that might stabilize its

[2]Sherman Maisel, *Managing the Dollar* (New York: W. W. Norton, 1973), p. 196.

currency. A nation can avoid politically unpopular options such as high interest rates, tax hikes, or cutbacks in government spending. It can also turn a blind eye to trade barriers, monopoly power, lax lending policies, and other constraints on productive growth. Hence the expectation of readily available bailouts may foster the very conditions that cause currency crises.

Future Bailouts? The decision to bail out a depreciating currency isn't as simple as it appears. To minimize the ill effects of bailouts, the IMF and other institutions typically require the nation in crisis to pledge more prudent monetary, fiscal, and trade policies. Usually there's a lot of debate about what kinds of adjustments will be made—and how soon. As long as the nation in crisis is confident of an eventual bailout, however, it has a lot of bargaining power to resist policy changes. Only after the IMF finally said no to further bailouts in 2001 did Argentina devalue its currency and pursue more domestic reforms.

SUMMARY

- Money serves the same purposes in international trade as it does in the domestic economy—namely, to facilitate specialization and market exchanges. The basic challenge of international finance is to create acceptable standards of value from the various currencies maintained by separate countries. LO22-1
- Exchange rates are the mechanism for translating the value of one national currency into the equivalent value of another. An exchange rate of $1 = 2 euros means that one dollar is worth two euros in foreign exchange markets. LO22-2
- Foreign currencies have value because they can be used to acquire goods and resources from other countries. Accordingly, the supply of and demand for foreign currency reflect the demands for imports and exports, for international investment, and for overseas activities of governments. LO22-1
- The balance of payments summarizes a country's international transactions. Its components are the trade balance, the current account balance, and the capital account balance. The current and capital accounts must offset each other. LO22-1
- The equilibrium exchange rate is subject to any and all shifts of supply and demand for foreign exchange. If relative incomes, prices, or interest rates change, the demand for foreign exchange will be affected. A depreciation is a

- change in market exchange rates that makes one country's currency cheaper in terms of another currency. An appreciation is the opposite kind of change. LO22-2
- Changes in exchange rates are often resisted. Producers of export goods don't want their currencies to rise in value (appreciate); importers and tourists dislike it when their currencies fall in value (depreciate). LO22-3
- Under a system of fixed exchange rates, changes in the supply and demand for a specific currency can't be expressed in exchange rate movements. Instead such shifts will be reflected in excess demand for or supply of that currency. Such market imbalances are referred to as balance-of-payments deficits or surpluses. LO22-2
- To maintain fixed exchange rates, monetary authorities must enter the market to buy and sell foreign exchange. To do so, deficit countries must have foreign exchange reserves. In the absence of sufficient reserves, a country can maintain fixed exchange rates only if it's willing to alter basic fiscal, monetary, or trade policies. LO22-3
- Flexible exchange rates eliminate balance-of-payments problems and the crises that accompany them. But complete flexibility can lead to disruptive changes. To avoid this contingency, many countries prefer to adopt managed exchange rates—that is, rates determined by the market but subject to government intervention. LO22-3

Key Terms

exchange rate
equilibrium price
balance of payments
trade deficit
depreciation (currency)
appreciation

foreign exchange markets
gold standard
market shortage
balance-of-payments deficit
balance-of-payments surplus

foreign exchange reserves
gold reserves
flexible exchange rates
managed exchange rates
devaluation

Questions for Discussion

1. Why would a decline in the value of the dollar prompt foreign manufacturers such as BMW to build production plants in the United States?   LO22-3
2. How do changes in the value of the U.S. dollar affect foreign enrollments at U.S. colleges?   LO22-3
3. How would rapid inflation in Canada affect U.S. tourism travel to Canada? Does it make any difference whether the exchange rate between Canadian and U.S. dollars is fixed or flexible?   LO22-2
4. Under what conditions would a country welcome a balance-of-payments deficit? When would it *not* want a deficit?   LO22-3
5. In what sense do fixed exchange rates permit a country to "export its inflation"?   LO22-1
6. In the World View on page 477, who is Farshad Shahabadi referring to as "everyone else"?   LO22-1
7. If a nation's currency depreciates, are the reduced export prices that result "unfair"?   LO22-3
8. How would each of these events affect the supply or demand for Japanese yen?   LO22-1
   (*a*) Stronger U.S. economic growth.
   (*b*) A decline in Japanese interest rates.
   (*c*) Higher inflation in the United States.
   (*d*) A Japanese tsunami.
9. Is a stronger dollar good or bad for the United States? Explain.   LO22-3
10. Why does the World View on page 483 say the undervalued yuan is "more bane than boom"?   LO22-3

---

web activities to accompany this chapter can be found on the Online Learning Center:
http://www.mhhe.com/schiller13e

mobile app Visit your mobile app store and download the Schiller: Study Econ app *today!*

LO22-2 1. According to the World View on page 474, which nation had
    (*a*) The cheapest currency? _____
    (*b*) The most expensive currency? _____

LO22-2 2. If a euro is worth $1.40, what is the euro price of a dollar? _____

LO22-3 3. If a pound of U.S. pork cost 40 rupiah in Indonesia before the Asian crisis, how much did it cost when the dollar value of the rupiah fell by 80 percent? _____

LO22-2 4. If a PlayStation 3 costs 20,000 yen in Japan, how much will it cost in U.S. dollars if the exchange rate is
    (*a*) 120 yen = $1? _____
    (*b*) 1 yen = $0.00833? _____
    (*c*) 100 yen = $1? _____

LO22-2 5. Between 1980 and 2003, by how much did the dollar appreciate (Figure 22.3)? _____%

LO22-1 6. If inflation raises U.S. prices by 3 percent and the U.S. dollar appreciates by 5 percent, by how much does the foreign price of U.S. exports change? _____%

LO22-2 7. According to the World View on page 474, what was the peso price of a euro in May 2011? _____

LO22-3 8. For each of the following possible events, indicate whether the global value of the U.S. dollar will A: rise or B: fall.
    (*a*) American cars become suddenly more popular abroad. _____
    (*b*) Inflation in the United States accelerates. _____
    (*c*) The United States falls into a recession. _____
    (*d*) Interest rates in the United States drop. _____
    (*e*) The United States experiences rapid increases in productivity. _____
    (*f*) Anticipating a return to the gold standard, Americans suddenly rush to buy gold from the two big producers, South Africa and the Soviet Union. _____
    (*g*) War is declared in the Middle East. _____
    (*h*) The stock markets in the United States collapse. _____

LO22-3 9. The following schedules summarize the supply and demand for trifflings, the national currency of Tricoli:

Triffling price (U.S. dollars per triffling)	0	$4	$8	$12	$16	$20	$24
Quantity demanded (per year)	40	38	36	34	32	30	28
Quantity supplied (per year)	1	11	21	31	41	51	61

Use these schedules for the following:
    (*a*) Graph the supply and demand curves on the next page.
    (*b*) Determine the equilibrium exchange rate. _____
    (*c*) Determine the size of the excess supply or excess demand that would exist if the Tricolian government fixed the exchange rate at $22 = 1 triffling. _____

(d) Which of the following events would help reduce the payments imbalance? Which would not? (A = helps; B = doesn't help)

  (i) Domestic inflation.　　_____

  (ii) Foreign inflation.　　_____

  (iii) Slower domestic growth.　　_____

  (iv) Faster domestic growth.　　_____

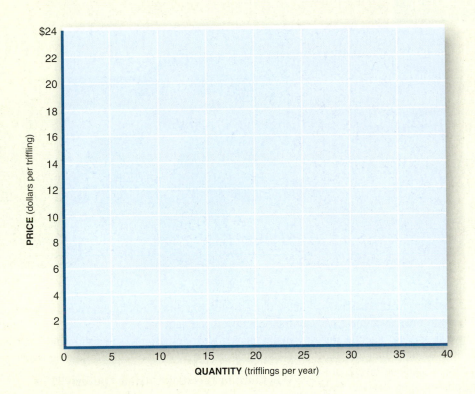

LO22-3　10. As shown in Table 22.1, in 2010 the United States was running a current account deficit. How would each of the following events affect the size of the current account deficit?

(a) U.S. companies, the largest investors in Switzerland, see even more promising investment opportunities there.　　_____

(b) The Netherlands, one of the largest foreign investors in the United States, finds investment opportunities less attractive.　　_____

(c) Unemployment and recession continue in the United States.　　_____

LO22-2　11. The following exchange rates were taken from ExchangeRate.com. On July 21, by how much did the dollar appreciate or depreciate against the

(a) Chinese yuan?　　_____

(b) Canadian dollar?　　_____

Currency Rates per 1.00 U.S. Dollar

	July 20	July 21
Chinese yuan (CNY)	6.458831	6.454755
Canadian dollar (CAD)	0.948479	0.945833

Global Poverty

Bono, the lead singer for the rock group U2, has performed concerts around the world to raise awareness of global poverty. He doesn't have a specific agenda for eradicating poverty. He does believe, though, that greater awareness of global poverty will raise assistance levels and spawn more ideas for combating global hunger, disease, and isolation.

The dimensions of global poverty are staggering. According to the World Bank, over a third of the world's population lacks even the barest of life's necessities. *Billions* of people are persistently malnourished, poorly sheltered, minimally clothed, and at constant risk of debilitating diseases. Life expectancies among the globally poor population still hover in the range of 40–50 years, far below the norm (70–80 years) of the rich, developed nations.

In this chapter we follow Bono's suggestion and take a closer look at global poverty. We address the following issues:

- **What income thresholds define "poverty"?**
- **How many people are poor?**
- **What actions can be taken to reduce global poverty?**

In the process of answering these questions, we get another opportunity to examine what makes economies "tick"— particularly what forces foster faster economic growth for some nations and slower economic growth for others.

AMERICAN POVERTY

Poverty, like beauty, is often in the eye of the beholder. Many Americans feel "poor" if they can't buy a new car, live in a fancy home, or take an exotic vacation. Indeed, the average American asserts that a family needs at least $35,000 a year "just to get by." With that much income, however, few people would go hungry or be forced to live in the streets.

Official Poverty Thresholds

To develop a more objective standard of poverty, the U.S. government assessed how much money a U.S. family needs to purchase a "minimally adequate" diet. Back in 1963 it concluded that $1,000 per year was needed for that purpose alone. Then it asked how much income was needed to purchase other basic necessities like housing, clothes, transportation, and so on. It figured all those *non*food necessities would cost twice as much as the food staples. So it concluded that a budget of $3,000 per year would fund a "minimally adequate" living standard for a U.S. family of four. That standard became the official **U.S. poverty threshold** in 1963.

Inflation Adjustments. Since 1963, prices have risen every year. As a result, the price of the poverty "basket" has risen as well. In 2010, it cost roughly $22,000 to purchase those same basic necessities for a family of four that cost only $3,000 in 1963.

   Twenty-two thousand dollars might sound like a lot of money, especially if you're not paying your own rent or feeding a family. If you break the budget down, however, it doesn't look so generous. Only a third of the budget goes for food. And that portion has to feed four people. So the official U.S. poverty standard provides only $5 per day for an individual's food. That just about covers a single Big Mac combo at McDonald's. There's no money in the poverty budget for dining out. And the implied rent money is only $700 a month (for the whole family). So the official U.S. poverty standard isn't that generous—certainly not by *American* standards (where the *average* family has an income of nearly $80,000 per year and eats outside their $200,000 home three times a week).

U.S. Poverty Count

The Census Bureau counted over 46 million Americans as "poor" in 2010 according to the official U.S. thresholds (as adjusted for family size). This was one out of seven U.S. households, for a **poverty rate** of roughly 15 percent. According to the Census Bureau, the official U.S. poverty rate has been in a narrow range of 11–15 percent for the last 40 years.

How Poor Is U.S. "Poor"?

Many observers criticize these official U.S. poverty statistics. They say that far fewer Americans meet the government standard of poverty and even fewer are really destitute.

In-Kind Income. A major flaw in the official tally is that the government counts only *cash* income in defining poverty. Since the 1960s, however, the U.S. has developed an extensive system of **in-kind transfers** that augment cash incomes. Food stamps, for example, can be used just as easily as cash to purchase groceries. Medicaid and Medicare pay doctor and hospital bills, reducing the need for cash income. Government rent subsidies and public housing allow poor families to have more housing than their cash incomes would permit. These in-kind transfers allow "poor" families to enjoy a higher living standard than their cash incomes imply. Adding those transfers to cash incomes would bring the U.S. poverty count down into the 9–11 percent range.

Material Possessions. Even those families who remain "poor" after counting in-kind transfers aren't necessarily destitute. Over 40 percent of America's "poor" families own their homes, 70 percent own a car or truck, and 30 percent own at least *two* vehicles. Telephones, color TVs, dishwashers, clothes dryers, air conditioners, and microwave ovens are commonplace in America's poor households.

---

poverty threshold (U.S.): Annual income of less than $22,000 for a family of four (2010, inflation adjusted).

poverty rate: Percentage of the population counted as poor.

in-kind transfers: Direct transfers of goods and services rather than cash, such as food stamps, Medicaid benefits, and housing subsidies.

America's poor families themselves report few acute problems in everyday living. Fewer than 14 percent report missing a rent or mortgage payment, and fewer than 8 percent report a food deficiency. So American poverty isn't synonymous with homelessness, malnutrition, chronic illness, or even social isolation. These problems exist among America's poverty population, but they don't define American poverty.

GLOBAL POVERTY

Poverty in the rest of the world is much different from poverty in America. *American poverty is more about* **relative** *deprivation than* **absolute** *deprivation. In the rest of the world, poverty is all about* **absolute** *deprivation.*

Low Average Incomes

As a starting point for assessing global poverty, consider how *average* incomes in the rest of the world stack up against U.S. levels. By global standards, the United States is unquestionably a very rich nation. As we observed in Chapter 2 (see the World View on page 32), U.S. GDP per capita is five times larger than the world average. Over three-fourths of the world's population lives in what the World Bank calls "low-income" or "lower-middle-income" nations. In those nations the *average* income is under $4,000 a year, less than *one-tenth* of America's per capita GDP. Average incomes are lower yet in Haiti, Nigeria, Ethiopia, and other desperately poor nations. By American standards, virtually all the people in these nations would be poor. By *their* standards, no American would be poor.

World Bank Poverty Thresholds

extreme poverty (world):
World Bank income standard of less than $1.25 per day per person (inflation adjusted).

Because national poverty lines are so diverse and culture-bound, the World Bank decided to establish a uniform standard for assessing global poverty. And it set the bar amazingly low. In fact, the World Bank regularly uses two thresholds, namely $1.25 per day for **"extreme" poverty** and a higher $2 per day standard for less "severe" poverty.

The World Bank thresholds are incomprehensibly low by American standards. How much could you buy for $1.25 a day? A little rice, maybe, and perhaps some milk? Certainly not a Big Mac. Not even a grande coffee at Starbucks. And part of that $1.25 would have to go for rent. Clearly this isn't going to work. Raising the World Bank standard to $2 per day (**severe poverty**) doesn't reach a whole lot further.

severe poverty (world):
World Bank income standard of $2 per day per person (inflation adjusted).

The World Bank, of course, wasn't defining "poverty" in the context of American affluence. They were instead trying to define a rock-bottom threshold of absolute poverty—a threshold of physical deprivation that people everywhere would acknowledge as the barest "minimum"—a condition of "unacceptable deprivation."

Global Poverty Counts

On the basis of household surveys in over 100 nations, *the World Bank classifies over a billion people as being in "extreme" poverty (<$1.25/day) and 2.5 billion people as being in "severe" poverty (<$2/day).*

Figure 23.1 shows where concentrations of extreme poverty are the greatest. Concentrations of extreme poverty are alarmingly high in dozens of smaller, less developed nations like Mali, Haiti, and Zambia, where average incomes are also shockingly low. However, the greatest *number* of extremely poor people reside in the world's largest countries. China and India alone contain a third of the world's population and half of the world's extreme poverty.

Table 23.1 reveals that the distribution of severe poverty (<$2/day) is similar. The incidence of this higher poverty threshold is, of course, much greater. Severe poverty afflicts over 80 percent of the population in dozens of nations and even reaches over 90 percent of the population in some (e.g., Burundi). By contrast, less than 14 percent of the U.S. population falls below the official *American* poverty threshold, and *virtually no American household has an income below the* **global** *poverty threshold.*

Analysis: Global poverty is defined in terms of absolute deprivation.

Number of People in Extreme Poverty
30 million
99 million
485 million
2 million
213 million
1,374 million

FIGURE 23.1
Geography of Extreme Poverty

Over a billion people around the world are in "extreme" poverty. In smaller, poor nations, deprivation is commonplace.

Source: *The World Bank, WDR2011 Data Set,* **data.worldbank.org.**

web analysis

For the latest facts on world poverty, visit **www.globalissues.org** and click on "Poverty Facts and Stats."

Social Indicators

The levels of poverty depicted in Figure 23.1 and Table 23.1 imply levels of physical and social deprivation few Americans can comprehend. Living on less than a dollar or two a day means always being hungry, malnourished, ill-clothed, dirty, and unhealthy. The problems associated with such deprivation begin even before birth. Pregnant women often fail to get enough nutrition or medical attention. In low-income countries only a third of all births are attended by a skilled health practitioner. If something goes awry, both the mother and the baby are at fatal risk. Nearly all of the children in global poverty are in a state of chronic malnutrition. At least 1 out of 10 children in low-income nations will actually die before reaching age 5. In the poorest sectors of the population, infant and child mortality rates are often two to three times higher than that. Children often remain unimmunized to preventable diseases. And AIDS is rampant among both children and adults in the poorest nations. All of these factors contribute to a frighteningly short life expectancy—less than half that in the developed nations.

Fewer than one out of two children from extremely poor households are likely to stay in school past the eighth grade. Women and minority ethnic and religious groups are often wholly excluded from educational opportunities. As a consequence, great stocks of human capital remain undeveloped: in low-income nations only one out of two women and only two out of three men are literate.

Persistent Poverty

Global poverty is not only more desperate than American poverty, but also more permanent. In India a rigid caste system still defines differential opportunities for millions of rich and poor villagers. Studies in Brazil, South Africa, Peru, and Ecuador document barriers

Country	Living in Severe Poverty	
	Percent	Number
Burundi	94%	8 million
Rwanda	90	9
Tanzania	88	39
Nigeria	84	130
Bangladesh	81	131
Ethiopia	78	65
India	76	878
China	36	479
World	**37%**	**2,506**

Source: *The World Bank, WDR2011 Data Set,* **data.worldbank.org.**

TABLE 23.1
Population in Severe Poverty
(<$2/day)

More than a third of the world's population has income of less than $2 per person per day. Such poverty is pervasive in low-income nations.

that block access to health care, education, and jobs for children of poor families. Hence inequalities in poor nations not only are more severe than in developed nations but also tend to be more permanent.

Economic stagnation also keeps a lid on upward mobility. President John F. Kennedy observed that "a rising tide lifts all boats," referring to the power of a growing economy to raise everyone's income. In a growing economy, one person's income *gain* is not another person's *loss*. By contrast, a stagnant economy intensifies class warfare, with everyone jealously protecting whatever gains they have made. The *haves* strive to keep the *have-nots* at bay. Unfortunately, this is the reality in many low-income nations. As we observed in Chapter 2 (Table 2.1), in some of the poorest nations in the world output grows more slowly than the population, intensifying the competition for resources.

GOALS AND STRATEGIES

Global poverty is so extensive that no policy approach offers a quick solution. Even the World Bank doesn't see an end to global poverty. The United Nations set a much more modest goal back in 2000.

The UN Millennium Goal

Millennium Poverty Goal:
United Nations goal of reducing global rate of extreme poverty to 15 percent by 2015.

The UN established a **Millennium Poverty Goal** of cutting the incidence of extreme global poverty in half by 2015 (from 30 percent in 1990 to 15 percent in 2015). Even that seemingly modest goal wouldn't greatly decrease the *number* of people in poverty. The world's population keeps growing at upward of 80–100 million people a year. By the year 2015, there will be close to 7.2 billion people on this planet. Fifteen percent of that population would still leave over a *billion* people in extreme global poverty.

Why should we care? After all, America has its own poverty problems and a slew of other domestic concerns. So why should an American—or, for that matter, an affluent Canadian, French, or German citizen—embrace the UN's Millennium Poverty Goal? For starters, one might embrace the notion that a poor child in sub-Saharan Africa or Borneo is no less worthy than a poor child elsewhere. And a child's death in Bangladesh is just as tragic as a child's death in Buffalo, New York. In other words, humanitarianism is a starting point for *global* concern for poor people. Then there are pragmatic concerns. Poverty and inequality sow the seeds of social tension both within and across national borders. Poverty in other nations also limits potential markets for international trade. Last but not least, undeveloped human capital anywhere limits human creativity. For all these reasons, the UN feels the Millennium Poverty Goal should be universally embraced.

Policy Strategies

To reach even this modest goal will be difficult, however. In principle, *there are only two general approaches to global poverty reduction:*

The End of Poverty?

- *Redistribution* of incomes within and across nations.
- *Economic growth* that raises average incomes.

The following sections explore the potential of these strategies for eliminating global poverty.

INCOME REDISTRIBUTION

Many people suggest that the quickest route to eliminating global poverty is simply to *redistribute* incomes and assets, both within and across countries. The potential for redistribution is often exaggerated, however, and its risks underestimated.

Within-Nation Redistribution

Take another look at those nations with the highest concentrations of extreme poverty. Tanzania is near the top of the list in Figure 23.1 and Table 23.1, with an incredible 68 percent of its population in extreme poverty and 88 percent in severe poverty. Yet the

WORLD VIEW

Glaring Inequalities

Inequality tends to diminish as a country develops. In poor nations, the richest tenth of the population typically gets 40 to 50 percent of all income—sometimes even more. In developed countries, the richest tenth gets 20 to 30 percent of total income.

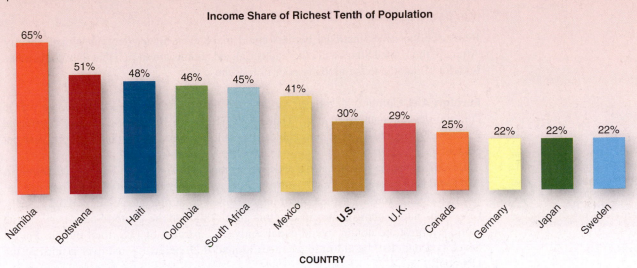

Income Share of Richest Tenth of Population

Namibia 65% • Botswana 51% • Haiti 48% • Colombia 46% • South Africa 45% • Mexico 41% • U.S. 30% • U.K. 29% • Canada 25% • Germany 22% • Japan 22% • Sweden 22%

COUNTRY

Source: *The World Bank, WDI2011 Data Set,* **data.worldbank.org.**

Analysis: The FOR WHOM question is reflected in the distribution of income. Although the U.S. income distribution is very unequal, inequalities loom even larger in most poor countries.

other 12 percent of the population lives fairly well, taking over 30 percent of that nation's income. So what would happen if we somehow forced Tanzania's richest households to share that wealth? Sure, Tanzania's poorest households would be better off. But the gains wouldn't be spectacular: the *average* income in Tanzania is less than $1,200 a year. Nigeria, Haiti, Zambia, and Madagascar also have such low *average* incomes that outright redistribution doesn't hold great hope for income gains by the poor. (See the World View above).

Economic Risks. Then there's the downside to direct redistribution. How is the income pie going to be resliced? Will the incomes or assets of the rich be confiscated? How will underlying jobs, stocks, land, and businesses be distributed to the poor? How will *total* output (and income) be affected by the redistribution? If savings are confiscated, people will no longer want to save and invest. If large, efficient farms are divided up into small parcels, who will manage them? After Zimbabwe confiscated and fragmented that nation's farms in 2000, its agricultural productivity plummeted and the economy collapsed. If the government expropriates factories, mills, farms, or businesses, who will run them? If the *rewards* to saving, investment, entrepreneurship, and management are expropriated, who will undertake these economic activities?

This is not to suggest that *no* redistribution of income or assets is appropriate. More progressive taxes and land reforms can reduce inequalities and poverty. But the potential of direct within-nation redistribution is often exaggerated. Historically, nations have often been forced to reverse land, tax, and property reforms that have slowed economic growth and reduced average incomes.

Expenditure Reallocation. In addition to directly redistributing private income and wealth, governments can also reduce poverty by reallocating direct government expenditures. As we observed in Chapter 1 (Figure 1.3), some poor nations devote a large share of output to the military. If more of those resources were channeled into schools, health services, and infrastructure, the poor would surely benefit. Governments in poor nations also tend to give priority to urban development (where the government and middle class reside), to the neglect of rural development (where the poor reside). Redirecting more resources to rural development and core infrastructure (roads, electricity, and water) would accelerate poverty reduction.

Across-Nation Redistribution

Redistribution *across* national borders could make even bigger dents in global poverty. After all, the United States and other industrialized nations are so rich that they could transfer a lot of income to the globally poor if they chose to.

Foreign Aid. Currently developed nations give poorer nations $80–$100 billion a year in "official development assistance." That's a lot of money. But even if it were distributed exclusively to globally poor households, it would amount to less than $35 per year per person.

Millennium Aid Goal:
United Nations goal of raising foreign aid levels to 0.7 percent of donor-country GDP.

Developed nations have set a goal of delivering more aid. The United Nations' **Millennium Aid Goal** is to raise foreign aid levels to 0.7 percent of donor-country GDP. That may not sound too ambitious, but it's a much larger flow than at present. As Table 23.2 reveals, few "rich" nations now come close to this goal. Although the United States is by far the world's largest aid donor, its aid equals only 0.21 percent of U.S. total output. For all developed nations, the aid ratio averages around 0.28 percent—just over a third of the UN goal.

Given the history of foreign aid, the UN goal is unlikely to be met anytime soon. But what if it were? What if foreign aid *tripled*? Would that cure global poverty? No. Tripling foreign aid would generate only $100 a year for each of the nearly 3 billion people now in global poverty. Even that figure is optimistic, as it assumes all aid is distributed to the poor in a form (e.g., food, clothes, and medicine) that directly addresses their basic needs.

Nongovernmental Aid. Official development assistance is augmented by private charities and other nongovernmental organizations (NGOs). The Gates Foundation, for example, spends upward of $1 billion a year on health care for the globally poor, focusing on treatable diseases like malaria, tuberculosis, and HIV infection (see the World View on the next page). Religious organizations operate schools and health clinics in areas of extreme poverty. The International Red Cross brings medical care, shelter, and food in emergencies.

TABLE 23.2
Foreign Aid

Rich nations give roughly $100–120 billion to poor nations every year. This is a tiny fraction of donor GDP, however.

Country	Total Aid ($ billions)	Percentage of Donor Total Income
Australia	$ 3	0.29%
Canada	4	0.30
Denmark	2	0.88
France	13	0.46
Italy	3	0.16
Japan	9	0.18
Norway	4	1.06
United Kingdom	11	0.52
United States	29	0.21
22-Nation Total	**$120**	**0.28%**

Source: *The World Bank, WDI2011 Data Set,* **data.worldbank.org.**

WORLD VIEW

The Way We Give

Philanthropy Can Step In Where Market Forces Don't

One day my wife Melinda and I were reading about millions of children dying from diseases in poor countries that were eliminated in this country. . . .

Malaria has been known for a long time. In 1902, in 1907, Nobel Prizes were given for advances in understanding the malaria parasite and how it was transmitted. But here we are a hundred years later and malaria is setting new records, infecting over 400 million people every year, and killing over a million people every year. That's a number that's increasing every year, and every day it's over 2,000 African children. . . .

And this would extend to tuberculosis, yellow fever, AIDS vaccine, acute diarrheal illnesses, respiratory illnesses; you know, millions of children die from these things every year, and yet the advances we have in biology have not been applied because rich countries don't have these diseases. The private sector really isn't involved in developing vaccines and medicines for these diseases because the developing countries can't buy them. . . .

And so if left to themselves, these market forces create a world, which is the situation today, where over 90 percent of the money spent on health research is spent on those who are the healthiest. An example of that is the billion a year spent on combating baldness. That's great for some people, but perhaps it should get behind malaria in terms of its priority ranking . . .

So philanthropy can step in where market forces are not there. . . . It can get the people who have the expertise and draw them in. It can use awards, it can use novel arrangements with private companies, it can partner with the universities. . . . And every year the platform of science that we have to do this on gets better.

—Bill Gates

Source: Speech at The Tech Museum, November 15, 2006. © Bill & Melinda Gates Foundation. Used with permission.

Analysis: When markets fail to provide for basic human needs, additional institutions and incentives may be needed.

web analysis

Go to **www.nptrust.org** and visit the "Charitable Giving Statistics" link for data on philanthropy in the United States.

As with official development assistance, the content of NGO aid can be as important as its level. Relatively low-cost immunizations, for example, can improve health conditions more than an expensive, high-tech health clinic can. Teaching basic literacy to a community of young children can be more effective than equipping a single high school with Internet capabilities. Distributing drought-resistant seeds to farmers can be more effective than donating advanced farm equipment (which may become useless when it needs to be repaired).

ECONOMIC GROWTH

No matter how well designed foreign aid and philanthropy might be, across-nation transfers alone cannot eliminate global poverty. As Bill Gates observed, the entire endowment of the Gates Foundation would meet the health needs of the globally poor for only one year. The World Bank concurs: "Developing nations hold the keys to their prosperity; global action cannot substitute for equitable and efficient domestic policies and institutions."[1] So as important as international assistance is, it will never fully suffice.

Increasing Total Income

The "key" to ending global poverty is, of course, **economic growth.** As we've observed, *redistributing existing incomes doesn't do the job;* total *income has to increase.* This is what economic growth is all about.

Unique Needs. The generic prescription for economic growth is simple: more resources and better technology. But this growth formula takes on a new meaning in the poorest

economic growth: An increase in output (real GDP); an expansion of production possibilities.

[1]World Bank, *World Development Report, 2006* (Washington, DC: World Bank, 2006), p. 206.

nations. Rich nations can focus on research, technology, and the spread of "brain power." Poor nations need the basics—the "bricks and mortar" elements of an economy such as water systems, roads, schools, and legal systems. Bill Gates learned this firsthand in his early philanthropic efforts. In 1996 Microsoft donated a computer for a community center in Soweto, one of the poorest areas in South Africa. When he visited the center in 1997 he discovered the center had no electricity. He quickly realized that growth policy priorities for poor nations are different from those for rich nations.

Growth Potential

The potential of economic growth to reduce poverty in poor nations is impressive. The 40 nations classified as "low-income" by the World Bank have a combined output of only $1 trillion. That's about twice the annual sales revenue of Walmart. "Lower-middle-income" nations like China, Brazil, Egypt, and Sri Lanka produce another $18 trillion or so of annual output. Hence every percentage point of economic growth increases total income in these combined nations by roughly $200 billion. According to the World Bank, if these nations could grow their economies by just 3.8 percent a year (an extra $760 billion of output in the first year and increasing thereafter), global poverty *could* be cut in half by 2015.

China has demonstrated just how effective economic growth can be in reducing poverty. Since 1990 China has been the world's fastest-growing economy, with annual GDP growth rates routinely in the 8–10 percent range. This sensational growth has not only raised *average* incomes but has also dramatically reduced the incidence of poverty. In fact, *the observed success in reducing global poverty from 30 percent in 1990 to 21 percent in 2010 is almost entirely due to the decline in Chinese poverty.* By contrast, slow economic growth in Africa, Latin America, and South Asia has *increased* their respective poverty populations.

Reducing Population Growth

China not only has enjoyed exceptionally fast GDP growth but also has benefited from relatively slow population growth (now around 0.8 percent a year). This has allowed *aggregate* GDP growth to lift *average* incomes more quickly. In other poor nations, population growth is much faster, making poverty reduction more difficult. As Table 23.3 shows,

TABLE 23.3
Growth Rates in Selected Countries, 2000–2009

The relationship between GDP growth and population growth is very different in rich and poor countries. The populations of rich countries are growing very slowly, and gains in per capita GDP are easily achieved. In the poorest countries, population is still increasing rapidly, making it difficult to raise living standards. Notice how per capita incomes are declining in many poor countries (such as Zimbabwe and Haiti).

	Average Annual Growth Rate (2000–2009) of		
	GDP	**Population**	**Per Capita GDP**
High-income countries			
Canada	2.1	1.0	1.1
France	1.5	0.5	1.0
United States	2.0	1.1	0.9
Japan	1.1	0.2	0.9
Low-income countries			
China	10.9	0.8	10.1
India	7.9	1.6	6.3
Ethiopia	7.5	2.8	4.7
Nigeria	6.6	2.4	4.2
Venezuela	4.9	1.7	3.2
Madagascar	3.6	2.9	0.7
Burundi	2.7	2.0	0.7
Haiti	0.7	1.8	−1.1
West Bank/Gaza	−0.9	3.8	−4.7
Zimbabwe	−7.5	0.9	−8.4

Source: *The World Bank, WDR2011 Data Set,* **data.worldbank.org.**

population growth is in the range of 2–3 percent in some of the poorest nations (e.g., Ethiopia, Nigeria, and West Bank/Gaza). ***Reducing population growth rates in the poorest nations is one of the critical keys to reducing global poverty.***

Birth control in some form may have to be part of any antipoverty strategy. In the poorest population groups in the poorest nations, contraceptives are virtually nonexistent. Yet within those same nations, contraceptive use is much more common in the richest segments of the population. This suggests that limited access, not cultural norms or religious values, constrains the use of contraceptives. To encourage more birth control, China also used tax incentives and penalties to limit families to one child.

Human Capital Development

Reducing population growth makes poverty reduction easier, but not certain. The next key is to make the existing population more productive—that is, to increase **human capital.**

human capital: The knowledge and skills possessed by the workforce.

Education. In poor nations, the need for human capital development is evident. Only 71 percent of the population in low-income nations completes even elementary school. Even fewer people are *literate*—that is, able to read and write a short, simple statement about everyday life (e.g., "We ate rice for breakfast"). Educational deficiencies are greatest for females, who are often prevented from attending school by cultural, social, or economic concerns (see the accompanying World View). In Chad and Liberia, fewer than one out of six girls completes primary school. Primary school completion rates for girls are in the 25–35 percent range in most of the poor nations of sub-Saharan Africa.

WORLD VIEW

The Female "Inequality Trap"

In many poor nations, women are viewed as such a financial liability that female fetuses are aborted, female infants are killed, and female children are so neglected that they have significantly higher mortality rates. The "burden" females pose results from social norms that restrict the ability of women to earn income, accumulate wealth, or even decide their own marital status. In many of the poorest nations, women

- Have restricted property rights.
- Can't inherit wealth.
- Are prohibited or discouraged from working outside the home.
- Are prohibited or discouraged from going to school.
- Are prevented from voting.
- Are denied the right to divorce.
- Are paid less than men if they do work outside the home.
- Are often expected to bring a financial dowry to the marriage.
- May be beaten if they fail to obey their husbands.

These social practices create an "inequality trap" that keeps returns on female human capital investment low. Without adequate education or training, they can't get productive jobs. Without access to good jobs, they have no incentive to get an education or training. This kind of vicious cycle creates an inequality trap that keeps women and their communities poor.

Source: The World Bank, *World Development Report 2006*, pp. 51–54. Used with permission.

Analysis: Denying women economic rights is not only discriminatory but reduces the amount of human capital available for economic growth.

In Niger and Mali, only one out of five *teenage* girls is literate. This lack of literacy creates an **inequality trap** that restricts the employment opportunities for young women to simple, routine, manual jobs (e.g., carpet weaving and sewing). With so few skills and little education, they are destined to remain poor.

The already low levels of *average* education are compounded by unequal access to schools. Families in extreme poverty typically live in rural areas, with primitive transportation and

inequality trap: Institutional barriers that impede human and physical capital investment, particularly by the poorest segments of society.

communication facilities. *Physical* access to schools itself is problematic. On top of that, the poorest families often need their children to work, either within the family or in paid employment. In Somalia, only 8 percent of poor young children attend primary schools; in Ethiopia, Yemen, and Mali, about 50 percent attend. These forces often foreclose school attendance for the poorest children.

Health. In poor nations, basic health care is also a critical dimension of human capital development. Immunizations against measles, diphtheria, and tetanus are more the exception than the rule in Somalia, Nigeria, Afghanistan, Congo, the Central African Republic, and many other poor nations. For all low-income nations taken together, the child immunization rate is only 67 percent (versus 96 percent in the United States). Access and education—not money—are the principal barriers to greater immunizations.

Water and sanitation facilities are also in short supply. The World Bank defines "adequate water access" as a protected water source of at least 20 liters per person a day within 1 kilometer of the home dwelling. We're not limited to indoor plumbing with this definition: a public water pipe a half mile from one's home is considered adequate. Yet only three out of four households in low-income nations meet even this minimum threshold of water adequacy (see the World View below). In Afghanistan, Ethiopia, and Somalia only one out of four households has even that much water access. Access to sanitation facilities (ranging from pit latrines to flush toilets) is less common still (on average one out of three low-income-nation households). In Ethiopia only 6 percent of the population is so privileged.

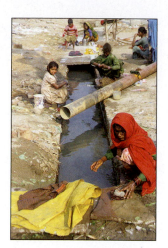

Analysis: Unsafe water is a common problem for the globally poor.

WORLD VIEW

Dying for a Drink of Clean Water

In the United States and Europe, people take it for granted that when they turn on their taps, clean water will flow out. But for those living in U.S. cities devastated by Hurricane Katrina, as in large parts of the world, obtaining safe water requires a constant struggle.

Water is essential to all aspects of life, yet 99 percent of water on Earth is unsafe or unavailable to drink. About 1.2 billion people lack safe water to consume, and 2.6 billion do not have access to adequate sanitation. There are also stark comparisons: just one flush of a toilet in the West uses more water than most Africans have to perform an entire day's washing, cleaning, cooking, and drinking.

Unsafe water and sanitation are now the single largest cause of illness worldwide, just as they have been a major threat to the health of people affected by Hurricane Katrina. A recent UN report estimated that

- At least 2 million people, most of them children, die annually from waterborne diseases such as diarrhea, cholera, dysentery, typhoid, guinea worm, and hepatitis, as well as such illnesses as malaria and West Nile virus carried by mosquitoes that breed in stagnant water.
- Many of the 10 million child deaths that occurred last year were linked to unsafe water and lack of sanitation. Children can't fight off infections if their bodies are weakened by waterborne diseases.
- Over half of the hospital beds in the developing world are occupied by people suffering from preventable diseases caused by unsafe water and inadequate sanitation.

When poor people are asked what would most improve their lives, water and sanitation are repeatedly one of the highest priorities. We should heed their call.

—Jan Eliasson and Susan Blumenthal

Source: *The Washington Post,* September 20, 2005, p. A23. From *The Washington Post,* September 20, 2005. Reprinted with permission by Jan Eliasson through Monica Lundkrist.

Analysis: Access to safe water and sanitation is one of the most basic foundations for economic growth. The UN's millennium water goal is to reduce by 2015 half the percentage of people without safe water.

When illness strikes, professional health care is hard to find. In the United States, there is one doctor for every 180 people. In Sierra Leone, there is one doctor for every 10,000 people! For low-income nations as a group, there are 2,500 people for every available doctor.

These glaring inadequacies in health conditions breed high rates of illness and death. In the United States, only 8 out of every 1,000 children die before age 5. In Angola, 260 of every 1,000 children die that young. For all low-income nations, the under-5 mortality rate is 13.5 percent (nearly one out of seven). Those children who live are commonly so malnourished (severely underweight and/or short) that they can't develop fully (another inequality trap).

AIDS takes a huge toll as well. Only 0.6 percent of the U.S. adult population has HIV. In Botswana, Lesotho, Swaziland, and Zimbabwe, over 25 percent of the adult population is HIV-infected. As a result of these problems, life expectancies are inordinately low. In Zambia, only 16 percent of the population lives to age 65. In Botswana, life expectancy at birth is 35 years (versus 78 years in the United States). For low-income nations as a group, life expectancy is a mere 57 years.

Rostow's Five Stages of Development

In view of these glaring human capital deficiencies, one might wonder how poor nations could possibly grow enough to reduce their extreme poverty. After surveying diverse growth experiences, Walt Rostow, an M.I.T. economist, discerned five distinct stages in the development process, as summarized in Table 23.4. Many of the poorest nations are still stuck in stage 1, the "traditional society," with minimal core infrastructure, especially in the rural areas where the poorest households reside. To get beyond that stage, poor nations have to create the "preconditions for takeoff"—to channel more resources into basic education and health services while dismantling critical inequality traps.

Meeting Basic Needs. *To get beyond Rostow's stage 1, poor nations must substantially improve the health and education of the mass of poor people.* Cuba was highly successful in following this approach. Although Cuba was a very poor country when Fidel Castro took power in 1959, his government placed high priority on delivering basic educational and health services to the entire population. Within a decade, health and educational standards approached those of industrialized nations.

Implied Costs. The amount of money needed to meet the basic needs of poor nations is surprisingly modest. Malaria vaccinations cost less than 20 cents a shot. Bringing safe water to the poor would cost around $4 billion per year. Bringing both safe water and sanitation would cost about $23 billion annually. Providing universal primary education would cost about $8 billion a year. These costs aren't prohibitive. After all, U.S. consumers spend

Walt Rostow distinguished these five sequential stages of economic development:
- Stage 1: *Traditional society*. Rigid institutions, low productivity, little infrastructure, dependence on subsistence agriculture.
- Stage 2: *Preconditions for takeoff*. Improved institutional structure, increased agricultural productivity, emergence of an entrepreneurial class.
- Stage 3: *Takeoff into sustained growth*. Increased saving and investment, rapid industrialization, growth-enhancing policies.
- Stage 4: *Drive to maturity*. Spread of growth process to lagging industrial sectors.
- Stage 5: *High mass consumption*. High per capita GDP attained and accessible to most of population.

Source: The World Bank, *World Development Indicators 2005*, Table 2.11a. **www.worldbank.org.**

TABLE 23.4
Five Stages of Economic Development

$20 billion a year on pet food and $100 billion on alcohol. The challenge for poor nations is to get the necessary resources applied to their basic needs.

Capital Investment

To reach stages 2 and 3 in Rostow's scenario, poor nations also need sharply increased capital investment in both the public and private sectors. Transportation and communications systems must be expanded and upgraded so markets can function. Capital equipment and upgraded technology must flow into both agricultural and industrial enterprises.

investment rate: The percentage of total output (GDP) allocated to the production of new plants, equipment, and structures.

Internal Financing. Acquiring the capital resources needed to boost productivity and accelerate economic growth is not an easy task. Domestically, freeing up scarce resources for capital investment requires cutbacks in domestic consumption. In the 1920s Stalin used near-totalitarian powers to cut domestic consumption in Russia (by limiting output of consumer goods) and raise Russia's **investment rate** to as much as 30 percent of output. This elevated rate of investment pushed Russia into stage 3, but at a high cost in terms of consumer deprivation.

Other nations haven't had the power or the desire to make such a sacrifice. China spent two decades trying to raise consumption standards before it gave higher priority to investment. Once it did so, however, economic growth accelerated sharply. Unfortunately, low investment rates continue to plague other poor nations.

microfinance: The granting of small ("micro"), unsecured loans to small businesses and entrepreneurs.

Pervasive poverty in poor nations sharply limits the potential for increased savings. Nevertheless, governments can encourage more saving with improved banking facilities, transparent capital markets, and education and saving incentives. And there is mounting evidence that even small dabs of financing can make a big difference. Extending a small loan that enables a poor farmer to buy improved seeds or a plow can have substantial effects on productivity. Financing small equipment or inventory for an entrepreneur can get a new business rolling. Such **microfinance** can be a critical key to escaping poverty (see the World View below).

WORLD VIEW

Muhammad Yunus: Microloans

Teach a man to fish, and he'll eat for a lifetime. But only if he can afford the fishing rod. More than 30 years ago in Bangladesh, economics Professor Muhammad Yunus recognized that millions of his countrymen were trapped in poverty because they were unable to scrape together the tiny sums they needed to buy productive essentials such as a loom, a plow, an ox, or a rod. So he gave small loans to his poor neighbors, secured by nothing more than their promise to repay.

Microcredit, as it's now known, became a macro success in 2006, reaching two huge milestones. The number of the world's poorest people with outstanding microloans—mostly in amounts of $15 to $150—was projected to reach 100 million. And Yunus, 66, shared the Nobel Peace Prize with the Grameen Bank he founded. The Nobel Committee honored his grassroots strategy as "development from below."

You know an idea's time has come when people start yanking it in directions its originator never imagined. Some, like Citigroup, are making for-profit loans, contrary to Yunus's break-even vision. Others, like Bangladesh's BRAC, are nonprofit but have a more holistic vision than Grameen, offering health care and social services in addition to loans.

Source: "The Best Ideas," *BusinessWeek*, December 18, 2006, pp. 96–106. Used with permission of Bloomberg L.P. Copyright © 2011. All rights reserved.

Analysis: Microloans focus on tiny loans to small businesses and farmers that enable them to increase output and productivity.

web analysis

Go to **www.grameenfoundation. org** for more information on microcredit.

Some nations have also used inflation as a tool for shifting resources from consumption to investment. By financing public works projects and private investment with an increased money supply, governments can increase the inflation rate. As prices rise faster than consumer incomes, households are forced to curtail their purchases. This "inflation tax" ultimately backfires, however, when both domestic and foreign market participants lose confidence in the nation's currency. Periodic currency collapses have destabilized many South and Central American economies and governments. Inflation financing also fails to distinguish good investment ideas from bad ones.

External Financing. Given the constraints on internal financing, poor nations have to seek external funding to lift their investment rate. In fact, Columbia University economist Jeffrey Sachs has argued that external financing is not only necessary but, if generous enough, also sufficient for *eliminating* global poverty (see the accompanying World View). As we've observed, however, actual foreign aid flows are far below the "Big Money" threshold that Sachs envisions. Skeptics also question whether more foreign aid would really solve the problem, given the mixed results of previous foreign aid flows. They suggest that more emphasis should be placed on increasing *private* investment flows. Private investment typically entails *direct foreign investment* in new plants, equipment, and technology, or the purchase of ownership stakes in existing enterprises.

WORLD VIEW

Jeffrey Sachs: Big Money, Big Plans

Columbia University economics professor Jeffrey Sachs has seen the ravages of poverty around the world. As director of the UN Millennium Project, he is committed to attaining the UN's goal of reducing global poverty rates by half by 2015. In fact, Professor Sachs thinks we can do even better: the complete *elimination* of extreme poverty by 2025.

How will the world do this? First, rich nations must double their foreign aid flows now, and then double them again in 10 years. Second, poor nations must develop full-scale, comprehensive plans for poverty reduction. This "shock therapy" approach must address all dimensions of the poverty problem simultaneously and quickly, sweeping all inequality traps out of the way.

Critics have called Sachs's vision utopian. They point to the spotty history of foreign aid projects and the failure of many top-down, Big Plan development initiatives. But they still applaud Sachs for mobilizing public opinion and economic resources to fight global poverty.

Source: Jeffrey Sachs, *The End of Poverty,* Penguin, 2006.

Analysis: World poverty can't be eliminated without committing far more resources. Jeffrey Sachs favors an externally financed, comprehensive Big Plan approach.

Agricultural Development

When we think about capital investment, we tend to picture new factories, gleaming office buildings, and computerized machinery. In discussing global poverty, however, we have to remind ourselves of how dependent poor nations are on agriculture. As Figure 23.2 illustrates, 65 percent of Somalia's income originates in agriculture. Agricultural shares in the range of 35–55 percent are common in the poorest nations. By contrast, only 1 percent of America's output now comes from farms.

Low Farm Productivity. What keeps poor nations so dependent on agriculture is their incredibly low **productivity.** Subsistence farmers are often forced to plow their own fields by hand with wooden plows. Irrigation systems are primitive and farm machinery is scarce or nonexistent. While high-tech U.S. farms produce nearly $50,000 of output per worker,

productivity: Output per unit of input—for example, output per labor-hour.

FIGURE 23.2
Agricultural Share of Output

In poor nations, agriculture accounts for a very large share of total output.

Source: *The World Bank, WDR2011 Data Set,* **data.worldbank.org.**

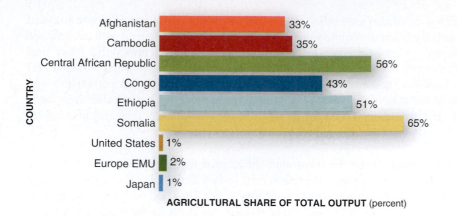

AGRICULTURAL SHARE OF TOTAL OUTPUT (percent)

Ethiopian farms produce a shockingly low $218 of output per worker (see Figure 23.3). Farmers in Zimbabwe produce only 313 kilograms of cereal per hectare, compared with 7,238 kilos per hectare in the United States.

To grow their economies—to rise out of stage 1—poor nations have to invest in agricultural development. Farm productivity has to rise beyond subsistence levels so that workers can migrate to other industries and expand production possibilities. One of the catapults to China's growth was an exponential increase in farm productivity that freed up labor for industrial production. (China now produces nearly 5,500 kilos of cereal per hectare.) To achieve greater farm productivity, poor nations need capital investment, technological know-how, and improved infrastructure.

Institutional Reform

The five stages of economic growth envisioned by Rostow imply significant discontinuities in the development process. Nations need some critical mass—some spark—to jump from one stage to the next. That's where the kind of "shock therapy" envisioned by Jeffrey Sachs comes in. However, not everyone embraces this view. Surely economic growth won't occur automatically, as centuries of global poverty make clear. But growth doesn't necessarily have to follow the sequence of Rostow's five stages either. Moreover, even a series of capital infusions (rather than one massive shock) might promote development.

The critical thing is to get enough resources and use them in the best possible way. To do that, **a *nation needs an institutional structure that promotes economic growth.***

Property Rights. Land, property, and contract rights have to be established before farmers will voluntarily improve their land or invest in agricultural technology. China saw how agricultural productivity jumped when it transformed government-run communal farms into local enterprises and privately managed farms, beginning in 1978. China is using the lessons of that experience to now extend ownership rights to farmers.

Analysis: Lack of capital, technology, and markets keeps farm productivity low.

FIGURE 23.3
Low Agricultural Productivity

Farmers in poor nations suffer from low productivity. They are handicapped by low education, inferior technology, primitive infrastructure, and a lack of machinery.

Source: *The World Bank, WDR2011 Data Set,* **data.worldbank.org.**

VALUE OF FARM OUTPUT PER WORKER (U.S. dollars)

Entrepreneurial Incentives. Unleashing the "animal spirits" of the marketplace is also critical. People *do* respond to incentives. If farmers see the potential for profit—and the opportunity to keep that profit—they will pursue productivity gains with more vigor. To encourage that response, governments need to assure the legitimacy of profits and their fair tax treatment. In 1992 the Chinese government acknowledged the role of profits and entrepreneurship in fostering economic advancement. Before then, successful entrepreneurs ran the risk of offending the government with conspicuous consumption that highlighted growing inequalities. The government even punished some entrepreneurs and confiscated their wealth. Once "profits" were legitimized, however, entrepreneurship and foreign investment accelerated, pushing China well into Rostow's stage 3.

Cuba stopped short of legitimizing private property and profits. Although Fidel Castro periodically permitted some private enterprises (e.g., family restaurants), he always withdrew that permission when entrepreneurial ventures succeeded. As a consequence, Cuba didn't advance from stage 2 to stage 3. Venezuela has recently moved further in that direction, expropriating and nationalizing private enterprises (see the accompanying World View), thereby discouraging private investment and entrepreneurship.

WORLD VIEW

Chávez Sets Plans for Nationalization

BOGOTA, Colombia, Jan. 8—Venezuelan President Hugo Chávez on Monday announced plans to nationalize the country's electrical and telecommunications companies, take control of the once-independent Central Bank, and seek special constitutional powers permitting him to pass economic laws by decree.

"We're heading toward socialism, and nothing and no one can prevent it," Chávez, who won a third term in a landslide election in December, said in a speech in Caracas, in the Venezuelan capital. . . .

Chávez also said Monday that the government would soon exert more control over the Central Bank, one of the few Venezuelan institutions that has shown itself to be independent of the Chávez administration. Two of the seven directors of the bank's board, including Domingo Maza Zavala, who often criticized government economic policy, are on their way out.

"The Central Bank must not be autonomous," Chávez said. "That is a neoliberal idea."

—Juan Forero

Analysis: By restricting private ownership, governments curb the entrepreneurship and investment that may be essential for economic development.

Equity. What disturbed both Castro and Venezuelan President Chávez was the way capitalism intensified income inequalities. Entrepreneurs got rich while the mass of people remained poor. For Castro, the goal of equity was more important than the goal of efficiency. A nation where everyone was equally poor was preferred to a nation of haves and have-nots. Chávez thought he could pursue both equity and efficiency with government-managed enterprises.

In many of today's poorest nations, policy interests are not so noble. A small elite often holds extraordinary political power and uses that power to protect its privileges. Greed restricts the flow of resources to the poorest segments of the population, leaving them to fend for themselves. These inequalities in power, wealth, and opportunity create inequality traps that restrain human capital development, capital investment, entrepreneurship, and ultimately economic growth.

Business Climate. To encourage capital investment and entrepreneurship, governments have to assure a secure and supportive business climate. Investors and business start-ups

FIGURE 23.4

Business Climates Affect Growth

Nations that offer more secure property rights, less regulation, and lower taxes grow faster and enjoy higher per capita incomes.

Source: Adapted from Heritage Foundation, *2011 Index of Economic Freedom*, p. 7. Washington, DC. Used with permission.

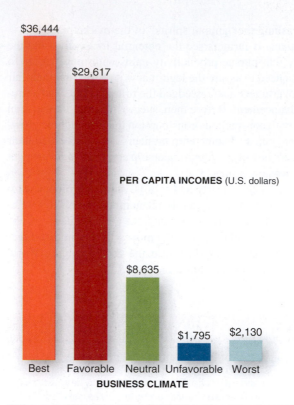

PER CAPITA INCOMES (U.S. dollars)

Best	$36,444
Favorable	$29,617
Neutral	$8,635
Unfavorable	$1,795
Worst	$2,130

BUSINESS CLIMATE

Note: Business climate in 183 nations gauged by 50 measures of government tax, regulatory, and legal policy.

want to know what the rules of the game are and how they will be enforced. They also want assurances that contracts will be enforced and that debts can be collected. They want their property protected from crime and government corruption. They want minimal interference from government regulation and taxes.

As the annual surveys by the Heritage Foundation document, nations that offer a more receptive business climate grow at a faster pace. Figure 23.4 illustrates this connection. Notice that nations with the most pro-business climate (e.g., Hong Kong, Singapore, Iceland, the United States, and Denmark) enjoy living standards far superior to those in nations with hostile business climates (e.g., North Korea, Congo, Sudan, Zimbabwe, and Myanmar). This is no accident; *pro-business climates encourage the capital investment, the entrepreneurship, and the human capital investment that drive economic growth.*

Unfortunately, some of the poorest nations still fail to provide a pro-business environment. Figure 23.5 illustrates how specific dimensions of the business climate differ across fast-growing nations (China) and perpetually poor ones (Cambodia and Kenya). A biannual survey of 26,000 international firms elicits their views of how different government policies restrain their investment decisions. Notice how China offers a more certain policy environment, less corruption, more secure property rights, and less crime. Given these business conditions, where would you invest?

The good news about the business climate is that it doesn't require huge investments to fix. It does require, however, a lot of political capital.

World Trade

comparative advantage: The ability of a country to produce a specific good at a lower opportunity cost than its trading partners.

When it comes to political capital, poor nations have a complaint of their own. They say that rich nations lock them out of their most important markets—particularly agricultural export markets. Poor nations typically have a **comparative advantage** in the production of agricultural products. Their farm productivity may be low (see Figure 23.3), but their low labor costs keep their farm output competitive. They can't fully exploit that advantage in export markets, however. The United States, the European Union, and Japan heavily

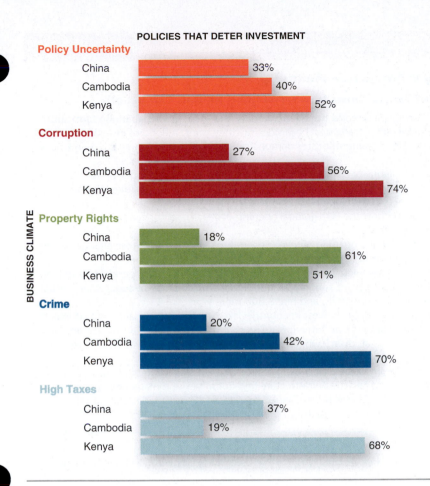

POLICIES THAT DETER INVESTMENT

BUSINESS CLIMATE

Policy Uncertainty
- China — 33%
- Cambodia — 40%
- Kenya — 52%

Corruption
- China — 27%
- Cambodia — 56%
- Kenya — 74%

Property Rights
- China — 18%
- Cambodia — 61%
- Kenya — 51%

Crime
- China — 20%
- Cambodia — 42%
- Kenya — 70%

High Taxes
- China — 37%
- Cambodia — 19%
- Kenya — 68%

FIGURE 23.5
Investment Climate

International investors gravitate toward nations with business-friendly policies. Shown here are the percentages of international firms citing specific elements of the business climate that deter their investment in the named countries.

Source: The World Bank, *World Development Indicators 2006*. **www.worldbank.org**.

subsidize their own farmers. This keeps farm prices low in the rich nations, eliminating the cost advantage of farmers in poor nations. To further protect their own farmers from global competition, rich nations erect trade barriers to stem the inflow of Third World products. The United States, for example, enforces an **import quota** on foreign sugar. This trade barrier has fostered a high-cost, domestic beet sugar industry (see the World View on the next page) while denying poor nations the opportunity to sell more sugar and grow their economies faster.

Poor nations need export markets. Export sales generate the hard currency (dollars, euros, and yen) that is needed to purchase capital equipment in global markets. Export sales also allow farmers in poor nations to expand production, exploit economies of scale, and invest in improved technology. Ironically, *trade barriers in rich nations impede poor nations from pursuing the agricultural development that is a* **prerequisite** *for growth.* The latest round of multilateral trade negotiations dragged on forever because of the resistance of rich nations to opening their agricultural markets. Poor nations plead that "trade, not aid" is their surest path to economic growth.

A 2004 study estimated that 440 million people would be lifted out of severe poverty if all trade barriers were dismantled. [2] China has demonstrated how a vibrant export sector can propel economic growth; South Korea, Taiwan, Malaysia, India, and Costa Rica have also successfully used exports to advance into the higher stages of economic growth. Mozambique is demonstrating how even a small window of export opportunity can make a real difference in investment and productivity rates (see the World View on the next page). Other poor nations want the same opportunity.

import quota: A limit on the quantity of a good that may be imported in a given time period.

[2] William Cline, *Trade Policy and Global Poverty* (Washington, DC: Institute for International Economics, 2004).

WORLD VIEW

African Sugar Production Ramps Up

EU Plan to Cut Tariffs Shows How Developing Nations Can Benefit

BRUSSELS—The developing world has been adamant that rich nations abandon farm subsidies in order to get a global trade deal both sides say they want. A flood of investment pouring into Southern Africa's sugar industry demonstrates why the poor countries won't back down on this demand.

The hundreds of millions of dollars being spent to ramp up African sugar production is a direct response to European Union plans to slash import duties and subsidies that for years have locked out farmers in developing countries. . . .

The expansion shows how the EU's gradual opening of its farm sector can boost production in some developing countries. . . .

The impact of the planned opening of the EU's sugar market suggests those changes could trigger significant investment in some of the world's poorest rural economies. . . .

Sugar concern Tongaat-Hulett Group Ltd. of South Africa says it will spend $180 million over the next two years to plant roughly an additional 21,250 acres of sugar cane, install modern technology in existing mills, and hire 8,800 more workers. . . .

"It's not easy to find reasons to invest in countries like Mozambique," said Tongaat-Hulett Chief Executive Peter Staude in an interview. "The civil war just ended, and there are land mines and machine guns all over." One of the company's executives was shot at recently when his plane landed near the sugar mill in Xinavane.

Two things made the investment possible, he said. One is that Mozambique has two functional harbors connected to rail lines, infrastructure that doesn't exist in many other poor African countries, Staude said. The other was the planned changes to EU sugar tariffs and subsidies.

"Above all, we want a platform to sell into the EU," he said.

—John W. Miller

Source: *The Wall Street Journal*, February 12, 2007, p. A4. Used with permission of Dow Jones & Company, Inc. via Copyright Clearance Center, Inc.

Analysis: Poor nations need access to markets in rich nations in order to encourage investment in domestic production. They demand "trade, not aid."

THE ECONOMY TOMORROW

Analysis: Markets exist but struggle in poor nations.

UNLEASHING ENTREPRENEURSHIP

The traditional approach to economic development emphasizes the potential for government policy to reallocate resources and increase capital investment. External financing of capital investment was always at or near the top of the policy agenda (see the World View on page 503). This approach has been criticized for neglecting the power of people and markets.

One of the most influential critics is the Peruvian economist Hernando de Soto. When he returned to his native Peru after years of commercial success in Europe, he was struck by the dichotomy in his country. The "official" economy was mired in bureaucratic red tape and stagnant. Most of the vitality of the Peruvian economy was contained in the unofficial "underground" economy. The underground economy included trade in drugs but was overwhelmingly oriented to meeting the everyday demands of Peruvian consumers and households. The underground economy wasn't hidden from view; it flourished on the streets, in outdoor markets, and in transport services. The only thing that forced this thriving economy underground was the failure of the government to recognize it and give it legitimate status. Government restrictions on prices, business activities, finance, and trade—a slew of inequality traps—forced entrepreneurs to operate "underground."

De Soto concluded that countries like Peru could grow more quickly if governments encouraged rather than suppressed these entrepreneurial resources. In his best-selling book, *The Other Path,* he urged poor countries to refocus their development policies. This "other path" entails improving the business climate by

- Reducing bureaucratic barriers to free enterprise.
- Spreading private ownership.
- Developing and enforcing legal safeguards for property, income, and wealth.
- Developing infrastructure that facilitates business activity.

Yunus's "microloans" (see the World View on page 502) would also fit comfortably on this other path.

De Soto's book has been translated into several languages and has encouraged market-oriented reforms in Peru, Argentina, Mexico, Russia, Vietnam, and elsewhere. In India the government is drastically reducing both regulation and taxes to pursue De Soto's other path. The basic message of his other path is that poor nations should exploit the one resource that is abundant in even the poorest countries—entrepreneurship.

SUMMARY

- Definitions of "poverty" are culturally based. Poverty in the United States is defined largely in *relative* terms, whereas global poverty is tied more to *absolute* levels of subsistence. LO23-1
- About 15 percent of the U.S. population (over 46 million people) are officially counted as poor. Poor people in America suffer from *relative* deprivation, not *absolute* deprivation, as in global poverty. LO23-1
- Global poverty thresholds are about one-tenth of U.S. standards. "Extreme" poverty is defined as less than $1.25 per day per person; "severe" poverty is less than $2 per day (inflation adjusted). LO23-1
- One billion people around the world are in extreme poverty; 2.5 billion are in severe poverty. In low-income nations global poverty rates are as high as 70–90 percent. LO23-2
- The United Nations' Millennium Poverty Goal is to cut the global poverty rate in half, to 15 percent by 2015. LO23-3

- Redistribution of incomes *within* poor nations doesn't have much potential for reducing poverty, given their low *average* incomes. *Across*-nation redistributions (e.g., foreign aid) can make a small dent, however. LO23-3
- Economic growth is the key to global poverty reduction. Many poor nations are stuck in stage 1 of development, with undeveloped human capital, primitive infrastructure, and subsistence agriculture. To grow more quickly, they need to meet basic human needs (health and education), increase agricultural productivity, and encourage investment. LO23-3
- To move into sustained economic growth, poor nations need capital investment and institutional reforms that promote both equity and entrepreneurship. LO23-3
- Poor nations also need "trade, not aid"—that is, access to rich nation markets, particularly in farm products. LO23-3

Key Terms

poverty threshold (U.S.)	Millennium Poverty Goal	investment rate
poverty rate	Millennium Aid Goal	microfinance
in-kind transfers	economic growth	productivity
extreme poverty (world)	human capital	comparative advantage
severe poverty (world)	inequality trap	import quota

Questions for Discussion

1. Why should Americans care about extreme poverty in Haiti, Ethiopia, or Bangladesh? LO23-2

2. If you had only $14 to spend per day (the U.S. poverty threshold), how would you spend it? What if you had only $2 a day (the World Bank "severe poverty" threshold)? LO23-1

3. If a poor nation must choose between building an airport, some schools, or a steel plant, which one should it choose? Why? LO23-3

4. How do more children per family either restrain or expand income-earning potential? LO23-3

5. Are property rights a prerequisite for economic growth? Explain. LO23-3

6. How do unequal rights for women affect economic growth? LO23-3

7. Could a nation reorder Rostow's five stages of development and still grow? Explain. LO23-3

8. How does microfinance alter prospects for economic growth? The distribution of political power? LO23-3

9. Can poor nations develop without substantial increases in agricultural productivity? (See Figure 23.2.) How? LO23-3

10. Would you invest in Cambodia or Kenya on the basis of the information in Figure 23.5? LO23-3

11. Why do economists put so much emphasis on entrepreneurship? How can poor nations encourage it? LO23-3

12. How do nations expect nationalization of basic industries to foster economic growth? LO23-3

13. If economic growth reduced poverty but widened inequalities, would it still be desirable? LO23-3

14. What market failure does Bill Gates (World View, p. 497) cite as the motivation for global philanthropy? LO23-3

 web activities to accompany this chapter can be found on the Online Learning Center: **http://www.mhhe.com/schiller13e**

 mobile app Visit your mobile app store and download the Schiller: Study Econ app *today!*

PROBLEMS FOR CHAPTER 23   Name: _____

LO23-1 1. Adjusted for inflation, the World Bank's threshold for "extreme" poverty is $1.25 per person per day.
- (*a*) How much *annual* income does this imply for a family of four? $_____
- (*b*) What portion of the official U.S. poverty threshold (roughly $22,000 for a family of four) is met by the World Bank's measure?   _____ %

LO23-2 2. Two and a half billion people are in "severe" poverty with less than $2 of income per day.
- (*a*) What is the maximum *combined* income of this "severely" poor population? $_____
- (*b*) What percentage of the world's *total* income (roughly $72 trillion) does this represent?   _____ %

LO23-2 3. In Namibia,
- (*a*) What percentage of total output is received by the richest 10 percent of households? (See World View, p. 495.)   _____ %
- (*b*) How much output did this share amount to in 2010, when Namibia's GDP was $12 billion? $_____
- (*c*) With a total population of 2 million, what was the implied per capita income of
    - (*i*) The richest 10 percent of the population? $_____
    - (*ii*) The remaining 90 percent? $_____

LO23-3 4. (*a*) How much foreign aid does the United States now provide? (See Table 23.2.) $_____
- (*b*) How much more is required to satisfy the UN's Millennium Aid Goal if U.S. GDP = $15 trillion? $_____

LO23-3 5. If the industrialized nations were to satisfy the UN's Millennium Aid Goal, how much *more* foreign aid would they give annually? (See Table 23.2.) $_____

LO23-3 6. According to Table 23.3, how many years will it take for per capita GDP to double in
- (*a*) China?   _____
- (*b*) Madagascar?   _____
- (*c*) Zimbabwe?   _____

LO23-3 7. (*a*) Which low-income nation in Table 23.3 has a GDP growth rate closest to that of the United States?   _____
- (*b*) How much faster is that nation's population growth?   _____ %
- (*c*) How much lower is its per capita GDP growth?   _____ %

LO23-3 8. According to the World View on page 497,
- (*a*) How much money is spent annually to combat baldness? $_____
- (*b*) How much medical care would that money buy for each child who dies from malaria each year? $_____

Chapter 1: Page 1 (top), Official White House photo by Pete Souza; Page 1 (middle), Blend Images/Getty Images; Page 1 (bottom), Monty Raukusen/Getty Images; Page 2, Official White House photo by Pete Souza; Page 10: AP Photo/Katsumi Kasahara; Page 20, VisionsofAmerica/ Joe Sohm/Photodisc/Getty Images

Chapter 2: Page 30, Monty Raukusen/Getty Images; Page 37 (left), Santokh Kochar/Getty Images; Page 37 (right), Photo by Gene Alexander, USDA Natural Resources Conservation Service; Page 40 (left), © Photodisc/Getty Images; Page 40 (right), © Copyright 1997 IMS Communications Ltd/Capstone Design. All Rights Reserved

Chapter 3: Page 45, Blend Images/Getty Images; Page 63, Bloomberg via Getty Images; Page 66, Owen Franken/Corbis

Chapter 4: Page 70, Hisham F. Ibrahim/Getty Images; Page 72, USGS photo by Don Becker; Page 72, AP Photo/WPSD Local 6; Page 74, Image Source/Corbis

Chapter 5: Page 91 (top), Fuse/Jupiterimages; Page 91 (middle), Michele Constantini/PhotoAlto/Corbis, Page 91 (bottom), Copyright Thomas Hartwell/2003; Page 92, Fuse/Jupiterimages; Page 99, PRNewsFoto/Porsche Cars North America; Page 105, Getty Images

Chapter 6: Page 116, Michele Constantini/PhotoAlto/Corbis; Page 121 (top), PhotoAlto/PictureQuest; Page 121 (bottom), McGraw-Hill Companies; Page 128, Thinkstock/JupiterImages; Page 131, © DAVID LEWIS/Reuters/Corbis

Chapter 7: Page 136, Copyright Thomas Hartwell/2003; Page 152, Bloomberg via Getty Images

Chapter 8: Page 163 (top), © The McGraw-Hill Companies, Inc./Lars Niki, photographer; Page 163 (middle), Author's Image/PunchStock; Page 163 (bottom), Library of Congress Prints and Photographs Division [LC-USZ62-63968]; Page 164, © The McGraw-Hill Companies, Inc./ Lars Niki, photographer; Page 169, Travelshots.com/Alamy; Page 174, Phillip Gould/Corbis

Chapter 9: Page 190, Author's Image/PunchStock; Page 195, Courtesy of Apple; Page 205 (top, bottom left, and bottom middle), Courtesy of Apple.; Page 205 (bottom right), Bloomberg via Getty Images; Page 209, AP Photo/Jeff Chiu

Chapter 10: Page 213, Library of Congress Prints and Photographs Division [LC-USZ62-63968]; Page 228, Getty Images

Chapter 11: Page 239, The McGraw-Hill Companies, Inc./Andrew Resek, photographer; Page 260, PRNewsFoto/AT&T Corporation

Chapter 12: Page 265, The McGraw-Hill Companies, Inc./Jill Braaten, photographer; Page 268, bobhdeering/Alamy

Chapter 13: Page 281 (top), BananaStock/Jupiterimages; Page 281 (middle), Bloomberg via Getty Images; Page 281 (bottom), Joseph Sohm-Visions of America/Getty Images, Page 282, BananaStock/ Jupiterimages

Chapter 14: Page 302, Bloomberg via Getty Images; Page 303, © Brand X Pictures/PunchStock

Chapter 15: Page 325, Joseph Sohm-Visions of America/Getty Images

Chapter 16: Page 341 (top), AP Photo; Page 341 (middle), Mark Richards/PhotoEdit; Page 341 (bottom), © Brand X Pictures/PunchStock; Page 342, AP Photo; Page 347, Courtesy of Monster.com; Page 353, Getty Images

Chapter 17: Page 366, Mark Richards/PhotoEdit

Chapter 18: Page 386, © Brand X Pictures/PunchStock; Page 390, Library of Congress Prints and Photographs Division [LC-USZ62-105062]

Chapter 19: Page 407 (top), Comstock/JupiterImages; Page 407 (middle), Jeffrey Hamilton/Digital Vision/Getty Images; Page 407 (bottom), © DreamPictures/Pam Ostrow/Blend Images LLC; Page 408, Jeffrey Hamilton/Digital Vision/Getty Images

Chapter 20: Page 427, © DreamPictures/Pam Ostrow/Blend Images LLC

Chapter 21: Page 443 (top), Ingram Publishing; Page 443 (middle), DAJ/Getty Images; Page 443 (bottom), AFP/Getty Images; Page 444, Ingram Publishing

Chapter 22: Page 470, DAJ/Getty Images

Chapter 23: Page 490, AFP/Getty Images; Page 492, © Digital Vision/ PunchStock; Page 500, Dr. Parvinder Sethi; Page 504, © The McGraw-Hill Companies, Inc./Barry Barker, photographer; Page 508, Author's Image/PunchStock

GLOSSARY

Note: Numbers in parentheses indicate the chapters in which the definitions appear.

absolute advantage: The ability of a country to produce a specific good with fewer resources (per unit of output) than other countries. (21)

acreage set-aside: Land withdrawn from production as part of policy to increase crop prices. (15)

antitrust: Government intervention to alter market structure or prevent abuse of market power. (4, 10, 11, 13)

appreciation: A rise in the price of one currency relative to another. (22)

average fixed cost (AFC): Total fixed cost divided by the quantity produced in a given time period. (7)

average total cost (ATC): Total cost divided by the quantity produced in a given time period. (7, 9, 10)

average variable cost (AVC): Total variable cost divided by the quantity produced in a given time period. (7)

balance of payments: A summary record of a country's international economic transactions in a given period of time. (22)

balance-of-payments deficit: An excess demand for foreign currency at current exchange rates. (22)

balance-of-payments surplus: An excess demand for domestic currency at current exchange rates. (22)

barriers to entry: Obstacles such as patents that make it difficult or impossible for would-be producers to enter a particular market. (9, 10, 11, 12, 13, 15)

bilateral monopoly: A market with only one buyer (a monopsonist) and one seller (a monopolist). (17)

bond: A certificate acknowledging a debt and the amount of interest to be paid each year until repayment; an IOU. (18)

breakeven level of income: The income level at which welfare eligibility ceases. (20)

budget constraint: A line depicting all combinations of goods that are affordable with a given income and given prices. (5)

capital: Final goods produced for use in the production of other goods, such as equipment and structures. (1)

capital gain: An increase in the market value of an asset. (18)

capital-intensive: Production processes that use a high ratio of capital to labor inputs. (2)

cartel: A group of firms with an explicit, formal agreement to fix prices and output shares in a particular market. (11)

cash transfers: Income transfers that entail direct cash payments to recipients, such as Social Security, welfare, and unemployment benefits. (21)

ceteris paribus: The assumption of nothing else changing. (1, 3, 5)

closed economy: A nation that doesn't engage in international trade. (21)

collective bargaining: Direct negotiations between employers and unions to determine labor market outcomes. (17)

comparative advantage: The ability of a country to produce a specific good at a lower opportunity cost than its trading partners. (21, 23)

competitive firm: A firm without market power, with no ability to alter the market price of the goods it produces. (8)

competitive market: A market in which no buyer or seller has market power. (9)

complementary goods: Goods frequently consumed in combination; when the price of good *x* rises, the demand for good *y* falls, *ceteris paribus*. (3, 6)

concentration ratio: The proportion of total industry output produced by the largest firms (usually the four largest). (11, 12)

constant returns to scale: Increases in plant size do not affect minimum average cost; minimum per-unit costs are identical for small plants and large plants. (7)

consumer surplus: The difference between the maximum price a person is willing to pay and the price paid. (5, 10)

consumption possibilities: The alternative combinations of goods and services that a country could consume in a given time period. (21)

contestable market: An imperfectly competitive industry subject to potential entry if prices or profits increase. (10, 11, 13)

corporate stock: Shares of ownership in a corporation. (18)

corporation: A business organization having a continuous existence independent of its members (owners) and power and liabilities distinct from those of its members. (18)

cost efficiency: The amount of output associated with an additional dollar spent on input; the MPP of an input divided by its price (cost). (16)

countercyclical payment: Income transfer paid to farmers for difference between target and support prices. (15)

coupon rate: Interest rate set for a bond at time of issuance. (18)

cross-price elasticity of demand: Percentage change in the quantity demanded of *X* divided by the percentage change in the price of *Y*. (6, 12)

cross-subsidization: Use of high prices and profits on one product to subsidize low prices on another product. (13)

current yield: The rate of return on a bond; the annual interest payment divided by the bond's price. (18)

default: Failure to make scheduled payments of interest or principal on a bond. (18)

demand: The willingness and ability to buy specific quantities of a good at alternative prices in a given time period, *ceteris paribus*. (3, 5)

demand curve: A curve describing the quantities of a good a consumer is willing and able to buy at alternative prices in a given time period, *ceteris paribus*. (3, 5, 6)

demand for labor: The quantities of labor employers are willing and able to hire at alternative wage rates in a given time period, *ceteris paribus*. (16, 17)

demand schedule: A table showing the quantities of a good a consumer is willing and able to buy at alternative prices in a given time period, *ceteris paribus*. (3)

depreciation (currency): A fall in the price of one currency relative to another. (22)

derived demand: The demand for labor and other factors of production results from (depends on) the demand for final goods and services produced by these factors. (16)

devaluation: An abrupt depreciation of a currency whose value was fixed or managed by the government. (22)

dividend: Amount of corporate profits paid out for each share of stock. (18)

dumping: The sale of goods in export markets at prices below domestic prices. (20)

economic cost: The value of all resources used to produce a good or service; opportunity cost. (7, 8)

economic growth: An increase in output (real GDP); an expansion of production possibilities. (1, 2, 23)

economic profit: The difference between total revenues and total economic costs. (8, 9, 12, 13, 15)

economics: The study of how best to allocate scarce resources among competing uses. (1)

economies of scale: Reductions in minimum average costs that come about through increases in the size (scale) of plant and equipment. (7, 10, 13)

effective tax rate: Taxes paid divided by total income. (19)

efficiency: Maximum output of a good from the resources used in production. (1, 7, 9)

efficiency decision: The choice of a production process for any given rate of output. (14, 16)

elasticity of labor supply: The percentage change in the quantity of labor supplied divided by the percentage change in wage rate. (16)

embargo: A prohibition on exports or imports. (21)

emission charge: A fee imposed on polluters, based on the quantity of pollution. (14)

entrepreneurship: The assembling of resources to produce new or improved products and technologies. (1)

equilibrium price: The price at which the quantity of a good demanded in a given time period equals the quantity supplied. (3, 9, 21, 22)

equilibrium wage: The wage rate at which the quantity of labor supplied in a given time period equals the quantity of labor demanded. (16, 17)

exchange rate: The price of one country's currency expressed in terms of another's; the domestic price of a foreign currency. (22)

expected value: The probable value of a future payment, including the risk of nonpayment. (18)

explicit costs: A payment made for the use of a resource. (7, 8)

exports: Goods and services sold to foreign buyers. (21)

external costs: Costs of a market activity borne by a third party; the difference between the social and private costs of a market activity. (14)

externalities: Costs (or benefits) of a market activity borne by a third party; the difference between the social and private costs (benefits) of a market activity. (2, 4)

extreme poverty (world): World Bank income standard of less than $1.25 per day per person (inflation adjusted). (23)

factor market: Any place where factors of production (e.g., land, labor, capital) are bought and sold. (3)

factors of production: Resource inputs used to produce goods and services, e.g., land, labor, capital, entrepreneurship. (1, 2, 7)

financial intermediary: Institution (e.g., a bank or the stock market) that makes savings available to dissavers (e.g., investors). (18)

fixed costs: Costs of production that don't change when the rate of output is altered, such as the cost of basic plants and equipment. (7, 8)

flat tax: A single-rate tax system. (19)

flexible exchange rates: A system in which exchange rates are permitted to vary with market supply-and-demand conditions; floating exchange rates. (22)

foreign exchange markets: Places where foreign currencies are bought and sold. (22)

foreign exchange reserves: Holdings of foreign currencies by official government agencies, usually the central bank or treasury. (22)

free rider: An individual who reaps direct benefits from someone else's purchase (consumption) of a public good. (4)

game theory: The study of decision making in situations where strategic interaction (moves and countermoves) occurs between rivals. (11)

Gini coefficient: A mathematical summary of inequality based on the Lorenz curve. (19)

gold reserves: Stocks of gold held by a government to purchase foreign exchange. (22)

gold standard: An agreement by countries to fix the price of their currencies in terms of gold; a mechanism for fixing exchange rates. (22)

government failure: Government intervention that fails to improve economic outcomes. (1, 4, 13, 14, 19)

gross domestic product (GDP): The total market value of all final goods and services produced within a nation's borders in a given time period. (2)

Herfindahl-Hirshman Index (HHI): Measure of industry concentration that accounts for number of firms and size of each. (11)

horizontal equity: Principle that people with equal incomes should pay equal taxes. (19)

human capital: The knowledge and skills possessed by the workforce. (2, 23)

implicit cost: The value of resources used, even when no direct payment is made. (7, 8)

import quota: A limit on the quantity of a good that may be imported in a given time period. (23)

imports: Goods and services purchased from international sources. (21)

income effect of higher wages: An increased wage rate allows a person to reduce hours worked without losing income. (16)

income elasticity of demand: Percentage change in quantity demanded divided by percentage change in income. (6, 15)

income quintile: One-fifth of the population, rank-ordered by income (e.g., top fifth). (2)

income share: The proportion of total income received by a particular group. (19)

income transfers: Payments to individuals for which no current goods or services are exchanged, such as Social Security, welfare, and unemployment benefits. (19, 20)

indifference curve: A curve depicting alternative combinations of goods that yield equal satisfaction. (5)

indifference map: The set of indifference curves that depicts all possible levels of utility attainable from various combinations of goods. (5)

inequality trap: Institutional barriers that impede human and physical capital investment, particularly by the poorest segments of society. (23)

inferior good: Good for which demand decreases when income rises. (6)

inflation: An increase in the average level of prices of goods and services. (4)

initial public offering (IPO): The first issuance (sale) to the general public of stock in a corporation. (18)

in-kind income: Goods and services received directly, without payment, in a market transaction. (19)

in-kind transfers: Direct transfers of goods and services rather than cash, such as food stamps, Medicaid benefits, and housing subsidies. (20, 23)

investment decision: The decision to build, buy, or lease plants and equipment; to enter or exit an industry. (8, 9)

investment rate: The percentage of total output (GDP) allocated to the production of new plants, equipment, and structures. (23)

labor force participation rate: The percentage of the working-age population working or seeking employment. (20)

labor supply: The willingness and ability to work specific amounts of time at alternative wage rates in a given time period, *ceteris paribus*. (16, 17, 20)

laissez faire: The doctrine of "leave it alone," of nonintervention by government in the market mechanism. (1, 13)

law of demand: The quantity of a good demanded in a given time period increases as its price falls, *ceteris paribus*. (3, 5, 6)

law of diminishing marginal utility: The marginal utility of a good declines as more of it is consumed in a given time period. (5)

law of diminishing returns: The marginal physical product of a variable input declines as more of it is employed with a given quantity of other (fixed) inputs. (7, 16)

law of supply: The quantity of a good supplied in a given time period increases as its price increases, *ceteris paribus*. (3, 6)

liquidity: The ability of an asset to be converted into cash. (18)

loan rate: The implicit price paid by the government for surplus crops taken as collateral for loans to farmers. (15)

long run: A period of time long enough for all inputs to be varied (no fixed costs). (7, 8)

long-run competitive equilibrium: $p = MC =$ minimum ATC. (9)

Lorenz curve: A graphic illustration of the cumulative size distribution of income; contrasts complete equality with the actual distribution of income. (19)

macroeconomics: The study of aggregate economic behavior, of the economy as a whole. (1)

managed exchange rates: A system in which governments intervene in foreign exchange markets to limit but not eliminate exchange rate fluctuations; "dirty floats." (22)

marginal cost (MC): The increase in total cost associated with a one-unit increase in production. (7, 8, 9)

marginal cost pricing: The offer (supply) of goods at prices equal to their marginal cost. (9, 10, 12, 13)

marginal factor cost (MFC): The change in total costs that results from a one-unit increase in the quantity of a factor employed. (17)

marginal physical product (MPP): The change in total output associated with one additional unit of input. (7, 16)

marginal rate of substitution: The rate at which a consumer is willing to exchange one good for another; the relative marginal utilities of two goods. (5)

marginal revenue (MR): The change in total revenue that results from a one-unit increase in the quantity sold. (8, 10)

marginal revenue product (MRP): The change in total revenue associated with one additional unit of input. (16, 17, 19)

marginal tax rate: The tax rate imposed on the last (marginal) dollar of income. (19, 20)

marginal utility: The change in total utility obtained by consuming one additional (marginal) unit of a good or service. (5)

marginal wage: The change in total wages paid associated with a one-unit increase in the quantity of labor employed. (17)

market demand: The total quantities of a good or service people are willing and able to buy at alternative prices in a given time period; the sum of individual demands. (3, 5)

market failure: An imperfection in the market mechanism that prevents optimal outcomes. (1, 4, 11, 13, 14, 19, 20)

market mechanism: The use of market prices and sales to signal desired outputs (or resource allocations). (1, 3, 4, 9)

market power: The ability to alter the market price of a good or service. (4, 8, 10, 12, 15, 17)

market share: The percentage of total market output produced by a single firm. (11)

market shortage: The amount by which the quantity demanded exceeds the quantity supplied at a given price; excess demand. (3, 22)

market structure: The number and relative size of firms in an industry. (8, 10)

market supply: The total quantities of a good that sellers are willing and able to sell at alternative prices in a given time period, *ceteris paribus*. (3, 9)

market supply of labor: The total quantity of labor that workers are willing and able to supply at alternative wage rates in a given time period, *ceteris paribus*. (16)

market surplus: The amount by which the quantity supplied exceeds the quantity demanded at a given price; excess supply. (3, 15, 16)

merit good: A good or service society deems everyone is entitled to some minimal quantity of. (4)

microeconomics: The study of individual behavior in the economy, of the components of the larger economy. (1)

microfinance: The granting of small ("micro"), unsecured loans to small businesses and entrepreneurs. (23)

Millennium Aid Goal: United Nations goal of raising foreign aid levels to 0.7 percent of donor-country GDP. (23)

Millennium Poverty Goal: United Nations goal of reducing global rate of extreme poverty to 15 percent by 2015. (23)

mixed economy: An economy that uses both market signals and government directives to allocate goods and resources. (1)

monopolistic competition: A market in which many firms produce similar goods or services but each maintains some independent control of its own price. (12)

monopoly: A firm that produces the entire market supply of a particular good or service. (2, 4, 8, 10)

monopsony: A market in which there's only one buyer. (17)

moral hazard: An incentive to engage in undesirable behavior. (20)

natural monopoly: An industry in which one firm can achieve economies of scale over the entire range of market supply. (4, 10, 13)

nominal tax rate: Taxes paid divided by taxable income. (19)

normal good: Good for which demand increases when income rises. (6)

normal profit: The opportunity cost of capital; zero economic profit. (8)

oligopolist: One of the dominant firms in an oligopoly. (11)

oligopoly: A market in which a few firms produce all or most of the market supply of a particular good or service. (11)

open economy: A nation that engages in international trade. (21)

opportunity cost: The most desired goods or services that are forgone in order to obtain something else. (1, 3, 4, 5, 7, 9, 13, 14, 21)

opportunity wage: The highest wage an individual would earn in his or her best alternative job. (16)

optimal consumption: The mix of consumer purchases that maximizes the utility attainable from available income. (5)

optimal mix of output: The most desirable combination of output attainable with existing resources, technology, and social values. (4)

optimal rate of pollution: The rate of pollution that occurs when the marginal social benefit of pollution control equals its marginal social cost. (14)

outsourcing: The relocation of production to foreign countries. (16)

par value: The face value of a bond; the amount to be repaid when the bond is due. (18)

parity: The relative price of farm products in the period 1910–1914. (15)

payoff matrix: A table showing the risks and rewards of alternative decision options. (11)

per capita GDP: The dollar value of GDP divided by total population; average GDP. (2)

perfect competition: A market in which no buyer or seller has market power. (8)

personal income (PI): Income received by households before payment of personal taxes. (19)

poverty gap: The shortfall between actual income and the poverty threshold. (20)

poverty rate: Percentage of the population counted as poor. (23)

poverty threshold (U.S.): Annual income of less than $22,000 for a family of four (2010, inflation adjusted). (23)

predatory pricing: Temporary price reductions designed to alter market shares or drive out competition. (11)

present discounted value (PDV): The value today of future payments, adjusted for interest accrual. (18)

price ceiling: An upper limit imposed on the price of a good. (3, 13)

price discrimination: The sale of an individual good at different prices to different consumers. (5, 10)

price/earnings (P/E) ratio: The price of a stock share divided by earnings (profit) per share. (18)

price elasticity of demand: The percentage change in quantity demanded divided by the percentage change in price. (6, 10, 15)

price elasticity of supply: The percentage change in quantity supplied divided by the percentage change in price. (6)

price-fixing: Explicit agreements among producers regarding the price(s) at which a good is to be sold. (11)

price floor: Lower limit set for the price of a good. (3)

price leadership: An oligopolistic pricing pattern that allows one firm to establish the (market) price for all firms in the industry. (11)

private costs: The costs of an economic activity directly borne by the immediate producer or consumer (excluding externalities). (14)

private good: A good or service whose consumption by one person excludes consumption by others. (4)

product differentiation: Features that make one product appear different from competing products in the same market. (11, 12, 13)

product market: Any place where finished goods and services (products) are bought and sold. (3)

production decision: The selection of the short-run rate of output (with existing plants and equipment). (8, 9, 10, 12, 14)

production function: A technological relationship expressing the maximum quantity of a good attainable from different combinations of factor inputs. (7)

production possibilities: The alternative combinations of final goods and services that could be produced in a given period with all available resources and technology. (1, 2, 21)

production process: A specific combination of resources used to produce a good or service. (16)

productivity: Output per unit of input—for example, output per labor-hour. (2, 7, 17, 23)

profit: The difference between total revenue and total cost. (7, 8, 15)

profit maximization rule: Produce at that rate of output where marginal revenue equals marginal cost. (8, 10)

profit per unit: Total profit divided by the quantity produced in a given time period; price minus average total cost. (9)

progressive tax: A tax system in which tax rates rise as incomes rise. (4, 19)

proportional tax: A tax that levies the same rate on every dollar of income. (4)

public choice: Theory of public sector behavior emphasizing rational self-interest of decision makers and voters. (4)

public good: A good or service whose consumption by one person does not exclude consumption by others. (4)

quota: A limit on the quantity of a good that may be imported in a given time period. (21)

regressive tax: A tax system in which tax rates fall as incomes rise. (4, 19)

regulation: Government intervention to alter the behavior of firms—for example, in pricing, output, or advertising. (13)

retained earnings: Amount of corporate profits not paid out in dividends. (18)

risk premium: The difference in rates of return on risky (uncertain) and safe (certain) investments. (18)

scarcity: Lack of enough resources to satisfy all desired uses of those resources. (1)

severe poverty (world): World Bank income standard of $2 per day per person (inflation adjusted). (23)

shift in demand: A change in the quantity demanded at any (every) price. (3, 5)

short run: The period in which the quantity (and quality) of some inputs can't be changed. (7, 8)

short-run competitive equilibrium: $p = $ MC. (9)

shutdown point: The rate of output where price equals minimum AVC. (8, 9)

size distribution of income: The way total personal income is divided up among households or income classes. (19)

social costs: The full resource costs of an economic activity, including externalities. (14)

social insurance programs: Event-conditioned income transfers intended to reduce the costs of specific problems, such as Social Security and unemployment insurance. (20)

substitute goods: Goods that substitute for each other; when the price of good x rises, the demand for good y increases, *ceteris paribus*. (3, 6, 13)

substitution effect of higher wages: An increased wage rate encourages people to work more hours (to substitute labor for leisure). (16)

supply: The ability and willingness to sell (produce) specific quantities of a good at alternative prices in a given time period, *ceteris paribus*. (3)

supply curve: A curve describing the quantities of a good a producer is willing and able to sell (produce) at alternative prices in a given time period, *ceteris paribus*. (8)

target efficiency: The percentage of income transfers that go to the intended recipients and purposes. (20)

tariff: A tax (duty) imposed on imported goods. (21)

tax base: The amount of income or property directly subject to nominal tax rates. (19)

tax elasticity of labor supply: The percentage change in quantity of labor supplied divided by the percentage change in tax rates. (20)

tax elasticity of supply: The percentage change in quantity supplied divided by the percentage change in tax rates. (19)

tax incidence: Distribution of the real burden of a tax. (19)

terms of trade: The rate at which goods are exchanged; the amount of good A given up for good B in trade. (21)

total cost: The market value of all resources used to produce a good or service. (7)

total revenue: The price of a product multiplied by the quantity sold in a given time period: $p \times q$. (5, 6, 8)

total utility: The amount of satisfaction obtained from entire consumption of a product. (5)

trade deficit: The amount by which the value of imports exceeds the value of exports in a given time period (negative net exports). (21, 22)

trade surplus: The amount by which the value of exports exceeds the value of imports in a given time period (positive net exports). (21)

transfer payments: Payments to individuals for which no current goods or services are exchanged, like Social Security, welfare, and unemployment benefits. (4)

unemployment: The inability of labor force participants to find jobs. (4)

union shop: An employment setting in which all workers must join the union within 30 days after being employed. (17)

unionization rate: The percentage of the labor force belonging to a union. (17)

unit labor cost: Hourly wage rate divided by output per labor-hour. (7)

utility: The pleasure or satisfaction obtained from a good or service. (5)

variable costs: Costs of production that change when the rate of output is altered, such as labor and material costs. (7, 8)

vertical equity: Principle that people with higher incomes should pay more taxes. (19)

voluntary restraint agreement (VRA): An agreement to reduce the volume of trade in a specific good; a "voluntary" quota. (21)

wage replacement rate: The percentage of base wages paid out in benefits. (20)

wealth: The market value of assets. (19)

welfare programs: Means-tested income transfer programs, such as welfare and food stamps. (20)

Note: **Bold** page numbers indicate definitions; page numbers followed by *n* indicate material in notes.

A

Absolute advantage
  absolute costs, 453
  defined, **453**
Accounting cost, economic cost versus, 151–152
Accounting profits, 167–168
Acer, 266
Acid rain, 303
Acohido, Byron, 228
Acquisition. *See* Mergers and acquisitions
Acreage set-asides, 331
Across-nation income redistribution, 496–497
Administrative costs, 288–289
Adolescents, demand and, 94
Advanced Micro Devices, 228
Advertising
  best global brands, 276
  caveat emptor and, 105–106
  future of economics and, 105–106, 274–276
  as nonprice competition, 257
AFL-CIO, 373–374
Aggregate decisions, 3–4
Agriculture. *See* Farming
Agriculture and Consumer Protection Act of
    1973, 334
AIDS, 501
Air pollution
  health effects of, 306
  types of, 303–304
Airline Deregulation Act of 1978, 293
Airlines, 230
  deregulation of, 293–294
  oligopoly and, 248, 255
Alberts, Sheklon, 417
Ali, Muhammad, 345
Alligator market, 130
Alling, William R., 229
Alternative production processes, 358
Aluminum Company of America (ALCOA), 259
American Airlines, 248, 255
American Association of Retired Persons (AARP), 438
American Bar Association (ABA), 242
American Enterprise Institute, 290
American Express, 242
American Federation of Labor-Congress of Industrial Organizations
    (AFL-CIO), 373–374
American Greetings, 242
American Home Products, 253, 266
American Medical Association (AMA), 242
American Milk Producers, 242
American Safety Razor, 242
American Tobacco Company, 257
Amgen, 36

Anheuser-Busch Cos., 242, 256, 471
Antitrust, 76–77
  contestability, 294
  defined, **76, 233, 258, 283**
  deregulation versus, 283–285
  enforcement of, 258–260
  Herfindahl-Hirshman Index, 259–260
  industry behavior and, 258–260
  industry structure and, 259
  objections to, 259
AOL-Time Warner, 242, 275
Apple Computer, Inc., 92, 98, 116, 164, 193, 200–201, 204–207,
    208–209, 239, 242, 269, 275, 276, 401, 471
Apple iPhone, 51, 92, 98, 116, 121, 127, 128, 195–197
Appleby, Julie, 225
Appreciation (currency), **476**
Argentina, currency devaluation, 485
Armey, Dick, 422
Asian crisis of 1997–1998, 325, 336, 478, 485
Ask.com, 242
Associated Press (AP), 413
AST, 204
Atari, 195, 203–204
AT&T, 51, 121, 233, 234–235, 241, 242, 260, 275, 276, 287, 291–292
Auction commissions, 242, 254
Average costs, 145–148, 149–151
Average fixed cost (AFC), 146–147
  defined, **146**
  falling, 146–147
Average total cost (ATC)
  in competitive markets, 198
  defined, **145, 198, 221**
  intersection with marginal cost, 149–151
  long-run, 152–153
  in monopoly, 221
  natural monopoly and, 283–284, 286
  u-shaped, 147
Average variable cost (AVC)
  defined, **146**
  rising, 147
  in shutdown decision, 180–181

B

Baby Boomers, 435, 439
Baby formula, price-fixing and, 253
Bahl, Kushe, 206
Bailouts, currency, 485–486
Baker, David R., 314
Balance of payments, 473–475, 482
  balance-of-payments deficit, 481
  balance-of-payments surplus, 481
  capital account balance, 475

Balance of payments—*Cont.*
    current account balance, 475
    defined, **474**
    exchange rates and, 480–485
    trade balance, 474–475
Ballor, Jordan, 82
Ballot-box economics, 85
Bangladesh, microloans in, 502
Barbaro, Michael, 380
Barclay's Bank, 471
Barnes and Noble, 273
Barriers to entry
    in agriculture, 326
    in competitive markets, 193, 198
    defined, **193, 217, 255, 268, 293, 326**
    deregulation and, 293–294
    in monopolistic competition, 268
    in monopoly, 217, 222, 223, 226–227, 293–294
    in natural monopoly, 293–294
    in oligopoly, 255–258
    types of, 255–258
Barriers to trade, 458–464
    comparative effects of, 461–463
    embargoes, 458–459
    nontariff barriers, 464
    quotas, 331, 461, 462–463
    tariffs, 459–460, 462, 508
    voluntary restraint agreements, 463–464
Becker, Gary S., 19, 113, 123, 479
Beech-Nut, 242
Beecham, 242
"Beggar they neighbor" policies, 460–461
Behavior. *See also* Industry behavior
    antitrust policy and, 258–259, 283
    consumer, 46, 92
    maximizing, 46
Bell, F. W., 120*n*
Benefits, external, 75–76
Berg, Cart, 304
Best Buy, 194
Bic, 242
Bilateral monopoly, 377–378
Birth control, 498–499
BlackBerry, 255
Bloated costs, 286–287, 293, 296
Bloomberg, Michael, 317
Blumenthal, Susan, 500
BMW, 472–473, 475, 480
Boeing Co., 230, 446
Bohlen, Celestine, 218
Bonds, 398–401
    bond issuance, 398–399
    bond referenda, 85
    bond trading, 399
    defined, **398**
    yields, 399–401
Bono, 490
Booms, 396–397
Borders, 273
Boston Tea Party of 1776, 459

BP, 20, 58, 59, 63, 243
BRAC, 502
Branca, Michael, 256
Brand image, in monopolistic competition, 268
Brand loyalty, in monopolistic competition, 268–270
Brazil, currency devaluation, 485
Breakeven level of income, 434
Bristol-Meyers Squibb, 253
British Petroleum (BP), 20, 58, 59, 63, 243
Brown & Williamson, 257
Budget constraint
    defined, **110**
    utility maximization and, 110–112
Burger King, 270, 273
Burlington-Northern, 291
Bush, George H. W., 320, 485
Bush, George W., 6, 16, 19–20, 416
Business. *See also* Entrepreneurship
    business climate, economic growth and, 505–506
    circular flow and, 47–48
    maximizing behavior of, 46
Business cycles
    Great Depression. *See* Great Depression
    Great Recession of 2008–2009. *See* Great Recession of 2008–2009
Busts, 396–397
"Buy American" policies, 336, 460, 471
Buyer concentration, 376

C
Cable Communications Policy Act of 1984, 295
Cable television, deregulation and, 295–296
Cable Television Consumer Protection and Competition Act of 1992, 295
Cadbury Schweppes, 242, 254
Campbell, 241, 242
Campbell Cereal Company, 256–257
Candy, price-fixing in, 254
Canon, 242
Cap-and-trade system, 313–314
Capital
    defined, **5**
    as factor of production, 4–5
Capital account balance, 475
Capital gains
    on corporate stock, 393
    defined, **393**
Capital-intensive production, 35
Capital investment, 502–503
Capital stock, 35
Caribou, 266
Carl XVI Gustaf, King, 479
Carl's Jr., 273
Carnation, 242
Carolina Power and Light Company, 314
Carson, John, 246
Cartels, 254
Carty, Sharon Silke, 182
Cash transfers, 428–429
Casio, 198, 242

Castro, Fidel, 459, 505
Caterpillar, Inc., 366, 372, 378–379, 446
Catfish farming, 177, 184, 190, 191, 326
Causation, graphs and, 26
Caveat emptor, 105–106
Central African Republic, health in, 500
Central American Free Trade Agreement (CAFTA), 466
CenturyLink, 242
Ceteris paribus
   defined, **19, 52, 98**
   individual demand and, 52, 98
   marginal utility and, 98
Chad, education in, 499
Change to Win Coalition, 374
Charpak, Georges, 479
Chávez, Hugo, 505
Chief executive officers (CEOs), pay caps for, 360–362
China
   dumping and, 457, 458
   economic growth and, 498–499, 504–506
   exchange rate intervention and, 483
   government failure and, 17
   gross domestic product (GDP) of, 32–33
   international trade and, 457, 458
   Kyoto Treaty and, 320
   production costs and, 136, 156
   reducing population growth, 498–499
   tariffs on, 459, 460
   trade barriers and, 507
   voluntary restraint agreements, 463
Chine Mobile, 276
Choice, 13–18
   balance and, 18
   in command economy, 14
   debates concerning, 14–16
   "for whom" decisions, 13
   government failure and, 17
   "how" decisions, 13
   in market economy, 13–14
   market failure and, 17
   in mixed economy, 14, 17
   "what" decisions, 13
Christie's, 242, 254
Chrysler, 456
Church & Dwight, 242
Cigarettes
   nonprice competition and, 257
   price elasticity of demand and, 121
   secondhand smoking and, 74–75
Circular flow, 47–48
   dollars and exchange, 48
   in factor markets, 47
   opportunity cost and, 48
   in product markets, 47
   supply and demand, 47–48
Citigroup, 502
Clayton Act of 1914, 233, 234, 258
Clean Air Act of 1970, 315
Clean Air Act of 1990, 315
Cline, Harry, 456

Cline, William, 507*n*
Clinton, Bill, 16, 123, 361–362, 485
Closed economy, 448
Coca-Cola Company, 239, 242, 246, 251, 266, 268, 269, 274–275, 276, 472
The Coffee Beanery, 266
Cold War, 250–251
Colgate-Palmolive, 242
Collective bargaining, 377–380
   defined, **378**
   final settlement in, 379–380
   possible agreements in, 378–379
   pressure to settle in, 379
College tuition, 253
Columbus, Christopher, 386–389, 397–398
Command-and-control system, 315
Command economy
   government failure and, 17
   in international economics, 15
   nature of, 14
Commodity Credit Corporation (CCC), 332–333
Communism, 14, 218
Communist Manifesto (Marx), 14
Communities and Small-Scale Mining (CASM), 131
Compaq, 204
Comparative advantage, 452–453
   absolute costs, 453
   defined, **452, 506**
   nature of, 452
   opportunity costs, 452
   pursuit of, 452–453
   regional trade pacts and, 465–466
   world trade and, 506–507
Compassion, Social Security and, 432
Competition
   in agriculture, 326
   import-competing industries, 456
Competitive equilibrium, 367
Competitive firms, 164–186. *See also* Competitive markets; Monopolistic competition
   defined, **171**
   determinants of supply, 182–185
   economic versus accounting profit, 166–168
   hiring decisions in, 352–355
   Internet-based price competition, 186
   investment decision, 181–182, 191–192
   market structure and, 169–170
   nature of perfect competition, 170–186
   production decision, 172–173, 197
   profit-maximizing rule, 174–179, 215
   profit motive, 165–166
   shutdown decision, 180–181, 203
Competitive markets, 190–209. *See also* Competitive firms; Monopolistic competition
   competitive process and, 204–207
   computers, 194–204
   defined, **193**
   electronics, 194, 206, 208–209
   market evolution, 195–197
   market supply curve, 191–194

Competitive markets—*Cont.*
microcomputers, 194–204
oligopoly versus, 251–253
production decision in, 197
Complementary goods, 51, 126–127
Compliance costs, 289
Computer industry. *See also* Internet; Technology
competitive markets, 194–204
entrepreneurship in, 194–204, 208–209
market power in, 217–222
monopoly and, 217–222
Concentration ratio, 241, 266–267, 294
Congo, health in, 500
Congressional Budget Office (CBO), 334
Constant returns to scale, 155
Consumer choice, 92–113
choosing among products, 101–105
consumer surplus, 99–100
demand curve, 95–99
determinants of demand, 93–95
market demand, 99
price discrimination, 101
Consumer demand, 93–99. *See also* Demand
cross-price elasticity of, 126–128, 269, 274
demand, defined, **94**
determinants of, 93–95
economic explanation for, 94–95
income elasticity of, 128–130, 328
key factors in, 94
price elasticity of, 117–128, 326–327
shifts in, 126
sociopsychiatric explanation for, 93
Consumer surplus, 99–100
defined, **226**
in monopoly, 226
Consumers
circular flow and, 47–48
maximizing behavior of, 46
Consumption (C), externalities in, 310
Consumption possibilities
defined, **448**–449
with trade, 449–451
without trade, 448–449
Contestable markets, 231–**232, 241, 294**
Continental Airlines, 248, 255
Coolidge, Calvin, 330
Coordination problems, in oligopoly, 253–255
Coors, 242
Copenhagen Accord (Copenhagen Climate Change Conference), 320
Core issues in economics, 2–21
basic decisions, 12–13
choice mechanisms, 13–18
economic growth, 12
economy is us, 3–4
individual versus aggregate decisions, 3–4
nature of economics, 18–20
production possibilities, 7–12, 13
scarcity, 4–6
Corning Inc., 458
Corporate social responsibility, 344

Corporate stock, 392–398
characteristics of, 392
defined, **392**
initial public offerings, 393
market fluctuations, 394–397
resource allocation and, 397–398
secondary trading, 393–394
stock returns, 392–393
Corporations. *See also* Stock market
corporate taxes, 80–81
defined, **392**
Cost-benefit analysis
of environmental protection, 317
government failure and, 84–85
valuation problems, 84–85
Cost efficiency
defined, **358**
labor market, 358
Costco, 194
Costs
balancing benefits and, 290–291
bloated, 286–287, 293, 296
of environmental regulation, 317–318
external, 75
market incentives versus, 433–434
output and, 172–173
of regulation, 288–291
in U.S. farm policy, 335
Council on Environmental Quality, 302
Countercyclical payment, 334
Coupon rate, 399
Craft unions, 368. *See also* Labor unions
Cranick, Gene, 73
Creative Technology, 208
Cross-price elasticity of demand
calculating, 127–128
defined, **128, 269**
in monopolistic competition, 269, 274
nature of, 126–128
Cross-subsidization, 293
CSX, 291
Cuba
economic growth in, 505
U.S. embargo of, 459
Curity, 242
Currency. *See also* Dollars; Exchange rates; Foreign exchange markets
appreciation of, 476
depreciation of, 475–476
devaluation of, 485–486
Current account balance, 475
Current yield, 399–401
Cyclical instability. *See* Great Recession of 2008–2009

D

Dairy products, Dairy Termination Program, 331
Dairymen, Inc., 242
Dannon, 266
Dean Foods, 242

Default
  bond, 399
  defined, **399**
Defense spending. *See also* War
  guns versus butter and, 7, 9–10
  production possibilities curve and, 9–10
Deficiency payments, in agriculture, 333
Deficits
  balance-of-payments, 481
  trade, 447, 475
Degrees of power, 240
Dell Computer, 36, 186, 204, 208, 239, 269, 270
Dell Inc., 182
Delta Air Lines, 248, 255
Demand, 48–55. *See also* Consumer demand; Demand curve
  ceteris paribus and, 52, 98
  defined, **48, 94**
  demand schedule, 49–50, 54–55
  determinants of, 51–52, 97–99
  equilibrium and, 59–63
  income elasticity of, 128–130, 328
  individual, 49–53
  inelastic, 326–328
  for labor, 347–352, 352–353, 367
  law of, 51, 98–99, 113
  movements in, 53
  price elasticity of, 225, 326–327
  shifts in, 52–53, 62, 105–106, 126
  in U.S. farm policy, 331–333
Demand curve, 50–51, 95–99
  advertising and, 105–106
  defined, **50, 98**–99, **113, 117**
  deriving, 112–113
  individual, 50–51
  kinked, 247–249
  labor, 348, 352–355
  in monopoly, 214
  price and, 97–99
  quantity and, 97–99
  utility theory, 95–97
Demand for labor, 367
Demand schedule, 54–55
  defined, **49**
  individual, 49–50
Demick, Barbara, 10
Deogun, Nikhil, 251
Depreciation (currency), **475**–476
Depression. *See also* Great Depression
  first farm depression (1920–1940), 329–330
  second farm depression (1980–1986), 335
Deregulation. *See also* Regulation
  antitrust versus, 283–285
  examples of, 291–297
  future of, 297–298, 336
  of U.S. farm policy, 336
Derived demand
  defined, **348**
  for labor, 347–348
Determinants of demand, 51–52, 97–99
Determinants of supply, 56, 182–185

Devaluation, **485**–486
Development. *See* Economic growth
Developmental patterns, 35
Dial, 242
Digital Equipment, 198
Diminishing marginal physical product of labor, 350–351
Diminishing marginal returns, 141
Diminishing marginal revenue cost of labor, 351–352
Diminishing marginal utility, 95–97
Direct government expenditures, 78
Direct income support, in agriculture, 334–335
Discover, 242
Diseconomies of scale, 155–156
Disney, 446–447
Disneyland, 167
Distribution control, as barrier to entry, 255–256
Dividends, 393
Dockery, Douglas, 306
Dollar costs, 143–151
  average costs, 145–148, 149–151
  cost summary, 149–151
  marginal costs, 148–151
  total cost, 143–145
Dollars. *See also* Currency; Exchange rates; Foreign exchange markets
  demand for, 471
  supply of, 472
  value of, 472–473, 477
Domino's, 52, 266
Dow, 446
Dumping, 457, 458
Dunkin' Donuts, 265, 267, 269, 273
Dunlop, 242
Duopoly, 240
Duracell, 242

E

E-commerce, 186
Eagle Snacks, 257
Earnings test, 436, 438
Eastman Kodak, 242
Economic cost
  accounting costs versus, 151–152
  defined, **152, 166**
Economic development. *See* Economic growth
Economic explanation for demand, 94
Economic growth
  agricultural development and, 503–504
  capital investment and, 502–503
  defined, **12, 33, 497**
  entrepreneurship and, 505, 508–509
  global poverty and, 497–507
  of government, 78–79
  human capital development in, 35, 499–501
  institutional reform and, 504–506
  population growth and, 33–34, 498–499
  Rostow's stages of development, 501–502
  world trade and, 506–507

Economic profits, 166–168
    in agriculture, 326
    in competitive markets, 192–193
    defined, **167, 193, 270, 285, 326**
    entry and exit in monopolistic competition,
       270–272
    unregulated behavior and, 285–286
    zero, 192–193, 206–207
Economics
    core issues in, 2–21
    defined, **5**–6
    ends versus means, 18
    future of. *See* Future of economics
    graphs in, 22–26
    international. *See* International economics
    macroeconomics versus microeconomics, 18–19.
       See also Macroeconomics;
Microeconomics
    nature of, 18–20
    normative versus positive analysis, 18
    politics versus, 19–20, 85
    theory versus reality, 19–20
Economies of scale, 154–156
    as barrier to entry, 217–218, 227
    constant returns to scale, 155
    defined, **154, 217, 284**
    diseconomies of scale versus, 155–156
    illustrated, 155
    market power and, 217–218, 227, 229–231
    monopoly and, 217–218, 284
    natural monopoly and, 284
Economist in Chief role, 2–3, 5
Education
    college tuition, 253
    as external benefit, 75–76
    human capital and, 35, 36, 499–500
    ivy league college price-fixing, 253
    price competition and, 253
Education gap, 35, 36
Effective tax rates, 415
Efficiency
    cost efficiency, 358
    costs of, 290
    defined, **10, 138, 206**
    efficiency decision, 307–308, 360
    environmental protection and, 307–308
    federal income taxes and, 412–414
    government failure and, 84
    in labor market, 358–360
    market economy and, 14
    minimum average cost, 206
    monopolistic competition and, 273–274
    in natural monopoly, 286
    price, 286
    production, 286
    production function and, 138–139
    production possibilities and, 10–11
    target, 429
    taxation and, 422–423
Efficiency decision, 307–308, **360**

Elasticity
    cross-price, 126–128, 269, 274
    determinants of, 122–123
    income elasticity of demand, 128–130, 328
    price elasticity of demand, 117–128, 225, 326–327
    price elasticity of supply, 130
    tax elasticity of supply, 412–414
Elasticity of labor supply, 347
Electric utility industry, 282
    cap-and-trade permits, 313–314
    deregulation of, 296–297
    oligopoly and, 253, 254
    profit maximization in, 308
Electronics. *See also* Computer industry
    competitive markets, 194, 206, 208–209
Eliasson, Jan, 500
Ellison, Larry, 342, 360
Embargoes, 458–459
Emission charges, 311–312
Employer power, 374–377
    in monopsony, 374–377
    potential use of, 376–377
Ends versus means, 18
Engardio, Pete, 194
Entergy, 308
Entrepreneurship
    in competitive firms, 168
    in computer industry, 194–204, 208–209
    defined, **5**
    economic growth and, 505, 508–509
    as factor of production, 4–5
    market power and, 229
    venture capital, 401–402
Entry and exit, 191–192, 203–204, 270–272
Entry barriers. *See* Barriers to entry
Entry effects, in monopolistic competition, 271–272
Environmental protection, 38, 302–321
    air pollution, 303–304, 306
    cost-benefit analysis of, 317
    future of, 319–320
    market failure and, 308–310
    market incentives for, 306–308
    pollution damages and, 305–306
    regulatory options, 311–315
    solid waste pollution, 305
    water pollution, 304–305, 500
Epson, 242
Equal pay, 353
Equilibrium, 59–63
    changes in, 61–63
    international trade and, 461–462
    labor market, 355–357, 367
    market clearing and, 59–60
    market mechanism and, 60
    market shortage, 60–61, 63
    market surplus, 60, 63, 330, 356
    in monopolistic competition, 272
    self-adjusting prices, 61
    of supply and demand, 59–63
Equilibrium price, 59, 191, 461, 473

Equilibrium wages, 355, 367
Equity. *See* Inequity
Ethanol, 329
Ethiopia, farm productivity in, 503–504
European Monetary Union (EMU), 484
European Union (EU)
   agriculture in, 333
   international trade and, 506–507
   nontariff barriers, 464
   voluntary restraint agreements, 463
   World Trade Organization (WTO) and, 465
Eveready, 242
Excess capacity, monopolistic competition and, 273
Exchange rates
   appreciation and, 475–476
   currency bailouts, 485–486
   defined, **471**
   depreciation and, 475–476
   devaluation, 485–486
   dollars and, 48
   exchange rate intervention, 480–485
   fixed, 480–484
   foreign exchange markets and, 471–475, 478–486
   international comparison of, 474
   market forces and, 476–478
   resistance to changes in, 478–480
   specialization and, 46
Excise taxes, 81
Exclusion, by labor unions, 371–372
Expectations
   in determining demand, 94, 107
   indifference curves and, 107
   individual demand and, 52
   profit, 394–395
Expected value
   defined, **391**
   in present value of future profits, 391
Explicit costs, 151, 166
Exports
   comparative export ratios, 446
   defined, **446**
   export industries, 456
   U.S., 446–447
External costs, 308
Externalities, 74–76
   benefits, 75–76
   in consumption, 310
   costs, 75
   defined, **38, 74, 308**
   environmental protection and, 308–310, 320
   inequity and, 77
   market power and, 76–77
   in production, 308–310
   secondhand smoking, 74–75
"Extreme" poverty (world), 492
ExxonMobil, 243, 269, 472

F

Facebook, 401–402
Factor markets, 47

Factor mobility, 36
Factors of production, 35–38. *See also* Capital; Entrepreneurship; Factor markets; Human capital; Labor force
   capital stock, 35
   defined, **4, 35, 137**
   described, 4–5
   government and, 37–38
   land, 4–5
   productivity and, 35–37
   striking a balance, 38
Faiola, Anthony, 246
Fairness, taxes and, 420–422
Fanelli, James, 74
Farm Act of 1990, 336
Farm Act of 2002, 337
Farm Act of 2008, 325, 337
Farm Act of 2012, 337
Farm Security Act of 1985, 336
Farm Security Act of 2001, 325
Farming, 325–338
   agricultural development and, 503–504
   catfish, 177, 184, 190, 191, 326
   destabilizing forces in, 326–328
   first farm depression (1920–1940), 329–330
   food shortage in North Korea, 10
   future of, 335–337
   international perspective on, 333, 456
   second farm depression (1980–1986), 335
   U.S. farm policy, 330–335
Federal Express, 36
Federal government. *See also* Federal income taxes; Regulation; United States economy
   direct expenditures of, 78
   growth of, 78–79
   income transfers of, 77, 78
Federal income taxes, 80, 411–417, 422–423
   efficiency and, 412–414
   equity and, 414–416
   flat tax, 422–423
   policies concerning, 416–417
   tax brackets and rates, 411–412
Federal Trade Commission Act of 1914, 233, 234, 258
Ferdinand, King, 386, 388, 389
Ferenczi, Peter, 260
Fields, W. C., 217
Financial intermediaries, 387
Financial markets, 386–403. *See also* International finance
   bond market, 398–401
   capital investment and, 502–503
   economic growth and, 502–503
   present value of future profits, 388–392
   role of, 387–388
   stock market, 392–398
   venture capital market, 401–402
Fines, pollution, 313
Firestone, 266
Firm demand, market demand versus, 171
Firm size
   in global perspective, 243
   in measuring market power, 241

Fischer, Edmond, 479
Fisher, Marc, 231
Fisher-Price, 266
Fixed costs (FC), 144, 172, 283–284
Fixed exchange rates, 480–484
Flat tax, 422–423
Flexible exchange rates, 484–485
Food. *See also* Farming
  government stockpiles, 332–333
  guns versus butter, 7, 9–10
  shortages in North Korea, 10
Food stamps. *See* Supplemental Nutrition Assistance Program (SNAP)
Food Workers, 373, 382
"For whom" decisions
  market outcomes and, 64
  nature of, 13, 30
  in the U.S. economy, 38–40
Ford, Henry, 196, 213, 232
Ford Motor Company, 196, 213, 232, 275, 456
Foreign aid, in across-nation income redistribution, 496–497
Foreign exchange. *See* Exchange rates; Foreign exchange markets
Foreign exchange markets, 471–475. *See also* Exchange rates
  balance of payments and, 473–475, 482
  currency bailouts, 485–486
  defined, **478**
  demand for dollars, 471
  equilibrium in, 461
  market dynamics, 475–478
  supply of dollars, 472
  value of the dollar, 472–473
Foreign exchange reserves, 481
Foreign trade. *See* International trade
Forero, Juan, 505
Frank, Robert, 256
Free rider, 72–73
Free-trade equilibrium, 462
Freedom to Farm Act of 1996, 325, 336
Freud, Sigmund, 94–95
Friedman, Milton, 422
Frito-Lay, 256, 257
Fujishige, Hiroshi, 167
Fullerton, Don, 312
Future of economics. *See also* Great Recession of 2008–2009
  advertising, 105–106, 274–276
  antitrust enforcement, 258–260
  competitive electronics markets, 208–209
  deregulation and, 297–298, 336
  ending global poverty, 41
  energy independence, 131
  farm policy, 335–337
  global competitiveness, 156–158
  greenhouse threat, 319–320
  international trade and, 465–466
  Internet-based price competition, 186
  monopoly and, 232–235
  organ transplants and, 64–66
  pay caps for executives, 360–362
  right-sizing government, 84–86
  solar power and, 20–21, 131
  taxation in, 422–423

  union mergers, 382
  venture capitalists, 401–402
Future profits, present value of, 388–392

G

Galles, Gary M., 463
Gambling, 82, 389–391
Game theory, 249–251
Gantt, Ray, 194
Gates, Bill, 234, 497, 498
Gates Foundation, 496–497
Gateway, 204, 269
GATT (General Agreement on Tariffs and Trade), 465
GDP. *See* Gross domestic product (GDP)
GDP per capita, 32–33
Gehrlein, Rachel, 304
Gen Corp., 242
Gender
  demand and, 93
  female "inequality trap" and, 499–500
General Agreement on Tariffs and Trade (GATT), 465
General Electric, 253, 254, 257, 276
General Foods, 256–257
General Mills, 239, 242, 257
General Motors Corp., 13, 182, 257, 275, 368, 369, 379, 399, 400–401, 456, 472
General Tire, 266
Gerber Products, 242
Gibson, 242
Gillette, 242
Gini coefficient, 411
Glaxo-Wellcome, 266
Global poverty, 490–509. *See also* Poverty
  American poverty, 430–434, 491–492
  defining, 492–494
  economic growth and, 497–507
  ending, 41
  entrepreneurship and, 508–509
  GDP in poor nations, 33–34
  goals and strategies concerning, 41, 494
  income distribution and, 39–41
  income redistribution and, 494–497
  measuring, 492–494
  persistent, 493–494
Global warming, 302, 304, 314, 319
Gold
  in exchange-rate intervention, 481–482
  gold reserves, 481–482
  gold standard, 480
  prices of, 131
Gold reserves, 481–482
Gold standard, 480
Goldman Sachs, 343
Goodyear, 266
Google Inc., 36, 235, 239, 241, 242, 276, 393–401, 402, 408
Government, 70–86
  circular flow and, 47–48
  factors of production and, 37–38
  failure of. *See* Government failure

federal. *See* Federal government
   growth of, 78–79
   local. *See* Local government
   market failure and, 71–78
   maximizing behavior of, 46
   regulation and. *See* Regulation
   "right"-sizing, 84–86
   role in command economy, 14
   role in market economy, 14
   state. *See* State government
   stockpiles of food, 332–333
   taxation and. *See* Taxation
Government failure, 82–84
   ballot-box economics and, 85
   cost-benefit analysis and, 84–85
   defined, **17, 82, 288, 315, 420**
   opportunity cost and, 84
   perceptions of waste, 83
   pollution and, 315
   public choice theory, 85–86
   taxes and, 420–422
Government regulation. *See* Regulation
Grameen Bank, 502
Graphs, 22–26
   causation and, 26
   linear versus nonlinear curves, 25–26
   shifts, 24–25, 126
   slopes, 23–24, 25, 126
Great Depression, 297–298
   "beggar thy neighbor" policies in, 460–461
   first farm depression and, 330, 335
   imperfect knowledge and, 20
   new government services during, 78
   union power and, 372
Great Recession of 2008–2009
   economic stimulus program, 19–20
   Economist in Chief role, 2–3, 5
   unemployment in, 11–12
Green, Mark J., 258*n*
Greenhouse effect, 302, 304, 314, 319–320
Grimaldi, James V., 233
Gross domestic product (GDP)
   defined, **31**
   growth of, 33
   international comparisons, 31–34
   mix of output, 34–35
   as output measure, 31–34
   per capita, 32–33
   in poor nations, 33–34
Guns versus butter, 7, 9–10
Gutierrez, Alec, 128

H

Hahn, Robert, 290
Hale, Ellen, 477
Hall, Maria C., 169
Hallmark, 242
Hand, Learned, 259
Hargreaves, Steve, 63*n*

Harrah's, 266
Harvard Center for Risk Management, 317
Hasbro, 266
Hawley, Willis, 460
Healey, James R., 182
Health
   air pollution and, 306
   human capital and, 500–501
Heilbroner, Robert, 70
Heinz, 242
Herfindahl-Hirshman Index (HHI), 259–260
Heritage Foundation, 16, 18, 37
Heritage Index of Economic Freedom, 16, 18
Hershey, 242, 254, 463
Hewlett-Packard, 195, 239, 242, 266, 269, 270
Hibbs, Jason, 73*n*
Historical record, of labor unions in the U.S., 372–374
Hoechst-Marion, 266
Holmes, Stanley, 267
Hoover, Herbert, 461
Hopkins, Jim, 402
Horizontal equity, 414
Horovitz, Bruce, 270
Housing market, property taxes and, 81, 184, 417–418
Houthakker, Hendrick S., 120*n*
"How" decisions
   factors of production, 35–38
   market outcomes and, 64
   nature of, 13, 30
   in the U.S. economy, 35–38
Human capital
   defined, **35, 499**
   economic growth and, 35, 499–501
   female "inequality trap" and, 499
   as source of economic growth, 35, 499–501
Hurricane Katrina, 500
Hynix, 254

I

IBM, 198, 204, 276
Imperfect knowledge, 20
Implicit costs, 151, 166
Import quotas, 331, **461–463, 507**
Imports
   defined, **445**
   import-competing industries, 456
   quotas, 331, 461–463, 507
   U.S., 445
In-kind income, 409
In-kind transfers, 77, 409, **428–429, 491**
InBev, 471
Income. *See also* Global poverty; Poverty
   in determining demand, 94, 107
   indifference curves and, 107
   labor's share of, 380–381
   leisure time versus, 343–345
   personal income (PI), 409
   size distribution of, 409–411
   wealth versus, 409

Income distribution, 38–40
  global inequality of, 39–41
  income quintile in, 39
  redistribution and poverty,
    494–497
  U.S., 39
Income effect of higher wages, 345–346
Income elasticity of demand, 128–130
  in agriculture, 328
  computing, 129–130
  defined, **129, 328**
  normal versus inferior goods, 130
Income quintile, 39
Income share, 410
Income taxes
  federal, 80, 411–417, 422–423
  state and local, 81
Income transfers, 77, 78
  defined, **419, 428**
  impact of, 419–420
Independence Air, 255
Index of Economic Freedom, 16, 18
India
  Kyoto Treaty and, 320
  wireless phones in, 206
Indifference curves, 107–113
  constructing, 107–109
  defined, **108**
  deriving demand curve from, 112–113
  indifference maps, 108–109
  price-quantity relationship in, 107–109
  utility maximization and, 110–112
Indifference maps, 108–109
Individual decisions, 3–4
Individual demand, 49–53
  ceteris paribus and, 52, 98
  demand curve, 50–51
  demand schedule, 49–50
  determinants of, 51–52, 97–99
  law of demand, 51, 98–99, 113, 117
  movements versus shifts in, 53
  nature of, 49
  shifts in, 52–53, 105–106
Industrial unions, 368. *See also* Labor unions
Industry behavior. *See also* Behavior
  antitrust policy and, 258–260
  in monopolistic competition, 268–274
  unregulated, 285–286
Industry structure, antitrust policy and, 259
Inefficiency
  in monopolistic competition, 273–274
  production possibilities and, 11
Inelastic demand, in agriculture,
  326–328
Inequality, taxes and, 419–420
Inequality trap, 499–500
Inequity, 77
  economic growth and, 505
  federal income taxes and, 414–416
Infant industries, 457

Inferior goods
  defined, **130**
  income elasticity of demand and, 130
Infineon, 254
Inflation
  defined, **78**
  in macro instability of markets, 78
  poverty and, 491
Initial public offerings (IPOs), 393
Inputs
  control of key inputs in monopoly, 227
  factors of production, 4–5
  labor market, 357–360
  varying levels of, 137–138
Institutional reform, 504–506
Intel Corporation, 228, 392–398
Interest rate effect, in present value of future profits, 390
Interest rates, in financial markets, 388
Internal financing, 502–503
International Brotherhood of Electrical Workers, 368
International Business Machines Corp., 198, 204, 276
International economics. *See also* International finance; International trade
  agriculture in, 333, 456
  best global brands, 276
  competitive markets in, 194, 206
  education gap in, 36
  ending global poverty, 41
  environmental protection and, 319
  exchange in, 46
  farm subsidies in, 333
  firm size in global perspective, 243
  global competitiveness of production costs, 156–158
  global inequality of income distribution, 39–40
  gross domestic product (GDP) in, 31–34
  Index of Economic Freedom, 16, 18
  labor market in, 346
  market versus command economies, 15
  maximizing behavior, 46
  monopoly in, 218
  outsourcing jobs and, 36–37
  pollution and, 303, 314
  price and, 63
  specialization in, 46
  taxation in, 413, 421
  terrorism and, 7, 457
  top tax rates, 421
International finance, 470–486. *See also* Financial markets
  exchange rates in, 471–475, 478–486
  market dynamics, 475–478
International Monetary Fund (IMF), 486
International Salt, 257
International trade, 444–467. *See also* Exports; Imports
  barriers to. *See* Barriers to trade
  comparative advantage and, 452–453
  economic growth and, 506–507
  equilibrium and, 461–462
  exchange rates in. *See* Exchange rates; Foreign exchange markets
  export ratios, 446
  future of, 465–466

motivation to trade, 448–452
mutual gains, 451–452
protectionism, 455–458
terms of trade, 453–455
trade balances, 447
U.S. trade patterns, 445–447
Internet
global competitiveness and, 157–158
price competition based on, 186
Investment decision
for competitive firms, 181–182, 191–192
defined, **181, 191**
Investment rate, 502–503
Invisible hand (Smith), 13–14, 17, 60
iPad, 208, 209
iPhone, 51, 92, 98, 116, 121, 127, 128, 195–197
iPod, 208
Isabella, Queen, 386

J

Jack in the Box, 273
Jackson, Thomas Penfield, 233
James, LeBron, 105, 342
Japan
international trade and, 506–507
U.S. as net debtor and, 479
JetBlue Airways, 248, 294
Job fairs, 343
Jobs, Steve, 92, 98, 116, 117, 123, 193, 195–197, 208, 401
Johnson & Johnson, 242, 275
Johnston, Summerfield K., Jr., 251
Jones, Calvin, 193

K

Das Kapital (Marx), 14
Kelloggs, 239, 242, 257
Kennedy, John F., 6, 494
Keynes, John Maynard, 5, 14
Kimberly-Clark, 242
Kinked demand curve, 247–249
Kinnaman, Thomas, 312
Kneale, Dennis, 204
Kodak, 242
Koenig, David, 248
Koerber, Kristine, 267
Kravenczynski, John, 353
Krebs, Edwin, 479
Krieg, Kenneth J., 230
Kyoto Treaty, 320

L

La, Howard, 343
Labor demand curve, 348, 352–355
Labor force, 342–362. *See also* Labor supply; Labor unions
as factor of production, 4–5
firm's hiring decision, 352–355
future of, 360–362

global competitiveness and, 156–158
government role and, 38
input choice in, 357–360
international comparisons, 346
labor demand and, 347–352
market equilibrium and, 355–357
market supply and, 346–347
outsourcing and, 36–37, 358
regional trade pacts and, 465–466
unit labor costs, 156
Labor force participation rate, 437
Labor supply, 343–346
backward-bending supply curve, 345–346
declining, 437
defined, **343, 367, 430**
of firm, 352
income versus leisure, 343–345
labor unions and, 367, 371
market, 352–355
tax elasticity of, 434
union wage goal, 371
Labor unions, 366–383
collective bargaining and, 377–380
employer power and, 374–377
examples of, 372–374
extent of power, 372–374
future of, 382
impact of, 380–382
mergers of, 382
objectives of, 368
potential use of power and, 369–372
types of, 368
Lackey, Kathleen, 66n
Lahart, Justin, 11
Laissez faire
antitrust versus regulation, 283
defined, **14, 283**
macroeconomics based on, 14
LaMonica, Paul, 223
Land, as factor of production, 4–5
Laser eye surgery, price-fixing and, 254
Law of demand, 51, 98–99, **113, 117**
Law of diminishing marginal utility, 95–97
Law of diminishing returns, 349–352
defined, **141, 351**
diminishing marginal physical product of labor, 350–351
diminishing marginal revenue product of labor, 351–352
Law of supply, 56, 130
Law of Unintended Consequences, 430
Lawsuits, as barrier to entry, 227
Legal framework, 37. *See also* Regulation
Leibowitz, Jon, 228
Leinwand, Donna, 58n
Leisure, income versus, 343–345
Leith, Scott, 269
Letendre, Gerry, 477
Lever Bros., 242
Lexmark, 242
Liberia, education in, 499
Limited liability, 392

Linear relationships, 25–26
Liquidity, 399
Live Nation Entertainment, 222, 223, 255–256, 257
Loan rates, 332–333
Loanable funds
   demand for, 391–392
   supply of, 388
Loans, microloans, 502–503
Local government
   growth of, 79
   taxation by, 81–82, 184, 417–418
Local labor markets, 367–368
Lockheed Martin Corp., 230
Lockout, 379
Logomasini, Angela, 317
Long run
   defined, **152, 181**
   investment decision in, 181–182
Long-run competitive equilibrium, 199–200
Long-run costs, 152–154
   average costs, 152–153
   investment decision and, 182
   marginal costs, 153
Loopholes, tax, 414, 416
L'Oreal, 275
Lorenz curve, 410–411
Lorillard, 242
Lotteries, 82, 389–391
Luhby, Tami, 343
Luxuries, necessities versus, 122

M

Machalaba, Daniel, 290
Mackey, Troy, 273
Macroeconomics
   defined, **18**–19
   resistance to exchange-rate changes, 478–480
Magnetek Inc., 229
Maisel, Sherman, 485, 485*n*
Managed exchange rates, 485
Manufacturer's Suggested Retail Price (MSRP), 99
Marcus, Rudolph A., 479
Marginal abatement costs, 313–314
Marginal cost (MC), 148–151
   competitive firms and, 172–173, 174–175
   defined, **143, 173, 191**
   intersection with average total cost, 149–151
   long-run, 153
   marginal cost curve, 183–184
   in market supply curve, 191
   natural monopoly and, 284
   resource computation, 148–149
   in shutdown decision, 180–181
Marginal cost pricing
   defined, **224, 273, 284**–285
   in monopolistic competition, 273
Marginal factor cost (MFC)
   defined, **376**
   in monopsony, 376, 377

Marginal physical product (MPP)
   defined, **140, 349**
   diminishing, 350–351
   diminishing marginal returns, 141
   falling, 142
   of labor, 156, 348–349, 350–351
   marginal productivity and, 140–141
   marginal resource cost and, 142–143
Marginal productivity, 140–141
Marginal rate of substitution, 112
Marginal resource cost, 142–143
Marginal revenue (MR)
   in competitive firms, 174
   defined, **174, 216**
   monopoly, 215–216, 220
   in shutdown decision, 180–181
Marginal revenue product (MRP)
   defined, **349, 376**
   diminishing, 351–352
   of labor, 349, 351–353, 360–362, 418
   in monopsony, 376–377
Marginal tax rates, 411–412, 413, 416, 421, **432**
Marginal utility (MU)
   defined, **95, 107**
   diminishing, 95–97
   equilibrium outcomes, 104–105
   indifference curves and, 107–109
   negative, 95–97
   prices and, 97–99, 111–112
   total utility versus, 95, 96
   utility maximization, 104, 111–112
Marginal wage, 369–370
Market clearing, 59–60
Market competition, monopoly compared with, 223–227
Market demand
   defined, **54, 99**
   firm demand versus, 171
   market demand curve, 54–55
Market economy
   efficiency and, 14
   government role in, 14
   in international economics, 15
   invisible hand (Smith), 13–14, 17, 60
   laissez faire, 14
   market failure and, 17
   market mechanism in, 14
Market equilibrium for labor, 342–362
   equilibrium wage, 355–356, 367
   minimum wages, 356–357
Market failure, 71–78. *See also* Antitrust; Regulation
   antitrust policy and, 258–260
   causes of, 71
   choice and, 17
   defined, **17, 71, 258, 283, 309, 411, 429**
   environmental protection and, 308–310
   externalities and, 74–76
   inequity and, 77
   macro instability and, 77–78
   market mechanisms and, 71
   market power and, 76–77

optimal mix of output, 71
public goods and, 72–74
social insurance programs and, 429
sources of, 71
Market fluctuations, in corporate stock, 394–397
Market incentives
costs versus, 433–434
for environmental protection, 306–308
social insurance programs and, 430–434
Social Security and, 437–438
Market mechanisms, 14, 60, 71, 205–206
Market outcomes, 63–64
"for whom" decision and, 64
"how" decision and, 64
optimal versus perfect, 64
organ transplants and, 64–66
"what" decision and, 63
Market participants
exchange and, 46
locating markets, 48
maximizing behavior, 46
specialization and, 46
Market power, 76–77, 213–236
in agriculture, 326
barriers to entry, 217, 226–227
characteristics of, 214–216
comparative perspective on, 223–227
computer industry, 217–222
consequences of, 76–77
defined, **76, 170, 214, 267, 326, 368**
determinants of, 240–241
inequity and, 76
labor unions and, 366, 367–368
limits to, 224–225
measures of, 241–243
in monopolistic competition, 267
in monopoly, 76–77, 213–236
pros and cons of, 228–232
restricted supply and, 76–77
Market share
allocation of, 254–255
battle for, 244–245
defined, **244**
in oligopoly, 244–245, 254–255
Market shortage, 60–61, 63, **481**
Market structure
competitive firms, 169–170
competitive markets, 190–209
defined, **169, 240**
degrees of power, 240
monopolistic competition, 266–268
monopoly, 213–236
oligopoly, 239–261
types of, 169–170, 240
Market supply
defined, **55, 191**
determinants of, 56
of labor, 346–347
market supply curve, 191–194
nature of, 56–58

Market supply curve, 191–194
barriers to entry, 193
entry and exit, 191–192
in perfect competition, 191–194
shifts in, 198–200, 202–203
tendency toward zero profits, 192–193
Market supply of labor, 346–347
Market surplus, 60, 63, **330, 356**
Marketing orders, 331
Markkula, A. C., 401
Marlboro, 276
Mars (company), 254
Mars missions, 6, 7
Marx, Karl, 14, 39
MasterCard, 242, 256
Material Enterprises Co., 287
Mattel, 203–204, 266
Mauer, Joe, 353
Maximizing behavior, 46
Mayfield, Mark, 177
Maza Zavala, Domingo, 505
McCain, John, 19–20
McCarthy, Joseph, 459
McCracken, Harry, 209
McDonald's, 266, 267, 269, 270, 273, 276, 446, 491
McGuinness, Paul, 413
McKinsey & Co., 206
Measurement problems, 241–243
Medicare, 429
Medina Sidonia, Duke of, 386
MegaMillions lottery, 389–391
Memory chips, price-fixing in, 254
Mercedes-Benz, 472–473
Merck, 266
Mergers and acquisitions
as barrier to entry, 227, 230, 231, 256–257
mergers of labor unions, 382
Merit goods, 77
Merle, Renae, 230
Merrell Dow, 266
Mexico
nontariff barriers, 464
production costs and, 156
MGM, 266
Michelin, 266
Microcomputer market, 194–204
Microeconomics
defined, **18**–19
resistance to exchange-rate changes, 478–480
Microfinance, 502–503
Micron, 254
Microsoft Corp., 122, 155, 232–235, 239, 240, 241, 242, 259, 276, 396, 498
Mid-America Dairies, 242
Millennium Aid Goal (United Nations), 496
Millennium Declaration (World Bank), 41
Millennium Poverty Goal (United Nations), 494, 503
Miller, John W., 508
Minimum average cost, 147–148, 206
Minimum wages, 356–357

Mining, 318
Minnesota Twins, 353
Mixed economy
    defined, **17**
    government failure and, 17
    market failure and, 17
    origins of concept, 14
Mohegan Sun, 266
Moiseyev, Michael R., 230
Monarch, 242
Monopolistic competition, 265–277
    advertising and, 274–276
    defined, **266**
    examples of, 266
    industry behavior and, 268–274
    market power in, 267
    market structure and, 266–268
Monopoly, 213–236, 240. *See also* Deregulation
    barriers to entry, 217, 222, 223, 226–227, 293–294
    computer industry and, 217–222
    defined, **38, 76, 169, 214**
    electric power, 296–297
    marginal revenue in, 215–216, 220
    market competition compared with, 223–227
    market power and, 76–77, 213–236
    natural, 77, 231, 282–298
    price discrimination in, 225–226
    price in, 215–216, 220–221
    production decision in, 218–220
    profit maximization, 215–217
    restricted supply and, 76–77
Monopoly franchises, 227
Monopsony, 374–377
    defined, **374**
    free agents in professional sports, 375
Montgomery, David, 344
Moral hazard, 432
Motorola, 127, 239
Mozilla, 242
Mullins, Marcy E., 292
Multilateral trade pacts, 465
Munster, Piper Gene, 121
Murray, Betty, 154
Mussenden, Sean, 121*n*

N

Nader, Ralph, 258
Nakashima, Ryan, 226
National Academy of Sciences, 320
National Biscuit Company, 257
National Center for Atmospheric Research, 320
National Football League, 368, 379
National Hockey League, 379
National Industrial Recovery Act (NIRA) of 1933, 372
National Labor Relations Board (NLRB), 374
National Mining Association, 318
National Oceanic and Atmospheric Administration, 319–320
National Organ Transplantation Act (U.S.), 65
National Restaurant Association, 357

National security. *See also* War
    international trade and, 457
    terrorist attacks of September 11, 2001, 7, 457
Natural monopoly, 282–298. *See also* Deregulation
    declining ATC curve, 283–284
    defined, **77, 231, 283**
    subsidies and, 286
    unregulated behavior, 284–285
NatWest Securities, 256
Necessities, luxuries versus, 122
Negative marginal utility, 95–97
Network economies, as barrier to entry, 258
New Deal, 16
New England Telephone & Telegraph, 287
New York City Taxi and Limousine Commission, 257
New York Telephone, 287
News Corp., 275
Nextel, 241
Nigeria, health in, 500
Nintendo, 122, 239, 241, 242
Nominal tax rates, 415
Nongovernmental organizations (NGOs), in across-nation income redistribution, 496–497
Nonlinear relationships, 25–26
Nonprice competition, as barrier to entry, 257
Nontariff barriers, 464
Norelco, 242
Norfolk-Southern, 291
Normal goods
    defined, **130**
    income elasticity of demand and, 130
Normal profit, 168
North American Free Trade Agreement (NAFTA), 465–466
North Korea
    cost of military in, 9–10
    food shortages in, 10
Northwest Airlines, 255
Nvidia, 228
Nynex, 287

O

Obama, Barack, 2–3, 6, 16, 19–20, 121, 315, 318, 320, 337, 357, 361, 362, 382, 409, 415–417, 459, 464
Office of Management and Budget (OMB), 316
Oil
    prices of, 58, 59, 63, 252, 254
    supply and demand for, 45, 58, 59, 63
Okun, Arthur M., 408
Old Age Survivors and Disability Assistance (OASDI), 435
Oligopolists, 244
Oligopoly, 239–261
    antitrust enforcement and, 258–260
    barriers to entry, 255–258
    behavior of, 243–247
    competition versus, 251–253
    coordination problems, 253–255
    defined, **240**
    examples of, 240–243
    game theory and, 249–251

kinked demand curve, 247–249
market share and, 244–245, 254–255
market structure, 240–243
retaliation and, 245–247
Oligopsony, 376
Oliveira, Nancy, 477
Oogav, Shy, 169
OPEC (Organization of Petroleum Exporting Countries), 252, 254, 335
Open economy, 451
Opportunity costs, 6–7
bond, 399
circular flow and, 48
comparative advantage, 452
defined, **6, 48, 79, 102, 138, 206, 285, 315, 452**
environmental protection and, 315
government failure and, 84
increasing, 9
in product markets, 102, 138–139
production function and, 138–139
production possibilities curve and, 7–12
solar power and, 20–21
taxation and, 79–80, 83–84
unregulated behavior and, 284–285
Opportunity wages, 361
Optimal consumption
defined, **103, 108**
equilibrium outcomes, 104–105
indifference curves and, 108
utility maximization and, 103–104, 110–112
Optimal mix of outputs, 71
Optimal rate of pollution, 316
Oracle, 36, 342, 360, 361–362
Organ transplants
market incentives and, 65
shortage of, 65
supply of organs, 64–66
zero price ceiling, 65
Organic pollution, 304–305
Organization of Petroleum Exporting Countries (OPEC), 252, 254, 335
Osgood, Charlie, 453
Other goods
change in price of, 126–128
in determining demand, 94, 107
indifference curves and, 107
Output
cost summary and, 149–151
costs and, 172–173
gross domestic product (GDP), 31–34
limits to, 5–6
military share of, 11
mix of, 31, 34–35, 71
in monopolistic competition, 270
in monopoly, 220
in oligopoly, 252–253
profit-maximizing rate of, 175–178
regulation of, 287–288
revenue and, 172
Outsourcing
defined, **358**
productivity and, 36–37

Ovation Pharmaceuticals, 225
Ownership
corporate stock, 392
property rights, 417–418
Ozone layer, 302, 303

P
P/E (price/earnings) ratio, **394**
Pabst, 242
Page, Larry, 408
Panasonic Corp., 194
Papa John's, 266
Paperworkers Union, 382
Par value, 398–399
Parity, 330
Parker, Suzy, 297
Patents, 226, 255
Paul, Ron, 270
Pawlosky, Mark, 169
Payne, Tommy, 121
Payoff matrix, 249–250
Payroll taxes, 418–419
cost of labor, 418–419
supply and, 185
tax incidence, 419
trade-offs, 438
Peet's, 266
Pentagon terrorist attack (2001), 7, 457
PepsiCo Inc., 239, 242, 246, 251, 266, 268, 269, 274
Per capita GDP, 32–33
Perfect competition, 170–186, 240
defined, **169**
market characteristics of, 193
market demand versus firm demand, 171
price takers, 170–171
structure of, 170
Perfume, price-fixing and, 253
Perrier, 266
Personal income (PI), 409
Pfizer, 242, 275
Philip Morris, 242
Philips, 194
Pillsbury, 242
Pizza Hut, 266
Players Association, 368
PlayStation 3, 122
Polaroid Corporation, 226
Policy constraints
global poverty and, 494
privatization of Social Security, 438–439
U.S. tax, 416–417
Politics
ballot-box economics, 85
economics versus, 19–20, 85
labor unions and, 382
monopoly and, 224
Pollution. See also Environmental protection
damages from, 305–306
government failure and, 315

Pollution—*Cont.*
 international economics and, 303, 314
 market failure and, 308–310
 market incentives and, 306–308
Poor nations, gross domestic product (GDP) of, 33–34
Popcorn test, of diminishing marginal utility, 95–97
Population growth, 33–34, 498–499
Poverty. *See also* Global poverty
 gross domestic product and, 33–34
 in-kind income and, 409, 491
 lotteries and, 82, 389–391
 in the U.S., 430–434, 491–492
 welfare programs and, 430–434
Poverty gap
 defined, **431**
 social insurance programs and, 431
Poverty rate, 491
Poverty threshold, 491
Predatory pricing, 255
Present discounted value (PDV), 389–390
Present value of future profits, 388–392
 demand for loanable funds, 391–392
 interest rate effects, 390
 time value of money, 389–390
 uncertainty, 390–391
Price. *See also* Inflation
 changes in, 355
 consumer demand and, 92, 97–99
 cross-price elasticity, 126–128
 equilibrium, 59, 191, 461, 473
 impact of labor unions on, 381
 Internet-based competition in, 186
 in macro instability of markets, 78
 marginal cost pricing, 206, 224, 273, 284–285
 marginal utility and, 97–99, 111–112
 market share and, 244–245
 monopoly, 215–216, 220–221
 oil, 58, 59, 63, 252, 254
 oligopoly, 243–249, 252–254
 of organ transplants, 65
 for pollution damages, 305–306
 price elasticity of demand, 117–128
 regulation of, 285–286, 293
 relative, 122–123
 role in terms of trade, 454–455
 self-adjusting, 61
 supply and demand and, 61, 63
 ticket scalping and, 61, 63
 in U.S. farm policy, 330, 334–335
 zero price ceiling and, 65
Price ceilings, 65, 296–297
Price competition, 201–202, 293
Price discrimination
 consumer choice and, 101
 defined, **101, 225**
 in monopoly, 225–226
Price/earnings (P/E) ratio, 394
Price efficiency, 286
Price elasticity of demand, 117–128
 in agriculture, 326–327

 defined, **117, 225, 326**
 determinants of elasticity, 122–123
 elastic versus inelastic demand, 119–121
 smoking and, 121
 total revenue and, 123–126
Price elasticity of supply, 130
Price-fixing
 defined, **253**
 examples of, 253–254
Price floors, 60
Price leadership, 254
Price premiums, in monopolistic competition, 270
Price regulation, 285–286, 293
Price signals, monopolistic competition and, 273–274
Price supports, in agriculture, 330–331
Price takers, 170–171
Private costs, 309
Private goods, 72
Privatization, of Social Security, 438–439
Procter & Gamble, 241, 242, 258, 275
Product differentiation
 defined, **246, 268, 293**
 in monopolistic competition, 268
 in natural monopoly, 293
 in oligopoly, 246–247
Product markets
 caveat emptor and, 105–106
 choosing among products, 101–105
 consumer demand in, 93–99
 consumer surplus and, 99–100
 costs of production, 136–158
 defined, **47**
 demand curve, 95–99
 determinants of demand, 93–95
 dollar costs, 143–151
 economic versus accounting costs, 151–152
 economies of scale, 154–156
 global competitiveness, 156–158
 income elasticity, 128–130
 indifference curves, 107–113
 long-run costs, 152–154
 marginal productivity, 140–141
 market demand and, 99
 price discrimination, 101
 price elasticity, 117–128
 production function, 137–140
 resource costs, 141–143
 shifts versus movements, 126
Production
 externalities in, 308–310
 in monopolistic competition, 267–268
Production costs, 136–158
 dollar costs, 143–151
 economic versus accounting, 151–152
 economies of scale, 154–156
 global competitiveness, 156–158
 long-run, 152–154
 marginal productivity, 140–141
 production function, 137–140
 resource costs, 141–143

Production decision
of competitive firms, 172–173, 197
defined, **172, 197, 219, 270, 307**
environmental protection and, 306–307
in monopolistic competition, 267–268, 270
in monopoly, 218–220
output and costs, 172–173
output and revenues, 172
Production function, 137–140
defined, **137**
efficiency and, 138–139
short-run constraints, 139–140
varying input levels, 137–138
Production possibilities, 7–12
cost of North Korea's military, 9–10
decisions concerning output choices, 13
defined, **7, 36, 448**
economic growth and, 12
efficiency and, 10–11
"for whom" decisions, 13
guns versus butter and, 7, 9–10
"how" decisions, 13
inefficiency and, 11
mechanisms of choice, 13–18
production possibilities curve, 7–8
production possibilities schedule, 7–8
public goods and, 73
with trade, 449–451
without trade, 448–449
unemployment and, 11–12
"what" decisions, 13
Production processes
alternative, 358
defined, **358**
Productivity, 35–37
changes in, 354
defined, **35, 138, 381, 503**
factor mobility and, 36
farm, 503–504
global competitiveness and, 156–158
impact of labor unions on, 380–382
marginal, 140–141
monopoly and, 224
outsourcing and, 36–37
technological advance, 36
trade, 36–37
Professional sports
collective bargaining in, 379
monopsony in, 375
pay in, 353
Profit maximization
competitive firms and, 174–179
monopoly, 215–217
Profit maximization rule, 175–**176, 215**
Profit per unit, 198
Profit squeeze, 207
Profit taxes, supply and, 185
Profits
in competitive markets, 198
defined, **141, 165, 335**

economic versus accounting, 166–168. *See also*
Economic profits
expectations for, 394–395
in monopolistic competition, 272
in monopoly, 221–222
in oligopoly, 251–253
other motivations versus, 165
present value of future, 388–392
in production decision, 197–198
profit motive, 165–166
regulation of, 286–287
in U.S. farm policy, 335
Progressive taxes, 80, 411–412, 435–436
Progresso, 242
Property rights, 504
Property taxes, 81, 184, 417–418
Proportional taxes, 80, 419
Protectionism, 455–458
dumping, 457, 458
export industries, 456
import-competing industries, 456
infant industries, 457
national security, 457
net gain, 456–457
terms of trade and, 458
Public choice theory, 85–**86**
Public goods, 72–74
defined, **72**
externalities and, 74–76
firefighting services, 73
free rider problem, 72–73
inequity and, 77
market power and, 76–77
private goods versus, 72
underproduction of, 73–74
Public sector. *See* Government

Q

Qing, Koh Gui, 483
Quaker Oats, 242, 257
Quality, deterioration of, 287–288
Quantity demanded, marginal utility and, 97–99
Quotas, import, 331, **461,** 462–463, 507

R

R. J. Reynolds, 257
Railroad Revitalization and Regulatory Reform Act
of 1976, 291
Railroads, deregulation and, 291
Ralcorp, 239, 242, 257
Ramus, Catherine, 344
Ray-O-Vac, 242
Reagan, Ronald, 16, 459, 485
Real Networks, 242
Recessions. *See* Great Recession of 2008–2009
Recycling, 312, 317
Regional trade pacts, 465–466
Regressive taxes, 80, 81, **417**–418

Regulation. *See also* Deregulation; Environmental protection
  antitrust versus, 283–285
  as barrier to entry, 257
  costs of regulation, 288–291
  defined, **283**
  employment in federal regulatory agencies, 289
  environmental protection options, 311–315
  farming, 330–335
  natural monopoly and, 282–298
  regulatory options, 285–288, 311–315
  role of, 37–38
Regulatory options
  "cap and trade," 313–314
  command-and-control, 315
  imperfect answers and, 288
  market-based, 311–313
  output regulation, 287–288
  price regulation, 285–286, 293
  profit regulation, 286–287
  tradable pollution permits, 313–314
Relative price, 122–123
Relative wages, 380
Remington, 242
Replacement workers, 372
Repurchase rates, in monopolistic competition, 269–270
Research and development, market power and, 228–229
Research in Motion, 255
Resource allocation
  financial markets and, 397–398
  guns versus butter, 7, 9–10
  solar power and, 20–21
Resource costs, 141–143
Response lags, 328
Retail Clerks, 382
Retained earnings, 393
Retaliation, in oligopoly, 245–247
Retirement age, Social Security and, 435
Revenue
  output and, 172
  from taxes, 79–80
  total, 172
Revolutionary War, 459
Reynolds American, 121, 242
Riedl, Brian, 337
Risk
  of competitive firms, 168
  in financial markets, 386, 387
  oligopoly and, 249
  of within-nation income redistribution, 495
Risk management, in financial markets, 388
Risk premiums
  defined, **388**
  in financial markets, 388
Romar Tissue Mills, 242
Roosevelt, Franklin D., 16, 332–333
Rostow, Walt, 501–502
Royal Caribbean Cruises, 313
Royal Crown, 242, 246
Royal Dutch/Shell, 243
Ruiz, Gerardo, 464

Russia
  Cold War and, 250–251
  currency bailouts, 485

S

Sabia, Joe, 357
Sachs, Jeffrey, 503, 503n
Safety
  government regulation of, 38
  trucking industry, 290
Sales taxes, 417–418
Samsung, 208, 254
Sandberg, Annette, 290
Satisfaction meter, 96
Scalping, 61, 63
Scarcity, 4–6
  defined, **4**
  factors of production and, 4–5
  guns versus butter and, 7, 9–10
  limits to output and, 5–6
  opportunity costs and, 6–7
Scarf, Herbert, 120n
Scheck, Justin, 182
Schimberg, Henry A., 251
Schmidt, Eric, 408
Scott, H. Lee, 380
Secondary trading, 393–394
Secondhand smoking, 74–75
Security. *See* National security
Self-adjusting price, 61
Seneca, 303
September 11, 2001 terrorist attacks, 7, 457
Service Corp. International, 154
Service Employees International Union, 368
Set-asides, 331
Severe poverty, 492
Sharp, 198
Sherman Act of 1890, 233, 234, 258
Shifts in demand, 52–53, 62, **105**–106, 126
Shifts in supply, 58, 62, 63, 328
Shirley, Mark, 130
Short run
  competitive firm output and costs in, 172
  defined, **139, 172**
  determinants of supply in, 183–184
  investment decision in, 181
  short-run constraints on production, 139–140
Short-run competitive equilibrium, 199
Short-run price, in monopolistic competition, 270
Shoven, John, 120n
Shutdown point, 181, 203
Sicher, John, 246
Sierra Leone, health in, 501
Singh, Ruchira, 206
Sirius, 231
Size distribution of income, 409–410
Skeen, Kerry, 255
Slopes, on graphs, 23–24, 25
Smith, Adam, 13–14, 17, 60, 166, 239

Smith, Brad, 235
Smog, 304
Smoking. *See* Cigarettes
Smoot-Hawley Tariff Act of 1930, 460, 461
Social costs, 309
Social insurance programs
    defined, **429**
    welfare versus, 429
Social networking, 401–402
Social Security, 435–438. *See also*
        Transfer payments
    compassion and, 437–438
    declining labor supply, 437
    earnings test, 436, 438
    privatization of, 438–439
    program features, 435–436
    Social Security taxes, 80, 419
    welfare versus, 429
    work disincentives, 436–437
Social Security taxes, 80, 419
Sociopsychiatric explanation for demand, 93
Solar power, 20–21, 131
Solid waste pollution, 305
Solsman, Joan E., 396
Somalia, health in, 500
Sony Corp., 122, 194, 208, 239, 241, 242
Sorensen, Charles F., 213*n*
Sotheby's, 242, 254
Soto, Hernando de, 508–509
South Korea, voluntary restraint agreements, 463
Southwest Airlines, 248
Soviet Union. *See* Russia
Spalding, 242
Specialization
    international trade and, 448
    market participants and, 46
Speculation, foreign exchange, 484–485
Sprint, 226, 241, 242, 255, 260
Staggers Rail Act of 1980, 291
Staples, 36
Starbucks, 36, 265–270, 273
State government
    growth of, 79
    taxation by, 81–82
Station, 266
Steelworkers, 382
Steinhauser, Gabriele, 235
Sterrett, David, 357
Stevens, C. R., 229
Stock market, 392–398
    averages, 398
    corporate stock, 392–398
    resource allocation and, 397–398
Stockpiles of food, 332–333
Stone, Tess, 51*n*
Stoner, Nancy, 304
Streitfeld, David, 184
Strikes, 379
Subsidies
    cross-subsidization, 293

as regulatory option, 286
    in U.S. farm policy, 333, 334, 336–337
Substitute goods, 126–127
    defined, **51, 126, 296**
    marginal rate of substitution, **112**
Substitution effect of higher wages, 345
Subway, 270
Sugar industry, 463, 508
Summit Technology, 242, 254
Sun Microsystems, 446
Sunbeam, 242
Suplee, Curt, 306
Supplemental Nutrition Assistance Program (SNAP), 409
Supply, 55–58
    defined, **48**
    determinants of, 56, 182–185
    equilibrium and, 59–63
    law of, 56, 130
    of loanable funds, 388
    market. *See* Market supply; Market supply curve
    restricted, 76–77
    shifts of, 58, 62, 63, 328
    tax elasticity of, 412–414
    in U.S. farm policy, 331
Supply and demand, 45–67. *See also* Demand; Supply
    circular flow and, 47–48
    demand, 48–55
    equilibrium, 59–63
    market outcomes, 63–64
    market participants, 46
    supply, 48, 55–58
Supply curve
    defined, **183**
    shifts in, 184, 198–200, 202–203
    short run, 183–184
    tax effects, 184–185
Surplus
    balance-of-payments, 481
    market, 60, 330
    trade, 447

T
T-Mobile, 242, 260
T-shirt market, 169, 186
Taiwan, voluntary restraint agreements, 463
Target, 194
Target efficiency, 429
Tariffs, 459–460, 462, 508
Tastes
    in determining demand, 93, 94, 107
    indifference curves and, 107
Tax base, 416
Tax elasticity of labor supply, 434
Tax elasticity of supply, 412–414
Tax incidence
    defined, **418**
    payroll taxes, 419
    property tax, 418
    sales tax, 417–418

Tax rates, marginal, 411–412, 413, 416, 421, 432
Taxation, 79–82, 408–423
  fairness and, 420–422
  federal, 80–81, 411–417, 422–423
  forms of income, 409
  future of, 422–423
  "green" taxes, 312
  inequality and, 419–420
  inequity and, 77, 414–416
  international perspective on, 413, 421
  international tax rates, 421
  marginal tax rates, 411–412, 413, 416, 421, 432
  nature of income, 409
  opportunity costs and, 79–80, 83–84
  payroll, 185, 418–419, 438
  property, 81, 184, 417–418
  sales, 417–418
  size distribution of income, 409–411
  state and local, 81–82, 184, 417–418
  supply curve effects, 184–185
Taylor, Lester D., 120n
Teamsters, 373, 382
Technology. See also Internet
  technological advance, 36, 326
Teenagers, demand and, 94
Telecommunications Act of 1996, 292, 295
Telephone service
  deregulation and, 291–292
  local, 292
  long distance, 292
Temporary Aid to Needy Families (TANF), 430, 434
Terms of trade, 453–455
  defined, 453
  improving, 458
  limits to, 453–454
  role of markets and prices in, 454–455
Terrorist attacks of September 11, 2001, 7, 457
Texas Instruments, 203–204, 242
Thatcher, Margaret, 333
Thermal pollution, 305
Ticket scalping, 61, 63
Ticketmaster, 222, 223, 226
Tim Horton's, 267
Time lags
  in agricultural supply, 328
  price elasticity of demand and, 123
Time limits, welfare programs and, 434
Time preferences, of financial markets, 388
Time value of money, present discounted value
    (PDV), 389–390
Time Warner, 242, 275
Tongaat-Hulett Group Ltd., 508
Toshiba Corporation, 239, 471
Total costs (TC), 143–145
  competitive firms and, 173
  defined, 143
  fixed costs, 144
  variable costs, 144–145
Total profit, 173
Total return, corporate stock and, 393

Total revenue, 101
  defined, 123, 172
  price elasticity of demand and, 123–126
Total utility
  defined, 95
  marginal utility versus, 95, 96
Total wages paid, 369–370
Toyota, 243, 379
Tradable pollution permits, 313–314
Trade, 36–37. See also International trade
Trade agreements, 465–466
Trade balance, 474–475
Trade barriers. See Barriers to trade
Trade deficits, 447, 475
Trade surplus, 447
Trade unions. See Labor unions
Training, as barrier to entry, 257
Transfer payments, 427–440. See also Social Security
  cash versus in-kind benefits, 428–429
  defined, 77
  of federal government, 77, 78
  impact of, 419–420
  in-kind transfers, 77, 409, 428–429, 491
  income transfers, 77, 78
  inequity and, 77
  major programs, 428–430
  Medicare, 429
  social insurance versus welfare, 429
  Social Security, 435–438
  transfer goals, 429
  unintended consequences of, 430
  welfare programs, 429, 430–434
Transportation costs
  nontariff barriers, 464
  regulation and, 290
Treasury bonds. See Bonds
Trucking
  safety rules in, 290
  trade unions, 373
Trujillo, Ron, 154
Tunks, Jeff, 58
Tyco, 266

U
U2 Ltd., 63, 413, 490
Uncertainty, in present value of future profits, 390–391
Unemployment
  defined, 78
  in the Great Recession of 2008–2009, 11–12
  in macro instability of markets, 77–78
  outsourcing jobs and, 36–37, 358
  production possibilities and, 11–12
  in the U.S., 11–12
Unemployment benefits. See Transfer payments
Unintended consequences, of transfer payments, 430
Union of Needletrades and Textile Employees, 373
Union Pacific, 291
Union shops, 372
Unionization rate, 373–374

Unit labor costs, 156
United Airlines, 248, 255, 294
United Auto Workers Union (UAW), 366, 368, 369, 372, 373, 374, 378–379, 382
United Fruit, 257
United Mine Workers, 373
United Nations, 319–320
   Intergovernmental Panel on Climate Change (IPCC), 319
   Millennium Aid Goal, 496
   Millennium Poverty Goal, 494, 503
United States economy, 30–42. *See also* Federal government; Regulation
   balance of payments, 473–475, 482
   central economic questions of, 30
   Copenhagen Accord, 320
   developmental patterns of, 35
   farm policy in, 330–335
   federal growth, 78–79
   federal taxes, 80–81, 411–417, 422–423
   "for whom" decisions in, 38–40
   global competitiveness and, 156–158
   Great Depression in. *See* Great Depression
   Great Recession of 2008–2009 in. *See* Great Recession of 2008–2009
   gross domestic product, 31–35
   guns versus butter in, 7, 9–10
   "how" decisions in, 35–38
   income distribution in, 39
   Index of Economic Freedom, 16
   international trade and, 506–507. *See also* International trade
   Kyoto Treaty and, 320
   limits to output, 5–6
   merit goods and, 77
   as mixed economy, 14, 17
   net debtor position of, 479–480
   pollution taxes and, 312
   poverty in, 430–434, 491–492
   Social Security. *See* Social Security
   state and local growth, 79
   taxation in. *See* Taxation
   trade patterns of, 445–447
   transfer programs, 428–430
   unemployment in, 11–12
   union power in, 372–374
   welfare programs, 430–434
   "what" decisions in, 31–35
U.S. Bureau of Labor Statistics, 93
U.S. Census Bureau, 409, 491
U.S. Department of Agriculture, 329, 334, 337
U.S. Department of Commerce, 463
U.S. Department of Defense, 230
U.S. Department of Justice, 38, 230, 231, 233, 234–235, 254, 256, 258–260
U.S. Department of Transportation, 290, 464
U.S. Environmental Protection Agency (EPA), 306, 314
U.S. Federal Communications Commission (FCC), 231, 287, 291–292, 295
U.S. Federal Trade Commission (FTC), 38, 225, 227, 228, 230, 257, 258
U.S. Food and Drug Administration (FDA), 298
U.S. General Accounting Office (GAO), 294

U.S. Interstate Commerce Commission (ICC), 291
U.S. National Organ Transplantation Act, 65
U.S. Rubber, 257
U.S. Steel, 257
Universal Manufacturing Corp., 229
US Airways, 248, 255
User fees, 312
Utility, 95
Utility maximization, 110–112
   consumer choice and, 102–104
   marginal utility (MU) and, 111–112
   optimal consumption and, 103–104, 110–111
Utility theory, 95–97
   law of diminishing marginal utility, 95
   maximization of utility, 104, 111–112
   popcorn test of, 95–97
   total versus marginal utility, 95, 96
   utility, defined, **95**

V

Valuation problems, government failure and, 84–85
Value of information, 396
Variable costs (VC), 144–145, **172**
Venture capital, 401–402
Verizon, 226, 241, 242, 255, 275
Vertical equity, 414
Via Technologies, 228
Visa, 242, 256
VISX, 242, 254
Vizio, 209
Voluntary restraint agreements, 463–464
Vonage, 226, 255
Voting, in ballot box economics, 85

W

Wage replacement rate, 435–436
Wages
   changes in wage rates, 353–354
   equilibrium, 355–356, 367
   impact of labor unions on, 380–382
   marginal, 369–370
   relative, 380
   substitution effect of, 345–346
Wagner Act, 372
Wales, David, 225
Walmart Stores Inc., 36, 243, 367–368, 380
Walt Disney Company, 167, 446–447
Wang, Aileen, 483
War. *See also* Defense spending; National security
   federal government expenditures and, 78, 79
   guns versus butter and, 7, 9–10
Ward. Michael, 120n
Warner-Lambert, 242
Warren, Earl, 259
Waste
   perceptions of government, 83
   solid waste pollution, 305
Water market, 269, 500

Water pollution, 304–305, 500
Wealth, 409
Wealth of Nations, The (Smith), 13–14
Weisman, Jonathan, 477
Welfare programs, 430–434
   benefit determination, 430–431
   defined, **429**
   social insurance versus, 429
   work incentive problem, 431–432
Wendy's, 270, 273
Western Electric, 233, 287
Westinghouse Electric Co., 194, 253, 254, 471
Weyerhaeuser, 446
"What" decisions
   market outcomes and, 63
   nature of, 13, 30
   in the U.S. economy, 31–35
Whoriskey, Peter, 460
Wildavsky, Ben, 375
Willamette Warriors, 453
Wilson, 242
Wind power, 131
Witherspoon, Reese, 342
Within-nation income redistribution,
   494–496
Wm. Wrigley, 242
Work disincentives, 436–437
World Bank, 33, 40, 41, 492–494
World Series, 444
World Trade Center terrorist attack
   (2001), 7, 457

World Trade Organization (WTO)
   nontariff barriers, 464
   protests, 465
World War I, 372
World War II, 10, 78, 79, 372
Wozniak, Steve, 195–197, 401

X

Xerox, 198
XM, 231

Y

Yahoo!, 242, 396
Yield
   bond, 399–401
   current, 399–401
Yoder, Stephen Kreider, 229
YouTube, 36, 402
Yunus, Muhammad, 502

Z

Zambia, health in, 501
Zero economic profit, 192–193, 206–207
Zimbabwe
   farm productivity in, 503–504
   gross domestic product (GDP) of, 33–34
   redistribution of income in, 495
   risk and, 388
Zuckerberg, Mark, 401–402

HOUSEHOLD INCOME AND POVERTY STATUS, 1980–2010

Year	Income (in 2010 dollars)		Mean Income, by Race				Number (in millions) and Percent of Persons in Poverty				
	Median	Mean	White	Black	Hispanic	Asian	All	White	Black	Hispanic	Asian
2010	49,445	67,530	73,439	44,780	51,540	84,828	46,180 (15.1)	19,599 (9.9)	10,675 (27.4)	13,243 (26.6)	1,729 (12.1)
2009	50,599	69,098	74,449	46,806	53,091	92,310	43,569 (14.3)	18,530 (9.4)	9,944 (25.8)	12,350 (25.3)	1,746 (12.5)
2008	50,939	69,290	75,039	47,122	52,224	87,275	39,829 (13.2)	17,024 (8.6)	9,379 (24.7)	10,987 (23.2)	1,576 (11.8)
2007	52,823	71,095	76,955	49,035	53,449	89,402	37,276	16,032 (8.2)	9,237 (24.5)	9,890 (21.5)	1,349 (10.2)
2006	52,124	71,988	77,584	48,800	54,691	95,479	36,460	16,013 (8.2)	9,048 (24.3)	9,243 (20.6)	1,353 (10.3)
2005	51,739	70,746	76,619	47,415	52,646	89,455	36,950 (12.6)	16,227 (8.3)	9,168 (24.8)	9,368 (21.8)	1,402 (11.1)
2004	51,174	69,796	75,327	46,902	52,955	88,323	37,040 (12.7)	16,908 (8.7)	9,014 (24.7)	9,122 (21.9)	1,201 (9.8)
2003	51,353	70,023	75,737	47,575	52,716	82,952	35,861 (12.5)	15,902 (8.2)	8,781 (24.4)	9,051 (22.5)	1,401 (11.8)
2002	51,398	70,114	75,281	48,492	54,401	84,894	34,570 (12.1)	15,567 (8.0)	8,602 (24.1)	8,555 (21.8)	1,161 (10.1)
2001	52,005	71,685	76,902	48,335	54,659	90,098	32,907 (11.7)	15,271 (7.8)	8,136 (22.7)	7,997 (21.4)	1,275 (10.2)
2000	53,164	72,339	77,305	49,604	55,681	92,169	31,581 (11.3)	14,366 (7.4)	7,982 (22.5)	7,747 (21.5)	1,258 (9.9)
1999	53,252	71,628	76,662	50,329	52,852	88,179	32,791 (11.9)	14,735 (7.7)	8,441 (23.6)	7,876 (22.7)	1,285 (10.7)
1998	51,944	69,270	74,731	45,604	51,136	80,428	34,476 (12.7)	15,799 (8.2)	9,091 (26.1)	8,070 (25.6)	1,360 (12.5)
1997	50,123	67,307	72,553	44,848	48,603	79,766	35,574 (13.3)	16,491 (8.6)	9,116 (26.5)	8,308 (27.1)	1,468 (14.0)
1996	49,112	65,207	69,848	44,917	47,054	78,247	36,529 (13.7)	16,462 (8.6)	9,694 (28.4)	8,697 (29.4)	1,454 (14.5)
1995	48,408	63,838	68,548	43,186	44,324	78,456	36,425 (13.8)	16,267 (8.5)	9,872 (29.3)	8,574 (30.3)	1,411 (14.6)
1994	46,937	62,750	67,184	42,568	45,945	76,487	38,059 (14.5)	18,110 (9.4)	10,196 (30.6)	8,416 (30.7)	974 (14.6)
1993	46,419	61,556	66,010	40,458	45,008	74,655	39,265 (15.1)	18,882 (9.9)	10,877 (33.1)	8,126 (30.6)	1,134 (15.3)
1992	46,646	59,137	63,378	38,750	43,884	71,333	38,014 (14.8)	18,202 (9.6)	10,827 (33.4)	7,592 (29.6)	985 (12.7)
1991	47,032	59,203	63,027	39,097	45,075	72,249	35,708 (14.2)	17,741 (9.4)	10,242 (32.7)	6,339 (28.7)	996 (13.8)
1990	48,423	60,487	64,321	40,128	45,236	75,056	33,585 (13.5)	16,622 (8.8)	9,837 (31.9)	6,006 (28.1)	858 (12.2)
1989	49,076	62,003	65,879	40,738	47,524	76,196	31,528 (12.8)	15,599 (8.3)	9,302 (30.7)	5,430 (26.2)	939 (14.1)
1988	48,216	60,245	64,097	39,807	46,034	71,445	31,745 (13.0)	15,565 (8.4)	9,356 (31.3)	5,357 (26.7)	1,117 (17.3)
1987	47,848	59,506	63,262	38,852	45,507		32,221 (13.4)	16,029 (8.7)	9,520 (32.4)	5,422 (28.0)	1,021 (16.1)
1986	47,256	58,382	62,020	38,401	43,983		32,370 (13.6)	17,244 (9.4)	8,983 (31.1)	5,117 (27.3)	
1985	45,640	58,167	59,611	37,383	42,171		33,064 (14.0)	17,839 (9.7)	8,926 (31.3)	5,236 (29.0)	
1984	44,802	54,894	58,152	35,910	42,232		33,700 (14.4)	18,300 (10.0)	9,490 (33.8)	4,806 (28.4)	
1983	43,453	52,649	(NA)	34,394	40,299		35,303 (15.2)	19,538 (10.8)	9,882 (35.7)	4,633 (28.0)	
1982	43,758	52,735	55,716	34,161	40,637		34,398 (15.0)	19,362 (10.6)	9,697 (35.6)	4,301 (29.9)	
1981	43,876	52,417	55,301	34,173	42,263		31,822 (14.0)	17,987 (9.9)	9,173 (34.2)	3,713 (26.5)	
1980	44,616	53,064	55,930	35,194	42,006		29,272 (13.0)	16,365 (9.1)	8,579 (32.5)	3,491 (25.7)	

Source: U.S. Bureau of the Census.

PRODUCTIVITY AND RELATED DATA, BUSINESS SECTOR 1970–2010 (2005 = 100)

Year	Output per Hour of All Persons	Output	Hours of All Persons	Compensation per Hour	Real Compensation per Hour	Unit Labor Costs
1970	48.6	30.3	62.2	14.4	66.3	29.7
1971	50.6	31.4	62.1	15.4	67.5	30.3
1972	52.2	33.4	64.0	16.3	69.6	31.3
1973	53.8	35.8	66.5	17.7	71.0	32.9
1974	52.9	35.2	66.6	19.4	70.1	36.7
1975	54.8	34.9	63.7	21.4	70.8	39.0
1976	56.6	37.2	65.8	23.2	72.7	41.1
1977	57.5	39.3	68.3	25.1	73.7	43.6
1978	58.1	41.8	71.8	27.3	74.9	46.9
1979	58.1	43.2	74.3	29.9	74.9	51.4
1980	58.0	42.7	73.6	33.1	74.6	57.0
1981	59.2	43.9	74.1	36.2	74.5	61.2
1982	58.7	42.5	72.5	38.8	75.4	66.1
1983	60.8	44.8	73.7	40.4	75.3	66.5
1984	62.4	48.7	78.0	42.1	75.4	67.5
1985	63.8	51.0	79.9	44.1	76.3	69.1
1986	65.7	52.9	80.5	46.4	78.8	70.6
1987	65.9	54.6	82.9	48.0	79.0	72.9
1988	66.9	57.0	85.2	50.5	80.1	75.6
1989	67.6	59.1	87.4	51.9	78.9	76.8
1990	69.0	60.0	86.9	55.2	80.0	80.0
1991	70.1	59.5	84.9	58.0	81.1	82.8
1992	73.0	61.8	84.7	61.1	83.3	83.7
1993	73.4	63.8	86.9	62.5	83.1	85.2
1994	74.0	66.9	90.4	63.4	82.6	85.7
1995	74.1	68.8	92.9	64.7	82.3	87.4
1996	76.2	71.9	94.4	66.9	82.9	87.8
1997	77.6	75.7	97.5	69.1	83.8	89.1
1998	79.9	79.4	99.4	73.3	87.7	91.8
1999	82.7	83.9	101.4	76.6	89.8	92.7
2000	85.6	87.7	102.4	82.3	93.3	96.1
2001	88.1	88.4	100.3	86.1	95.0	97.7
2002	92.1	90.1	97.8	88.8	96.3	96.4
2003	95.6	92.9	97.2	93.0	98.7	97.3
2004	98.4	96.7	98.3	96.2	99.5	97.8
2005	100.0	100.0	100.0	100.0	100.0	100.0
2006	100.9	103.1	102.1	103.8	100.5	102.8
2007	102.5	105.2	102.6	108.1	101.8	105.4
2008	103.6	104.2	100.5	111.5	101.1	107.6
2009	107.3	100.4	93.6	113.6	103.4	105.9
2010	111.1	104.4	93.9	116.2	104.1	104.6

Source: *Economic Report of the President, 2011.*

Stock prices and yields, 1969–2010

Year	Common stock prices — Dow Jones industrial average	Common stock yields — Dividend-price ratio	Common stock yields — Earnings-price ratio	10 year Treasury bond (to yield)
1969	876	3.24	6.08	6.67
1970	753	3.83	6.45	7.35
1971	884	3.14	5.41	6.16
1972	950	2.84	5.50	6.21
1973	923	3.06	7.12	6.84
1974	759	4.47	11.59	7.56
1975	802	4.31	9.15	7.99
1976	974	3.77	8.90	7.61
1977	894	4.62	10.79	7.42
1978	820	5.28	12.03	8.41
1979	844	5.47	13.46	9.44
1980	891	5.26	12.66	11.46
1981	932	5.20	11.96	13.91
1982	884	5.81	11.60	13.00
1983	1,190	4.40	8.03	11.10
1984	1,178	4.64	10.02	12.44
1985	1,328	4.25	8.12	10.62
1986	1,792	3.49	6.09	7.68
1987	2,275	3.08	5.48	8.39
1988	2,060	3.64	8.01	8.85
1989	2,508	3.45	7.42	8.49
1990	2,678	3.61	6.47	8.55
1991	2,929	3.24	4.79	7.86
1992	3,284	2.99	4.22	7.01
1993	3,522	2.78	4.46	5.87
1994	3,793	2.82	5.83	7.09
1995	4,493	2.56	6.09	6.57
1996	5,742	2.19	5.24	6.44
1997	7,441	1.77	4.57	6.35
1998	8,625	1.49	3.46	5.26
1999	10,464	1.25	3.17	5.65
2000	10,734	1.15	3.63	6.03
2001	10,188	1.32	2.95	5.02
2002	9,226	1.61	2.92	4.61
2003	8,993	1.77	3.84	4.01
2004	10,317	1.72	4.89	4.27
2005	10,548	1.83	5.36	4.29
2006	11,409	1.87	5.78	4.80
2007	13,170	1.86	5.29	4.63
2008	11,253	2.37	3.54	3.66
2009	8,876	2.40	1.86	3.26
2010	10,663	1.98		3.22

Source: *Economic Report of the President, 2011.*

—Corporate profits with inventory valuation and capital consumption adjustments, 1959–2009
(Billions of dollars)

Year	Corporate profits with inventory valuation and capital consumption adjustments	Taxes on corporate income	Corporate profits after tax with inventory valuation and capital consumption adjustments — Total	Corporate profits after tax with inventory valuation and capital consumption adjustments — Net dividends	Undistributed profits with inventory valuation and capital consumption adjustments
1959	56	24	32	13	19
1960	54	23	31	13	18
1961	55	23	32	14	18
1962	63	24	39	15	24
1963	69	26	43	16	26
1964	76	28	48	18	30
1965	87	31	56	20	36
1966	93	34	59	21	39
1967	91	33	58	22	37
1968	99	40	59	23	36
1969	95	40	55	24	31
1970	84	35	49	24	25
1971	98	38	60	25	35
1972	112	42	70	27	43
1973	125	50	76	30	46
1974	116	53	63	33	30
1975	135	52	83	33	50
1976	163	65	98	39	59
1977	192	74	118	45	73
1978	217	85	132	51	81
1979	223	90	133	57	76
1980	201	87	114	64	50
1981	226	84	142	74	68
1982	210	66	143	78	65
1983	264	81	184	83	100
1984	319	98	221	91	130
1985	330	99	231	98	133
1986	319	110	210	106	104
1987	369	130	238	112	126
1988	433	142	291	130	161
1989	427	146	280	158	123
1990	438	145	292	169	123
1991	451	139	313	181	132
1992	479	149	331	188	143
1993	542	171	371	203	168
1994	600	194	407	285	172
1995	697	219	478	254	224
1996	786	232	554	298	257
1997	868	246	622	334	288
1998	802	248	553	352	202
1999	851	259	593	337	255
2000	818	265	553	378	175
2001	767	204	563	371	192
2002	886	193	694	399	294
2003	993	243	750	425	325
2004	1,231	300	924	540	384
2005	1,448	399	1,034	577	457
2006	1,669	475	1,200	702	498
2007	1,511	446	1,065	795	271
2008	1,263	308	954	798	157
2009	1,758	255	1,003	719	284

Source: *Economic Report of the President, 2011.*

U.S. INTERNATIONAL TRANSACTIONS 1980–2010 (MILLIONS OF DOLLARS) CREDITS (+), DEBITS (−)

Year	Goods[1] Exports	Imports	Net	Services Net military transactions	Net travel and transportation receipts	Other services, net	Balance on goods and services	Income receipts and payments Receipts on U.S. assets abroad	Payments on foreign assets in U.S.	Net	Unilateral transfers, net[3]	Balance on current account
1980	224,250	−249,750	−25,500	−1,822	−997	8,912	−19,407	72,606	−42,532	30,073	−8,349	2,317
1981	237,044	−265,067	−28,023	−844	144	12,552	−16,172	86,529	−53,626	32,903	−11,702	5,030
1982	211,157	−247,642	−36,485	112	−992	13,209	−24,156	86,200	−56,412	29,788	−17,075	−11,443
1983	201,799	−268,901	−67,102	−563	−4,227	14,124	−57,767	84,200	−53,700	31,500	−17,718	−43,985
1984	219,926	−332,418	−112,492	−2,547	−8,438	14,404	−109,073	104,756	−74,036	30,720	−20,598	−98,951
1985	215,915	−338,088	−122,173	−4,390	−9,798	14,483	−121,880	93,679	−73,087	20,592	−22,700	−123,987
1986	223,344	−368,425	−145,081	−5,181	−8,779	18,474	−140,566	91,186	−79,095	12,091	−24,679	−153,154
1987	250,208	−409,765	−159,557	−3,844	−8,010	18,098	−153,313	100,511	−91,302	9,209	−23,909	−168,013
1988	320,230	−447,189	−126,959	−6,320	−3,013	20,435	−115,856	129,366	−115,722	13,644	−25,988	−128,201
1989	359,916	−477,665	−117,749	−6,749	3,551	27,805	−93,142	161,287	−141,463	19,824	−26,169	−99,486
1990	387,401	−498,435	−111,034	−7,599	7,501	30,270	−80,861	171,742	−143,192	28,550	−26,654	−78,965
1991	414,083	−491,020	−76,937	−5,274	16,561	34,516	−31,135	149,214	−125,084	24,130	10,752	3,747
1992	439,631	−536,528	−96,897	−1,448	19,969	40,191	−38,185	132,427	−109,101	23,325	−33,154	−48,013
1993	456,943	−589,394	−132,451	1,385	19,714	42,185	−69,166	134,545	−110,255	24,290	−37,113	−81,989
1994	502,859	−668,690	−165,831	2,570	16,305	49,767	−97,189	165,838	−148,744	17,094	−37,583	−117,678
1995	575,204	−749,374	−174,170	4,600	21,772	52,729	−95,069	211,920	−186,880	25,040	−35,188	−105,217
1996	612,113	−803,113	−191,000	5,385	25,015	57,731	−102,869	226,271	−201,743	24,528	−38,862	−117,203
1997	678,366	−876,485	−198,119	4,968	22,152	63,952	−107,047	261,026	−240,371	20,655	−41,292	−127,684
1998	670,416	−917,112	−246,696	5,220	10,210	68,113	−163,153	258,648	−251,751	6,897	−48,435	−204,691
1999	698,034	−1,034,345	−336,310	−7,245	6,836	72,481	−264,239	293,925	−280,037	13,888	−50,428	−300,779
2000	784,181	−1,230,413	−446,233	−6,610	2,714	71,349	−378,780	350,918	−329,864	21,054	−58,645	−416,371
2001	730,277	−1,152,257	−421,980	−8,398	−3,217	69,201	−364,393	290,797	−259,075	31,722	−64,487	−397,158
2002	696,268	−1,171,613	−475,345	−12,761	−4,334	71,916	−420,524	280,942	−253,544	27,398	−64,948	−458,074
2003	728,258	−1,269,802	−541,544	−17,062	−12,249	76,671	−494,183	320,456	−275,147	45,309	−71,794	−520,668
2004	819,870	−1,485,501	−665,631	−17,232	−15,328	88,846	−609,345	413,739	−346,519	67,219	−88,362	−630,488
2005	909,016	−1,692,817	−783,801	−15,512	−13,121	98,258	−714,176	535,263	−462,905	72,358	−105,772	−747,590
2006	1,035,868	−1,875,324	−839,456	−11,652	−9,743	101,611	−759,240	682,221	−634,136	48,085	−91,481	−802,636
2007	1,160,366	−1,983,558	−823,192	−10,701	4,576	127,217	−702,099	829,602	−730,049	99,553	−115,548	−718,094
2008	1,304,896	−2,139,548	−834,652	−13,375	19,103	130,122	−698,802	796,528	−644,554	151,974	−122,026	−668,854
2009	1,068,499	−1,575,443	−506,944	−13,378	14,951	130,463	−374,908	588,203	−466,783	121,419	−124,943	−378,432
2010	1,288,699	1,934,555	−645,856	−12,908	20,384	138,354	−500,027	663,240	−498,016	165,224	−136,095	−470,898

Source: *Economic Report of the President, 2009* and U.S. Bureau of Economic Analysis.